WORKING WOMEN
Past, Present, Future

WORKING WOMEN
Past, Present, Future

INDUSTRIAL RELATIONS RESEARCH ASSOCIATION SERIES

The Bureau of National Affairs, Inc., Washington, D.C.

Library of Congress Cataloging-in-Publication Data

Working women: past, present, future.

(Industrial Relations Research Association series)
Includes index.
1. Women—Employment—United States—History.
2. Sex discrimination in employment—United States—
History. I. Koziara, Karen Shallcross. II. Moskow,
Michael H. III. Tanner, Lucretia Dewey. IV. Series.
HD6095.W735   1987   331.4'0973   87-9410
ISBN 0-87179-547-7
ISBN 0-913447-34-X (soft)

Printed in the United States of America
International Standard Book Number 0-87179-547-7 (hardcover)
0-913447-34-X (softcover)

Contents

Working Women—A Summary of Research Knowledge and Research Needs

KAREN SHALLCROSS KOZIARA*
MICHAEL H. MOSKOW**
LUCRETIA DEWEY TANNER***

For the first time the Industrial Relations Research Association is publishing a volume in its research series that is devoted exclusively to women in the work force. With this book the Association recognizes that women have entered the labor force in unprecedented numbers and changed it dramatically. This change has enormous implications for labor and industrial relations practitioners and researchers alike. The discipline's predominant focus on blue-collar male unionized workers must now shift to include studying, teaching, and working with women in white- and pink-collar jobs.

Working women became a topic of major research interest during the 1960s, and that interest continued during the 1970s and 1980s. The result of this research is a rich literature on employment issues such as labor force participation, wages, occupations, public policy, and women's status in both employer and labor organizations.

These research efforts originally addressed broad themes. Recently, however, narrower research questions have been studied, and much recent research focuses on specific topics, such as the measurement of comparable worth, the attitudes of men and women toward work, and labor market and retirement experiences of women and men. The trend toward increasingly specific research issues makes this an ideal time to step back and review the existing literature and to identify some remaining unanswered questions. An objective of the editors of this volume was to provide an analytical overview of the current status of working women based on the research of the past two

---

*Professor of Human Resource Administration, Temple University.
**Vice President, Strategy and Business Development, Premark International, Inc.
***Executive Director, Advisory Committee on Federal Pay.

decades. Another objective was to review the existing research, to identify its major contributions and shortcomings, and to suggest what directions research should take in the next decade. Our goal was a readable volume, useful to a wide audience of people knowledgeable about industrial relations, but not particularly familiar with research on working women. In the IRRA tradition, this volume combines disciplines, bringing together the views of economists, historians, sociologists, psychologists, and business scholars on various aspects of women in the working world.

Each author was selected because of a unique expertise and was given a free hand to discuss prior research, to supplement it with new material if possible, and to offer suggestions for additional research. Each saw the challenge differently, and the resulting chapters are both different and complementary. The several themes that emerged are summarized in the following section.

Working Women: Past and Present

Women shared the work of providing food and clothing and child rearing with their spouses throughout history. With the coming of the Industrial Revolution and its need for labor outside the home, women and children came into the factory system. Subsequently, as noted in the Foner and the Marshall and Paulin chapters, women made great strides during wars, moving into more skilled and higher-paying jobs. As servicemen returned, however, women—white and black— dropped back to their lower-status, unskilled positions. It is only in recent history that women became a sizable segment of the work force and made inroads into previously all-male occupations.

Virtually every chapter of this volume addresses this enormous influx of women into the work force. Half of the currently employed are women. Both married and single women work primarily because of economic necessity and because of a change in society's preferred life-styles.

The tired stereotype of women working only until marriage is long gone, even among women in middle- and upper-income families. For example, one recent survey of graduates of women's colleges in the years 1967 and 1977 found that 78 percent were working for pay, and that more recent graduates married and started families after establishing their careers.

Women in Traditionally Male Jobs

Increasing numbers of women are entering traditionally male-dominated professions. Twenty or even 10 years ago there were few women engineers, dentists, attorneys, or physicians. Yet in the early

1980s they entered these fields in substantial numbers. In 1982–1983, for example, 36 percent of all law degrees, 27 percent of medical degrees, 17 percent of dental degrees, and 12 percent of engineering degrees went to women. There are also increasing numbers of women in academia, as discussed by Bognanno.

In actual numbers professional women remain a small portion of the total female work force. As noted by Colwill, Dipboye, and others, sex stereotypes and absence of role models make it difficult for women to advance into these higher paid, more prestigious jobs. As society's views change and more women enter these fields and become visible, however, barriers weaken, in turn encouraging others to consider these previously predominantly male occupations.

Women have not made substantial inroads into craft, skilled, and other high-paying blue-collar jobs. Relatively few women are in apprenticeship programs, and even after they achieve training and credentials, they are replaced during downturns in the economy by workers with more seniority.

Job or Sex Segregation

This volume's authors often refer to sex or job segregation. The concentration of men and women in different jobs is rooted in history and culture, and to a great extent has been deliberate. Women were encouraged to enter the nurturing professions—teaching, nursing—and discouraged from entering the sciences. These patterns are fully described throughout this volume, but little is known about the extent to which women and men will select occupations in a barrier-free society.

Women's Earnings

Women's earnings remain in the range of 60–65 percent of men's on average. This earnings gap is particularly visible among middle-aged women. The earnings of young women are almost equivalent to those of men of the same age, but women need more education than men to achieve comparable earnings. The Shaw and Shaw chapter characterizes women in the 40–64 age group as holding service and low-paid retail sales jobs. While these authors write about working women, these same women, in retirement, become recipients of Social Security benefits and often fall into the elderly poor category.

Minority Women

Malveaux and Wallace discuss the problems of black and other minority workers. Minority women have moved out of household work and now, along with white women, hold predominantly clerical jobs.

Distinctions exist within these clerical jobs, with blacks more likely to work as file clerks and typists and whites as bank tellers, secretaries, and receptionists.

Some minority women have gained economically from union and association membership. A greater proportion of blacks than whites in the labor force are union members, according to Needleman and Tanner, and they have gained leadership skills and demonstrated abilities in these organizations.

Women's Work and the Family

Because the largest increase in labor force participation is among women with young children, researchers have focused attention on this and its long-range implications for society. As documented in both the Marshall and Paulin and the Blau and Ferber chapters, only recently have researchers and policy-makers taken notice of the problems faced by working women and their families. As outlined in Koziara's chapter, public policy is only beginning to address work and family issues, and many questions remain about the appropriate government role in providing services for working parents.

The United States does not provide government-supported child care or require employers to provide parental leave, as noted in Cook's international comparisons. Not only is this a women's issue, it also has widespread implications for the family and society. Woman's dual role, or her "double burden" as wage-earner and homemaker, exerts pressures on families. The Voydanoff chapter suggests part-time jobs as a way to reduce stress and increase family harmony. Yet, because of economic need, personal preference, limited access to employee benefits, and employer reluctance to make work-schedule accommodations, part-time employment is not generally a viable solution.

To some people, the rise of women's employment seems a leading cause of family breakups. But the research shows tradeoffs, with both benefits and disadvantages. Women's work adds substantially to family economic well-being. At the same time, working wives do 50 percent less housework and their families probably eat more tuna surprises. The effect of a working wife on the divorce rate is mixed, and there is no indication that children of working mothers turn out better or worse than those of nonworking mothers.

Evidence suggests that divorce virtually assures a decline in a woman's living standard, in contrast to her former husband's gain. The women's movement has successfully fought for equality, but many middle-aged and older women have not benefited from the equal opportunity movement. Societal pressures for traditional education and occupations prevailed when this group would have most benefited from change, and affirmative action laws arrived too late. The earnings gap will not be closed for them.

The Need for Additional Research

All of the authors contributing to this volume identify future research needs. First and foremost, Colwill urges all researchers, whatever their discipline, to write in everyday layman's language so that the research can be understood and translated into policy.

Stereotyping and its implications are repeatedly mentioned as subjects for additional research. How does stereotyping—feminine characteristics of nurturing and helplessness and masculine traits of aggressiveness—restrict women's ability to enter the upper echelons of the corporate world? Are women who display male characteristics rejected because these unexpected traits are not valued in women?

While aggregated data show the numbers of women entering various occupations, more information is needed on life-styles. Evidence now indicates that men and women are offered similar salaries on entry into professions. What will their lifelong experience be? Will women and men have similar career advancement and compensation over the long run?

An important and relatively unexplored area has to do with women's preferences in our society. Do those who have more limited aspirations reflect the influence of societal stereotypes, or do they have a sincere desire for a life-style different from that of men? What choices would women make in a barrier-free society?

Existing research also largely ignores women entrepreneurs, inventors, and performing artists. We know very little about women in these risk-taking occupations. The information available about these women is largely biographical and anecdotal rather than analytical or systematic. It is a promising area for future research.

Additional research is needed about the barriers minority women face in education and in the job market. What effects has public policy had on their employment opportunities, and what policies could be undertaken to enhance those opportunities?

Pay equity or comparable worth has become an exciting issue in discussions about women's pay. As editors, we purposefully did not include a separate chapter on this emotionally charged issue, but it is discussed by some of the authors. As noted, virtually all states have researched the issue and a few are implementing adjustments. Questions remain, however. How have these pay-equity adjustments affected the work force—both those granted the increases and the nonrecipients? Has pay equity affected the private sector? If so, why and how?

New evidence suggests that technological change is reducing the demand for clerical workers, and some claim that it may in the future reduce the number of jobs in female-dominated occupations. Researchers should be alert to these changes. How will technology affect the job market, educational requirements, family income, and the creation of other jobs?

While women have joined unions and their share of the total U.S. union movement is growing, most women workers are not union members. If women are favorably disposed toward unions, as research suggests, why aren't more of them represented by unions or unionlike organizations?

Women have entered the labor force at an extremely fast pace. Research, however, is slow. It requires time and effort to identify problems and carry out the necessary data-gathering. Actual publication presents another lengthy lag. The changes brought about by women's entry into the world of work, the effects on their families, their successes and failures may go undetected by the slow pace of research. Findings may be outdated by the time they are published. This is a concern that needs to be addressed by all researchers.

Working Women: The Future

The editors are impressed by the enormous progress made by women in improving the level and the quality of their participation in the work force. Women are working in unprecedented numbers in almost every occupation, and the gap between male and female pay appears to be narrowing. Observers can disagree about whether progress has been "fast enough," but the fact remains that practices are changing and the direction is positive.

Progress in the future undoubtedly will be easier for young women. They have the advantage of wider employment options and higher relative pay as compared with their predecessors. Older women have a longer way to go to catch up. The process of changing practices and attitudes is inevitably uneven, and our expectation is that progress will be slower for older women.

Likewise, questions remain about the future of women in female-dominated jobs. What impact will technology have on these jobs? Will pay equity become widespread and, if it does, will it help or hurt women?

All in all, the future looks brighter than the past for working women. The advances made in the past two decades are unlikely to be reversed, and further improvement is expected during the rest of the century. Much of the research summarized by the various authors focuses on how much the labor status of working women has changed.

We think that future changes may prove to be equally pronounced and exciting.

Chapter Highlights

Employment and Earnings of Women: Historical Perspective

Marshall and Paulin trace the evolution of women's work from preindustrial society to the present. From the earliest periods, women's work was considered peripheral to and of less value than men's. In the preindustrial United States women worked in agricultural and homemaking pursuits within their immediate families. Work for wages was rare until young unmarried women moved into factories on the eve of the emerging industrial world. This began a trend that shows no sign of ending.

The authors cite three factors that brought women into the world of work in great numbers: (1) the increased number of women in the population, (2) wartime demand for labor, and (3) married women's economic needs. Occupational segregation has existed throughout U.S. history. In 1900, approximately 90 percent of all working women were in 25 of 252 occupations; in 1940, 90 percent were in 11 of 451 occupations. Although new job opportunities in male occupations became available during wars, gains made by both white and black women were lost in the postward periods.

Dramatic changes in women's employment came after World War II, particularly during the 1960s and 1970s. Women's labor force participation increased, from 34 percent in 1950 to more than 53 percent in 1983. Women are still found in traditionally female occupations, but there are also more women in the nontraditional areas of medicine, law, and accounting.

Even though employed wives earn less than men, they contribute significantly to family incomes. The median income for a working couple was $23,000 in 1978, compared with $17,000 for families with only the husband working. In the same year, dual-earner families were less likely to fall below the official poverty line; families headed by women were most likely to be in that category. While women have made some progress toward integrating occupations, they are a long way from equality.

Occupations and Earnings of Women Workers

In their review of the literature on male and female occupational distribution and earnings, Blau and Ferber find little change in the patterns despite the great influx of women into the labor force. This is clearly because of occupational segregation by sex on all levels, including the professions. Although women did achieve some integration in predominantly male professions between 1970 and 1980, they made little progress in the blue-collar occupations during the same period. Segregation continues to exist even within occupations. For example, the proportion of females with tenure at universities is half that of their male counterparts. Although the earnings gap continues, the authors believe there is a trend toward narrowing the differentials.

Education has a strong positive effect on the income of both men and women, but women need to have more education to achieve the same earnings as men. Young women earn almost as much as men their age in the same occupation.

Older women's earnings continue to show a wide gap in relation to men's, but things may be changing. Data indicate that young women are likely to retain their substantial improvements in relative earnings as they age. This trend will be reinforced as they choose the less traditional jobs and spend more time working.

There are two broad explanations for the sex differences in occupations and earnings of men and women: (1) the human capital explanation, and (2) the labor market discrimination explanation. The human capital theory suggests that people are rewarded for investing in education and job training. Labor market theories assume that employers, customers, and coworkers have discriminatory tastes, even when male and female workers have equal qualifications.

Blau and Ferber state that if the human capital theory is correct, women will choose which occupations to enter and there is no need for concern. If, however, their choices reflect socialization, change will be slow and public policy should focus on education. If there is labor market discrimination, the crucial question becomes whether women have equal opportunity. Available information suggests that both education and discrimination are explanatory factors.

Future research should explain experience at the firm level and over time. More needs to be known about career choices and feedback effects. Will women invest in education and training if they know that they will earn less than men with the same education and training? If a woman earns less than a man, whose career will take precedence in family decisions? If it is his, will he be the more experienced and marketable job-seeker?

Women's Work, Family, and Health

Voydanoff explores the relationships between the working woman's employment demands, her family, and her health. Women's contribution to the family income and standard of living is substantial, especially among full-time workers and those in low-income families. Research indicates that later marriage, later first birth, higher educational attainment, and lower fertility are associated with labor force participation and attachment, higher status jobs, and economic well-being. In addition, women employed outside the home are healthier, both physically and mentally, than homemakers. It may be a self-selection process, with women in poor health and mothers with disabled children less likely to work.

The standard of living of many families increases, although the demands of work create strains in a two-earner family. The effects of a wife's employment on divorce are mixed. On the one hand, employment provides independence which can affect the decision about staying married. On the other hand, added income improves the quality of family life.

The interrelationships between working and spillover effects into family life suggest that the number of hours worked is directly related to family conflict, strain, and the probability of divorce. Greatest marital satisfaction and positive mental health are generally associated with part-time work. Alternative work schedules show mixed results. Flextime reduces stress for women without children, but not for those with major child-care responsibilities.

Voydanoff also discusses the two-career families where the husband and wife work in different locations. The effects of commuter marriages vary according to the length of time apart and are more successful when couples are older, married longer, and free from child-care responsibilities.

Men and Women in Organizations: Roles and Status, Stereotypes and Power

Colwill sets the stage for more detailed discussions of women who work by laying out the basic assumptions that follow them into the workplace—the belief that women are somehow inferior. She outlines sex-stereotyping in society and on the job. While stereotyping helps us define our complex world, broadly categorizing men and women with different attributes leads to simplification and erroneous assumptions. Although sex roles vary from time to time, Colwill notes one consistent feature: "[A]ll things feminine have been seen as inferior to men. . . . The obvious corollary of this truism is that the organizational roles played by men have been the important work roles of the society—the work roles most highly rewarded with money and prestige."

Examinations of peoples' attitudes show that women are viewed as nurturing, emotional, and nimble-fingered, while men are seen as aggressive, adventuresome, and physically strong. These beliefs prejudice how we think of men and women and our predictions of how they might perform on the job, thus discriminating against women in certain job assignments, particularly managerial positions.

Stereotyping influences the relative power of the sexes—personal, interpersonal, and organizational. Men and women use power differently. Women are more likely to employ indirect power and personal resources, such as affection and helplessness, to achieve goals. Men are more likely to use direct power, such as issuing orders, and concrete resources, such as money. The masculine power strategies are more effective for both sexes.

As current outmoded management techniques are reexamined, however, power, too, will be redefined, and the new definitions may move away from the male "good" and the female "bad" ways of using power. Will future researchers examine stereotyping and its impact on job selection for women and men who enter nontraditional jobs in order to make the research available to practitioners? Colwill urges that research reports be written for the lay person, or else the good work done will not be generally known.

Problems and Progress of Women in Management

Dipboye finds more women in management today than 10 or 20 years ago, but they are still a distinct minority, particularly at higher levels. He offers little hope for any change in the immediate future. Although women managers now are progressing faster than their predecessors, they do not move up the ladder as quickly as their male counterparts. There is evidence that college students have unfavorable attitudes toward women in management.

Why? Sex stereotypes exist. The typical woman is seen as emotional, sensitive, warm, gentle, patient, and understanding. Men are seen as aggressive, rational, confident, tough, individualistic, and enterprising—attributes of a successful manager but not those of the stereotypical woman.

Unlike nonmanagerial women, managerial women's traits deviate markedly from those of the "typical" female. Women in management score higher on measures of masculine personality traits than do women in traditionally female occupations. On the issue of how women in management perform, Dipboye looks at subordinates' satisfaction with managers. The findings are mixed. Subordinates of female supervisors are equally satisfied or only slightly less satisfied. They are less satisfied when a woman boss has less influence than a man. Another common index of effectiveness is managers' ratings. Here women receive ratings as favorable as those of men.

Women wanting managerial careers may confront barriers from "gatekeepers"—recruiters, personnel officers, and others. There is bias against female applicants. On the job a woman faces other barriers limiting her advancement: (1) exclusion from the informal relations with male peers, (2) no available mentors, (3) inequitable compensation, and (4) biases in job assignments and promotions. Evidence also suggests that women may be given dead-end jobs.

Women and the American Labor Movement: A Historical Perspective

Foner's chapter traces women's early involvement in union activity. He describes women as denied basic political rights and barred from craft jobs, but there was some banding together in the needle trades and textile firms for self-protection in the 1830s. The first recorded strike in which women participated occurred in 1825 among the tailoresses of New York who sought higher wages. A formal organization was established six years later. Other isolated instances of organizing and strike activity took place during the same period, but no lasting organization of women workers emerged.

Foner chronicles the rise and fall of organizations of women, paralleling the formation and disbanding of early labor organizations. The Knights of Labor achieved some gains for women and minorities, but that organization's decline left their status virtually unchanged.

The craft-oriented American Federation of Labor (AFL) was not interested in women's concerns. Most women worked in unskilled jobs and were excluded from the crafts. The AFL's concession to women workers was to organize them in separate federal labor unions. The women's response was to form their own organizations, such as the Women's Trade Union League.

The Committee for Industrial Organization (CIO) had greater participation of women in auxiliaries and as strikers and organizers. During World War II, women's union membership climbed to 3.5 million. These gains turned out to be permanent.

Women in Unions: Current Issues

This chapter is a review of the current status of women in unions, including membership, bargaining demands, and leadership positions. According to Needleman and Tanner, as of 1984 every third union member was a woman. Over the years, women became members of a number of unions and associations. Nonetheless, eight organizations represent about 60 percent of all unionized women. The authors discuss women in a few predominantly female-organized occupations—flight attendants, health-care workers, and teachers.

Women share some of the traditional concerns of organized men, such as wages and working conditions. New wage issues surfaced in recent years, the most important of which is pay equity or comparable worth. Public-sector unions are actively pursuing this goal-concept and almost every state is reviewing its job classification system.

Although there have been women union members for over a century, they have only recently begun to enter the leadership circles. In the past decade their presence grew steadily in locals and at the regional levels, and in the 1980s they even entered national leadership positions. The same stereotypes and barriers to women in the corporate executive world exist in labor organizations. The Coalition of Labor Union Women, founded in 1978, serves as a catalyst to union women's efforts to achieve power and policy-making positions and to pursue their interests.

The authors stress the need for ongoing research to produce membership data for individual unions and associations. Information is also needed about women in elected and appointed positions at all levels of the organizations. Finally, Needleman and Tanner speculate on the future of unionism and women's stake in its continuation as an effective institution.

Professional Careers for Women in Industrial Relations

In this chapter devoted to women in industrial relations, Gray supplements existing research with original findings. As she explains, the industrial relations profession is diverse and includes many disciplines—economics, sociology, management, psychology, law, history, and social psychology. She looks at where women are in the profession.

Despite increased job opportunities in the 1980s, women are clustered in low-paying jobs. Gray notes that while women appear to be making progress, with the largest advancement coming in the administrative and technical areas of personnel, there is little change on the labor relations side. "Women are not visible in the prestigious decision-making circles of labor policy committees in the Business Round Table, the National Association of Manufacturers, and the U.S. Chamber of Commerce and rarely represent employers at the bargaining table."

According to Gray, women seeking a professional career in personnel fare relatively better in government than in private industry. Even there, however, the median salaries for women fall 20 percent below those of men.

She looks closely at women in government regulatory agencies, labor education, and labor unions, and among neutrals and those on college faculties, to assess their representation. While women are present, their numbers are usually small and they are absent from the upper levels of the power structures. Improvements are being made, but they come slowly.

Women in Professions: Academic Women

Bognanno's chapter provides an overview of the status of academic women. In the recent past far fewer women than men were tenured full professors at universities, and the university world was often hostile to aspiring women academics. However, the percentage of women in higher education increased substantially between 1970 and the present, and there are indications that young women with Ph.D.s no longer face the disadvantages in finding employment at universities that their predecessors confronted.

Nonetheless, research shows that differences persist between academic men and women in rank, income, and tenure status. Do these differences reflect individual differences in discipline, years of continuous service, and academic performance, or do they reflect discriminatory treatment? Although research provides no clear-cut answers, recent studies suggest that affirmative action does not reduce faculty quality and that the research productivity of young male and female assistant professors is essentially the same.

Similarly, the impact of equal employment opportunity policies on university hiring and promotion policies remains unclear. These policies rarely directly affect the decentralized university decision-making process, but they may create a climate in which gender discrimination is brought to consciousness and thus monitored. It is likely that the increasing number of faculty and administrative women in universities also will affect the decision-making process, an interesting example of feedback effects.

For academic women the future appears more promising than the past. Their numbers and status are increasing, a trend likely to continue as women invest in more higher education and if the university "scramble" for qualified faculty, predicted by some, occurs in the 1990s. The development of policies against sexual harassment, admittedly more important to students than to faculty women, is another sign that universities are becoming more hospitable places for women.

Minority Women in the Workplace

Malveaux and Wallace take a broad and critical look at the research on black, Asian, Hispanic, and Native American women. About 20 percent of all women in the labor force are members of these minority groups.

Black women's occupations changed between 1960 and 1981. Black women moved out of private household jobs and into clerical and retail sales positions, they increased their representation in "traditionally female" professional occupations like nursing and noncollege teaching, and they began to enter the traditional professional and managerial jobs as well.

Most women work as clericals regardless of race. Within clerical occupations, however, there are racial differences. White women are overrepresented in such jobs as bank teller, secretary, and receptionist, while black women are overrepresented as file clerks, typists, and social welfare clerical assistants. Many black women have low-paying jobs, which has serious implications for the 42 percent of black families headed by females.

The authors suggest supply- and demand-side strategies to improve the labor market status of minority women. Supply-side strategies include apprenticeship programs to enter blue-collar jobs, educational access programs, and other types of training. Unfortunately, these efforts, the authors note, do not guarantee jobs. Demand-side approaches may be more successful. These methods include litigation, organization, and legislation.

From Midlife to Retirement: The Middle-Aged Woman Worker

Women's midlife work concerns are overlooked by researchers, according to Shaw and Shaw. Despite deficiencies and the need for more research in the future, some of the studies now available provide a profile of the middle-aged working woman.

Today's middle-aged women, defined as those age 40–64, grew up in an era hostile to working women, when the emphasis was placed on traditional mother-housewife roles. Most began work before the equal opportunity legislation of the 1960s, and their career opportunities were limited to a few traditional jobs. Their work patterns vary. The single largest group is labor force reentrants, with intermittent workers nearly as large, and continuous workers also constituting a sizable portion of the total.

These women are less likely to hold professional and managerial jobs and more likely to hold retail sales or service jobs. They earn less than men due to a combination of factors—less work experience and training, and sex, race, and age discrimination.

The authors find that most women have a mixture of economic and noneconomic motives for working. They note that more than half of the middle-aged women would work even if they could live comfortably without doing so.

On an optimistic note, Shaw and Shaw predict that the future may not mirror the past. Today's women in their twenties and thirties have more opportunity to choose nontraditional jobs, the earnings gap is narrowing, and women have fewer children and remain in the work force longer. These trends must be carefully observed by future researchers.

*International Comparisons: Problems and Research
in the Industrialized World*

Women's labor force participation is increasing in most Western industrialized economies, but women hold low-paid jobs, with little training and few promotional opportunities available. Cook sees the "double burden"—working outside the home and maintaining the traditional housewife role—as the most important issue facing women. The Scandinavian countries are almost alone in recognizing the problem and having legislation to encourage equality in household and child-rearing responsibilities, including paternal leaves.

If women researchers did not study and point out the needs of women workers, their problems would go unnoticed. Research efforts have been instrumental in bringing about government policy shifts, accepting women as a permanent part of the labor force, and providing equal employment opportunity.

Some specific areas of policy shifts are recognition of the need for child care, extension of maternal and paternity leaves, new health and safety standards, and equal pay for work of equal value. Flexibility in work scheduling has been promoted and adopted. Shorter hours is a primary European trade union issue, both as a response to rising unemployment and as a way of coping with the double-burden issue. Part-time work is another response. Although largely confined to Scandinavian countries and to Australia, it is widely accepted there. Virtually all industrialized countries except Japan have made accommodations to working women. Cook suggests that additional research is needed on the health and stress problems of women workers and their trade union roles.

Women and Work: The Evolving Policy

The public policy treatment of women workers in the United States evolved from employment restrictions in the 1800s to protectionism in the early 20th century, as Koziara notes. It was not until the 1960s that the Equal Pay Act and Title VII of the Civil Rights Act outlawed sex discrimination in the terms and conditions of employment.

The impact of outlawing sex discrimination in employment is far-reaching and ongoing. Women now have access to jobs previously closed to them. They are protected from practices such as employment evaluations based on marital status and pregnancy that reduced job security and limited occupational advancement. Sexual harassment, once considered amusing, is illegal and is rapidly becoming an anathema to employers.

Public policy has been extremely influential in defining the status of working women. However, the laws covering women workers change slowly because they reflect widely held norms of appropriate sex roles in our society. The slow pace of change also reflects the fragmented policy-formation process and a reactive rather than proactive approach to social issues. Changes in policies affecting women workers historically resulted from coalition-building, supportive research, and political pressure.

Important policy issues remain, many of them practically and philosophically complex. For example, the pay-equity issue raises questions about how wages are set in our society. Also at issue is how to balance equal opportunity with the different roles that men and women often play at work and at home. Is equal treatment an appropriate standard, or should policy specifically address the needs of families and working parents?

These are some of the policy questions for the next decade. As in the past, our answers will come slowly. However, those answers, once framed, will affect the labor force, employers, individual workers, unions, workplace norms, and the very fabric of our society. They are exciting questions, and the answers will both challenge and change us.

CHAPTER 1

Employment and Earnings of Women: Historical Perspective

RAY MARSHALL*
BETH PAULIN**

The increasing labor force participation of women is perhaps the most important labor market development of the century. Women always worked, of course, but in the preindustrial society the family was the basic producing unit and the work of women was an integral part of that unit. Industrialization caused an expansion of the labor market and made economic activity increasingly external to the family. In the new division of labor, women were considered peripheral and temporary participants in the male-dominated market economy. Decisions concerning wages and other conditions of employment were made on the assumption that men would be the main wage earners. Hence, market values gave inadequate attention to the importance of home work. This "traditional model" described the dominant features of labor market patterns in the United States until the 1960s.

The increased labor force participation of women has changed the character of the work force. Women are no longer peripheral, but integral parts of the work force. Most women spend more time working than they do bearing children, and male and female expectations about self-realization from jobs and careers are converging. Unfortunately, conditions of employment continue to assume that women are still temporary, peripheral labor force participants.

The causes of today's male-female occupational and earnings patterns are deeply rooted in history, social attitudes, and power relations between labor and management and between workers themselves— both in the workplace and in society at large. Thus, in order to fully understand these patterns, it is important to look at the historical emergence of women's work and wages.

---

*Professor of Economics and Public Affairs, L.B.J. School of Public Affairs, University of Texas.
**Ph.D. candidate in economics, University of Texas.

This chapter begins with a look at preindustrial society, a period when the majority of the population was involved in agricultural labor and home manufacture and when women's legal, political, and personal rights were sharply curtailed. This was a period when domestic life was almost indistinguishable from economic life—the period of the family economy.

We next consider industrial society, which emerged in force sometime around the mid-1800s. This period is characterized by growing dependence on wage labor, the separation of economic life from family life, the division and further subdivisions of the production process following the dicta of scientific management, the progress of technology, and the embodiment of that technology in new machinery. Also included in this period is the emergence of internal labor markets and the growing interdependence of world economies. We divide the industrial period into three subsections for analysis: pre-World War II, World War II, and post-World War II. The purpose of the division is twofold. First, it facilitates our desire to emphasize the differences in the preconceptions about women's work before the war and women's actual effort during the war. Second, we can better emphasize the changing power relations that emerged as a result of these contradictions.

After a discussion of the current status of women workers in the 1980s, we look ahead and conjecture about women's future in an economy transformed by international competition, technological change, and changing labor markets. Special attention is paid to the growth of the service sector where the majority of women still find employment. Finally, we end with a brief discussion of some important public policy issues for women today.

Women and Work in Preindustrial Society

United States preindustrial society encompasses the period from colonization to the mid-1800s. Various changes took place throughout the span of over 200 years and, as is typical for a country so large, all regions did not share the same experiences at the same points in time.

Economically, the preindustrial period is generally characterized by the predominance of agricultural activity, domestic manufacture, unstable markets, labor shortages (especially in the crafts and trades), indentured servitude, and slavery. A more dynamic description would call attention to the nascent movement away from agriculture and toward production for money wages. Also included would be the effects of population growth: markets increasing in number, size, and stability; the disappearance of labor shortages and indentured servitude; and the growing scarcity of good farmland in the Northeast and mid-Atlantic states, pushing some people west and others into the cities.

Sociologically, the period is characterized by the "entrepreneurial spirit" and the desire to accumulate wealth, individual freedom (at least for the propertied white man), and strict patriarchal relations that denied women political, legal, economic, and personal rights.[1] Social interaction among individual family members was virtually indistinguishable from the economic. There was an unmistakable economic character in family life and, likewise, a conspicuous family character to economic life. Outside the towns, social interaction was limited by the physical distance between farms and the amount of time needed to perform the tasks required for the self-sufficiency of the family. Thus, except for the occasional outing or Sunday religious service, personal contacts were pretty much confined to the family unit. This was especially true for women.

Most women in preindustrial society married, and in so doing relinquished the few rights they possessed as single women:

> A woman ceased to exist if she married, for she and her spouse became one flesh and the flesh was his. The husband had the right to chastise his wife physically, and he had exclusive rights to any property she might have owned as a single woman, to her dower, and to any wages and property that might come to her while she was his wife. In short, like slave or servant women, married women whether rich or poor were legal non-entities. (Foner, 1979, p. 11.)

There are conflicting accounts of women's role in production during this period.[2] Some sources claim that women were restricted from certain jobs or occupations, while others list a variety of "nontraditional" occupations within which women worked.[3] As contradictory as the evidence first appears, closer inspection of the social aspects of work as opposed to the technical reveals the existence of a fundamental line of demarcation between jobs performed by men and those performed by women. Let us focus on the technical aspects of women's work.

Technically, married women's work in the family economic unit generally involved cloth production and sewing, the making of soap and bedding, the growing of food in family plots, and service to the family as cook and nurse. The extent to which a woman was individually responsible for the clothing, feeding, and general care of her family depended upon the family's level of success or failure in produc-

---

[1] See Matthaei (1982), pp. 22–28, for further discussion.

[2] This scarcity of reliable broad-based data forces reliance on a wide range of evidence from diversified sources. To illustrate, the first Census was not taken until 1780, and it was not until 90 years later that published Census reports included the number of women working in the various occupations.

[3] See Matthaei (1982), Buckley (1977), and Campbell (1972).

tion for exchange. There were times when women's work also included working shoulder-to-shoulder with men. Labor scarcity, especially acute in the colonial period, had the magnetic effect of drawing women into the same line of work as the men in the family.

Occasionally women were forced to work for money income; either their husbands or fathers were unable to provide the needed cash for family necessities, or the women had lost their husbands through death, desertion, or divorce. Before the first factories, a woman earned income or the equivalent by selling or trading fruits and vegetables or domestic manufacture such as soap, clothing, and cloth. Sometimes women would take in boarders, set up taverns, or establish "dame" schools. There were also cases where women would step into the shoes of a deceased or ill husband or father and continue on in his craft alone.[4] However, the majority of single women and divorced or widowed women with no children hired themselves out as domestic servants.

Women's work was thus integral to the family economy and frequently included "men's work." The *meaning* of women's work was very different, however, as a refocusing on the social aspects clearly elucidates. We have already pointed out the extent to which women were denied full participation in the community, both legally and politically. As a consequence, a woman's power over her own destiny was restricted. Women were forced to depend upon men to represent them in society and to define for them their place within it. This included the definition of their work and the value placed upon it. To quote Julie Mathaei (1982, p. 31): "Unlike her husband, a woman did not exist as an individual in the public sphere; rather she defined herself in relation to the members of her family, as the wife of her husband and the mother of her children." As a wife and mother, "[h]er work was to fill their needs, her life and work were, hence, defined by their needs." Women worked, then, not for their own self-advancement in the larger community, but rather for the self-sufficiency of the family: "[A] wife's involvement was qualitatively different. . . . He worked as a property owner and family head . . . she as a homemaker, in order to aid her family" (p. 32).

In other words, he worked from a position of power, she from a position of subordination. Thus, although there were many instances when women entered men's public sphere, it should not be misconstrued as an indication of a more egalitarian society. First, as we have just mentioned, focusing attention on the technical aspects of work as opposed to the social relations surrounding that work tends to obstruct the fundamental difference between the work of women and

---

[4] This was about the only way a woman could enter a craft or trade.

men. Second, the flow of women into men's jobs was not reciprocated by the flow of men into women's jobs. Ordinarily men did not perform women's work if a woman was present. And finally, the available wage data support the idea of unequal wages based in patriarchal power relations that were transposed upon the labor market. Although occupational breakdowns within the factories are impossible due to the lack of comprehensive data, we do know that wages paid to women at the close of the preindustrial period were almost always 20 to 50 percent lower than those of males. In the Maryland textile mills, for example, weekly wages for men in 1831 averaged $3.87, while those for women averaged $1.91. Wages in Virginia reflected the same gender-based differential. Male operatives earned $2.73 a week, while women earned $1.58 (U.S. Department of Labor, Bureau of Labor Statistics, 1934, p. 93).

An 1832 report to the U.S. House of Representatives, presented by Secretary of the Treasury Louis McLane, showed numerous instances of women receiving considerably lower wages than men within the same establishment. One example was of 100 tailoring shops in Boston that paid 50 cents a day to their 1,300 women employees, while their male employees received $2.00 a day.[5] Reports such as this would later lead the U.S. Commissioner of Labor to conclude that women's low wages were the result of the fact that women "had come into industry from a general subjection to man . . . which he thought was enough in itself to keep her wages low" (Baker, 1964, p. 80).

Gradually, as we approach the end of the preindustrial period, we find that many more forms of home production followed textiles out of family production and into the market. As women were released from some of their domestic activities, women—primarily the young and single—moved into the factories, taking jobs in textiles, boots and shoes, sewing, and tailoring. Other women increased their activity in the putting-out system as the economy passed through the transition from household to factory production. Nonetheless, the proportion of all women involved in wage labor during the preindustrial period was still very small, and the majority of women who worked outside the home did so as domestic servants—as remained the case until 1940.

Women in Industrial Society

Occupational Structure and Wages Before World War II

The next period begins where the last left off, with the transfer of manufacture from the home to the factory. It includes the structural

---

[5] Louis McLane, *Statistics of Manufactures in the U.S.*, Vol. 1 (Washington: 1833), p. 465. Cited in Buckley (1977), p. 36.

realignments that occurred with the development of the industrial market system and ends on the eve of the Second World War.

The economic character of this period underwent a vast transition from one dependent upon agriculture and the extractive industries to one dependent on manufacture, construction, and transportation, and later to one that included commerce, trade, and the service industries. Introduction of the embodiment of technological advance in new machinery brought about the manufacture of goods capable of being produced more quickly and at a lower cost than ever before. At the same time population growth and improvements in transportation provided both new markets for these goods and a pool of available labor from which the emerging enterprises could draw. Never again would work life and family life be so intertwined as it was in preindustrial society.

As the production process moved into the factories, workers were subject to long hours, low wages, poor working conditions, and precarious employment. The competitive pursuit of profits enticed firms to seriously consider Frederick Taylor's (1967, first published in 1911) research in time and motion studies. Scientific management techniques were implemented in an effort to increase management's control and to reduce the workers' power in the production process.

The fragmentation of labor envisioned by Taylor's methods enabled employers to substitute machines and unskilled or semiskilled labor for skilled workers. Tensions built up within the working class as skilled workers, most of whom were white males, bitterly resented being displaced by women, children, and recent immigrants who made up the bulk of the unskilled labor force. Not only were these men losing their power over capital, but their conditions—as well as their status—were also threatened by women, children, and "foreigners."

In an effort to save their jobs and their status, skilled workers formed craft unions. These unions had a legitimate fear that women's entrance into a trade would pull down all wages in that trade. There were only two ways to prevent this from happening: They could allow women into the unions and fight for equal pay, or they could prevent women from entering the trade in the first place. The first option was inconsistent with the dominant patriarchal power relations and so the craft unions adopted the second strategy. A most striking example of the implementation of this strategy occurred in 1907, when the Molder's Union, in order to prevent women from entering their trade, imposed a hefty fine of $50 on any male union member who gave instructions to a female laborer (Foner, 1979, p. 319).

Economic realignments were accompanied by modifications in political, legal, and social institutions. Politically, modifications were largely superficial. Women and blacks were enfranchised, but their political power was diluted in part by the strong hold that white males had on the political machinery. Women and blacks made "some" inroads into local governing bodies, but their representation at higher levels of government and in the courts was virtually nil. It would take years for women (and blacks) to accumulate the political power necessary to have much effect on public policy.

Legally, changes occurred in the regulation of business and labor, but many of these changes served only to reinforce the status quo. Federal laws were passed to prevent monopolies and business mergers in restraint of trade, but these measures often were used against labor and its organizations. Under the Norris-LaGuardia Act of 1932 and the National Labor Relations Act of 1935, labor was subject to harsh treatment by legal authorities and the courts.

Women gained some power from changes in the legal structure, but the power was not used to its full potential largely because of the unyielding rules that emanated from the social system. These rules defined the social position of men and women and were affected by the Victorian attitudes expressed in novels, sermons, and etiquette books. All stressed women's devotion to the family and warned of the dangers of women's work outside the home. Women were repeatedly told they could realize their "womanliness" through an extension of their biological role as the bearer and nurturer of children. The only morally acceptable role for a woman was that of serving her family: to be "submissive and patient and to cultivate and spread virtue" (Foner, 1979, p. 38). Women were thus discouraged from working in the public sphere, although there were many times when it became economically imperative for them to do so.

Despite the idealized picture of women transmitted from the vestiges of the Victorian era, the hostility of male unions to women workers, and a period of intolerable working conditions, the proportion of all females in the labor force almost doubled, from 9.7 percent in 1870 to almost 20 percent in 1940. By 1940 almost one-fourth of the labor force was composed of women—compared with less than one-seventh of the labor force in 1870 (see Table 1).

The entrance of women into the labor force can be attributed to three salient factors: demographics, war, and an increase in the labor force participation of married women.

The role of demographics lies in the redistribution of women in the various age categories and in population growth. Typically, the majority of the labor force is drawn from that part of the population ages 20–64. From 1870 to 1940 the proportion of women in this age group increased noticeably. By 1940 it included almost all women, up from less than one-half in 1870. Add in the fact that the female population tripled in these 70 years, and one can account for both the

TABLE 1
The Female Labor Force: 1870–1940

Year	Total Number of Women Workers in the Labor Force	Percent of Female Population	Labor Force Participation Rate[a]	Women as a Percent of the Labor Force
1870	1,917,446	9.7%	13.3%	14.8%
1880	2,647,157	10.7	14.7	15.2
1890	4,005,532	13.1	17.4	17.2
1900	5,114,461	14.3	20.4	18.1
1910	7,788,826	16.7	25.2	20.9
1920	8,429,707	17.1	23.3	20.4
1930	10,396,000	17.8	23.6	21.9
1940	13,015,000	19.8	25.7	24.4

Source: U.S. Department of Labor, Women's Bureau, Women's Occupations Through Seven Decades, Bull. 218 (1947): p. 34.

[a] Labor force for the years 1870 to 1890 includes those 10 years of age and older. Labor force for the years 1900 to 1940 includes those 14 years of age and older. Labor force for 1930 is estimated.

increasing proportion of women in the labor force and their increasing numbers.

While the female population was tripling in size and reshuffling its distribution among age groups, married women, who made up the majority of the female population, were increasing their labor force participation by more than 170 percent. The proportion of all married women in the labor force increased from 5.6 percent in 1900 to 15.2 percent in 1940. Looking at this phenomenon from a different perspective, we see that married women made up 15 percent of the female labor force in 1870 and 35.5 percent in 1940.

Several interrelated factors contributed to the rise in the labor force participation of married women. Among them were mandatory schooling for young children and a decline in fertility rates. Both served to open the way for more freedom of movement outside the home. Rebecca Farnham, writing for the Women's Bureau in 1939, suggested that the predominant factor, however, was "the inadequacy of men's earnings in modern times, when most workers have no land or home industry to support wages" (Farnham, 1939, p. 8). To substantiate her claim, she pointed out that even at the peak of prosperity in 1929, the average American family had only 75 percent of the income necessary to provide the minimum of adequate living. Of city workers not on relief, only two-thirds had enough income to meet the minimum living requirements.[6] Farnham's point is a good one. The urban

___

[6] Married women also increased their labor force participation during the Great Depression when many husbands were without work. Many married women found jobs as office workers in the growing service sector.

family, if unable to be supported by the male head, was forced to send its female members into the workplace. Rural families were not exempt, although they were more self-sufficient in their ability to provide food and clothing.[7]

The final factor affecting women's labor force participation was war. Although Census data on the numbers of women working in the different occupations were not compiled until 1870, various reports indicate that the Civil War, as well as World War I, had a positive impact on women's market work.[8] As a result of the Civil War, women increased their numbers in the teaching and nursing professions and in clothing manufacture, while World War I lured women into industries where only a negligible number of them previously had worked. For example, before World War I, 7 percent of the wage-earners in the iron and steel mills were women. During the war, 16 percent were women (Farnham, 1939, p. 3). The same occurred in chemicals, where the proportion of women increased from 3.5 percent of the labor force to 13 percent, and in metal factories and foundries, where the percentage of women grew from 15 to 21 percent (Farnham, 1939). Women also entered lumber mills, auto and aircraft factories, and electrical, munitions, and war supplies industries. Increasing numbers of women became telegraph operators and office workers, while even more became nurses and teachers.

Women's occupational gains in the typically male industries during the war were almost transitory in nature. Return to peacetime production meant a return to "women's work" for many of the newly employed women and those who followed them. A comparison of the top 10 occupations for women in 1870 and 1940, along with some figures on occupational segregation, substantiate this claim.

The top 10 occupations for women in 1870 and 1940 are given in Table 2. Of all women who were gainfully employed in 1870, 88 percent were in these 10 occupations (Hooks, 1947, p. 52). Women as a percentage of all workers in the top 10 occupations for women in 1940 are given in parentheses following the occupation.

It is obvious that women worked in occupations that were a reflection of the jobs they had done previously in the family economy. Even in the "newer" occupations, women were required to perform their preindustrial familiar tasks of nurturing and mothering.

Occupational segregation was prevalent throughout the entire period. In 1900, 90.2 percent of the women who worked were in 25 of

---

[7] In rural areas most married women who participated in the labor force did so as "putting out" workers, while the daughters traveled to the cities to work in factories or as domestics. This was particularly true earlier in this period and became less common as the transition from home to factory was completed.

[8] See Hooks (1947), Farnham (1939), and Pidgeon (1937).

TABLE 2
The Top Ten Occupations for Women: 1870 and 1940

1870

1. Domestic servants
2. Agricultural laborers
3. Tailoresses and seamstresses
4. Milliners, dress, and mantua makers
5. Teachers (not specified)
6. Cotton mill operatives
7. Laundresses
8. Woolen mill operatives
9. Farmers and planters
10. Nurses

1940

1. Servants, private family (91.3%)
2. Stenographers, typists, and secretaries (93.5%)
3. Teachers[a] (75.7%)
4. Clerical and kindred[a] (35.7%)
5. Saleswomen[a] (40.8%)
6. Bookkeepers, accountants, and cashiers (62.1%)
7. Operatives, apparel and accessories (77.5%)
8. Housekeepers, private family (99.2%)
9. Waitresses, except private family (67.6%)
10. Trained nurses and student nurses (97.9%)

Sources: 1870: U.S. Department of Labor, Women's Bureau, *Women's Occupations Through Seven Decades*, Bull. 218 (1947): p. 52. 1940: U.S. Department of Commerce, Bureau of the Census, *16th Census of the United States: 1940*, Population, Vol. III, The Labor Force, Part I, U.S. Summary, Table 58 (Washington: U.S. Government Printing Office, 1943).
    [a] Not elsewhere classified.

252 occupations. Forty years later the percentage had dropped only slightly to 86.7 percent (Hooks, 1947, p. 66). A more detailed accounting of occupations in 1940 revealed that in 11 out of 451 occupations, 90 percent of all employed persons were women. In 27 other occupations women were in the majority. These occupations make up the bulk of employment opportunities for women. By way of contrast, in 89 out of 451 occupations, 90 percent or more of the people employed were men; in 9 occupations men made up the entire work force.[9]

Black women also entered new occupations and industries throughout the period, but were held back by the color of their skin. Before the Civil War there were few blacks in manufacturing and mechanical pursuits. Part of this resulted from the fact that 90 percent

───────

[9] The nine occupations were railroad conductors, baggagemen, locomotive engineers, locomotive firemen, railroad and car shop mechanics and repairmen, railroad brakemen, railroad switchmen, firemen in fire departments, and soldiers, sailors, marines, and members of the Coast Guard.

of the black population lived in the South, where industrial development lagged behind the North and where mechanical jobs were
defined as white men's jobs. Most blacks lived on plantations and
participated in the economy as agricultural laborers and household
servants. After the Civil War and as late as 1910, 95 percent of all black
women continued to work in agriculture and in domestic and personal
service. Up until World War I, the only manufacturing industry to
employ large numbers of black women were the cigar and cigarette
industries (Farnham, 1939, p. 59).

As white women left their traditional jobs for the new job opportunities during World War I, black women filtered in through the
bottom of the occupational hierarchy. Their greatest gains were in
textile and clothing, food industries, tobacco factories, and wood product manufacture. After the war, many of these gains were lost as white
women moved back into their prewar occupational slots. Black women
maintained a small increase in the trades, professions, and clerical
occupations, but in 1930 nine out of ten black women were employed
once again in agriculture and domestic and personal service.[10]

It was not until the 16th Census of the United States in 1940 that
detailed wage data were published. Previously, information on wages
by sex, industry, and occupation was limited and discordant, if it
existed at all. Consistent throughout, however, is the fact that females
were always paid lower wages than males. Without knowing the
number of hours worked and the detailed occupational employment, it
is difficult to determine how much of the differential was due to these
aforementioned factors and how much was due to the stereotype of
women working either to supplement a father's or husband's income or
to earn "pin money."

Data are available, however, from the 1940 Census on the distribution of wages among men and women in the same detailed
occupations who worked full-time during the previous year, and they
indicate that even when hours and weeks of work are considered,
wages of women still fall below those of men. Men worked both more
hours per week and months per year than did women: 69.7 percent of
the men employed in 1939 worked for 9–12 months, whereas
64.4 percent of the women did so. Likewise, 36.7 percent of the men
worked 45 hours a week or more, compared with 28.5 percent of the
women. Nevertheless, a more detailed breakdown in the distribution
of income by sex and occupation for those who worked full-time in 1939
reveals that in every occupation female income is more heavily skewed

---

[10] Five one-hundredths of black women workers were in tobacco, clothing (including home),
food, and textile manufacture. The same percentage were in trade, clerical, transportation and
communications, teaching, nursing, and acting.

toward the lower end of the pay scale. Even in those occupations where wages are very low, the proportion of women in the lower income category exceeds that of men (see Table 3).

As factories and businesses expanded and merged in the late 1800s and early 1900s, the wage relationships between segregated men's and women's jobs became institutionalized in the personnel policies of firms. Job ladders were established within firms and wage scales were set up to reflect one's position in the firm's hierarchy. These wage scales reflected the social value placed on women's work and hence institutionalized the relative wage rates for men's and women's work. The most notorious and widely publicized case of this was with Westinghouse, whose company manual stipulated that the lowest paid male job was not be paid a wage below that of the highest paid female job, *regardless of the job content and value to the firm* ("Westinghouse Industrial Relations Manual: Wage Administration," Nov. 1, 1938, and Feb. 1, 1939, cited in Heen, 1984).

Union contracts also served to institutionalize the socially determined wage structure. For example, in 1913 the International Ladies' Garment Workers' Union signed a contract that formally recognized the division of labor within the ladies' garment industry. Known as the "Protocol in Dress and Waist Industry," the contract limited women to the less skilled jobs and stipulated that the highest paid female could not earn more than the lowest paid male (Foner, 1979).

The Impact of World War II

The Second World War had a double-edge effect on the United States. Advancement in technology occurred at a rapid pace, while more than 10 million draftees were inducted into the armed forces.[11] It is against this backdrop that women made some of their most impressive gains in terms of labor force participation, occupational integration, and earnings.

Women made many advances into male jobs after the bombing of Pearl Harbor. Prior to that, however, women's labor was neglected. From the summer of 1940, when the United States launched the defense program, to the attack on Pearl Harbor, there was no appreciable advance in women's employment.

> Comparatively few women were hired by defense plants, primarily because of the large backlog of unemployed men on which the expanding munitions industries could draw. . . .[12] Moreover, there was encoun-

---

[11] A total of 16,354,000 U.S. citizens served in the armed forces during World War II.

[12] *Author's note*—In June of 1940, 5.9 million men were unemployed. By July of that year, the number had increased to 6.3 million. Even in June of 1941 over 4 million men were still without work. As for the employment of women, 11.9 million were employed in January 1942, the same number as in the preceding June (Robinson, 1943, p. 651).

TABLE 3
Occupational Income Distribution for Full-Time Workers by Sex, 1939

Occupation	Sex	Income Category			
		I	II	III	IV
College presidents, professors, and	F	21.9%	28.7%	45.1%	2.6%
instructors	M	9.6	13.5	59.5	15.9
Librarians	F	30.3	53.5	14.6	0.1
Social and welfare workers	F	15.5	66.4	15.7	0.4
	M	9.5	54.0	32.4	3.1
Teachers (other than art and music, college professors and instructors; including county agents)	F	33.2	37.3	27.3	0.4
	M	15.0	36.3	44.2	3.2
Bookkeepers, accountants, cashiers, ticket agents	F	50.4	44.8	3.2	0.1
	M	13.4	47.9	33.8	2.6
Office machine operators	F	32.5	65.8	0.7	—
	M	21.0	70.8	7.0	0.3
Stenographers, typists, secretaries	F	37.7	56.9	4.1	0.1
	M	18.2	52.2	24.1	3.9
Telegraph operators	F	29.4	65.9	3.4	—
	M	4.6	58.2	35.9	0.2
Telephone operators	F	47.3	50.2	1.6	—
	M	27.0	41.8	28.7	0.7
Laundry operators and laundresses (excluding family)	F	94.5	4.8	—	—
Charwomen, janitors, and porters	F	89.0	10.3	0.1	—
	M	35.5	59.9	1.1	—
Elevator operators	F	82.0	17.4	0.2	—
	M	38.5	59.9	1.1	—
Servants (excluding private family)	F	95.9	2.9	0.1	—
	M	80.7	18.1	0.5	—
Farm laborers (wage workers) and farm foremen	F	94.0	1.2	—	—
	M	92.1	4.9	0.4	—

Operatives and Kindred (Not Elsewhere Classified) by Industry

Manufacturing:					
Food and kindred products	F	81.8	17.5	0.1	—
	M	26.8	64.8	7.5	—
Tobacco manufacture	F	88.0	11.5	0.1	—
	M	59.0	37.1	2.1	0.1
Cotton manufacture	F	95.5	4.2	—	—
	M	82.4	16.9	0.4	—
Silk and rayon	F	90.0	9.4	—	—
	M	54.0	43.4	2.1	—

TABLE 3 (*Continued*)

Occupation	Sex	Income Category I	II	III	IV
Woolen and worsted	F	79.5%	19.9%	0.1%	—
	M	38.8	58.2	17.6	0.1
Knit goods	F	84.6	14.7	0.1	—
	M	40.1	46.6	17.6	—
Lumber, furniture, and lumber products	F	82.2	16.8	0.1	—
	M	50.1	46.4	2.5	—
Paper, paper products, and printing	F	80.5	18.6	0.2	—
	M	22.3	67.7	9.2	—
Chemicals and petroleum and coal	F	69.6	29.6	0.2	0.1
products	M	11.7	73.6	14.0	0.1
Rubber products	F	66.4	32.9	0.2	—
	M	12.2	73.3	13.8	0.1
Footwear, except rubber	F	87.1	14.8	0.1	—
	M	43.4	53.7	2.4	0.1
Leather and leather products, except	F	85.2	17.7	0.1	—
footwear	M	28.7	65.3	4.3	0.2
Stone, clay, and glass products	F	77.1	28.3	0.1	—
	M	22.6	67.9	8.7	0.1
Iron, steel, nonferrous metal products and	F	66.0	33.0	0.2	—
machinery	M	17.0	73.0	17.5	0.1
Transportation equipment[a]	F	45.0	53.8	0.8	—
	M	30.6	66.6	2.1	0.1

Nonmanufacturing Industries and Services

Domestic	F	97.0	1.5	—	—
	M	84.5	13.3	0.7	—
Protective services	F	28.7	46.9	23.1	0.2

Source: U.S. Department of Commerce, Bureau of the Census, *10th Census of the United States: 1940*, Population, Vol. III, The Labor Force, Part I, U.S. Summary, Table 73 (Washington: U.S. Government Printing Office, 1943).

Note: Income categories I–IV correspond to $1–999, $1,000–1,999, $2,000–4,999, and $5,000 and up, respectively. Percentages across occupations may not total 100 due to rounding and a small percentage of nonrespondents. No entries are recorded when the percentage is less than 0.1.

[a] Excludes auto and auto equipment.

tered in many quarters a definite discrimination against women as munitions workers, based on traditional prejudice and fear that they lacked mechanical ability despite their proved skill along such lines in the manufacture of armaments in 1917–1918. (Robinson, 1943, p. 651).

After December 7, 1941, this all began to change rapidly. From 1940 to the peak of women's war employment in July 1944, the number of women in the labor force increased by more than 6 million, to 20.6 million, an increase of almost 50 percent (Pidgeon, 1946, p. 1). In June 1940 women made up 24.7 percent of the civilian labor force. By

July 1945 this had increased to 35 percent. In 1944, for the first time in American history, the number of married women exceeded the number of single women in the labor force. Married women were 44 percent of the female labor force that year, while single women made up 43 percent. The remaining 13 percent were widowed and divorced women (see Table 4).

Women filled the slots left open by the men in the armed forces, as well as those created specifically to fill the material needs of the war. Women made their greatest gains in the categories of operatives and kindred, craftsmen, foremen, and laborers except farm, and clerical and kindred (see Table 5). Among the various industries in which women worked, the greatest increase in numbers of women employed occurred in manufacturing, the most marked of which was direct war industries.

Black as well as white women made work-related gains during World War II. As was the case with the First World War, black women tended to filter up through the bottom of the occupational hierarchy, first entering those jobs left by white women and then moving into the expanded war-production industries.

The employment of black women increased from 1.5 to 2.1 million from April 1940 through April 1944 (Blood, 1945, p. 17). The distribution of black women among occupations was much more diverse than ever before. There was a significant decrease in the proportions of black women who were farm workers and domestic service workers and an increase in the proportions who were industrial workers, personal and other service workers, clerical and sales, and proprietors, managers, and officials, although the gain in the latter category was slight.

As women and blacks became more integrated occupationally during the war, various contradictions emerged. Women and blacks were called into the war industries by an emotional appeal to their

TABLE 4

Marital Status of Women Workers Before, During, and After World War II

Marital Status	Percent of All Women of Each Marital Status Who Worked				Percent Distribution of Women Workers			
	1940	1944	1947	1949	1940	1944	1947	1949
All	28%	32%	30%	31%	100%	100%	100%	100%
Single	49	55	52	51	49	43	38	33
Married	17	23	22	24	36	44	46	51
Widowed/divorced	33	32	36	35	15	13	16	16

Source: U.S. Department of Labor, Women's Bureau, Handbook of Facts on Women Workers, Bull. 237 (1950): p. 16.

TABLE 5
Occupational Status of Women Workers Before, During, and After World War II

Occupation Group	Percent of All Workers			Percent Distribution by			Change in No.
	1940	1945	1947	1940	1945	1947	1940–1947
All employed women	26%	36%	28%	100%	100%	100%	+32.6
Clerical and kindred	53	70	59	21	25	26	+63.2
Operatives and kindred	26	38	28	18	24	22	+56.2
Domestic service	94	94	92	18	9	11	−19.5
Professional and semiprofes-sional	45	46	40	13	8	10	−1.9
Service (except domestic)	40	48	44	11	10	11	+31.1
Sales	28	54	40	7	8	8	+59.0
Farmers and farm workers	8	22	12	6	10	6	+31.9
Proprietors, man-agers, officials (except farm)	12	17	14	4	4	5	+73.3
Craftsmen, fore-men, laborers (except farm)	3	5	2	2	2	1	+45.5

Source: U.S. Department of Labor, Women's Bureau, *Handbook of Facts on Women Workers*, Bull. 225 (1948): pp. 2–3.

patriotism, an appeal to help their country in the fight for freedom and equality. But how much freedom and equality was available to these groups in their very own country? Women and blacks had heretofore been shut out of many occupations and industries or relegated to the low-level jobs. In many states women were not allowed to dispose of any property without their husband's signature or consent, to enter into contracts, or even to gain legal guardianship of their children. Blacks were not allowed to eat in certain restaurants, sleep at certain hotels, live in certain neighborhoods, or ride in the front of the bus. Indeed, despite the patriotic appeal of a war to make the world safe for democracy, it required considerable protest—including a threatened march on Washington—for blacks to get the right to work in defense plants in other than custodial jobs.

    This contradiction also presented itself in the wages paid to women and blacks for performing the same jobs as white males. Employers continued their practice of exploiting the social conditions of women and blacks, paying them low wages. The extent of this practice became all the more apparent when the National War Labor Board (NWLB) was established in 1942 to regulate wages in the war industries. NWLB personnel uncovered the gross inequities in wage payments and eventually issued General Order 16, permitting companies to equalize male and female wage rates. Compliance was voluntary, however.[13]

Male unions also joined the NWLB in the effort to equalize wages, although not always for altruistic reasons. Male unions feared that, as a result of the new training and skills acquired by women and blacks, employers would either replace white men with the cheaper labor of women and blacks, or use them as wage-cutters. Other unions were interested in helping their female and black members. The International Union of Electrical Workers, for example, pushed for not only equal pay for equal work, but equal pay for comparable work, recognizing that many jobs were labeled "women's" jobs and were paid less regardless of their technical content.

The success of the NWLB and the various unions and women's groups that lobbied for equal pay varied. In general, equal pay was achieved in those industries where there was strong union backing. By 1947 nine states had adopted equal pay legislation, although in two— Illinois and Michigan—the law applied only in manufacturing.[14]

Other types of pay legislation affecting women included minimum wage laws. The Fair Labor Standards Act of 1938 provided minimum wage protections for women engaged in interstate commerce or in the manufacture of goods that moved in interstate commerce. A year later the Supreme Court first recognized the right of a state to pass a minimum wage law for women and by 1947, 26 states had enacted such legislation. Of these, four had minimum wage laws that extended to men (Connecticut, New York, Massachusetts, and Rhode Island).

Other legislation having an indirect effect on women's wages included laws regulating hours of work, weight-lifting limits, rest periods, night work, meal periods, and a day of rest. The intention of protective legislation for women was not to provide the employer with an excuse for not hiring women, although this was the unfortunate result in many cases where the protective legislation did not cover male workers.

At war's end there was still a wage differential between men and women in the same occupation, the same age group, the same industries, and the same occupations within the same industries. Data on these facts are found in Tables 6, 7, and 8.

---

[13] Equal pay was compulsory only when the NWLB ruled on the issue in a specific disputed case brought before the board.

[14] The other seven states with equal-pay laws were Massachusetts, Montana, New Hampshire, New York, Pennsylvania, Rhode Island, and Washington.

TABLE 6
Median Year's Earnings of Men and Women by Chief Occupational Groups: 1946

| | Median Year's Earnings of: | |
Occupation Group	Women	Men
Proprietors, managers, officials	$1,671	$3,087
Craftsmen, foremen, and kindred	1,568	2,433
Semiprofessionals	1,548	2,356
Professionals	1,501	3,345
Clerical and kindred	1,480	2,246
Operatives and kindred	1,114	2,067
Laborers (except mine)	1,024	1,413
Salespersons	754	2,142
Service workers (except domestic)	662	1,665
Domestic service workers	373	465

Source: U.S. Department of Labor, Women's Bureau, Handbook of Facts on Women Workers, Bull. 225 (1948): p. 20.

The Postwar Period

The most dramatic changes in women's employment policies have come since World War II, especially during the 1960s and 1970s when a combination of economic, social, and technological changes greatly transformed women's role in the economy. From being a peripheral or temporary part of the labor force during the early part of the century, women became permanent and integral participants in the labor mar-

TABLE 7
Median Year's Earnings of Men and Women Wage and Salary Workers by Chief Industry Groups: 1946

| | Median Year's Earnings of: | |
Industry Group	Women	Men
Government	$1,795	$2,453
Transportation, communications, other public utilities	1,471	2,398
Manufacturing	1,341	2,225
Durable	1,439	2,230
Nondurable	1,286	2,216
Finance, insurance, real estate	1,301	2,518
Business and repair service	1,299	1,939
Professional and related services	1,254	1,965
Wholesale trade	1,009	2,272
Retail trade	785	1,796
Amusement, recreation	608	1,561
Personal and domestic service	472	1,295

Source: U.S. Department of Labor, Women's Bureau, Handbook of Facts on Women Workers, Bull. 225 (1948): p. 20.

TABLE 8

Median Year's Earnings of Women and Men, All Workers and Full-Time Workers, by Age: 1946[a]

Age Group	All Workers		Full-Time	
	Women	Men	Women	Men
Under 20	$ 461	$ 406	—	—
20, under 25	1,135	1,247	—	—
25, under 35	1,102	2,098	$1,698	$2,493
35, under 45	1,288	2,535	1,809	2,837
45, under 55	1,209	2,575	1,719	2,823
55, under 65	966	2,285	1,543	2,558
65 and older	427	1,625	1,188	2,129

Source: U.S. Department of Labor, Women's Bureau, Handbook of Facts on Women Workers, Bull. 225 (1948): p. 21.

[a] No figures are entered when the number in the sample is too small to compute a median.

ket. The traditional model was dominant as late as 1950, when 70 percent of American households were headed by men whose income was the sole source of family support; by 1985 less than 15 percent of American households fit this model.

Between 1973 and 1983, over 60 percent of the gain in the work force came from women who increased their labor force participation by 13.7 million, compared with an increase of 8.4 million by men. The labor force participation rate for women rose from 33.9 percent in 1950 to more than 53 percent in 1983, while the rate for men declined from 86.4 percent in 1950 to 77.2 percent in 1980. Women increased their proportion of the total labor force from 29.6 percent in 1950 to 44 percent today.

The rapid increase in the labor force participation of women is shown in Table 9, which also indicates that younger women have higher labor force participation rates than their mothers and grandmothers. Female labor force participation rates tend to decline in the 25–34 age category and then to increase for older age groups.

About half of the absolute increase in the labor force participation by women was among the relatively young, those 25–34 years of age. As Table 10 shows, most mothers of children under 18 and two-thirds of mothers with children 6–18 were in the work force in 1984, regardless of their marital status. Of course, divorced and separated mothers are more likely to work than those who are married with husbands present.

There is some debate over whether the great increase in the number of working mothers has had a negative impact on childrearing. However, the mother's self-image and the family's economic and emotional well-being undoubtedly are conditioned by the ability of the mother and father to work. A paid job has become an important

TABLE 9
Labor Force Participation of Women 20 Years of Age and Over
Annual Averages, Selected Years, 1955–1984

Year of Birth	1955 Age	1955 Rate	1960 Age	1960 Rate	1965 Age	1965 Rate	1970 Age	1970 Rate	1975 Age	1975 Rate	1979 Age	1979 Rate	1984 Age	1984 Rate
1961–1965													20–24	70.4
1956–1960											20–24	69.1	25–29	70.4
1951–1955									20–24	64.1	25–29	65.7	30–34	69.1
1946–1950							20–24	57.8	25–29	57.0	30–34	61.9	35–39	70.2
1941–1945					20–24	50.0	25–29	45.2	30–34	51.7	35–39	63.4	40–44	70.1
1936–1940			20–24	46.2	25–29	38.9	30–34	44.7	35–39	54.9	40–44	63.9	45–49	66.2
1931–1935	20–24	46.0	25–29	35.7	30–34	38.2	35–39	49.2	40–44	56.8	45–49	60.4	50–54	59.4
1926–1930	25–29[a]	35.3	30–34	36.3	35–39	43.6	40–44	52.9	45–49	55.9	50–54	56.5	55–59	49.8
1921–1925	30–34	34.7	35–39	40.8	40–44	48.5	45–49	55.0	50–54	53.3	55–59	48.7	60–64	33.4
1920 or before:														
1916–1920	35–39	39.2	40–44	46.8	45–49	51.7	50–54	53.8	55–59	47.9	60–64	33.9		
1911–1915	40–44	44.1	45–49	50.7	50–54	50.1	55–59	49.0	60–64	33.3	65–69	15.3		
1906–1910	45–49	45.9	50–54	48.8	55–59	47.1	60–64	36.1	65–69	14.5	70+	4.7		
1901–1905	50–54	41.5	55–59	42.2	60–64	34.0	65–69	17.3	70+	4.8				
1896–1901	55–59	35.6	60–64	31.4	65–69	17.4	70+	5.7						
1895 or before	60–64	29.0	65–69	17.6	70+	6.1								
	65–69	17.8	70+	6.8										
	70+	6.4												

Sources: U.S. Department of Labor, Women's Bureau, *United Nations Decade for Women, 1976–1985; Employment in U.S.* (Washington: U.S. Government Printing Office, July 1985); U.S. Department of Labor, Bureau of Labor Statistics, *Perspectives on Working Women: A Databook*, Bull. 2080 (Washington: U.S. Government Printing Office, October 1980).

[a] Note how the groups' labor force participation rate (LFPR) can be followed through time; in 1955, 35.3 percent of 25–29 year olds were in the work force; by 1984 the LFPR of this age group was 70.4.

TABLE 10
Participation Rates[a] for Women with Children, by Marital Status
and Age of Children

	No Children Under 18			Children Ages 6–18			Children Under 6		
Year	M	Sep.	Div.	M	Sep.	Div.	M	Sep.	Div.
1960	34.7	n/a	n/a	39.0	n/a	n/a	18.6	n/a	n/a
1970	42.2	52.3	67.7	49.2	60.6	82.4	30.4	45.4	63.3
1980	46.0	58.9	71.4	61.7	66.3	82.3	45.1	52.2	68.8
1981	46.3	59.9	72.4	62.5	70.0	83.4	47.8	51.0	65.4
1982	46.2	57.5	71.6	63.2	68.4	83.6	48.7	55.2	67.2
1983	46.4	55.6	71.7	63.8	68.7	83.2	49.9	53.8	68.7
1984	47.1	59.3	70.6	65.4	70.2	84.1	51.8	54.0	67.9

Source: U.S. Bureau of the Census, Statistical Abstract of the U.S.: 1985 (105th ed.). (Washington: 1984).
Note: M = married, husband present; Sep. = separated; Div. = divorced.
[a] Percentage of women in each specific category in the labor force.

symbol of self-worth and personal independence for women—even though most women work for economic reasons. The mechanization of household work and increasing life expectancy have created much more time for women to pursue careers. Around 1900 the average life expectancy for a woman was 47 years, 18 of which were spent in childbearing; by 1980 life expectancy was 77 years, only 10 of which were devoted to childbearing (although more are devoted to child rearing).

Because minorities have different life expectancies, the impact of trends can be seen more clearly by looking at the experiences of white women. In 1900, the life expectancy for a white woman was about 64 years. She could expect, on the average, to be widowed at 52 and die before her last child left home. In 1980, a white woman who married at 22 could expect to live about 79.4 years and to stop having children at age 30. Her last child would leave home when she was 48. However, there was a 47.4 percent chance that her first marriage would end in divorce. Davis and van den Oever (1982) observe: "Underlying demographic changes thus force women to reduce the importance of marriage in their lives. The prospect is that two-thirds of their adult years will be spent without children in the household and half to two-thirds without a husband."

As a consequence of the increased labor force participation of women, job practices and family practices became more closely related. The absence of such family-enhancing policies as flexible working time, child-care facilities, and maternity leave has a strong impact on American families and, in turn, probably has important effects on delinquency, the development of children, and other social problems.

The greater availability of such social services probably is a major reason for the superior earnings positions of women in other industrialized countries. Such services as child allowances, health care, child care, pregnancy leave, and flexible working time all facilitate the continuity of employment by women and, therefore, their more equal wage-earning profiles. Of course the opportunities for women were also aided by tighter labor markets in Europe during most of the postwar period. In addition, European school children typically spend more hours and days in school than do American children—240 days versus 160 in the United States—resulting in less need for child-care facilities for school-age children.

The increased labor force participation by women has been accompanied by other important trends that interact to condition the nature and extent of employment opportunities for women:

1. Declining fertility rates have been an important trend reflecting and affecting changes in women's employment. The average birthrate has declined from 22.3 per thousand in the 1935–1955 period to 19.5 per thousand between 1955 and 1978 and is expected to be 15.8 for 1975 through 1995 to 2000 (Marshall, 1979). These declines in birthrates reflect changing employment and life-styles for women. They mean that more time can be devoted to work outside the home. These declining fertility rates also mean that there will be less job competition in the future from domestic population increases. Moreover, declining birthrates, if sustained, would imply an aging population.

Related to the decline in fertility rates is the fact that young women are delaying marriage. In 1960 only 28.4 percent of 20- to 24-year-old women had never been married; by 1983 this proportion had increased to 55.5 percent.

2. There have been some significant changes in the age composition of the work force, and these will continue during the 1980s. Youth job pressure will be relieved somewhat by the fact that 4 million fewer 16- to 24-year-olds will enter the work force during the 1980s. The most dramatic change will be in the 25–44 age group, reflecting the aging of the postwar baby boom generation. In 1975 there were only 39 million people in this category; by 1990 there will be more than 60 million. This will greatly intensify job competition in this group, as it will constitute over half the work force in 1990. Intensified competition for jobs could make this group less supportive of affirmative action programs for women and minorities unless special efforts are made to gain their support.

There are also those who believe that the decline in the number of 16- to 24-year-olds will create labor shortages among young workers. We do not share this belief because these projections are based on the native-born population. If we are unable to control illegal immigration, there will be a continuing influx of undocumented workers in the secondary labor market where many young workers are concentrated. If, however, temporary labor shortages should occur among young people, it would improve their relative earnings and lead to improvements in the nature of jobs they hold. Moreover, some projections of labor shortages among young workers assume a continuation of patterns of "male" and "female" jobs. These shortages could be overcome and labor markets made more efficient by the reduction of labor market segregation. Unfortunately, however, analysts probably are correct in assuming that these patterns will change relatively slowly.

The changing age composition will also result in a growing proportion of older women in the population. Greater attention to the special needs of this group will be required. These needs include the ability to work, but also special income support for those who cannot work or who have inadequate retirement systems because those systems have discriminated against women. Older workers also have special housing and health needs.

3. Technological changes have had important effects on the employment of women, especially in shifting the occupation mix more toward the services, which represented almost three-fourths of the American labor force in 1985. Technological changes also have lengthened female life expectancy, reduced the number of years spent in childbearing, and the time required for housework, and have greatly increased the time women have for labor market work.

Although women accounted for 68 percent of the increase in white-collar employment, they remained heavily concentrated in traditionally female occupations. In 1983, women constituted 80 percent of all administrative support (including clerical) workers, but only 8 percent of precision production, craft, and repair workers; they were 70 percent of retail and personal sales workers, but only 32 percent of managers, administrators, and executives.

Despite the fact that a large percentage of women remained in traditional occupations, there were significant relative increases in nontraditional areas like medicine, law, and accounting. In 1970, 60 percent of all female professional and technical workers were in the traditional occupations of nursing and noncollege teaching; this number had dropped to about 52 percent by 1979.

Table 11 gives a more detailed breakdown of the occupational distribution of employed women between 1950 and 1981. Women have increased their proportion in professional and managerial jobs, while there has been a slight decrease in sales and significant declines in the private household, operatives, and farm categories. The number of women in craft jobs has increased, especially since 1960.

TABLE 11
Occupational Distribution of Employed Women, Annual Averages,
Selected Years 1950–1981

Occupation	1950	1960	1970	1979	1981	Women as % of All Workers in Occ., 1981
Total (in 1,000s)	17,340	21,874	29,667	40,446	42,145	42.9
Percent	100.0	100.0	100.0	100.0	100.0	—
Professional/technical	12.5	12.4	14.5	16.1	17.0	44.7
Managerial, administrative except farm	4.4	5.0	4.5	6.4	7.4	27.4
Sales	8.7	7.7	7.0	6.9	6.8	45.4
Clerical	27.8	30.3	34.5	35.0	34.7	80.5
Craft	1.5	1.0	1.1	1.8	1.9	6.3
Operatives, including transport	19.6	15.2	14.5	11.5	9.7[a]	39.8
Nonfarm laborers	0.8	0.4	0.5	1.3	1.2	11.5
Service, except private household	12.4	14.8	16.5	17.2	17.1	59.3
Private household	8.7	8.9	5.1	2.6	2.3	96.5
Farm and farm managers	3.6[b]	.5	.3	.3	.4	11.3
Farm laborers and supervisors		3.2	1.5	.9	.8	25.7

Sources: U.S. Department of Labor, Bureau of Labor Statistics, *Perspectives on Working Women: A Databook,* Bull. 2080 (October 1980); for 1980 data, U.S. Department of Labor, Women's Bureau, *Equal Employment Opportunity for Women: U.S. Policies* (1982).
[a] 1981 data exclude transportation.
[b] 1950 data include farm and farm managers and laborers and supervisors.

According to data from the Equal Employment Opportunity Commission, the proportions of the total professional labor force represented by different groups were as follows:

	1966	1979
White women	13.0%	31.6%
Black women	0.6	2.2
Black men	0.7	1.9
White men	83.5	58.9
Other, including Asian and Hispanic Americans and American Indians	2.2	5.4

As these data show, white women have made particularly impressive gains in broad professional occupations. However, considerable job segregation exists within these broad classifications.

4. The trends toward higher inflation and unemployment also have important implications for the employment of women. The inflationary biases built into traditional management macroeconomic demand policies were aggravated by external shocks to the economy during the 1970s. The monetarist policies adopted to reduce inflation have greatly increased unemployment. Structural unemployment was already serious for the United States and other countries, especially Third World countries, and is likely to continue to be a worldwide problem, at least for the rest of this century. High levels of unemployment limit the nature and extent of jobs available to women at the very time that increasing unemployment of other family members puts greater pressure on women to work.

The unemployment rates for women generally have been higher than those for men overall—5.9 percent and 4.4 percent in 1970—but the differential was eliminated during 1980. The 1981–1982 recession was unique in that while previous recessions (1961–1962 and 1970–1971, for example) temporarily halted the increase in women's labor force participation and increased the unemployment differentials between men and women, the labor force participation rate continued to increase during the 1981–1982 recession and the unemployment rate for men rose faster than that for women.

However, women have been much more vulnerable than men to increasing unemployment in the managerial and administrative occupations. In October 1982, when overall unemployment in the category was 3.6 percent, the unemployment rate of women was 4.7 percent. At the same time the overall unemployment rates were 9.8 percent for men and 8.6 percent for women.

5. Another important trend is the declining rate of productivity growth, which reduces the competitiveness of American firms, makes it difficult to improve real incomes, and aggravates social tensions. Real wages in the United States declined during the 1970s, but real per capita incomes were sustained by the increased employment of women. Obviously, this is a self-limiting process because not many families have additional wives they can send into the work force. In the future, therefore, greater attention will have to be given to improving productivity as a way of increasing incomes or preventing them from declining.

The reasons for the decline in productivity are not well understood, but many experts give heavy weight to capital formation and the American management system. While these and other factors are important, probably the most important causes of changes in our productivity are uncoordinated, discontinuous, and unstable national economic policies.

6. The internationalization of the American economy has intensified competition. As the policies of multinational corporations have
become increasingly important factors in the labor market, competition between workers in the United States and other countries
(especially low-wage Third World countries) has increased, with the
result that the traditional authoritarian "scientific management" system is being challenged and American firms are finding it necessary to
pay much more attention to efficiency and productivity. Internationalization has also contributed to unemployment among women
who are heavily concentrated in the industries most vulnerable to
competition, even though in the recessions of 1979–1980 and
1981–1982, as noted earlier, most of the increase in unemployment was
in male-dominated industries.

At the beginning of the 1980s, despite some occupational upgrading, women had about the same earnings relative to men as they had at
the beginning of the 1970s. Women who worked full-time in 1963
earned about 63 percent as much as men. Although women came close
to achieving parity in some newer occupations such as computer
science, most of them had the lower-paying jobs in each occupation.
This is especially unfortunate since most women work because of
economic need. Almost two-thirds of all women in the civilian labor
force in March 1984 were either single (26 percent), divorced (11 percent), widowed (5 percent), separated (4 percent), or had husbands
whose 1983 incomes were less than $15,000 (19 percent).

Despite their lower relative earnings, working wives make substantial contributions to family incomes. In the 51 percent of families
where both husbands and wives worked, median income was $23,000
in 1978, compared with $17,000 for families where only the husband
worked. Working wives who were employed all year contributed
38 percent to family income, but they contributed only 11 percent to
family income where they worked part-time or less than 26 weeks full-
time.

The dual-earner family became dominant during the 1970s. In
1920 only 9 percent of wives were employed. A dramatic increase in
the number of working wives occurred during the late 1960s; by 1968,
45 percent of all families were dual-earners, and only the husbands
worked in 31 percent (Hayghe, 1981). There was a tendency for wives
to work in the same general occupational category as their husbands. A
study of dual-earner families showed that they usually were younger,
58 percent had children under age 18 (as contrasted with 60 percent of
traditional families), were better educated, were more prevalent
among black than among white or Hispanic couples, and had 20 percent higher incomes than traditional families, primarily because of the
wives' earnings.

Incomes of dual-earner families are much less likely to be below the official poverty line than are those of traditional families (1.8 vs. 5.5 percent in 1978). Among dual-earner families, those below the poverty line tend to be younger and have less education, but a major reason for their poverty is that they work less than those whose incomes are above the poverty line. In 1978, 62 percent of husbands and 22 percent of wives in dual-earner families worked full-time 40 weeks or more; the comparable figures for nonpoor dual-earner families were 88 percent for husbands and 51 percent for wives.

Unemployment has a particularly severe effect on the earnings of dual-earner families if it is the husband who becomes unemployed. In the second quarter of 1980, median weekly earnings of dual-earner families were $532, compared with only $375 for the traditional family. However, if the husband was unemployed, median weekly family income fell to about $190. If the wife was unemployed, median weekly family income fell to $310, but where both spouses were working and another member of the household was unemployed, it averaged between $570 and $580.

Table 12 shows poverty to be heavily concentrated among blacks and women. Families headed by white women are almost three times as likely to be poor as those headed by white men (27.1 vs. 10.4 percent), and those headed by black women are about five times as likely to be poor as those headed by white men (51.7 vs. 10.4 percent).

The extent of the feminization of poverty is suggested by the fact that in 1983 almost half of all poor people in the United States lived in families headed by women. That year 36 percent of families headed by women were poor, contrasted with only 13 percent of families headed by men and 7 percent of married couple families. The reasons for the greater incidence of poverty in female-headed households are the

TABLE 12
Poverty Rate by Type of Family, 1984

Family Type	Poverty Rate (Percent)
White families	9.1
Married-couple families	8.3
Male households, no wife	10.4
Female households, no husband	27.1
Black families	30.9
Married-couple families	13.8
Male households, no wife	23.8
Female households, no husband	51.7

Source: U.S. Bureau of the Census, Current Population Reports, "Money Income and Poverty Status of Families and Persons in the U.S.," Series P-60, No. 149, 1984.

concentration of women in low-paying jobs, inadequate pension provisions for women, and the fact that divorce often reduces women to poverty. This condition is rendered most serious in the many cases where mothers with children receive no support payments from absent fathers (see Table 13).

One of the reasons for women's lower earning rates is their concentration in low-paying jobs. Moreover, the age-earnings profiles for women are flat relative to those of men; they peak much earlier. One explanation for this pattern, advanced by human capital theorists, is that women anticipate periods of withdrawal from the labor market for childbearing and therefore choose occupations where the withdrawal penalties are low and lifetime earnings growth is relatively low (Mincer and Polachek, 1974, 1978; Polachek, 1976, 1979, 1981).

However, this theory has been challenged by studies that attribute the sex-earnings ratios more to employment policies and labor market discrimination and less to choices made by women.[15] These studies show that women lose relatively little from withdrawal and recoup their losses relatively fast when they reenter the work force. A more plausible explanation for the lower job growth of women is the fact that they have less seniority in the labor force and interrupt their job tenure for childbearing. Employers apparently structure jobs for women to accommodate this pattern and provide less opportunity for on-the-job training that leads to higher-paying jobs. The experience factor, moreover, is becoming more favorable for women because the main reason for their increased labor force participation rate is not *new entry* rates, but the fact that *experienced women are reentering or never leaving* the work force (Barrett, 1980).

TABLE 13
Child Support Payments to Mothers from Absent Fathers, 1983

| | Mothers Receiving No Payments (1,000s) | | Mothers Receiving Some Payments | |
| | | | No. Receiving Payments (1,000s) | Mean Yearly Income from Child Support |
Number of Own Children	Awarded but Not Received	Not Awarded		
1	433	1,938	1,497	$1,779
2	375	1,088	1,092	2,782
3	127	429	332	2,943
4 or more	23	241	118	3,705

Source: U.S. Bureau of the Census, Current Population Reports, "Child Support and Alimony," Series P-23, No. 141, 1983.

---

[15] For reviews of these theories, see Hartmann and Reskin (1983).

While labor market factors account for some of the male-female earnings differential, careful studies have found that *less than half of the gross earnings differentials* can be accounted for by such human capital factors as education, training, experience, and skill (Hartmann and Reskin, 1983). The large unexplained residual is attributable to overt and institutional discrimination, especially job segregation.

As noted, there have been large earnings differentials between predominantly male and female occupations. A 1981 study of 1970 data found that workers in predominantly female occupations earn on average $4,000 less than those in predominantly male occupations (Treiman and Hartmann, 1981). Of course, some of these earnings differentials can be explained by the characteristics of occupations in which men and women are concentrated, but the impact of occupational segregation appears to be larger the more detailed the occupational classification; the most detailed Census data make it possible to attribute more than one-third of the sex differential to job segregation. This is probably an underestimate because the earnings in different occupations are themselves affected by job segregation. It has been found, for example, that earnings differentials by sex are largest in those occupations dominated by males (Treiman and Hartmann, 1981), even though the highest-paying occupations for women are those dominated by men.

These trends suggest that women have made some progress toward integrating occupations but are a long way from equality. While conclusive proof is not available, there is little doubt that a major factor responsible for the integration of nontraditional occupations has been pressure from the federal government to enforce antidiscrimination legislation and the affirmative action requirements for government contractors. Surveys suggest that women in managerial positions, in particular, feel that discrimination is the main barrier to their advancement and that during the 1980s "businesses sense less federal pressure to hire and promote women as part of affirmative action requirements" (Lublin, 1982).

A favorable factor in the future employment of women in professional, technical, and managerial positions is the increasing proportion of them with college and professional degrees. Women earned 8 percent of the law degrees in 1970 and 48 percent in 1980; for medical degrees the increase was from 10 to 33 percent, and for MBAs it was from 3 to 21 percent. For undergraduate degrees as well, there is increasing convergence by sex.

The median educational levels of women and men have been about equal since 1970; both had medians of 12.2 in 1970 and 12.6 in 1979, and in March 1984 the median for women was 12.7 years and for men it was 12.8. There have been marked declines in the proportions of women (30.6 in 1970 and 14.4 in March 1984) and men (37.3 in 1970 and 18.0 in 1984) in the labor force who had completed less than four years of high school and marked increases in the proportions who had completed four years of college—for women, 10.7 percent in 1970 and 22.2 percent in 1984, and for men, 14.2 percent in 1970 and 27.9 percent in 1984.

Data on the proportion of women who have had four or more years of college indicate significant differences by age groups, with more young women than men ages 18–24 having four or more years of higher education, but larger proportions of men than of women in the older categories with equivalent education. More men than women in every age category did not complete four years of high school, as is indicated in the following summary:

Age and Sex	Percent of Labor Force with:	
	Less than Four Years of High School	*Four Years of College*
18–24 years		
Women	14.7	9.4
Men	23.9	8.4
25–34 years		
Women	11.2	24.7
Men	13.2	27.8
35–64 years		
Women	22.6	15.2
Men	27.5	22.2

(*Source:* Bureau of Labor Statistics, *Employment in Perspective: Working Women,* Report 650, 2nd quarter 1981).

Women college graduates earned only slightly more than men high school dropouts in 1983—$14,679 and $12,117, respectively. Women high school graduates working full-time year-round had an average income lower than that of fully employed men who had completed less than four years of elementary school.

To some extent, occupational and earnings differences reflect differentials in education as well as in continuity of employment and work experience. However, there is no doubt that a large residual, estimated by one study to be between one-half and one-third of the earnings differentials between men and women, cannot be accounted for after controlling for these factors (U.S. Department of Labor, Women's Bureau, 1979; *Economic Report of the President,* 1974, p. 155). Studies that do control for educational attainment show wide differentials in earnings and career patterns between men and women.

A 1980 study by Susan Bailey and Barbara Burrell found that seven years after graduating from Harvard Law School, *25 percent of men and only 1 percent of women were partners in law firms.* The average salaries of graduates of the Harvard School of Public Health were $37,800 a year for men and $21,300 for women. This survey examined the careers of 1972 graduates of Harvard's schools of law, dentistry, design, divinity, education, public health, and arts and sciences seven years after students were awarded advanced degrees. Women graduates had consistently lower salaries regardless of marital or family status. The study concluded that there was "convincing evidence that subtle biases continue to constrain the career development of many women."

However, the main determinants of future employment growth for women will be the growth of nonprofessional occupations because that is where most of the jobs are. These will, in turn, depend on general economic conditions and the extent to which women are able to break into nontraditional occupations.

Another determinant of the future economic prospects for women will be their relationship with unions. Although unions have been male-dominated institutions in the United States and abroad, women are increasing their membership in absolute numbers. Unions are major economic and political forces, and their policies will affect female as well as male workers. The objectives of some unions will sometimes conflict with those of women's groups—like the establishment of goals and timetables in the construction industry or when women's groups challenge established union seniority systems in order to improve job opportunities for women—but there will be broad, overlapping interests between unions and women's groups, making their cooperation mutually advantageous. An illustration of the kinds of things unions can and have done to promote female (and, therefore, their own) economic interests is illustrated by the pay equity, comparable worth, or "equal pay for work of equal value" issue which has become a major economic goal for women in the 1980s.

Conclusions

Despite dramatic increases in the labor force participation rates of women and substantial relative changes in their occupational positions, they have yet to achieve equality in the labor market. The disadvantages they suffer generally are an inheritance from the past when women's legal and personal rights were closely circumscribed by law and custom. This burden of history was carried over into the industrial market economy in which women initially were considered temporary, peripheral participants in a male-dominated economy.

A number of factors have contributed to women's increased labor force participation, including technological changes that gave women more control over the number of children they might have, their increased life expectancy, the mechanization of household work, and an increase in the number of nonhousehold jobs considered "suitable" for women. These changes were accompanied by rising living standards and changing social attitudes about "women's work" and the place of women in society. Other factors contributing to the improvement of women's employment position were their rising education levels, tight labor markets, especially during wars, and the civil rights movement which focused public attention on employment discrimination against women as well as minorities.

Despite considerable progress, important labor market disadvantages for women remain, especially in occupational segregation and pay. Labor market factors provide an explanation for some of the pay differential, but even the most objective studies find a large part of it unexplained. There can be little question that discrimination accounts for much of this residual.

Efforts to reduce discrimination against women must be based on a clear understanding of the reasons for discrimination and what is required for change. The concept of discrimination that seems most compatible with reality is one that perceives it as based on a combination of status and economic interests. Status is a very strong human motivator. It enters into employment through job hierarchies. Race and sex enter this hierarchical relationship because women and blacks have been considered "inferior" people whose inclusion will denigrate high-status jobs. Economic interests enter because participants in employment relationships use discrimination for their own economic motives—preservation of jobs for incumbents, increased power to protect jobs and working conditions, or profit maximization. Managers, for example, can reduce labor costs by discriminating against women; their status considerations are revealed by their reluctance to hire women in managerial lines. Of course, management's ability to discriminate against women reduces men's ability to improve their conditions.

Discrimination may be overt or institutional. Overt discrimination is where specific employment decisions are made on the basis of some factor other than merit or qualifications. Institutionalized patterns do not require specific decisions; they are based on prevailing ideas of "status" or the proper occupations and pay for men and women. These patterns are institutionalized because even the victims of discrimination ordinarily adjust to them.

Discriminatory patterns are changed and perpetuated by moral, economic, physical, or political power—defined as the ability to create or to prevent change. Because discrimination is hard to define in a democratic society, those interested in change usually attempt to employ moral power. However, moral power, while very potent in the long run, tends to be less effective than other tactics in the short run. Nevertheless, the history of discrimination suggests that the burden of initiating and carrying through the processes that eliminate discrimination must rest with the victims. Nobody else is likely to assign as high a priority to eliminating discrimination.

National policy must give greater weight to women's issues because the effective and equitable development of female human resources will have important implications for the nation's political, social, and economic health.

The federal government's antidiscrimination and economic and social policies have helped to improve the economic position of women as well as minorities. However, antidiscrimination policies, though necessary, have not been sufficient to improve the conditions of women and minorities. Cooperative relationships between the civil rights enforcement agencies and between these agencies and the private sector are desirable objectives, but there will always be some who will not cooperate; therefore, voluntary efforts must be backed by sufficient penalties to encourage cooperation and deter violation. The arguments about quotas and reverse discrimination are false issues that divert attention from the real problem—the need to take *positive measures* to break down *institutional patterns* of discrimination against people for reasons unrelated to their merit and ability. Goals and timetables are not quotas, and special programs to help people overcome the consequences of past discrimination are not necessarily reverse discrimination.

The United States derives rich benefits from being a multiracial, multicultural society. But it is hard to see how we can derive the benefits of such a system and avoid dangerous and debilitating social strife without equal opportunity, and it is hard to see how equal opportunity can be a reality in the face of institutionalized discrimination without affirmative action.

But antidiscrimination programs are not sufficient if significant improvements are to be made in the economic conditions of women. General economic policies to reduce unemployment and foster full utilization of our resources and special targeted programs to deal with the needs of particular groups also are required. High unemployment levels create great difficulty for women in particular. Both the 1981 tax and subsequent spending cuts probably adversely affected women, as they are heavily concentrated in low-income jobs that did not benefit from the reduction in taxes and which bore the main brunt of cuts in human resource development programs. Over 70 percent of the program cuts now in place fall on low-income groups. These include education, job-training, Medicaid, housing aid, food stamps, school nutrition, aid to poor families with children, energy assistance, and unemployment compensation.

Finally, there is a need for the United States to develop more systematic policies to deal with the reality that women are permanent and integral parts of the labor force and that the "traditional" pattern of men being the only family income-earners is obsolete. This requires particular attention to the labor market needs of women at different stages in their lives: career selection and development, childbearing and reentry into the work force, ability to enter nontraditional jobs, a policy with respect to child care for working mothers (especially low-income working mothers), health care for women and children, and special housing, income support, and health care needs of older women whose proportion of the population will be increasing. There also is a need to require divorced fathers to provide more support for their children.

References

Bailey, Susan, and Barbara Burell. *Second Century Radcliffe News*, Winter 1980.
Baker, Elizabeth. *Technology and Women's Work*. New York: Columbia University Press, 1964.
Barrett, Nancy. "Productivity Impact of the Housework Shift." Washington: U.S. Department of Labor, May 1980.
Blood, Kathryn. *Negro Women War Workers*. U.S. Department of Labor, Women's Bureau, Bull. 205. Washington: U.S. Government Printing Office, 1945.
Branson, William H. "Trends in United States International Trade and Investment Since World War II." In *The American Economy in Transition*, ed. Martin Feldstein. Chicago: University of Chicago Press, 1980. Pp. 183–257.
Buckley, J.E. "Equal Pay in America." In *Equal Pay for Women*, ed. Barrie O. Pettman. Washington: Hemisphere Publishing Corp., 1977. Pp. 35–61.
Campbell, Helen. *Women Wage Earners*. Boston: Roberts Brothers, 1893. Reprint—New York: Arno Press, 1972.
Davis, Kingsley, and Pietronella van den Oever. "The Demographics of Feminism." *Washington Times*, July 1, 1982.
Economic Report of the President. Washington: U.S. Government Printing Office, 1974.
Farnham, Rebecca. *Women at Work: A Century of Industrial Change*. U.S. Department of Labor, Women's Bureau, Bull. 161. Washington: U.S. Government Printing Office, 1939.
Foner, Philip S. *Women and the American Labor Movement*, Vol. 1. New York: Free Press, 1979.
Freeman, Richard B. "The Evolution of the American Labor Market, 1948–1980." In *The American Economy in Transition*, ed. Martin Feldstein. Chicago: University of Chicago Press, 1980. Pp. 349–96.
Hartmann, Heidi I. "Capitalism, Patriarchy, and Job Segregation by Sex." In *Women and the Workplace*," eds. Martha Blaxall and Barbara Reagan. Chicago: University of Chicago Press, 1976. Pp. 137–169.

Hartmann, Heidi I., and Barbara F. Reskin. "Job Segregation: Trends and Prospects." Washington: National Academy Press, 1983.

Hayghe, Howard. "Husbands and Wives as Earners." *Monthly Labor Review* 104 (February 1981): pp. 46–59.

Heen, Mary. "A Review of Federal Court Decisions Under Title VII of the Civil Rights Act of 1964." In *Comparable Worth and Wage Discrimination: Technical Possibilities and Political Realities*, ed. Helen Remick. Philadelphia: Temple University Press, 1984. Pp. 197–219.

Hooks, Janet M. *Women's Occupations Through Seven Decades*. U.S. Department of Labor, Women's Bureau, Bull. 218. Washington: U.S. Government Printing Office, 1947.

Lublin, Joanna S. "White Collar Cutbacks Are Falling More Heavily on Women than Men." *Wall Street Journal*, November 9, 1982.

Marshall, Ray. "Productivity and Human Resources." Working paper, EPC, UNA, 1979.

Matthaei, Julie A. *An Economic History of Women in America*. New York: Schocken Books, 1982.

Mincer, Jacob, and Solomon W. Polachek. "Women's Earnings Reexamined." *Journal of Human Resources* 13 (Winter 1978): pp. 118–34.

––––––. "Family Investments in Human Capital: Earnings of Women." *Journal of Political Economy* 82 (March-April 1974): pp. S76–S108.

Pidgeon, Mary Elizabeth. *Changes in Women's Occupations: 1940–1950*. U.S. Department of Labor, Women's Bureau, Bull. 253. Washington: U.S. Government Printing Office, 1954.

––––––. *Employment of Women in the Early Postwar Period*. U.S. Department of Labor, Women's Bureau, Bull. 211. Washington: U.S. Government Printing Office, 1946.

––––––. *Women in the Economy of the United States of America*. U.S. Department of Labor, Women's Bureau, Bull. 155. Washington: U.S. Government Printing Office, 1937.

Polachek, Solomon W. "Occupational Self-Selection: A Human Capital Approach to Sex Differences in Occupational Structure." *Review of Economics and Statistics* 63 (February 1981): pp. 60–69.

––––––. "Occupational Segregation Among Women: Theory, Evidence, and a Prognosis." In *Women in the Labor Market*, eds. Cynthia B. Lloyd, Emily S. Andrews, and Curtis L. Gilroy. New York: Columbia University Press, 1979.

––––––. "Occupational Segregation: An Alternative Hypothesis." *Journal of Contemporary Business* (Winter 1976): pp. 1–12.

Robinson, Mary. "Women Workers in Two Wars." *Monthly Labor Review* 60 (October 1943): pp. 650–71.

Taylor, Frederick Winslow. *The Principles of Scientific Management*. New York: Norton, 1967.

Treiman, Donald J., and Heidi I. Hartmann, eds. *Women, Work, and Wages: Equal Pay for Jobs of Equal Value*. Committee on Occupational Classification and Analysis, Assembly of Behavioral and Social Sciences, National Research Council. Washington: National Academy Press, 1981.

U.S. Bureau of the Census. *Statistical Abstract of the U.S.: 1985* (105th ed.). Washington: U.S. Government Printing Office, 1984.

––––––. *Historical Statistics of the U.S.: Colonial Times to 1970, Bicentennial Edition*, Part 2. Washington: U.S. Government Printing Office, 1975.

U.S. Department of Labor, Bureau of International Labor Affairs. *Demographic and Occupational Characteristics of Workers in Trade-Sensitive Industries*. Economic Discussion Paper No. 2, 1980.

U.S. Department of Labor, Bureau of Labor Statistics. *Occupational Outlook Quarterly* 29, No. 2 (Summer 1985).
———. Occupational Outlook Quarterly 28, No. 1 (Spring 1984).
———. *Occupational Outlook Handbook*, 1984–85 ed. Bull. 2205. Washington: U.S. Government Printing Office, April 1984.
———. *History of Wages in the U.S. from Colonial Times to 1928*. Bull. 604. Washington: U.S. Government Printing Office, 1934.
U.S. Department of Labor, Women's Bureau. "Facts of Women Workers." Washington: U.S. Government Printing Office, 1984.
———. *Time of Change: 1983 Handbook on Women Workers*. Washington: U.S. Government Printing Office, 1983.
———. *Equal Employment Opportunity for Women: U.S. Policies*. Washington: U.S. Government Printing Office, 1982.
———. *The Employment of Women: General Diagnosis of Development and Issues*. Washington: U.S. Government Printing Office, April 1979.
———. *Handbook of Facts on Women Workers*. Bull. 237. Washington: U.S. Government Printing Office, 1950.
———. *Handbook of Facts on Women Workers*. Bull. 225. Washington: U.S. Government Printing Office, 1948.
———. *Women's Work in the War*. Bull. 193. Washington: U.S. Government Printing Office, 1942.

CHAPTER 2

Occupations and Earnings of Women Workers

FRANCINE D. BLAU*
MARIANNE A. FERBER**

Despite the dramatic influx of women into the labor market during this century, the differences in occupational distribution and earnings between men and women have changed relatively little. Data demonstrating this are presented in the first section of this chapter. However, these data do suggest that although progress has been fairly modest, the pace of change accelerated during the 1970s and early 1980s, providing grounds for cautious optimism regarding further narrowing of gender differentials in the future.

Beginning in the 1960s a number of explanations were proposed for sex differences in occupations and earnings. We discuss them briefly in the second section. In the third section we focus on the large empirical literature that has resulted from efforts to test competing explanations for these differentials. Lastly, we consider the implications of what we have learned and make some suggestions for additional research.

Differences in Occupations and Earnings: An Overview

Occupational Segregation

The most casual inspection of the labor market reveals that men and women tend to be employed in different occupations (see Table 1). In both 1972 and 1984, women were heavily concentrated in the administrative support (including clerical) and service occupations. Together these two categories accounted for 48 percent of women

---

* Professor of Economics and Labor and Industrial Relations, University of Illinois, Urbana-Champaign.

** Professor of Economics, University of Illinois, Urbana-Champaign.

Note: We would like to thank the editors of this volume for helpful comments and suggestions. Portions of this chapter draw upon Chapters 6 and 8 of Francine D. Blau and Marianne A. Ferber, *The Economics of Women, Men, and Work* (Englewood Cliffs, NJ: Prentice-Hall, © 1986). Reprinted by special permission of Prentice-Hall.

TABLE 1
Occupational Distribution of Men and Women, 1972 and 1984
(annual averages)

Occupational Category	1972			1984		
	% of Male Labor Force in Occupation	% of Female Labor Force in Occupation	Women as a % of Workers in Occupation	% of Male Labor Force in Occupation	% of Female Labor Force in Occupation	Women as a % of Workers in Occupation
Executive, administrative, and managerial	11.5	4.9	19.7	13.0	8.5	33.6
Professional specialty	9.7	12.4	44.0	11.6	14.0	48.5
Technicians and related support	2.3	2.4	38.4	2.8	3.3	48.1
Sales occupations	10.0	11.1	40.5	11.1	13.1	47.9
Administrative support, including clerical	6.4	31.5	75.0	5.7	29.1	79.9
Service occupations	8.3	21.2	61.1	9.4	18.7	60.8
Precision production, craft, and repair	19.4	1.7	4.8	20.2	2.4	8.5
Operators, fabricators, and laborers	25.9	13.4	24.1	21.1	9.6	26.0
Farming, forestry, and fishing	6.4	1.9	15.4	5.1	1.2	15.6
Total employed	100.0	100.0	38.0	100.0	100.0	43.7

Sources: U.S. Department of Labor, Bureau of Labor Statistics, *Employment and Earnings* (January 1984), Table 1, pp. 14–16; and U.S. Department of Labor, Bureau of Labor Statistics, *Employment and Earnings* (January 1985), Table 21, p. 175, and Table 22, pp. 176–80.

workers in 1984. Men were heavily represented in executive, administrative, and managerial positions, and even more so in precision
production, craft, and repair occupations, the strongholds of skilled
blue-collar workers, as well as farming, forestry, and fishing.

While the situation was roughly similar in both years, Table 1
reveals that there were some improvements. Women were less concentrated in administrative support and service occupations in 1984
than they had been in 1972. They also had made considerable inroads
into executive and managerial jobs, increasing their share of such
positions from 20 percent in 1972 to 34 percent in 1984. Nonetheless,
the figures in Table 1 amply demonstrate that considerable gender
differences in occupational distribution remain.

The data on major occupations in Table 1 do not reveal the full
extent of occupational segregation by sex. For example, among sales
workers, women tend to be employed as retail sales clerks, while men
are more likely to be manufacturing sales representatives. Among
professionals, women are concentrated in the traditionally female
professions—librarian, nurse, prekindergarten, kindergarten, and
elementary school teacher. Men are more likely to be in the traditionally male professions, including engineer, lawyer, and physician.

These differences between men and women are often referred to
as "occupational segregation" by sex. The degree of such segregation
can be measured by an index developed by Duncan and Duncan
(1955). It indicates the percentage of women, or men, who would have
to change jobs in order to duplicate the distribution of the other
group.[1] This index would be equal to zero if women (or men) composed
the same proportion of workers in each occupation as they composed in
the labor force as a whole.[2] At the other extreme, the index would be
equal to 100 if there were only male or only female workers employed
in each occupation.

A number of studies have calculated the index of segregation
using the more detailed breakdown of occupations for various Census
years. The precise number of job categories distinguished has varied,
but it is at least 300 in the early years and well in excess of 400 for the
more recent period. Gross (1968) calculated the index of occupational
segregation for each Census year from 1900 to 1960. The figures were
66.9 percent in 1900 and 68.4 in 1960, and they varied little over the

---

[1] The index is defined as follows:
$$s = \tfrac{1}{2} \Sigma \quad M_i - F_i$$
where M_i = the percentage of the male labor force in occupation i and F_i = the percentage of the
female labor force in occupation i.

[2] Or, looking at it another way, the index would be equal to zero if the same percentage of
female and male workers were employed in each occupation.

whole period.[3] These figures are not entirely reliable because of recurrent changes in the Census classification scheme. Blau and Hendricks (1979) suggested that the tendency to create more detailed classifications may have provided an upward bias over time. In order to determine possible changes in occupational segregation with somewhat greater precision, they relied on only 183 occupations for which it was possible to obtain comparable data for the 1950–1970 period. They found that the index rose slightly (by 1.1 percentage points) between 1950 and 1960, then dropped by 3.1 percentage points between 1960 and 1970.

More recent work suggests that the decline after 1960 may have been the beginning of a trend rather than merely another fluctuation. Beller (1984) found that the decrease in segregation accelerated during the 1970s, declining by 6.7 percentage points between 1972 and 1981.[4] Further, she discovered that the index was lower and had decreased somewhat more rapidly for younger cohorts in the 1970s.

The decline in occupational segregation during the 1970s was concentrated in traditionally male professional and managerial jobs. While many professions remained disproportionately male or female in 1980, a comparison of the data for that year with 1970 shows that women made notable progress in precisely those professional occupations that were most predominantly male in 1970. For example, the representation of women increased from 5 to 14 percent for lawyers, from 11 to 28 percent for operations and systems researchers and analysts, from 12 to 24 percent for pharmacists, and from 5 to 13 percent for veterinarians. There were similar large increases in many executive, administrative, and managerial occupations during this period. Extreme examples are a rise in the proportion of women from 0 to 26 percent for administrators, public administration; from 0 to 9 percent for administrators, protective services; and from 8 to 18 percent for managers, marketing, advertising, and public relations. Evidence that segregation is likely to decrease further is provided by developments in higher education where the influx of women into formerly male-dominated fields has been rapid, in some instances even dramatic. For example, among bachelor degree recipients the proportion of women rose by more than 400 percent in all fields where they composed less than 15 percent in 1970–1971.

Whatever evidence there is of a recent and impending decline in occupational segregation, men and women continued to experience a

---

[3] If any pattern might be noted, it is that there was a decline in the index during the two decades which included World War I, to 65.7 percent, and World War II, to 65.6 percent, when women tended to work in nontraditional jobs.

[4] Beller relied on data from the Current Population Survey conducted monthly by the Bureau of the Census.

very different occupational distribution in the early 1980s even in terms of broad categories, as we saw in Table 1, let alone when more detailed occupations are considered. It was still the case that more than 60 percent of women (or men) would have had to change jobs in 1981 for the occupational distributions of the two groups to be the same. In particular, thus far women have failed to make much progress in integrating the traditionally male-dominated blue-collar occupations.

Segregation Within Occupations

Not only are there differences in the distribution of men and women among occupations, there are also differences in the specific jobs they do within occupations and where they do them. We shall examine available evidence on both these issues.

There is considerable evidence of what is often termed vertical segregation. University faculties provide a good illustration. Among full-time faculty in institutions of higher education in 1981, only 10 percent of full professors and 21 percent of associate professors, but 36 percent of assistant professors and 51 percent of instructors and lecturers were women. The importance of this becomes especially obvious in view of the association of the two highest ranks with tenure, while other ranks provide no comparable job security. Almost 60 percent of male faculty, but only half that proportion of female faculty, have reached that privileged level. This ratio has remained about the same since the middle 1970s.

Another example of a hierarchy, though one that combined vertical with occupational segregation, is the Federal Civil Service, which uses grades. While all Civil Service jobs have job security after a probationary period, grades have a strong association with salary as well as with prestige and power. More than 70 percent of those in the six lowest ranks are women; their percentage in the highest seven ranks is 10 percent.

These two cases are particularly clear-cut, but they are illustrative of a widespread phenomenon. Though women's representation among managers and officials increased considerably in recent decades, their representation in top positions continues to be extremely sparse.

In addition to working at different levels within occupations, men and women are also frequently segregated by industry and even by firm. It has been noted, for instance, that the proportion of women assemblers is far higher in the electrical machinery equipment and supplies industry than in motor vehicles and motor vehicle equipment. Similarly, women make up a far larger proportion of drivers of school buses than of mass transit buses. A common example of individual firms hiring members of only one sex to do work that is widely performed by both is that of establishments employing only men or only women to wait on tables.

One study of employment patterns of male and female office workers in three large northeastern cities revealed a strong and consistent pattern of sex segregation by establishment among workers in the same occupational categories (Blau, 1977). More recently, Baron and Bielby (1984) reported that of over 400 work organizations in their sample, 59 percent were perfectly segregated by sex—no men and women shared the same job title—and in the remainder of the firms the median amount of segregation was 84.1 percent. Such findings make it clear to what extent it is still unusual for workers of both sexes to do the same work, side-by-side. Beyond that, there is some concern that occupations which have become integrated as the result of an influx of women may once again become segregated, as men move out or reduce their entry (Reskin and Roos, forthcoming).

Historically, there have been a number of occupations that were initially male but came to be female. Two of the best-known examples are primary school teachers and secretaries. Some recent examples of changeovers in the sex composition of occupational categories include computer operators (women made up 33.9 percent of these workers in 1970, but 59.1 percent in 1980) and insurance adjusters, where the percentage of women rose from 29.6 to 60.2. In some cases such trends are associated with technological changes that reduce the need for knowledge and judgment in the occupation (Reskin and Roos, forthcoming).

Changes in Occupational Segregation: An Appraisal

While a variety of developments bear watching before we may reach firm conclusions on the consequences for women of recent declines in occupational segregation, it is very likely that much of the observed decline does represent enhanced labor market opportunities for women and that the decrease will continue in the future. The group that can most readily respond to new opportunities, given the difficulty in changing occupations in midcareer, is younger women. And, indeed, the decrease in occupational segregation is particularly pronounced for this group. This means that change is necessarily something of a slow process, but may be expected to gain momentum as more recent cohorts of women who are less occupationally segregated replace the older ones.

The Earnings Gap

The most widely used measure of the earnings gap is the ratio of annual earnings of full-time, year-round female as compared with male workers. Table 2 shows the relevant data since 1955 when this information first became available. There are at least two ways of looking at

TABLE 2

Median Annual and Usual Weekly Earnings of
Full-time Women Workers as Percent of Men's Earnings,
Selected Years, 1955–1985

	Annual[a]	Weekly[b]
1955	63.9	—
1960	60.8	—
1965	60.0	—
1970	59.4	62.3
1975	58.8	62.0
1976	60.2	62.2
1977	58.9	61.9
1978	59.7	61.3
1979	60.0	62.4
1980	60.2	63.4
1981	59.2	64.6
1982	61.7	65.0
1983	63.6	65.6
1984	63.7	67.8
1985	—	68.2

Sources: U.S. Bureau of Labor Statistics, U.S. Working Women: A Databook (1955–1975), Bulletin 1977; Earl F. Mellor, "Investigating the Differences in Weekly Earnings of Women and Men," Monthly Labor Review 107 (June 1984): pp. 17–28 (weekly earnings 1970–1983); U.S. Bureau of the Census, Current Population Reports, Consumer Income Series P-60, Money Income of Households, Families, and Persons in the United States (annual earnings 1976–1984), various issues; Bureau of National Affairs, Inc., Daily Labor Report, No. 23 (February 4, 1986) (weekly earnings 1984–1985).

[a] Includes year-round, full-time workers only. Includes income from self-employment.

[b] Includes all full-time workers, regardless of weeks worked. Excludes income from self-employment.

this information. One is that, although there have been some modest fluctuations during the intervening years, the ratio was virtually the same in 1984 as in 1955. Alternatively, it may be noted that there was an increase, albeit a slow and unsteady one, from 58.9 percent in 1977 to 63.7 percent in 1984.

This interpretation gains further credence from the second series in Table 2, which shows the ratio of usual weekly earnings. These data have only more recently become available. It will be noted that in each year the earnings ratio computed on the basis of weekly earnings is slightly higher than the annual figure.[5] More important, there was a

---

[5] The reasons for the differences in the weekly and annual series are discussed in Rytina (1983). Women's weekly earnings are estimated to be an even higher percent of men's, even among full-time workers (those working 35 hours or more per week) when an adjustment is made for hours worked. O'Neill (1985) reports a figure of 72 percent for 1983 after this adjustment. This figure must, however, be viewed with some caution because of the inevitable lack of accuracy of estimates of hours worked (see Borjas, 1980).

fairly steady upward trend from 61.3 percent in 1978 to 68.2 percent in 1985, averaging about one percentage point per year.

On the basis of these data, we tentatively conclude that a trend toward a narrowing of sex differentials in earnings began in the late 1970s or early 1980s (see also O'Neill, 1985; Blau and Beller, 1984; and Smith and Ward, 1984). Nonetheless, given the persistence of a substantial earnings gap between women and men, it is interesting to examine the situation for workers with various levels of schooling and in different age groups.[6] As we shall see, consideration of the latter topic provides clues to the expected behavior of the male-female earnings gap in the future. Unfortunately, the relevant data are available only for income, not earnings. The former includes such items as interest, dividends, and transfer payments as well as earnings. But for the great majority of the employed population these items are quite small.[7]

As can be seen in Table 3, education has a strong positive effect on the income of both groups, but it takes considerably more years of schooling for women to achieve the same earnings as men. For instance, in both 1967 and 1983, males with only an elementary school education earned more than female high school graduates, while male high school graduates had higher incomes than women who had completed college. Also, there was no clear tendency for women's earnings relative to men's to increase with years of schooling. Hence, a rising level of education for both men and women cannot be expected of itself to reduce the income gap. Despite the similarities in the patterns of sex differentials in the two years, it is worth noting that the ratio of women's as compared with men's income increased for all levels of schooling between 1967 and 1983.

Over the life cycle women earned less than men in all age groups, but the extent to which this is the case varies considerably. In 1983 the differential was only 4 percent for the youngest group, ages 15–19, but increased steadily to 44 percent for those between ages 40 and 54.[8] Does this merely indicate that men's earnings tend to rise more steeply with age than do women's, or does it show that young women are doing better now than their predecessors did? The data for one point in time do not enable us to answer this question. Information in Table 4, however, does help to shed some light on this subject.

---

[6] Minority women are discussed in Malveaux and Wallace, Chapter 10 of this book. Therefore we do not consider differences by race here.

[7] In 1982, for instance, when median earnings were $21,077 for men and $13,014 for women, the corresponding figures were $21,655 and $13,663 for income. Accordingly, women's earnings were 62 percent of men's, while women's income was 63 percent of men's.

[8] The narrower income gap after age 54 may be explained by the larger proportion of men who partially retire for a time before entirely leaving the labor market. This often involves a reduction in earnings, even when they continue to work at least 35 hours per week (Honig, 1983).

TABLE 3
Median Income for Men and Women
Working Year-Round, Full-Time, by Years of Schooling,
1967 and 1983[a]

Years of Schooling	1967			1983		
	Income		Women's Income as Percent of Men's	Income		Women's Income as Percent of Men's
	Men	Women		Men	Women	
Elementary						
Less than 8	$ 4,831	$2,820	58.4%	$14,093	$ 9,385	66.6%
8	6,133	3,343	54.5	16,438	10,337	62.9
High school						
1–3	6,891	3,704	53.8	17,685	11,131	62.9
4	7,732	4,499	58.2	21,823	13,787	63.2
College						
1–3	8,816	5,253	59.6	24,613	16,536	67.2
4	11,571	6,796	58.7	29,892	18,452	61.7
5 or more	12,510	7,823	62.5	34,643	22,877	66.4

Source: U.S. Bureau of the Census, Current Population Reports, Consumer Income Series P-60, No. 145, Money Income of Households, Families, and Persons in the United States.
[a] Data refer to workers 25 years of age and older.

The data, which focus on adults in the prime working years, show that young women's incomes were a higher percent of men's than were those of older women in each year. But it is also the case that the ratio of women's to men's earnings was higher for each age group in 1983 than it had been in 1967 and 1973. The gains were most pronounced for the 25–34 age group whose relative income increased by almost 11 percentage points between 1973 and 1983. This suggests clear improvements in women's, especially young women's, relative earnings over

TABLE 4
Median Income of Women Working Year-Round,
Full-Time as Percent of Men's Income, by Age

Age	1967	1973	1983
25–34	62.2%	62.6%	73.3%
35–44	55.1	52.5	61.3
45–54	54.0	52.3	56.2

Source: U.S. Bureau of the Census, Current Population Reports, Series P-60, Money Income of Households, Families, and Persons in the United States, various issues.

time rather than merely life-cycle effects. When we examine how specific cohorts fared over the period, we find that while the income of the 35–44 age group was a smaller percent of men's in 1983 than that of the 25–34 age group in either of the previous years, the difference is quite modest. Moreover, the fact that the income of the 45–54 age group was actually a slightly larger percent of men's income than that of the 35–44 group in either of the prior years is most encouraging.

We conclude that younger women are likely to retain a substantial amount of the improvement in their relative earnings as they age. Moreover, the observation that young women are now entering less traditional occupations and are spending more time in the labor market reinforces our conclusion that they are likely to continue faring better than their predecessors at each point of the life cycle. As this occurs, the overall sex gap in earnings, and income, should decline considerably more as earlier cohorts of women with relatively low earnings are replaced increasingly by the more recent cohorts with higher earnings.

Explanations of Sex Differences in Occupations and Earnings

There is no question that the work women and men do and the rewards they receive continue to be substantially different. There is, on the other hand, considerable disagreement about the reasons why this is the case. The explanations may, generally, be divided into two broad categories, one emphasizing differences in voluntary decisions of individual workers, the other focusing on differences in the treatment women and men receive in the labor market.

The Human Capital Explanation

A variety of supply-side explanations could be offered to account for sex segregation by occupation and industry, including sex differences in tastes for various types of work. We focus here on the human capital explanation since it has received the most attention. The neoclassical human capital theory essentially originated in the early 1960s with the work of Theodore Schultz (1961) and Gary Becker (1964), even though there were several forerunners. The core of this approach is the view that people spend on themselves in diverse ways, not for the sake of present enjoyment, but in order to obtain higher pecuniary and nonpecuniary returns in the future (Blaug, 1976, p. 829).[9] The application of this model to explain differences in occupations and earnings relies crucially on the assumption that men's and

---

[9] This review article provides an excellent evaluation of the work of the human capital school.

women's life-styles differ in ways the model itself does not explain, but which greatly influence returns to investments in human capital.[10]

Men are expected to enter the labor force and remain in it until retirement age. Hence, any increase in the wage rate resulting from additional skills they acquire will have a positive effect on earnings throughout their lifetime.[11] Women, on the other hand, are expected to work for pay only intermittently, giving priority to family responsibilities as they arise. Consequently they will, at best, reap the rewards of their investment for a shorter time and may find their human capital depreciating while they are not employed. As a result, men and women make different amounts of investment and choose different types of occupations.

Similarly, employers will hire men in preference to women for positions that involve a great deal of on-the-job training and investment in firm-specific human capital. Like the choices of workers themselves, these decisions of employers are a rational response to the voluntary preferences of men and women for different life-styles.

This, in a nutshell, is the model developed by such scholars as Polachek (1981), Landes (1977), Zellner (1975), and Mincer and Polachek (1974) to explain sex differences in occupations and earnings. Men are expected to be found in occupations that require relatively large amounts of job-oriented education and on-the-job (particularly firm-specific) training, but that also offer high rewards for the accumulated human capital. Women, on the other hand, tend to opt for jobs where general education, useful also to the homemaker, is utilized, and where there are no severe penalties for work interruptions. In return they accept lower earnings and less upward mobility.

Theories of Labor Market Discrimination

The foundation for the neoclassical analysis of labor market discrimination was laid by Becker (1957). This model assumes that employers, customers, and coworkers may have discriminatory tastes, even when male and female workers are perfect substitutes (equally productive).[12] Employers with these tastes will hire women workers only at a wage discount large enough to compensate for the disutility of employing them. Employers may also pay women less if discriminating customers will make purchases from women only at a lower price. Last, female employees may receive lower remuneration if discrimi-

---

[10] Discriminatory socialization prior to entry into the labor market is not ruled out, but this theory, like our chapter, is concerned only with the labor market itself.

[11] Presumably their pension will increase along with earnings.

[12] Like most other theories of discrimination, this one was developed to explain racial differences, but may be equally well applied to sex differences.

nating coworkers have to be more highly compensated for working with them or, as Bergmann and Darity (1981) suggested, become demoralized and less productive because of the presence of women.

While this type of discrimination does not necessarily predict occupational segregation, such segregation can occur if tastes for discrimination vary across occupations. This is entirely plausible once it is recognized that employers are more likely to be willing to hire a woman for a clerical job than for construction work, and that many consumers may be more willing to have a woman sell them dinnerware than a car. Furthermore, it is widely believed that men are far more willing to have women as subordinates rather than as peers or supervisors.

To the extent that wages are flexible, as assumed in neoclassical models, only firms where tastes for discrimination are unusually large would fail to hire women at the lower prevailing wages. This raises doubts whether the large amount of occupational segregation we observe can be accounted for in this way, since it would require all, or virtually all, employers to have such large discriminatory tastes. However, it does seem plausible that variation across employers in their tastes for discrimination could help to explain the significant amount of segregation by firm (and industry) that exists. At the same time the possibility for complete segregation by firms alleviates the need for wage differentials between equally qualified men and women, unless tastes for discrimination are very widespread. That is, women could work only for nondiscriminatory employers or only with nondiscriminatory male coworkers.

In any case, in this model segregation is not a cause of the earnings differential, but rather in some respects a substitute for it. Bergmann (1974), on the other hand, developed a model that assigns a central place to segregation in bringing about the pay gap. Here discriminatory tastes result not only in men and women being employed in different occupations, but demand for labor in the female sector is assumed to be small relative to the supply of female labor. Further, employers who hire women at low wages will find it profitable to utilize more labor-intensive methods, causing these workers to be less productive. This "crowding hypothesis" provides a persuasive explication of the consequences of segregation, regardless of its cause.

The problem still remains that in a competitive economy, nondiscriminating firms, producing at a lower cost, could drive the higher-cost discriminatory enterprises out of business. An obvious answer is that sufficient elements of monopoly power exist to permit discrimination to continue.

Monopoly power may exist both in the product market and in the labor market.[13] Madden's (1973) theory, based on a monopsony model, also can explain lower wages of women. A firm has monopsony power when it is a large buyer of labor relative to the size of the particular market.

To see how this can adversely affect women, consider the not uncommon case of a one-university town. In the past when the husband's job prospects usually determined family location, the faculty wife with a Ph.D. had little choice but to take whatever the university offered her; most considered themselves fortunate if they were able to obtain employment at all. Even the growing numbers of egalitarian Ph.D. couples cannot entirely avoid this problem. In order to change jobs, they must find *two* acceptable alternatives in a single location. This will obviously be harder to do than to find *one* desirable alternative. Thus the Ph.D. couple will have fewer options than those with only one Ph.D. in the family. (Similar problems arise for other two-career couples. We use this illustration because the mobility of academic couples tends to be less than that of most others.) While among Ph.D. couples both the husband's *and* the wife's salary may be adversely affected, since women with Ph.D.s are more likely than men Ph.D.s to have a Ph.D. spouse, this factor may be expected to have a larger adverse effect on academic women as a group than on academic men.[14]

If the supply of female labor is less elastic than that of male labor, the employer with monopoly power in the labor market will maximize profits by paying women less than men. The important question here is whether such a differential in elasticities is likely to exist. Madden (1973) offers the monopsony model as a general explanation for the earnings gap and some tentative empirical support for this model is provided by Cardwell and Rosenzweig (1980). However, it seems likely, as suggested by the example above, that the monopsony explanation is more applicable to specific occupations and labor markets than to the aggregate differential. For a fuller discussion, see Blau (1984a).

A second approach to explaining the long-run existence of discrimination is the notion of statistical discrimination (Aigner and Cain,

---

[13] While monopoly power in the labor market has been emphasized in the sex discrimination literature, monopoly power in the product market is another possibility that has been considered. Becker (1957) hypothesized that, on average, employer discrimination would be less severe in competitive than in monopolistic industries because the former cannot afford to indulge discriminatory tastes at the expense of efficiency. Some support has been obtained for this prediction. See, for example, Hannan and Ashenfelter (1983).

[14] For evidence that both men and women with a spouse who was also a faculty member were paid less, see Ferber and Loeb (1974).

1977; Arrow, 1972; Phelps, 1972). It may take two forms, both of which assume imperfect information. First, employers may assume, rightly or wrongly, that women are, on the average, less productive and therefore hire them only at lower wages, if at all. This is clearly discriminatory if the employer's perception is wrong. Even if the employer's view is correct, judging each individual not in terms of his or her own potential, but in terms of group averages, may be regarded as discriminatory from a normative perspective. Second, employers may accept women to be equal with men, on the average, but assume that they are less predictable. If such employers are risk-averse, the result will be much the same as if they believed women were less qualified.

In view of the real difficulties in correctly evaluating a potential employee's qualifications, let alone predicting his or her performance, it is not unreasonable to conclude that employers are likely to rely on such tenuous indicators as group averages. In times of rapid change it is also quite likely that the information they tend to rely on may be out of date. Arrow (1972, 1976) further helps to explain the existence of discrimination in the long run. The contribution of his perceptual equilibrium model is that it introduces a feedback mechanism. When employers, for whatever reason, put women into poorer, low-paying jobs, women have little incentive to invest in themselves or to become stable employees. This is a simple case of the self-fulfilling prophecy.

Institutional models, such as the internal labor market analysis or the dual labor market model (Doeringer and Piore, 1971; Piore, 1971)[15] give a more explicit role to the traditions and norms of the workplace. Blau and Jusenius (1976) suggest that their main contribution is to clarify the relationship between sex differentials in earnings and occupational segregation. They argue that under the administered system of internal labor markets firms attach wage rates to occupational categories rather than to individuals (see also Thurow, 1975). Under such circumstances the employer can pay women less only by assigning them to lower-paid job categories and by assigning lower values to predominantly female jobs. Women are likely to be assigned to categories perceived to fit their average characteristics (statistical discrimination). This, in turn, is likely to influence their behavior and productivity (Arrow's perceptual equilibrium). If women are relegated to a relatively few types of jobs, crowding can also play a part.

Radicals argue further that employers as a group benefit from such segmentation of the labor force by sex and race because it prevents workers from seeing their common interests and establishing solidarity. These divisive strategies would thwart unionization and other

---

[15] See also Cain (1976).

attempts of workers to share power (Gordon, Edwards, and Reich, 1982; Gordon, 1972). Radical feminists also suggest that to explain sex segregation one must take into account not only capitalism, but also patriarchy, which is defined as a system of male oppression of women (Milkman, 1980; Hartmann, 1976).[16] In this view, male workers as well as male capitalists participate in holding women back in the labor market in order to maintain power within the family (Hartmann, 1981). They point to the role of male trade unions in maintaining occupational segregation as evidence for this.

Institutional analyses bring to the fore an important point about the nature of discrimination: Labor market discrimination against women is not necessarily the outcome of conscious, overt acts by employers. Once men and women are channeled into different types of entry jobs, the normal, everyday operation of the firm—"business as usual"—will virtually ensure sex differences in productivity, promotion opportunities, and pay. This is termed institutional discrimination. Even sex differences in initial occupational assignment may be in part due to traditional policies that tend to work against women, like referrals from current male employees or an informal network of male colleagues at other firms, sexist recruitment materials picturing women in traditionally female jobs and men in traditionally male jobs, and lack of encouragement of female applicants to broaden their sights from traditional areas.[17]

A variety of economic theories have been suggested in this section to answer the question of who discriminates, why, and how. Employers, coworkers, and customers may have tastes for discrimination; employers may judge individuals by the group they belong to; the real problems may be caused by the crowding of women into a few sectors or the failure to give women the opportunity to enter jobs that have career ladders. Efforts to distinguish among these theories empirically are still in their infancy because the primary emphasis in empirical work has been on testing for the existence of discrimination. Indeed, it may be unreasonable to expect that some day one theoretical approach will be identified as "correct." Each of these explanations contributes to our understanding of a complex reality, where factors keeping women in sex-segregated and poorly paid jobs, rather than being mutually exclusive, are far more likely to have reinforced each other.

Feedback Effects

If labor market discrimination exists, it is expected to adversely affect the economic status of women directly by producing differences

---

[16] See also Strober (1984).
[17] See Roos and Reskin (1984) for a description of business practices that tend to adversely affect women.

in economic outcomes between men and women that are not due to differences in productivity or qualifications. That is, men and women who, in the absence of discrimination, would be equally productive and receive the same pay (or be in the same occupation), do not receive equal rewards.

If such differences in the treatment of equally qualifed men and women are widespread and persistent, the behavior of women is likely to be adversely affected. Productivity differences among workers reflect, in part, decisions they make as to whether to continue schooling, participate in training programs, remain continuously in the labor force, etc. Faced with labor market discrimination, women may have less incentive to make such human capital investments. To the extent that such *indirect* or *feedback effects* of labor market discrimination exist, they are also expected to lower the economic status of women relative to men (Lundberg and Startz, 1983; Weiss and Gronau, 1981; Blau, 1977; Bergmann, 1976; Ferber and Lowry, 1976; Strober, 1976). Arrow's (1972, 1976) notion of perceptual equilibrium discussed above is an example of the operation of feedback effects.

Much of the theoretical and virtually all of the empirical work on labor market discrimination has focused on its more readily measured *direct* effects—that is, on pay or occupational differences between equally well-qualified (potentially equally productive) men and women. We follow this emphasis below. However, it is important to recognize that the *full* impact of discrimination also includes any feedback effects on women's behavior that result from their being less well qualified than men.

Empirical Findings

As noted above, most empirical research focuses on the question of whether and to what extent labor market discrimination against women (or minorities) exists. This is the most fundamental issue, both for better understanding the determinants of women's status in the labor market and for deciding upon appropriate policies. Less attention is devoted to choosing among alternative models of discrimination or identifying the importance of feedback effects. However, even relatively straightforward attempts to test for the existence of discrimination are extremely difficult.

In this section we examine the evidence for the existence of discriminatory pay differentials with both time-series and cross-sectional data. Second, we explore the available literature concerning the role of and causes for occupational segregation. In the next section we point out the main unresolved questions and suggest what types of future research would be most helpful.

Discrimination in Earnings: Time-Series Data

Some evidence regarding the relative merits of the human capital and discrimination explanations for the earnings gap comes from time-series data. As we have seen, despite substantial increases in women's labor force participation rates, not until the late 1970s were there signs that the ratio of female to male earnings was beginning to turn up. Recent studies by O'Neill (1985) and Smith and Ward (1984) argue that this stability is, however, consistent with the human capital explanation for the pay gap.

Both O'Neill and Smith and Ward emphasize that women's labor force participation rate is increased by flows of relatively inexperienced new entrants into the labor force, as well as by an increased propensity of women to remain in the labor force more permanently. While the latter works to increase the average experience of women relative to men, the former works to reduce it. Data presented by O'Neill on job tenure and by Smith and Ward on work experience suggest that there was a widening of the experience gap in the 1960s (relative to the 1950s).[18] They also point out that the educational attainment of women declined relative to men during this period, in part because the female labor force became less selective of highly educated women. Thus, they find the lack of progress of women workers during the 1960s explicable in terms of these human capital factors.

Since the late 1960s, however, evidence suggests that women workers' qualifications are increasing relative to men's. Though women workers' median educational attainment declined slightly relative to men's, their fields of study and propensity to pursue college and graduate education have become more similar to men's (Blau and Ferber, 1986). Further, average experience of women workers increased slightly during the 1970s, the gains being largest among younger women (O'Neill, 1985; Smith and Ward, 1984). And, as O'Neill points out, the weekly earnings series shows a decline in the earnings gap dating from the mid to late 1970s (see also

---

[18] A unique feature of the Smith and Ward (1984) study is their use of simulations to estimate average work experience of various age cohorts of women workers and the female population. For the late 1960s and the 1970s, O'Neill (1985) presents experience data from the National Longitudinal Surveys of younger and older women. Data are available only for particular age groups and years. It is unfortunate that neither study presents data on (or estimates of) the average work experience of male workers. Increased educational attainment probably reduced the average experience of male workers due to later school-leaving ages. In addition, especially during the late 1960s and 1970s, cohort effects most likely reduced the average experience of male workers. Specifically, the number of younger workers with relatively little experience increased as the baby boom group entered the labor market, while declining participation (increased retirement) rates reduced the size of the more experienced group.

Table 2).[19] O'Neill and Smith and Ward also see human capital factors as playing a role in the especially large gains of younger women over the past 10 to 15 years (see Table 4), since their age group is the one that has made the greatest improvements in their qualifications relative to men.

Smith and Ward further argue that the *timing* of the largest narrowing of the earnings gap in the early 1980s casts doubt on antidiscrimination policies as a causal factor because these programs were cut back by the Reagan Administration. They think this points to the importance of human capital factors. Consistent with this interpretation, they argue that government interference is neither necessary to nor helpful in improving women's labor market position.

However, at least two questions may be raised regarding their conclusion. First, it is not at all clear that the largest narrowing of the differential occurred in the early 1980s. Smith and Ward rely on the annual earnings series in reaching this conclusion, but, as may be seen in Table 2, the annual and weekly earnings series do not agree in this respect. Second, even if we focus solely on the annual earnings series, we are hard pressed to explain the stability of the earnings gap in the 1970s in the face of women workers' increasing experience. An alternative explanation for the particularly large relative increases shown by the annual earnings series in 1982 and 1983 is the recession. Overtime, more prevalent among men than women, tends to be cut back in a recession. Occasional overtime pay is included in the annual earnings series but not in the weekly earnings data (which refer to usual earnings).

Nonetheless, the work of O'Neill and of Smith and Ward presents convincing evidence that the human capital interpretation makes a substantial contribution to explaining the earnings gap and its recent narrowing. This does not, however, rule out discrimination as a continuing cause of the earnings differential, which remains substantial. Moreover, these developments are also consistent with possible diminution in discrimination, perhaps caused by equal opportunity legislation (Beller, 1979). Younger women would benefit most from such a decline since they are most able to take advantage of new opportunities by acquiring the necessary training.[20] Indeed, their growing human capital investments may be in part a *response* to their expectations of lessened labor market discrimination in comparison to earlier cohorts. The timing of the influx of women into higher education and male fields and the rapid increase in the labor force participa-

---

[19] O'Neill finds a reduction in the annual earnings series dating from the same point after an adjustment is made for sex differences in hours worked.

[20] Freeman (1973) makes a similar argument as to why the black-white differential among males narrowed more among younger blacks in the 1970s.

tion of younger women in the 1960s and 1970s are consistent with this hypothesis.

It seems reasonable to view trends in sex differentials in earnings as part of a long-term cumulative process in which women's improved job qualifications and reduced labor market discrimination reinforce each other. The precise timing of this improvement may never be fully understood. It should, however, become apparent before long whether the optimism of O'Neill and of Smith and Ward, which we cautiously share, that progress has indeed begun and may well accelerate in the future is justified.

Discrimination in Earnings: Cross-Sectional Data

More evidence on the relative importance of human capital factors versus discrimination is provided by cross-sectional studies. As we have seen, labor market discrimination may be defined as a situation where two equally qualified individuals are treated differently solely on the basis of characteristics not relevant to job performance, such as sex and race. As noted above, this definition does not take into account possible feedback effects, when individuals faced with lower returns are likely to accumulate less human capital. While such secondary effects may be quite important, they are also particularly intractable, and most empirical work does not focus on them. But even this involves problems.

In the absence of direct measures of discrimination, the residual approach is usually employed. That is, the portion of the earnings gap that can be explained by a variety of available productivity-related variables is estimated. It is then assumed that the remaining unexplained portion represents the effects of discrimination. In the context of regression equations estimated for men and women separately, the portion of the differential associated with sex differences in the *means* of the explanatory variables (or endowments) is attributed to nondiscriminatory factors, while the portion associated with sex differences in the *coefficients* (or returns), including the constant term, is attributed to discrimination (Blinder, 1973; Oaxaca, 1973). Depending, however, on which variables are included, the level of discrimination may be either over- or underestimated.

On the one hand, overestimates of discrimination may occur if important determinants of (or proxies for) productivity are omitted from the analysis and if men are more qualified with respect to such factors. Omitted variables are often a problem because we generally do not have information on all the relevant qualifications of individuals. Some factors that affect earnings, like motivation and effort, are not easily quantified. Others—field of specialization in school, for example—may be unavailable in a particular data set. Some portion of the earnings differential which is found to be "unexplained" may in fact be due to such factors.

This difficulty was recognized all along, but recently has received particular attention. It has been suggested (Kamalich and Polachek, 1983; Roberts, 1980) that this problem could be solved by using a "reverse regression," where wage is the independent variable and an index of qualifications is the dependent variable. It turns out, however, that this method is not clearly superior and may be as much subject to biases as the traditional approach (Blau and Kahn, 1985; Goldberger, 1984).

In the absence of direct measures of productivity and improved proxies, questions about possible upward bias in the conventional method of measuring discrimination are likely to persist. At the same time, it is important to recognize that this conventional approach may also have an opposite bias. As noted above, some of the lower qualifications of women may directly result from labor market discrimination. For example, qualified women may be excluded from training programs or denied higher-level jobs. While resulting sex differences in qualifications could accurately reflect productivity differences, these productivity differences (and consequent differences in pay) would be due to labor market discrimination. This raises the question of whether it is appropriate to include variables such as occupation, industry, and academic rank which may themselves be tainted by discrimination. When such variables are controlled for in the analysis, the impact of discrimination on earnings is underestimated. Further, feedback effects of labor market discrimination on women's behavior and choices are also neglected by such analyses.

Given these opposing considerations, it is not clear whether estimates of discrimination are likely to be too high or too low. In any case, the uncertainties need to be kept in mind when considering the available evidence. It must also be noted that estimates of discrimination are likely to vary depending on the group examined and the variables controlled for. We shall concentrate on studies using national samples.[21]

Early research, using data with no information on labor force experience, explains only a small part of the earnings gap. Thus Fuchs (1971), using 1960 Census data, accounted for only 3 to 15 percent of the differential. Oaxaca (1973), using data from the 1967 Survey of Economic Opportunity, left unexplained 80 percent of the pay differential between white men and women and 94 percent of the differential between black men and women.

---

[21] For more extensive reviews, including some occupation-specific studies, see Blau (1984a), Treiman and Hartmann (1981), Lloyd and Niemi (1979), and Kohen (1975).

More recently, longitudinal data providing information about work experience became available. Mincer and Polachek (1974) were the first to utilize information on work experience and work interruptions from the National Longitudinal Surveys (NLS) data. They accounted for 45 percent of the pay gap between white married men and women, ages 30 to 44—the group they examined. Mincer and Polachek tried to avoid the problem of joint determination of earnings and experience (i.e., feedback effects) by using a two-stage procedure. Unfortunately, serious questions have been raised about the adequacy of their adjustment (Blau, 1984a; Mincer and Polachek, 1978; Sandell and Shapiro, 1978). Thus the potential importance of feedback effects has not been determined.

Subsequent studies have confirmed the importance of work history information. This is illustrated in Table 5 which presents the results of a study by Corcoran and Duncan (1979), one of the most recently conducted investigations incorporating work histories.[22] It is impressive in the long list of controlled variables (see the notes to Table 5), including years of training completed on the current job as well as variables reflecting work experience, years out of the labor force since completing school, and indicators of labor force attachment. Again, however, this study does not take feedback effects into account.

As might be expected, sex differences in work history and on-the-job training accounted for a substantial portion of the wage gap: 39 percent of the differential between white women and white men and 22 percent of the (larger) differential between black women and white men. On the other hand, indicators of labor force attachment, such as absenteeism and placing constraints on job location or hours, did not play an important role in explaining wage differences, because these variables were not very strongly related to the wages of either men or women.

Differences in formal education, while relatively important in explaining racial differences in pay, accounted for little of the wage gap between white women and white men. This is not surprising in that, within race groups, there is relatively little difference in median educational attainment between men and women. However, as we have seen, there are, even now, substantial differences between men and women in fields of study that may be important in explaining the

---

[22] A more recent study by Salvo and McNeil (1984), using data collected by the Bureau of the Census in 1979, found that the human capital variables (i.e., labor market experience, work interruptions, and education) explained only 15 percent of the earnings gap, considerably less than the Corcoran and Duncan (1979) study. This is probably because the Salvo and McNeil study lacked information on job tenure and on-the-job training, and thus did not include them as explanatory variables.

TABLE 5

Percentages of the Wage Gap Between White Men and
Other Groups of Workers Explained by
Differences in Qualifications, 1975[a]

	Black Men	White Women	Black Women
Years of formal education	38%	2%	11%
Years of training completed on current job	15	11	8
Other work history[b]	3	28	14
Indicators of labor force attachment[c]	−3	3	−1
Unexplained	47	56	68
Total[d]	100	100	100
Wage differential[e]	23%	36%	43%

Source: Corcoran and Duncan (1979), pp. 8, 18.

[a] Includes workers ages 18–64.

[b] Includes controls for years out of the labor force since completing school, years of work experience before present employer, preemployer work experience squared, years with current employer prior to current position, years of posttraining tenure on current job, and proportion of total working years that were full-time.

[c] Includes controls for hours of work missed due to illness of others in 1975, hours of work missed due to own illness in 1975, limits placed on job hours or location, and plans to stop work for nontraining reasons.

[d] Net of effect of city size and southern residence.

[e] Computed on the basis of the geometric means of the hourly wage for each group.

pay differential. In a rare study by Daymont and Andrisani (1983) that did include such information, it was found that, in 1979, differences in college major explained almost half of the earnings differential between recent male and female college graduates. While these results suggest the importance of this factor, disentangling the issue of field of study from sex composition of the occupation is no easy matter.

The findings of Corcoran and Duncan and of other similar studies suggest that differences in qualifications do indeed play a large role in producing pay differences between men and women, but by no means provide a full explanation. Such studies must be interpreted with some caution since they are subject to the biases discussed earlier, including the larger problem of feedback effects. Some evidence consistent with the importance of feedback is found in studies of sex differences in quitting. As discussed earlier, employers may be reluctant to hire women for jobs requiring considerable firm-specific training (or pay them less for such jobs) because they believe women workers are more likely to quit than male workers. Although women on average do have higher quit rates, they are no more likely to quit than comparable men when personal and job characteristics are controlled (Blau and Kahn,

1981; Viscusi, 1980).[23] Further, the explanation for average sex differentials in quit rates was found to be differences in characteristics of the jobs men and women hold, rather than their personal characteristics.

The evidence reviewed here does not prove that there is discrimination, let alone enable us to measure it with any precision. It does, however, strongly suggest that both human capital factors and labor market discrimination in all likelihood play a role in producing the wage gap, and it is not unreasonable to attribute as much as half the sex differential to discrimination. Additional evidence that labor market discrimination exists is provided by the many court cases in which employers have been found guilty of sex discrimination in pay or have reached out-of-court settlements with the plaintiffs. In any case, given the feedback mechanisms where discrimination influences the amount of human capital accumulated, and where disparities in the amounts of human capital provide a rationale for some of the discrimination, it may not be appropriate to treat the two as completely separate and independent alternatives.

Occupational Segregation and Earnings

As was pointed out previously, occupational segregation by sex is a particular concern because it is believed to be related to the sex earnings differential. This may be caused by less on-the-job training and lesser incentives for worker stability in female jobs and/or by overcrowding. Once again, however, there are serious obstacles in attempts to derive precise empirical estimates of these relationships.

The first problem is that most of the available data, even those on detailed Census categories, tend to aggregate some male and female jobs into single occupations (Baron and Bielby, 1984). Also, there is considerable segregation by firm even within occupations (Baron and Bielby, 1984; Blau, 1977). Thus, reliance on the available information on occupations tends to lead to an underestimation of the impact of segregation on earnings.

Second, there is a conceptual problem when using differences in women's earnings in male and female occupations to measure the impact of segregation on earnings. Even when women work in male jobs, the lower-paying alternatives they face in the female sector may reduce the wage at which they are willing to work. Thus, occupational segregation may lower wages of women in *both* male *and* female jobs. If this is so, then measuring the impact of segregation by contrasting

---

[23] Similarly, Osterman (1979) found no sex differences in absenteeism, all else equal, for a sample of professional workers.

wages of women in male and female jobs would result in an underestimation.

Nor is the use of male rather than female earnings an entirely
acceptable solution. Men may work in female occupations because
they have strong preferences for that type of work, because of bad luck
or poor information, or because they found a particular niche in which
they receive pay comparable to what they could earn in the male
sector. If the third explanation is true, there would be a downward bias
in estimates of the impact of occupational segregation on earnings.

A third consideration may work in the opposite direction. Workers in higher-paying, predominantly male occupations, or firms, may
have unmeasured characteristics that make them more productive.
What appear to be occupation (or firm) effects on wages may actually be
unmeasured productivity differences.[24]

For all these reasons the available findings must be viewed as
somewhat tentative. Nonetheless, an examination of the resulting
estimates is instructive. These suggest that occupational differences
are a significant factor in explaining the gender pay gap.

Using 1980 Census data, Treiman and Hartmann (1981) conclude
that between 35 and 39 percent of the earnings differential is related to
the occupational distribution of men and women. Similarly, Oaxaca
(1973) found that job characteristics accounted for some 20 to 35 percent of the discriminatory pay gap. Further, a number of studies,
including England (1982), Cabral, Ferber, and Green (1981), Jusenius
(1977), Ferber and Lowry (1976), and Stevenson (1975), found that as
the percentage of female workers in an occupation increases, all else
being equal, earnings decline. Last, when extremely detailed occupational categories within a single firm that closely approximate the
employer's own job titles are used, they reveal a considerably greater
impact of occupation on wages than do aggregate analyses. For example, Blau (1984b) reported that 76 percent of the unexplained pay
differential between men and women was due to sex differences in
distribution among occupational categories within a firm.

Causes of Occupational Segregation

While occupation appears to be a factor in producing the pay
differential, considerable controversy surrounds the causes of this
segregation. Again, the potential candidates are women's and men's
voluntary choices versus labor market discrimination.

As discussed earlier, human capital theorists argue that since
women generally anticipate shorter and less continuous work careers

---

[24] See Blau (1984b) for a fuller discussion of these issues.

than do men, it will be in their interest to choose female occupations that presumably require less human capital investments and have lower wage penalties for time spent out of the labor force. While there is evidence consistent with this view (Polachek, 1981), most studies do not support this thesis. For example, England (1982) found that women's earnings did not show lower rates of depreciation or appreciation in female than in male occupations. Indeed, her findings were that women earned less in female jobs at all levels of experience, and she concluded that women cannot maximize lifetime earnings by choosing female occupations.[25] Nonetheless, further study may reveal greater support for the investment hypothesis. Further, existing evidence does not rule out the importance of other supply-side factors in the family, school, or media that may encourage men and women to aspire to and train for "sex-appropriate" work.

On the demand side, employers may contribute to occupational segregation by discriminating against equally qualified women in hiring, placement, access to training programs, and promotion to traditionally male jobs. There is evidence consistent with the existence of discrimination in a number of studies, including Olson and Becker (1983), Cabral, Ferber, and Green (1981), Duncan and Hoffman (1979), Kanter (1977).[26] Further, as with pay discrimination, support for the view that discrimination plays some part is found in the many cases in which employers were found guilty of discrimination or settled out of court.

Research Needs and Policy Implications

As we have seen, much knowledge has been accumulated, but even more remains to be learned, about the reasons for existing differences in labor market outcomes for women and men. Thus far, research has focused on the crucial policy-related issue of the importance of human capital and other supply-side factors versus discrimination in producing the earnings gap.

To the extent that the human capital explanation is correct, one may conclude that women's position in the labor market is determined by their own voluntary choices and that there is no cause for further concern. Alternatively, it may be argued that their choices are, at least in part, caused by differentiated socialization and education of men and women. In this case one might, for instance, advocate policies that assure equal treatment in schools and encourage women to widen their aspirations, since those who accept primary responsibility for home-

---

[25] See also Corcoran, Duncan, and Ponza (1984) and Abowd and Killingsworth (1983).
[26] For reviews of the literature on this topic, see England (1984) and Roos and Reskin (1984).

making are at greater risk because they are dependent upon the continuation of the family unit. However, there still would be no reason
for interference in the labor market.

The situation is quite different if there is labor market discrimination. The crucial question here is whether one gives precedence to the
right of people to choose their associates freely in whatever manner
they wish or the right of individuals to equal opportunity. Those who
object to treatment of persons as members of groups, rather than in
terms of their own ability to perform a job, will, of course, be inclined
to opt for the latter.

It is unfortunate, although perhaps not surprising, that despite
the vast amount of research on this topic, there is no complete consensus on the question of whether or not labor market discrimination
exists. Based on available information, our own view, with which we
suspect many would concur, is that both human capital factors and
labor market discrimination play a role in producing the observed
differences. This provides a rationale for government policies aimed at
combating discrimination in both educational institutions and the
labor market. And, indeed, there has been evidence of a modest
amount of success for both types of policies (Beller, 1982, 1979).

To be more helpful to policy-makers, future research could concentrate on a number of areas. First, more finely honed methods could
be constructed for testing the varying models of discrimination. The
process through which various causes of discrimination may interact
and reinforce each other needs to be better understood.

Progress may well involve more work on individual enterprises,
including an examination of personnel practices with respect to hiring,
pay, and promotion. A comparison of these policies across firms and
over time may shed light on the most effective firm-level policies for
improving the status of women, another important goal of future
research.[27] Establishment data may also further the development of
better measures of job performance, and thus better estimates of
discrimination.

A second useful focus of future research is on the determinants of
career choices of women and the process of career development in
general. This would involve a better understanding of how the nature
of work differs between typically male and typically female jobs, how
these differences relate to pay structure,[28] and what factors govern
access to positions in each sector. The results of such research would be

---

[27] For an excellent review of what has been learned thus far from studies of this type, see
O'Farrell and Harlan (1984).

[28] For some examples of useful research in this area, see Ferber and Spaeth (1984), England,
Chassie, and McCormack (1982), and Roos (1981).

very useful in determining both the desirability and the most effective form of government intervention.

Finally, we need to know a great deal more about the nature and magnitude of feedback effects: the influence of labor market discrimination on women's human capital investments and job qualifications. While public attention often focuses on the social costs of combating discrimination or "reverse discrimination,"[29] negative feedback effects and the wastage of human resources they entail are potentially serious and often overlooked social costs of continuing discrimination.

Feedback effects could greatly magnify the impact of even a modest amount of direct discrimination. Assume, for instance, that a woman earns only somewhat less than a man with equal qualifications. When two such people make the decision on how to share household responsibilities, they maximize income by having the man specialize in market work. Hence, he acquires more experience and gets more on-the-job training, and in time his qualifications may be considerably better than hers.

Moreover, such behavior encourages statistical discrimination which, in turn, increases the earnings gap. Finally, young women and their parents who are aware of this situation have less incentive to invest in human capital than do young men and their families.

Thus, feedback effects can produce a "vicious circle" in which labor market discrimination discourages women from investing in themselves and women's lesser qualifications provide a rationale for discrimination. By the same token, however, improvements in women's labor market position are also likely to be cumulative. Hence, if market discrimination accounts for only a small part of women's inferior economic status and/or if appropriate policies initially make only small improvements, even a small step in the right direction should eventually result in a much larger step for womankind.

References

Abowd, John, and Mark R. Killingsworth. "Sex Discrimination, Atrophy, and the Male-Female Wage Differential." *Industrial Relations* 22 (Fall 1983): pp. 387–402.

Aigner, Dennis J., and Glen G. Cain. "Statistical Theories of Discrimination in Labor Markets." *Industrial and Labor Relations Review* 30 (January 1977): pp. 175–87.

---

[29] Available evidence from statistical studies does not support the concern over reverse discrimination. See, for example, Leonard (1984, 1985), Ferber and Green (1982). Similarly, a survey conducted by the Center for National Policy Review found that virtually all the employers included in a sample of government contractors stated that no lowering of employment standards was necessary to achieve the company's affirmative action objectives. Interestingly enough, it was found that, in most companies, affirmative action programs had brought about an improvement in personnel management systems (reported by Bureau of National Affairs, Inc., 1983).

Arrow, Kenneth. "Economic Dimensions of Occupational Segregation: Comment I."
    Signs: Journal of Women in Culture and Society 1, Pt. 2 (Spring 1976):
    pp. 233–37.
_____. "Models of Job Discrimination." In Racial Discrimination in Economic Life,
    ed. Anthony J. Pascal. Lexington, MA: D.C. Heath, 1972. Pp. 83–102.
Baron, James N., and William T. Bielby. "A Woman's Place Is With Other Women:
    Sex Segregation in the Workplace." In Sex Segregation in the Workplace: Trends,
    Explanations, Remedies, ed. Barbara F. Reskin. Washington: National Academy
    Press, 1984. Pp. 25–55.
Becker, Gary S. Human Capital: A Theoretical and Empirical Analysis, With Special
    Reference to Education. New York: Columbia University Press, 1964.
_____. The Economics of Discrimination. Chicago: University of Chicago Press,
    1957.
Beller, Andrea H. "Trends in Occupational Segregation by Sex and Race, 1960–1981."
    In Sex Segregation in the Workplace: Trends, Explanations, Remedies, ed. Bar-
    bara F. Reskin. Washington: National Academy Press, 1984. Pp. 11–26.
_____. "The Impact of Equal Opportunity Policy on Sex Differentials in Earnings and
    Occupations." American Economic Review 72 (May 1982): pp. 171–75.
_____. "The Impact of Equal Employment Opportunity Laws on the Male/Female
    Earnings Differential." In Women in the Labor Market, eds. Cynthia B. Lloyd,
    Emily S. Andrews, and Curtis L. Gilroy. New York: Columbia University Press,
    1979. Pp. 304–30.
Bergmann, Barbara R. "Reducing the Pervasiveness of Discrimination." In Jobs for
    Americans, ed. Eli Ginzberg. Englewood Cliffs, NJ: Prentice-Hall, 1976.
    Pp. 120–41.
_____. "Occupational Segregation, Wages and Profits When Employers Discrimi-
    nate by Race or Sex." Eastern Economic Journal 1 (April–July 1974): pp. 103–10.
Bergmann, Barbara R., and William Darity, Jr. "Social Relations in the Workplace and
    Employer Discrimination." In Proceedings of the 33rd Annual Meeting, Indus-
    trial Relations Research Association, 1980. Madison, WI: IRRA, 1981.
    Pp. 155–62.
Blau, Francine D. "Discrimination Against Women: Theory and Evidence." In Labor
    Economics: Modern Views, ed. William A. Darity, Jr. Boston: Kluwer-Nijhoff,
    1984a. Pp. 53–90.
_____. "Occupational Segregation and Labor Market Discrimination." In Sex Segre-
    gation in the Workplace: Trends, Explanations, Remedies, ed. Barbara F. Reskin.
    Washington: National Academy Press, 1984b. Pp. 117–43.
_____. Equal Pay in the Office. Lexington, MA: D.C. Heath, 1977.
Blau, Francine D., and Andrea H. Beller. "Trends in Earnings Differentials by Sex
    and Race, 1971–1981." Paper presented at the American Economic Association
    meetings, Dallas, December 1984.
Blau, Francine D., and Marianne A. Ferber. The Economics of Women, Men, and
    Work. Englewood Cliffs, NJ: Prentice-Hall, 1986.
Blau, Francine D., and Wallace E. Hendricks. "Occupational Segregation by Sex:
    Trends and Prospects." Journal of Human Resources 14 (Spring 1979):
    pp. 197–210.
Blau, Francine D., and Carol L. Jusenius. "Economists' Approaches to Sex Segrega-
    tion in the Labor Market: An Appraisal." Signs: Journal of Women in Culture and
    Society 1 (Spring 1976): pp. 181–99.
Blau, Francine D., and Lawrence M. Kahn. "The Use of Reverse Regression in Test-
    ing for Discrimination." Southern Economic Journal (April 1985): pp. 1121–26.

_____. "Race and Sex Differences in Quits by Young Workers." *Industrial and Labor Relations Review* 34 (July 1981): pp. 563–77.

Blaug, Mark. "The Empirical Status of Human Capital Theory: A Slightly Jaundiced Survey." *Journal of Economic Literature* 14 (September 1976): pp. 827–55.

Blinder, Alan S. "Wage Determination: Reduced Form and Structural Estimates." *Journal of Human Resources* 8 (Fall 1973): pp. 436–55.

Borjas, George J. "The Relationship Between Wages and Weekly Hours of Work: The Role of Division Bias." *Journal of Human Resources* 15 (Summer 1980): pp. 409–23.

Bureau of National Affairs, Inc. *Employee Relations Weekly*, September 12, 1983.

Cabral, Robert, Marianne A. Ferber, and Carole A. Green. "Men and Women in Fiduciary Institutions: A Study of Sex Differences in Career Development." *Review of Economics and Statistics* 63 (November 1981): pp. 573–80.

Cain, Glen G. "The Challenge of Segmented Labor Market Theories to Orthodox Theory: A Survey." *Journal of Economic Literature* 14 (December 1976): pp. 1215–57.

Cardwell, Lucy A., and Mark R. Rosenzweig. "Economic Mobility, Monopsonistic Discrimination and Sex Differences in Wages." *Southern Economic Journal* 46 (April 1980): pp. 1102–17.

Corcoran, Mary, and Greg J. Duncan. "Work History, Labor Force Attachment, and Earnings Differences Between Races and Sexes." *Journal of Human Resources* 14 (Winter 1979): pp. 3–20.

Corcoran, Mary, Greg J. Duncan, and Michael Ponza. "Work Experience, Job Segregation, and Wages." In *Sex Segregation in the Workplace: Trends, Explanations, Remedies*, ed. Barbara F. Reskin. Washington: National Academy Press, 1984. Pp. 171–91.

Daymont, Thomas N., and Paul J. Andrisani. "Why Women Earn Less Than Men: The Case of Recent College Graduates." In *Proceedings of the 36th Annual Meeting, Industrial Relations Research Association, 1982*. Madison, WI: IRRA, 1983. Pp. 425–35.

Doeringer, Peter B., and Michael J. Piore. *Internal Labor Markets and Manpower Analysis*. Lexington, MA: D.C. Heath, 1971.

Duncan, Greg J., and Saul Hoffman. "On-the-Job Training and Earnings Differences by Race and Sex." *Review of Economics and Statistics* 61 (November 1979): pp. 594–603.

Duncan, Otis Dudley, and Beverly Duncan. "A Methodological Analysis of Segregation Indexes." *American Sociological Review* 20 (April 1955): pp. 210–17.

England, Paula. "Socioeconomic Explanations of Job Segregation." In *Comparable Worth and Wage Discrimination: Technical Possibilities and Political Realities*, ed. Helen Remick. Philadelphia: Temple University Press, 1984.

_____. "The Failure of Human Capital Theory to Explain Occupational Sex Segregation." *Journal of Human Resources* 17 (Summer 1982): pp. 358–70.

England, Paula, Marilyn Chassie, and Linda McCormack. "Skill Demands and Earnings in Female and Male Occupations." *Sociology and Social Research* 66 (January 1982): pp. 147–68.

Ferber, Marianne A., and Carole A. Green. "Traditional or Reverse Sex Discrimination? A Case Study of a Large Public University." *Industrial and Labor Relations Review* 35 (July 1982): pp. 550–64.

Ferber, Marianne A., and Jane W. Loeb. "Professors, Performance and Rewards." *Industrial Relations* 13 (February 1974): pp. 67–77.

Ferber, Marianne A., and Helen M. Lowry. "The Sex Differential in Earnings: A Reappraisal." *Industrial and Labor Relations Review* 29 (April 1976): pp. 377–87.

Ferber, Marianne A., and Joe L. Spaeth. "Work Characteristics and the Male-Female Earnings Gap." *American Economic Review* 74 (May 1984): pp. 260–64.

Forbes, Benjamin, and James E. Piercy. "Running to the Top: Executive Women in 1983 and Beyond." *Business Horizons* 26 (September-October 1983): pp. 38-47.

Fraker, Susan. "Why Women Aren't Getting up to the Top." *Fortune* 109 (April 16, 1984): pp. 40–45.

Freeman, Richard B. "Changes in the Labor Market for Black Americans, 1948–1972." *Brookings Papers on Economic Activity* (1:1973): pp. 67–120.

Fuchs, Victor R. "Differences in Hourly Earnings Between Men and Women." *Monthly Labor Review* 94 (May 1971): pp. 9–13.

Goldberger, Arthur S. "Redirecting Reverse Discrimination." *Journal of Business and Economic Statistics* 2 (April 1984): pp. 114–16.

Gordon, David M. *Theories of Poverty and Underemployment.* Lexington, MA: D.C. Heath, 1972.

Gordon, David, Richard Edwards, and Michael Reich. *Segmented Work, Divided Workers: The Historical Transformation of Labor in the United States.* Cambridge: Cambridge University Press, 1982.

Gross, Edward. "Plus Ça Change . . . ? The Sexual Structure of Occupations Over Time." *Social Problems* 16 (Fall 1968): pp. 198–208.

Hannan, Timothy H., and Orley Ashenfelter. "Sex Discrimination and Market Concentration: The Case of the Banking Industry." Paper presented at the American Economic Association meetings, December 1983.

Hartmann, Heidi I. "The Family as the Locus of Gender, Class, and Political Struggle: The Example of Housework." *Signs: Journal of Women in Culture and Society* 6 (Spring 1981): pp. 366–94.

———. "Capitalism, Patriarchy, and Job Segregation by Sex." In *Women and the Workplace: The Implications of Occupational Segregation,* eds. Martha Blaxall and Barbara B. Regan. Chicago: University of Chicago Press, 1976. Pp. 136–69.

Honig, Marjorie. "Partial Retirement in the Labor Market Behavior of Older Women." Unpublished paper, 1983.

Jusenius, Carol L. "The Influence of Work Experience, Skill Requirement, and Occupational Segregation on Women's Earnings." *Journal of Economics and Business* 29 (Winter 1977): pp. 107–15.

Kamalich, Richard F., and Solomon W. Polachek. "Discrimination: Fact or Fiction? An Examination Using an Alternative Approach." *Southern Economic Journal* 49 (October 1983): pp. 450–61.

Kanter, Rosabeth M. *Men and Women of the Corporation.* New York: Basic Books, 1977.

Kohen, Andrew I., with S.C. Breinich and P. Shields. "Women and the Economy: A Bibliography and a Review of the Literature on Sex Differentiation in the Labor Market." Center for Human Resource Research, College of Administrative Science, Ohio State University, 1975.

Landes, Elizabeth M. "Sex Differences in Wages and Employment: A Test of the Specific Capital Hypothesis." *Economic Inquiry* 15 (October 1977): pp. 523–38.

Leonard, Jonathan S. "What Promises Are Worth: The Impact of Affirmative Action Goals." *Journal of Human Resources* 20 (Winter 1985): pp. 1–20.

———. "Antidiscrimination or Reverse Discrimination: The Impact of Changing Demographics, Title VII, and Affirmative Action on Productivity." *Journal of Human Resources* 19 (Spring 1984): pp. 145–74.

Lloyd, Cynthia B., and Beth T. Niemi. *The Economics of Sex Differentials.* New York: Columbia University Press, 1979.

Lundberg, Shelly, and Richard Startz. "Private Discrimination and Social Intervention in Competitive Labor Markets." *American Economic Review* 73 (June 1983): pp. 340–47.

Madden, Janice F. *The Economics of Sex Discrimination*. Lexington, MA: D.C. Heath, 1973.

Malkiel, Burton G., and Judith A. Malkiel. "Male-Female Pay Differentials in Professional Employment." *American Economic Review* 63 (September 1973): pp. 693–705.

Milkman, Ruth. "Organizing the Sexual Division of Labor: Historical Perspectives on 'Women's Work' and the American Labor Movement." *Socialist Review* 49 (January-February 1980): pp. 95–150.

Mincer, Jacob, and Solomon W. Polachek. "An Exchange: Theory of Human Capital and the Earnings of Women: Women's Earnings Reexamined." *Journal of Human Resources* 13 (Winter 1978): pp. 118–34.

———. "Family Investments in Human Capital: Earnings of Women." *Journal of Political Economy* 82 (March-April 1974): pp. S76–S108.

Oaxaca, Ronald. "Sex Discrimination in Wages." In *Discrimination in Labor Markets*, eds. Orley Ashenfelter and Albert Rees. Princeton, NJ: Princeton University Press, 1973. Pp. 124–51.

O'Farrell, Brigid, and Sharon L. Harlan. "Job Integration Strategies: Today's Programs and Tomorrow's Goals." In *Sex Integration in the Workplace: Trends, Explanations, Remedies*, ed. Barbara F. Reskin. Washington: National Academy Press, 1984. Pp. 267–91.

Olson, Craig A., and Brian E. Becker. "Sex Discrimination in the Promotion Process." *Industrial and Labor Relations Review* 36 (July 1983): pp. 624–41.

O'Neill, June. "The Trend in the Male-Female Wage Gap in the United States." *Journal of Labor Economics* 3, Pt. 2 (January 1985 Supp.): pp. S91–S116.

Osterman, Paul. "Sex Discrimination in Professional Employment: A Case Study." *Industrial and Labor Relations Review* 32 (July 1979): pp. 451–64.

Phelps, Edmund S. "The Statistical Theory of Racism and Sexism." *American Economic Review* 62 (September 1972): pp. 659–61.

Piore, Michael J. "The Dual Labor Market: Theory and Implications." In *Problems in Political Economy: An Urban Perspective*, ed. David M. Gordon. Lexington, MA: D.C. Heath, 1971. Pp. 90–94.

Polachek, Solomon W. "Occupational Self-Selection: A Human Capital Approach to Sex Differences in Occupational Structure." *Review of Economics and Statistics* 63 (February 1981): pp. 60–69.

Reskin, Barbara F., and Patricia A. Roos. "Status Hierarchies and Sex Segregation." In *Ingredients for Women's Employment Policy*, eds. Christine Bose and Glenna Spitze. Albany, NY: State Univ. of New York Press, forthcoming.

Roberts, Harry. "Statistical Biases in the Measurement of Employment Discrimination." In *Comparable Worth: Issues and Alternatives*, ed. E. Robert Livernash. Washington: Equal Employment Opportunity Commission, 1980. Pp. 173–95.

Roos, Patricia A. "Sex Stratification in the Workplace: Male-Female Differences in Economic Returns to Occupation." *Social Science Research* 10 (September 1981): pp. 195–224.

Roos, Patricia A., and Barbara F. Reskin. "Institutional Factors Contributing to Sex Segregation in the Workplace." In *Sex Segregation in the Workplace: Trends, Explanations, Remedies*, ed. Barbara F. Reskin. Washington: National Academy Press, 1984. Pp. 235–60.

Rytina, Nancy. "Comparing Annual and Weekly Earnings From the Current Population Survey." *Monthly Labor Review* 106 (April 1983): pp. 32–38.

Salvo, Joseph J., and John M. McNeil. *Lifetime Work Experience and Its Effect on Earnings: Retrospective Data from the 1979 Income Survey Development Program.* U.S. Bureau of the Census, Current Population Report, Series P-23, No. 136. Washington: June 1984.

Sandell, Steven H., and David Shapiro. "An Exchange: Theory of Human Capital and the Earnings of Women: A Reexamination of the Evidence." *Journal of Human Resources* 13 (Winter 1978): pp. 103–17.

Schultz, Theodore W. "Investment in Human Capital." *American Economic Review* 51 (March 1961): pp. 1–17.

Smith, James P., and Michael P. Ward. *Women's Wages and Work in the Twentieth Century.* Santa Monica, CA: Rand Corporation, October 1984.

Stevenson, Mary H. "Relative Wages and Sex Segregation by Occupation." In *Sex, Discrimination, and the Division of Labor*, ed. Cynthia B. Lloyd. New York: Columbia University Press, 1975. Pp. 175–200.

Strober, Myra H. "Toward Dimorphics: A Summary Statement to the Conference on Occupational Segregation." *Signs: Journal of Women in Culture and Society* 1 Pt. 2 (Spring 1976): pp. 293–302.

————. "Toward a General Theory of Occupational Sex Segregation: The Case of Public School Teaching." In *Sex Segregation in the Workplace: Trends, Explanations, Remedies*, ed. Barbara F. Reskin. Washington: National Academy Press, 1984. Pp. 144–56.

Thurow, Lester C. *Generating Inequality.* New York: Basic Books, 1975.

Treiman, Donald J., and Heidi I. Hartmann, eds. *Women, Work, and Wages: Equal Pay for Jobs of Equal Value.* Washington: National Academy Press, 1981.

Viscusi, W. Kip. "Sex Differences in Worker Quitting." *Review of Economics and Statistics* 62 (August 1980): pp. 388–98.

Weiss, Yoram, and Reuben Gronau. "Expected Interruptions in Labour Force Participation and Sex-Related Differences in Earnings Growth." *Review of Economic Studies* 58 (October 1981): pp. 607–19.

Zellner, Harriett. "The Determinants of Occupational Segregation." In *Sex, Discrimination, and the Division of Labor*, ed. Cynthia B. Lloyd. New York: Columbia University Press, 1975. Pp. 125–45.

CHAPTER 3

Women's Work, Family, and Health

PATRICIA VOYDANOFF*

The study of relationships between work, family, and health among women has emerged and evolved over the past 25 years as the percentage of women in the labor force has increased (Voydanoff, 1984a; Kanter, 1977). Before this research began it was generally believed that work and family life were separate domains of life having little influence on each other. This perceived separation was tied to beliefs regarding the roles of men and women. According to traditional sex-role ideology, men are breadwinners performing instrumental duties outside the home and women are wives and mothers performing expressive duties inside the home. Research in the social sciences reflected this view. Issues regarding work were studied among men and research on family life was based on samples of women. Unemployment was viewed as a problem among men, while employment was seen as problematic among women (Feldberg and Glenn, 1979).

As increasing numbers of married women and mothers entered the labor force, questions were raised regarding the effects of women's outside employment on their traditional roles and responsibilities. The first studies, beginning in the late 1950s and early 1960s, focused on the effects of mothers' employment on their children's development. In recent years research has begun to examine the effects of women's employment on health and other aspects of family life. The impact of family characteristics and demands on women's labor force participation is also a current topic of interest.

During the past few decades, research on men has addressed different issues. Research during and since the Depression of the 1930s has examined the effects of men's unemployment on health and family life. Since the early 1960s, changing orientations to work have led to the recognition that working affects other aspects of men's lives such as leisure and overall quality of life. More recently, working

---

*Center for the Study of Family Development, University of Dayton, Ohio.

conditions and occupational stress have been studied as health risks and sources of stress for men and their families.

This chapter reviews and integrates what is known about relationships between work, family, and health among women. More importantly, it presents a framework for the analysis of these issues that highlights gaps in our knowledge and suggests directions for future research. The framework is built upon two major approaches used to investigate linkages among work, family life, and health. The "direct effect" approach is used to examine relationships among work, family, and health. First, the effects of family and health on women's labor force participation are reviewed. This is followed by an analysis of the impacts of women's employment status and working conditions on health and family life. The "joint effects" approach is used to examine the combined effects of work and family roles on work, family, and health outcomes. The major types of joint effects include the impact of performing multiple work and family roles on health and family life; the effects of the combined work characteristics of husbands and wives on health and family life; and work/family role coordination over the life course. The findings of the review are followed by an assessment of the current state of knowledge and recommendations for future research.

Because we are concerned with relationships between work and family, most of the research reviewed deals with women who are married and/or have children. Since relationships between work, family, and health for women are intertwined with those of men, the review incorporates data for men where appropriate.

Effects of Marriage, Parenthood, and Health on Women's Labor Force Participation

Recent evidence documents several ways in which family life and health affect the extent of women's labor force participation. The most important of these influences include (1) economic need, (2) constraints of the husband's occupation, (3) family life-cycle stage, and (4) physical health. This section reviews the literature on the effects of these factors on women's labor force participation.

These factors differ in their effects on women's work lives. Economic need increases women's labor force participation, while the constraints of husbands' occupations, family demands associated with family life-cycle stages, and poor physical health restrict participation. Data indicate a recent shift in the relative influence of these factors in the direction of increased labor force participation. The number of married women and mothers in the labor force has grown dramatically since World War II. In 1940 about 15 percent of married women were in the labor force; this rate increased to 24 percent in 1950, 31 percent in 1960, 41 percent in 1970, and 52 percent in 1983. Until the mid-1970s, wives without children under 18 had higher rates of labor force participation than mothers. Since then, however, mothers have had a higher rate; in 1983, 57 percent of mothers with children under 18 were in the labor force compared with 47 percent of wives without children. The rates of women with preschool children also have been increasing rapidly. In 1983, 50 percent of mothers whose youngest child was under 6 were in the labor force compared with 30 percent in 1970 and 19 percent in 1960. Forty-five percent of mothers whose youngest child is 1 year old and under were in the labor force; by the time the youngest child is 2 years old, a majority of married women are working or looking for work (Waldman, 1983).

The Provision of Economic Resources

Most women work to provide income for themselves or their families. They are either members of two-earner families or are sole support for themselves or their children. Two-thirds of employed women are single, divorced, widowed, separated, or married to men earning less than $10,000 per year (Mortimer and Sorensen, 1984).

In 1984 more than half of working wives were married to men earning less than $20,000 per year (Mortimer and Sorensen, 1984). Income levels vary considerably among traditional-earner families in which only the husband is employed and two-earner families in which both the husband and wife are employed. In 1978 the median family income for two-earner families was $22,730; the comparable figure for traditional-earner families is $18,900. Women's contribution is larger than it appears because men in two-earner families earn less than those in traditional-earner families—$14,900 compared with $16,000. Traditional-earner families were more likely to be below the poverty line in 1978; 5.5 percent were poor compared with 1.8 percent of two-earner families (Hayghe, 1981). This difference is larger in 1980; 7.2 percent of traditional-earner families were poor compared with 2.1 percent of two-earner families (Hayghe, 1982).

Women's contribution to the total income and standard of living of their families is substantial especially among full-time workers and those in families with relatively low incomes. In 1978 working wives contributed 26 percent to family income. This figure varies, however, according to the extent of labor force participation. Wives working full-time year-round contributed 40 percent to family income; those working full-time between 27 and 49 weeks contributed 30 percent; and those working up to half a year full-time or 1 to 52 weeks part-time contributed approximately 11 percent (Johnson, 1980).

Women's earnings have differing effects on the family's economic situation depending on the level of the husband's earnings. Oppenheimer (1982) reports that wives' earnings serve as a functional alternative to husbands' upward occupational mobility by raising family income to the category of higher-paid occupations. Employed women whose husbands earn relatively high incomes are able to improve the relative earnings status of their families. However, when husbands earn at the highest levels, most women are not able to earn enough to substantially improve their family's economic situation (Coser, 1985). In addition, incomes of women married to men with low earnings serve to maintain rather than improve the family's relative economic status (Paulson, 1982).

Female-headed families are often completely dependent on women's earnings or government transfer payments. In 1984 approximately 20 percent of families with children were maintained by the mother alone. This figure has doubled since 1970 mainly in response to the rising divorce rate. Almost half of these families maintained by women alone live below the poverty level (Hayghe, 1984). The number of one-parent families maintained by men is much smaller and these families are much less likely to be poor. In 1978, 42 percent of female-headed families were poor compared with 15 percent of male-headed one-parent families (Waldman et al., 1979).

The high rate of poverty among female-headed families is related to rates of labor force participation and income level. Female-headed families are less likely to have a wage earner than two-parent families. Over 90 percent of two-parent families have earners, while the figures for female-headed families are 78 percent in families with one child and 43 percent in families with four or more children (Hayghe, 1984). Female-headed families are also less likely to have more than one earner in the home. However, even when earners are present in female-headed families, family income is lower than for other families. In 1978 the average income in female-headed families with a working mother was $8,900, 40 percent that of two-earner families and 54 percent that of single-parent families headed by working fathers (Johnson, 1980). These patterns are related to the concentration of women in low-paying jobs and the lack of adequate child care for working mothers.

Wives' Participation in Their Husbands' Work

While the need to provide economic resources encourages a woman's employment, participating in her husband's work may limit the labor force participation of some wives—that is, they may not work outside the home, they may work part-time, or they may have low attachment to the labor force. The wives of professionals and managers often assist their husbands' careers by entertaining business associates, performing household and childbearing tasks, attending work-related social functions, and making business contacts through volunteer work in the community. These activities provide career advantages to husbands and improve the family's status in the community (Coser, 1985; Papanek, 1979). This contribution of unpaid labor by women has been referred to as a two-person career—that is, an occupation in which the wife has well-defined duties that are an integral part of her husband's occupation (Papanek, 1973). Occupations that fit the two-person career model include business executives, politicians, ministers, the self-employed, the military, and diplomats. Wives' participation is increased by work situations that involve men working at home, men using the home for business purposes, living in an institutional setting, or wives working alongside their husbands or serving as a proxy for their husbands (Finch, 1983).

Several aspects of two-person careers may limit the extent to which wives participate in the labor force: the level of economic rewards obtained by successful husbands, geographic mobility, demands on their time, and lack of control over the scheduling of time (Mortimer, Hall, and Hill, 1978). The high levels of income earned by men in two-person careers and the economic status derived from wives' participation combine to decrease the relative economic and status contributions that wives could make to their families through their own labor force participation (Coser, 1985).

Family Life-Cycle Stage

Family responsibilities associated with childbearing and child-rearing are a second family limitation on wives' labor force participation and attachment. A substantial amount of research has attempted to disentangle reciprocal relationships between childbearing and labor force participation, performance, and attachment. This research suggests that childbearing decreases labor force participation in the early stages of the work/family life cycle. However, after the early years of childbearing, labor force experience is associated with decreased fertility. The short-run effects of fertility lessen as children grow older, while the effects of initial employment and reduced fertility stimulate later employment (Felmlee, 1984; Cramer, 1980). Research documents a complex process through which marriage at a later age, later first birth, higher educational attainment, and lower fertility are associated with labor force participation and economic well-being (Hofferth, 1984; Hanson, 1983; Moore and Hofferth, 1979).

Relatively few women work continuously over the total period during which they are employed. Data from the Panel Study of Income Dynamics indicate that 21 percent of married women ages 18–47 were continuously employed between 1968 and 1978. Approximately 44 percent were employed for 7 of the 10 years (Masnick and Bane, 1980). However, the work-life expectancies of men and women are converging. In 1977 the average man of age 16 was expected to be in the labor force for 38 years; the comparable figure for women was 28 years. The average work-life duration for women has increased 12 years since 1970, while that of men has remained fairly constant. The average man enters the labor force 3 times during his life, while the average woman enters 4.5 times. Men's intermittent participation in the labor force ends earlier than women's. By age 25, men are expected to enter the labor force 1.1 more times versus 2.7 additional entries for women (Smith, 1982).

Young women's intermittent participation in the labor force is closely tied to childbearing. The length of time out of the labor force varies according to the number of children and the age of the youngest child when the mother returns to work. Waite, Haggstrom, and Kanouse (1985) report that most married women are working before their first pregnancy. The rate decreases during pregnancy so that by the month the child is born only one-fifth are still employed. By two years after the birth, the employment rate has increased to 60 percent of its previous level. Leaving employment is a more frequent response to the first pregnancy than is a reduction in hours.

McLaughlin (1982) has shown that the extent of decrease in employment before the first birth and the increase following the birth vary according to education, prebirth labor force experience, and economic need. Labor force participation rates are higher before and after birth among those with high levels of education and labor force experience. Economic need is not associated with more rapid withdrawal before the birth, but is positively associated with returning to work following the birth. Among older women, intermittent work histories are associated with family responsibilities, poor health, high family income, migration, and involuntary unemployment (Shaw, 1982).

Family responsibilities are also related to trends in part-time employment among women. Since 1965 the number of voluntary part-time workers has increased considerably. Much of this increase has occurred among women, especially among married women and mothers of children under 18. It has been greatest among women 18 to 44 years old. In 1977, 58 percent of female part-time workers were between the ages of 23 and 54 (Barrett, 1979). Despite the growth in part-time employment, the proportion of women working full-time has remained relatively stable at about two-thirds (Masnick and Bane, 1980). In addition, the percentage of mothers working full-time, year-round has increased from 32 in 1970 to 35 in 1977 (Waldman et al., 1979).

The concept of the life-cycle squeeze is useful in illustrating the interaction between economic need and family life-cycle stage in relation to wives' employment. A life-cycle squeeze is a period in which a family's economic needs and aspirations are relatively greater than its resources. Oppenheimer (1982) has documented two life-cycle squeezes during which husbands' earnings are likely to fall short of satisfying the life-cycle aspirations of the family. These periods are early adulthood when couples are establishing households and having children while husbands' earnings are still relatively low, and later adulthood when peak child-rearing expenses associated with adolescence are not matched by sufficient earnings increases. Oppenheimer (1974, 1979, 1982) suggests that these life-cycle squeezes are powerful determinants of wives' labor force participation during the two squeeze periods when economic costs are relatively high and time demands from children are relatively low (Oppenheimer, 1982). More recent data indicating rapid increases in the labor force participation of mothers with young children suggest that differences in participation by life cycle stage are decreasing.

Health and Women's Labor Force Participation

Women employed outside the home are healthier than homemakers. Employed women report fewer chronic illnesses, activity limitations, and doctor's visits and are less likely to rate their health as poor or fair (Verbrugge, 1982a; Nathanson, 1980; Waldron, 1980). Women reporting poor health or limited activity due to health problems are less likely to join and more likely to leave the labor force (Waldron et al., 1982). Verbrugge (1985) attributes this relationship to social selection since those with poor health are likely to avoid or limit obligations, become upset about their roles and reduce their activities, and work short or irregular job schedules. This explanation is supported by data indicating that health is more strongly related to employment than family status. Verbrugge (1983) suggests that selection is stronger for employment than for family status since the labor market filters strongly on health factors.

Women's work lives also are influenced by the health of others in the family. When children, elderly parents, or spouses are ill, handicapped, or disabled, women are the major care givers. In many cases, providing this care restricts women's labor force participation and the type of jobs they hold. Mothers of disabled children have lower levels of labor force participation and are less likely to become employed as their children become older. Employed mothers of disabled children earn less than other mothers; this earnings differential is greatest among mothers of school-age children (Baldwin and Glendinning, 1983). Single women caring for elderly parents are less likely to be employed than male care givers regardless of economic need. Many of these women quit working before retirement age (Wright, 1983). Brody (1985) reports that 28 percent of nonworking care givers had quit their jobs to care for their elderly mothers. An additional one-fourth were considering quitting work and many had reduced their work hours. Reduced labor force participation among care givers is partially attributable to the lack of other sources of care such as day care and respite care.

Summary

This section demonstrates complex relationships among marriage, parenthood, health, and women's work outside the home. Most women work because of economic need. Their earnings support single-parent families and improve the standard of living of two-earner families. Women also contribute to the economic well-being of their families by unpaid work of benefit to their husbands' careers. Women's family responsibilities limit their labor force participation. However, economic pressures to work often are greater when family responsibilities are more demanding—that is, when there are young children or ill family members requiring care. Working women are usually healthier than homemakers, suggesting that poor health limits labor force participation for some women. Thus, family and health factors both encourage and constrain women's labor force participation over the life course.

The Effects of Women's Employment on Family Life and Health

During the past 20 years a great deal of research has been conducted on the effects of women's employment on family life. This research examines the effects of women's employment on family formation and stability, household division of labor and husband-wife relationships, and family size and child development. Much of this work focuses on employment per se—that is, whether a woman is employed outside the home or is a full-time homemaker. Several comprehensive reviews of this research have been published in recent years (Moore and Sawhill, 1984; Moore, Spain, and Bianchi, 1984; Bronfenbrenner and Crouter, 1982; Hoffman, 1979; Moore and Hofferth, 1979; Rallings and Nye, 1979). Since space limitations prevent a thorough examination of this extensive literature, the following discussion draws on these reviews.

Family Formation and Stability

Female employment is related to the postponement of marriage—that is, marrying at a later age; however, it is not related to remaining single. Data on the effects of wife employment on divorce are mixed. The results may be explained by two counteracting processes, the independence effect and the income effect. The independence effect suggests that since working women can support themselves, they are less likely to marry for economic reasons or to escape their parental homes. In addition, women in unhappy marriages may be more likely to divorce if they can support themselves. The income effect suggests that working women are more likely to marry because their income makes marriage affordable and increases their desirability as marriage partners. The income of working wives also may prevent divorce by improving the quality of family life (Moore and Sawhill, 1984; Moore and Hofferth, 1979).

Household Division of Labor and Husband-Wife Relationships

Employed women spend approximately 50 percent less time in family work (housework and child care) than full-time homemakers. Since husbands and children do not compensate for the lower amount of time spent by employed women, families with working wives spend less total time on family work. This difference is accounted for by lowered standards and increased efficiency in housework and limited outside child-care assistance. Over the past several years husbands slowly have begun to increase the amount of time they spend in housework and child care. Men do relatively more housework before the birth of the first child and after grown children have left home. However, since this change is occurring equally in families with employed wives and full-time homemakers, it is not associated with wife employment. Employed wives spend more total time in paid work and family work than men and full-time homemakers (Szinovacz, 1984; Miller and Garrison, 1982; Moore and Hofferth, 1979; Rallings and Nye, 1979).

Working wives have higher levels of marital power than full-time homemakers, especially in the area of financial decision-making. This difference has been explained by the resource theory of power. This theory suggests that the level of marital power is associated with the relative amounts of income, occupational prestige, contacts, and other socioeconomic resources provided by the husband and wife. Since employed wives are able to provide more of these resources than full-time homemakers, their power relative to their husbands' is greater (Moore and Hofferth, 1979; Rallings and Nye, 1979).

Data on the effects of wife employment on marital satisfaction are mixed and complex. Employed wives have higher levels of marital satisfaction than homemakers under certain conditions, namely, if they have high levels of education, are working out of choice, are working part-time, and/or receive approval and support from their husbands. Wives who have low incomes, are working out of necessity, and/or hold undesirable jobs have lower marital satisfaction than full-time homemakers. Some husbands of employed wives have lower levels of marital satisfaction than husbands of full-time homemakers. These findings have been attributed to a relative loss of power and status, demands to participate in household work, and a disruption in traditional routines. However, men whose wives are working out of choice or are working part-time have higher levels of marital satisfaction than husbands of housewives (Moore and Hofferth, 1979; Rallings and Nye, 1979).

Family Size and Child Development

An earlier section referred to reciprocal relationships between female employment and family size and focused on the influence of fertility on labor force participation. However, female employment also negatively affects family size (Felmlee, 1984; Cramer, 1980). Women who are working or planning to work report wanting and planning to have fewer children (Moore, Spain, and Bianchi, 1984).

Due to the early concern about the possible negative effects of maternal employment on children, research has examined its numerous possible impacts on children, including academic achievement, independence, and sex-role attitudes. The most consistent finding from this research is that maternal employment per se has no pervasive negative consequences for children. In general, the children of working mothers do well in school, have high achievement motivation, are relatively independent, and have relatively egalitarian sex-role norms. As with marital satisfaction, several conditions associated with maternal employment are significant. Children do better if their mothers work out of choice, like their work, and provide high-quality supervision. One still unexplained negative effect of maternal employment has been reported: middle-class sons of working mothers tend to have low achievement levels (Moore and Sawhill, 1984; Moore, Spain, and Bianchi, 1984; Bronfenbrenner and Crouter, 1982; Hoffman, 1979).

Physical Health

As reported earlier, women employed outside the home are healthier than homemakers. Much of this relationship can be accounted for by selection—that is, women in poor health are less likely to be employed. Longitudinal data indicate that employment per se has little direct effect on subsequent health changes (Waldron et al., 1982).

Several studies have examined the combined effects of work and family roles on physical health. Verbrugge (1983) reports that being employed, married, and a parent are independently related to positive health outcomes among women. Women with all three roles report the highest levels of health, while those with none have the poorest health; these effects are additive rather than interactive. These results differ from those of Nathanson (1980) who, in addition to finding positive main effects for marital status, children, and employment, also reports significant positive interactions for children × employment and marital status × children.

In contrast, Woods and Hulka (1979) find that role density—that is, the number of role responsibilities—is positively related to physical symptoms. Family responsibilities are of major importance, especially having three or more children or an ill spouse. Haynes and Feinleib (1980) report high rates of coronary heart disease among clerical workers and women with three or more children. Rates are especially high among clerical workers who also are married with children. Thus, although multiple roles tend to have positive effects on health, specific combinations of work and family roles have negative consequences.

A more detailed analysis of the combined effects of work-role characteristics and family demands on health has been presented by Verbrugge (1985). Poor health is associated with several role burdens including irregular or short work schedules, dissatisfaction with work and other major roles, few or many time constraints, few or many family dependents, and few role involvements and responsibilities. She interprets these direct and curvilinear relationships in terms of social selection and social causation. Social selection accounts for relationships between few responsibilities and poor health since the unhealthy are unable to engage in as many activities as the healthy. Social causation explains relationships between high levels of responsibility and poor health because of the stress associated with high demands.

Mental Health

Good mental health is higher among employed women than among full-time homemakers. Warr and Parry's review (1982) indicates that employed women have significantly higher psychological well-being in half of 38 studies and nonsignificantly higher well-being in the other half; no studies reported higher well-being among homemakers. Findings reported by Kessler and McRae (1982) suggest that the relationship between mental health and employment is weaker than that for physical health. However, it is more attributable to the effects of employment on mental health and less a result of selection than is the case for physical health. It is also strongly affected by family characteristics and attitudes toward working. Husband's assistance with housework and children and favorable attitudes toward working are negatively related to depression and psychophysical symptoms (Waldron and Herold, 1986; Keith and Schafer, 1983; Ross, Mirowsky, and Huber, 1983; Kessler and McRae, 1982).

Relationships among work, family, and mental health are generally similar to those reported for physical health. Being married, being employed outside the home, and being a parent are independently associated with lower levels of depression (Kandel, Davies, and Raveis, 1985; Gore and Mangione, 1983; Aneshensel, Frerichs, and Clark, 1981). Married and employed women also have fewer psychophysical complaints; however, having children under 18 at home is accompanied by more complaints (Gore and Mangione, 1983).

The findings for performing multiple roles are mixed. Kandel, Davies, and Raveis (1985) find that women who are married, working, and parents have the lowest levels of depression, while those who are single, not working, and not parents have the highest levels. This result contrasts with the findings of Aneshensel, Frerichs, and Clark (1981) who report no additional reduction in depression from being employed and being married or a parent. More detailed analyses reveal complex interactions among the three roles in relation to depression. Kandel, Davies, and Raveis (1985) find that being employed buffers the effects of marital stress on depression, while parenthood exacerbates the effects of occupational stress. Cleary and Mechanic (1983) report similar results. They find that marital status is less strongly related to depression among employed women than among homemakers. However, having children at home is positively related to depression among employed women. Gove and Geerken (1977) indicate that psychiatric symptoms increase monotonically with an increase in the number of children among employed women but not among homemakers.

Thus, to understand the impact of multiple roles on mental and physical health it is necessary to look beyond the number and type of roles women perform and to study the complex relationships among them. The conditions under which enacting multiple roles is associated with negative health needs further analysis. The balance of demands and rewards associated with each role and interactions among them must be assessed to increase our understanding of these complexities.

Summary

This research focused on the effects of women's employment per se on health and family life. The effects cannot be understood fully, however, without examining specific conditions associated with employment. Unfortunately, most research in this area deals with samples of men or samples undifferentiated by sex. The next section reviews the available data regarding the effects of work-role characteristics on health and family life among samples of employed women.

Women's Work-Role Characteristics, Health, and Family Life

Several conditions associated with performing a job may spill over into family life or affect mental and physical health. Spillover refers to the generalization of characteristics from one life domain to another—for example, individuals experiencing stress at work are tense and tired at home. Spillover can be either positive or negative. With positive spillover, satisfaction or stimulation in one role generates energy and interest in other areas of life. In negative spillover, problems and stress in one role drain and preoccupy the individual, making it difficult to perform the other role adequately. This process can also have negative impacts on mental and physical health.

Research on men indicates that work-role characteristics vary in the extent to which they evoke positive or negative spillover. Intrinsic characteristics, such as autonomy, and attitudes, such as job satisfaction and involvement, show positive or curvilinear relationships with quality of family life and health. Other work-role characteristics place demands and limits on an individual's work behavior that must be accommodated; they do not imply initiative or direct involvement on the individual's part. Two characteristics of this type have a negative influence on health and the quality of family life: (1) the amount and scheduling of work time, and (2) job demands.

Amount and Scheduling of Work Time

The effects of the total number of work hours vary according to the outcome being examined. Women's work hours are directly related to work/family conflict and strain (Pleck and Staines, 1985; Katz and Piotrkowski, 1983; Keith and Schafer, 1983) and to the probability of divorce, especially among middle-income families and families in which the husband disapproves of his wife's employment (Spitze and South, 1985). Other studies find that number of work hours is associated with lower levels of spousal interaction, but is not related to the quality of marital and family relations (Pleck and Staines, 1985; White, 1983; Piotrkowski and Crits-Christoph, 1981). The number of hours worked is associated with depression and other psychological distress symptoms and with high diastolic blood pressure, but not with levels of serum cholesterol (Keith and Schafer, 1983; Sorensen et al., 1983).

Data on part-time work complement these findings. As mentioned earlier, working part-time is generally associated with marital satisfaction. In addition, the mental health of women working part-time is equal to or higher than levels for homemakers and women working full-time; however, part-time work is not related to physical health (Hauenstein, Kasl, and Harburg, 1977; Welch and Booth, 1977). Thus, although working per se and working part-time are associated with positive health and family outcomes, working long hours has negative consequences.

The most extensive study reporting on the impact of women's work schedules on family life (Pleck and Staines, 1985) finds that working variable days or weekends and working nonday and variable shifts are positively but not significantly related to work/family conflicts, but are not related to family adjustment. White (1983) reports a negative relationship between an irregular work schedule and the amount of spousal interaction. Piotrkowski, Stark, and Burbank (1983) find weak positive relationships between working a nonday shift and anxiety, psychosomatic and physical complaints, and work/family conflict.

Studies of alternative work schedules reveal mixed results. Lee (1983) finds that flextime reduces stress regarding child care and socialization, but makes no difference in stress associated with household chores. Bohen and Viveros-Long (1981) demonstrate that flextime is associated with less job/family-role strain among women without children, but is not effective in reducing strain among parents with major responsibility for child care. A study of nurses with children under 18 indicates that a compressed workweek schedule (three 12-hour days) is associated with less job/family-role strain, better job/family management, more time spent with children, and less time spent with spouse (Sorenson, 1984).

Job Demands

Limited research has located a wide range of job demands that influence work/family relationships and health. The following are the most significant correlates of work/family conflict and family-role strain: amount of physical and mental effort, being required to work hard and fast, heavy workload, lack of autonomy, and dangers in the physical environment (Katz and Piotrkowski, 1983; Piotrkowski, Stark, and Burbank, 1983; Pleck, 1979). In addition, a small-scale study by Piotrkowski, Stark, and Burbank (1983) reports relationships between lack of control, poor supervisor relations, job insecurity, and dangers in the physical environment with anxiety and psychosomatic and physical complaints.

Limited data indicate that large numbers of women are employed in occupations that may expose them to specific physical, chemical, and biological hazards (Waldron, 1980). For example, clerical workers are exposed to chemicals from copying and duplicating machines and strain associated with working at video display terminals. Health-care workers are subject to the risk of infectious diseases, back strain from lifting patients, and exposure to anesthetic gases. Women working in dry-cleaning and laundry establishments have high levels of cancer mortality. Women in the textile industry who work with cotton fibers risk the development of brown lung and byssinosis. Beauticians have an increased risk of respiratory disease because of exposure to hairsprays. The available data do not permit a precise estimate of the effects of occupational hazards on women's health. Waldron (1980) concludes that, although many women work in relatively safe environments, a substantial fraction are exposed to serious health hazards.

The few studies that examine the joint effects of work-role characteristics and family structure demands on quality of family life among women reveal that both work and family characteristics are related to work/family conflict (Cooke and Rousseau, 1984; Katz and Piotrkowski, 1983; Keith and Schafer, 1980). These variables include work hours, job involvement, job autonomy, time expectations at work, marital status, and number and ages of children. A study of working parents reports that family demands explain more variance in time shortage, while work-role characteristics explain more variance in job tension (Kelly and Voydanoff, 1985; Voydanoff and Kelly, 1984). The most extensive study including both work and family characteristics indicates that work-role characteristics and family structure demands have additive effects on work/family conflict and marital/ family satisfaction—that is, the variables make independent contributions to quality of family life (Voydanoff, 1984b). The effect of work-role characteristics and family demands do not have interactive effects in which work-role characteristics exacerbate the effects of family demands on family life or vice versa.

Job Satisfaction

Among the intrinsic and attitudinal aspects of work, only job satisfaction has been examined among women. Katz and Piotrkowski (1983) report a significant negative correlation between job satisfaction and family-role strain. A second study (Piotrkowski and Crits-Christoph, 1981) finds direct relationships between positive job mood and marital satisfaction, satisfaction with family relations, and positive home mood for low-status women. For high-status women, only positive home mood is directly related to job satisfaction; the other two correlations are negative. These findings support the idea that moderate levels of job satisfaction and other indicators of psychological involvement in work have positive effects on family life. However, at the highest levels, satisfaction with and involvement in work may be associated with a lack of participation in family life and other negative effects.

Job satisfaction is more consistently related to mental and physical health among women. Keith and Schafer (1983) report a negative correlation between job satisfaction and depression. Kessler and McRae (1982) find that employed women who are satisfied with their jobs have low levels of psychological distress, while those who are dissatisfied have high levels. A comprehensive analysis of job satisfaction and physical health reports consistent though generally not significant positive relationships between job satisfaction and a wide range of indicators of physical health (Verbrugge, 1982b).

This research generally supports the findings on men regarding the impact of work-role characteristics on health and quality of family life. However, the lack of research in this area among women precludes precise conclusions and generalizations.

Joint Effects of Husbands' and Wives' Work-Role Characteristics on Family Life

As indicated above, women's family demands and health have direct effects on labor force participation, and conditions associated with employment directly influence health and family life. In addition to these direct effects, work and family characteristics have joint effects on health and family life. These joint effects are examined in the next two sections. First, we look at the effects of husbands' and wives' combined work-role characteristics on family life among two-earner families. These combined characteristics also may influence health; however, no studies documenting these effects could be located. Three major aspects of husbands' and wives' combined work-role characteristics are related to the nature and quality of family life: relative socioeconomic attainment of husbands and wives, work-related geographic mobility and commuter marriage, and amount and scheduling of work time.

Relative Socioeconomic Attainment of Husbands and Wives

Limited data suggest that when wives are more successful than their husbands, the effects on the quality of family life are negative. For example, Hornung and McCullough (1981) report lower levels of marital satisfaction among achievement-oriented men whose wives have more education than expected in relation to their own educational level. However, women with "overeducated" husbands have higher levels of marital satisfaction. In addition, husbands, but not wives, are dissatisfied with their marriages when their wives' occupations are higher than expected based on the husband's educational level. A second study, using a different sample, reports that the likelihood of life-threatening family violence increases among couples in which the woman's occupation is higher than expected in relation to her husband's occupation (Hornung, McCullough, and Sugimoto, 1981).

Philliber and Hiller (1983) report that women in nontraditional occupations in 1967 were more likely to have divorced, to have left the labor force, or to have shifted to a lower-status position by 1974 than women in traditional occupations in 1967. Being in a nontraditional occupation is more strongly related to these changes than the relative status of the husbands' and wives' occupations.

Work-Related Geographic Mobility and Commuter Marriage

When a member of a two-career or two-earner family chooses or is required to make a work-related move, the normal stresses associated with such moves in one-earner families are increased. Although some husbands are refusing transfers and passing up opportunities to move because of their wives' careers, the effects on women are greater. Women move more often to accommodate their spouses' job transfers and changes than men do (Foster, Wallston, and Berger, 1980; Duncan and Perrucci, 1976). These moves have negative effects on wives' employment status, weeks worked, and earnings; however, limited research suggests that these effects disappear after two years (Spitze, 1984; Lichter, 1983).

In recent years, an alternative to one spouse's moving to accommodate the career of the other has emerged—a commuter marriage in which spouses work in different locations during the week and reunite on weekends. These separations differ from an earlier type associated with traditionally male occupations such as merchant marine, entertainer, athlete, politician, and the military in that they derive from the combined demands of two occupations. The effects of commuter marriage vary according to several family and work characteristics. Commuter marriages are more successful among families in which the two jobs are relatively close to each other, length of periods apart are relatively short, both spouses are strongly career-oriented, at least one spouse has an established career, and the couples are older, married longer, and free from child-rearing responsibilities (Gerstel and Gross, 1983, 1984; Gross, 1980; Kirschner and Walum, 1978).

Amount and Scheduling of Work Time

Little information is available about the effects of the combined hours worked by husbands and wives on family life. Dempster-McClain and Moen (1983) report that marital satisfaction is highest among couples with reduced hours—that is, the husband works full-time or extended hours and the wife works part-time—and is lowest for couples with extended hours in which both work at least full-time and one or both work overtime or hold second jobs. The pattern of reduced hours is associated with the lowest levels of work/family interference for women and the highest levels for men. A higher total number of hours worked by a couple is related to less time spent with children and lower family satisfaction for men and women and to work/family interference among women; however, total hours are not related to marital happiness or satisfaction (Kingston and Nock, 1985).

Data on the effects of joint work schedules are also limited. Kingston and Nock (1985) report that the length of the family workday—that is, the total number of hours that at least one spouse is at work—is related to more time spent on chores and less free time spent with spouse among women and higher family satisfaction among men. The length of the workday is not related to marital happiness or satisfaction. Perry-Jenkins (1985) finds that the length of the family workweek is negatively related to the frequency of leisure activities with spouse and/or children and to the number of joint positive interactions with spouse among parents but not among nonparents. A third study (Staines and Pleck, 1983) reveals interactions between husbands' and wives' shifts in relation to husband's schedule conflict. The influence of husbands' nonday and variable shifts on schedule conflict is exacerbated when wives also work nonday or variable shifts.

Research on the effects of combined husband-wife work characteristics on family life reveals that they are diverse. However, because research of this type is in its infancy, it is impossible to draw firm and specific conclusions regarding the nature and extent of these effects.

Women's Work and Family Role Coordination Over the Life Course

At some time in their lives most women are workers, wives, and mothers. Many women perform all three roles simultaneously. The adequate performance of each role depends on the demands, responsibilities, time, energy, and commitment associated with the others. The demands associated with women's work and family roles vary over the life course. For example, women beginning careers while raising young children are likely to experience role overload. In the early stages of a career, workers are highly involved in their work as they establish themselves as full members of their occupations (Hall and Hall, 1979). At the same time, young children demand much time, attention, and energy (Aldous, 1978). Working parents of school-age children find it difficult to participate in the school and community activities that often occur during working hours (Harry, 1976). About the time that middle-aged women with grown children begin to establish new or second careers, many become responsible for the care of elderly parents (Brody, 1985). In this section we discuss two of the major adaptations women use to address the overload and conflicting demands associated with traditional work and family career patterns: sequential work/family role staging and symmetrical work/family role allocation (Voydanoff, 1980, 1985).

Sequential Work/Family Role Staging

In sequential staging an individual alternates work and family responsibilities over some portion of the life course. The alternative is simultaneous staging in which both work and family activities are pursued continuously with minimal interruptions for childbearing (Sorensen, 1983; St. John-Parsons, 1978; Elder, 1977; Bernard, 1971). Sequential staging of work and family responsibilities is the modal pattern among women (Chenoweth and Maret, 1980). The following types of sequential work/family participation are most common: (1) conventional, in which a woman quits working when she marries or has children and does not return to work; (2) early interrupted, in which she stops working for childbearing early in her career and then returns; (3) late interrupted, in which she establishes a career, quits for a period of childbearing, and then returns; and (4) unstable, in which she alternates between full-time homemaking and paid employment. These patterns vary in their effects on women's earnings over the life course. Wives who remain employed during childbearing earn more at midlife than those who interrupt their careers and those who enter the labor force during and following childbearing (Van Velsor and O'Rand, 1984).

Most sequencing occurs as women adjust their labor force participation to demands associated with family career stages, especially childbearing (Moen, 1982; Waite, 1980). The choice between early and later parenthood is a major element of role staging. This decision involves several trade-offs in the performance of work and family activities over the life course (Wilkie, 1981). Early parenthood increases economic pressures on the family; however, it also provides an opportunity for women to formulate future career goals. Women who establish careers before childbearing often find it easier to return to a desirable position than those interrupting earlier. Some women prefer to raise children when they are younger and more compatible in age and interests with other child-rearing families; others choose to assume parenting responsibilities later when there is less pressure to advance in a career for both parents (Daniels and Weingarten, 1982; Hall and Hall, 1979; Bernard, 1978).

The increasing numbers of women who are committed to working over the life course find it difficult to engage in extensive work/family-role staging. Many of these women perform two full-time jobs—one at work and one at home. This situation prompts the perception that the division of work and family responsibilities between men and women is unfair and stimulates calls for the husbands of employed women to do more family work.

Symmetrical Work/Family Role Allocation

Symmetrical role allocation involves a relatively interchangeable division of labor in which both husbands and wives are employed outside the home and perform family work. In a symmetrical pattern of role allocation, husbands perform more family work and women perform more work-related duties than in traditional role allocation. The relative commitment to work and family careers by husbands and wives is more balanced; men increase their accommodation to family needs while women accommodate more to outside work demands (Bailyn, 1978; Young and Willmott, 1977).

Wives in symmetrical families are coproviders with major responsibility for contributing economically to the family. Men whose wives share the provider role have more flexibility to pursue satisfying work and develop a broader range of interests, relationships, and identities. In addition, in symmetrical families husbands move beyond "helping" their wives with family work and assume responsibility in this area. Both responsibilities and task performance are more symmetrical.

Despite the need among employed women for this type of role allocation, progress toward its achievement has been slow. Recent data suggest a slight increase in the amount of time husbands of employed women spend in family work, although women still spend more time than men. The major contributor to symmetry in family work is the decreased amount of time spent by women (Szinovacz, 1984; Pleck 1983). Many men and some women resist major changes in the direction of symmetrical role allocation (Lein, 1979; Tognoli, 1979).

Issues for Future Research

Research on women's work, family, and health has developed unevenly. Some areas have been explored in detail while others remain relatively neglected. All have unanswered questions of importance to our understanding of linkages between work, family, and health among women.

Research on the effects of marriage, parenthood, and health on women's labor force participation has focused on the role of economic need in encouraging such participation and the role of family demands, responsibilities associated with husbands' careers, and poor health in restricting labor force participation. However, this research does not address several important issues regarding the influence of family demands on women's work. Although family characteristics and demands influence labor force participation at a given time, they do not explain much of the persistent gap between men's and women's earnings and occupational attainments.

Most research on family demands focuses on the care of young children. Little is known about the effects of caring for children with special needs or caring for spouses, elderly parents, and other family members who are ill or disabled. Recent statistics indicate that reducing labor force participation to care for young children is becoming less common; however, few studies assess the effects of this increased labor force attachment on other aspects of women's work such as aspirations and long-term earnings and attainments. We also need more work that analyzes the joint impacts of economic need and family demands on women's work. The life-cycle squeeze is a promising start in this direction. Lastly, research examining family influences on productivity, satisfaction, and work involvement is almost nonexistent.

Until recently, studies of the effects of women's work on family life and health were limited to relationships between employment status and family and health outcomes, such as family formation and stability, the nature and quality of husband-wife relationships, family size and children's development, and mental and physical health. Some of this research has also examined contingent effects, such as whether the woman is working by choice, part-time versus full-time employment, extent of spouse support, having a favorable attitude toward working, and the number and ages of children. However, few studies look at the effects of conditions associated with various jobs on women's health and family life. The research reviewed above on work hours and scheduling, job demands, and job satisfaction is, with few exceptions, based on small unrepresentative samples and a narrow range of work-role characteristics. Research on job stress and unemployment, which is quite extensive among men, is in its infancy among women. These gaps hinder the development of effective employment policies to address issues of importance to working women and their families.

In addition, more needs to be done to establish causal direction and reciprocal effects in relationships among women's work, family, and health. First steps have been taken regarding relationships between women's labor force participation and fertility and physical health. This research demonstrates complex reciprocal relationships influenced by other factors, such as the effects of age at first birth and education on the relationship between fertility and women's labor force participation. Other relationships can be expected to be reciprocal, such as those between family demands and satisfaction and work productivity, satisfaction, and involvement.

Research based on the joint-effects approach is even more limited. Work on the influence of combined husband-wife work-role characteristics on family life is just beginning; it is nonexistent regarding women's health. Initial work in this area looks at the relative attainments of husbands and wives and geographic mobility. A few studies examine the effects of husbands' and wives' combined work hours and scheduling on family life; however, work on the effects of combined job demands, satisfaction, and involvement has not yet begun. Despite the complexities involved, future research in this area should provide a broader understanding of the interrelationships among work, family, and health for both women and men. It also will fill gaps in areas where more is known about women than about men, and vice versa.

When we look at research on the effects of women performing multiple roles, the picture changes somewhat. Work in this area is more extensive among women than men. It examines the impact of women's combined work and family responsibilities on mental and physical health and quality of family life. However, it is still difficult to distinguish between the positive and negative main effects of multiple roles and their interactive effects. Although this research shows mixed results, it does establish that the effects of multiple roles are not exclusively positive or negative. As in other areas, we need to establish the conditions under which they are positive, negative, or mixed.

Research on women's coordination of work and family roles over the life course also is in an early stage of development. Major patterns of work/family-role staging have been documented; however, these patterns gloss over the many variations women use to coordinate work and family demands. In addition, although these patterns have been examined in relation to women's rates of labor force participation, their effects on health and quality of family life have not been assessed. Men's relatively low levels of participation in household work and child-rearing are shown to be a factor in the slow development of symmetrical work/family-role allocation between men and women. However, we have no compelling explanations of why women's increased labor force participation is not met with increased male participation in family work.

These gaps suggest important areas for future research. In addition, the implications of changing patterns in women's work and family lives for the nature and quality of both women's and men's lives need further study. First, the provider role, the traditional mainstay of men's participation in family life, is increasingly being shared by women. Most women in two-earner and single-parent families work because of economic need; their families cannot be supported solely by a man working outside the home. We need more information about the implications of this change for employers, employment policy, work-ers' health and well-being, and the nature and quality of family life.

Second, the increased employment of wives means that a growing number of families have no adult at home full-time. This development has significant implications for many aspects of "women's work," including child care, care of other dependents such as elderly parents, the provision of social support, and unpaid work in the community. We are just beginning to assess the effects of this change and to formulate policies and programs to accommodate the increased need for alter-native types of dependent and community care.

These changes mean that the basis for both men's and women's participation in work and family life is changing. Men are no longer the sole economic providers and women are no longer at home to care for their families full-time. It is not sufficient to view these as women's issues that affect men only as husbands of working women. The analy-sis of work, family, and health must move beyond an examination of women's roles and assume a broader perspective in which these issues are recognized as relevant to both men and women. As long as employ-ment policies regarding issues such as flextime, part-time work, and parental leaves are based on the assumption that these policies are relevant only to women, women will be at a disadvantage in the employment arena.

References

Aldous, Joan. *Family Careers: Developmental Change in Families.* New York: Wiley, 1978.

Aneshensel, Carol S., Ralph R. Frerichs, and Virginia A. Clark. "Family Roles and Sex Differences in Depression." *Journal of Health and Social Behavior* 22 (December 1981): pp. 379–93.

Bailyn, Lotte. "Accommodation of Work to Family." In *Working Couples*, eds. R. and R. Rapoport. New York: Harper & Row, 1978. Pp. 159–74.

Baldwin, Sally, and Caroline Glendinning. "Unemployment, Women and Their Dis-abled Children." In *A Labour of Love*, eds. J. Finch and D. Groves. Boston: Rout-ledge and Kegan Paul, 1983. Pp. 53–71.

Barrett, Nancy S. "Women in the Job Market: Unemployment and Work Schedules." In *The Subtle Revolution*, ed. Ralph Smith. Washington: Urban Institute, 1979. Pp. 63–98.

Bernard, Jessie. "'Contingency' or 'Career' Schedules for Women." In *Increasing Student Development Options in College*, guest ed. D.E. Drew. Washington: Jossey-Bass, 1978. Pp. 27–37.

———. *Women and the Public Interest.* Chicago: Aldine, Atherton, 1971.

Bohen, Halcyone H., and Anamaria Viveros-Long. *Balancing Jobs and Family Life.* Philadelphia: Temple University Press, 1981.

Brody, Elaine M. "Parent Care as a Normative Family Stress." *Gerontologist* 25 (1985): pp. 19–29.

Bronfenbrenner, Urie, and Ann C. Crouter. "Work and Family Through Time and Space." In *Families That Work*, eds. S.B. Kamerman and S.D. Hayes. Washington: National Academy Press, 1982. Pp. 39–83.

Chenoweth, Lillian C., and Elizabeth Maret. "The Career Patterns of Mature American Women." *Sociology of Work and Occupations* 7 (May 1980): pp. 222–51.

Cleary, Paul D., and David Mechanic. "Sex Differences in Psychological Distress among Married People." *Journal of Health and Social Behavior* 24 (June 1983): pp. 111–21.

Cooke, Robert A., and Denise M. Rousseau. "Stress and Strain from Family Roles and Work-Role Expectations." *Journal of Applied Psychology* 69 (1984): pp. 252–60.

Coser, Rose Laub. "Power Lost and Status Gained: The American Middle-Class Husband." Paper presented at the Annual Meeting of the American Sociological Association, 1985.

Cramer, James C. "Fertility and Female Employment: Problems of Causal Direction." *American Sociological Review* 45 (April 1980): pp. 167–90.

Daniels, Pamela, and Kathy Weingarten. *Sooner or Later: The Timing of Parenthood in Adult Lives*. New York: Norton, 1982.

Dempster-McClain, Donna I., and Phyllis Moen. "Work-Time Involvement and Preferences of Employed Parents." Paper presented at the Annual Meeting of the National Council on Family Relations, 1983.

Duncan, R. Paul, and Carolyn Perrucci. "Dual Occupation Families and Migration." *American Sociological Review* 41 (April 1976): pp. 252–61.

Elder, Glen H., Jr. "Family History and the Life Course." *Journal of Family History* 2 (Winter 1977): pp. 279–304.

Feldberg, Roslyn L., and Evelyn Glenn. "Male and Female: Job Versus Gender Models in the Sociology of Work." *Social Problems* 26 (June 1979): pp. 524–38.

Felmlee, Diane H. "A Dynamic Analysis of Women's Employment Exits." *Demography* 21 (May 1984): pp. 171–83.

Finch, Janet. *Married to the Job: Wives' Incorporation in Men's Work*. London: George Allen & Unwin, 1983.

Foster, Martha A., Barbara S. Wallston, and Michael Berger. "Feminist Orientation and Job-Seeking Behavior among Dual-Career Couples." *Sex Roles* 8 (1980): pp. 59–65.

Gerstel, Naomi, and Harriet Gross. *Commuter Marriage*. New York: Guilford, 1984.
_____. "Commuter Marriage: Couples Who Live Apart." In *Contemporary Families and Alternative Lifestyles*, eds. E.D. Macklin and R.H. Rubin. Beverly Hills, CA: Sage, 1983. Pp. 180–93.

Gore, Susan, and Thomas W. Mangione. "Social Roles, Sex Roles and Psychological Distress." *Journal of Health and Social Behavior* 24 (December 1983): pp. 300–12.

Gove, Walter R., and Michael R. Geerken. "The Effect of Children and Employment on the Mental Health of Married Men and Women." *Social Forces* 56 (September 1977): pp. 66–85.

Gross, Harriet. "Dual-Career Couples Who Live Apart: Two Types." *Journal of Marriage and the Family* 42 (August 1980): pp. 567–76.

Hall, Francine S., and Douglas T. Hall. *The Two-Career Couple*. Reading, MA: Addison Wesley, 1979.

Hanson, Sandra L. "A Family Life-Cycle Approach to the Socioeconomic Attainment of Working Women." *Journal of Marriage and the Family* 45 (May 1983): pp. 323–38.

Harry, Joseph. "Evolving Sources of Happiness for Men Over the Life Cycle: A Structural Analysis." *Journal of Marriage and the Family* 38 (May 1976): pp. 289–96.

Hauenstein, Louise S., Stanislav V. Kasl, and Ernest Harburg. "Work Status, Work Satisfaction, and Blood Pressure among Married Black and White Women." *Psychology of Women Quarterly* 1 (1977): pp. 334–39.

Hayghe, Howard. "Working Mothers Reach Record Number in 1984." *Monthly Labor Review* 107 (December 1984): pp. 31–34.

———. "Dual-Earner Families: Their Economic and Demographic Characteristics." In *Two Paychecks: Life in Dual-Earner Families*, ed. J. Aldous. Beverly Hills, CA: Sage, 1982. Pp. 27–40.

———. "Husbands and Wives as Earners: An Analysis of Family Data." *Monthly Labor Review* 104 (February 1981): pp. 46–52.

Haynes, Suzanne G., and Manning Feinleib. "Women, Work and Coronary Heart Disease." *American Journal of Public Health* 70 (1980): pp. 133–41.

Hofferth, Sandra L. "Long-Term Economic Consequences for Women of Delayed Childbearing and Reduced Family Size." *Demography* 42 (May 1984): pp. 141–55.

Hoffman, Lois Wladis. "Maternal Employment: 1979." *American Psychologist* 34 (October 1979): pp. 859–65.

Hornung, Carlton A., and B. Claire McCullough. "Status Relationships in Dual-Employment Marriages: Consequences for Psychological Well-Being." *Journal of Marriage and the Family* 43 (February 1981): pp. 125–41.

Hornung, Carlton A., B. Claire McCullough, and Taichi Sugimoto. "Status Relationships in Marriage: Risk Factors in Spouse Abuse." *Journal of Marriage and the Family* 43 (August 1981): pp. 675–92.

Johnson, Beverly L. "Marital and Family Characteristics of the Labor Force, March 1979." *Monthly Labor Review* 103 (April 1980): pp. 48–52.

Kandel, Denise B., Mark Davies, and Victoria H. Raveis. "The Stressfulness of Daily Social Roles for Women." *Journal of Health and Social Behavior* 26 (March 1985): pp. 64–78.

Kanter, Rosabeth M. *Work and Family in the United States: A Critical Review and Agenda for Research and Policy.* New York: Russell Sage Foundation, 1977.

Katz, Mitchell H., and Chaya S. Piotrkowski. "Correlates of Family Role Strain among Employed Black Women." *Family Relations* 32 (July 1983): pp. 331–39.

Keith, Pat M., and Robert B. Schafer. "Employment Characteristics of Both Spouses and Depression in Two-Job Families." *Journal of Marriage and the Family* 45 (November 1983): pp. 877–84.

———. "Role Strain and Depression in Two-Job Families." *Family Relations* 29 (October 1980): pp. 483–88.

Kelly, Robert F., and Patricia Voydanoff. "Work/Family Role Strain among Employed Parents." *Family Relations* 34 (July 1985): pp. 367–74.

Kessler, Ronald C., and James A. McRae, Jr. "The Effect of Wives' Employment on the Mental Health of Married Men and Women." *American Sociological Review* 47 (April 1982): pp. 216–27.

Kingston, Paul William, and Steven L. Nock. "Consequences of the Family Work Day." *Journal of Marriage and the Family* 47 (August 1985): pp. 619–29.

Kirschner, Betty F., and Laurel Walum. "Two-Location Families." *Alternative Lifestyles* 1 (November 1978): pp. 513–15.

Lee, Robert A. "Flextime and Conjugal Roles." *Journal of Occupational Behavior* 5 (1983): pp. 297–315.

Lein, Laura. "Male Participation in Home Life." *Family Coordinator* 28 (October 1979): pp. 489–95.

Lichter, Daniel T. "Socioeconomic Returns to Migration among Married Women." *Social Forces* 62 (December 1983): pp. 487–503.

Masnick, George, and Mary Jo Bane. *The Nation's Families: 1960–1990.* Cambridge, MA: Joint Center for Urban Studies of MIT and Harvard University, 1980.

McLaughlin, Steven D. "Differential Patterns of Female Labor-Force Participation Surrounding the First Birth." *Journal of Marriage and the Family* 44 (May 1982): pp. 407–20.

Miller, Joanne, and Howard H. Garrison. "Sex Roles: The Division of Labor at Home and in the Workplace." *Annual Review of Sociology* 8 (1982): pp. 237–62.

Moen, Phyllis. "Continuities and Discontinuities in Women's Labor Force Activity." Paper presented at the Annual Meeting of the American Sociological Association, 1982.

Moore, Kristin A., and Sandra L. Hofferth. "Effects of Women's Employment on Marriage: Formation, Stability and Roles." *Marriage and Family Review* 2 (1979): pp. 27–36.

Moore, Kristin A., and Isabel V. Sawhill. "Implications of Women's Employment for Home and Family Life." In *Work and Family: Changing Roles of Men and Women,* ed. P. Voydanoff. Palo Alto, CA: Mayfield, 1984. Pp. 153–171.

Moore, Kristin A., Daphne Spain, and Suzanne Bianchi. "Working Wives and Mothers." In *Women and the Family: Two Decades of Change,* eds. B.B. Hess and M.B. Sussman. New York: Haworth, 1984. Pp. 77–98.

Mortimer, Jeylan T., Richard Hall, and Reuben Hill. "Husbands' Occupational Attributes as Constraints on Wives' Employment." *Sociology of Work and Occupations* 5 (August 1978): pp. 285–313.

Mortimer, Jeylan T., and Glorian Sorensen. "Men, Women, Work, and Family." In *Women in the Workplace: Effects on Families,* eds. K.M. Borman, D. Quarm, and S. Gideonese. Norwood, NJ: Ablex Publishing Corp., 1984. Pp. 139–67.

Nathanson, Constance A. "Social Roles and Health Status among Women: The Significance of Employment." *Social Science and Medicine* 14A (1980): pp. 463–71.

Oppenheimer, Valerie K. *Work and the Family: A Study in Social Demography.* New York: Academic Press, 1982.

––––––. "Structural Sources of Economic Pressure for Wives to Work: An Analytical Framework." *Journal of Family History* 4 (Summer 1979): pp. 177–97.

––––––. "The Life-Cycle Squeeze." *Demography* 11 (February 1974): pp. 227–45.

Papanek, Hanna. "Family Status Production." *Signs: Journal of Women in Culture and Society* 7 (1979): pp. 775–81.

––––––. "Men, Women, and Work: Reflections on the Two-Person Career." *American Journal of Sociology* 78 (January 1973): pp. 852–72.

Paulson, Nancy. "Change in Family Income Position: The Effect of Wife's Labor Force Participation." *Sociological Focus* 15 (April 1982): pp. 77–91.

Perry-Jenkins, Maureen. "The Relationship Between the Family Work Week and Marital Companionship: Implications for Workplace Policy." Paper presented at the Annual Meeting of the National Council on Family Relations, 1985.

Philliber, William W., and Dana V. Hiller. "Relative Occupational Attainments of Spouses and Later Changes in Marriage and Wife's Work Experience." *Journal of Marriage and the Family* 45 (February 1983): pp. 161–70.

Piotrkowski, Chaya S., and Paul Crits-Christoph. "Women's Jobs and Family Adjustment." *Journal of Family Issues* 2 (June 1981): pp. 126–47.

Piotrkowski, Chaya A., Evan Stark, and Maz Burbank. "Young Women at Work: Implications for Individual and Family Functioning." *Occupational Health Nursing* (November 1983): pp. 24–29.

Pleck, Joseph H. "Husband's Paid Work and Family Roles: Current Research Issues." In *Research in the Interweave of Social Roles: Families and Jobs,* Vol. 3, eds.

Helena Z. Lopata and Joseph H. Pleck. Greenwich, CT: JAI Press, 1983. Pp. 251–333.

———. "Work-Family Conflict: A National Assessment." Paper presented at the Annual Meeting of the Society of the Study of Social Problems, 1979.

Pleck, Joseph H., and Graham L. Staines. "Work Schedules and Family Life in Two-Earner Couples." *Journal of Family Issues* 6 (March 1985): pp. 61–82.

Rallings, E.M., and F. Ivan Nye. "Wife-Mother Employment, Family, and Society." In *Contemporary Theories about the Family*, eds. W.R.. Burr et al. New York: Free Press, 1979. Pp. 203–226.

Ross, Catherine E., John Mirowsky, and Joan Huber. "Dividing Work, Sharing Work, and In-Between." *American Sociological Review* 48 (December 1983): pp. 809–23.

Shaw, Lois B. *Unplanned Careers: The Working Lives of Middle-Aged Women.* Lexington, MA: D.C. Heath, 1982.

Smith, Shirley J. "New Worklife Estimates Reflect Changing Profile of Labor Force." *Monthly Labor Review* 105 (March 1982): pp. 15–20.

Sorensen, Annemette. "Women's Employment Patterns After Marriage." *Journal of Marriage and the Family* 45 (May 1983): pp. 311–21.

Sorensen, Glorian, et al. "Gender Differences in the Relationship Between Work and Health." Paper presented at the Annual Meeting of the American Sociological Association, 1983.

Sorenson, Ruth S. "The Impact of Compressed Work Week on Families." Paper presented at the Annual Meeting of the National Council on Family Relations, 1984.

Spitze, Glenna. "The Effect of Family Migration on Wives' Employment: How Long Does It Last?" *Social Science Quarterly* 65 (March 1984): pp. 21–36.

Spitze, Glenna, and Scott J. South. "Women's Employment, Time Expenditure, and Divorce." *Journal of Family Issues* 6 (September 1985): pp. 307–29.

St. John-Parsons, Donald. "Continuous Dual-Career Families." *Psychology of Women Quarterly* 3 (Fall 1978): pp. 30–42.

Staines, Graham L., and Joseph H. Pleck. *The Impact of Work Schedules on the Family.* Ann Arbor: University of Michigan, 1983.

Szinovacz, Maximiliane E. "Changing Family Roles and Interactions." In *Women and the Family: Two Decades of Change*, eds. B.B. Hess and M.B. Sussman. New York: Haworth Press, 1984. Pp. 163–201.

Tognoli, Jerome. "The Flight from Domestic Space: Men's Role in the Household." *Family Coordinator* 28 (October 1979): pp. 599–607.

Van Velsor, Ellen, and Angela M. O'Rand. "Family Life Cycle, Work Career Patterns and Women's Wages at Midlife." *Journal of Marriage and the Family* 46 (May 1984): pp. 365–73.

Verbrugge, Lois M. "Role Burdens and Physical Health of Women and Men." Paper presented at the Annual Meeting of the American Sociological Association, 1985.

———. "Multiple Roles and Physical Health of Women and Men." *Journal of Health and Social Behavior* 24 (March 1983): pp. 16–30.

———. "Women's Social Roles and Health." In *Women: A Developmental Perspective*, eds. P.W. Berman and E.R. Ramey. Washington: National Institutes of Health, 1982a. Pp. 49–78.

———. "Work Satisfaction and Physical Health." *Journal of Community Health* 7 (1982b): pp. 262–83.

Voydanoff, Patricia. Work and Family Life. Beverly Hills, CA: Sage, forthcoming.

———. "Work/Family Linkages over the Life Course." *Journal of Career Development* 12 (September 1985): pp. 23–32.

_____. *Work and Family: Changing Roles of Men and Women*. Palo Alto, CA: Mayfield, 1984a.

_____. "Work Role Characteristics, Family Structure Demands, and Quality of Family Life." Paper presented at the Annual Meeting of the National Council on Family Relations, 1984b.

_____. "Work/Family Life Cycles." Paper presented at the Theory and Methods Workshop, National Council on Family Relations, 1980.

Voydanoff, Patricia, and Robert F. Kelly. "Determinants of Work-Related Family Problems among Employed Parents." *Journal of Marriage and the Family* 46 (November 1984): pp. 881–92.

Waite, Linda J. "Working Wives and the Family Life Cycle." *American Journal of Sociology* 86 (September 1980): pp. 272–94.

Waite, Linda J., Gus W. Haggstrom, and David E. Kanouse. "Changes in the Employment Activities of New Parents." *American Sociological Review* 50 (April 1985): pp. 263–72.

Waldman, Elizabeth. "Labor Force Statistics from a Family Perspective." *Monthly Labor Review* 106 (December 1983): pp. 16–20.

Waldman, Elizabeth, Allyson S. Grossman, Howard Hayghe, and Beverly L. Johnson. "Working Mothers in the 1970's: A Look at the Statistics." *Monthly Labor Review* 102 (October 1979): pp. 39–49.

Waldron, Ingrid. "Employment and Women's Health: An Analysis of Causal Relationships." *Journal of Health Services* 10 (1980): pp. 434–54.

Waldron, Ingrid, and Joan Herold. "Employment, Attitudes Toward Employment, and Women's Health." *Women & Health* 2 (1986): pp. 79–98.

Waldron, Ingrid, Joan Herold, Dennis Dunn, and Roger Staum. "Reciprocal Effects of Health and Labor Participation in Women: Evidence from Two Longitudinal Studies." *Journal of Occupational Medicine* 24 (1982): pp. 126–32.

Warr, Peter, and Glenys Parry. "Paid Employment and Women's Psychological Well-Being." *Psychological Bulletin* 91 (1982): pp. 498–516.

Welch, Susan, and Alan Booth. "Employment and Health among Married Women with Children." *Sex Roles* 3 (1977): pp. 385–97.

White, Lynn K. "Determinants of Spousal Interaction: Marital Structure or Marital Happiness." *Journal of Marriage and the Family* 45 (August 1983): pp. 511–19.

Wilkie, Jane R. "The Trend Toward Delayed Parenthood." *Journal of Marriage and the Family* 43 (August 1981): pp. 583–91.

Woods, Nancy F., and Barbara S. Hulka. "Symptom Reports and Illness Behavior among Employed Women and Homemakers." *Journal of Community Health* 5 (1979): pp. 36–45.

Wright, Fay. "Single Careers." In *A Labour of Love*, eds. J. Finch and D. Groves. Boston: Routledge & Kegan Paul, 1983. Pp. 89–105.

Young, Michael, and Peter Willmott. *The Symmetrical Family*. New York: Penguin Books, 1977.

CHAPTER 4

Men and Women in Organizations: Roles and Status, Stereotypes and Power

NINA L. COLWILL*

The past two decades have not been kind to industrial relations people. Equality by sex in the workplace was conceptualized in the 1960s, greatly complicating the lives of those who perform the workplace appraisals of women and men. Equal opportunity in employment became the watchword of the 1970s, only to be replaced in many organizations with affirmative action programs (Quaintance, 1984), and every-step-of-the-way performance appraisal became a more and more complex statistical, ethical, legal, and managerial decision-making process (Schneier and Beatty, 1984). To keep pace with the changing demands of the workplace, the industrial relations expert has had to have at least a passing knowledge of yet another area: the social psychology of organizational functioning. This chapter addresses the issues facing men and women in today's organizations through the eyes of a social psychologist, through roles and status, stereotypes and power.

Roles and Status, Women and Men

We all play many roles every day, but the phrase "playing roles" does not mean to imply that the process is ingenuine or that role players are pretentious. Let's look, for example, at a few of the roles played by a dual-career couple, Susan McTaggart and Bob Cunningham. When Susan is representing a client in court, she's Ms. S.W. McTaggart, the lawyer; when she rocks her baby and sings him to sleep, she's Mummy, the devoted mother. When she jogs with her old

*Associate Professor, Department of Business Administration, University of Manitoba.
Note: Many of the concepts and some of the very words in this chapter have been liberally lifted from *The New Partnership: Women and Men in Organizations* (Colwill, 1982) and from several articles written for *Business Quarterly.* I wish to express my appreciation to Mayfield Publishing Company and to *Business Quarterly.*

97

high school classmates, she's Suzie, the light-hearted friend. When Bob is designing a building for a client, he's R.M. Cunningham, the architect; when he golfs on Saturday morning, he's Bob Cunningham, the golfer; when he visits his mother, he's Bobby, her son. He's all of these people and many more—Susan's husband, their children's father, the United Way Chair—and the very different behaviors he and Susan exhibit in these situations speak not of their hypocrisy, but of the power of the social context.

Although no one role is more genuine, more "Susan" or more "Bob" than any of the others, some of Susan's and Bob's roles are less important than others and none are as important, as salient, or as encompassing as their male and female sex roles. Sex roles organize so much of their experience and interact so well with their other social and working roles that they form one of the most crucial elements of their self-concepts.

Sex Roles: So Dear to Our Hearts

Sex roles are rooted in our history; they're defined by our religions; they're delineated by our legal systems; they're reinforced by our cultures. Sex-role socialization, the process by which we learn our sex roles, continues from birth to death, at home, at school, at work, and in all social settings. This socialization begins so early and is so subtle that one can rarely remember the origins of the beliefs and attitudes that form the basis of one's sex role. We each have an idiosyncratic set of beliefs and attitudes that give our own sex role the appearance of uniqueness, but there is a basic belief system for each culture that is dominant enough to guarantee that by age 3 most children will be able to describe accurately components of the male and female sex role as complex as "father" and "mother" (Emmerick, 1959).

Because the logic behind our sex roles is tenuous at best, it is difficult to argue with articulation for their existence. Historically, people have rarely tried. Instead they have treated sex roles as moral lessons: ladies must go first; women belong in the home; men should pay for the date; men should walk on the street side of the sidewalk. As moral lessons, our sex roles have been adequately monitored by guilt and fear and their salience and importance elevated even higher. In our achieving society, however, there is another role that rivals even the sex role in importance: the work role.

Organizational Roles: Bread, Butter, and a Niche in the Working World

- "What do you do?"
- "What is he?"

Few people reading this book would wonder at the meaning of these questions, for we have all learned that they refer to job titles and, by implication, to the roles that accompany those titles. It is extremely difficult for North Americans to be comfortable with anyone until they know what sex role and what work role that person should be playing. This information is not considered to be irrelevant in social, nonwork situations, for we have come to define the essence of human beings in terms of these two roles.

Sex roles have varied from time to time and from place to place, but with one consistent feature: in virtually every society throughout history women and all things feminine have been seen as inferior to men and all things masculine. The obvious corollary of this truism is that the organizational roles played by men have been the important work roles of the society—the work roles most highly rewarded with money and prestige. Historically this situation has been exacerbated by the overcrowding of female work ghettos and by the trade unions and universities that controlled access to male work roles (Cohen, 1984).

Until very recent history, the sex roles that our society had agreed upon as culturally appropriate blended very nicely with the sex roles that people played at work. Throughout the centuries and across a variety of cultures, men have usually performed the strenuous jobs that require cooperative effort and mobility, and women have performed jobs of isolation and low mobility. Even within manufacturing societies, men and women have tended traditionally to make the tools of their respective trades (D'Andrade, 1966). Women, who were socially defined as the nurturant, supportive care givers of the home, have replayed this helpmate role in another costume in the 20th century workplace as nurses, secretaries, sales clerks, and primary school teachers. High school girls have rarely chosen to be engineers, and their brothers seldom consider nursing, because engineering is not consistent with the female sex role and nursing is not consistent with the male sex role.

It is theoretically possible for a strong division of labor to exist, yet for female and male workers to enjoy equal prestige and equal pay—for men and women to play separate but equal roles. Unfortunately, it doesn't often work that way, for men tend to be seen as defining the norm and women tend to be seen as deviating from it. As the classic ingroup-outgroup model indicates, outgroup members and their work are evaluated with negative prejudices and ingroup members and their work are viewed with positive prejudices (Janis, 1971). That's why the notion of "separate but equal" doesn't work very well: the more stereotypes we hold about the differences between women and men, the more reasons we have to believe that men are superior to women.

Thus a division of labor by sex serves to increase the status gap between women and men, and any profession "begins to tilt, like a neighborhood" (Steinem, 1983) when it becomes more than one-third female.

This occupational prestige imbalance has resulted in pay inequities which have been attacked by equal pay legislation and, more recently, by equal pay for work of equal value or "comparable worth" guidelines. During the early 1980s the battle has raged over this issue (Robb, 1985; Nelson, Opton, and Wilson, 1983; Milkovich, 1982), and the late 1980s should see an increase in research interest in the topic. The research will be no easy task, for researchers will have to separate the concepts of sex and occupation in order to view the worth of work independent of the sex of the incumbent—a monumental task for any well-socialized adult (Colwill, 1984). It remains to be seen whether the research findings and the success of comparable worth legislation weakens or strengthens the division of labor by sex. One thing is certain: we will have to reevaluate a host of sex-role stereotypes before dramatic change can occur.

Sex-Role Stereotypes: Our Perceptions of Women and Men

The most sex-role liberated among us have a private closet of sex-role stereotypes, and industrial relations experts are no exception. Our examination of this problem will begin with a definition of three terms: sex-role stereotypes, sex prejudice, and sex discrimination. A *sex-role stereotype* is merely a belief about women or men: women are nurturant, emotional, and nimble-fingered, for instance; men are aggressive, adventuresome, and physically strong. By itself, a stereotype is a relatively harmless belief that can be changed by facts that refute it. Stereotypes, however, usually become paired with strong emotional evaluations to form attitudes. One such attitude—*sex prejudice*—is a prejudgement about the way women and men will think or behave as a function of their sex. A prejudice is much more harmful than a mere stereotype, because its strong emotional and evaluative component guarantees that it will be difficult to alter by facts alone and because it so often leads to *sex discrimination*—the more favorable treatment of one sex.

It seems, then, that sex discrimination must begin with a sex-role stereotype. But why do we stereotype people? We use stereotypes the way we use any other belief system or information-processing system—for efficiency. We are constantly bombarded by sights, sounds, and smells, and we need complex information-processing systems to screen this multiplicity of information, to order it, and to classify it. Without such systems, our lives would be a chaotic blur of sights, sounds, and ideas. Without rules of order and classification, we could never learn complex subjects like mathematics, and we would have no frameworks for the millions of bits of information we learn daily about a wide variety of topics.

Like any other classification scheme or belief system, stereotypes lose their efficiency when they become too simplistic or too general. It might be very useful to hold a stereotype about people who carry bicycle chains and switchblades, but our stereotypes about broad classes of people like accountants, blacks, women, and men are usually more trouble than they're worth. There are wide variations within these groups, and our general stereotypes can't possibly capture all of the important variables.

In spite of the relative inefficiency of sex-role stereotypes, we work very hard to maintain them—to maintain a sense of order in our universe, however inaccurate that order may be. We reinterpret situations, make invalid assumptions about people's motives, and, if everything else fails, reassure ourselves that we have found "the exception that proves the rule." Because sex-role stereotypes seldom exist in isolation, because they usually attach themselves to strong emotional values to form prejudices, our investment in maintaining these beliefs is usually very high.

Although we tend to assume that sex-role stereotypes are rapidly disintegrating, Dubno's (1985) longitudinal study of MBA students' attitudes toward female executives indicates that this is not, in fact, the case. Between 1975 and 1983, the male MBA students in his study retained their consistently negative attitudes toward women as managers, and female MBA students remained significantly more positive than their male counterparts.

Sex-role stereotypes about managers don't always favor men. In fact, female managers have been evaluated more positively than their male counterparts by female MBA students (Mickalachki and Mickalachki, 1984) and by female managers (Jabes, 1980). It may be that men and women prefer to be managed by members of their own sex, thereby dispelling the notion that nobody wants a female boss.

It is possible that people—even managers and future managers—think in hypothetical terms about men and women in management when they are asked to evaluate male and female managers. When they are faced with actual managers in a real-world situation, however, sex may not be as important a variable as one might expect. We know, for instance, that men and women who have been managed by women have fewer sex-role stereotypes about female managers (Ezell, Odewahn, and Sherman, 1981), and although the managers in Deaux's (1979) study demonstrate slightly more positive attitudes toward the male managers under their jurisdiction, no sex difference was found in the ratings of Terborg and Shingledecker's (1983) nonmanagement employees when the researchers balanced for type of job and managerial level. Furthermore, as Gerdes and Garber's (1983) study of managers' ratings of male and female engineers indicates, sex is more likely to be used as a discriminating variable when there is insufficient information to make a decision based on competence. This finding, which has been replicated in other contexts (e.g., Hodgins and Kalin, 1985), demonstrates the importance for researchers of isolating the myriad variables affecting discrimination and the necessity for human resource managers to gather as much data as possible before making personnel decisions.

Colwill and Josephson's (1983) study of a large Canadian government department suggests that men and women interpret women's lack of representation in management and in technical positions very differently. Men are more likely to believe that the disproportionately low number of women in management is a function of women's intrinsic characteristics, while women consider the sex difference in managerial representation to be due to external factors such as discrimination. This is not a surprising finding; it is logical that men and women would choose a sex-role stereotype about women's skills and barriers that would render themselves blameless for women's lack of representation in managerial and technical positions. However, these data should serve as a reminder that we all have heavy investments in our stereotypes and that the process of attitude change will be slow enough to accommodate all the face-saving techniques that must occur along the way. Researchers have two roles in this process: the role of monitors, continuing to measure attitude change throughout the years ahead, and the role of change agents, disseminating their research findings in a palatable form that will jar and debunk our stereotypes.

Where will the sex-role stereotyping literature go from here? Gone are the days when respondents will blatantly describe their sex-role stereotypes to researchers without blinking an eye. It is clear that researchers will have to employ more and more sophisticated techniques if they hope to collect sex-role stereotyping data from a very sophisticated public. No longer can they expect their respondents to believe that "there are no right or wrong answers," for it is becoming increasingly clear that the people who do this type of research consider sex-role stereotyping to be wrong.

Unobtrusive measures will have to be used if researchers hope to gather valid information about sex-role stereotypes in the workplace. In one such study the grading and regrading of actual university projects was examined, and it was discovered that a bias in favor of men existed among graders who did not know the students personally and had no previous experience with their capabilities (Bradley, 1984). In another field study, Levinson (1975) had his sociology students make job enquiries over the telephone in response to 256 different newspaper advertisements for jobs. The students worked in male-female teams of two, with the "sex-role inappropriate" partner (e.g., male applying for a secretarial position or female applying for a pest-control position) making the first enquiry and the "sex-role appropriate" partner (female secretary and male pest-controller) making the same job enquiry a half-hour later. One-third of the employers in this study exhibited blatant sex discrimination, some even acknowledging that they were breaking the law with statements like: "Well, I can't turn you down because you're a girl. But really, I think you're barking up the wrong tree."

Research in the area of unbiased selection is bound to continue over the next decade, for the legal and methodological questions in this area have hardly begun to be answered (Quaintance, 1984), and many human resource managers are still operating under myths about employee selection that were established during the past two decades and rarely tested (Schmidt and Hunter, 1983). But the research cannot stop at performance appraisal. Nine years ago Schein (1978) recognized the fact that the sex-role stereotyping literature had ground to a halt in the study of employee selection decisions and that little attention had been focused on the impact of stereotypes in the daily functioning of women in the workplace. Today there is some research evidence that speaks to that issue. It is known, for instance, that women tend to believe that they are being treated justly even when they are not—that it is merely other women who are discriminated against (Crosby, 1984). Women also learn to cope with discrimination by accommodation, and female job applicants have been shown to change their behavior, without being fully aware of doing so, in order to accommodate what they believe to be the interviewer's sex-role stereotypes (von Baeyer, Sherk, and Zanna, 1981). We know little, however, about the organizational behavior of men as a function of stereotypes about them, and both male and female reactions require further exploration if we are to fully understand the effects of sex-role stereotyping. One route is through the study of power.

Power

A bright, articulate female consultant is making a presentation to a group of men seated around a boardroom table. She pauses and gestures with her glasses to accent a dramatic point in her discussion. Suddenly a man who has been watching her intently interrupts: "You look completely different without your glasses."

Two strangers, a woman and a man, board a plane. Both are dressed in gray wool suits and both carry leather briefcases. They sit beside each other without speaking and begin their paperwork. Presently, a flight attendant offers them magazines. The man chooses *Time*; the woman chooses *Business Week*. He turns to her with a pleasant smile and says: "I've never seen a girl read *Business Week* before."

Both of these women have been gently robbed of the same commodity—power. They have intruded into masculine territory and have been reminded that they are viewed as pretenders. The woman in the boardroom has been informed that she is a sex object, and the woman on the plane has been told that she is a little girl.

If one accumulates the multitude of definitions of power that exist, they seem to fall into a hierarchy ranging from personal power at the microlevel, through interpersonal power, to organizational power at the macrolevel. *Personal power* is probably best conceptualized by Rotter's (1966) notion of locus of control: feeling in control of one's environment. To feel personally powerful is to feel good about oneself. To define *interpersonal power*, we turn to Johnson's (1976) power definition, which can best be described as "influence": the ability to get another person to do or to believe something he or she would not have done or believed spontaneously. Note that this definition focuses on the attitudes and the behavior of the person being influenced. Finally, for *organizational power* we look to Kanter's (1977) definition of power as the ability to mobilize resources. To Kanter, power is energy in the physical sense of the word. Power is access to the means for doing what needs to be done.

Personal Power: Feeling Good About Oneself

Although power is typically conceptualized in terms of other people, there are also individual differences in feelings of powerfulness that have direct bearing on organizational functioning. Julian Rotter (1966) was the first psychologist to attempt to quantify this attitude toward personal power with a test that is now known as Rotter's Internal-External (I-E) Locus of Control Scale. People who score on the "Internal" end of Rotter's scale tend to see themselves as being in charge of their own fates. "Externals," on the other hand, believe that their lives are controlled externally, by forces in the environment beyond their control, by luck, or by powerful others.

Rotter's I-E Scale is of particular interest to us here because of the large number of studies showing scores on the test to be related to various organizational behaviors and because research has often demonstrated sex differences in the measure. To name a few of the work-related correlates with locus of control, Internals are more likely to attribute their successes to skill rather than to luck (Phares, 1976); are less likely to bow to social pressure (Ryckman, Rodda, and Sherman, 1972); are better able to influence others (Phares, 1976); and are less likely to rely upon coercion in their influence attempts (Goodstadt and Hjelle, 1973). Also of interest in this context is the traditional finding that males are more Internal than females (e.g., McGinnies et al., 1974).

Over the next few years the research on sex differences in locus of control will necessarily become more complex and will employ several variables in interaction with each other. It has already been demonstrated that the male-internal, female-external model is too simplistic—that the locus of control interacts with other variables such as self-esteem (Harrison, Guy, and Lupfer, 1981) in such a way that one cannot meaningfully discuss sex differences per se.

Interpersonal Power: Getting Our Own Way

Sex differences in interpersonal power have been represented by two different literatures. One literature, addressing *power bases or power resources*, grew from the classic work of French and Raven (1959) in which the specific, often conscious, bases of the power used by individuals were examined to determine which were more effective under which conditions. A second literature, on the *communication of power*, grew from what can best be described as a stereotyping literature in which the traits, behaviors, and appearance of people were studied and manipulated in order to understand an influence process which is often outside our awareness. These two literatures often overlap, for it is difficult to isolate the ascribed, the acquired, the subconscious, the stereotype, and the conscious awareness, and the arbitrary distinction imposed here is somewhat artificial.

Power Bases and Power Resources. In 1959, French and Raven developed a model that differentiated five different bases of power: reward, punishment, legitimate, expert, and referent power (see Table 1 for descriptions). In 1965, Raven added a sixth power base, information power, which he considered to be a separate concept. Although French and Raven did not conceptualize their bases of power as necessarily referring to organizations, and certainly not to business in particular, their classic analysis has received its most devoted audience in the organizational and business literature and the bases of power have most often been described in organizational terms, as they are here.

Over the decade that followed French and Raven's classic papers, surprisingly few of the hundreds of studies of the bases of power explored sex differences. Dunn (1972) did study perceptions about the appropriateness of reward and punishment as power strategies for

TABLE 1
French and Raven's Six Bases of Power

Power Base	Typical Organizational Use
Reward power	The power to bestow organizational rewards
Punishment power	The power to withhold or remove organizational power
Legitimate power	Authority conferred by organizational title
Expert power	Power gained through special expertise
Referent power	Power gained through attraction or perceived similarity
Information power	Power gained through the possession of information that is sought by others

Source: Colwill (1982), p. 93.

women and men, and learned that concrete rewards and coercion are perceived to be masculine modes of influence. Rosen and Jerdee (1973) were also able to demonstrate that male-dispensed rewards were more effective influence tools than were rewards given by women. It was really Johnson's (1976) work, however, that gave birth to an area in which power bases and power strategies were studied as sex-role issues.

Using Dunn's rationale, Johnson argued that the division of labor by sex has accorded very different types of power resources to women and men, and she set out to derive a model based on French and Raven's analysis that would summarize the ways in which men and women exert power. Her research indicates that there are at least three power dimensions along which men and women tend to differ and are perceived to differ:

1. Men are more likely to exert *direct* power by openly and overtly issuing orders or requests; women are more likely than men to employ *indirect* power techniques, the goal of which is to conceal the source of influence from the person being influenced.

2. Men are more likely to bargain with *concrete resources* like money, strength, and knowledge in their influence attempts; women tend to employ *personal resources* such as affection or approval that depend upon personal relationships for their maintenance.

3. Men tend to stress their own *competence* when trying to influence others, by drawing attention to their expertise, information, or physical strength; women are more likely to employ *helplessness*— to stress their weakness or their incompetence.

Although Johnson's research indicates that women and men have different power sources available to them, she speculated that there would be different short-run and long-run consequences for employing "masculine" and "feminine" power strategies (see Table 2), and some attempts have been made to test the effectiveness of these strategies for women and men. Using videotapes of men and women delivering speeches on "masculine" (gun control) or "feminine" (day-care centers) topics in a helpless or competent manner, Falbo, Hazen, and Linimon (1982) found that speakers using the "sex-role appropriate" power base were better liked and were seen as more competent and better qualified. However, the speakers of either sex speaking on either topic were seen as more qualified when using the competent rather than the helpless power base. The latter finding is consistent with research employing in-basket tasks in two different studies in which sex, status, and power strategies of the main actor were manipulated (Colwill, Perlman, and Spinner, 1982, 1983); the power strategies labeled by Johnson as "masculine" were more effective for women *and* men.

Johnson's model has yet to be tested in an actual organizational setting, with women and men at different organizational levels in various occupations engaged in their day-to-day routines. We know that there are sex-role stereotypes about power resources and that

TABLE 2
Johnson's Three Dimensions of Power

Typically Masculine Power Strategies	Typically Feminine Power Strategies	Short-Run Advantages of Feminine Power Strategies	Long-Run Disadvantages of Feminine Power Strategies
Direct	Indirect	The person influenced may believe it was her/his own idea.	If effective in the short run, this strategy has concealed your power.
Concrete rewards	Personal rewards	People who like you may be easily influenced by your affection and attention.	Your span of influence is very narrow—dependent upon the goodwill and affection of others.
Competence	Helplessness	Tends to work very well for women, who may be seen as legitimately helpless in many situations.	May leave you feeling helpless. Others may come to see you as weak and incompetent.

Source: Colwill (1982), p. 98.

university students do not debunk these stereotypes, but it has been demonstrated that "feminine" power strategies tend to be less effective than "masculine" power strategies for women and men. It has yet to be determined if sex is as important a determinant as organizational status in the choice of power strategies, if Johnson's "masculine" power strategies are more effective in written and oral communication in all organizational contexts for both women and men, and if the short-run and long-run consequences of various influence attempts will be different in the "real world."

Power and Stereotypes: The Communication of Interpersonal Power. We gain and lose interpersonal power, not only through our conscious power strategies, but through the myriad messages we convey to others, *verbally* (the words we say), *paraverbally* (the way we say the words we say), and *nonverbally* (communication without words). The people with whom we interact use these communications to help organize us on a hierarchy of status, and our influence over them may be more a function of these stereotypes than of the actual power resources we are consciously employing.

Power bases and power resources, discussed in the last section, tend to be communicated *verbally*. It is through words that we are direct or indirect, that we bargain with concrete or personal resources, and that we stress our helplessness or our competence. But other, less conscious communications also take place verbally. For example, there is evidence that women and men speak very different English, a phenomenon that has come to be known as "genderlect" (Dickerson, cited in Kramer, 1974), with women being more likely to use tag questions ("You will come, *won't you?*"), qualifiers ("This product is *perhaps* the best on the market"), superlatives ("*the most wonderful*"), and such explicit words as "mauve," "ecru," and "lovely" (Eakins and Eakins, 1978; Lakoff, 1975). Because there is evidence that the language traditionally used by women is less effective than the language traditionally used by men (Sztaba and Colwill, 1986), there is every reason to believe that we communicate our relative power and powerlessness through our "masculine" and "feminine" language.

The verbal communication of men's power and women's relative powerlessness also takes the form of sexist language in four different ways (Colwill, 1983): (1) through the use of masculine words, supposedly to refer generically to both sexes ("draftsman" to refer to men and women who do drafting, "chairman" to refer to men and women who chair—but never "cleaning lady" to refer to men and women who clean); (2) through the use of high-status titles for men and low-status titles for women of the same status (Mr. Smith and Betty, girl and man); (3) through the use of different words to describe women and men performing the same task (manager and manageress, lawyer and lady lawyer, nurse and male nurse); and (4) by reinforcing a sex-role stereotype ("When a man hires a secretary, he should choose her with care").

Sexist language is often considered to be a petty issue and is the butt of hundreds of jokes. (As a feminist living in Manitoba, can you imagine how often someone has said to me: "I suppose you'd like to change the name of our province to Personitoba"?) There is, however, strong evidence that sexist language perpetuates sexism. In a study examining this effect, Briere and Lanktree (1983) manipulated the pronouns in one paragraph of the APA Ethical Standards of Psychologists (from "he," to "he or she" or "she or he"). They asked psychology students to read the paragraph and to comment on the attractiveness of psychology as a career for women or men. Students who had read the masculine pronoun version of the Ethical Standards paragraph rated psychology as a less attractive profession for women—a powerful effect for a petty variable!

At the *paraverbal* level, power and powerlessness are also being communicated by men and women. Men interrupt more than women do (96 percent of all interruptions in Zimmerman and West's [1975] study), and women allow themselves to be interrupted more than men do (100 percent in the same study). Women are also more likely than men to yield, to agree, and to praise; men talk at greater length and make more suggestions (Lockheed and Hall, 1976). It would not be surprising, given these sex differences in paraverbal behavior, if men left mixed-sex interactions feeling much more powerful than the women with whom they communicated.

There is a strong relationship between the verbal and the paraverbal behaviors of men and people of high status; men and high-status people are more direct, speak more simply and forcefully, are more likely to be referred to by their last name and title, are more likely to interrupt, and are less likely to be interrupted (Henley, 1977). Similarly, there is a strong relationship between the *nonverbal* behavior of men and the nonverbal behavior of people of high status. Men and high-status people tend to lean back in their chairs, to sit in asymmetrical positions, and to relax their hands and necks. Women and low-status people tend to demonstrate greater body rigidity and to take up less physical space by holding their legs together and their arms closer to their bodies—what has come to be known as a "ladylike position" (Mehrabian, 1971, 1972; Birdwhistle, 1970). Physical space is also allotted according to status and sex. People of higher status are typically given larger work areas—a bigger office and a bigger desk—and are accorded greater personal space. Similarly, women are accorded less personal space than men, for both males and females stand closer to women and touch them more than they touch men (Henley, 1977).

It has long been recognized that people are treated differently as a function of their physical attractiveness (Berscheid and Walster, 1974), and common sense tells us to make the most of our own physical attributes in order to increase our interpersonal power. In recent years a literature has emerged showing an employee evaluation and hiring advantage for physically attractive people (Cash, Gillen, and Burns, 1977; Dipboye, Arvey, and Tersptra, 1977). More recent research indicates, however, that while physical attractiveness is a consistent advantage for men, it appears to be a disadvantage for women if they are already seen as incompetent (Holahan and Stephan, 1981) and no advantage if they are seeking a managerial position (Heilman and Saruwatari, 1979). As researchers delineate more of the parameters of what has come to be known as "beautyism," their work will help human resource managers to sort through their own stereotypes.

In recent years the attainment of interpersonal power through status and physical attractiveness has focused on dress. The last word on dressing for interpersonal power comes from John Molloy, whose model rests on the assumption that we will become what we appear to be. By asking subjects to evaluate people wearing a variety of different clothes, he has been able to describe the ideal male (Molloy, 1975) and female (Molloy, 1977) business uniform—the outfit that best conveys status, authority, and credibility. The watchwords for men and women are identical: expensive, simple, and conservative, with natural fibres. His cautions to women are more complex, however; they must not be too feminine, reminding the world that they are women (no frills, accenting frivolity; no vests, accenting breasts), and never must they appear too masculine, suggesting that they are cute imitations of men (no ties, no fedoras, no pant suits).

Ours is a society in which first impressions are considered to be very important, a society in which the handshake has been given the status of a personality test. It's not surprising, therefore, that the social sciences are rife with studies demonstrating that people from all walks of life form and act upon these impressions very rapidly. Thus, our social psychological literature and our intuition combine to make Molloy's message a popular one, and there are few business people who deliberately ignore his advice. Yet while Molloy's research on initial impression does seem to indicate that he has delineated the perfect business uniforms for women and men, it has yet to be demonstrated that the long-term consequences of dressing for success are as dramatic as he would have us believe. In one study that addressed this issue, albeit a generation ago, clothing—at least for men—was a significant factor only in judging strangers (Hoult, 1954).

The next research step in the communication-of-power literature will undoubtedly address the long-run consequences of stereotypes on power and the ability of individuals to increase their interpersonal power by deliberately manipulating their verbal, paraverbal, and non-verbal behavior. Henley (1977) has suggested that the latter is not as easily accomplished as one might imagine—that women who adopt the communication styles of men and high-status people, for instance, are seen not as powerful, but as sexy. Thus, the woman who stands with her hands on her hips, speaks in a deep voice, and invades the personal space of men may find herself being perceived, not as a person of superior status, but as a sex object.

Is the notion of a high-status woman so incongruous that people must search for alternative explanations? Are women assumed to have low status unless it has been concretely demonstrated otherwise? Are men assumed to have high status unless their dress, their occupation, or their speech exposes them as low-status people? Are we more likely to use nonverbal cues to stereotype men, requiring factual information about women before we can assign them a high status? These questions and questions about the long-term consequences of high- and low-status behavior have yet to be addressed empirically. When they are, human resource managers will be in a much better position to evaluate the extent to which stereotypes about power are influencing personnel decisions in their organizations.

Organizational Power: Mobilizing Resources

Most of the textbooks on power that are used in management studies today (see, e.g., Mintzberg, 1983; Pfeffer, 1981) address the issues of personal and interpersonal power primarily as routes to organizational power, for the mobilization of resources is ultimately the power issue of concern in organizations. To the managers in Kanter's (1977) famous study of the multinational conglomerate "Indsco," the credibility of a manager is an extremely important factor in defining that person as organizationally powerful, and credibility can relate to a variety of organizational, interpersonal, and personal variables, not the least of which is sex.

The power research of the next decade should begin to tie together the three types of power delineated here, for their distinction, as mentioned earlier, has always been an arbitrary one. The research of the next decade should begin to test some of the intuitions about power: that people who feel personally powerful are better able to influence others; that those high in personal power can more easily mobilize organizational resources; and that those who influence others can better mobilize resources.

Power: The Infinite Resource

Throughout the previous discussion of power, there have been several allusions to the notion that power can be conceptualized as a finite or as an infinite resource. Power is typically viewed as a scarce resource, not to be given away too freely. We speak of "stealing power," "usurping power," and "power struggles," and most treatments of organizational power assume that a win-lose game is being played. During the next decade, however, new theoretical frameworks for power will be sought, and as some of the more antiquated models of management are being reexamined, so too will the notion of power as a finite resource come under scrutiny.

The area of power has many implications for industrial relations. Human resource management decisions are explicitly or implicitly based upon individual differences in all three types of power: attitudes toward one's own power, the ability to influence others, and the ability to mobilize resources. Research on quantifiable measures of personal, interpersonal, and organizational power will enable human resource managers to make better and better decisions. As so many of our other resources become limited, the reconceptualization of power as an infinite resource could open new channels of communication for union and management.

Trends of the 1970s, Trends of the 1980s

The sex-role-in-business issue of the 1970s was, indisputably, women in management; hundreds of articles and dozens of books dissected the female manager, examined men's and women's attitudes toward her, and studied and advised upon her competence, her clothing, her family life, her sex life, her ambitions, and her probable future. In the late 1980s and early 1990s, female managers should enjoy a well-deserved rest from the questionnaires and microphones of social scientists, for the focus of research on sex roles in business will shift to women in female work ghettos, to women in male-dominated trades, and to men in female-dominated occupations.

The Secretarial Position

Secretaries, who have labored invisibly for decades, will soon be discovered by researchers who will recognize the gold mine of research opportunities in the secretarial position: attitudes toward secretaries; the effects of secretaries' behavior on themselves, their bosses, and their organizational units; the ideal traits of a good secretary. There has been a well-publicized shortage of secretaries for several years (Stead, 1980), and a crisis is facing a management that has failed to recognize the inappropriateness of its expectations for secretaries: an expectation for them to be, on the one hand, capable of managerial decision-making and, on the other hand, disinterested in promotion (Colwill, 1985). During the next few years pioneer companies will make their first halting steps toward using the secretarial position as a training ground for management, and researchers will descend upon these organizations to monitor the progress of what will appear to be an avant garde idea.

Women in Trades

During the next decade we should see the day when female executive appointments fail to warrant newspaper headlines. We are far from observing such blasé attitudes toward women in trades, however. Women have been edging their way into offices, into educational systems, and into hospitals for decades, successfully employing a foot-in-the-door technique that has allowed men to accommodate themselves to their presence, establishing themselves solidly in positions of subservience and nurturance before suggesting that equality by sex might be in order. But no one has ever pretended that women are welcome in the trades. There are no slots for women in the trades. There has been no need for nurturance in carpentry, plumbing, and metalworking, and subservient positions are usually filled by male apprentices, by male students who are financing their training for their real occupational goal, or by young men who are "finding themselves."

In many ways the notion of women in trades presents the ultimate assault on male and female organizational roles, for it challenges our society's most basic attitudes about physical strength; endurance; technical, mechanical, and spatial skills; and (no, it is not dead) chivalry. The lack of research on women in trades has not gone unnoticed (O'Farrell, 1982; Walshok, 1981), and profitable research directions of the future should move beyond anecdotes and tabulation and into the empirical study of role conflicts, coworker and client attitudes, and the efficacy of special programs for women in trades.

Men in Female-Dominated Occupations

A third problem area of sex-role research for the 1980s will focus on men in female-dominated occupations: nurses, infant-care workers, home economists, and secretaries. The row that these men hoe may be tougher than that of their nontraditional female counterparts because they must fight against the stereotypes of those who step out of their sex roles combined with a stereotype that women in male-dominated occupations do not have to face—the stereotypes associated with those who emulate their status inferiors.

There have been numerous speculations and numerous assumptions about the family backgrounds, the sexual orientation, and the career possibilities of men in female-dominated occupations, but little research. If unemployment increases and sex roles continue to dissolve, men will seek work where it is still available—in the female-dominated occupations. If history runs true to form, they will succeed in raising the status and the financial worth of these occupations. Undoubtedly, researchers will follow them, documenting, questioning, collecting, interpreting, and helping to pave the way for the next generation.

New Directions

If researchers wish to be pacesetters of sex-role change in the workplace, rather than mere recorders, we will see a new kind of research in the next decade. Researchers will tackle our most basic assumptions about women and men, slowly separating occupational roles from sex roles and power from stereotypes. They must be prepared to create and employ new methodologies with subjects who are well versed in the concepts of sex roles and stereotypes. With powerful statistical tools and large national samples at their disposal, researchers must learn to listen to individual respondents, taping interviews, asking open-ended questions, employing postexperimental questionnaires.

Whatever techniques researchers employ in the future, they must learn to write in the language of the intelligent layperson, for if their findings are hidden in esoteric journals, they will be closely guarded secrets that have no impact on the sex-role changes to come. For changes will continue. With or without research, sex roles will be extricated from occupational roles, power will be reconceptualized, sex stereotypes will become merely amusing, sex discrimination will be socially punished. Research can channel the process, can organize the outcomes, can render change less painful. Research can inform, can point our thoughts in new directions, pairing hitherto unrelated variables and separating hitherto inseparable factors. There is an honesty that emerges from good research based on valid assumptions and accomplished with integrity—a truth that no storyteller, no philosopher, no artist can replicate. During the next decade industrial relations experts will continue to benefit from this truth, and if researchers apply skill in communication and human resource managers apply skill in the implementation, so will men and women in the workplace.

References

Bersheid, E., and E.H. Walster. "Physical Attractiveness." In *Advances in Experimental Social Psychology*, Vol. 7, ed. L. Berkowitz. New York: Academic Press, 1974. Pp. 158–215.

Birdwhistle, R.L. *Kinesics and Context*. Philadelphia: University of Pennsylvania Press, 1970.

Bradley, C. "Sex Bias in the Evaluation of Students." *British Journal of Social Psychology* 23 (1984): pp. 146–53.

Briere, J., and C. Lanktree. "Sex-Role Related Effects of Sex Bias in Language." *Sex Roles* 9 (1983): pp. 625–32.

Cash, T.F., B. Gillen, and D.S. Burns. "Sex and Beautyism in Personnel Consultant Decision-Making." *Journal of Applied Psychology* 62 (1977): pp. 301–11.

Cohen, M. "Problems of Women at Work." In *Public Personnel Update*, eds. M. Cohen and R.T. Golembiewski. New York: Marcel Dekker, 1984.

Colwill, N.L. "The Secretarial Crisis: Toward Evolution or Extinction?" *Business Quarterly* 50 (2) (1985): pp. 12–14.

————. "Equal Pay for Work of Equal Value: Are Women Worth Less than Men?" Proceedings of the Economic Council of Canada, Colloquium on the Economic Status of Women in the Labour Market, Ottawa, November 1984.

————. "Sexist Language: Sex Role Liberation's Pettiest Issue?" *Business Quarterly* 48 (2) (1983): pp. 6, 20.

————. *The New Partnership: Women and Men in Organizations.* Palo Alto, CA: Mayfield Publishing Co., 1982.

Colwill, N.L., and W.L. Josephson. "Attitudes Toward Equal Opportunity in Employment: The Case of One Canadian Government Department." *Business Quarterly* 48 (1) (1983): pp. 87–93.

Colwill, N.L., D. Perlman, and B. Spinner. "'Masculine' and 'Feminine' Power Styles of Female Secretaries and Regional Managers: An In-Basket Task." Paper presented at Canadian Psychological Association 44th Annual Conference, Winnipeg, Manitoba, June 10, 1983.

————. "Effective Power Styles for Women and Men: A Test of Johnson's Model." CPA Section on Women, Canadian Psychological Association 43rd Annual Conference, June 8, 1982.

Crosby, F. "The Denial of Personal Discrimination." *American Behavioral Scientist* 27 (1984): pp. 371–86.

D'Andrade, R.G. "Sex Differences and Cultural Institutions." In *The Development of Sex Differences*, ed. E.E. Maccoby. Stanford, CA: Stanford University Press, 1966. Pp. 174–204.

Deaux, K. "Self-Evaluations of Male and Female Managers." *Sex Roles* 5 (1979): pp. 571–80.

Dipboye, R.L., R.D. Arvey, and D.E. Terpstra. "Sex and Physical Attractiveness of Raters and Applicants as Determinants of Resume Evaluations." *Journal of Applied Psychology* 62 (1977): pp. 288–294.

Dubno, P. "Attitudes Toward Women Executives: A Longitudinal Approach." *Academy of Management Journal* 28 (1985): pp. 235–39.

Dunn, L.A. "Consideration of Variables in Reward and Coercive Influence Attempts." Unpublished manuscript, Tufts University, Medford, MA, 1972.

Eakins, B.W., and R.G. Eakins. *Sex Differences in Human Communication.* Boston: Houghton Mifflin, 1978.

Emmerick, W. "Parental Identification in Young Children." *Genetic Psychological Monographs* 60 (1959): pp. 257–308.

Ezell, H.F., C.A. Odewahn, and J.D. Sherman. "The Effects of Having Been Supervised by a Woman on Perceptions of Female Managerial Competence." *Personnel Psychology* 34 (1981): pp. 291–99.

Falbo, T., M.D. Hazen, and D. Linimon. "The Costs of Selecting Power Bases or Messages Associated With the Opposite Sex." *Sex Roles* 8 (1982): pp. 147–57.

French, F.R.P., and B. Raven. "The Bases of Social Power." In *Studies in Power.* Ann Arbor, MI: Institute for Social Research, 1959. Pp. 150–67.

Gerdes, E.P. and D.M. Garber. "Sex Bias in Hiring: Effects of Job Demands and Applicant Competence." *Sex Roles* 9 (1983): pp. 307–19.

Goodstadt, B.E., and L.A. Hjelle. "Power to the Powerless: Locus of Control and the Use of Power." *Journal of Personality and Social Psychology* 27 (1973): pp. 190–96.

Harrison, B.G., R.F. Guy, and S.L. Lupfer. "Locus of Control and Self-Esteem as Correlates of Role Orientation in Traditional and Nontraditional Women." *Sex Roles* 7 (1981): pp. 1175–87.

Heilman, M.E., and L.R. Saruwatari. "When Beauty Is Beastly: The Effects of Appearance and Sex on Evaluations of Job Applicants for Managerial and Non-managerial Jobs." *Organizational Behavior and Human Performance* 23 (1979): pp. 360–72.

Henley, N.M. *Body Politics: Power, Sex and Nonverbal Communication.* Englewood Cliffs, NJ: Prentice-Hall, 1977.

Hodgins, D.C., and R. Kalin. "Reducing Sex Bias in Judgments of Occupational Suitability by the Provision of Sex-Typed Personality Information." *Canadian Journal of Behavioral Science* 17 (1985): pp. 346–58.

Holahan, C.K., and C.W. Stephan. "Why Beauty Isn't Talent: The Influence of Physical Attractiveness, Attitudes Toward Women and Competence on Impression Formation." *Sex Roles* 7 (1981): pp. 867–76.

Hoult, T.F. "Experimental Measurement of Clothing as a Factor in Some Social Ratings of Selected American Men." *American Sociological Review* 19 (1954): pp. 324–28.

Jabes, J. "Casual Attributions and Sex-Role Stereotypes in the Perceptions of Female Managers." *Canadian Journal of Behavioural Science* 12 (1980): pp. 52–63.

Janis, I.L. "Groupthink." *Psychology Today* 5 (6) (1971): pp. 43–44, 46, 74–76.

Johnson, P. "Women and Power: Towards a Theory of Effectiveness." *Journal of Social Issues* 32 (1976): pp. 99–110.

Kanter, R.M. *Men and Women of the Corporation.* New York: Basic Books, 1977.

Kramer, C. "Women's Speech: Separate but Unequal?" *Quarterly Journal of Speech* 60 (1974): pp. 14–24.

Lakoff, R. *Language and Women's Place.* New York: Harper & Row, 1975.

Levinson, R.M. "Sex Discrimination and Employment Practices: An Experiment With Unconventional Job Enquiries." *Social Problems* 22 (1975): pp. 533–43.

Lockheed, M.E., and K.P. Hall. "Conceptualizing Sex as a Status Characteristic: Application to Leadership Training Strategies." *Journal of Social Issues* 32 (1976): pp. 111–24.

McGinnies, E., L.A. Nordholm, C.D. Ward, and D.L. Bhanthumnavin. "Sex and Cultural Differences in Perceived Locus of Control Among Students in Five Countries." *Journal of Consulting and Clinical Psychology* 42 (1974): pp. 451–55.

Mehrabian, A. *Nonverbal Communication.* Chicago: Aldine-Atherton, 1972.

————. "Verbal and Nonverbal Interaction of Strangers in a Waiting Situation." *Journal of Experimental Research in Personality* 5 (1971): pp. 127–38.

Mickalachki, D.M., and A. Mickalachki. "MBA Women: The New Pioneers." *Business Quarterly* 49 (1) (1984): pp. 110–15.

Milkovich, G.T. "Comparable Worth: The Emerging Debate." in *Perspectives on Personnel/Human Resources Management,* rev. ed., eds. H.G. Heneman III and D.P. Schwab. Homewood, IL: Richard D. Irwin, 1982. Pp. 374–85.

Mintzberg, H. *Power in and Around Organizations.* Englewood Cliffs, NJ: Prentice-Hall, 1983.

Molloy, J.T. *The Women's Dress for Success Book.* New York: Collier Macmillan, 1977.

_____. *Dress for Success*. New York: P.H. Wyden, 1975.

Nelson, B.A., E.M. Opton, Jr., and T.E. Wilson. "Wage Discrimination and Title VII in the 1980s: The Case Against 'Comparable Worth'." In *Contemporary Problems in Personnel*, 3d ed., eds. K. Pearlman, F.L. Schmidt, and W.C. Hamner. New York: John Wiley & Sons, 1983. Pp. 66–82.

O'Farrell, B. "Women and Nontraditional Blue-Collar Jobs in the 1980s: An Overview." In *Women in the Workplace*, ed. P.A. Wallace. Boston: Auburn House, 1982. Pp. 135–65.

Pfeffer, J. *Power in Organizations*. Marshfield, MA: Pitman Publishing, 1981.

Phares, E.J. *Locus of Control in Personality*. Morristown, NJ: General Learning Press, 1976.

Quaintance, M.K. "Moving Toward Unbiased Selection." In *Public Personnel Update*, eds. M. Cohen and R.T. Golembiewski. New York: Marcel Dekker, 1984.

Raven, B.H. "Social Influence and Power." In *Current Studies in Social Psychology*, eds. I.D. Steiner and M. Fishbein. New York: Holt, Rinehart & Winston, 1965.

Robb, R.E. "Equal Pay Policy." In *Towards Equity*, Proceedings of a Colloquium on the Economic Status of Women in the Labour Market. Ottawa: Economic Council of Canada, 1985. Pp. 61–70.

Rosen, B., and T.H. Jerdee. "The Influence of Sex-Role Stereotypes on Evaluations of Male and Female Supervisory Behavior." *Journal of Applied Psychology* 57 (1973): pp. 44–48.

Rotter, J. "Generalized Expectations for Internal vs. External Control of Reinforcement." *Psychological Monographs* 80 (1966): pp. 1–28.

Ryckman, R.M., W.C. Rodda, and M.F. Sherman. "Locus of Control and Expertise Relevance and Determinants of Changes in Opinion About Student Activism." *Journal of Social Psychology* 88 (1972): pp. 107–14.

Schein, V.E. "Sex Role Stereotyping, Ability and Performance: Prior Research and New Directions." *Personnel Psychology* 31 (1978): pp. 259–67.

Schmidt, F.L., and J.E. Hunter. "New Research Findings in Personnel Selection: Myths Meet Realities in the '80's." In *Contemporary Problems in Personnel*, 3d ed., eds. K. Pearlman, F.L. Schmidt, and W.C. Hamner. New York: John Wiley & Sons, 1983. Pp. 98–103.

Schneier, C.E., and R.W. Beatty. "Performance Appraisal and the Law." In *Public Personnel Update*, eds. M. Cohen and R.T. Golembiewski. New York: Marcel Dekker, 1984.

Stead, B.A. "The National Secretarial Shortage: A Management Concern." *MSVC Business Topics* (February 1980): pp. 43–47.

Steinem, G. "Perspectives on Women in the 1980s: The Baird Poskanzer Memorial Lecture." In *Perspectives on Women in the 1980s*, eds. J. Turner and L. Emery. Winnipeg: University of Manitoba Press, 1983. Pp. 14–27.

Sztaba, T.I., and N.L. Colwill. "Genderlect and Perceptions: Does It Pay to Be a Lady?" Unpublished manuscript, University of Manitoba, 1986.

Terborg, J.R., and P. Shingledecker. "Employee Reactions to Supervision and Work Evaluation as a Function of Subordinate and Manager Sex." *Sex Roles* 9 (1983): pp. 813–24.

Von Baeyer, C.L., D.L. Sherk, and M.P. Zanna. "Impression Management in the Job Interview: When the Female Applicant Meets the Male (Chauvinist) Interviewer." *Personality and Social Psychology Bulletin* 7 (1981): pp. 45–51.

Walshok, M.L. *Blue-Collar Women*. Garden City, NY: Anchor Press/Doubleday, 1981.

Zimmerman, D.H., and C. West. "Sex Roles, Interruptions and Silences in Conversation." In *Language and Sex: Difference and Dominance*, eds. B. Thorne and N. Henley. Rowley, MA: Newbury House, 1975. Pp. 105–129.

CHAPTER 5

Problems and Progress
of Women in Management

ROBERT L. DIPBOYE*

Within the short space of approximately 10 years the study of
women in management has emerged as a major area of research in
organizational behavior and management. During this period, reviews
of the literature appeared on an almost yearly basis (Wortman, 1982;
Bass, 1981; Nieva and Gutek, 1981; L.K. Brown, 1979; S.M. Brown,
1979; Kanter, 1977a; Larwood and Wood, 1977; Terborg, 1977;
O'Leary, 1974). The past decade also saw the formation of the Women
in Management division within the Academy of Management, the
addition of courses on women in management in business school
curricula, and an increasing number of consultants, how-to books, and
training programs providing advice on how to cope with the special
problems associated with women in management. The topic deserves
the attention it has received. The movement of women into management has the potential of fundamentally changing the way management is conceptualized and practiced. In this chapter I will review the
research that has appeared over the past decade, point out some of its
strengths and weaknesses, and suggest new directions for future
research.

How Much Progress Have Women Made?

In seeking an answer to this question, one finds both good and bad
news. The good news is that there are clearly more women in management today than there were 10 or 20 years ago. In 1960 women
composed less than 6 percent of the executive, administrative, and
managerial occupational group in the U.S. Census. This percentage
had risen to 18.5 by 1970 and to 30.5 by 1980 (U.S. Department of
Commerce, 1984). Even after correcting for changes that were made in
the Census Bureau's occupational classification system, the propor-

---

*Professor, Department of Psychology and the Jones School of Administrative Science, Rice
University.

tional gains that women made in the managerial category were larger than in any other major occupational group (Rytina and Bianchi, 1984). Corresponding to the increased representation of women in management, the general public has become more accepting since the 1960s of the idea that women should have vocational and educational opportunities equal to those of men (Mason, Czajka, and Arber, 1976).

The bad news is that women are still a distinct minority in management, particularly at the higher levels, and there are signs that this situation will continue for some time to come. According to one estimate, 49,000 men and only 1,000 women held top policy-making jobs in major corporations in 1984 (*Business Week*, 1984). Although women managers may be progressing at a faster pace than their predecessors (Rogan, 1984b), they do not appear to be moving up the hierarchy as rapidly as their male counterparts (Olson and Becker, 1983; Stewart and Gudykunst, 1982; Smith, 1979). For example, Olson and Becker (1983) examined rates of promotion between 1973 and 1977 among 408 men and women from the Quality of Employment Panel and found that if women had been held to the same standards as men, 32 percent would have been promoted instead of only 19 percent. Barbara Everitt Bryant, senior vice president at Market Opinion Research Co., observes that "although business began recruiting and promoting women in substantial numbers in the early 1970s—far enough back to give them time for considerable career advancement— they account for only a tiny percentage of upper management" (*Business Week*, 1984, p. 126). Fraker (1984, p. 40) reports that executive recruiters she interviewed could not identify any women who might become a president or chief executive in a Fortune 500 company: "Even companies that have women in senior management privately concede that those women aren't going to occupy the chairman's office."

The gains women have made in occupying positions on corporate boards appear even smaller than at the top management levels. Only 367 women, compared with 15,500 men, hold board positions in the top 1,300 public companies in the United States, and among the 6,543 directorships in the Fortune 500, a mere 2.8 percent are occupied by women (*Business Week*, 1984). The lack of women on boards is not surprising considering that board positions are usually filled from the ranks of senior management in other firms, and there are still very few women at the highest levels. Elgart (1983, p. 121) claims that there are qualified women, however, and they have been systematically excluded from directorships. Consequently, corporate boards retain "the historic white male profile that has existed since the days when boards were invented."

Even if women are still underrepresented in management, the hope remains that rapidly changing attitudes will soon bring full equality of opportunity for women in management. As shown in a recent replication of a 1965 *Harvard Business Review* survey, men and women have become more accepting of women in management (Sutton and Moore, 1985). The percentage of managers who were strongly favorable toward women in management rose from only 9 percent in 1965 to 33 percent in 1985 among the male managers, and from 48 to 68 percent among the female managers. The percentage agreeing that they personally would feel comfortable working for a woman rose from 27 to 47 percent among the male managers and from 75 to 82 percent among the female managers. Perhaps the most dramatic change was in beliefs regarding women's desire for management responsibilities. In 1965, 54 percent of the male managers and 50 percent of female managers agreed that women rarely expect or want authority. In the 1985 survey these percentages had dropped dramatically to 9 percent for the men and 4 percent for the women.

Despite the softening of bias against women in management, there is still reason for pessimism. A substantial minority of male and female college students (Dubno, 1985; Helmreich, Spence, and Gibson, 1984; Tomkiewicz and Brenner, 1982) and managers (Sutton and Moore, 1985; Fernandez, 1981; Rosen and Jerdee, 1978; Terborg et al., 1977) continue to hold unfavorable attitudes toward women managers. There is even evidence from surveys conducted in several universities that the number of female students favorable toward women in management has actually declined slightly from the mid-1970s, although women continue to hold generally favorable attitudes (Dubno, 1985; Helmreich, Spence, and Gibson, 1984). Also, expectations that new generations of male managers will radically expand the opportunities of women may be overly optimistic in light of some evidence that male college students are less accepting of women in nontraditional roles than are either female college students (Dubno, 1985; Helmreich, Spence, and Gibson, 1984; Tomkiewicz and Brenner, 1982; Crino, White, and De Sanctis, 1981) or male managers (Crino, White, and De Sanctis, 1981). Although younger managers tend to be more accepting of women as managers than do older managers, the differences among age groups that have been reported are too small to justify the conclusion that male managers now moving up in the ranks will be more supportive of women than the older managers they are replacing (Sutton and Moore, 1985).

Sex Stereotyping as the Primary Roadblock

As Nieva and Gutek (1981) have noted, there are at least four levels at which one may explain why women are underrepresented in management and are making painfully slow progress in rising to top positions. At the individual level, female deficiencies in knowledge, skill, and personality as well as male and female attitudinal biases have been hypothesized to prevent women from entering and succeeding in management. At the interpersonal level, men and women have been seen as having to adopt social roles that are inconsistent with the integration of women into a traditionally male domain such as management. A group-level explanation has been that men tend to exclude women from the informal relationships critical to the acquisition of power and influence in organizations. Finally, structural characteristics of organizations have been seen as blocking the upward aspirations of women.

Regardless of whether the individual, group, role, or structure is seen as the primary cause, a psychological construct frequently implicated in theoretical discussions of women's status in management is the *sex stereotype*. Two types of stereotypes have been distinguished (Terborg, 1977). Sex-characteristic stereotypes are beliefs regarding what attributes or behaviors are *characteristic* of men or women. Sixty to 70 percent of respondents have been shown to attribute to the "typical woman" socioemotional traits such as emotional, sensitive, warm, gentle, patient, and understanding, whereas they attribute to the "typical man" task-oriented traits such as aggressive, rational, confident, tough, individualistic, and enterprising (Williams and Best, 1982; Spence and Helmreich, 1978). Women also tend to be stereotyped as generally less work-oriented in their attitudes and values and more concerned with the extrinsic aspects of the job (Rosen and Jerdee, 1973). The attributes assigned to the successful manager differ from those assigned to the typical woman (Massengill and DiMarco, 1979; Powell and Butterfield, 1979; Rosen and Jerdee, 1978; Schein, 1973, 1975). A second type of stereotype is the sex-role stereotype which dictates how men and women *should* behave and attributes they *should* possess. The most frequent theme in the literature appears to be that sex-role and sex-characteristic stereotypes overlap—what men and women *are* is the way they *should* be.

In individual-level explanations of women's underrepresentation in management, stereotypes are seen to play a crucial role. It has been hypothesized that many women do not aspire to managerial careers because they have incorporated traditional stereotypes into their self-concepts. Those who do aspire to become managers must overcome stereotypes which place the female manager in the position of being damned if she does and damned if she doesn't. She may not be taken seriously by superiors, subordinates, peers, and clients whose perceptions and evaluations are biased by the stereotypes they have of women. If she succeeds in breaking through those sex-characteristic stereotypes and is seen as acting as a manager should, she runs the risk of violating sex-role stereotypes that dictate that women should not act "like men." Even when social roles, organizational structures, and informal group relations are presented as the primary causes, stereotyping is often seen as at least a concomitant factor that helps to rationalize and perpetuate women's low status.

How Valid Are Sex-Characteristic Stereotypes?

Many discussions of women in management begin with the assumption that stereotypes are totally erroneous. Rather than being a mere aberration, however, stereotyping is a normal and even a helpful process through which humans make sense of their social environment. Although a stereotype is inherently inaccurate to the extent that it is extended to all members of a group, a stereotype often possesses a "kernel" of truth. In evaluating the validity of the stereotype that women are less qualified than men for managerial positions, one needs to compare men and women on the traits and behaviors they bring to the managerial role, the behaviors they actually exhibit in the performance of the role, and, most important, the effectiveness with which they perform the managerial role.

Research with Nonmanagerial Women

Trait Differences. In comparing men and women in general on the attributes thought to be characteristic of successful managers, men often appear to differ from women in ways that provide some support for traditional stereotypes. Men appear more aggressive, dominant, and competitive than women at all ages (Maccoby and Jacklin, 1974). Women tend to score higher on self-report measures of the need to affiliate (Hoyenga and Hoyenga, 1979) and empathy for others (Eisenberg and Lennon, 1983). Women also have been shown to be less confident of succeeding (Lenney, 1977) and more likely to conform to group pressures (Eagly and Carli, 1981), particularly when performing a "masculine" task with male coworkers. Moreover, women tend to rate themselves higher on stereotypic feminine traits and lower on stereotypic masculine traits than do men (Spence and Helmreich, 1978; Heilbrun, 1976; Bem, 1974; Constantinople, 1973). One can also find *weak* support in research with nonmanagerial samples for the stereotypes that working women are less involved in their jobs (Golembiewski, 1977) and less committed to their organizations (Bruning and Snyder, 1983; Graddick and Farr, 1983; Golembiewski, 1977). Finally, minimal sex differences in the preferences for job attributes are often found that support some stereotypes of women, but both males and females are usually found to value the intrinsic aspects of their jobs more than the extrinsic aspects (Lacy, Bakemeier, and Shepard, 1983).

Behavioral Differences. Male and female college students do not appear to differ to any substantial degree on the decisions they make in hypothetical cases (Dobbins et al., 1983; Pence et al., 1982; Heilman and Guzzo, 1978). Consistent differences have been found between male and female students, however, in laboratory research examining actual behavior in leadership roles. Women are less likely to attempt to influence or dominate task activities when placed in a mixed-sex group (Kimble, Yoshikawa, and Zehr, 1981) or in a supervisory role (Instone, Major, and Bunker, 1983; Ayers-Nachamkin et al., 1982). Even women who are high on dominance, as measured by a self-report personality questionnaire, appear likely to take the follower role when working with a low dominance male (Carbonell, 1984; Megargee, 1969). Another consistent laboratory finding is that women tend to follow a norm of equality and administer rewards equally among subordinates, whereas men tend to follow an equity norm and distribute rewards according to level of individual performance (Major and Deaux, 1982). Finally, women appear less assertive than men in their speech, with men generally speaking louder and interrupting others more frequently. For example, O'Barr and Atkins (1980) observed that women in courtroom settings tend to use hedges, tag questions, question intonations, hypercorrect grammar and pronunciation, and other speech forms that lessen their power and influence.

Research with Managerial Women

, *Trait Differences.* Unlike nonmanagerial women, managerial women deviate markedly from stereotypes of the "typical female." Women in management tend to score higher on measures of "masculine" personality traits than women in traditionally female occupations (Waddell, 1983; Brenner, 1982; Morrison and Sebald, 1974). Similar differences are found between female college students majoring in management and those in more traditional college majors (Steinberg and Shapiro, 1982; Foster and Kolinko, 1979; Pfeifer and Shapiro, 1978; Wertheim, Widon, and Wortzel, 1978). On the other hand, few differences on trait measures are typically found between men and women who aspire to managerial positions (Miner and Smith, 1982; Foster and Kolinko, 1979; Wertheim, Widon, and Wertzel, 1978) or actually occupy managerial roles (Cook and Mendelson, 1984; Harlan and Weiss, 1982; Wood and Greenfield, 1976, 1979; Miner, 1974, 1978). For example, Harlan and Weiss (1982) compared the traits of 50 male and 50 female managers who had been matched on level, responsibility, and functional area. They found that managers of both sexes had high power and achievement needs, high self-esteem, and high motivation to manage, with females differing little from their male counterparts on this profile. Women who are highly educated (Brenner, 1982), work in traditionally male work settings (Moore and Rickel, 1980), and are at higher levels of management (Moore and Rickel, 1980) appear to conform more to the stereotype of the successful manager and less to the traditional female stereotype than do women with less education, working in traditionally female settings, and at lower levels of management.

Female managers also appear to be quite similar to male managers in the value they place on intrinsic and extrinsic aspects of the job (Brief, Rose, and Aldag, 1977; Brief and Oliver, 1976). When differences are found in work-related values, they typically are either inconsistent with the traditional stereotypes of women (Donnell and Hall, 1980) or trivial in magnitude (Watson and Ryan, 1979). The longer women are in managerial positions, the less likely they are to differ from their male counterparts in their job involvement and their value for intrinsic and extrinsic job features (Gomez-Mejia, 1983).

Behavioral Differences. In contrast to research on the behavior of nonmanagerial men and women, the research on the leadership behavior of men and women who are actually in managerial positions has yielded little in the way of consistent findings. Much of this research has shown that male and female supervisors do not differ in how they are described by their subordinates on such dimensions as initiation of structure and consideration (Osburn and Vicars, 1976; Day and Stogdill, 1972), production versus people orientation (Donnell and Hall, 1980), power and influence (Rice, Instone, and Adams, 1984), and participation (Donnell and Hall, 1980). Likewise, studies have shown that male and female managers do not differ in their attitudes toward performance appraisal (Lovrich and Jones, 1983), their preferred styles of handling interpersonal conflict (Renwick, 1977), and their decision-making processes (Muldrow and Bayton, 1979).

In contrast to these studies, other researchers have found differences in the leadership behavior of men and women. There is some evidence that female supervisors are described as higher in the initiation of structure but equally considerate (Bartol and Wortman, 1975; Petty and Lee, 1975), less willing to share information with colleagues (Donnell and Hall, 1980), more Machiavellian (Chonko, 1982), and closer in their supervision and more prone to playing favorites (South et al., 1982). There is also evidence that female managers show more consideration (Petty and Bruning, 1980; Adams, 1978) and participation (Jago and Vroom, 1982), but the same level of structuring (Petty and Bruning, 1980; Adams, 1978) as male managers. A recent experiment (Steckler and Rosenthal, 1985) found that female MBAs communicated less competently than male MBAs when they role-played phone conversations with a peer, but more competently than the males in role-playing conversations with subordinates and supervisors.

How Do Men and Women Actually Perform in the Managerial Role? A more important issue than the traits and behaviors of men and women in management is how they actually perform as managers. One potential index of effectiveness is subordinate satisfaction with the manager, and here again the findings are quite mixed. Subordinates of female supervisors have been known to be equally satisfied (Adams, 1978; Osborn and Vicars, 1976; Bartol and Wortman, 1975) or only slightly less satisfied (Adams, Rice, and Instone, 1984; Rice, Instone, and Adams, 1984; Rousell, 1974) with the supervision they receive than the subordinates of male supervisors. There is also evidence that employees who have had a female supervisor are more positive toward women in management than are those who have never had a female supervisor (Ezell, Odewahn, and Sherman, 1981).

The satisfaction of subordinates with a supervisor depends to a large extent on the supervisor's style of supervision. It is not clear from past research whether the effectiveness of various leadership styles differs as a function of the sex of the leader. Although Petty and his associates (Petty and Miles, 1976; Petty and Lee, 1975) found that structuring on the part of the supervisor was associated with decreased satisfaction among male subordinates of female supervisors and increased satisfaction among male subordinates of male supervisors, Petty and Bruning (1980) failed to replicate these findings. Kanter (1977a) has suggested that if female supervisors tend to be less effective than male supervisors, it is not because of differences in their styles as much as differences in the formal and informal influence that is associated with their positions. In support of this contention, South et al. (1982) found that to the extent female supervisors had less influence than their male counterparts, subordinates with female supervisors tended to have less job satisfaction and lower group morale than those with male supervisors.

A more common index of effectiveness than subordinate satisfaction is the direct rating of the manager's effectiveness. Female managers tend to receive ratings that are as favorable as those received by male managers, regardless of whether the evaluator is a subordinate (Fernandez, 1981; Deaux, 1979; Moses and Boehm, 1975). There is some evidence based on opportunistic samples from individual firms that women receive higher ratings than men. Peters et al. (1984) found this with ratings of store managers by their immediate supervisors. Similarly, Tsui and Gutek (1984) found that when performance evaluations of middle-level women managers were compared with the evaluations of their male colleagues, the women received significantly higher performance ratings from their peers and tended to receive higher ratings from supervisors and subordinates. Despite the fact that women are seen by others as performing as well or even better than their male counterparts, there is some indication that they tend to see themselves as performing more poorly than their male peers (Deaux, 1979). For example, Izraeli (1985) found in a study of Israeli union officials that the self-ratings of the amount of influence wielded were lower among female leaders than among male leaders.

Summary

There is some evidence that nonmanagerial women may, indeed, differ from men in their traits and behaviors in ways that provide support for traditional stereotypes. These differences are typically too small to be of much practical significance. Moreover, women who are attracted to a managerial role appear to deviate markedly from this stereotype. Whether they had these managerial characteristics to begin with or they changed in that direction as a consequence of their socialization in the managerial role has yet to be determined. An answer to this question will require cross-sectional and longitudinal studies in which males and females are compared on managerial traits and behaviors as early as the elementary or secondary school years and changes are tracked through college, postgraduate MBA work, and into the different stages of their organizational careers. Future research should also give more attention to sex differences in the performance of other internal and external roles that managers must perform rather than continuing to focus exclusively on the supervisory role. More attempts should be made to observe actual behavior of male and female managers in field settings rather than relying as much on retrospective descriptions by subordinates and others. Finally, attention needs to be given to the differences in formal and informal power possessed by men and women managers in order to test the claim that the amount of power associated with the position is a more important determinant of managerial effectiveness than the traits and behaviors of the manager (South et al., 1982; Kanter, 1977a).

The Biases of Women Against a Managerial Career

The research on characteristics of managerial and nonmanagerial women suggests that aspiring managerial women are as likely as aspiring managerial men to possess the requisite traits of the successful manager and to achieve success in management. Nevertheless, the research on nonmanagerial women suggests one reason why women continue to be underrepresented in management. Regardless of the validity or invalidity of the stereotypes of women, many women appear to have been socialized to conform to traditional female stereotypes and, consequently, have much more limited occupational aspirations than do men. Thus, women are not only systematically excluded from entering management, but the total pool of qualified women is smaller than it should be because of the biases of many women against a managerial career. Marini and Brinton (1984) analyzed data from a national survey conducted in 1978 and found that 86 percent of young men between 14 and 22 years of age aspired to male occupations and only 4.1 percent to female occupations, whereas 52 percent of young women aspired to female occupations and only 34 percent aspired to male occupations. Young women also appear less likely than young men to aspire to a managerial career (Fottler and Bain, 1980; McCall and Lawler, 1976; Barnett and Tagiuri, 1973; Miner and Smith, 1969). Moreover, boys are likely to aspire to specific careers, such as engineering, that provide a greater likelihood of entry to managerial careers.

The higher managerial aspirations of men even appear among men and women in traditionally female occupations. For example, Auster (1978) found that out of 15 nursing specialties, male nursing students ranked administration as the most preferred, whereas women nursing students ranked it only 12th. Once they have decided on a managerial career, women still tend to have lower aspirations than do men. In a survey of 4,191 managers from 12 companies, Fernandez (1981) found that the percentage of men aspiring to the fifth or sixth level of management ranged from a high of 52 percent among blacks to a low of 23 percent among Asians. In comparison, the percentage of women aspiring to the same levels ranged from a high of 21 percent among the blacks to a low of 4 percent among the Native Americans.

Biases in the Hiring and Recruiting of Women

It is clear that one reason for the underrepresentation of women in management is that many women who would have succeeded in management have taken themselves out of the competition. It is equally clear, however, that women who aspire to management positions confront an additional barrier in the form of bias against women in the judgments made by corporate recruiters, personnel officers, and others in "gatekeeping" positions and in the instruments they use to assess managerial talent. Again, stereotypes are commonly seen as the source of these biases.

Biographical Data

Regardless of the specific techniques employed by an organization to screen and select managers, biographical data on the applicant in the form of résumés or application information are usually considered at some point in the process. Stereotypes possessed by recruiters and others in gatekeeping roles have been hypothesized to bias their judgments of women applying for managerial positions.

In support of the stereotype hypothesis, female applicants for managerial positions tend to be rated as less qualified than male applicants with identical résumés (Siegfried, 1982; Cann, Siegfried, and Pearce, 1981; Dipboye, Arvey, and Terpstra, 1977; Dipboye, Fromkin, and Wiback, 1975; Rosen and Jerdee, 1974b). Bias against women appears more likely when there is ambiguity as to the relevance of her credentials to the position (Heilman, 1984), when there are fewer than 25 percent female applicants (Heilman, 1980), and when the position requires supervision of male subordinates (Rose and Andiappan, 1978). A spouse, child, and an undergraduate business degree appear to favor a male candidate more than a female candidate (Renwick and Tosi, 1978). Whereas being physically attractive appears to help the chances of a male managerial candidate, it may actually hurt the chances of a female candidate by making salient feminine stereotypes (Heilman and Saruwatari, 1979). At least two other studies, however, have found that very attractive managerial candidates are rated as more qualified than less attractive candidates regardless of sex (Dipboye, Arvey, and Terpstra, 1977; Dipboye, Fromkin, and Wiback, 1975).

There have been at least three studies that have failed to find sex bias with persons in actual decision-making roles (Hitt, Zikmund, and Pickens, 1982; Oliphant and Alexander, 1982; Rosen and Mericle, 1979). Despite these findings, bias against female applicants has been found frequently enough with subjects other than students to suggest that the findings of sex bias in past research cannot be readily dismissed as nongeneralizable. Bias against female applicants has been found with college recruiters (Dipboye, Fromkin, and Wiback, 1975), managers (Gerdes and Garber, 1983), and school administrators (Frasher, Frasher, and Wims, 1982). Additionally, personnel officers in companies have been shown less likely to respond and less likely to respond favorably to an unsolicited résumé from a female candidate for a professional position than from a male candidate with similar credentials (Firth, 1982; McIntyre, Moberg, and Posner, 1980). Levinson (1982) found that in 28 percent of phone conversations in which females sought a "male-typed" job in response to an advertisement, the response on the part of the employer was clearly discriminatory. In one case the male caller was encouraged by the owner of a restaurant to interview for a managerial position, but the woman "was told she would be better suited now for positions such as hostess, cashier, or waitress" (p. 53). Clear-cut discrimination was even more common, however, against males applying for female jobs (44 percent) than it was for females applying for male jobs.

Face-to-Face Interviews

Before companies actually hire managerial candidates, they usually require more information than is typically found in a résumé. The effects of stereotypes may be much less pronounced as the result of information provided in a face-to-face interview. Indeed, in laboratory research with videotaped (Dipboye and Wiley, 1977), scripted (Dipboye and Wiley, 1978), and face-to-face interviews (Baron, 1982), female candidates tend to be rated the same as male candidates. The personality of the interviewer is likely to moderate the extent to which bias occurs against females in evaluations of interviews. For example, one study found that highly authoritarian persons were biased against a female applicant for a managerial position despite the additional information afforded by a videotaped interview (Simas and McCarrey, 1979).

Scored Biographical Information

Instead of relying on the subjective judgments of the interviewer, an alternative is to develop an objective scoring key in which individual items of biographical information obtained through applications, résumés, or interviews are weighted according to the extent to which they discriminate successful from unsuccessful managers. Scored biographical inventories can effectively forecast the success of a variety of employees, including managers. Because many of these inventories were developed to forecast the success of male managers, they can adversely affect the hiring of women (Reilly and Chao, 1982). Nevertheless, it is possible, as Ritchie and Boehm (1977) demonstrated at AT&T, to develop biographical instruments that are both valid and free of sex bias.

Assessment Centers

Another commonly used technique for evaluating managerial candidates is the assessment center. In the typical assessment center, candidates perform exercises (leaderless group discussions, in-basket exercises, role plays, formal presentations) that tap cognitive and interpersonal skills related to management effectiveness (organization and planning skills, decisiveness, fluency of written and oral communications). Because the measures of performance on these exercises are subjective, stereotypes may still enter into assessment-center evaluations. Nevertheless, men and women do not differ in either the level of assessments they receive or the predictive validity of these assessments (Thornton and Byham, 1982).

Paper-and-Pencil Tests

Ghiselli (1973) has reported that paper-and-pencil tests of intellectual ability, spatial and mechanical abilities, and perceptual abilities predict proficiency in managerial positions with correlations of approximately .21 to .30, and personality tests predict proficiency with correlations of .21 to .28. Validities of this level can prove quite useful given the low cost of testing, a low selection ratio, and a low base rate of success in the position. Whether paper-and-pencil measures adversely affect the hiring of women depends on which measures are used. Women tend to score substantially lower on spatial-ability and quantitative-ability tests (Maccoby and Jacklin, 1974). Also, as previously noted, they have been found to score lower on self-report measures of personality (e.g., aggression, self-confidence, independence) that are commonly used to assess managerial potential. On the other hand, women often score higher on measures of verbal ability (Maccoby and Jacklin, 1974) and social sensitivity (Hoffman, 1977). Whether these various measures predict the success of male and female managers any differently has yet to be researched.

Summary

Among the instruments for selecting managerial candidates, the subjective evaluations of paper credentials appear to be the most vulnerable to the biasing effects of sex stereotypes. Although assessment centers, scored biographical inventories, and paper-and-pencil tests also have the potential of screening out a disproportionate number of women, they appear to present fewer problems because of their greater objectivity. Numerous gaps remain in the research on sex-bias in the selection and recruitment of women managers. Virtually no research has been done on the biases that can enter into the recruitment of managerial candidates. Also, past research has focused on single techniques when the typical practice is to use multiple techniques to screen and select managers. Research is needed on how biases that exist in the early phases of the selection/recruitment process may influence subsequent evaluations.

Biased Treatment of Women Managers

Once women have taken managerial positions, they still may face other barriers that limit their career advancement. These include exclusion from informal relationships with male peers, biases in the perception and evaluation of their performance in supervisory roles, inequitable compensation, greater conflicts between work and family roles, sexual harassment, lack of sponsors, and biases in job assignments. As in the case of biases in selection and recruitment, stereotyping is commonly discussed as the root cause of the unfair treatment of women managers.

Biases in Job Assignments and Promotions

An important determinant of a manager's career success appears to be the extent to which job assignments and promotions he or she receives are challenging and conducive to the development of managerial skills. Laboratory research has shown that male managers (Mai-Dalton and Sullivan, 1981) and college students (Mai-Dalton and Sullivan, 1981; Taylor and Ilgen, 1981; Terborg and Ilgen, 1975) are less likely to assign a female subordinate to a challenging task than they are a male subordinate. Consistent with these laboratory findings, Fernandez (1981) found that a substantial proportion of the managers he surveyed (34 percent) believed that most female managers are placed in dead-end jobs. Unfortunately, this survey did not examine whether male managers are any less likely to "get stuck" than their female counterparts. Other surveys providing this comparison suggest that women are perceived as more likely than men to receive assignments that are less beneficial to their careers. Rosen, Templeton, and Kichline (1981) surveyed 117 female managers and 117 male managers a few years after receiving their MBAs and found that women were more likely to report that the job assignments they had been given had kept many of them from developing social networks. One of the more frequent complaints among the women was that they were "drowning in details of the work, while male colleagues are out making contacts, forming coalitions, and increasing visibility." Similarly, Strober (1982) found in a 1978 survey of 1974 MBA graduates of Stanford that fewer women (75 percent) than men (91 percent) reported that their job was a satisfactory stepping-stone to their desired future position.

Other evidence suggests that men progress more in responsibility and authority when they are promoted than do women. Stewart and Gudykunst (1982) found that the number of promotions received and the hierarchical level attained by managers in an organization were positively related ($r = .41$) for men, but were unrelated ($r = .03$) for women. After controlling the variance due to length of tenure, age, and years of education, female employees were found to receive more promotions than males, but to occupy lower positions in the hierarchy than their male counterparts.

In a study involving a more representative sample of working people, Wolf and Fligstein (1979) found that control over hiring, firing, and pay was much more likely to accompany a higher status job for a man than for a woman. Even those women who rise to top levels of management still may not possess the same authority and responsibility usually thought to accompany such positions. Some indication of this was provided by a recent attempt of the Gallup organization to draw a nationwide sample of women with the title of vice president or higher. The initial sample of over 2,000 women had to be reduced to less than 800 because, according to the pollster, "Many of them, despite their titles, worked at relatively low levels" (Rogan, 1984c, p. 35). Because only female managers were surveyed in this study, one cannot determine the extent to which male managers have titles that are more lofty than their duties. Nevertheless, other studies that have provided male-female comparisons suggest that women managers may not be assigned the same responsibilities as their male colleagues. Harlan and Weiss (1982), for example, compared matched samples of managerial women and men in two retail organizations and found that 40 percent of the men and 22 percent of the women in one organization and 67 percent of the men and 50 percent of the women in the second organization reported having responsibility for $1 million or more of the company's assets. Similarly, Strober (1982) found in the 1978 follow-up that 43 percent of the male MBAs from the Stanford class of 1974 and 13 percent of the women had authority to approve expenditures in excess of $100.

The Lack of Sponsors for Women

Some evidence suggests that successful managers tend to have someone in the organization who acts as a sponsor and mentor (Hunt and Michael, 1983). Fernandez (1981) found that the managers in his survey ranked performing well, work experience, and having a sponsor as the first, second, and third most important factors in obtaining desired positions. It has been suggested that one of the barriers faced by women managers is that they have difficulty in finding a sponsor or mentor. In support of this, Fernandez (1981) found that 44 percent of the managers in his survey believed that women have a harder time than white men in finding a mentor. Also, Rosen, Templeton, and Kichline (1981) found that more male managers (62 percent) than female managers (50 percent) said that there was someone in the organization who had taken a special interest in their careers. If a woman is to have a high-level sponsor, in most cases it will be a male manager. This presents the protégée and the mentor with all the problems that typically accompany male-female relationships (Fitt and Newton, 1981). In contrast to the evidence that women are less likely to acquire mentors, Strober (1982) found that the women in her sample were somewhat more likely than the men to have a mentor and that having a mentor was unrelated to managerial success for both male and female managers.

Relationships With Peers

An important part of most managers' jobs is relating to other managers at their level. Recent surveys indicate that women confront more problems in developing effective working relationships with male managers who are their peers. The percentage of female managers saying that they currently feel or have felt cut off from informal relationships with their male colleagues has ranged from 60 to 67 percent (Rogan, 1984b; Fernandez, 1981; Rosen, Templeton, and Kichline, 1981). In the Fernandez survey, 57 percent of white male managers agreed that female managers are often excluded from informal work networks by men. Thirty-five percent of white female managers and 39 percent of white male managers agreed that female managers have difficulty initiating informal work-related activities such as lunch dates and drinks after work because of the possible misinterpretation of these invitations as sexual advances.

Biases in the Compensation of Women Managers

Just as in other occupational areas, the salaries of women lag behind those of men. As of March 1983, women in executive, administrative, and managerial occupations earned 60 percent of what men in these occupations earned (U.S. Department of Commerce, 1984, p. 41). There is evidence that women at higher occupational levels are less satisfied with their pay than are men (Varca, Shaffer, and McCauley, 1983). In addition, survey results suggest that women managers attribute this gap to biases against women in pay administration. Seventy percent of the 722 female executives polled in a recent Gallup survey agreed that they have felt that they were being paid less than a man of equal ability (Rogan, 1984d). These views do not appear to be shared by the male counterparts. In a 1965 *Harvard Business Review* survey of managers, 84 percent of women managers and 50 percent of male managers agreed that a woman executive is invariably paid less than her male counterparts. In a 1985 replication of this survey, 73 percent of the women executives, but only 34 percent of the male executives, agreed with this statement.

In one of the few published attempts to determine the source of the gender gap in pay, Siegelman, Milward, and Shepard (1982) found a yearly salary differential of $5,343 between male and female administrators at the University of Kentucky. A differential of $2,011 still remained after controlling for the responsibility level of the jobs. In a more rigorous analysis of male and female Stanford MBAs, Strober (1982) found that the greater tendency of women to stop working for a period during their careers and the tendency of women to be segregated in jobs in lower-paying industries were the two factors that accounted for most of the differences between the sexes in their 1978 salaries. At least two laboratory experiments have also been conducted in an attempt to examine whether women managers who are comparable to men on all dimensions are still discriminated against in the administration of rewards. One experiment found that women were discriminated against (Dipboye, Arvey, and Terpstra, 1977), whereas the other found little evidence of bias (Rose and Stone, 1978).

One likely source of at least some of the gap in salary may be the lower aspirations and expectations of women. Major and Konar (1984) surveyed 83 students enrolled in a management internship program during 1980 and found that the mean salary that men expected to earn during their first working year was $18,516 compared with $15,805 for women. The mean salary they expected to earn at the peak of their careers was $64,482 for men and $42,188 for women. Strober (1982) found some evidence that women continue to have lower salary aspirations after entering the managerial ranks. She first surveyed Stanford MBAs at the time they graduated in 1974 and accepted their first positions. Although there were no significant differences in the starting salaries of men and women, the mean highest salary "hoped for" in their careers was $81,471 among the women and $135,083 among the men. In a 1978 follow-up to this earlier survey, Strober (1982) found that not only were women earning about 80 percent of what their male classmates earned, but the gender gap in salary aspirations had actually widened as the result of four years of work experience. The mean response of the women when asked for the highest salary they "hoped for" in their career was $115,305, whereas the mean response of the men to the same question was $269,479.

Consistent with the differences in aspirations, Lyson (1984) found that women preparing for traditionally male jobs expressed more concern for the intrinsic aspects of the job and less concern for extrinsic aspects (particularly pay) than did men. According to Lyson's analysis, the greater concern of men for the extrinsic factors may mean that men are quicker and more likely to seize opportunities that lead to positions of authority and prestige, while their female counterparts revel in the work itself. The findings of Strober's (1982) survey of 1974 Stanford MBAs support this contention to some extent. The men ranked attainment of wealth as significantly more important than did the women in the 1978 follow-up, whereas the women ranked independence, compatibility with coworkers, and location for spouse as more important than did the men.

Biases in the Perception and Evaluation of Women Managers

As discussed earlier, people may be less likely to recognize leadership on the part of a woman because of sex-characteristic stereotypes that bias their perceptions. A woman who clearly displays leadership, however, runs the risk of violating sex-role stereotypes that proscribe aggressive or dominant behavior on the part of a woman. The typical approach to testing the effects of stereotypes on the perception and evaluation of leader behavior has been to hold constant the behavior of managers in scenarios (usually written) while manipulating the sex of the manager. The results that have emerged from this research have been neither clear nor consistent. Some research has shown that the sex of the leader has no effect on perceptions or evaluations of the leader (Butterfield and Powell, 1981; Dennis and Alvares, 1977; Hall and Hall, 1976). On the other hand, Wiley and Eskilson (1982) found that managers who were told that a person in a script was male tended to describe him as more powerful, higher in corporate position, and warmer than did the managers who were told that the person was female.

Similarly, research has yielded mixed support for the hypothesis that managers are evaluated more favorably if their behavior is congruent with sex-role stereotypes than if their behavior is incongruent with these stereotypes. Some support for this hypothesis has been found in experiments with college students (Bartol and Butterfield, 1975; Rosen and Jerdee, 1973), blue-collar workers (Haccoun, Haccoun, and Salay, 1978), and managers (Jago and Vroom, 1982; Wiley and Eskilson, 1982). Other studies have found that relative to a man who exhibits "masculine" behavior such as assertiveness or anger, a woman who exhibits the same behavior is evaluated as favorably (Trempe, Rigny, and Haccoun, 1985; Solomon et al., 1982) or more favorably (Moore, 1984; Mai-Dalton, Feldman-Summers, and Mitchell, 1979). In the research in which the ratings of performance and promotability have been examined, some studies have shown bias against women (Frasher, Frasher, and Wims, 1982; Rosen and Jerdee, 1974a, 1974b), some have shown bias in favor of women (London and Stumpf, 1983), and still others have shown no bias (Stumpf and London, 1981).

Surprisingly, most studies have ignored the prior attitudes of subjects toward women in management. Two studies in which prior attitudes were measured found that those who were favorably disposed toward women in management were more likely to perceive a female manager's behavior in terms that were consistent with their attitudes (Rice, Bender, and Vitters, 1980; Garland and Price, 1977).

Role Conflicts as Barriers to Women Managers

Women in general experience more role conflicts than do their male counterparts, and this role conflict serves as another barrier to women managers seeking to advance in their careers. A major source

of role conflict appears to be conflict between household responsibilities and organizational duties. Even women managers as high as
the vice presidential level report that they carry a disproportionate
share of the responsibility for home chores (Rogan, 1984a). Strober
(1982) found in her 1978 survey of the 1974 Stanford MBA graduates
that the women managers mentioned discrimination and conflict with
family roles (e.g., integrating own career with spouse's career) as the
most serious problems they expected to face in achieving their career
goals. Men were more likely to mention the "problems of managing"
and "getting stuck" as the most serious they would confront.

There are several ways in which role conflict may adversely affect
the career success of a woman manager. Research has shown that
women with high levels of role conflict tend to have lower job satisfaction (Andrisani and Shapiro, 1978) and job involvement (Herman and
Gyllstrom, 1977; Gordon and Hall, 1974; Matthews, Collins, and
Cobb, 1974). Whether role conflict has a similar effect among men
managers as well cannot be determined on the basis of present
research, but it appears that managerial women may at least experience more ambivalence regarding the importance of their managerial
careers than men because of these conflicts (Chusmir, 1982). Cooper
and Davidson (1982) claim on the basis of a study of managers in the
United Kingdom that female managers are more likely than male
managers to show symptoms of stress, such as headaches, cigarette
smoking, drug and alcohol abuse, and marital problems, because of
their greater role conflicts. Probably the most damaging effect of the
female manager's role conflicts is to prevent her from taking promotions that involve relocations. Surveys have shown that women managers are less likely to accept a promotion that requires relocation
(Breen, 1983) and are more likely than men to accommodate their
careers to their spouse's (Rosen, Templeton, and Kichline, 1981).
Also, 41 percent of the men but only 25 percent of the women in a
recent survey of managers said that their families would support a
promotion requiring a relocation (Breen, 1983). Conflicts such as these
are probably a major factor in accounting for the very low percentage of
women (3 percent, according to one estimate) who are international
managers (Adler, 1984).

Remedies

There has been a considerable amount of discussion of how to
reduce the barriers to women who aspire to managerial positions, but
very few studies that attempt to actually evaluate these remedies. The
five general strategies that have received the most attention are
(1) affirmative action in hiring and recruitment; (2) training of men and

women to reduce the influence of sex-role stereotypes and improve their managerial skills; (3) legal remedies such as lawsuits; (4) structural changes in organizations; and (5) entrepreneurship.

Affirmative Action in Hiring, Recruitment, and Promotion

In a recent Conference Board survey, the companies that were successful in affirmative action programs aimed at improving job opportunities for women were found to have top management which was clearly committed to improving the opportunities for women, line managers who were held accountable for meeting EEO requirements, and EEO departments with authority over the staffing process (Schaeffer and Lynton, 1979). Furthermore, these organizations were likely to train women in the knowledge and skills needed to make them promotable and were likely to train managers in interviewing and selection techniques. One strategy for increasing opportunities for women in management was to drop the MBA degree as a prerequisite for management positions. Several organizations were found to have done this with no apparent ill effects. With the percentage of women in MBA programs having grown from only 4 percent in 1972 to over 25 percent in 1985 (Warsh, 1985), this proposal may be somewhat outdated.

Both men and women in management appear to accept the effectiveness of civil rights legislation and other legal intervention in providing equal opportunity for women. In a 1965 *Harvard Business Review* survey, 71 percent of men and 55 percent of women rejected the idea that new laws would expedite progress of women in management. In a 1985 replication of this survey, only 16 percent of the men and 26 percent of the women believed that civil rights laws have had no impact on equal opportunity. Nevertheless, neither men nor women appear receptive to affirmative action when it is implemented through preferential treatment. In a recent Gallup survey of 1,562 adults, 85 percent of the men and 84 percent of the women said that ability should be the main consideration and only 9 percent of the men and 11 percent of the women said there should be preferential treatment to correct past discrimination (*Gallup Report*, 1984). Fernandez (1981) found that 47 percent of white male managers believed that affirmative action has hurt their chances for promotion and 84 percent believed that it had lowered general hiring and promotion standards. Moreover, women leaders who are believed to have been selected as leaders on the basis of their sex have been shown to have received lower evaluations from their subordinates than women who are believed to have been selected on the basis of ability and those believed to have been selected on the basis of a random draw (Jacobson and Kock, 1977). In another study, women managers who believed that they had been hired on the basis of their sex, in comparison with those who believed they had been hired for their ability, education, or experience, were found to report less commitment to their organizations, less satisfaction with their work, supervisor, coworkers, and the overall job, and more role conflict and ambiguity (Chacko, 1982).

Special Training for Men and Women

Training is one of the most frequently discussed strategies for improving the status of women in management (Hartnett and Novarra, 1980; Larwood, Wood, and Interlied, 1978). Fernandez (1981) found that 42 percent of the white male managers in his sample believed that women need special training, whereas only 30 percent of white women and 28 percent of black women felt that women needed such training. On the other hand, 44 percent of white men, 42 percent of white women, and 56 percent of black women believed that white male managers needed special training. The topics that were mentioned most frequently by managers as areas in which women need training included technical skills (59 percent), dealing with male subordinates and peers (48 percent), and understanding the political aspects of management (23 percent). Men, on the other hand, were seen as needing training in overcoming their biases and stereotypes toward women and minorities (32 percent), understanding problems specific to women and minorities (14 percent), and human relations (13 percent).

Despite the proliferation of training to eliminate bias among men and provide managerial skills for women, relatively few attempts to evaluate special training for men and women have been reported in the literature. The few that have been published do not appear particularly supportive of their effectiveness (Dunnette and Motowidlo, 1982; White, Crino, and De Sanctis, 1981; Rader, 1979).

Structural Changes

Kanter (1977a) has presented the interesting thesis that equality for women in organizations can only be achieved by implementing structures that improve the quality of work life of both men and women. To empower lower-level managers, she recommends such structural changes as assigning senior managers to serve as sponsors of lower-level managers, reducing the number of levels of management, and the creation of autonomous work units to increase the formal and informal power of women in low-level managerial positions. Other structural changes recommended by Kanter (1977a) are the hiring and placement of managerial women in batches to avoid tokenism, and extending managerial career paths to traditionally female occupations such as clerical work. Strober (1975) recommended that organizations accommodate their policies and structures to the family roles of the female manager. Among the suggestions she made were extended leaves for women managers in the childbearing years; the creation of part-time, lower-level, and middle-level managerial positions; the elimination of the requirement that a manager relocate geographically as a condition for promotion; flexible work schedules; and day-care arrangements.

Some corporations are beginning to reconsider their transfer policies. Also, an increasing number of organizations have experimented with flexible work schedules and vouchers for child care. Nevertheless, few organizations have actually restructured in the ways suggested by Kanter (1977a), Strober (1975), and others. Most continue to have structures and policies that favor the manager with a stay-at-home spouse and that present special role conflicts for the married female manager.

Legal Remedies

A variety of legal remedies are available to women who believe that they are being unfairly discriminated against, including the 1964 Civil Rights Act, Executive Order 11246, the Federal Equal Pay Act of 1963, the Equal Employment Act of 1972, Title IX of the Education Amendments of 1972, and the fair employment practice laws that are on the books in at least four-fifths of the states. Although legal remedies have been used successfully to increase opportunities for women in management (Larwood and Wood, 1977), it is a high-risk alternative. Judges have been reluctant to hold up for scrutiny the techniques that organizations use to select and promote managers (Bartholet, 1982). Viewed from a strictly utilitarian perspective, filing a discrimination suit against an employer is not a wise decision in most situations, given the high cost and low probability of success (Gleason, 1984).

Entrepreneurship

If women with managerial aspirations cannot find opportunities within male-dominated organizations that fit their aspirations, then perhaps they should start their own businesses. There is some evidence that this is already occurring (Bettner and Donahue, 1983). Since 1970 the increase in the number of self-employed women has been at a rate that is five times that of men and three times as fast as the total increase in women wage-earners (Becker, 1984). Since 1977 the number of firms owned by women has increased almost 33 percent, and approximately a third of new firms founded each year are started by women (Gregg, 1985).

Most of the empirical work on women entrepreneurs has consisted of attempts to establish a profile of the typical or successful female entrepreneur (Waddell, 1983) and anecdotal evidence on the factors relating to success and failure of women entrepreneurs. Some of the special problems said to hamper the female entrepreneur are lack of business knowledge in areas such as finance, marketing, and purchasing; second-class treatment by the financial community; failure to delegate; lack of feedback from clients; difficulties in recruiting male employees; and conflicting marital roles (Cuba, DeCenzo, and Anish, 1983). Work in this area has yet to go much beyond the level of anecdotal evidence, however.

The increasing number of female entrepreneurs is an interesting and important trend. It should be recognized, however, that the percentage increases look quite large because they are computed against a very small base. Moreover, female enterpreneurship is not likely to represent a major solution to the problem of underrepresentation of women in management, given the high failure rate of new businesses. Increased opportunities will be needed within existing corporations for women to make significant gains in management.

Summary

As may be seen from the preceding review, research on women in management has burgeoned over the past decade. Not surprisingly, the research on women in management continues to focus more on their problems than on their progress. Women continue to be underrepresented in management, and several factors have received attention from researchers as possible explanations. One major factor is that women as a group are not as likely as men to aspire to managerial careers. Another barrier is bias against women in the methods used to select managers in organizations. Once they enter a managerial position, discriminatory treatment may present further roadblocks to their advancement. Bias in the perception and evaluation of their performance of the managerial role has been hypothesized as serving as one such roadblock. Other problems believed to confront women are exclusion from informal relationships, assignment to dead-end jobs, inequitable compensation, role conflicts, and lack of a sponsor or mentor.

A variety of remedies have been recommended as means of increasing the representation and status of women in management. Affirmative action in the recruitment, hiring, and promotion of women can succeed in bringing substantial numbers of women into the managerial ranks, but there also appear to be some negative consequences of affirmative action in the form of male resentment of preferential treatment and demoralization of women who think they have been hired because of their sex rather than their ability. Training programs aimed at eliminating the stereotypes of men and women and instilling the necessary behavioral skills in women have been popular approaches, but their benefits may not justify their considerable costs. Structural changes have great potential for profoundly improving the status of women, but few of the proposals made to increase opportunities for women and accommodate to their special problems appear to have been implemented.

Where Should Future Research Go?

Despite the large volume of research on women in management that has been conducted over the past decade, investigators have focused on relatively few issues, primarily at the individual level of analysis, and have left untouched many important questions at the intergroup, interpersonal, and structural levels. One possible reason for the narrowness of past research is the overreliance on what I will call "stereotype-fit" models (Dipboye, 1985). People are hypothesized to possess stereotypes of women and these stereotypes guide their perception, evaluation, and treatment of women. Fundamentally, these stereotype models are cognitive models, in that they view discrimination against women as something that is done with good, albeit misguided, intentions. For example, a woman may be discriminated against in the hiring process because she is perceived to possess attributes of the "typical woman" and anticipated to achieve less success in the managerial role than a man with equivalent qualifications. She is rejected, not so much because of prejudice against women as the desire to hire the person best qualified for the job.

As important as stereotypes are, there are also emotional, social, and behavioral factors that can account for discrimination against women in management and that have been largely ignored in past research. The power of women managers can be eroded by irrational fears and anxieties of being led by a woman as well as by the sexual feelings that invariably enter into male and female relations. Habitual and often mindless patterns of behavior that men and women exhibit in interacting with each other are another potential deterrent for women. For example, there is seldom a conscious intent behind the subtle verbal and nonverbal ways in which men dominate and women submit in the course of conversing with each other. These communication styles still can have the effect of eroding the power and influence of women. Finally, the behavior and attitudes of organization members are shaped to a large extent by the social roles they occupy. These roles, in turn, are defined by the expectations that persons inside and outside the organization communicate to them regarding what is appropriate and what is inappropriate conduct. For example, a woman may be held back in promotion decisions not so much because of the individual stereotypes of her superior or the traits and behaviors of the woman, but because the culture of the organization communicates both overtly and covertly that men and not women should be on the fast track. The findings of research that ignores the influence of the organizational context on individual decisions are not totally irrelevant, but they must be tempered by the realization that decisions are often shaped by formal and informal social constraints.

The call for research on the affective, social, and behavioral factors does not mean that stereotypes should be ignored by investigators. To the contrary, more research is also needed on stereotypes. Future research, however, should pay more attention to individual differences in the stereotypes held by raters. Only a few researchers have included such measures despite the evidence that individual differences account for a substantial proportion of variance in perceptions and evaluations of women (Rice, Bender, and Vitters, 1980; Simas and McCarrey, 1979; Garland and Price, 1977).

Researchers should also move away from the rather outdated emphasis on global stereotypes of the "typical woman" and incorporate recent developments in social psychological research and theory. Research has shown that people do not appear to have as strong a conception of women in general or men in general in the 1980s as they did when the first sex stereotype studies were conducted in the 1950s (Ashmore, 1981). Also, global stereotypes do not appear to influence judgments except under conditions in which little or no information other than sex is available on the stimulus person (Locksley et al., 1980). As more individuating information becomes available, more specific stereotypes appear to become influential. There is also increasing evidence that people are less likely to think in terms of global categories of men and women than they are of subcategories. In one recent study, Noseworthy and Lott (1984) had subjects name as many different types of women as they could think of and found five fairly distinct subtypes: housewife, career woman, sex object, athlete, and "libber." They found that whereas the stereotypes of the career woman and the athlete were quite different from the stereotype of women in general, the stereotypes of housewife and sex object were quite similar to the traditional female stereotype. Ashmore (1981) found evidence that students subtype both men and women. In describing women, they appeared to use such subcategories as the girlfriend, the neurotic, the nurturing woman, the submissive woman, the wallflower, and the upper-class young woman. In describing men, students used such subcategories as the tough guy, the pain in the ass, the businessman, the egotist, the student body president, and the male chauvinist. These subcategories appear to influence perceptions and evaluations more than the general categories of "all men" or "all women."

A logical extrapolation from the research and theory in basic social psychology is that general stereotypes of the typical woman have less influence on the perception and evaluation of women in management than the more specific categories. Because they are more specific does not mean that they are any less insidious, however, as seen by subtypes such as the "overcontrolling woman" or the "Queen Bee." Future research needs to delineate some of the more common subcategories that persons in organizational settings use in the perception of males and females, the factors influencing whether they become salient, and their effects on the careers of men and women managers.

Conclusions

When one compares the blatant bias against women that was prevalent in past years with what it has been during the past two decades, there is little doubt that the status of women in management has improved dramatically. Despite these gains, management is still a male domain and is likely to remain so for quite some time. One major conclusion of the present review is that women continue to face barriers that prevent many of them from entering and succeeding in managerial careers. The barriers appear to have changed, however, becoming more complex and subtle over the years. Whereas the major problem confronting women in the past was unmitigated bias, the situation they confront today could be best described as one of ambivalence. For example, there are far fewer raging bigots in the ranks of male managers today, but even egalitarian males may have mixed feelings about bringing more women into management in the face of what appears to be a shrinking demand for middle-level managers. Likewise, more women aspire to managerial careers, but many of those who have taken advantage of these opportunities in the past decade are now facing difficult choices involving trade-offs between career and family. Another major conclusion is that the stereotype-fit models dominating past work are too simplistic to contribute significantly to the understanding and solution of problems such as these. If the literature on women in management is to advance over the next decade, theories will be needed that better capture the complexity of the problems that men and women face in their careers today.

References

Adams, E.F. "A Multivariate Study of Subordinate Perceptions of and Attitudes Toward Minority and Majority Managers." *Journal of Applied Psychology* 63 (June 1978): pp. 277–88.

Adams, J., R.W. Rice, and D. Instone. "Follower Attitudes Toward Women and Judgments Concerning Performance by Female and Male Leaders." *Academy of Management Journal* 27 (September 1984): pp. 636–43.

Adler, N.J. "Women in International Management: Where Are They?" *California Management Review* 26 (Summer 1984): pp. 78–89.

Andrisani, P.J., and M.B. Shapiro. "Women's Attitudes Toward Their Jobs: Some Longitudinal Data on a National Sample." *Personnel Psychology* 31 (Spring 1978): pp. 15–34.

Ashmore, R.D. "Sex Stereotypes and Implicit Personality Theory." In *Cognitive Processes in Stereotyping and Intergroup Behavior*, ed. D.L. Hamilton. Hillsdale, N.J.: Lawrence Erlbaum, 1981. Pp. 37–82.

Auster, D. "Occupational Values of Male and Female Nursing Students." *Sociology of Work and Occupations* 5 (May 1978): pp. 209–33.

Ayers-Nachamkin, B., C.H. Cann, R. Reed, and A. Horne. "Sex and Ethnic Differences in the Use of Power." *Journal of Applied Psychology* 67 (August 1982): pp. 464–71.

Barnett, R.C., and R. Tagiuri. "What Young People Think About Managers." *Harvard Business Review* 51 (No. 3, 1973): pp. 106–18.

Baron, A.S. "What Men Are Saying About Women in Business." *Business Horizons* 25 (January-February 1982): pp. 10–14.

Bartholet, E. "Application of Title VII to Jobs in High Places." *Harvard Law Review* 95 (March 1982): pp. 947–1027.

Bartol, K.M., and D.A. Butterfield. "Sex Effects in Evaluating Leaders." *Journal of Applied Psychology* 61 (August 1976): pp. 446–54.

Bartol, K.M., and M.S. Wortman, Jr. "Males vs. Female Leaders: Effects on Perceived Leader Behavior and Satisfaction in a Hospital." *Personnel Psychology* 28 (Winter 1975): pp. 533–47.

Bass, B.M. *Stogdill's Handbook of Leadership Research.* New York: Free Press, 1981.

Becker, E.H. "Self-Employed Workers: An Update to 1983." *Monthly Labor Review* 107 (July 1984): pp. 14–19.

Bem, S.L. "The Measurement of Psychological Androgyny." *Journal of Consulting and Clinical Psychology* 42 (April 1974): pp. 155–62.

Bettner, J., and C. Donahue. "Now They're Not Laughing (Not Just a Corporate Bureaucrat but the Boss of Her Own Business)." *Forbes* 132 (November 1983): pp. 116–19.

Breen, G.E. *Middle Management Morale in the '80s.* New York: American Management Association, 1983.

Brenner, D.C. "Relationship of Education to Sex, Managerial Status, and the Managerial Stereotype." *Journal of Applied Psychology* 67 (June 1982): pp. 380–83.

Brief, A.P., and R.L. Oliver. "Male-Female Differences in Work Attitudes Among Retail Sales Managers." *Journal of Applied Psychology* 61 (August 1976): pp. 526–28.

Brief, A.P., G.L. Rose, and R.J. Aldag. "Sex Differences in Preferences for Job Attributes Revisited." *Journal of Applied Psychology* 62 (October 1977): pp. 645–46.

Brown, L.K. "Women and Business Management." *Signs: Journal of Women in Culture and Society* 5 (Winter 1979): pp. 266–88.

Brown, S.M. "Male Versus Female Leaders: A Comparison of Empirical Studies." *Sex Roles* 5 (October 1979): pp. 595–611.

Bruning, N.S., and R.A. Snyder. "Sex and Position as Predictors of Organizational Commitment." *Academy of Management Journal* 26 (September 1983): pp. 485–91.

Business Week. "You've Come a Long Way, Baby—But Not as Far as You Thought." October 1, 1984: pp. 126–31.

Butterfield, D.A., and G.N. Powell. "Effect of Group Performance, Leader Sex, and Rater Sex on Ratings of Leader Behavior." *Organizational Behavior and Human Performance* 28 (August 1981): pp. 129–41.

Cann, A., W.D. Siegfried, and L. Pearce. "Forced Attention to Specific Applicant Qualifications: Impact on Physical Attractiveness and Sex of Applicant Biases." *Personnel Psychology* 34 (Spring 1981): pp. 65–75.

Carbonell, J.L. "Sex Roles and Leadership Revisited." *Journal of Applied Psychology* 69 (February 1984): pp. 44–49.

Chacko, T.I. "Women and Equal Employment Opportunity: Some Unintended Effects." *Journal of Applied Psychology* 67 (February 1982): pp. 119–23.

Chonko, L.S. "Are Purchasing Managers 'Machiavellian'?" *Journal of Purchasing and Materials Management* 13 (Winter 1982): pp. 15–20.

Chusmir, L.H. "Job Commitment and the Organizational Woman." *Academy of Management Review* 7 (October 1982): pp. 595–602.

Constantinople, A. "Masculinity-Femininity: An Exception to the Famous Dictum?" *Psychological Bulletin* 84 (November 1973): pp. 389–407.

Cook, S.H., and J.L. Mendelson. "The Power Wielders: Men and/or Women Managers?" *Industrial Management* 26 (March-April 1984): pp. 22–27.

Cooper, C.L., and M.J. Davidson. "The High Cost of Stress on Women Managers." *Organizational Dynamics* 10 (Spring 1982): pp. 44–53.

Crino, M.D., M.C. White, and C.L. De Sanctis. "A Comment on the Dimensionality and Reliability of the Women as Managers Scale (WAMS)." *Academy of Management Journal* 24 (December 1981): pp. 866–76.

Cuba, R., D. DeCenzo, and A. Anish. "Management Practices of Successful Female Business Owners." *American Journal of Small Business* 8 (Fall 1983): pp. 40–46.

Day, D.R., and R.M. Stogdill. "Leader Behavior of Male and Female Supervisors: A Comparative Study." *Personnel Psychology* 25 (Summer 1972): pp. 353–60.

Deaux, K. "Self-Evaluations of Male and Female Managers." *Sex Roles* 5 (October 1979): pp. 571–80.

Dennis, L., and K.M. Alvares. "Effects of Sex on Descriptions and Evaluations of Supervisory Behavior in a Simulated Industrial Setting." *Journal of Applied Psychology* 62 (August 1977): pp. 405–10.

Dipboye, R.L. "Some Neglected Variables in Research on Discrimination in Appraisals." *Academy of Management Review* 10 (January 1985): pp. 116–27.

Dipboye, R.L., R.D. Arvey, and D.E. Terpstra. "Sex and Physical Attractiveness of Raters and Applicants as Determinants of Resume Evaluations." *Journal of Applied Psychology* 62 (June 1977): pp. 288–94.

Dipboye, R.L., H.M. Fromkin, and K. Wiback. "Relative Importance of Applicant Sex, Attractiveness, and Scholastic Standing in Evaluation of Job Applicant Resumes." *Journal of Applied Psychology* 60 (February 1975): pp. 39–43.

Dipboye, R.L., and J.W. Wiley. "Reactions of Male Raters to Interviewee Self-Presentation Style and Sex: Extensions of Previous Research." *Journal of Vocational Behavior* 13 (October 1978): pp. 192–203.

————. "Reactions of College Recruiters to Interviewee Sex and Self-Presentation Style." *Journal of Vocational Behavior* 10 (February 1977): pp. 1–12.

Dobbins, G.N., R.G. Pence, J.A. Orban, and J. Sgro. "The Effects of Sex of the Leader and Sex of the Subordinate on the Use of Organizational Control Policy." *Organizational Behavior and Human Performance* 32 (December 1983): pp. 325–43.

Donnell, S.M., and J. Hall. "Men and Women as Managers: A Significant Case of No Significant Difference." *Organizational Dynamics* 8 (Spring 1980): pp. 60–77.

Dubno, P. "Attitudes Toward Women Executives: A Longitudinal Approach." *Academy of Management Journal* 28 (March 1985): pp. 235–39.

Dunnette, M.D., and S.J. Motowidlo. "Estimating Benefits and Costs of Antisexist Training Programs in Organizations." In *Women in the Work Force*, ed. H.J. Bernardin. New York: Praeger, 1982. Pp. 156–82.

Eagly, A.H., and L.L. Carli. "Sex of Researchers and Sex-Typed Communications as Determinants of Sex Differences in Influenceability: A Meta-Analysis of Social Influence Studies." *Psychological Bulletin* 90 (July 1981): pp. 1–20.

Eisenberg, N., and R. Lennon. "Sex Differences in Empathy and Related Capacities." *Psychological Bulletin* 94 (July 1983): pp. 100–31.

Elgart, L.D. "Women on 'Fortune 500' Boards." *California Management Review* 25 (Summer 1983): pp. 121–27.

Ezell, H.F., C.A. Odewahn, and J. Sherman. "The Effects of Having Been Supervised by a Woman on Perceptions of Female Managerial Competence." *Personnel Psychology* 34 (Summer 1981): pp. 291–99.

Fernandez, J.P. *Racism and Sexism in Corporate Life.* Lexington, MA: Lexington Books, 1981.

Field, H.S., and W.H. Holley. "Subordinates' Characteristics, Supervisors' Ratings, and Decisions to Discuss Appraisal Results." *Academy of Management Journal* 20 (June 1977): pp. 315–21.

Firth, M. "Sex Discrimination in Job Opportunities for Women." *Sex Roles* 3 (August 1982): pp. 891–902.

Fitt, L.W., and D.A. Newton. "When the Mentor Is a Man and the Protegee a Woman." *Harvard Business Review* 59 (March-April 1981): pp. 56–60.

Foster, L.W., and T. Kolinko. "Choosing to Be a Managerial Woman: An Examination of Individual Variables and Career Choice." *Sex Roles* 5 (October 1979): pp. 627–34.

Fottler, M.E., and T. Bain. "Sex Differences in Occupational Aspirations." *Academy of Management Journal* 23 (March 1980): pp. 144–49.

Fraker, S. "Why Women Aren't Getting to the Top." *Fortune* 109 (April 16, 1984): pp. 40–45.

Frasher, J.M., D.S. Frasher, and F.B. Wims. "Sex-Role Stereotypes in School Superintendents' Personnel Decisions." *Sex Roles* 3 (February 1982): pp. 261–68.

Frodi, A., J. Macaulay, and P.R. Thome. "Are Women Always Less Aggressive than Men? A Review of the Experimental Literature." *Psychological Bulletin* 84 (July 1977): pp. 634–60.

Gallup Report. "Substantial Majority of Americans Oppose Affirmative Action." No. 224 (May 1984).

Garland, N., and H.H. Price. "Attitudes Toward Women in Management and Attributions for Their Success and Failure in a Managerial Position." *Journal of Applied Psychology* 62 (February 1977): pp. 29–33.

Gerdes, E.P., and D.M. Garber. "Sex Bias in Hiring: Effects of Job Demands and Applicant Competence." *Sex Roles* 9 (March 1983): pp. 307–19.

Ghiselli, E.E. "The Validity of Aptitude Tests in Personnel Selection." *Personnel Psychology* 26 (Winter 1973): pp. 461–78.

Gleason, S.E. "The Decision to File a Sex Discrimination Complaint in the Federal Government: The Benefits and Costs of 'Voice.'" In *Proceedings of the 36th Annual Meeting, Industrial Relations Research Association*, 1983. Madison, WI: IRRA, 1984. Pp. 187–97.

Golembiewski, R.T. "Testing Some Stereotypes About the Sexes in Organizations: Differential Centrality of Work?" *Human Resources Management* 16 (Winter 1977): pp. 21–24.

Gomez-Mejia, L.R. "Sex Differences During Occupational Socialization." *Academy of Management Journal* 26 (September 1983): pp. 492–99.

Gordon, F.C., and D.T. Hall. "Self-Image and Stereotypes of Femininity: Their Relationship to Women's Role Conflicts and Coping." *Journal of Applied Psychology* 59 (April 1974): pp. 241–43.

Graddick, M.M., and J.L. Farr. "Professionals in Scientific Disciplines: Sex-Related Differences in Working Life Commitments." *Journal of Applied Psychology* 68 (November 1983): pp. 641–45.

Gregg, G. "Women Entrepreneurs: The Second Generation." *Across the Board* 22 (January 1985): pp. 10–18.

Haccoun, D.M., R. Haccoun, and G. Salay. "Sex Differences in the Appropriateness of Supervisory Styles: A Non-Management View." *Journal of Applied Psychology* 63 (February 1978): pp. 124–27.

Hall, F.S., and D.T. Hall. "Effects of Job Incumbents' Race and Sex on Evaluations of Management Performance." *Academy of Management Journal* 19 (September 1976): pp. 476–81.

Harlan, A , and C.L. Weiss. "Sex Differences in Factors Affecting Managerial Career Advancement." In *Women in the Workplace*, ed. P.A. Wallace. Boston: Auburn House, 1982. Pp. 59–100.

Hartnett, O., and V. Novarra. "Single Sex Management Training and a Woman's Touch." *Personnel Management* 12 (March 1980): pp. 32–35.

Heilbrun, A.B., Jr. "Measurement of Masculine and Feminine Sex Role Identities as Independent Dimensions." *Journal of Consulting and Clinical Psychology* 44 (April 1976): pp. 183–90.

Heilman, M.E. "Information as a Deterrent Against Sex Discrimination: The Effects of Applicant Sex and Information Type on Preliminary Decisions." *Organizational Behavior and Human Performance* 33 (April 1984): pp. 174–86.

————. "The Impact of Situational Factors on Personnel Decisions Concerning Women: Varying the Sex Composition of the Applicant Pool." *Organizational Behavior and Human Performance* 26 (December 1980): pp. 386–95.

Heilman, M.E., and R. Guzzo. "The Perceived Cause of Work Success as a Mediator of Sex Discrimination in Organizations." *Organizational Behavior and Human Performance* 21 (June 1978): pp. 346–57.

Heilman, M.E., and K. Kram. "Self-Derogating Behavior in Women—Fixed or Flexible: The Effects of Co-Workers' Sex." *Organizational Behavior and Human Performance* 23 (December 1978): pp. 497–507.

Heilman, M.E., and L.R. Saruwatari. "When Beauty Is Beastly: The Effects of Appearance and Sex on Evaluations of Job Applicants for Managerial and Non-managerial Jobs." *Organizational Behavior and Human Performance* 23 (June 1979): pp. 360–72.

Helmreich, R.L., J.T. Spence, and R.H. Gibson. "Sex-Role Attitudes: 1972–1980." *Personality and Social Psychology Bulletin* 8 (December 1984): pp. 656–63.

Herman, J.B., and K.K. Gyllstrom. "Working Men and Women: Inter- and Intra-Role Conflict." *Psychology of Women Quarterly* 1 (Summer 1977): pp. 319–33.

Hitt, M.A., W.S. Zikmund, and D.A. Pickens. "Discrimination in Industrial Employment: An Investigation of Race and Sex Bias Among Professionals." *Work and Occupations* 9 (May 1982): pp. 217–31.

Hoffman, M.L. "Sex Differences in Empathy and Related Behaviors." *Psychological Bulletin* 84 (July 1977): pp. 712–22.

Hoyenga, K.B., and K.T. Hoyenga. *The Question of Sex Differences*. Boston: Little Brown & Co., 1979.

Hunt, D.M., and C. Michael. "Mentorship: A Career Training and Development Tool." *Academy of Management Review* 8 (July 1983): pp. 475–86.

Instone, D., B. Major, and B.B. Bunker. "Gender, Self-Confidence, and Social Influence Strategies." *Journal of Personality and Social Psychology* 44 (February 1983): pp. 322–33.

Izraeli, D.N. "Sex Differences in Self-Reported Influence Among Union Officers." *Journal of Applied Psychology* 70 (February 1985): pp. 148–57.

Jacobson, M.B., and J. Effertz. "Sex Roles and Leadership Perceptions of the Leaders and the Led." *Organizational Behavior and Human Performance* 12 (January 1974): pp. 383–97.

Jacobson, M.E., and W. Kock. "Women as Leaders: Performance Evaluation as a Function of Method of Leader Selection." *Organizational Behavior and Human Performance* 20 (October 1977): pp. 149–57.

Jago, A.G., and V.H. Vroom. "Sex Differences in the Incidence and Evaluation of Participative Leader Behavior." *Journal of Applied Psychology* 67 (December 1982): pp. 776–83.

Kanter, R.M. *Men and Women of the Corporation.* New York: Basic Books, 1977a.

———. "Some Effects of Proportion on Group Life: Skewed Sex Ratios and Responses to Token Women." *American Journal of Sociology* 82 (No. 5, 1977b): pp. 965–90.

Kimble, C.E., J.S. Yoshikawa, and H.D. Zehr. "Vocal and Verbal Assertiveness in Same-Sex and Mixed-Sex Groups." *Journal of Personality and Social Psychology* 40 (June 1981): pp. 1047–54.

Lacy, W.B., J.L. Bakemeier, and J.M. Shepard. "Job Attribute Preferences and Work Commitment of Men and Women in the United States." *Personnel Psychology* 36 (Summer 1983): pp. 315–29.

Larwood, L., and M.M. Wood. *Women in Management.* Lexington, MA: Lexington Books, 1977.

Larwood, L., M. Wood, and S.D. Inderlied. "Training Women for Management: New Problems, New Solutions." *Academy of Management Review* 3 (September 1978): pp. 584–93.

Lenney, E. "Women's Self-Confidence in Achievement Settings." *Psychological Bulletin* 84 (January 1977): pp. 1–17.

Levinson, R.M. "Sex Discrimination and Employment Practices: An Experiment with Unconventional Job Inquiries." In *Women and Work: Problems and Perspectives,* eds. R. Kahn-Hut, A.N. Daniels, and R. Colvard. New York: Oxford University Press, 1982. Pp. 54–65.

Locksley, A., E. Borgida, N. Brekke, and C. Hepburn. "Sex Stereotypes and Social Judgment." *Journal of Personality and Social Psychology* 39 (November 1980): pp. 821–31.

London, M., and S.A. Stumpf. "Effects of Candidate Characteristics on Management Promotion Decisions: An Experimental Study." *Personnel Psychology* 36 (Summer 1983): pp. 241–59.

Lovrich, N.P., Jr., and C.E. Jones. "Affirmative Action, Women Managers, and Performance Appraisal: Simultaneous Movement in Conflicting Directions?" *Review of Public Personnel Administration* 3 (Summer 1983): pp. 3–19.

Lyson, T.A. "Sex Differences in the Choice of a Male or Female Career Line." *Work and Occupations* 11 (May 1984): pp. 131–46.

Maccoby, E.E., and C.N. Jacklin. *The Psychology of Sex Differences.* Palo Alto, CA: Stanford University Press, 1974.

Mai-Dalton, R.R., S. Feldman-Summers, and T.R. Mitchell. "Effects of Employee Gender and Behavioral Style on the Evaluations of Male and Female Banking Executives." *Journal of Applied Psychology* 64 (April 1979): pp. 221–26.

Mai-Dalton, R.R., and J.J. Sullivan. "The Effects of Manager's Sex on the Assignment to a Challenging or Dull Task and Reasons for the Choice." *Academy of Management Journal* 24 (September 1981): pp. 603–12.

Major, B., and K. Deaux. "Individual Differences in Justice Behavior." In *Equity and Justice in Social Behavior*, eds. J. Greenberg and R. Cohen. New York: Academic Press, 1982. Pp. 43–76.

Major, B., and E. Konar. "An Investigation of Sex Differences in Pay Expectations and Their Possible Causes." *Academy of Management Journal* 27 (December 1984): pp. 777–92.

Marini, M.M., and M.C. Brinton. "Sex Typing in Occupational Socialization." In *Sex Segregation in the Workplace: Trends, Explanations, Remedies*, ed. B.F. Reskin. Washington: National Academy Press, 1984. Pp. 192–231.

Mason, K.O., J.L. Czajka, and S. Arber. "Change in U.S. Women's Sex-Role Attitudes, 1964–1974." *American Sociological Review* 41 (August 1976): pp. 573–96.

Massengill, D., and N. DiMarco. "Sex-Role Stereotypes and Requisite Management Characteristics: A Current Replication." *Sex Roles* 5 (October 1979): pp. 561–70.

Matthews, J.J., W.E. Collins, and B.B. Cobb. "A Sex Comparison of Reasons for Attributions in Male Dominated Occupations." *Personnel Psychology* 1 (Winter 1974): pp. 535–41.

McCall, M.W., and E.E. Lawler. "High School Students' Perceptions of Work." *Academy of Management Journal* 19 (March 1976): pp. 17–24.

McIntyre, S.D., J. Moberg, and B.Z. Posner. "Preferential Treatment in Preselection Decisions According to Sex and Race." *Academy of Management Journal* 23 (December 1980): pp. 738–49.

Megargee, E.I. "Influence of Sex Roles in the Manifestation of Leadership." *Journal of Applied Psychology* 53 (December 1969): pp. 377–82.

Miner, J.B. "The Miner Sentence Completion Scale: A Reappraisal." *Academy of Management Journal* 21 (June 1978): pp. 283–94.

———. "Motivation to Manage Among Women: Studies of College Students." *Journal of Vocational Behavior* 5 (April 1974): pp. 241–50.

Miner, J.B. and N.R. Smith. "Decline and Stabilization of Managerial Motivation Over a 20-Year Period." *Journal of Applied Psychology* 67 (June 1982): pp. 297–305.

———. "Managerial Talent Among Undergraduate and Graduate Business Students." *Personnel and Guidance Journal* 47 (December 1969): pp. 995–1000.

Moore, D.P. "Evaluating In-Role and Out-of-Role Performers." *Academy of Management Journal* 27 (September 1984): pp. 603–18.

Moore, L.M., and A.U. Rickel. "Characteristics of Women in Traditional and Nontraditional Managerial Roles." *Personnel Psychology* 33 (Summer 1980): pp. 317–33.

Morrison, R.F., and M.L. Sebald. "Personal Characteristics Differentiating Female Executives From Female Non-Executive Personnel." *Journal of Applied Psychology* 59 (October 1974): pp. 656–59.

Moses, J.L., and V.R. Boehm. "Relationship of Assessment Center Performance to Management Progress of Women." *Journal of Applied Psychology* 60 (August 1975): pp. 527–29.

Muldrow, T.W., and J.A. Bayton. "Men and Women Executives and Processes Related to Decision Accuracy." *Journal of Applied Psychology* 64 (February 1979): pp. 99–106.

Nieva, V.F., and B.A. Gutek. *Women and Work: A Psychological Perspective.* New York: Praeger, 1981.

Noseworthy, C.M., and A.J. Lott. "The Cognitive Organization of Gender-Stereotypic Categories." *Personality and Social Psychology Bulletin* 10 (September 1984): pp. 474–81.

O'Barr, W.B., and B.K. Atkins. "Women's Language or Powerless Language?" In *Women and Language in Literature and Society*, eds. S. McConnell, R. Borker, and N. Furman. New York: Praeger, 1980. Pp. 93–110.

O'Leary, V.E. "Some Attitudinal Barriers to Occupational Aspirations in Women." *Psychological Bulletin* 81 (November 1974): pp. 809–26.

Oliphant, V.N., and E.R. Alexander III. "Reactions to Resumes as a Function of Resume Determinateness, Applicant Characteristics, and Sex of Raters." *Personnel Psychology* 35 (Winter 1982): pp. 829–42.

Olson, C.A., and B.E. Becker. "Sex Discrimination in the Promotion Process." *Industrial and Labor Relations Review* 36 (July 1983): pp. 624–41.

Osborn, R., and W. Vicars. "Sex Stereotypes: An Artifact in Leader Behavior and Subordinate Satisfaction Analysis?" *Academy of Management Journal* 19 (September 1976): pp. 439–49.

Pence, E.C., W.C. Pendleton, G.H. Dobbins, and J.A. Sgro. "Effects of Causal Explanations and Sex Variables on Recommendations for Corrective Actions Following Employee Failure." *Organizational Behavior and Human Performance* 29 (April 1982): pp. 227–40.

Peters, L.H., E.J. O'Connor, J. Weekley, A. Pooyan, B. Frank, and B. Erenkrantz. "Sex Bias and Managerial Evaluations: A Replication and Extension." *Journal of Applied Psychology* 69 (May 1984): pp. 349–52.

Petty, M., and N.S. Bruning. "A Comparison of the Relationships Between Subordinates' Perceptions of Supervisory Behavior and Measures of Subordinates' Job Satisfaction for Male and Female Leaders." *Academy of Management Journal* 23 (December 1980): pp. 717–25.

Petty, M.M., and G.K. Lee. "Moderating Effects of Sex of Supervisor and Subordinate on Relationships Between Supervisory Behavior and Subordinate Satisfaction." *Journal of Applied Psychology* 60 (October 1975): pp. 624–28.

Petty, M.M., and R.H. Miles. "Leader Sex-Role Stereotyping in a Female Dominant Work Culture." *Personnel Psychology* 29 (Autumn 1976): pp. 393–404.

Pfeifer, P., and S.J. Shapiro. "Male and Female MBA Candidates: Are There Personality Differences?" *Business Quarterly* 43 (April 1978): pp. 77–80.

Powell, G.N., and D.A. Butterfield. "The 'Good Manager': Masculine or Androgynous?" *Academy of Management Journal* 22 (June 1979): pp. 395–403.

Rader, M.H. "Evaluating a Management Development Program for Women." *Public Personnel Management* 8 (May-June 1979): pp. 138–45.

Reilly, R.R., and G.T. Chao. "Validity and Fairness of Some Alternative Employee Selection Procedures." *Personnel Psychology* 35 (Winter 1982): pp. 1–62.

Renwick, P.A. "Effects of Sex Differences on the Perception and Management of Superior-Subordinate Conflict: An Exploratory Study." *Organizational Behavior and Human Performance* 19 (August 1977): pp. 403–15.

Renwick, P.A., and H. Tosi. "The Effects of Sex, Marital Status, and Educational Background on Selection Decisions." *Academy of Management Journal* 21 (March 1978): pp. 93–103.

Rice, R.W., L.R. Bender, and A.C. Vitters. "Leader Sex, Follower Attitudes Toward Women, and Leadership Effectiveness: A Laboratory Experiment." *Organizational Behavior and Human Performance* 25 (February 1980): pp. 46–78.

Rice, R.W., D. Instone, and J. Adams. "Leader Sex, Leader Success, and Leadership Process: Two Field Studies." *Journal of Applied Psychology* 69 (February 1984): pp. 12–31.

Ritchie, R.J., and V.R. Boehm. "Biographical Data as a Predictor of Women's and Men's Management Potential." *Journal of Vocational Behavior* 11 (December 1977): pp. 363–68.

Rogan, H. "Executive Women Find It Difficult to Balance Demands of Job, Home." *Wall Street Journal*, October 30, 1984a, pp. 35, 55.

———. "Young Executive Women Advance Farther, Faster than Predecessors." *Wall Street Journal*, October 26, 1984b, p. 31.

———. "Top Women Executives Find Path to Power Is Strewn with Hurdles." *Wall Street Journal*, October 25, 1984c, p. 35.

———. "Women Executives Feel that Men Both Aid and Hinder Their Careers." *Wall Street Journal*, October 19, 1984d, pp. 31, 44.

Rose, G.L., and P. Andiappan. "Sex Effects on Managerial Hiring Decisions." *Academy of Management Journal* 21 (April 1978): pp. 104–12.

Rose, G.L., and T.H. Stone. "Why Good Job Performance May (Not) Be Rewarded: Sex Factors and Career Development." *Journal of Vocational Behavior* 12 (April 1978): pp. 197–207.

Rosen, B., and Jerdee, T.H. "Identifying and Coping With Backlash to Affirmative Action Programs." *Business Horizons* 22 (February 1979): pp. 15–20.

———. "Perceived Sex Differences in Managerially Relevant Characteristics." *Sex Roles* 4 (December 1978): pp. 837–43.

———. "Effect of Applicant's Sex and Difficulty of Job on Evaluations of Candidates for Managerial Positions." *Journal of Applied Psychology* 59 (August 1974a): pp. 511–12.

———. "Influence of Sex-Role Stereotypes on Personnel Decisions." *Journal of Applied Psychology* 59 (February 1974b): pp. 9–14.

———. "The Influence of Sex-Role Stereotypes on Evaluations of Male and Female Supervisory Behavior." *Journal of Applied Psychology* 57 (February 1973): pp. 44–48.

Rosen, B., and M. Mericle. "Influence of Strong Versus Weak Fair Employment Policies and Applicant's Sex on Selection Decisions and Salary Recommendations in a Management Simulation." *Journal of Applied Psychology* 64 (August 1979): pp. 435–39.

Rosen, B., N.C. Templeton, and K. Kichline. "First Few Years on the Job: Women in Management." *Business Horizons* 24 (December 1981): pp. 26–29.

Rousell, C. "The Relationships of Sex of Department Heads to Department Climate." *Administrative Science Quarterly* 19 (June 1974): pp. 211–20.

Rytina, N.F. "Earnings of Men and Women: A Look at Specific Occupations." *Monthly Labor Review* 105 (April 1982): pp. 25–31.

Rytina, N.F., and S.M. Bianchi. "Occupational Reclassification and Changes in Distribution by Gender." *Monthly Labor Review* 107 (March 1984): pp. 11–17.

Schaeffer, R.G., and E.F. Lynton. *Corporate Experiences in Improving Women's Job Opportunities.* New York: The Conference Board, 1979.

Schein, V.E. "Relationship Between Sex Role Stereotypes and Requisite Management Characteristics Among Female Managers." *Journal of Applied Psychology* 60 (June 1975): pp. 340–44.

———. "The Relationship Between Sex Role Stereotypes and Requisite Management Characteristics." *Journal of Applied Psychology* 57 (April 1973): pp. 95–100.

Shinar, E.H. "Sexual Stereotypes of Occupations." *Journal of Vocational Behavior* 7 (August 1975): pp. 99–111.

Siegelman, L., H.B. Milward, and J.M. Shepard. "The Salary Differential Between Male and Female Administrators: Equal Pay for Equal Work?" *Academy of Management Journal* 25 (September 1982): pp. 664–71.

Siegfried, W.D. "The Effects of Specifying Job Requirements and Using Explicit Warnings to Decrease Sex Discrimination in Employment Interviews." *Sex Roles* 8 (January 1982): pp. 73–82.

Simas, K., and M. McCarrey. "Impact of Recruiter Authoritarianism and Applicant Sex on Evaluation and Selection Decisions in a Recruiter Interview Analogue Study." *Journal of Applied Psychology* 64 (October 1979): pp. 483–91.

Smith, C.B. "Influence of Internal Opportunity Structure and Sex of Worker on Turnover Patterns." *Administrative Science Quarterly* 24 (September 1979): pp. 362–81.

Solomon, L.J., K.A. Brehony, E.D. Rathblum, and J.A. Kelly. "Corporate Managers' Reactions to Assertive Social Skills Exhibited by Males and Females." *Journal of Organizational Behavior Management* 4 (Fall-Winter 1982): pp. 49–63.

South, S., C.M. Bonjean, J. Corder, and W.T. Markham. "Sex and Power in the Federal Bureaucracy." *Work and Occupations* 9 (May 1982): pp. 239–54.

Spence, J.T., and R.L. Helmreich. *Masculinity and Femininity: Their Psychological Dimensions, Correlates, and Antecedents.* Austin: University of Texas, 1978.

Steckler, N.A., and R. Rosenthal. "Sex Differences in Nonverbal and Verbal Communication With Bosses, Peers, and Subordinates." *Journal of Applied Psychology* 70 (February 1985): pp. 157–63.

Steinberg, R., and S. Shapiro. "Sex Differences in Personality Traits of Female and Male Master of Business Administration Students." *Journal of Applied Psychology* 67 (June 1982): pp. 306–10.

Stewart, L.P., and W.B. Gudykunst. "Differential Factors Influencing the Hierarchical Level and Number of Promotions of Males and Females Within an Organization." *Academy of Management Journal* 25 (September 1982): pp. 586–97.

Strober, M.H. "The M.B.A.: Same Passport to Success for Women and Men?" In *Women in the Workplace,* ed. P.A. Wallace. Boston: Auburn House, 1982. Pp. 25–44.

———. "Bringing Women into Management: Basic Strategies." In *Bringing Women into Management.* ed. M.H. Strober. New York: McGraw-Hill, 1975. Pp. 77–96.

Stumpf, S.A., and M. London. "Capturing Rater Policies in Evaluating Candidates for Promotion." *Academy of Management Journal* 24 (December 1981): pp. 752–66.

Sutton, C.D., and K.K. Moore. "Executive Women—20 Years Later." *Harvard Business Review* 63 (September-October 1985): pp. 42–66.

Taylor, M.S., and D.R. Ilgen. "Sex Discrimination Against Women in Initial Placement: A Laboratory Investigation." *Academy of Management Journal* 24 (December 1981): pp. 859–65.

Terborg, J.R. "Women in Management: A Research Review." *Journal of Applied Psychology* 62 (December 1977): pp. 647–64.

Terborg, J.R., and D.R. Ilgen. "A Theoretical Approach to Sex Discrimination in Traditionally Masculine Occupations." *Organizational Behavior and Human Performance* 13 (June 1975): pp. 352–76.

Terborg, J.R., L.H. Peters, D.R. Ilgen, and F. Smith. "Organizational and Personal Correlates of Attitudes Toward Women as Managers." *Academy of Management Journal* 20 (March 1977): pp. 89–100.

Thornton, G.C., III, and W.C. Byham. *Assessment Centers and Managerial Performance.* New York: Academic Press, 1982.

Tomkiewicz, J.B., and O.C. Brenner. "Organizational Dilemma: Sex Differences in Attitudes Toward Women Held by Future Managers." *Personnel Administrator* 27 (July 1982): pp. 62–65.

Trempe, J., A. Rigny, and R.R. Haccoun. "Subordinate Satisfaction With Male and Female Managers: Role of Perceived Supervisory Influence." *Journal of Applied Psychology* 70 (February 1985): pp. 44–47.

Tsui, A.S., and B.A. Gutek. "A Role Set Analysis of Gender Differences in Performance, Affective Relationships, and Career Success of Industrial Middle Managers." *Academy of Management Journal* 27 (September 1984): pp. 619–35.

U.S. Department of Commerce, Bureau of the Census. *Statistical Abstract of the United States*, 105th edition. Washington: U.S. Government Printing Office, 1984.

Varca, P., G.S. Shaffer, and C.D. McCauley. "Sex Differences in Job Satisfaction Revisited." *Academy of Management Journal* 26 (June 1983): pp. 348–53.

Waddell, F.T. "Factors Affecting Choice, Satisfaction, and Success in the Female Self-Employed." *Journal of Vocational Behavior* 23 (December 1983): pp. 294–304.

Warsh, D. "Study Updates Data on Professional Women." *Houston Chronicle*, December 30, 1985.

Watson, J.G., and E.J. Ryan. "A Comparative Study of the Personal Values of Female and Male Managers." *Journal of Psychology* 102 (April 1979): pp. 307–16.

Wertheim, E.G., C.S. Widon, and L.H. Wortzel. "Multivariate Analysis of Male and Female Professional Career Choice Correlates." *Journal of Applied Psychology* 63 (April 1978): pp. 234–42.

Wexley, K.N., and E.D. Palakos. "The Effects of Perceptual Congruence and Sex on Subordinates' Performance Appraisals of Their Managers." *Academy of Management Journal* 26 (December 1983): pp. 666–76.

_____. "Sex Effects on Performance Ratings in Manager-Subordinate Dyads: A Field Study." *Journal of Applied Psychology* 67 (August 1982): pp. 433–39.

White, M.C., M.D. Crino, and G.L. De Sanctis. "A Critical Review of Female Performance, Performance Training, and Organizational Initiatives Designed to Aid Women in the Work-Role Environment." *Personnel Psychology* 34 (Summer 1981): pp. 227–48.

Wiley, M.C., and A. Eskilson. "Interaction of Sex and Power Base on Perception of Managerial Effectiveness." *Academy of Management Journal* 25 (September 1982): pp. 671–77.

Williams, J.E., and D.L. Best. *Measuring Sex Stereotypes: A Thirty-Nation Study.* Beverly Hills, CA: Sage Publications, 1982.

Wolf, W.C., and N.D. Fligstein. "Sex and Authority in the Workplace: The Causes of Sexual Inequality." *American Sociological Review* 44 (April 1979): pp. 235–52.

Wood, M., and S. Greenfield. "Fear of Success in High Achieving Male and Female Managers in Private Industry vs. the Public Sector." *Journal of Psychology* 103 (Spring 1979): pp. 289–97.

_____. "Women Managers and Fear of Success." *Sex Roles* 2 (Spring 1976): pp. 375–87.

Wortman, M.S., Jr. "An Overview of the Research on Women in Management: A Typology and a Prospectus." In *Women in the Work Force*, ed. R.J. Bernardin. New York: Praeger, 1982.

CHAPTER 6

Women and the American Labor Movement: A Historical Perspective

PHILIP S. FONER*

Working women do not occupy an important place in most histories of the American labor movement. Yet women have been active on their own behalf since the earliest days of the factory system, often against what must have seemed insurmountable odds. Far from being passive, many women were militant and aggressive in their attempts to improve their working conditions. In a number of important industries, it was the militancy and perseverance of women workers that laid the foundations of trade unionism—this, in the face of the double obstacle of employer-public hostility and the indifference of most male-dominated unions.

The earliest years of women's efforts to improve their wages and working conditions were marked by spontaneous strikes in the needle trades and textile factories. Few lasting organizations appeared in the 1820s and 1830s. By the 1840s a permanent class of factory workers had appeared, and both men and women united to achieve a 10-hour day. Women, however, won their greatest gains during wartime. During periods of the Civil War, World War I, and World War II, women were needed to fill the jobs vacated by men who went off to war. It was during these periods that some labor unions took a greater interest in women's concerns and recruited them into their organizations. They feared that women's lower wages would make them more attractive as permanent employees to the exclusion of returning servicemen.

After each war, however, and despite women's union membership, they were forced to give up their jobs and reluctantly returned to the lower-paying traditionally female occupations.

This chapter traces the isolated events of women's uprisings, their formation of organizations, their gains during wartime, and their subsequent retreats. The road has been long and never easy, but theirs is an inspirational story.

---

* Professor Emeritus of History, Lincoln University, Pennsylvania.

First Strikes and Unions

In the 1820s and 1830s thousands of women first became wage earners in the needle trades and textile factories. Denied the right to vote, these women could not participate directly in politics. Nor could they establish themselves among the craft organizations of the skilled male workers. They were, therefore, forced to rely on their own forces to achieve better working conditions, higher wages, and a shorter workweek.

The first strike in which women alone participated occurred in 1825. This was the strike of the tailoresses of New York for higher wages. Six years later their efforts took the form of sustained activity. On February 11, 1831, the United Tailoresses Society of New York was organized. In June, the Society prepared its own list of wages and declared that its members would not work for less than the amount listed. When the employers rejected the new scale, the United Tailoresses—1,600 strong—went on strike. They continued to hold out through June and July, but appeals to male trade unions to boycott employers who refused to accept the proposed scale were in vain. On July 25, 1831, the tailoresses voted to return to work and to "draw up an Address to the public stating their reasons for adopting this cause." They announced that, despite the defeat, they would continue to meet and would even launch a cooperative clothing establishment. But the project never became a reality, and the last heard of the organization was an announcement of a meeting held on September 5, 1831.[1]

The first citywide federation of working women, embracing women from several trades, was the Female Improvement Society for the City and County of Philadelphia, organized in June 1835. Committees were chosen from each trade to draw up wage scales. A special committee was appointed to protest the low pay received by women sewing Army clothes and to call upon the Secretary of War to remedy the situation. Although the Secretary refused to take any action, the women did win a series of wage increases from private employers.[2]

Early in 1834 about a thousand women shoebinders met and formed the Female Society of Lynn and Vicinity for the Protection of Female Industry. Every member pledged to work only at agreed-upon wages, and they would be censured or expelled for violating this pledge.[3] Once organized, the women shoebinders of Lynn went out on strike for a new wage scale. The strike continued for more than two

---

[1] *National Gazette*, April 23, 1825; New York *Daily Sentinel*, February 12, March 5, June 12, 14, 16, July 21, 22, 26, September 5, 1831; New York *Working Man's Advocate*, August 31, 1831; Sumner (1910–1913), p. 132.
[2] New York *Working Man's Advocate*, June 9, 23, 1835; Sumner (1910–1913), p. 125.
[3] *Lynn Record*, January 8, 1834.

months, and in this case the women were supported throughout by the men's Cordwainers' Union, whose members raised funds for the strikers and agreed not to work for any shoe manufacturer who did not meet the women's demands. The Female Society announced in March 1834 that the employers had agreed to most of its demands, and the shoebinders returned to work with a new wage scale. Unfortunately, by June 1834 the very existence of the Female Society was reported to be threatened, as most of its members were working "under price" or not paying dues.[4]

Few lasting organizations of women workers emerged in this period. The women's organizations were even shorter-lived than the men's trade unions, usually being formed during a time of struggle and then fading after a strike was won or lost. It was an experience to be repeated many times throughout American labor history.

The first report in American history by male trade unionists that dealt with women workers was presented at the third convention of the National Trades' Union in 1836. It recommended that men admit women into their unions or encourage women to form separate unions. But the committee presenting the report viewed their suggestions as only a temporary solution. The real solution for women workers was inherent in their nature: "The physical organization, the natural responsibilities, and the moral sensibility of women, prove conclusively that her labors should be only of a domestic nature." Hence, the committee urged male trade unionists to "act the part of men" and seek the gradual destruction of the "unnatural policy of placing females in a different element from that designed by nature."[5]

Whatever the attitude of male workers, women would continue to enter the work force in increasing numbers. Women composed nearly 60 percent of the 67,000 textile workers in 1830, and their number increased during the next decade. In the 1830s most factory women came to the New England mills from nearby farms, and their earnings in the factories were not their sole means of support. They reacted to declining wages with demonstrations of protest, but when their demands were rejected, they often left the factories and returned to their parents' farms.

Female Labor Reform Associations

A more or less permanent working class gradually emerged in the factories during the 1840s. A good many New England farmers had lost

---

[4] *Lynn Record*, March 12, 1834; Dawley (1977), pp. 16–18; Foner (1947), pp. 60–64; Andrews and Bliss, (1911), pp. 41–44.

[5] "Report of the Committee on Female Labor to the National Trades' Union," *National Laborer*, November 12, 1836, reprinted in Commons et al., eds. (1910), Vol. 1, pp. 291–93.

their land during the depression of 1837–1840. "As the New England farms disappeared," writes Norman F. Ware, "the freedom of the mill operatives contracted. They could no longer escape. . . . A permanent factory population became a reality" (Ware, 1924, p. 24). These workers became fully committed to improving their conditions systematically rather than through brief "turnouts." This was reflected in the formation of the first unions of female factory workers—the Female Labor Reform Association.

The first and most important Female Labor Reform Association was organized in Lowell, Massachusetts, by 12 workers in the cotton mills; Sarah G. Bagley was elected president. Within six months membership had grown to 500 and was rising steadily.[6] Representatives of the Lowell Association attended meetings of factory women in the mill towns of Manchester, Dover, and Nashua, New Hampshire, and in each place a Female Labor Reform Association was organized. The Lowell union also contacted factory women in western Pennsylvania, and the Female Labor Reform Association of Allegheny and Pittsburgh was soon formed (Foner, 1977, pp. 65–68). The influence of the Lowell women extended also to working women in the trades. The Female Industrial Association of New York, organized in 1845, included representatives of almost all of the women's trades: tailoresses, shirtmakers, bookbinders and stitchers, capmakers, strawmakers, dressmakers, and lacemakers.[7]

The issue that united working women and working men of the 1840s was the struggle for the 10-hour day. While many mechanics had achieved the 10-hour day during the 1830s, the New England workers had not shared these gains. Too, many who had earlier won the 10-hour day subsequently lost it during the economic crisis (Foner, 1977, pp. 102–3, 115–18, 130, 160, 163). Most workers—male mechanics and female operatives alike—still worked 12 to 14 hours a day.

In 1840 the 10-hour day was established for federal government employees by executive order of President Martin Van Buren. To accomplish the same thing for employees of private companies required involving the state legislatures that had chartered the companies. In the drive for the 10-hour day sparked by the Lowell Female Labor Reform Association, the mill towns were blanketed with petitions to the Massachusetts legislature, and Sarah G. Bagley and other factory women appeared at the hearings held by the Committee on Manufacturing of the Massachusetts House of Representatives. Their testimony provided a dramatic picture of the working life of a female factory operative. Despite the overwhelming evidence presented by

---

[6] *Voice of Industry*, May 29, June 5, 10, 12, 1845; Andrews and Bliss (1911), pp. 71–72.
[7] *Voice of Industry*, September 5, November 7, 1845.

witnesses supporting the need for a 10-hour day, the investigating committee, in its report, opposed any legislation.[8]

Only in New Hampshire was the crusade for a 10-hour law successful. There the campaign was headed by the Female Labor Reform Associations of Manchester, Dover, and Nashua, and the male operatives and mechanics. But at the insistence of employers, clauses were inserted into the 10-hour law that permitted employers to draw up special contracts with workers for more than 10 hours. Even before the law was passed, employers submitted these contracts to their workers and informed them that they had the alternative of signing and continuing to work, or refusing to sign and being jobless. For a time the workers refused to sign, but in the end they had to submit. Workers who still refused to sign were discharged, and when they went elsewhere to seek employment, they found all doors closed to them.

The failure of the 10-hour movement of the 1840s was an important factor in the decline and disappearance of the Female Labor Reform Associations. Another contributing factor was the replacement of the factory women by the wives and daughters of Irish immigrants. Coming poverty-stricken to the United States, in seeking work they were forced to accept whatever conditions were imposed upon them. In time they, too, would organize unions and battle for better conditions.[9]

Ten-hour laws were passed in a number of states in the 1850s, but like those of the 1840s they were meaningless because they had the "special contract" feature. Nevertheless, because of the 10-hour movement, in which women workers continued to play an important role, the hours of labor were reduced. In 1830 the average working day had been 12½ hours. By the 1880s, the 10-hour day was prevalent in most of American industry, but for two decades the demand of organized labor, including organized women workers, was for an 8-hour day (Foner, 1947, pp. 213–16).

Lynn Shoemakers' Strike

The biggest strike in American history before the Civil War took place in Lynn, Massachusetts, where the shoeworkers were seeking an increase in wages. In 1860 the workshops and factories of Lynn produced four and one-half million pairs of shoes, but the shoeworkers' wages had been sharply reduced. Men were earning $3 a week. Wages for women were even lower; many of them earned as little as $1 a week and worked as long as 16 hours a day.

---

[8] *Voice of Industry*, January 15, June 15, 1845; Massachusetts House, General Court, House Document No. 5, 1845, pp. 1–6, 15–17; Massachusetts, Senate, General Court, Senate Document No. 81, 1846, pp. 19, 21; Foner (1977), pp. 108–20, 236–42.
[9] *Voice of Industry*, July 29, 1847; Foner (1977), pp. 266–70, 290–310.

When the manufacturers turned down the workers' request for higher wages, the male shoeworkers struck on Washington's birthday, 1860. Two weeks later the women shoebinders and stitchers of Lynn joined the strike.[10]

"The great feature of Wednesday, March 7, was the women's procession," began an account in the *Lynn Weekly Reporter*. Despite a driving snowstorm, the procession of 800 women strikers, escorted by a detachment of musket-bearing militia and the Lynn Cornet Band, marched for several hours through Lynn's major thoroughfares. At the head of the procession they carried a banner with the inscription, "American Ladies Will Not Be Slaves. Give Us Fair Compensation, And We Labour Cheerfully."[11]

On April 10, after 30 manufacturers had signed a written agreement advancing wages over 10 percent, more than a thousand men and women went back to work. The employers, however, refused to recognize the unions that had been organized during the strike. The shoeworkers, in turn, announced that their principal objective—fair remuneration for their labor—had been achieved and that, having formed a permanent association for the protection of their interests during the strike, they would continue the struggle until the employers recognized their organization. Although they did not invite the binders and other women shoeworkers into their association, they expressed gratitude to them for their devotion to the labor cause and announced their determination to work jointly with them and any organizations they might form.[12]

During the Civil War (1861–1865), women played an increasingly important role in the production of goods. Because of the shortage of male workers and the wartime industrial expansion, more than 100,000 new jobs were available for women in factories, sewing rooms, and arsenals. For the first time women were employed as government clerks, being hired in 1862 by General Elias Spinner, Treasurer of the United States, for the Treasury Department. Congress appropriated funds for the salaries of these women in 1864, but the appropriation set a maximum of $600 a year for female government clerks, while male clerks earned from $1,200 to $1,800 (Baker, 1977, pp. 83–85; Montgomery, 1967, pp. 34–35).

Private employers drew the appropriate conclusion and began to hire women in print and cigar shops, telegraph offices, department stores, and light manufacturing plants at no more than 50 percent of the wages men received for the same work. Indeed, it was predicted

---

[10] Dawley (1977), pp. 38–64; Massachusetts, Bureau of Statistics of Labor, *Eleventh Annual Report*, 1880, pp. 17–19; *Lynn News, Lynn Weekly Reporter*, February 23, April 7, 1860.

[11] *Lynn Weekly Reporter*, March 10, 17, 1860; *Lynn News*, March 7, 1860.

[12] *Lynn Weekly Reporter*, April 14, 21, 1860.

that, if the trend continued, men's wages would be brought down to the level of women's by the end of the war. [13]

This prospect compelled the labor movement to take greater interest in women workers and to pay more attention to the improvement of their working conditions. Hence, when working women's unions were formed in a number of cities during the war, they received the cooperation of many of the local working men's unions. [14] Most of the working women's unions vanished before the war's end, but the Working Women's Protective Union, organized by philanthropists in New York City, Chicago, Detroit, and St. Louis, to provide legal protection for working women, especially seamstresses, remained in existence until the 1880s. [15]

National Labor Union

Seventy-seven delegates representing 13 states and the District of Columbia met in Baltimore on August 20, 1866, and formed the National Labor Union. None was a woman or represented an organization with a large female membership. But the convention pledged "individual and undivided support to the sewing women, factory operatives and daughters of toil" and made it clear that, in so doing, it was not acting solely out of sympathy with the working women, but also in the interest of male workers. An *Address of the National Labor Congress to the Workingmen of the United States* appealed to them to protest against the exploitation of working women "and lend their powerful influence to effect a reform, and in no manner can they do more thoroughly than by aiding in the formation of those labor associations in which experience has demonstrated their own safety lies."[16]

Implementation of the *Address* was left to the various trade unions. Only one union responded—the Cigar Makers' International Union. In fact, the cigarmakers amended their constitution, which had prohibited women from membership, and in 1867 became the first national union to admit women. It admitted blacks to membership at the same time. [17]

At the 1868 convention of the National Labor Union, the Committee on Female Labor urged the extension of the eight-hour day demand to women workers, equal pay for equal work, and trade unions

---

[13] *New York Tribune*, October 9, 14, 1863, March 22, 1964; *New York Herald*, November 14, 1863.

[14] *Fincher's Trades' Review*, November 21, 28, 1863, June 29, 1864.

[15] *New York Sun*, November 5, 11, December 17, 1863; *New York Tribune*, December 9, 1879, January 19, 1881.

[16] "Resolutions of the Founding Convention of the National Labor Union," in Commons et al., eds. (1910), Vol. 9, p. 135; "Address of the National Labor Congress to the Workingmen of the United States," Chicago, 1867.

[17] *Workingman's Advocate*, April 12, 19, 26, 1867; Andrews and Bliss (1911), pp. 91–96.

for working women. It also encouraged women "to learn trades, engage in business, join our labor unions, or form protective unions of their own, and use every other honorable means to persuade or force employers to do justice to women by paying them equal wages for equal work." While the National Labor Union was unwilling to accept a Committee's recommendation that women should secure the ballot, the rest of the report was adopted. The National Labor Union thus became the first labor federation in world history to vote for equal pay for equal work.[18]

Although, as we have seen, only one NLU-affiliated union, the Cigar Makers, admitted individual women to membership, the action of the 1868 convention encouraged a group of women reformers—led by suffrage pioneer Susan B. Anthony—to proclaim an alliance of women and labor and praise the National Labor Union in the columns of the feminist weekly, *The Revolution*. Unfortunately, a conflict emerged between the NLU and the women reformers at the 1869 convention over the seating of Anthony as a delegate. Her opponents claimed that she had acted as a recruiter of strikebreakers during a printers' strike. In defense, she maintained that this was the only way women could get experience, but this argument did not persuade the majority of delegates and the final vote was 63 to 28 to reject Anthony's credentials. This brought the alliance of women reformers and trade union leaders to an end. However, before the NLU passed out of existence, it did affirm and reaffirm its position in favor of economic rights of working women, including their right to receive pay equal to men's for equal work.[19]

Knights of Labor

In 1869 nine Philadelphia garment cutters, whose union had been shattered and its members blacklisted, formed a secret society which they named the Noble Order of the Knights of Labor. Its founder, Uriah H. Stephens, placed great emphasis on labor solidarity and encouraged an organization which would "include men and women of every craft, creed, and color . . ." (Foner, 1947, pp. 433–37). But Stephens was so obsessed with the value of secrecy and with the sexist view that women could not keep secrets, that while he mentioned women, he did not advocate opening membership to them. They were excluded from the Knights of Labor for more than a decade. In Sep-

---

[18] *Proceedings of the Second Session of the National Labor Congress in Convention Assembled at New York City, September 21, 1868,* Philadelphia, 1868, p. 4; Dubois (1975), pp. 206–208; Kugler (1954), p. 93.
    [19] *Workingman's Advocate,* September 4, 1869; Dubois (1975), pp. 268–72; Montgomery (1967), pp. 398–99; Kugler (1954), pp. 98–102.

tember 1881, the Knights repudiated secrecy, thus removing one obstacle to the admission of women. Also influencing the movement toward women's eventual membership was the fact that the 1880 Census revealed that in the preceding decade the number of females over 15 years of age employed in manufacturing had increased 64 percent, while the number of males over 16 years of age had increased by less than 25 percent. The 2,647,000 women gainfully employed in 1880 constituted 15.2 percent of the nation's work force, and employers were continuing to hire women, at lower wages, to replace men. By 1890 there were 4,005,500 gainfully employed women—17.2 percent of the total labor force (U.S. Department of Labor, Women's Bureau, 1948, p. 1; 1947, pp. 208–23).

In an effort to protect men's wages from the lower wages paid to working women, the Knights included in its constitution, adopted in 1878, a provision that one of its goals would be to secure "for both sexes equal pay for equal work." Three years later it added the provision for the admission of women (Foner, 1955, p. 61).

Garfield Assembly 1684, the first local composed exclusively of women (in this case shoeworkers), was chartered in September 1881. One other local was formed in 1881; there were 3 in 1882, 9 in 1883, 13 in 1884, 46 in 1885, and 121 in 1886. The organizational structure of the Knights of Labor provided for two types of local assemblies—trades and mixed. When a small community did not contain a sufficient number of workers in a particular trade to form a separate local, it formed a mixed local, including all eligible Knights. Many of the mixed locals had only women members.[20]

Figures on the number of women workers of the Knights of Labor vary, but the most acceptable estimate is that in 1886, when the organization's membership was at its highest point, there were about 50,000 women members, or 8 or 9 percent of the total. A breakdown of the occupations of the women members in 1886 reveals that 19 of the 96 assemblies listed were composed of shoeworkers; 17 of mill operatives; 12 of housekeepers; 5 each of sewers, tailoresses, and laundresses; 4 each of knitters, collar and shirt ironers, and dress- and cloakmakers; 2 each of hatters, weavers, and paper-box makers; and 1 each of bookbinders, carpetmakers, cigarmakers, farmers, feather curlers, gold cutters, lead pencil workers, and rubber workers.[21]

While the Knights did not wage a consistent campaign to eliminate racism in its ranks, it did bring large numbers of black workers into the predominantly white labor movement for the first time. It has

[20] Terence V. Powderly to John A. Forsythe, May 28, 1884, Terence V. Powderly Papers, Catholic University of America.

[21] "Report of the General Instructor and Director of Women's Work," *Proceedings of the General Assembly of the Knights of Labor*, 1869, pp. 4–5.

been estimated that of a total membership exceeding 700,000 in 1886, no fewer than 60,000 were black. A number of locals of black women were organized in Atlanta, Richmond, Durham, Memphis, Raleigh, and Jacksonville, usually composed of domestic workers and seamstresses. Nearly all of these locals were segregated, as were locals of black male Knights, but there were a few integrated locals of female workers in the South. Ida B. Wells, famous as a crusader against lynching, wrote in the *Memphis Watchman* in 1887:

> I was fortunate enough to attend a meeting of the Knights of Labor. . . . I noticed that everyone who came was welcomed and every woman from black to white was seated with the courtesy usually extended to white ladies alone in this town. It was the first assembly of the sort in this town where color was not the criterion to recognition as ladies and gentlemen. Seeing this I could listen to their enunciation of the principle of truth and accept them with a better grace.[22]

In spite of the hostility of its leadership to the strike as a weapon, the Knights of Labor obtained its greatest membership gains as a result of its role during strikes. The 1884 strikes of women members in the textile mills of Fall River and Worcester, Massachusetts, in the hat factories of South Norwalk, Connecticut, of tobacco workers in the Durham, North Carolina, plant of W. Duke & Co., and the 1885 strike of women Knights in the carpet-weaving industry were outstanding for the militancy and perseverance of the strikers.[23] Women Knights and wives of male members were also of great assistance to men engaged in strikes. They helped on the picket lines, gave scabs the "ditch-degree" and "water-cure" (throwing strikebreakers into ditches, dousing them with dishpans of water), and in Cleveland's Rolling Mill strike, they threw stones and pieces of slag at both strikebreakers and police who protected them.[24]

"Women as Boycotters" was the title of an article dealing with the effectiveness of the boycott as used by the Knights. The writer noted that since women did all or most of the buying for the family, it was they who determined the success or failure of a boycott. He cited the case of grocers who refused to sell the bread of an antiunion baker and pointed out that "it was the women Knights who visited his business and successfully forced compliance with the boycott" (Gordon, 1975, pp. 213–14).

The highest post occupied by women in the Knights of Labor was that of master workman of a District Assembly. The first to gain this post was Elizabeth Rodgers, who was chosen master workman of a

---

[22] *Memphis Watchman*, quoted in *New York Freeman*, January 15, 1887; Foner (1982), pp. 46–50.
[23] *New York Times*, February 22, 1885, June 6, 1886; *Yonkers Statesman*, February 27, March 6, May 15, 22, August 22, 29, 1885; Levine (1984), pp. 88–102; Foner (1955), pp. 63–64.
[24] *John Swinton's Paper*, May 24, June 7, 1885.

Chicago women's assembly in 1881 and master workman of District No. 24 in the same city in 1886. She presided over the entire Knight's organization in the Chicago area outside the stockyards, and her district encompassed 50,000 men and women. In reporting the selection of "A Woman Master Workman," the *New York Times* observed that although Rodgers was only 39 and the mother of 11 children, 8 of whom were living, she had "yet managed to make a reputation as a labor reformer."[25]

Leonora M. Barry, who headed a District Assembly of nearly a thousand women Knights in upstate New York, was also elected a master workman in 1886. Elizabeth Morgan was elected master workman of Local Assembly No. 1789 of Chicago in 1887, and Mary Elizabeth Lease—the famous female orator who urged Kansas farmers to "raise less corn and more hell"—was elected master workman of "one of the largest local assemblies in the state of Kansas" in 1891.[26]

The Knights of Labor began a rapid decline after 1886. The employers' tremendous counteroffensive following the Haymarket Affair of May 4, 1886, wiped out the Knights' substantial membership gains and left many locals in severe distress. Lockouts, blacklists, arrests, and imprisonment were used to drive workers out of the organization. By 1895 the membership had plummeted to 20,000, and although the Knights of Labor continued to exist thereafter, it ceased to be a viable labor organization (Foner, 1955, pp. 151–71).

For a brief period, the Knights of Labor broke down sex, ethnic, race, trade, and skill barriers in an attempt to mobilize men and women, black and white, skilled and unskilled, in a union of all the workers. While the events of this brief period did not fundamentally change the status and conditions of working women, they did create a kind of "labor feminism," advocating equal wages for men and women and equal rights within the organization, and they did bring forth a number of female labor leaders who were to carry their knowledge and experience with them into the next period in the history of organized labor and the woman worker (Levine, 1984, pp. 108–10; McCreesh, 1975, p. 49).

American Federation of Labor

Even while the Knights of Labor was disintegrating, the new American Federation of Labor was experiencing a slow but steady growth. First organized as the Federation of Organized Trades and Labor Unions of the United States and Canada, it was renamed in

---

[25] *New York Times*, August 31, 1886; James (1975), pp. 408–409.
[26] *Journal of United Labor*, June 23, 1887; James (1975), p. 409.

1886. By 1892 the number of member unions had increased from the original 13 to 40 (Foner, 1955, pp. 132–44; 1947, pp. 518–24).

No women were present at the founding convention of the Federation in 1881, but at its 1882 gathering the organization extended an invitation to all women's organizations to join and assured them that they would be represented at future sessions "upon an equal footing with trade organizations of men." At its next convention, the organization drafted "An Address to Working Girls and Women" urging them to organize and unite with the federation in establishing the principle that "equal amounts of work should bring the same prices whether performed by man or woman."[27]

But the AFL made little progress in organizing women during the 1880s. Only two national affiliates, the Cigar Makers' International Union and the Typographical Union, accepted women as members, and others actually passed resolutions prohibiting women from joining. Only one woman delegate appeared at any AFL convention prior to 1891, and women were conspicuously absent at meetings of affiliated local unions (Foner, 1955, pp. 189–90).

Women workers, being relatively unskilled, did not fit into the AFL craft unions, and to the degree that they were organized in the early years of the federation, they were often in separate unions. The women frequently complained that they got the worst end in such an arrangement, since "the men think that the girls should not get as good work as the men and should not make half as much money as a man."[28] Very few women were willing to join the separate unions, and the plan was quickly abandoned.

Instead, the AFL established federal labor unions for women workers. The first and most important was the Ladies' Federal Labor Union No. 2703 in Chicago, organized in June 1888 by Elizabeth Chambers Morgan, wife of Chicago's leading socialist, Thomas P. Morgan. It was a mixed union, composed of typists, seamstresses, dressmakers, clerks, music teachers, candymakers, gummakers, and other female workers. It received an AFL charter the year it was organized (Scharnau, 1973, pp. 340–44; Ritter, 1971, pp. 242–44).

Other federal labor unions of women workers came into being in the 1890s in Toledo, Ohio, Terre Haute, Indiana, and Emporia, Kansas, and were chartered by the AFL. The AFL also directly chartered unions of women workers in a special industry, such as the union of collar and shirt workers in Troy, New York. By November 1891 there were six unions in the collar, cuff, and shirt industry of Troy, all

---

[27] *Proceedings of the Federation of Organized Trades and Labor Unions of the United States and Canada*, 1882 Convention, pp. 16, 19, 20, 23; 1883 Convention, pp. 13, 15, 19.

[28] Mary Meenin to Chris Evans, June 20, 1892, American Federation of Labor Correspondence, AFL Building, Washington, D.C. (hereinafter cited as AFL Correspondence).

affiliated with the AFL. Several unions of female operatives in the industry were also organized in the principal shirt manufacturing centers of Albany, Cohoes, Glens Falls, and Greenwich, New York.[29]

A significant event in 1891 was the affiliation with the AFL of a national union with a substantial number of women members—the United Garment Workers of America, the first national union in the men's clothing industry. The women's garment industry, on the other hand, had neither a national union in the 1890s nor very many women members in those local unions that did exist (McCreesh, 1975, pp. 65–70).

In April 1892, Samuel Gompers, the first president of the AFL and, with the exception of one year (1895), the head of the Federation until his death in 1924, appointed Mary E. Kenney as a general organizer, with no limitation on the trades in which she would do her organizing work. Working with Leonora O'Reilly, an Irish garment worker, Kenney helped organize Local 16 of the United Garment Workers. She also helped organize women workers in Boston. But on September 30, the AFL refused to renew her commission as general organizer, pleading financial distress.[30]

The AFL remained without a woman general organizer until December 1893 when Gompers commissioned Miss E.E. Pitt, a member of the Typographical Union in Boston, and instructed her to begin "organizing women regardless of their trades or callings." In January 1894, Gompers recommended to the AFL Executive Council that four additional women organizers be appointed, but his proposal was quickly rejected. Moreover, Pitt's work as an organizer was cut short, and in the fall of 1894 the Federation was again without a woman general organizer. To be sure, most of the national trade unions in the AFL were basically craft in structure and were interested in the organization of skilled workers. They persistently ignored the resolutions adopted at Federation conventions calling for the organization of women workers. Except for adopting routine resolutions sympathetic to women, the AFL paid almost no attention to the needs of five million female workers and continued to ignore them until the twentieth century.[31]

Even more women entered the labor force during the first decade of the new century. They could be found in the former male-domi-

---

[29] *Troy Daily Times*, November 23, 1891; Troy *Northern Budget*, January 6, 11, February 1, November 20, 1891.

[30] Mary K. O'Sullivan, "Autobiography," manuscript in Arthur and Elizabeth Schlesinger Library on the History of Women in America, Radcliffe College, Cambridge, Massachusetts, pp. 1–67, 88–89, 98–99; Mary E. Kenney to Samuel Gompers, May 18, September 1892, and Chris Evans to Gompers, October 1, 1892, AFL Correspondence; McCreesh (1975), pp. 62, 69.

[31] Samuel Gompers to E.E Pitt, December 29, 1893, Samuel Gompers Letter Books, Library of Congress, Manuscripts Division; Gompers (1925), Vol. 1, pp. 480–82.

nated industries such as commerce, transportation, and communications and were predominant in such trades as steam laundries, retail sales, food processing, and many branches of light manufacturing, especially garments. In 1910 in New York City, almost 60 percent of immigrant women worked for wages. The indifference of the AFL to organizing women workers and the dramatic increase in their numbers combined to bring about the founding, in 1903, of the first national body dedicated to organizing women workers—the National Women's Trade Union League (Foner, 1979, pp. 257–58).

Women's Trade Union League

A number of settlement houses had been established in the large cities during the 1890s. Several of them were hostile to trade unions and refused to support the labor movement, but this was not true of the large social settlements. Labor unions met regularly at Chicago's Hull House, at Denison House and South End House in Boston, and at University and Henry Street Settlements in New York, and many union locals of women were founded at these locations. Eventually the settlement workers won the support and cooperation of young, militant working women in their effort to organize unions of women workers (Davis, 1967).

In 1902, William English Walling, the son of a prominent doctor and grandson of a Kentucky millionaire, became a resident of University Settlement. Convinced that working women could organize effectively and fight for decent conditions, and having read accounts of the British Women's Trade Union League, which had been founded in 1874 and had had considerable success in organizing women workers (or so it was reported in the United States), he decided to study its work at firsthand. With the support of Lillian Wald and Florence Kelley of the Henry Street Settlement, he went to England in 1903 to learn more about the League.[32]

Walling met members of the British Trade Union League and other trade union leaders and found that the organization encouraged women to join existing men's unions. He was especially impressed by the fact that the British League united both upper-class and working-class women in a common fight to organize women into their own unions and integrate them into established men's locals. He was persuaded that a similar organization could improve the conditions for American working women, and he carried the idea back to the United States.

---

[32] Biographical sketch of William English Walling in National Women's Trade Union League Papers, Box 1, Library of Congress, Manuscripts Division (hereinafter referred to as NWTU Papers).

Filled with enthusiasm, Walling went to Boston in November 1903 to attend the AFL convention. He and Mary Kenney O'Sullivan worked out a tentative plan for a new organization designed specifically to help working women enter unions, and they arranged a meeting in Faneuil Hall to which they invited AFL Executive Council members and convention delegates whose trades included large numbers of women (Boone, 1942, pp. 20–26).

After several meetings with AFL delegates and Boston settlement workers, the Women's Trade Union League was organized with a set of officers and a constitution. Mary Morton Kehew, a wealthy Bostonian and former president of the General Federation of Women's Clubs, was selected as the League's first president and Mary Kenney O'Sullivan as secretary. Jane Addams of Hull House agreed to serve as the League's vice-president.[33]

The constitution of the new organization stated that its objective "shall be to assist in the organization of women workers into trade unions." (Shortly thereafter, the following words were added: "and thereby to help secure conditions necessary for healthful and efficient work and to obtain a just return for such work.") Anyone was eligible to be a member upon declaring "himself or herself willing to assist those trade unions already existing, which have women members and to aid in the formation of new unions of women wage workers." Nonunion members (called "allies" because of the antilabor connotation of the term "nonunionist") were eligible not only to join the League, but to hold any office. However, the constitution stipulated that membership on the Executive Board was to be divided as follows: "The majority . . . shall be women who are, or have been, trade unionists in good standing, the minority of those well known to be earnest sympathizers and workers for the cause of trade unionism."[34]

Branches were soon formed in New York, Boston, and Chicago. In 1905 the center of League power shifted from New York to Chicago when Ellen M. Henrotin, a wealthy Chicago woman, was chosen national president, a post she held until 1907. That year Margaret Dreier Robins replaced Henrotin as president of the national League and served in that capacity until 1922.

In 1907–1908 the New York League reported, "While the Women's Trade Union League has been working for the organization of women into trade unions, it was recognized that the direct work of organization will be done by the women themselves and that its own

---

[33] "Report of the Meeting Held to Organize the Women's Trade Union League," Box 1, NWTU Papers. The name was changed to National Women's Trade Union League in 1907.

[34] *Constitution of the National Women's Trade Union League of America Adopted in Faneuil Hall, Boston, November 17–19, 1903.* The original is in NWTU Papers, Box 25.

work is largely educational."[35] A year later, in 1909, a revolution began in the garment trades that was to prove the validity of this estimate.

Uprising of the Garment Workers

On November 24, 1909, 18,000 shirtwaist makers in Manhattan and Brooklyn walked out of nearly 500 shops. By the end of the day, more than 20,000 workers were on strike, protesting wages averaging $5 for 56 to 59 hours of work each week, with only the usual rate for overtime, as well as tyrannical bosses, pettiness, espionage, favoritism, rudeness, and discourtesy. Manufacturers charged for needles and thread (often as much as $1.50 per week) and for electric power, the chairs the workers used, and lockers in the shops—all at a substantial profit to themselves. They fined their employees for being a few minutes late and for accidentally spoiling a piece of clothing (McCreesh, 1975, pp. 162–63; Berman, 1956, pp. 72–73; Levine, 1924, pp. 144–48).

Local 25 of the International Ladies' Garment Workers' Union had jurisdiction over the shirtwaist makers. Founded in 1906, the local had failed to attract many members, and just before the strike, membership had barely reached 800. Nevertheless, unrest had been building steadily. The union and the New York Women's Trade Union League called a meeting of shirtwaist makers on November 29, 1909, at Cooper Union, and after two hours during which speakers urged caution and moderate action, Clara Lemlich, a young worker, leaped to her feet and asked for the floor. Speaking in impassioned Yiddish, the native tongue of the majority of the shirtwaist workers, she declared, "I move we go on a general strike." A vote was taken immediately, and 3,000 voices shouted unanimous approval. The news of the vote was relayed to other halls where the shirtwaist makers had gathered. There also the strike vote was ratified.[36]

Thus began the famous labor struggle that has become known as the "Uprising of the Twenty Thousand." From November 1909 through February 1910, young women workers tied up the garment industry. By December 22, more than 700 pickets had been arrested; 19 were sentenced to the workhouse on Blackwell's Island on charges of disorderly conduct and vagrancy, and the rest were fined. But the arrests and imprisonment failed to dampen the strikers' spirit. The New York Women's Trade Union League capitalized on the fact that the majority of the strikers were women. It enrolled women into

---

[35] *Annual Report of the Women's Trade Union League of New York, 1907–1908*, p. 5.
[36] New York *Call*, August 27, September 6, 8, 16, October 12–22, 1909; McCreesh (1975), pp. 162–67; Berman (1956), pp. 78–79; Levine (1924), p. 149.

Local 25, raised funds, provided publicity, furnished bail for the arrested strikers, and organized marches and rallies in support of the strike. Some League members, including those from the upper class, walked the picket lines and went to jail with the strikers.[37]

Although the shirtwaist makers did not win their major demand for a union shop, they did achieve a reduction in working hours, time and a half for overtime, and removal of many of the employers' petty impositions. Most important, nearly 20,000 workers had joined Local 25 and 10,000 had become members of Philadelphia's Local 15 which had also joined the strike. They planted the seeds for permanent unionism in the garment trades—for women and men alike.[38]

The "Uprising of the Twenty Thousand" served as a catalyst for workers in other branches of the industry. In July 1910, 60,000 workers employed in the cloak-and-suit branch went on strike, and after nine weeks of bitter struggle, the "Protocol of Peace," as the agreement was called, won for the workers a reduction in hours, bonus pay for overtime, 10 legal holidays, improvements in sanitary conditions, and a provision for wage settlements to be made in each shop by negotiation. The settlement had important implications for unskilled women workers, since the agreement covered the wages and conditions of every worker in the trade, from skilled tailors to finishers (Dubofsky, 1968, pp. 186–95; Berman, 1956, pp. 150–53; Levine, 1924, pp. 168–93).

Also in 1910, Chicago garment workers—40,000 strong of whom 10,000 were women—brought production in the men's wear industry to a standstill and laid the foundation for the Amalgamated Clothing Workers Union.[39]

A general strike occurred in the New York fur industry on June 20, 1912, when more than 8,000 workers—2,000 of them women—walked out of 500 shops. The strike lasted 13 weeks and ended in victory. The fur workers obtained a reduction in hours, time and a half for overtime, 10 paid holidays, wages to be paid weekly and in cash—and union recognition. It was a historic agreement—the first thus far achieved in the revolt of the garment workers (Foner, 1950, pp. 39–52).

At the 1913 convention of the National Women's Trade Union League, Rose Schneiderman, a garment worker and ILGWU organizer, cited the gains that workers had made in the women's clothing

---

[37] *New York Times*, December 28, 1909; New York *Call*, November 26–29, 1909; Adams (1966), pp. 105–106; Clark and Wyatt (1910), pp. 70–86.

[38] *Philadelphia Public Ledger*, February 7, 8, 1910; New York Times, December 21, 24, 1909, January 4, 6, 1910; Berman (1956), p. 103; Scott (1910), pp. 48–58.

[39] *Chicago Daily Socialist*, October 22–28, 1910; McCreesh (1975), pp. 189–93; Zaretz (1934), pp. 73–90.

industry in the years since the uprising of the shirtwaist makers. She pointed out that in September 1909, just a few months before the shirtwaist strike, approximately 3,000 women belonged to unions in the garment trades. A year later, 16,716 women were enrolled as members. By September 1913, New York State trade union records listed 63,872 women as members in New York City needle trades' unions. Moreover, at least 60,000 women had gained a nine-hour day and a half-holiday on Saturday. They earned at least 20 percent more than they had in the years before the wave of strikes, and they had established reasonably stable trade unions to which they could turn for assistance. Indeed, it was these struggles that turned the shells of unions into mass organizations, thereby laying the foundation for lasting organizations in the women's and men's clothing industries and for the widespread unionization of women workers (Foner, 1979, p. 373).

The Industrial Workers of the World

Outside the garment trades, however, the vast majority of women workers were still unorganized. As a substantial portion of these women were unskilled workers and factory operatives, they continued to be ignored by the craft unions of the American Federation of Labor which concentrated on organizing skilled workers—especially white male skilled workers. However, the Industrial Workers of the World (IWW) had come into existence in 1905 after many progressive-minded elements in the labor and socialist movements reached the conclusion that industrial unionism was superior to craft unionism in the struggle against highly concentrated organizations of employers, and that it was impossible to convert the conservative AFL into an organization that could achieve real benefits for the majority of working men and women. In the eyes of these elements, there was a clear need for a new labor organization that "would correspond to modern industrial conditions and through which [the working people] might finally secure complete emancipation from wage-slavery for all workers."[40]

The IWW repeatedly emphasized that women were in industrial life to stay: "They cannot be driven back to the home. . . . They are part of the army of labor." There was only one thing to be done: "Organize them with the men, just as they work with the men." Male workers were urged, "Don't fight against women labor; women find it necessary to work. . . . They work because they have got to make a

---

[40] *Proceedings of the First Convention of the Industrial Workers of the World*, New York, 1905, p. 82.

living." At times the IWW spokesmen contradicted themselves on the question of women workers, arguing that married women should not enter industry, but in the main their treatment of the woman worker differed from that of the AFL. They were not content merely to lament the status of working-class women in industrial society; they set out to organize the women.[41]

IWW initiation fees and dues were kept very low in order to make membership more readily available to the masses of low-paid, unskilled workers. Dues for women workers were much lower than those of men, one of many indications that the IWW favored female participation and was determined not to discriminate against women workers as the AFL had done.[42] Another indication was that the IWW cleared the way for women to play an active role in the organization. There were a number of women organizers, and in 1909 Elizabeth Gurley Flynn became a member of the General Executive Board, a position no woman had ever occupied in the AFL (Baxandall, 1975, p. 98; Flynn, 1955, pp. 13–54).

Women were active in many IWW strikes, and their role in the great Lawrence strike of 1912 made the difference between success and failure.

The Lawrence Strike

When the Italian workers at the Washington woolen mill in Lawrence, Massachusetts, opened their pay envelopes on January 12, 1912, they found that their wages had been reduced by an amount equivalent to two hours' work, or as the workers put it, by "four loaves of bread." The wages of these men and women were already at the starvation level, and suddenly all the years of suffering from lack of food, miserable housing, inadequate clothing, poor health, and the tyranny of foremen came to a head and erupted in an outburst of rage against the machines—the symbol of the bosses' repression. The workers ran from room to room, stopping the motors, cutting the belts, tearing the cloth, breaking the electric lights, and dragging the other operatives from the looms. Within a half-hour, work came to a standstill.

The strike spread quickly, and by Saturday night, January 13, an estimated 20,000 textile workers had left their machines. Two days later Lawrence was an armed camp. Police and militia guarded the

---

[41] Flynn, "Women in Industry Should Organize," *Solidarity*, June 1, 1911; Elizabeth Gurley Flynn, "Women and Unionism," *Solidarity*, May 27, 1891; Foner (1965), pp. 127–30.
    [42] *Proceedings of the Second Annual Convention of the Industrial Workers of the World*, Chicago: IWW, 1906, pp. 96–97.

mills throughout the night. The Battle of Lawrence, one of the epic struggles between capital and labor, was on![43]

Since the AFL United Textile Workers had totally ignored the unskilled immigrants, who were the vast majority among the Lawrence workers, the strikers called on the IWW for help. Joseph J. Ettor, accompanied by Arturo Giovannitti, editor of *Il Progresso* and secretary of the Italian Socialist Federation, came immediately, and on January 13, under Ettor's leadership, the spontaneous outburst quickly gave way to a methodical strike organization rarely paralleled in the annals of the American labor movement.

To get around the city authorities' prohibition of gatherings in front of the mills, the strike committee, representing each of the 30 different nationalities, developed the ingenious strategy of the moving picket line. Day after day, for 24 hours a day, long lines of pickets moved in an endless chain around the mill district to discourage strikebreakers. Each picket wore a white ribbon or card that said, "Don't Be a Scab." No one could get through the lines without being accosted. What is more, the chain did not violate the law because the strikers did not mass in front of the mills.[44]

The women strikers and the wives of the male strikers trod the frozen streets alongside the men and often occupied the front ranks in demonstrations and parades. Expectant mothers and women with babies in their arms marched with the others, carrying signs reading "We Want Bread and Roses Too." This slogan inspired one of the great songs of the Lawrence strike, which has since come to symbolize women workers and their struggles. The opening section reads:

As we come marching, marching
    In the beauty of the day
A million darkened kitchens
    A thousand mill lofts gray
Are touched with all the radiance
    That a sudden sun discloses
For the people hear us singing:
    "Bread and Roses! Bread and Roses!"

(Kornbluh, 1964, p. 196.)

Anna La Pizza, a 34-year-old Italian woman, was shot through the heart and killed on January 29. Even though 19 witnesses testified that they had seen a soldier murder La Pizza, Ettor and Giovannitti were arrested, imprisoned, and removed from the strike leadership. William D. ("Big Bill") Haywood and Elizabeth Gurley Flynn took over.[45]

---

[43] *Lawrence Evening Tribune*, December 22–28, 1911, January 11–14, 1912; Cole (1963), pp. 100–10; Levine (1936), pp. 32–36.
[44] *Lawrence Evening Tribune*, January 14, 10, February 24, 1912; Foner (1965), pp. 315–23.
[45] *Lawrence Evening Tribune*, February 24, 1912; New York *Call*, February 24, 1912; Haywood (1929), p. 249.

Soon Gurley Flynn came to symbolize the leadership that women could exercise in a labor struggle. She was responsible for fund-raising and support work, and she also took charge of what came to be called the "Lawrence Children's Crusade," probably the most publicized episode connected with the strike. From the beginning, the Italians had considered sending their children to the homes of Italian Socialist Federation members in other cities. The majority of the strikers voted in favor of the exodus proposal. Gurley Flynn arranged the transportation; she placed the children from 4 to 14 years of age in suitable homes provided by Socialist women in New York and other cities.

The exodus of the children eased the relief burden, while it also attracted sympathy for the strikers' cause. The mill owners, disturbed by the unfavorable publicity they were receiving, determined to put an end to further departures. As the children were assembling at the Lawrence railroad station on February 24, the police sought to block them from boarding the cars that would carry them to Philadelphia. The mothers and the children were dragged to a military truck, and even clubbed, regardless of their panic-stricken cries. Fifteen children and eight adults, including pregnant mothers, were arrested, thrust into patrol wagons, and taken to the police station.

As the nation's press headlined the news of the police brutality, protests swept the nation and even carried over to Europe. Petitions poured into Congress demanding an investigation of the Lawrence strike. A congressional investigation was undertaken, as was one by the U.S. Commissioner of Labor. [46]

After eight weeks, without a break in the strikers' ranks, the mill owners began to negotiate with the strike committee. The committee reported to the strikers the employers' offer of 25 percent wage increases for the lowest-paid workers, with a decreasing percentage increase for the higher-paid workers. All were to get time and a quarter for overtime, and the companies promised no discrimination against strikers. On March 14, 1912, 20,000 strikers voted unanimously to accept the offer and go back to work. [47]

In an article entitled "The Women of Lawrence," the *Industrial Worker*, an official IWW publication, gave chief credit for the unprecedented victory to the bravery and enthusiasm of the women strikers and the strikers' wives. The tribute was merited. On many occasions, women had taken over the picket lines, refusing to shrink before police and troop brutality. Arrested and jailed, they refused to allow the IWW to spend money in their defense, but served their

---

[46] *Solidarity*, March 2, 1912; New York *Call*, February 8, March 6, 1912; *Lawrence Evening Tribune*, February 10, 18, 1912.

[47] *Lawrence Sun*, May 14–15, 1912; New York *Call*, March 14–15, 1912; Foner (1965), pp. 340–42.

terms and then returned to the picket lines. The determination and militancy of the women strikers were decisive in the final victory.[48]

At the end of the strike, more than 10,000 Lawrence textile workers were members of the IWW. Within two years the number had declined to 1,500. To a great extent the employers' offensive was responsible for the loss of IWW membership in Lawrence. However, IWW policies contributed substantially to accelerating the decline. Because it was primarily interested in unionizing during strikes, the IWW failed to build a strong permanent union, and it left the workers without effective leadership. In too many other strikes these weaknesses reemerged and were important factors in IWW membership losses following great gains (Foner, 1965, pp. 360–80).

World War I

With the United States' declaration of war against the Central Powers (Germany and her allies) on April 6, 1917, and the nation's entrance into the conflict, female labor became a national necessity. Almost 10 million American women were to enter gainful employment before the armistice—at least 3 million of them in factories and over 1 million in jobs directly connected with the production of war equipment. One hundred thousand women operated long-distance and intracity transport vehicles; 250,000 fabricated textiles (including items from tents to uniforms); and at least 100,000 were forging metal products. Further, female hands would play an essential role in providing sufficient food, clothing, and housing to equip 4 million men in service at domestic installations and overseas battlefields (Van Kleeck and McDowell, 1920, pp. 11–93).

"Female Labor Arouses Hostility and Apprehension in Union Ranks," declared *Current Opinion* in April 1918. It reported that a conflict had emerged between leaders of organized labor and of women's groups. While the AFL and most of its affiliated unions were emphasizing that there was no need for women workers to enter occupations traditionally held by men, leaders of the Women's Trade Union League were stressing that America's entry into the war meant that "women will find new avenues of employment—industries formerly closed to them will open their doors, and they will be drawn from unimportant industries to those essential to our national existence." To the male trade unionists, with some exceptions, this development meant an inevitable lowering of wage scales, but League spokespersons argued that the answer lay in unionizing the new women workers and establishing the "same wage scale for women and

---

[48] *Industrial Worker*, July 25, 1912; Steinberg (1975), pp. 74–76.

men." Only in this way, they insisted, could men be sure that when they came back from military service, they would not find "that not only have their places been taken, but wages cut."[49]

A resolution was introduced at the 1918 AFL convention calling "upon the officers and organizers of the affiliated national unions to make every effort to bring these women [who had newly entered industries] into the organizations of the representative crafts to which the men whose places they have taken, are members." The resolution was referred to the Executive Council for implementation, but the Council confined itself to seeking opinions from the officers of all unions as to the most effective way of achieving the intent of the resolution. The replies satisfied the Executive Council that these unions were doing all that was necessary "to safeguard and protect the rights of women wage workers and maintain standards." It thereupon assured working women that, together with these unions, the AFL Executive Council "will make every effort to give wholehearted support to the endeavor to organize the women workers of America to bring them the full fruition of organized effort that they may be accorded as a right, equal pay for equal work with men." At the same time, the Executive Council pledged that, together with the affiliated unions, it would organize and protect the interests of "colored workers."[50]

The latter pledge was never kept. When World War I came to an end on November 11, 1918, AFL membership was 4,726,748, up from 2,072,702 in 1916. Few of these new members were black, and fewer still were black women. While black women were excluded from nearly all AFL unions, white women's relationships with these organizations varied. In the case of women streetcar conductors (or conductorettes, as they called themselves), the locals of the Amalgamated Association of Street and Railway Employees of America, affiliated with the AFL, with one exception, conducted campaigns to prevent the employment of conductorettes and to encourage the dismissal of those already working. Only in Kansas City did the union men welcome the conductorettes into their local and insist that the guaranteed minimum pay of the women be raised to equal the wage of the men.[51]

Where women had been welcomed into unions during the war, they accepted the invitation gladly and made important contributions to advancing the interests of both themselves and men, and together they obtained better working conditions. Where they were confronted with union opposition, women defended their own special interests.

---

[49] *Current Opinion*, April 1918, pp. 292–93; *New York Times*, December 16, 1917.
[50] *Proceedings of the American Federation of Labor Convention*, 1918, pp. 202, 219; *Proceedings*, 1919, pp. 188–89.
[51] "Controversies Regarding the Right of Women to Work as Conductors," (1921), pp. 2–22; Foner (1982), pp. 136–43; Greenwald (1980), pp. 150–74; Finney (1957), p. 146–88.

Too often the opposition of male workers and their unions led many women to consider trade unionism and sex discrimination as synonymous. But the war also gave many women their first contact with labor organizations, and this contact brought them the advantages of trade union protection. By 1920, 8 percent of trade union members were female, and 6.6 percent of all working women were organized—a fivefold increase in a decade (Wolman, 1924, p. 162).

Postwar Developments

Unfortunately, during the demobilization and reconstruction following the war, women workers were unable to obtain the protection of trade unions. With rare exceptions, the male unionists were indifferent to the women's efforts to maintain the gains they had made during the war. In the AFL's proposals for postwar America, made public in late December 1918, the only concern expressed over the possibility of employment dealt with returning servicemen who, it was stated, should be aided by the government in their efforts to find work. Nothing was said about jobs for women workers. Trade unions, the national government, and state governments cooperated in supporting the veterans who demanded their former jobs. Together, they took up the cry: "The women must go!" And go they did. Most women workers were shut out of the work they had performed so effectively during the war.[52]

Although the war years had seen a growth in trade union membership among women workers, the Women's Bureau of the Department of Labor reported in 1920 that "many women are not included in the membership of the big international unions."[53] Events soon disclosed that further progress in organizing women workers into unions was to be exceedingly difficult. A committee of the National Women's Trade Union League met with the AFL Executive Council on August 23, 1921, to discuss the issuance of charters to groups of women not admitted to membership in the international unions of their trade. Nothing came of the discussion, and when the League appealed to the Council to issue charters to women if they were excluded by affiliates, the proposal was rejected. In 1924 eight international unions—barbers, carpenters, molders, teamsters, blacksmiths, longshoremen, miners, and seamen—acknowledged that they officially opposed the admission of women, but no word of criticism came from the AFL leadership.[54]

---

[52] *Proceedings of the American Federation of Labor Convention,* 1919, pp. 70–80; *New York Times,* February 1, October 10, 1919.

[53] *Labor,* December 25, 1920.

[54] Wolfson (1926), p. 71; Henry (1923), p. 102; *New Republic,* August 3, 1921, pp. 265–67.

At the 1925 AFL convention, the Executive Council authorized the new president, William Green, "to work out a plan" for the unionization of women workers. The plan proposed provided that the various unions in a given locality should make an intensive joint drive to organize women under their jurisdiction. The overall direction of the organizing campaign was placed in the hands of Edward F. McGrady, the AFL's legislative agent and top organizer. But McGrady did little to organize women workers. As he told representatives of the Women's Trade Union League, "[W]omen could not be organized; women do not want to be organized; women had been organized at great trouble and expense, and their unions had not lasted." McGrady's advice to the League was "to forget all this business, and leave the labor movement to men." "It will not be for another twenty-five or fifty years before we can even begin to organize women," he concluded (Craton, 1927, pp. 312–13; Wolfson, 1926, p. 75). At the 1926 AFL convention, President Green acknowledged that the campaign had failed, and he urged that organizing efforts among women workers be abandoned in favor of an educational effort (Chafe, 1972, pp. 120–31).

The entire August 1929 issue of the *American Federationist* was devoted to this educational effort, with the lead editorial stressing the principle that legislation was no substitute for union protection and urging the affiliated unions to undertake campaigns to recruit working women. But leading AFL organizers still insisted that it would take from 25 to 50 years before a campaign to unionize the working women could even begin (Wolfson, 1929, pp. 120–31).

Role of the Communists

A movement did exist, however, which was proving that the AFL approach was simply an excuse for inactivity. The Trade Union Educational League (TUEL), composed of communist men and women, was organizing thousands of women and leading them in strikes. The TUEL won the support of men and women who were not communists, and together they fought the male-dominated union bureaucracies of the International Ladies' Garment Workers' Union, the International Fur Workers' Union, and the Amalgamated Clothing Workers. It was also active in the drive to organize the unorganized textile workers in Passaic, New Jersey, and New Bedford and Fall River, Massachusetts (Foner, 1980, pp. 153–224).

In 1928 the communists abandoned their attempt to establish a progressive trade union program in the AFL and dissolved the Trade Union Educational League, replacing it with the Trade Union Unity League (TUUL). With their new organization, they focused their

efforts on achieving organization of the unorganized through independent industrial unions. The TUUL announced that the unionization of women workers was a key problem of American labor: "The
trade union leaders have altogether failed to defend the interests of
women workers, barring them from the unions and discriminating
against them in industry as they have done against the youth, the
Negroes, and the foreign-born." The new industrial union movement
called for equal pay for equal work and a general increase in women's
wages in keeping with the rise in the cost of living; a minimum wage for
women workers in agriculture and domestic service; the establishment
of a seven-hour day and a five-day week, with a six-hour day for harmful
and strenuous occupations; an annual full month's holiday with pay;
the prohibition of night work and work in particularly difficult and
harmful occupations; maternity leave on full pay for eight weeks before
and eight weeks after confinement for all women wage earners; and
paid intervals of not less than half an hour for nursing mothers every
three-and-a-half hours during the working day in special rooms to be
set aside for feeding their infants. It also called upon employers to
establish nurseries, to be under the management of the workers and
their organizations but at no cost to them, and to install special dressing
rooms, washrooms, and showers in the factories as well as a sufficient
number of seats for the women workers and office employees. Finally,
"all forms of social insurance against unemployment, old age, sickness,
etc., shall cover not only the industrial women but all women working
for wages." To further this program, the most supportive of women
workers adopted up to this time by an American labor organization, the
TUUL established a National Women's Department, organized
women's commissions in the trade unions, and held trade union conferences for women workers.[55]

The National Textile Workers' Union, the Needle Trades' Workers' Industrial Union, the Cannery-Agricultural Workers' Industrial
Unions, and other affiliates of the TUUL organized women workers—
black, white, and Hispanic—in the South, East, and West (Foner,
1980, pp. 224–55). But the most effective organizing among women
workers was done by a new industrial union movement which came
into existence in 1935—the Committee for Industrial Organization,
which three years later became the Congress of Industrial Organizations (CIO).

The Congress of Industrial Organizations

After passage of the National Industrial Recovery Act in June
1933, including Section 7(a) affirming the right of workers to join

---

[55] *The Trade Union Unity League: Methods and History*, New York, n.d., pp. 26–27; *Daily
Worker*, September 6, October 9, 14, 1929.

"unions of their own choosing," local industrial unions were formed all over the country, and they requested admission into the AFL. The Federation, determined to maintain the principle of organization by crafts, issued federal charters to organizations of unskilled and semi-skilled workers in the rubber, auto, steel, electrical, and other mass-production industries. However, these were only temporary charters, regarded as a device for holding on to the newly organized industrial locals until a way could be found to divide them up among the various craft unions. Since many AFL leaders did not consider unskilled workers worth organizing, they hoped that in the process these workers would fall by the wayside (Tomlins, 1979, p. 1033).

Disillusionment with the AFL's policy of federal unions spread rapidly among the new unionists in the mass-production industries, and many of the organizations formed during the union boom of the early New Deal disintegrated. At the 1933 AFL convention, Elizabeth Christman, speaking on behalf of the Women's Trade Union League, pleaded with the delegates to take immediate action to organize the five million women in industry. Many women were now in the mass-production industries, she pointed out, but the AFL policy of craft exclusiveness was unsuited to the organization of these industries. Christman offered an industrial union resolution, but it never even came to a vote. A year later, at the 1934 AFL convention, John L. Lewis of the United Mine Workers, a leading champion of industrial unionism, argued vigorously that it offered the only suitable way to organize the mass-production industries. A compromise resolution was adopted that appeared to accept the principle of industrial unionism, but it contained a rider limiting the scope of such unions.[56]

The refusal of the AFL leadership to alter the union structure to meet the needs of the vast majority of the workers in the mass-production industries produced a heated battle at the 1935 convention. A majority of the Committee on Resolutions opposed issuing industrial-type charters covering the rubber, auto, radio, and other industries. A minority, lead by John L. Lewis, insisted that "in the great mass production industries . . . industrial organization is the only solution." After the convention rejected the industrial union resolution by a vote of 1,820,000 to 1,090,000, the advocates of industrial unionism met separately and set up the Committee for Industrial Organization to encourage the formation of industrial unions that were to affiliate with the AFL (Morris, 1938, pp. 212–16).

The AFL Executive Council and the Committee leaders negotiated off and on over the next year, culminating in the Council's

---

[56] *New York Times*, October 4, 1933; *Proceedings of the American Federation of Labor*, 1933, pp. 84–89; *Proceedings*, 1934, pp. 120–36.

expulsion, in September 1936, of all but two international unions that were Committee members. Efforts to patch up the break were fruitless, and in 1938 the Committee changed its name to the Congress of Industrial Organizations.

There were no specific references to women in the statements launching the Committee, but it was obvious that unionization along industrial lines would require the cooperation and participation of women workers, many of whom were excluded from the craft unions. Also, two of the most powerful of the CIO unions, the Amalgamated Clothing Workers and the International Ladies' Garment Workers' Union, were in industries that employed substantial numbers of women, and the growth of these unions since 1933 indicated even to the most skeptical that women indeed could be unionized.

The CIO began a series of organizing campaigns in 1936–1937 in the rubber, auto, and steel industries, among packinghouse and textile workers, and in the electrical, radio, shipbuilding, and communications industries, among others. Many of these campaigns did not directly involve women because few of them were employed in the industries, but women did play a crucial role in these organizing drives.

Women's auxiliaries were indispensable in the sit-down strike of rubber workers in Akron, Ohio, in 1936 and in the General Motors sit-down strike of 1936–1937 in Flint, Michigan. The women fed the strikers daily, set up a first-aid station where they nursed casualties, distributed literature, ran around-the-clock picket lines, and took charge of publicity. The women also ran a day-care center for the children of striking mothers, established a welfare committee and a speakers' bureau, and visited wives who opposed the sit-down to try to convince them to support their husbands (Foner, 1980, pp. 300–14).

The General Motors workers and their womenfolk fought the giant corporation from December 30, 1936, to February 11, 1937, and won an agreement which recognized the United Auto Workers as the collective bargaining representative for its members. The company agreed not to interfere with the right of its employees to join the union (Foner, 1980, pp. 312–14; Fine, 1969, pp. 304–6).

As strikers, women were involved in 87 sit-downs in Detroit alone in the two weeks after the GM victory.[57] The general strike against all the hosiery mills in the Reading, Pennsylvania, area in March 1937 also took the form of a sit-down. Many of the strikers were women, and other women—wives of the men on strike—organized auxiliaries and provided hot meals and other assistance to the strikers. The strike ended on April 23 with a wage scale acceptable to the American Federation of Hosiery Workers, union recognition, and arbitration of

---

[57] *Detroit Free Press*, May 7, 1937; *Daily Worker*, March 6, 1937.

disputes. It was the first collective bargaining agreement with major plants in the hosiery industry.[58]

During 1937 there were 477 sit-down strikes involving more than 300,000 workers. Many of the strikers were women who adopted this technique in hospitals, drug companies, restaurants, five-and-ten-cent stores, and other locations where they were employed.[59]

Largely as a result of CIO organizing drives, 800,000 women were union members in 1940, a sevenfold increase in six years as contrasted with a tripling of the number of organized males over the same period. To be sure, 800,000 was still only a minority of the 11 million women workers, but it was the largest number of female members of unions up to this time.[60]

World War II

In the year preceding the Japanese attack on Pearl Harbor and the U.S. Declaration of War against Japan, Germany, and Italy, comparatively few women were hired by defense plants although the war was on in Europe and American industries were tooling up. But with Pearl Harbor, the increasing labor demands, coupled with the effects of the draft, compelled the employment of many women. Between 1940 and 1945, the number of women in the labor force expanded from less than 14 million to slightly more than 20 million. At the peak, in 1945, women made up 38 percent of the work force, as compared with 25 percent before the war.[61]

In general, the CIO unions opened their doors to women during as before the war. In the AFL, as we have seen, there were a number of unions that had denied women admission. Pressured by both the government and the women workers themselves, a number of these unions—the International Association of Machinists, the Molders and Foundry Workers, the Iron Shipbuilders and Helpers, the Ironworkers, and the Carpenters and Joiners—revised their admission policies after Pearl Harbor. The International Brotherhood of Boilermakers, the most intransigent of the AFL unions, refused to reverse its opposition to women members until the fall of 1942.[62]

The Railroad Brotherhoods also proved to be among the most unyielding to pressures to abandon their opposition to women, but by the war's end not only had all AFL and CIO unions admitted women,

---

[58] *Daily Worker*, March 3, 1937; *Hosiery Worker*, March 5, April 9, 30, 1937; *Reading Times*, March 26, 1937.
[59] *CIO News*, September 17, 1938; *Daily Worker*, September 15, 1938.
[60] *CIO News*, May 21, 1938.
[61] *New York Times*, April 29, 1945; June 12, 1940; "Women at War," *Life*, June 5, 1944, p. 74.
[62] *Monthly Labor Review* (1942), p. 1006; *Labor*, September 22, 1942; Staub (1973), pp. 195–96.

but even the transportation brotherhoods had opened their doors at least a crack. As far as black women were concerned, the doors of many unions remained tightly closed. The CIO, with many black members and a national commitment to job equality, attacked this discrimination. While the AFL opposed discrimination in theory, individual union affiliates practiced it repeatedly. In June 1942 *Fortune* reported that 19 international unions, 10 of them affiliated with the AFL (but none with the CIO), practiced discrimination against black workers. Even when unions had nondiscrimination pledges in their charters, they continued to employ subtle means to exclude blacks.[63]

Great Rise in Women's Union Membership

Women's membership in unions had skyrocketed during the war. The Women's Bureau of the Department of Labor put the increase at from approximately 800,000 before the war to 3,500,000 at the end of 1944. Of this number, about 1,500,000 were in the CIO and 1,300,000 in the AFL. The rest were organized in independent unions. The total represented about 20 percent of the 18,600,000 women employed in all industries as of October 1944. As *Labor*, the organ of the railroad unions, declared: "Unionism is no longer a man's world. Over 3,000,000 women workers now carry union cards."[64]

Despite improvements in attitudes, the relations between unions and women workers during the war years were not always harmonious. A Women's Bureau agent reported that "union contracts often openly discriminate against women in such matters as wage rates and seniority rights, or, if the contract does not discriminate, it fails to call for equality so that discrimination results in practice." The Women's Bureau concluded that in spite of wartime gains and modifications, union contracts remained generally "inadequate for women."[65]

Many unions circumvented equal pay for equal work by negotiating differentials under a job classification system or by accepting lower wages for women when they worked in a shop separate from men. Unions often used seniority rights to restrict the employment of women, specifying in their contracts that the heaviest and dirtiest work should be given to new employees, while the lighter and easier jobs were to go only to those who had many years of service. This situation made it difficult to employ women in the industry. Some unions failed to grant women full union status and benefits, or allowed women to be

---

[63] *Fortune*, June 1942, p. 73; Foner (1982), pp. 256–57.
[64] U.S. Department of Labor Women's Bureau, Union Series No. 5 (1946), p. 146; *Labor*, May 24, 1946; *New York Times*, September 30, 1943; Wolfson (1943), pp. 54–56.
[65] Memo from Alice Angus to Miss Miller, July 26, 1944, File "Union Study, 1944," Container 19, Accession 55-A-556, National Archives; Staub (1973), pp. 205, 208.

admitted only for the duration of the war. Moreover, while national unions generally agreed to the principle of equality, locals often reacted differently.[66]

The key to women's problems with unions was the failure of the war emergency to erase old fears and suspicions that unions harbored about women workers. Many male union members were opposed to the employment of women in the persistent irrational belief that, regardless of the wartime emergency and their own financial need, women still belonged in the home, and bringing them into industry would result in lowered pay scales. Unions often thought of women as merely "until" workers. "They are always working until they get married, until they have a baby, until the house is paid off. . . ." Why spend money, time, and energy organizing such temporary workers? (Foner, 1980, pp. 387–88).

By no means, then, did World War II settle problems between unions and women workers. But some permanent gains were made. Many trade unionists came to accept women in both the work force and the union movement. The war period offered the first real opportunity for great numbers of women and unions to come together and gain some understanding of their common problems. For the first time, too, many trade union leaders began to bargain collectively for such female demands as rest periods, clean washrooms, day-care centers, and maternity leaves, as well as wages, hours, and working conditions.

Out of World War II there emerged, for the first time in American history, a mass movement of three million women trade unionists!

References

Adams, Graham, Jr. *Age of Industrial Violence, 1910–1915*. New York: Columbia University Press, 1966.

Andrews, John B., and Helen Bliss. *History of Women in Trade Unions, 1825 to the Knights of Labor*, Vol. 10 of U.S. Congress, Senate, "Report on Conditions of Women and Child Wage Earners in the United States," Senate Document 645, 61st Cong., 2d Sess., 1911.

Baker, Ross K. "Entry of Women into Federal Job World at a Price." *Smithsonian* 8 (July 1977): pp. 83–85.

Baxandall, Rosalyn Fraad. "Elizabeth Gurley Flynn, The Early Years." *Radical America* 8 (January-February 1975): pp. 90–102.

Berman, Hyman. "Era of the Protocol, A Chapter in the History of the International Ladies' Garment Workers' Union, 1910–1916." Ph.D. dissertation, Columbia University, 1956.

---

[66] U.S. Department of Labor, Women's Bureau (1945); Staub (1973), pp. 206–207; "Women and the Unions, January 19, 1944," Accession 68-A-6357, RG86, National Archives; Otto S. Beyer, "Restriction on Employment of Women Resulting from Seniority Rules and Similar Provisions in Collective Bargaining Agreements," July 12, 1943, General Classified Historical Records, Section RG211, National Archives.

Boone, Gladys. *The Women's Trade Union League in Great Britain and the United States of America.* New York: Columbia University Press, 1942.

Chafe, William H. *The American Woman: Her Changing Social, Economic, and Political Roles, 1920–1970.* New York: Oxford University Press, 1972.

Clark, Sue Aimsley, and Elizabeth Wyatt. "The Shirtwaist Makers and Their Strike." *McClure's Magazine* 36 (November 1910): pp. 70–86.

Cole, Donald B. *Immigrant City: Lawrence, Massachusetts, 1845–1921.* Chapel Hill: University of North Carolina Press, 1963.

Commons, John R., et al., eds. *A Documentary History of the American Industrial Society.* Cleveland: World Publishing Co., 1910.

"Controversies Regarding the Right of Women to Work as Conductors." In *Women Street Car Conductors and Ticket Agents.* Washington: U.S. Government Printing Office, 1921. Pp. 2–3.

Craton, Ann Washington. "Organizing the Woman Worker." *Nation* (March 23, 1927): pp. 312–13.

Davis, Allen F. *Spearheads for Reform: The Social Settlement and the Progressive Movement, 1890–1914.* New York: Columbia University Press, 1967.

Dawley, Alan. *Class and Community: The Industrial Revolution in Lynn.* Cambridge, MA: Harvard University Press, 1977.

Dubofsky, Melvyn. *When Workers Organize: New York City in the Progressive Era.* Amherst: University of Massachusetts Press, 1968.

Dubois, Ellen. "A New Life: The Development of an American Woman Suffrage Movement, 1860–1869." Ph.D. dissertation, Northwestern University, 1975.

Fine, Sidney. *Sit-Down: The General Motors Strike of 1936–1937.* Ann Arbor: University of Michigan Press, 1969.

Finney, John D., Jr. "A Study of Negro Labor During and After World War I." Ph.D. dissertation, Georgetown University, 1957.

Flynn, Elizabeth Gurley. *I Speak My Own Piece: The Autobiography of the "Rebel Girl."* New York: International Publishers, 1955.

Foner, Philip S. *Organized Labor and the Black Worker, 1619–1981.* New York: International Publishers, 1982.

————. *Women and the American Labor Movement: From World War I to the Present.* New York: Free Press, 1980.

————. *Women and the Labor Movement: From Colonial Times to the Eve of World War I.* New York: Free Press, 1979.

————. *The Fur and Leather Workers Union.* Newark: Norden Press, 1950.

————. *History of the Labor Movement in the United States,* Vols. 1, 2, 4. New York: International Publishers, 1947, 1955, 1965.

Foner, Philip S., ed. *The Factory Girls: A Collection.* Urbana: University of Illinois Press, 1977.

Gompers, Samuel. *Seventy Years of Life and Labor,* Vol. 1. New York: E.P. Dutton, 1925.

Gordon, Michael A. "The Labor Boycott in New York City, 1880–1886." *Labor History* 16 (Spring 1975): pp. 184–229.

Greenwald, Maurine Weinder. *Women, War, and Work: The Impact of World War I on Women Workers in the United States.* Westport, CT: Greenwood Press, 1980.

Haywood, William D. *Bill Haywood's Book: The Autobiography of William D. Haywood.* New York: International Publishers, 1929.

Henry, Alice. *Women and the Labor Movement.* New York: George H. Doran, 1923.

James, Edward T. "More Corn, Less Hell, A Knights of Labor Glimpse of Mary Elizabeth Lease." *Labor History* 16 (Summer 1975): pp. 408–24.

Kornbluh, Joyce L., ed. *Rebel Voices: An I.W.W. Anthology*. Ann Arbor: University of Michigan Press, 1964.

Kugler, Israel. "The Women's Rights Movement and the National Labor Union, 1866–1872." Ph.D. dissertation, New York University, 1954.

Levine, Irving. "The Lawrence Strike." Master's thesis, Columbia University, 1936.

Levine, Louis. *The Women's Garment Workers*. New York: B.W. Huebsch, 1924.

Levine, Susan. *Labor's True Woman: Carpet Weavers, Industrialization and Labor Reform in the Gilded Age*. Philadelphia: Temple University Press, 1984.

McCreesh, Carolyn Daniel. "On the Picket Lines: Militant Women Campaign to Organize Garment Workers, 1882–1919." Ph.D. dissertation, University of Maryland, 1975.

Montgomery, David. *Beyond Equality: Labor and the Radical Republicans*. New York: Alfred A. Knopf, 1967.

Monthly Labor Review. "Admission of Women to Union Membership." 55 (November 1942): pp. 100–06.

Morris, James O. *Conflict Within the AFL: A Study of Craft Versus Industrial Unionism, 1901–1938*. Ithaca, NY: Cornell University Press, 1938.

Ritter, Ellen M. "Elizabeth Morgan: Pioneer Female Labor Agitator." *Central States Speech Journal* 22 (Fall 1971): pp. 228–49.

Scharnau, Ralph. "Elizabeth Morgan, Crusader for Labor Reform." *Labor History* (Summer 1973): pp. 340–51.

Scott, Marian F. "What the Women Strikers Won." *Outlook* 95 (July 12, 1910): pp. 480–88.

Staub, Eleanor. "United States Government Policy Toward Civilian Women During World War II." Ph.D. dissertation, Emory University, 1973.

Steinberg, Linda. "Women Workers and the 1912 Textile Strike in Lawrence, Massachusetts." Unpublished paper, Hampshire College, April 28, 1975.

Sumner, Helen. *History of Women in Industry in the United States*, Vol. 9 of U.S. Congress, Senate, "Report on Conditions of Women and Child Wage Earners in the United States," Senate Document 645, 61st Cong., 2d Sess., 1910–1913.

Tomlins, Christopher L. "AFL Unions in the 1930's: Their Performance in Historical Perspective." *Journal of American History* 65 (March 1979): pp. 1021–42.

U.S. Department of Labor, Women's Bureau. *Handbook of Facts on Women Workers*. Bull. 225. Washington: U.S. Government Printing Office, 1948.

———. *Women's Occupations Through Seven Decades*. Bull. 218. Washington: U.S. Government Printing Office, 1947.

———. *Women's Stake in Unions*. Series No. 5. Washington: U.S. Government Printing Office, 1946.

———. *Status of Women in Unions in War Plants*. Series No. 1. Washington: U.S. Government Printing Office, 1945.

Van Kleeck, Mary, and Mary McDowell. *The New Position of Women in American Industry*. U.S. Department of Labor, Women's Bureau, Bull. 12. Washington: U.S. Government Printing Office, 1920.

Ware, Norman J. *The Industrial Worker, 1840–1860*. New York: Little Brown, 1924.

Wolfson, Theresa. "Aprons and Overalls in War." *Annals of the American Academy of Political and Social Science* 228 (September 1943): pp. 46–58.

———. "Trade Union Activities of Women." *Annals of the American Academy of Political and Social Science* (May 1929): 127–39.

———. *The Woman Worker and the Trade Unions*. New York: International Publishers, 1926.

Wolman, Leo. *The Growth of American Trade Unions, 1880–1923*. New York: National Bureau of Economic Research, 1924.

Zaretz, Charles Elbert. *The Amalgamated Clothing Workers of America*. New York: Ancon Publishing, 1934.

CHAPTER 7

Women in Unions:
Current Issues

RUTH NEEDLEMAN*
LUCRETIA DEWEY TANNER**

The focus of this chapter is on current issues and problems facing women in unions. Specifically, we discuss membership trends, identify bargaining issues, and trace the status of women in leadership positions. Among the pertinent questions addressed are: Do women join unions—why or why not? To what extent do women hold leadership positions at all levels of the organizations? What are women's collective bargaining concerns? What does the future hold for women and the labor movement?

Background and Membership Trends

Women joined the labor force in great numbers during World War II, and by the war's end, some three million of them were union members. With the nation's return to peace, however, they gave up their jobs to returning servicemen, just as they had following past wars, and for the most part they went back to being full-time homemakers or to the traditional female occupations of typist, clerical worker, sales clerk, nurse, teacher, waitress, and household worker. The civil rights and the women's movements of the 1960s and 1970s combined with economic necessity to bring substantial numbers of women back into the labor force. Unionization expanded at all levels of government, and a number of public-sector bargaining laws were enacted. Professional associations became more unionlike as their professional and economic concerns merged in formal relationships. It is against this background that we discuss the modern woman union member.

---

*Coordinator, Division of Labor Studies, Indiana University Northwest.
**Executive Director, Advisory Committee on Federal Pay.
Note: Tanner's comments in this chapter are her own opinions and are not those of the
Advisory Committee or the U.S. government.

Researchers have generally concluded that the number of female union members, while increasing in absolute and relative terms, has not kept pace with their entry into the labor force (LeGrande, 1978; Bergquist, 1974; Dewey, 1971). Our data for the number of women members begin with 1956, as shown in Table 1.[1] In that year there were 21.5 million women in the civilian labor force, accounting for close to one-third of all workers. By 1978 they numbered 42.6 million, or almost 42 percent of the civilian labor force. Statistics for 1985, as shown in Table 2, indicate that their labor force participation rate was even higher—46 percent. In 1956 there were 3.2 million women union members (14.9 percent of the labor force), and although their number had increased to 5.7 million by 1985, the percentage of female union members in the labor force had declined to 13.2 percent.[2]

The statistics clearly show, however, that the proportion of women among all union members is increasing. For example, in 1977, 28 percent of all union members were women; in 1985 the figure was 34 percent (see Table 2). This growth can be attributed to two factors—more women were joining unions and, equally important, union membership had declined by 10 percent in industries where most

---

[1] Longitudinal comparisons are becoming increasingly difficult for a number of reasons. The Bureau of Labor Statistics has long been the source of information and other data compiled from questionnaires returned to the Bureau by the various organizations. BLS expanded and refined its statistics in the post-World-War-II period (Mitchell, 1985), adding data on women union members in 1956 and on associations in 1970. In 1980 it combined the union and association data under the broad category of labor organizations and then divided the aggregate numbers into two groups. Although these data are the best available, they are subject to interpretation. For example, unions differed in whom they included in membership counts. Also, some were reluctant to report total membership, while others tended to inflate membership figures.

In early 1982 BLS announced that its biennial *Directory of National Unions and Employee Associations*, a primary source of information on labor organizations, was being discontinued for budgetary reasons. The Bureau of National Affairs, Inc. (BNA) contracted with BLS to use the 1980 questionnaires, and it published the *Directory of U.S. Labor Organizations, 1982–83*. The total number of women union members was included in that edition, but there were no major breakdowns of union membership by sex, industry, state, white-collar, or organization size in BNA's subsequent 1984–1985 edition.

BLS now relies on the U.S. Department of Commerce, Bureau of the Census, for official data, and a new series, containing annual averages of union membership for 1983 and 1984, was published in the January 1985 issue of the BLS publication *Employment and Earnings*; 1984 and 1985 membership statistics appear in the January 1986 issue. Census data are based on a survey of about 65,000 households in 629 areas. Because of survey and definitional differences between BLS and Census data, as well as the reported decline in the total number of union members, the Census figures show a lower membership count of about 2 million in 1984.

[2] Despite this apparent decline in the number of union members as a proportion of the civilian labor force, one factor that was not apparent in the earlier statistics and is not included in the Current Population Survey data in Table 2, is the persistent increase in women's membership in associations. Table 1 shows women's membership in unions and in unions and associations combined. The difference between the two is 1 million in 1970; by 1978 the difference had increased to 1.6 million. Thus, it is possible that the figures for union membership alone in Table 2 understate the number of women members by about 2 million, a reversal of what appears to be a downward trend. Table 1 shows that a higher proportion of women in the labor force were union and association members in 1978 than in previous years. This difference is attributed to the exclusion of union members outside the United States up to 1976 and their inclusion in the 1978 totals.

TABLE 1
Labor Force Participation and National Union and Association
Membership of Women, Selected Years 1956–1978
(totals in millions)

Year	Civilian Labor Force			Membership—Unions and Associations		
	Total	Women	Percent Women	Total Women	Percent Women	Women Membership as a % of All Women in Labor Force
1970	82.7	31.5	38.1	5.0	23.9	16.0
1972	86.5	33.3	38.5	5.3	24.9	16.0
1974	91.0	35.8	19.4	5.7	25.0	15.8
1976	94.8	38.4	40.5	6.1	26.7	15.9
1978	102.3	42.6	41.6	6.9	28.1	16.6
				Membership—Unions		
1956	66.6	21.5	32.2	3.2	18.5	14.9
1958	67.6	22.1	32.7	3.1	18.2	13.8
1960	69.6	23.2	33.4	3.1	18.3	13.1
1962	70.6	24.0	34.0	3.1	18.6	12.8
1964	73.1	25.4	34.8	3.2	19.1	12.5
1966	75.8	27.3	36.0	3.4	19.3	12.6
1968	78.7	29.2	37.1	3.7	19.5	12.5
1970	82.7	31.5	38.1	4.0	20.7	12.6
1972	86.5	33.3	38.5	4.2	21.7	12.6
1974	91.0	35.8	39.4	4.3	21.3	11.9
1976	94.8	38.4	40.5	4.3	22.2	11.3
1978	102.6	42.6	41.6	5.3	24.2	12.4

Sources: Data are taken from several sources and may not be completely compatible.
1956–76 data are from LeGrande (1978); 1978 data are from U.S. Department of Labor, Bureau of
Labor Statistics, *Directory of National Unions and Employee Associations, 1979* (1980).

trade unionists were male. Even among women, membership in absolute numbers has declined by 176,000, or 3 percent, between 1983
and 1985.

Most of these female members can be found in only a few unions.
According to Dewey (1971), women members of no more than 21
unions accounted for three-quarters of all female trade unionists in
both 1958 and 1968. Four unions accounted for almost half of them.
During that decade, unions with women members represented workers in a variety of major employment areas—metals and machinery,
clothing, communications, transportation, services, trade, and government. By 1978 it was apparent that women were becoming members of more unions. As shown below, the number and percentage of
unions representing no women or having less than 10 percent of their
membership female decreased over the 22-year period.

TABLE 2
Employment of Wage and Salary Workers
by Union Affiliation and Sex, 1977, 1983, 1985

	1977	1983	1985
	(in millions)		
Total employed	81,334	88,290	94,521
Union members	19,335	17,717	16,996
Percent of total	26.5	20.1	18.0
Women employed	32,940	40,433	43,506
Percent of total employed	40.5	45.8	46.0
Women union members	5,329	5,908	5,732
Percent of total employed	16.2	14.6	13.2
Percent of total membership	27.6	33.3	33.7
Women members by race			
White	4,307	4,710	4,501
Black	1,021	1,020	1,058
Hispanic	—	336	333

Sources: For 1977 data, Earnings and Other Characteristics of Organized Workers, May 1977, BLS Report No. 556 (1979); for 1983 data, Employment and Earnings (January 1985), p. 206; for 1985 data, Employment and Earnings (January 1986), p. 213.

Unions reporting an all-male membership in both 1956 and 1978 were the Brotherhood of Maintenance of Way Employees; the Brotherhood of Locomotive Engineers; the United Slate, Tile and Composition Roofers, Damp and Waterproof Workers Association; and the Flight Engineers International Association. It should be pointed out, however, that these unions represent workers in occupations where women traditionally have not been employed (LeGrande, 1978).

Despite the growing dispersion of women among the 208 unions and associations, large numbers of female union members continue to be concentrated in only a few organizations. Eight of them, each with 300,000 or more women members, represent a combined total of 3.8 million women, or close to 60 percent of the total number of female trade unionists. These organizations are the National Education Association (NEA); the International Brotherhood of Teamsters,

	1956	% of Total	1978	% of Total
Total unions and associations	188	100	208	100
No women members	51	27	18	9
Under 10 percent	54	29	60	29

Sources: LeGrande (1978); U.S. Department of Labor, Bureau of Labor Statistics, Directory of National Unions and Employee Associations, 1979 (1980).

Chauffeurs, Warehousemen and Helpers of America (IBT); the American Federation of State, County and Municipal Employees (AFSCME); the United Food and Commercial Workers Union (UFCWU); the Amalgamated Clothing and Textile Workers Union (ACTWU); the Service Employees International Union (SEIU); the International Brotherhood of Electrical Workers (IBEW); and the American Federation of Teachers (AFT). Table 3 lists 47 organizations having at least 10,000 female members and the proportion of women in each.

Women have not made significant inroads into the higher-paying craft and construction jobs and the unions that represent these workers. A 1982 Equal Employment Opportunity Commission (EEOC) report shows that in 1979 only 5 percent of the 176,829 apprentices were women. Unions participating in job-referral programs at that time had a combined membership of 2.2 million, of whom 254,341 were women and 563,122 were black or Hispanic. The building trades unions claimed a combined membership of 1.5 million, including 24,000 women. Although most of the unions participating in the job-referral programs were in the building trades, there were few women apprentices. Rather, most of the women participated in the job-referral programs offered by the Hotel and Restaurant Employees Union (HREU), the International Ladies' Garment Workers' Union (ILGWU), the Teamsters, and the Retail Clerks International Union, now part of the UFCWU (Equal Employment Opportunity Commission, 1982).

Profile of a Woman Member

Approximately three of every five female union members are between the ages of 25 and 44; 15 percent are older and 10 percent are younger (this age distribution applies to male unionists as well). A majority of both female and male union members are white, but it should be noted that only 18 percent of all white wage and salary workers who are potential union members actually join unions. The proportions for blacks and Hispanics are far higher. About 30 percent of all employed black men are union members, the highest proportion of any group. Hispanic men rank second with 24 percent, followed by black women, 22 percent; white men, 22 percent; Hispanic women, 16 percent; and white women, 12 percent.

The industry with the highest proportion of women union members—about one-third—is federal, state, or local government where most of the employment and membership growth has occurred within the past 20–25 years. Ranking almost as high is the degree of organizations in transportation, communications, and public utilities, with a heavy concentration in the telecommunications systems. Another

TABLE 3
Approximate Number and Percent of Women in National Unions
and Employee Associations with 10,000 or More Women Members, 1978

Organization	Number of Women Members	Women as Percent of Total Union Membership
AFL-CIO		
Actors	36,000	46
Flight Attendants	17,000	90
Automobile Workers[a]	165,000	11
Bakery, Confectionary[b]	56,000	34
Chemical Workers	13,000	20
Clothing, Textile	331,000	66
Communications Workers	259,000	51
Electrical Workers (IBEW)	304,000	30
Electrical Workers (IUE)	102,000	40
Garment Workers	23,000	92
Glass, Bottles	25,000	38
Government Workers (AFGE)	130,000	49
Hotel & Restaurant	181,000	42
Industrial Workers	31,000	38
Ladies Garment	279,000	80
Laundry, Dry Cleaning	16,000	94
Leather Goods, Plastic	18,000	60
Machinists	119,000	13
Newspaper Guild	12,000	—
Office Employees	66,000	61
Oil Chemical	27,000	10
Postal Workers	80,000	33
Railway Clerks	49,000	26
Retail Clerks[c]—Food & Commercial	480,000	39
Retail, Wholesale	79,000	40
Service Employees	313,000	50
Shoe, United[d]	17,000	69
State, County	408,000	40
Steelworkers	163,000	13
Teachers	300,000	60
Theatrical, Stage Workers	12,000	16
Toys Union[e]	13,000	53
Transport Workers*	23,000	15
Upholsterers	14,000	28
Unaffiliated		
Distributive Workers*	16,000	40
Electrical Workers (UE)	42,000	25
Federal Employees (NFFE)	26,000	50
Government Workers (NAGE)	45,000	29
Longshoremen, Warehousemen*	4,000	18
Postmasters League*	10,000	50
Retail Workers	15,000	70
Teamsters	481,000	25

TABLE 3 (*Continued*)

Organization	Number of Women Members	Women as Percent of Total Union Membership
Employee Associations		
Classified School Employees	96,000	64
Education Association*	1,240,000	66
Licensed Practical Nurses	18,000	98
Nurses Association	181,000	96
University Professors*	16,000	23

Sources: U.S. Department of Labor, Bureau of Labor Statistics, *Directory of National Unions and Employee Associations, 1979* (1980). For those entries marked by *, the source was the 1977 *Directory*.
  a In 1978, UAW was unaffiliated; it reaffiliated with the AFL-CIO in July 1981.
  b Merged to form the United Bakery, Confectionary and Tobacco Workers International Union, February 1978.
  c Merged with the Meat Cutters and Butcher Workmen of North America to form the United Food and Commercial Workers International Union, August 1979.
  d Merged to form the Amalgamated Clothing and Textile Workers Union, March 1979.
  e Name changed to International Union Novelty Production Workers, February 1978.

19 percent of women members are employed in manufacturing industries, as shown in Table 4.

Membership varies by industry and by occupation within each industry. In 1980, for example, only 19 percent of all clerical workers were union members, yet 49 percent were organized in transportation and utilities and 43 percent in all levels of government. Forty-two percent of women in government managerial and professional occupations held union memberships, compared with 34 percent of the men (Adams, 1985). Thus, the profile of today's union member suggests that she is more likely to be white (although more employed black women are members), between the ages of 25 and 44, and working either for the government or in the transportation, communications, and public utilities industries.

A Closer Look at Women Members

Although a number of unions have women members, occupational segregation still determines, to a great degree, whether a woman will be a union member. The following summaries highlight the concerns of women members in selected occupations and industries.

Airlines—Flight Attendants. The airline industry provides some good examples of the problems women face in unions and in the work force. Few, if any, women belong to the Air Line Pilots Association

TABLE 4
Employed Wage and Salary Workers by Union Membership,
Industry, and Sex, September 1984

	Total Employed (in millions)	Percent Union Members	
		Men	Women
All industries	91,331	23.3	14.1
Private sector			
Total[1]	75,582	20.5	9.5
Mining	903	21.4	2.1
Construction	4,413	26.1	4.9
Manufacturing	20,038	30.2	18.9
Transportation, communication, and public works	5,414	42.5	32.1
Wholesale and retail trade	18,680	9.8	6.4
Finance, insurance, and real estate	5,753	3.5	2.2
Service	18,948	8.7	6.3
Government	15,748	38.9	33.1

Source: Adams (1985), p. 29.
[1] Includes agriculture, forestry, and fisheries not shown separately.

(ALPA). By contrast, until very recently the occupation of cabin attendant (or stewardess) was female-dominated. Although the number of attendants is small compared with most occupations, this group shows the evolution of work attitudes—from acceptance of short-term employment to full-scale job commitment. These changes have led to unionization and away from male dominance within the pilots' union and in negotiations, with the flight attendants becoming an important force in collective bargaining and gaining recognition within the labor community.

Until 1942 women were excluded from membership in the pilots' union by its constitution. Both the pilots and the industry were opposed to having women in the cockpit, except to serve coffee or tea. During the early years of aviation, female cabin attendants were trained nurses, but as the industry's technology advanced, the job requirements changed and hiring was then limited to only young, well-groomed, attractive, unmarried women. "The vestal virgins of the air were not expected to stay beyond the usual tenure of eighteen months before they found suitable husbands" (Nielsen, 1982).

Overtime pay, grievances, and unjust dismissals prompted some of the attendants to organize their own unions during the mid-1940s. The first contracts between a carrier and the stewardess-steward craft, signed in 1946, limited flight hours, granted access to personnel files, and eliminated arbitrary disciplinary actions and dismissals.

Collective bargaining alone, however, could not change the "no marriage" rule, and groups turned to the Equal Employment Opportunity Commission, which determined in 1968 that the rule was based on sex discrimination and violated Title VII of the Civil Rights Act of 1964. In 1982 a federal district judge ruled that those attendants who had left United Airlines involuntarily in the 1960s could be reinstated with the seniority they had at the time they left (Nielsen, p. 93).

By the early 1970s the question of whether sex was a bona fide occupational qualification for the job was no longer an issue, and during the decade most U.S. carriers gave up the 32–35 maximum age requirement for flying. A district court ruled in 1979 that United discriminated against women in the application of its maximum weight regulation (Nielsen, p. 100).

As flight attendants won the right to remain employed despite age and marital status, they became more job conscious and concerned with long-range goals, including pensions. As an example, in 1968 only 5 percent of the Pan Am flight attendants were married, only 600 were over 30, and 90 percent were female. By early 1977, 40 percent were married, 2,200 were over 30, 40 percent were in the pension plan, and 10 to 15 percent were male (Kahn, 1980).

The relationship between the pilots' and the attendants' organizations had been tenuous at best. Although the pilots chartered the Air Line Stewards and Stewardesses Association (ALSSA), albeit reluctantly, in 1946, and later, in 1950, the independent Airline Stewardesses joined ALSSA to become part of the pilots' organization, this affiliation became a source of friction for both groups. The stewardesses did not want to be dominated by the pilots, and the pilots were concerned that since the stewardesses outnumbered them, they could end up controlling the union. Between 1973 and 1975, the flight attendants gained the transfer of certified bargaining rights from the pilots' union to their own group. Finally, the uneasy alliance was terminated when the Association of Flight Attendants sought and received a separate charter from the AFL-CIO in 1984 and became the only federation affiliate headed by a woman.[3]

The current issue facing the flight attendants, pilots, and employees in other industries as well, is the spread of the two-tier wage structure. Under this plan, newly hired employees receive less than the full rate and may or may not attain the same rate as senior people, depending on the negotiated terms. Faced with deregulation, intense nonunion competition, and the need to hold down costs, carriers have successfully instituted two-tier pay systems. Yet, reports indicate that

---

[3] *Flightlog*, Association of Flight Attendants, Winter 1985, p. 5.

along with savings have come higher turnover rates, recruiting and morale problems, and friction within the work force (Wessel, 1985).

Health-Care Workers. The already sizable health-care industry has continued to grow; it accounted for approximately 11 percent of the 1984 GNP and 8 percent of nonagricultural employment.[4] The work force is predominantly female (about 76 percent of the 8 million employees), with blacks and Hispanics being overrepresented as well. About 17 percent of all hospital workers and 11 percent of those employed in other health services are members of minority groups.[5] The industry structure is a pronounced pyramid, with highly paid physicians, professionals, and dentists at the top, nurses and pharmacists in the middle, and large numbers of low-skill, low-wage employees at the bottom. Until recently, most physicians and other highly paid professionals were male.

Widespread collective bargaining in hospitals, nursing homes, and other health-care facilities is a contemporary development. Until the late 1960s only about 9 percent of all hospital workers were represented by labor organizations; in 1977 the figure was 20 percent, and in some areas, such as San Francisco and the Bay area, Minneapolis-St. Paul, and New York City, the figures are now much higher (Miller, 1980). According to current estimates, 13 percent of private and 37 percent of public medical-sector workers are organized.[6]

One study identified 40 organizations in the health field, although three unions dominate—the Service Employees International Union, AFL-CIO (SEIU), Local 1199 National Union of Hospital and Health Care Employees, and state affiliates of the American Nurses Association (Tanner, Weinstein, and Ahmuty, 1979).

SEIU's involvement in the health-care industry dates from the early 1930s, and the union represents the largest number of health-care workers—currently about 300,000 people. Most of them are aides, orderlies, kitchen help, and maintenance workers, but the union also has organized significant numbers of technical and professional employees, including registered nurses and doctors.

Local 1199, originally a small union of 5,000 pharmacists and drug-store employees in New York City, began organizing health-care workers in 1958 and perhaps more than any other union is identified with merging the civil rights and union movements. The best example of this merging of interests occurred in Charleston, South Carolina,

---

[4] *Statistical Abstract,* 1986.
[5] U.S. Department of Labor, Bureau of Labor Statistics, *Employment and Earnings* (January 1985), Table 28, p. 189.
[6] Bureau of National Affairs, Inc., *Government Employee Relations Report* (GERR), Vol. 23, No. 1123, p. 1089.

when a strike of 400 hospital workers, almost all of them black, spread across the city and captured the nation's attention. In this 1969 strike the Southern Christian Leadership Conference and Local 1199 forged an alliance that gained a wage increase and other benefits for the workers and provided an example of what could be achieved by united action (Foner, 1980). Expanding from the New York City area, Local 1199 organized up and down the East Coast. Like the SEIU, it represents both professional and nonprofessional hospital workers.

Nursing, along with teaching, is one of the few professions that has long been open to women, and today both are still predominantly female. The American Nurses Association (ANA), founded in 1896, considered itself a professional organization for many years and was ambivalent about assuming a role in collective bargaining. Its California affiliate, however, negotiated a first contract with the San Francisco Bay Hospitals in 1946. The ANA maintained an official no-strike policy until 1968; in 1984 it went on record as strongly supporting the Minnesota nurses' 39-day strike, the longest in its history. The primary issue in this strike was job security and rules governing layoffs.[7]

While wages are clearly the top issue in health-care negotiations for all groups, union security, working conditions, hours of work, and the grievance procedure are also important topics. Patient-care issues and the formation of formal committees to discuss ongoing concerns are also on the nurses' agenda for bargaining. They, too, have joined the pay equity controversy and sued the State of Illinois, although a federal district court dismissed the case.[8]

As already noted, health care has been a growth industry. However, recent government efforts to curb rising health-care costs may motivate a leveling-off or even a decline in employment. As economy measures and hospital closings increase, job protection is becoming a primary issue, as it has been in other declining industries. It may even become the dominant issue around the country, and the Minneapolis nurses' strike over jobs may be a forecast of the severity of future disputes.

The Public Sector. As public-sector employment grew in the 1960s and 1970s, union membership at the federal, state, and local levels accelerated. Even in the 1980s when union membership in general was declining, the public-sector unions, while not making the giant strides they once did, at least maintained a steady proportion of the work force as members.

By way of example, in 1956 only 5 percent of all union members— less than 1 million out of a total 18.1 million—were government

---

[7] GERR, Vol. 22, No. 1072, pp. 1434–35.
[8] *American Nurses Ass'n v. Illinois*, 606 F. Supp. 1313, 37 FEP Cases 705 (D. Ill. 1985).

employees; by 1968, membership in public-sector unions had increased to 2.2 million, or 11 percent of the total (Cohany and Dewey,
1970), and by 1984 there were 5.7 million government workers who
were union members, or one-third of the 17.4 million total. Half of the
public-sector work force are women, although the percentages vary by
level of government. Thirty-five percent of federal government employees are women; the figure for the state level is 46 percent, and for
the local level it is 56 percent.

The surge of union organization in the public sector can be attributed to several factors. One was the militancy of the civil rights
movement, dramatized by the 1968 walkout of sanitation workers in
Memphis, Tennessee. A second was President Kennedy's Executive
Order 10988 in 1962, sanctioning unionization only in the federal
government but having an impact as well on other levels of government. Third was the fact that public-sector wages were falling behind
those paid in the private sector and also were failing to keep pace with
inflation. States, too, enacted laws permitting public employees to
organize and bargain collectively. By 1984, 40 states and the District of
Columbia had enacted such legislation, and 10 of them even permitted
strikes under certain conditions (U.S. Department of Labor, Labor
Management Services Administration, March 1981).

Several public employee unions have had dramatic growth rates.
Membership in the American Federation of State, County and Municipal Employees (AFSCME) increased from 212,000 to over 1 million
in just two decades at a time when most other unions were losing
members. AFSCME, with a cross-section of state and local government workers in its ranks, represents growing numbers of women,
now more than 400,000 in a total membership of some 900,000 (see Table 3). Equally impressive have been the gains of the two major
teachers' organizations.

Teaching. Classroom teaching is another of the few professions
where women were welcomed. Societal changes and declines in real
income and status in the 1960s led teachers to organize in large numbers. The National Education Association (NEA) and the American
Federation of Teachers, AFL-CIO (AFT) grew from a combined membership of 1.2 million in 1968 to 2.2 million in 1984.[9] Until the late
1960s, the NEA considered itself a professional association and reluctantly engaged in collective bargaining. But NEA's posture changed,
and the two organizations of teachers, frequently the subject of merger

---

[9] The 2.2 million figure is based on membership for the two groups reported in the BNA
publication, *Directory of U.S. Labor Organizations,* 1984–85 edition. AFT reported 574,000
members, and the NEA, 1,641,000.

rumors, have many similarities, although they still maintain an adversarial relationship.

The teaching profession has come under severe attack in recent years. A decline in the quality of teachers has been alleged, and their competence in the classroom has been questioned in several reports.[10] Both the NEA and the AFT have responded to the charges by expressing their concern for quality education, including recruiting and retaining quality teachers, limiting class sizes, and gaining control over the classroom environment and curriculum as well as for the improvement in pay levels.

With the renewed focus on education, not unlike that of the post-Sputnik era of the 1960s, the teacher organizations have publicized their depressed salary levels as compared with those of other professions, and the need for increases. A 1983–1984 study by the NEA found that the average base salary of its 1.7 million members was $14,500 and urged a base of $24,000.[11] During its convention, the AFT called for increases of at least $6,000 to $8,000 in the pay of beginning teachers. It also advocated eliminating the current 10 to 20 years it takes to reach the top of the grade and compressing the number of annual pay adjustments into 3 to 5 years instead.

Merit or incentive pay to reward outstanding teachers has been forced upon both organizations as a primary bargaining agenda item, although both initially opposed or were unreceptive to the concept. However, the public's strong stand favoring the improvement of education, better teachers, and higher test scores persuaded them to change positions on the issue of merit pay.[12]

Bargaining Issues

Are women's concerns the same as men's? Evidence suggests that the answer is both yes and no. History shows that early efforts to organize women in the needle trades, the garment industry, and more recently in health care and teaching focused on wages, promotions, job training, and improving working conditions—the same issues that prompted men to organize. Women, however, also have specific needs, such as the elimination of discrimination, equal pay for work of equal or comparable value, protection against harmful work environments and sexual harassment, provision of child care, and flexible working arrangements. Some of the major issues are discussed in the following sections.

---

[10] GERR, Vol. 21, No. 1012, p. 1002, and Vol. 23, No. 1105, p. 394.
[11] GERR, Vol. 22, No. 1364, p. 1379.
[12] GERR, Vol. 22, No. 1077, p. 1662; Richburg (1985).

Earnings

While union membership affects the status of women in many ways, perhaps it can best be seen in the large and pervasive income disparities between union members and other employed women. Women members earn about 26 percent more than nonmembers. It is also true, however, that the earnings of men are consistently and disproportionately higher than those of women, whether union members or not; they were in 1966 and 1970 (Raphael, 1974) and they continued to be in 1983–1984 (Adams, 1985).

There is a distinct hierarchy of earnings for all men and women, organized or not, with men—white, black, and Hispanic—earning more than women—white, black, or Hispanic. A deviation occurred in 1985, when unionized Hispanics earned $10 a week more than black union members. It should be noted, however, that when the wages of white men and women union members are compared, the women's wages are 75 percent of male wages; for nonunion women, the figure is 68 percent. Black and Hispanic female union members also earn more than their unorganized counterparts—27 and 25 percent more, respectively. However, the gap between unionized black men and women is 20 percent; for Hispanics it is 38 percent.

The greatest financial benefits from union membership appear to go to Hispanic and black men as well as to all women, with white males trailing.

Pay Equity

Pay equity or comparable worth is the most controversial and emotionally charged issue to emerge in recent years. Critics call it a "looney tunes idea" and an attempt to "redistribute the wealth." Supporters embrace it as one of the most important issues facing women and the family in this decade.

The issue has captured labor's as well as the public's interest. Some unions use pay equity as a device for rallying support, launching campaigns, and energizing a labor movement looking for a focus. They are pursuing pay equity at the bargaining table, through legislation, and, where necessary, in the courts.

One pay-equity pioneer is the American Federation of State, County and Municipal Employees. Its most dramatic and landmark case involved the State of Washington. Under pressure from AFSCME, the state agreed in 1974 to commission a study to determine whether pay inequities existed between male and female state employees. The study found that there were substantial inequities in the pay for male- and female-dominated jobs having comparable numbers of evaluation points. When the state refused to correct the inequities,

AFSCME filed a suit with the Equal Employment Opportunity Commission and in a federal district court. Initially the court supported the union's position, but that decision was overturned in 1985. Rather than continue litigation, the parties reached an out-of-court settlement establishing a $42 million fund to correct differentials.

AFSCME's 1977 strike against the City of San Jose, California, to achieve pay equity also focused national attention on the pay-differential issue. After a nine-day strike, the parties agreed to study the city's internal pay system. This evaluation showed that female jobs paid an average of 18 percent less than male jobs of equal value. During negotiations, the city agreed to provide $1.5 million for adjustments amounting to 5 to 15 percent over the two-year period of the contract for the 60 female-dominated job classifications, in addition to a general across-the-board increase for the entire bargaining unit. More recent contracts between the local and the city provide for additional pay-equity adjustments.[13]

The Service Employees International Union has also been actively pursuing pay-equity issues for its members, winning important court cases in California. That this issue is attracting increasing attention is indicated by a 1984 Bureau of National Affairs, Inc., survey which showed that more than 20 states had enacted legislation to study the problem or had begun to eliminate pay inequities. Numerous bills have been introduced in Congress, including some that could affect private-sector pay systems.[14]

The issue of pay equity has generally been confined to the public sector which is highly organized and where there are substantial numbers of women workers and union members. Whether this issue will spread more generally into the private sector is still unclear. Except in certain industries, women are less organized and may not be represented in sufficient numbers for pay equity to be at the top of the list of bargaining demands. Yet this issue may spur the formation of "9 to 5" type organizations which eventually could affiliate with established unions. While the final chapter on pay equity has not been written, it is clear that the issue will not disappear.

Discrimination

Unions reflect society's values and thus were slow to support equal employment opportunity for women. Before the Civil Rights Act of 1964, some unions and employers negotiated separate male and female classifications and senority lists. Eventually these unions re-

---

[13] GERR, Vol. 23, No. 1118, pp. 889–90.
[14] Bureau of National Affairs, Inc., "Pay Equity and Comparable Worth," a BNA Special Report (August 1984). For further discussion of pay equity, see Koziara, Chapter 13.

versed their opposition, and today many are staunch advocates of women's rights. This change in outlook is demonstrated by the fact that almost all collectively bargained contracts now contain provisions against discrimination. A Bureau of National Affairs, Inc., survey of 400 contracts—a cross-section by geographic area, union, and industry—showed an increase of antidiscrimination clauses over the years. Guarantees of equal opportunities appeared in 69 percent of the agreements in 1970, 83 percent in 1975, and 94 percent in 1983.[15]

Women members have also sought enforcement of their rights through the grievance procedure, by filing charges with federal and state agencies, by taking their cases to court, and by turning to the Equal Employment Opportunity Commission to bring suits against unions. Although the number of charges of the latter type increased eightfold between 1970 and 1982, it still represents only 3 percent of the total number of complaints received by the EEOC from the private and public sectors combined.[16]

Sexual Harassment

Under Title VII of the Civil Rights Act of 1964, sexual harassment is prohibited as a type of sex discrimination. Those seeking redress in court under this title usually have been victims of sexual harassment by another individual. Yet it is interesting to note that arbitration cases involving sexual harassment in the private sector are less often based on grievances filed by victims, but rather more frequently involve grievances challenging the discharge or discipline of an employee for misconduct—alleged sexual harassment. While many arbitrators have upheld the discharge or discipline, others have reduced the penalty (Elkouri and Elkouri, 1985).

According to one study, most of the victims are clerical workers and more than half are sole supporters of their families. At least 10 states and the District of Columbia have adopted laws or regulations prohibiting sexual harassment in the workplace (Smith, 1983).

Unions have been active in sensitizing their members to the sexual harassment issue. An example of such activity is the videotape on sexual harassment in the workplace developed by the United Auto Workers (interviews).

Child Care/Parental Leave

Another issue facing working women is the problem of finding suitable child care. Almost universally, women are coping on an indi-

---

[15] Bureau of National Affairs, Inc., *Basic Patterns in Union Contracts*, 11th ed. (Washington: 1986) pp. 130–31.
[16] Equal Employment Opportunity Commission, *17th Annual Report* (Washington: April 1983).

vidual basis—considering themselves fortunate when they find good dependable care and distraught when none is available.

One Bureau of Labor Statistics study of large and medium-sized firms found that child care (full or partial defrayment of the cost of nursery, day-care, or babysitter services for employees' children) was an almost nonexistent benefit, available to only 1 percent of workers.[17] According to another study, by the Employee Benefit Research Institute, only 1,800 of the nation's 6 million employers offered child-care services in 1984.[18] However, they found that this small number represented a threefold increase since 1982, and they predict that over the next decade, as the female work force expands and the child population rises, more employers will be offering child-care benefits. Those few employers with such programs in place point to the advantages—a decrease in employee turnover and absenteeism, improved morale and motivation, and an aid in attracting new employees.

With these advantages known, why is the benefit not more widely offered? One reason is that only 4 to 10 percent of all employees need child care at any given time. A survey of women, both trade unionists and the general public, found that neither group believed that child care was a pressing problem, although they favored a national, federally subsidized, day-care program for children under school age (Nelson, 1986). Women generally have been reluctant to place children—particularly very young children—in centers, preferring care in their own homes or in someone else's home nearby.

Unions have not actively pressed for this benefit, except on a piecemeal basis. The Amalgamated Clothing and Textile Workers Union operates five centers that are funded by an employer payroll tax.[19] The New York City Service Employees Associations, affiliated with AFSCME, negotiates with the state for four day-care centers.[20] The American Federation of Government Employees plans to operate child-care centers in three cities where there are large numbers of federal employees.[21]

As child care becomes a family issue, a new concern is for "parental leave."[22] The United Mine Workers, a union historically with few women members and no publicly stated commitment to social issues, was one of a number of unions strongly favoring passage of a 1985 bill that would have required employers to allow up to 18 weeks of unpaid leave to enable a parent to care for a newborn, newly adopted, or ill

---

[17] *Employee Benefits in Industry 1980*, Bull. 2107 (Washington: U.S. Department of Labor, Bureau of Labor Statistics, September 1981).

[18] "Employers Offer More Child Care," *New York Times*, May 16, 1985.

[19] See Ratner and Cook (1981).

[20] GERR, Vol. 22, No. 1046, p. 135, and Vol. 23, No. 1128, pp. 1243–44.

[21] *Federal Employees News Digest*, February 18, 1985, p. 4.

[22] For further discussion of this issue, see Koziara, Chapter 13, in this volume.

child. Although only 1,500 of 250,000 UMW members are women, their local unions and the national convention supported parental leave as a national bargaining goal (Mann, 1985).

Health and Safety

Health and safety have long been union concerns, and organized labor has campaigned actively for protective legislation, reduced hours, overtime penalties, protective clothing, and clean and hazard-free workplaces. Recent technological change and the growing use of video display terminals (VDTs) raise questions about the impact of the technologies on the operator's health. Some coordinated efforts have been developed to regulate the uses of VDTs and to safeguard employees using them. In 1983, SEIU and the 9 to 5, National Association of Working Women, launched an 18-state "Campaign of VDT Safety." The Communications Workers and the Newspaper Guild have lobbied in at least six states. Success was achieved in New Mexico when the governor issued a regulation affecting 4,600 state workers.[23]

Other Issues

The preceding discussion only touches on some of the major issues that are of concern to women workers. Among others that should be added are: general economic conditions, including inflation and unemployment, the adequacy of pension plans, shorter workweeks, and comprehensive health insurance coverage. And there are more. Women are seeking respect and the elimination of favoritism. They are concerned about the nature and amount of work and about the atmosphere of the workplace, and they seek maternity benefits, promotional opportunities, and on-the-job training.

Women in Leadership Positions

Women are barely visible at the union movement's national level, but increasing numbers of them are appearing in leadership positions in locals and in regional organizations. Pressures on unions to include women in important decision-making positions within international unions and employee associations are greater than ever before. In fact, every major union has been affected to some degree by the grass-roots drive for visible female representation. This is partly because female union membership is rising more rapidly than male membership and because unions are focusing their organizing campaigns on women workers. In addition, women have built networks within unions, taken

---

[23] GERR, Vol., 23, No. 1109, pp. 556–57.

advantage of leadership training programs, and captured significant numbers of local leadership posts.

Because of the lack of relevant statistics, there is no accurate measure of women's progress over the past decade.[24] The 1978 national survey conducted by the Bureau of Labor Statistics found women occupying 25 percent of the leadership positions in associations, but only 6.6 percent in unions.[25] The percentage of female leaders in unions and associations combined was 10.7 (Schwartz and Hoyman, 1984).

In the decades of the 1950s and 1960s, the proportion of women in top leadership posts remained relatively stable, at 4.7 percent (Dewey, 1971). By the early 1970s, 7 percent of the national leadership was female (Kenneally, 1981; Bergquist, 1974); the number had inched up to 10.7 percent by 1978.[26] The percentages after 1970, however, include employee associations like the National Education Association and the American Nurses Association which have significantly higher percentages of women members and leaders than do unions (LeGrande, 1978; Bergquist, 1974; Dewey, 1971).

It is important to note that many of the gains were in appointive, not elective, positions, For example, in 1968 there were 48 women who had been elected or appointed to positions in international unions, 12 more than in 1958. The recorded increase, however, was the result of a change in Department of Labor data. Three new departments (legal, legislative, and public relations) had been added to the base, and all of the women in these positions had been appointed (Dewey, 1971). In fact, the number of women in elective positions dropped from 13 to 12 between 1958 and 1968 and all 12 were secretary-treasurers. By 1976 there were 9 more women in leadership positions, for a total of 57, only 7 of whom had been elected. The rest had been appointed (see Table 5). Employee associations, not unions, accounted for the increase in the number of elected women leaders (LeGrande, 1978).

At the highest echelon of the AFL-CIO, the national Executive Council, 2 women served in 1985 and a third was elected in 1987, along with 35 white males. To bring about the inclusion of women on the Council, the AFL-CIO set up a special subcommittee in 1979. This

---

[24] As previously noted, the Bureau of Labor Statistics stopped collecting data on female union membership and leadership in 1980. Most unions have not updated records, and among those who have, many choose not to release the information. Much of the data collected for this section of the chapter comes from interviews with high-ranking union officers. Since many requested anonymity, interview citations do not include name and date.

[25] This figure represents top officers only. If female representation on executive boards is added to totals, then associations have 35.5 percent female representation, and unions have 7.2 percent (Schwartz and Hoyman, 1984, p. 70).

[26] There are still some unions with more than 70 percent female membership that have less than 10 percent female leadership at national and regional levels (Baden, 1986).

TABLE 5
Selected Union Offices Held by Women,
by Election or Appointment, 1958, 1968, 1972, 1976[a]

	1958	1968	1972	1976
Total positions held by women	36	48	37	57
Total women	32	38	33	47
Elected				
President	2	0	2	2
Secretary-treasurer	11	12	13	7
Appointed				
Director of organizing	1	2	0	2
Research director	8	5	3	7
Research & education director	2	0	0	1
Education director	3	1	3	4
Director of social insurance	5	14	6	8
Editor	4	6	3	7
Legal activities	[b]	1	1	1
Legislative activities	[b]	3	3	7
Public relations activities	[b]	4	3	7

Sources: U.S. Department of Labor, Bureau of Labor Statistics, *Directory of National Unions and Employee Associations*, 1969, 1977, 1979; Dewey (1971), p. 45; Bergquist (1974), p. 7; LeGrande (1978), p. 13.
[a] Includes unions affiliated and not affiliated with the AFL-CIO.
[b] Not surveyed in 1958.

group, composed of 15 senior Council members, was charged with recommending measures to improve the representation of women and minorities. The Council adopted a plan to set aside two seats, one for a woman and one for a minority representative, thereby permitting an exception to the rule that Executive Council members be international union presidents and that no union hold more than one seat. In 1980, Joyce Miller, president of the Coalition of Labor Union Women (CLUW) and a vice president of the Amalgamated Clothing and Textile Workers Union, was elected to the Council; this was followed in 1981 by the appointment of Barbara Hutchinson, a black woman, who is vice president of the American Federation of Government Employees and director of its Women's Department. In 1987, the Council elected Lenore Miller, the new president of the Retail, Wholesale, and Department Store Union.[27]

At the present time no AFL-CIO regional director is female, and of the Federation's affiliates, only one, the Association of Flight Attendants, has a female international president. Only one head of an AFL-CIO department is a woman, but as education director she plays a

---

[27] See *New York Times*, February 18, 1987; *Wall Street Journal*, August 22, 1980; *AFL-CIO News*, August 22, 1980; and *Time of Change* (1983), p. 50.

critical role in promoting educational programs for women union members. Affiliates of the Associated Actors and Artists of America, the Screen Actors Guild, and the Actors Equity Association, have had female presidents.

There is no separate women's department in the AFL-CIO, but there is a Coordinator of Women's Affairs in the Civil Rights department. This position was established by resolution at the 1975 AFL-CIO convention, and at the same time the Federation adopted a six-point program calling for full participation of women in affiliated unions, for child-care legislation, and for passage of the Equal Rights amendment.[28]

The number of female leaders as well as members has been increasing in several unions. Heading the list is the Flight Attendants, where women hold more than 90 percent of the top positions—56 out of 62 executive board members (Schwartz and Hoyman, 1984). The percentage of female AFT leaders rose from 25 percent in 1980 to 32 percent in 1985; 11 of 34 top officers and executive board members are women. In addition, three of the six appointed assistants to the AFT president are women, and 40 percent of all national standing committees are headed by women (AFT Fact Sheet, undated). The number of women in AFSCME top leadership positions increased by three, a gain from 3 to 14 percent (Baden, 1986), and women hold one-third of the NEA executive board positions and one-half of the seats on the board of directors (Schwartz and Hoyman, 1984).

A recent survey of 15 unions and 2 associations, each with at least 100,000 female members, documents increases in the number of women leaders between 1979 and 1985 (Baden, 1986). In Table 6, current figures are compared with those collected for CLUW's 1980 study, *Absent from the Agenda.*

Very little documentation exists about women leaders at the regional and local levels. Only a few unions maintain, or release, these records (interviews). However, it has been reported that 15 percent of the presidents of Communications Workers (CWA) locals are women, 12 percent of Electrical Workers (IUE) locals are headed by women, and 5 percent of Machinists (IAM) locals have female presidents. In AFSCME, 33 percent of the union's 3,500 locals have women presidents, and 50 percent of all local officers are female (Baden, 1986; interviews). Black women hold a significant number of these positions, reflecting both a high level of activism among black women as well as AFSCME's commitment to race and sex equality.

Although no data are available on the percentage of black women holding national union office, a relatively large number of them are in

---

[28] See AFL-CIO (1975); Amendment to AFL-CIO Constitution.

TABLE 6
Female Officers and Governing Board Members

Union	Total Number of Officers		Number of Women Officers		Percent Female Officers		Percent Female Union Members	
	1979	1985	1979	1985	1979	1985	1979	1985
ACTWU	41	34	6	3	15	9	66	65
AFGE	18	19	0	2	0	10	49	26
AFSCME	29	28	1	4	3	14	40	45
AFT	32	34	8	11	25	32	60	60
CWA	17	18	0	1	0	6	51	52
HREU	22	24	1	2	4	8	42	50
IAM	11	11	0	0	0	0	13	15
IBEW	24	23	0	0	0	0	30	30
IBT	21	21	0	0	0	0	25	26
ILGWU	26	24	2	3	7	13	80	85
IUE	25	26	1	2	4	8	40	40
SEIU	46	50	7	9	15	18	50	50
UAW	26	25	1	1	3	4	11	13
UFCW	55	—	2	—	3	—	39	—
USWA	29	30	0	0	0	0	13	10
NEA	9/145a	9/121	5/75	3/61	55/51	33/50	75	60

Sources: For 1979, U.S. Department of Labor, Bureau of Labor Statistics, Directory of National Unions and Employee Associations, 1979; Coalition of Labor Union Women, Absent from the Agenda (1980). For 1985, Baden (1986); interviews.
ª First numbers are NEA executive committee members; second numbers are members of NEA board of directors.

prominent positions. They are represented among the top female officers of the Teamsters, IUE, Government Workers (AFGE), and the former Amalgamated Meat Cutters Union, now merged with the United Food and Commercial Workers; they also hold many of the second-level leadership positions in public-sector unions such as AFSCME and in industrial unions like the United Auto Workers (UAW).[29]

Female representation is more visible in AFL-CIO state federations. Not a single woman held the post of president or secretary-treasurer in any of these federations in 1968, but by 1985 Colorado, Connecticut, Georgia, and Pennsylvania had female secretary-treasurers and in 1986 Connecticut had a female state president. In 1972 only 9 of the 173 officers and board members of state labor councils were women, but by 1985 almost every state had at least one female board member (Schwartz and Hoyman, 1984). A number of state federations also have established special committees and programs for women workers; these include the California AFL-CIO's special Women's Activities Department, organized in 1976, and the Kentucky AFL-CIO's annual women's school, cosponsored with the state university's labor education program.[30]

Even more marked is the increasing number of women elected to local area central labor councils. There is at least one woman president of a central labor council in half the states, and a dozen have more than one (AFL-CIO, 1985b). Of the 26 central labor bodies in California, for example, 12 are headed by women (Franklin, 1983), and 4 of Indiana's 32 central labor bodies have a woman in the top post.

Although most international unions do not have special departments or bureaus for women members, virtually every one has designated a department or an individual to handle women's affairs; often it is the civil rights, human relations, or community service department. However, women's departments have been established by many of the largest unions, including AFGE, AFSCME, AFT, American Postal Workers' Union, CWA, IUE, UFCW, and UAW. The Service Employees International Union is now setting up a Women's Advisory Committee (Baden, 1986; interviews).

Another important indication of resource commitment to female members is the number of women on national level staffs. The CLUW

---

[29] The U.S. Commission on Civil Rights' 1982 study of 12 international unions showed that women held 7 percent of the vice presidential positions (out of 184); 1 percent were held by black women. Of the 294 executive board members, 4 percent were white women, 2 percent were black women, and less than 1 percent were Hispanic women.

[30] Washington State's Labor Council created a standing Women's Committee that has held conferences every two years since 1976. The Wisconsin State AFL-CIO created its Women's Committee in 1970 and holds conferences in alternate years (Franklin, 1983; Bergquist, 1974). The Pennsylvania AFL-CIO also has a Women's Committee.

estimate in *Absent from the Agenda* (1980) was that 16 percent of staff members were women; the update study (1985) doubles that figure. A major contributor to the increase is the rapidly expanding number of women organizers. For example, District 925, an affiliate of SEIU, has an organizing and field staff composed of 19 people, 17 of them women. Public-sector and health-care unions, in particular, have increased their organizing activities and are relying more and more on women representatives. When the totals for national headquarters and field staff (nonclerical) are combined, 35 percent of SEIU's staff representatives are women. For the AFT the figure is 34 percent, for CWA 24 percent, and for the Teamsters, 11 percent. The NEA's staff is 58 percent female (Baden, 1986).

Coalition of Labor Union Women

While many factors contribute to the improving status of women in unions, the Coalition of Labor Union Women has served as a leading catalyst. Its 1974 founding convention was the culmination of years of organizing efforts among rank-and-file women attempting to strengthen their voice within the labor movement.[31] Although international unions did not initially endorse CLUW, the new organization quickly demonstrated its effectiveness and achieved official recognition from the labor movement (Wertheimer and Nelson, 1975). CLUW opened discussions on women's issues and female representation at the 1975 AFL-CIO national convention, ensuring passage of the six-part program mentioned earlier. It also helped establish the staff position of Coordinator of Women's Affairs.

At the 1979 AFL-CIO convention, CLUW president Joyce Miller addressed the plenary, and Federation president Lane Kirkland announced the commitment of the Executive Council "to explore in depth and with seriousness of purpose ways and means by which this great contribution and role of women and minorities might be better reflected" in the Executive Council (*AFL-CIO American Federationist*, 1979).

CLUW's stated objectives include: (1) organize unorganized women workers, (2) promote affirmative action for women on the job and in the union, (3) encourage political action and press for legislation, and (4) increase participation of women within their unions. Also important is CLUW's commitment to racial equality, demonstrated by the composition of its leadership and membership (Seifer and Wertheimer, 1979; CLUW Constitution). Six of the top 12 officers are minority women, and minorities constitute just under 50 percent of

---

[31] See Weiner (1985), Quin (1984), Schwartz and Hoyman (1984), Seifer and Wertheimer (1979), and Sexton (1974).

the 200-member national executive board. CLUW estimates its minority membership to be 40 to 50 percent (Coalition of Labor Union Women; 1984a; interview).

More than 60 international unions and employee associations have representatives active in CLUW. Membership climbed from 5,500 in 1977 to more than 18,000 in 1985, and 75 chapters are working in 32 states. Activities range from direct support in union organizing drives to lobbying and extensive national educational efforts. CLUW has strengthened organized labor's ties to women's and civil rights groups and worked to extend the reach of labor's coalition-building efforts. CLUW's educational and training materials are used by unions and university labor education programs throughout the country to increase the numbers of active and qualified women unionists (Coalition of Labor Union Women, 1984b; Franklin, 1983). What is perhaps most important, CLUW acts as a national group and information network available to union women at every level.

Obstacles to Leadership

Today's union leaders express concern about the lack of female participation, but this lament is not new. At the turn of the century, local officers complained about women's lack of interest in union affairs. At the same time, it was also common to exclude women and members of minority groups from certain crafts and unions, to reserve leadership and staff positions for men only, and even to urge women to withdraw from the labor force altogether (Kessler-Harris, 1982; Foner, 1980; Tax, 1980; Baxandall, Gordon, and Reverby, 1976). These early trade union discriminatory practices reflected social attitudes and, to some extent, these views are still contributing to a male-dominated culture within many unions.

A few barriers to participation that women commonly mention are lack of self-confidence, inconvenient meeting times and places, and apprehension about attending meetings alone (UCLEA, Committee on Trade Union Women, 1982; Wertheimer and Nelson, 1975).

In addition, many stereotypes of women workers that contributed to their isolation from union life in the past were only recently challenged by union women activists, by women's and civil rights movements, and by sociologists and psychologists. Studies indicate, however, that these stereotypes still influence union members and officers. Among these views are: women are in the work force only temporarily; women are harder to organize; women are more concerned with the home and family than with the workplace and the union; and women lack the assertiveness, skills, and objectivity to be good leaders (Weiner, 1985; Feldberg and Glenn, 1982; Kanter, 1982, 1977a, 1977b, 1977c, 1976; Boyd, 1981; Hochschild, 1973).

To understand the problems women face in attempting to attain leadership positions, we need to examine both barriers to membership participation in general and union, job, and family-related obstacles affecting women in particular, including the impact of gender-based stereotypes of how women and men interact and how both judge a woman's potential and ability as a leader.

Membership Barriers. The issue of membership involvement has been important since the 1950s. Almost all studies written then and in the 1960s focus on men; yet the obstacles to membership involvement they identified continue to plague both women and men.[32] To a great extent these barriers evolved in response to changes in trade union structure and organization. For example, in order to bargain effectively with large corporations, many unions adopted structures that concentrated key decision-making functions at top leadership levels. Complex laws, procedures, and reporting requirements reinforced the trend toward centralization. Reliance on binding arbitration to resolve workplace problems also shifted the locus of activity and power away from the membership. As a result, the rank-and-file's direct involvement in local and especially in national union affairs decreased (Brody, 1980; Green, 1980; Montgomery, 1979). In addition, as long as the leadership was able to win acceptable wages and benefits at the bargaining table—the case until the late 1970s—many members saw the union as a service rather than as a membership organization. Union meetings attracted fewer and fewer members, and member apathy came to head the list of labor leadership's concerns (Freeman and Medoff, 1984; interviews).

A generally accepted measurement of union participation relies on three primary activities: holding office, serving on committees, and attending meetings. Other factors taken into account include a member's voting habits, willingness to read union literature, and use of the grievance procedure. Members are most likely to participate if their activity has observable effects on decision making; they are informed about union affairs; they are part of a work group that is homogeneous in pay, skills, and background; they are on personal terms with others involved in the union; and they hold a job with relatively high pay and status.[33]

Job dissatisfaction tends to *decrease* union participation. In fact, studies show that the more satisfied workers are with their jobs, the

---

[32] See Miles and Ritchie (1968), Solomon and Burns (1963), Barbash (1961), Kassalow (1961, 1966), Landsberger and Hulin (1961), Spinrad (1960), Seidman et al. (1958), Form and Dansereau (1957), Sayles and Strauss (1953), and Seidman, London, and Karsh (1950).

[33] See UCLEA, Committee on Trade Union Women (1982), Boyd (1981), Wertheimer and Nelson (1975), Spinrad (1960), Sayles and Strauss (1953), and Seidman, London, and Karsh (1950).

greater the likelihood of union involvement. Workers with skilled positions far outnumber the unskilled in leadership positions. Company departments with a high rate of grievances resolved favorably for union members also have a larger number of union activists (Boyd, 1981; Spinrad, 1960).

In Wertheimer and Nelson's 1975 study of trade union participation in New York City locals, both men and women ranked "the need for more information" as a leading obstacle to their increased involvement. Members felt they did not know enough about the union and did not understand *what* they could accomplish by participating, or *how* they could be useful.

At times members were discouraged from seeking office because they believed there were no openings. Leadership turnover varies dramatically from one local to another, and the turnover rate tends to decline at higher levels of the union hierarchy. Still, the turnover rate among national leaders was 20 percent a year between 1948 and 1967, significantly higher than for most organizations. But since most of the openings resulted from retirements and it is customary for leaders to select their successors from a limited pool of white male officers similar to themselves, this turnover rate does not translate into significant changes in the overall *composition* of leadership. Even though the turnover rate climbed to 25 percent in the past decade, due to deaths and retirements, most international officers and AFL-CIO Executive Council members have held their jobs for more than 10 years. Only 12.5 percent of the changes in leadership between 1971 and 1978 were the result of the defeat of an incumbent.[34]

Infrequency of turnover, while affecting every member's chance of winning a high office, has an especially adverse impact on women and minorities trying to break into the leadership circle. Women— minority women in particular—are less likely to have personal ties to current union leaders (usually white males) because women rarely belong to the same work group, department, or classification. In addition, women do not hold the skilled jobs from which most leaders come, and they experience greater job dissatisfaction due to the unskilled and low-status nature of traditionally female jobs.

Barriers Women Face. The traditional path to union office presents women with another set of barriers. Local level leadership comes from the ranks. Members usually follow a career ladder from shop-floor representative or steward up to the executive board or top office (Schwartz and Hoyman, 1984; Koziara, Bradley, and Pierson, 1982).

---

[34] There were 175 changes in top positions between 1971 and 1979—30 percent due to retirements, 35 percent to resignations or failure to seek reelection, 10 percent to death, and 12.5 percent to defeat in a contested election.

Incumbent presidents average 17 years in their locals, 15 years in some office, and between two and three positions prior to becoming president. Most top officers initiate their union activity during their first few years on the job and maintain their involvement thereafter. Although women today enter the work force at approximately the same time as men do and remain almost as long, this pattern is relatively new for them. From 1900 through the 1950s, a 26-year differential existed between the labor force attachment of men and women. The gap began to narrow substantially in 1970 and had dropped to 10 years by 1977 (Smith, 1982). It continues to narrow now that women are remaining in the work force during childbearing years. The number of interruptions and the average length of a woman's worklife formerly excluded her from the group taking the path to higher office, but that is now changing.

Who gets elected often depends less on the actual skills needed than on how members perceive both the job requirements and the candidates and what members consider important leadership traits. "One of the primary barriers to increasing the participation of women," writes Rosabeth Moss Kanter, leading authority on sex roles and behavior in organizations, "is the existence and persistence of cultural stereotypes." Although Kanter focuses on corporate behavior, her findings apply to other organizations, including unions. Consistently, traits relating to competence are considered male and those related to emotion, female. Not only are the traits attributed to women valued more negatively by society, but women internalize these negative feelings and, as a result, have a more denigrating self-concept than men (Kanter, 1977c; Wertheimer and Nelson, 1975; Broverman et al., 1972). That may account for why many women as well as men view men as better leaders and thus are hesitant to run for office. More women than men—in fact, most women—cite the lack of self-confidence as the chief barrier to their assuming greater responsibility in their unions.

Moreover, people display less confidence when performing a job usually associated with the other sex (Koziara and Pierson, 1981b). Wertheimer and Nelson found that women have difficulty envisioning themselves as leaders and fall victim to the "unexamined assumptions of men toward women's union role" (1975, p. viii).

In one study of women in leadership, Karen Koziara and David Pierson (1981a) identified three requirements for union office: (1) perceived negotiation and interpersonal skills; (2) perceived knowledge of industrial relations; and (3) members' views of the access they will have to the officers once elected. In the case of negotiation and interpersonal skills, for example, members will probably favor an effective and strong spokesperson—someone who is assertive and self-confident and commands respect, based on personal stature as well as on job status. As indicated above, virtually all research on stereotypes shows that these basic leadership attributes are assigned to men—by both women and men.[35] Men are considered "tougher" in bargaining situations (Falk, 1975); they are "characterized as aggressive . . . having better judgment and more intelligence than women" (Koziara and Pierson, 1981a) and more likely to have skilled, higher-paying jobs.

A knowledge of industrial relations, a second requirement for union office, can be measured by years of service and number of prior union positions held. Until recently, few women matched the "qualifications" of their male counterparts. Accessibility, the third factor, may also favor male candidates. It is measured by subjective rather than objective tests of a person's willingness to listen or respond to rank-and-file members. Members seem to feel that they have greater access to someone who works in their own department, belongs to their own political caucus, or socializes with them after hours. Jobs such as maintenance or inspection, which enable workers to move throughout the plants, thus making them "more accessible," are commonly held by men.

In addition, if women constitute a minority of the work force, a female leader may be perceived as representing a "special interest group"—the other women workers. A male leader is more likely to be perceived as representing all members of the bargaining unit. For minority women, these assumptions are even more restrictive. Members of male-dominated union committees, for example, were polled as to why it was important to have women/men on the committee. In response, 77 percent said that women were needed to represent the women, while only 28 percent said that men were needed to represent other men (Izraeli, 1984).

In ranking the barriers to their own increased participation, union women activists stress personal factors above all others—lack of confidence, home responsibilities, inconvenient meeting times, spouse's attitude, and child-care concerns.

Another difficult barrier to overcome is women's minority status within most active union circles, especially at regional and national levels. Studies indicate the importance of "relative numbers on interaction" (Kanter, 1977b). The small number of women—their "token status" in top leadership positions—ensures high visibility and, therefore, creates serious performance pressures. How a female leader performs may become a yardstick for evaluating how other women will or should perform. On the one hand, there is pressure to overachieve;

---

[35] See Koziara and Pierson (1981a, 1981b), Kanter (1977b), Falk (1975), Broverman et al. (1972), Megargee (1969), and Morris and Hackman (1969).

on the other, there is pressure to keep a "low profile" so that peers and superiors are not threatened (Izraeli, 1984; Kanter, 1977b).

A woman leader may also have to make special adjustments to fit into a male-dominated environment. She may be expected to ignore statements prejudicial to other women and/or to accept a stereotyped role within the group—for example, a coffee server or loyal supporter (Kanter, 1977b).

Most women union leaders, both white and minority, occupy token positions ("token" by virtue of their relative numbers, not on the basis of their qualifications or ability to influence policy). Research suggests that they must work hard to overcome certain behavior patterns and cultural stereotypes that interfere with job performance. These efforts translate into increased job-related stress. Most active union women, moreover, have both home and family respon-sibilities.[36] To add the burden of having to disprove stereotypes, excel to demonstrate competence, and cope with demeaning remarks about themselves and other women makes the road to leadership difficult. That so many women are, in fact, advancing on that road is a tribute to their perseverance and commitment to unionism.

Leadership Training Programs

Recommendations for increasing the number of women leaders range from minor adjustments in union practices to major policy revisions. Measures local unions can and have adopted without bylaw changes include ore convenient meeting times and locations, provi-sion for child care during union affairs, recognition for women already involved, and an emphasis on positive role models for women.

The barriers more difficult to cope with are rooted in past discrim-inatory practices, cultural stereotypes, and numerical minority status; these require a more organized and protracted effort. Overcoming women's own lack of self-confidence is an equally difficult, long-term task, and to deal with this unions have turned to membership educa-tion and leadership training.

A leadership training debate has emerged over whether separate training for women workers is more effective than mixed-group educa-tion. Union leaders are divided on this issue. Unions committed to training female members have held mixed programs on the impor-tance of women's concerns to the union, while using separate sessions to facilitate leadership training.

---

[36] The Wertheimer and Nelson (1975) demographic data and the surveys from UCLEA-sponsored summer schools for women indicate that a majority of women union activists are mothers. Of the 1982 participants in the Southern school, 20 percent reported having children under age 5 and 45 percent had children age 6 and over (Catlett, 1986; UCLEA, Committee on Trade Union Women, 1982).

Labor education for women workers has a very long history, dating back to the 1920s and the Bryn Mawr Women's Summer School. More contemporary pioneering efforts originated at Cornell University's New York City campus and at the University of Michigan in Ann Arbor. Both programs focus on women and work and include in their offerings a variety of courses and conferences designed for women workers. An important component of each program is a special course to train and develop the skills of minority women.

To expand training opportunities for women in a favorable learning environment, the University and College Labor Education Association (UCLEA) Committee on Trade Union Women initiated regional week-long summer schools in 1975. A most significant innovation in programming for women workers, the schools have attracted more than 4,500 women unionists as students; they take place annually in four regions and are jointly sponsored by the AFL-CIO Education Department and CLUW. Ten years ago, at the first schools, the majority of women paid their own way and less than half held union offices; today 95 percent are supported by their local unions, and close to 90 percent hold some union office, from international representative or local president to steward or committee member (Needleman, 1985).

Institutions affiliated with the UCLEA have also expanded their women's programs over the past decade. By 1985, 53 percent of the university and college labor education centers sponsored noncredit courses for women workers; approximately half have been initiated since 1975 (Haddad, 1985). A further indication of the growing commitment to women's programming is the increase in the number of female full-time professional staff members. In 1973 only 10.5 percent of the instructional personnel in labor education at universities and colleges were women; that figure reached 30.5 percent in 1985 (Nelson, 1985).

The CLUW Center for Education and Research has developed some of the best training materials to date for union women. In 1979 the Center launched its Empowerment of Union Women project to "research and monitor the status of women in national union leadership positions in American unions." Its first publication, *Absent from the Agenda* (1980), provided information on women in top union offices, the percentage of female members, and existing resources and departments responsible for administering women's programs. Its 1982 publication, the *Empowerment Handbook*, is a compilation of resource materials to help union women understand their history, their union, and the AFL-CIO. The *Handbook* also includes information women need to attain leadership positions, to set up and run women's committees, to defend their rights on the job, and to bargain over issues of concern. The second phase of the CLUW program focused on leadership training and led to the 1983 publication of *Color Me Union*, a model training program for union women.

Women and the Future of Unions

History tells us that women became union members, participated, and held responsible positions first in auxiliaries, then in local unions, and more recently at the national level. During the 1960s and 1970s they entered the work force in unprecedented numbers and behaved like men in their labor market attachment and concerns about pay and benefits. They joined unions, but not to the extent that they entered the labor force. Why not? Research indicates that women do not hold negative views of unions, so what accounts for the failure of so many of them to join?

This is only one of a number of questions calling for further research. For example, we need to learn more about women's role in unions and in leadership positions. Have union training programs helped? How effective are union women's departments? More generally, it would be useful to find out why minority women are more likely than other women to join unions. What issues are important to women, and how might these concerns be translated into bargaining demands? What techniques have been used by those associations and unions that have been successful in recruiting women members, and why couldn't other organizations adopt the same or similar approaches?

The AFL-CIO also is seeking answers to questions of this type as they apply to all union and prospective union members. Of primary concern is an explanation for the drop in overall union membership and how the decline might be reversed. This was the assignment of the Committee on the Evolution of Work, established by the Federation in 1982 to review changing economic and social conditions and recommend how unions might adapt to them. Among the Committee's suggestions were that unions should identify particular issues, such as pay equity and health and safety, that are of concern to workers and develop new benefits and services outside the collective bargaining structure.

The labor movement might look to the agendas of some of the women's groups for models of how to incorporate these recommendations in union programs. An organization of office workers, 9 to 5, identifies issues important to women employed by a particular company and attempts to resolve them outside formal collective bargaining. The teachers' and nurses' associations are examples of organizations that adapted their programs as the needs and interests of their memberships changed over a period of years.

As in the past, women have much to gain from being part of the larger labor movement. The unions also benefit from having women members, not only in the numbers they represent nationally and at the bargaining table, but also from the increasing contributions of women in leadership positions at all levels of the organizations.

References

Adams, Larry T. "Changing Employment Patterns of Organized Workers." *Monthly Labor Review* 108 (February 1985): pp. 25–31.

AFL-CIO. *The Changing Situation of Workers and Their Unions.* Report of the Committee on the Evolution of Work, February 1985a.

———. Organizations Affiliated With the AFL-CIO. Washington: January 19, 1985b.

———. Convention Proceedings and Resolutions, 1975.

AFL-CIO Fact Sheet. "Women Leadership in the AFT." undated.

AFL-CIO Federationist. December 25, 1979, p. 25.

AFL-CIO News. "Frank Emig Named to Head Community Services Department." January 19, 1985, p. 3.

AFL-CIO News Service. "AFL-CIO Convention Calls for All-Out Fight for Women's Rights." October 7, 1985.

Agassi, Judith Buber. *Comparing the Work Attitudes of Men and Women.* Lexington, MA: Lexington Books, 1982.

Antos, Joseph, Mark Chandler, and Wesley Mellow. "Sex Differences in Union Membership." *Industrial and Labor Relations Review* 33 (January 1980): pp. 162–69.

Baden, Naomi. "Developing an Agenda Expanding the Role of Women in Unions." *Labor Studies Journal* 10 (Winter 1986): pp. 229–49.

Barbash, Jack. *Labor's Grass Roots: A Study of the Local Union.* New York: Harper & Bros., 1961.

Baxandall, Rosalyn, Linda Gordon, and Susan Reverby. *America's Working Women: A Documentary History—1600 to the Present.* New York: Random House, 1976.

Bergquist, Virginia A. "Women's Participation in Labor Organizations." *Monthly Labor Review* 97 (October 1974): pp. 3–9.

Bidol, Patricia. *Improving Local Union Women's Committees.* Union Minorities/ Women Leadership Training Project, University of Michigan, and Program on Women and Work, Institute of Labor and Industrial Relations, University of Michigan-Wayne State University, 1981.

Blum, Albert A. *White-Collar Workers.* New York: Random House, 1971.

Boyd, Marilyn S. *Women's Liberation Ideology and Union Participation: A Study.* Saratoga, CA: Century Twenty One Publishing, 1981.

Brody, David. *Workers in Industrial America: Essays on the 20th Century Struggle.* New York: Oxford University Press, 1980.

Broverman, Inge K., Susan Raymond Vogel, Donald M. Broverman, Frank E. Clarkson, and Paul S. Rosenkrantz. "Sex-Role Stereotypes: A Current Appraisal." *Journal of Social Issues* 28(2) (1972): pp. 59–78.

Bureau of National Affairs, Inc., (BNA). "Two-Tier Wage Plans." In *Collective Bargaining Negotiations and Contracts.* Washington: BNA, February 14, 1985. No. 1036.

Business Week. "Little Room at the Top for Labor's Women." May 28, 1966, p. 62.

Catlett, Judith L. "After the Good-Byes: A Long-Term Look at the Southern School for Union Women." *Labor Studies Journal* 10 (Winter 1986): pp. 300–11.

Coalition of Labor Union Women (CLUW). *CLUW Directory,* 1984a.
_____. *Color Me Union,* 1983.
_____. "Empowerment of Union Women Projects: 1984 Annual Report," submitted to Carnegie Corporation of New York, December 1984b.
_____. *Empowerment Handbook.* Washington: CLUW, 1982.
_____. *Absent from the Agenda.* Washington: Center for Education and Research, CLUW, 1980.
Cohany, Harry P. "Membership of American Trade Unions, 1960." *Monthly Labor Review* 84 (December 1961): pp. 1299–1306.
Cohany, Harry P., and Lucretia M. Dewey. "Union Membership Among Government Employees." *Monthly Labor Review* 93 (July 1970): pp. 15–20.
Cook, Alice H. "Women and American Trade Unions." *Annals of the American Academy of Political and Social Science* (January 1968): pp. 124–31.
DeFronzo, James. "Class Identification among Working Wives: Educational Attainment and Union Membership, but *not* Occupational Prestige." *Psychological Reports* 49 (August 1981): pp. 171–77.
Dewey, Lucretia M. "Women in Labor Unions." *Monthly Labor Review* 94 (February 1971): pp. 42–48.
Dickason, Gladys. "Women in Labor Unions." *Annals of the American Academy of Political and Social Science* 251 (May 1947): pp. 70–78.
Douty, H.M. "Prospects for White-Collar Unionism." *Monthly Labor Review* 92 (January 1969): pp. 31–34.
Elkouri, Frank, and Edna A. Elkouri. *How Arbitration Works,* 4th ed. Washington: BNA Books, 1985.
Equal Employment Opportunity Commission (EEOC). *Job Patterns for Minority and Women in Apprenticeship Programs and Referral Unions, 1979.* Washington: EEOC, 1982.
Falk, Gail. "Sex Discrimination in the Trade Unions: Legal Resources for Change." In *Women: A Feminist Perspective,* ed. Jo Freeman. Palo Alto, CA: Mayfield Publishing Co., 1975. Pp. 254–76.
Feldberg, Roslyn L., and Evelyn Nakano Glenn. "Male and Female: Job Versus Gender Models in the Sociology of Work." In *Women and Work,* eds. Rachel Kahn-Hut, Arlene Kaplan Daniels, and Richard Colvard. New York: Oxford University Press, 1982. Pp. 65–80.
Foner, Philip S. *Women and the American Labor Movement: From World War I to the Present.* New York: Free Press, 1980.
Form, William H., and H. Dirk Dansereau. "Union Member Orientation and Patterns of Social Integration." *Industrial and Labor Relations Review* 10 (October 1957): pp. 3–12.
Franklin, Barbara Hayes. *Leadership Training for Union Women: 33 Program Ideas.* Washington: Center for Education and Research, CLUW, 1983.
Freeman, Richard B., and James L. Medoff. *What Do Unions Do?* New York: Basic Books, 1984.
Green, James R. *The World of the Worker: Labor in Twentieth Century America.* New York: Hill and Wang, 1980.
Haddad, Carol. "Ten-Year Report on Women's Labor Education at UCLEA-Affiliated Institutions." Presented at the National University and College Labor Education Association Annual Meeting, March 1985.
Hochschild, Arlie Russell. "A Review of Sex Role Research." *American Journal of Sociology* 78(4) (1973): pp. 1011–29.
Izraeli, Dafna N. "The Attitudinal Effects of Gender Mix in Union Committees." *Industrial and Labor Relations Review* 37 (January 1984): pp. 212–21.

Johnson, Gloria E., and Odessa Komer. "Education for Affirmative Action." In *Labor Education for Women Workers*, ed. Barbara Wertheimer. Philadelphia: Temple University Press, 1981. Pp. 204–16.

Kahn, Mark L. "Airlines." In *Collective Bargaining: Contemporary American Experience*, ed. Gerald G. Somers. Madison, WI: Industrial Relations Research Association, 1980. Pp. 315–72.

Kanter, Rosabeth Moss. "The Impact of Hierarchical Structures on the Work Behavior of Women and Men." In *Women and Work*, eds. Rachel Kahn-Hut, Arlene Kaplan Daniels, and Richard Colvard. New York: Oxford University Press, 1982. Pp. 234–47.

———. *Men and Women of the Corporation*. New York: Basic Books, 1977a.

———. "Some Effects of Proportions on Group Life: Skewed Sex Ratios and Responses to Token Women." *American Journal of Sociology* 82 (March 1977b): pp. 965–90.

———. "Women in Organizations: Sex Roles, Group Dynamics, and Change Strategies." In *Beyond Sex Roles*, ed. Alice G. Sargent. St. Paul: West Publishing Co., 1977c. Pp. 371–86.

———. "The Policy Issues: Presentation VI." *Signs: Journal of Women in Culture and Society* 2 (Spring 1976): pp. 282–91.

Kassalow, Everett M. "Canadian and U.S. White-Collar Union Increases." *Monthly Labor Review* 91 (July 1968): pp. 41–45.

———. "White-Collar Unionism in the United States." In *White-Collar Trade Unions: Contemporary Developments in Industrialized Countries*, ed. Adolf Sturmthal. Urbana: University of Illinois Press, 1966. Pp. 305–64.

———. "Organization of White-Collar Workers." *Monthly Labor Report* 84 (March 1961): pp. 234–38.

Kenneally, James J. *Women and American Trade Unions*. Montreal: Eden Press Women's Publications, 1981.

Kessler-Harris, Alice. *Out to Work: A History of Wage-Earning Women in the U.S.* New York: Oxford University Press, 1982.

———. "Where Are the Organized Women Members?" *Feminist Studies* 3 (1975): pp. 92–110.

Kistler, Alan. "Union Organizing: New Challenges and Prospects." *Annals of the American Academy of Political and Social Science* 473 (May 1984).

Koziara, Karen S., and David A. Pierson. "Barriers to Women Becoming Union Leaders." In *Proceedings of the 33rd Annual Meeting, Industrial Relations Research Association, 1980*. Madison, WI: IRRA, 1981a. Pp. 48–54.

———. "The Lack of Female Union Leaders: A Look at Some Reasons." *Monthly Labor Review* 104 (May 1981b): pp. 30–32.

Koziara, Karen S., Mary I. Bradley, and Donald A. Pierson. "Becoming a Union Leader: The Path to Union Office." *Monthly Labor Review* 105 (February 1982): pp. 44–46.

Koziara, Karen S., and Patrice J. Insley. "Organizations of Working Women Can Pave the Way for Unions." *Monthly Labor Review* 105 (June 1982): pp. 53–54.

Landsberger, Henry A., and Charles L. Hulin. "A Problem for Union Democracy: Officers' Attitudes Toward Union Members." *Industrial and Labor Relations Review* 14 (April 1961): pp. 419–31.

LeGrande, Linda H. "Women in Labor Organizations: The Ranks Are Increasing." *Monthly Labor Review* 101 (August 1978): pp. 8–14.

Lockheed, Marlaine E. "The Modification of Female Leadership Behavior in the Presence of Males." *Research in Education* (1975): pp. 111–23.

Lockheed, Marlaine E., and Katherine Patterson Hall. "Conceptualizing Sex as a Status Characteristic: Applications to Leadership Training Strategies." *Journal of Social Issues* 32 (Summer 1976): pp. 111–24.

Lohman, Mark Rodney. "Changing a Racial Status Ordering for Means of Role Modeling." Ph.D. dissertation, Stanford University, 1970.

Mann, John. "Parental Leave Needed." *Washington Post*, October 25, 1985.

Maupin, Joyce. *Working Women and Their Organizations: 150 Years of Struggle.* Berkeley, CA: Union Wage Educational Committee, 1974.

Megargee, Edwin I. "Influence of Sex Roles on the Manifestation of Leadership." *Journal of Applied Psychology* 53 (1969): pp. 377–82.

Miles, Raymond E., and J.B. Ritchie. "Leadership Attitudes Among Union Officials." *Industrial Relations* (October 1968): pp. 108–17.

Miller, Edwin L. "Job Attitudes of National Union Officials: Perceptions of the Importance of Certain Personality Traits as a Function of Job Level and Union Organizational Structure." *Personnel Psychology* 19 (Winter 1966): pp. 398–410.

Miller, Joyce. "Allies in the Future." *AFL-CIO American Federationist* (December 1979): pp. 24–25.

Miller, Richard U. "Hospitals." In *Collective Bargaining: Contemporary American Experience*, ed. Gerald G. Somers. Madison, WI: Industrial Relations Research Association, 1980. Pp. 373–433.

Mitchell, Daniel J.B. "Gaps in Minority Wages and Industrial Relations." *Monthly Labor Review* 108 (June 1985): pp. 33–34.

Montgomery, David. *Workers' Control in America.* Cambridge: Cambridge University Press, 1979.

Morris, Charles G., and J. Richard Hackman. "Behavioral Correlates of Perceived Leadership." *Journal of Personality and Social Psychology* 13 (1969): pp. 350–61.

Neary, H. James. "American Trade Union Membership in 1962." *Monthly Labor Review* 87 (May 1964): pp. 501–507.

Needleman, Ruth. "UCLEA-AFL-CIO Regional Summer Schools—A True Success Story." Slide show script, March 1985.

Nelson, Anne H. "A Union Woman's Influence." *Labor Studies Journal* 10 (Winter 1986): pp. 312–24.

———. "Women Representation on the Staff of UCLEA Institutes." Report to the UCLEA Annual Meeting, March 1985.

Newman, Winn. "Pay Equity Emerges as a Top Labor Issue in the 1980s." *Monthly Labor Review* 105 (April 1982): pp. 49–51.

Nielsen, Georgia Pointer. *From Sky Girl to Flight Attendant.* Ithaca, NY: ILR Press, Cornell University, 1982.

Quin, Liz. "The Taking of Power: Separatism as a Response to Oppression." Unpublished paper, November 1984.

Rankin, Theresa. "Can the Union Make Us Strong?" *Quest* 5(4) (1982): pp. 13–24.

Raphael, Edna E. "Working Women and Their Membership in Labor Unions." *Monthly Labor Review* 97 (May 1974): pp. 27–33.

Ratner, Ronnie Sternberg, and Alice Cook. "Women, Unions and Equal Employment Opportunity." Working Paper No. 3, Center for Women in Government, January 1981.

Richburg, Keith B. "NEA Leader to Promote Test for New Teachers." *Washington Post*, May 14, 1985.

Roberts, Markley. "The Future Demographics of American Unionism." *Annals of the American Academy of Political and Social Science* 473 (May 1984): pp. 23–32.

Rozen, Frieda Schoenberg. "Promoting and Recruiting: Reaching the Target Audience." In *Labor Education for Women Workers*, ed. Barbara Wertheimer. Philadelphia: Temple University Press, 1981. Pp. 37–41.

Sayles, Leonard R., and George Strauss. *The Local Union: Its Place in the Industrial Plant*. New York: Harper & Bros., 1953.

Schwartz, Arthur B., and Michele M. Hoyman. "The Changing of the Guard: The New American Labor Leader." *Annals of the American Academy of Political and Social Science* 473 (May 1984): pp. 64–75.

Seaberry, Jake. "Two-Tiered Wages: More Jobs vs. More Worker Alternation." *Washington Post*, April 7, 1985.

Seidman, Joel, Jack London, and Bernard Karsh. "Leadership in a Local Union." *American Journal of Sociology* 56 (November 1950): pp. 229–37.

Seidman, Joel, Jack London, Bernard Karsh, and Daisy L. Tagliacozzo. *The Worker Views His Union*. Chicago: University of Chicago Press, 1958.

Seifer, Nancy, and Barbara Wertheimer. "New Approaches to Collective Power: Four Working Women's Organizations." In *Women Organizing: An Anthology*, eds. Bernice Cummings and Victoria Schuch. Metuchen, NJ: Scarecrow Press, 1979. Pp. 152–83.

Sexton, Patricia Cayo. *The New Nightingales: Hospital Workers, Unions, New Women's Issues*. New York: Enquiry Press, 1982.

———. "Workers (Female) Arise: On Founding the CLUW." *Dissent* 21 (Summer 1974): pp. 380–95.

Slater, Carol. "Class Differences in Definition of Role and Membership in Voluntary Associations among Urban Married Women." *American Journal of Sociology* 65 (May 1960): pp. 616–19.

Smith, Robert Ellis. *Work Rights*. New York: E.P. Dutton, 1983.

Smith, Shirley J. "New Worklife Estimates Reflect Changing Profile of Labor Force." *Monthly Labor Review* 105 (March 1982): pp. 15–20.

Solomon, Benjamin, and Robert K. Burns. "Unionization of White-Collar Workers: Extent, Potential, and Implications." *Journal of Business* 36 (April 1963): pp. 141–65.

South, Scott J., Charles M. Bonjean, William T. Markham, and Judy Corder. "Female Labor Force Participation and the Organizational Experiences of Male Workers." *Sociological Quarterly* 24 (Summer 1983): pp. 367–80.

Spinrad, William. "Correlates of Trade Union Participation: A Summary of the Literature." *American Sociological Review* 25 (April 1960): pp. 237–44.

Tanner, Lucretia Dewey, Harriet Weinstein, and Alice Ahmuty. *Impact of the 1974 Health Amendments to the National Labor Relations Act on Collective Bargaining in the Health Care Industry*. Federal Mediation and Conciliation Service, 1979 (under contract with and published by Labor Management Services Administration, U.S. Department of Labor).

Tarr-Whelan, Linda. "Women Workers and Organized Labor." *Social Policy* 9 (May–June 1978): pp. 13–17.

Tax, Meredith. *The Rising of the Women*. New York: Monthly Review Press, 1980.

Torres, Ida. "Grievance Handling for Women Stewards." In *Labor Education for Women Workers*, ed. Barbara Wertheimer. Philadelphia: Temple University Press, 1981. Pp. 182–93.

UCLEA, Committee on Trade Union Women. "Surveys and Evaluations from Regional Summer Schools for Women Workers," 1982.

U.S. Department of Labor, Bureau of Labor Statistics. *Directory of National Unions and Employee Associations*. Washington: U.S. Government Printing Office, 1969, 1977, 1979, 1981.

U.S. Department of Labor, Labor Management Services Administration. "Summary of Public Sector Labor Relations Policies," March 1981.

U.S. Department of Labor, Women's Bureau. *Time of Change: 1983 Handbook on Women Workers.* Bull. 298. Washington: U.S. Government Printing Office, 1983.

Walker, Laura T. "Increasing Women's Participation in Their Unions through Education and Training." Washington: Center for Education and Research, Coalition of Labor Union Women, April 1984.

————. "Increasing Women's Participation in Their Unions through Education and Training." Update on the Empowerment of Union Women Project. Washington: Center for Education and Training, Coalition of Labor Union Women, July 1984.

Weiner, Lynn Y. *From Working Girl to Working Mother: The Female Labor Force in the United States, 1820–1980.* Chapel Hill: University of North Carolina, 1985.

Wertheimer, Barbara M., ed. *Labor Education for Women Workers.* Philadelphia: Temple University Press, 1981.

Wertheimer, Barbara M. "The United States of America." In *Women and Trade Unions in Eleven Industrialized Countries,* eds. Alice H. Cook, Val R. Lorwin, and Arlene Kaplan Daniels. Philadelphia: Temple University Press, 1984. Pp. 286–311.

Wertheimer, Barbara M., and Anne H. Nelson. *Trade Union Women: A Study of Their Participation in New York City Locals.* New York: Praeger, 1975.

Wessel, David. "Two Tier Pay Spreads, but Pioneer Firms Found Problems." *Wall Street Journal,* October 14, 1985.

CHAPTER 8

Professional Careers for Women in Industrial Relations

LOIS S. GRAY*

An increasing number of women are preparing for careers in industrial relations as evidenced by their enrollment in university industrial relations centers. What are their career prospects in this predominantly "male" field? While the number and percentage of women employed by corporate personnel and industrial relations departments, labor unions, government, and nonprofit organizations, and in other IR-related occupations have risen dramatically over the past 15 years, most of the jobs, particularly the top jobs, are held by men. This was not always the case. In the early evolution of this field, women played a prominent role. Their visibility declined as the field expanded. Why? And what accounts for the renewed interest and recognition today?

The search for answers to these questions led to a review of the literature and relevant statistics; interviews with knowledgeable observers, including women who are achievers; contacts with professional associations and with universities offering IR degrees; and, finally, a mail survey of graduates from Cornell's School of Industrial and Labor Relations.

A look at career prospects in the industrial relations field raises questions of definition that have continued to plague scholars. As a body of knowledge, IR draws on a variety of disciplines, including economics, industrial sociology, psychology, labor law, history, group dynamics, game theory, and social psychology. Its day-to-day workings are carried out by what John Dunlop calls the "actors" or participants in industrial relations activity, which include "(1) managers and their hierarchical superiors, (2) workers and trade union represen-

* Professor and Associate Dean, New York State School of Industrial and Labor Relations, Cornell University.
Note: The writer acknowledges the assistance of Heinz D. Meyer, a Ph.D. candidate at the NYSSILR, Cornell University, in data collection and analysis.

tatives, and (3) regulatory rule makers representing some form of government" (Greenwald, 1980, p. 591).

Some of the "actors" perform executive or line functions, and still others function as independent professionals (arbitrators, attorneys, and consultants). These functions are performed in a wide variety of organizational settings, including business, nonprofit, government, union, and individual or corporate operations. In addition to the "actors" are the teachers who train them and the researchers who write about and for them. Heterogeneity complicates analysis of career patterns and prospects.

Given the diversity of the field, it is fair to conclude that industrial relations is whatever industrial relations specialists do. Membership of the Industrial Relations Research Association (IRRA), a self-selected group of practitioners who identify with the field as a profession, provides one guide to what IR specialists are doing now. Categories of employment reported in the 1984 IRRA Directory include arbitration, consulting, government, legal, personnel/labor relations, union, academic, and "others" (not defined). Currently, 14.2 percent of IRRA members are women, up from 6.4 percent in 1972 (Industrial Relations Research Association, 1972, 1984).

Let us examine what is known about various segments of the IR profession to see where the women are. This chapter summarizes what is known about careers for women in personnel and human resource management, government regulatory agencies, labor education, labor unions and employee organizations, labor dispute settlement, and college faculties. There is substantial information, including published research, with respect to the first category—personnel and human resource management—but little about careers for women in the other fields.

A summary of the results of a survey of graduates of Cornell's School of Industrial and Labor Relations will illustrate one method for obtaining further information. Questions for research will be suggested.

Personnel and Human Resource Management

The largest single field of employment of women IRRA members is personnel and human resource management in business. During the past 15 years, women have been entering this field in increasing numbers, but women are not new to this occupation. As a matter of fact, women were prominent in its early history.

In the late 19th century the personnel movement in U.S. industry was largely "welfarism," that is, activities for "employee betterment." Hence, it was considered "women's work," similar to social work. Not surprisingly, employers turned to women to provide desired recreational, health, and welfare services, particularly in relation to the special needs of young women workers who were entering employment in those years. These early personnel jobs, which sometimes carried the title of "social secretary" or "matron," were seen as calling for "womanly qualities," with women functioning as counselors and protectors.

Even with the advent of "scientific management" with its emphasis on systematic selection, training, time and motion study, and wage and salary systems, women continued to play an important role. Among the pioneers were women with engineering degrees.

In 1921 Dr. Elizabeth K. Adams wrote that personnel management was "a new profession for women" and concluded that it was a field for which women were "especially well qualified." Major contributors to the literature of that era were Dr. Katherine Blackford on selection, Lillian Gilbreth on work efficiency, and Josephine Goldmark on hours of work.

In the 1920s, when employers organized to combat unionization under "The American Plan," personnel management broadened its scope to encompass labor relations, a function that called for analytical, confrontational, and negotiating qualities associated with "men's work." The leading postwar study of the role of women in the personnel field concluded that the opportunity for women to advance "seems to have declined in the last forty-five years even though the absolute number of these jobs has increased" (Miller and Coghill, 1964, p. 42).

In the 1950s women were found to be entering personnel through secretarial and clerical positions, while men were initially hired as interviewers. Exceptions were those women who were recruited during World War II, a time when male applicants were in short supply, and who were, therefore, hired for positions above the clerical level and moved up in personnel jobs formerly reserved for men. Women were perceived to be adept at handling details and working directly with other women. In the retail, banking, and insurance industries there were segregated personnel jobs, with women handling the problems of women and men those of men.

A 1956 study in New York City found few women in top personnel positions in heavy industry or in collective bargaining regardless of industry (Lynch, 1956). A 1963 study of the same group reported similar findings, with almost half the women in employment and personnel services. The majority of the respondents did not believe their chances for promotion to be "favorable" (Merkel, 1963). Advice to aspirants during the 1950s and 1960s was, "Get what education you can with an emphasis on psychology and then train to be a very good secretary and work for a personnel director" (Lynch, 1956).

A national survey in 1969 (members of the International Association of Personnel Women (IAPW), which attracted leading practitioners in this field) concluded that, while women were well represented in the personnel field as compared with other sectors of management, "their scope was somewhat limited." The majority (53 percent of the total) were concerned only with the employment function (recruiting, interviewing, selecting, and transferring employees). Counseling accounted for another 19 percent, and general personnel administration for 28 percent. Labor relations (negotiating and interpreting the labor agreement, participating in grievance procedures, arbitration, and conciliation) was a function performed by only 4 percent of the personnel women surveyed (Kay, 1969). When they were studied again in 1976, the distribution of IAPW members had changed little.

The late 1970s and early 1980s were years of rapid change in women's personnel roles. First, the numbers increased, as reflected in IRRA membership affiliations.[1] Second, the 1970s brought an influx of young, better educated, less experienced, and more highly paid women into personnel careers, which altered the profile of the typical personnel woman and the type of work available to her (Doll et al., 1982).

According to the 1970 Census, more than 13,000 women were employed as personnel and labor relations managers, holding full-time positions in business, industry, government, and nonprofit organizations. By 1980, the number was almost five times larger, and the proportion as compared with men in this occupation jumped from 21 to 36 percent of the total.

Despite women's increasing opportunities for careers in this field, they continued to be clustered in the low-paid jobs; women constituted more than half of those personnel and labor relations managers earning less than $17,499, and only 5 percent of them were in the over $50,000 bracket. The average salary of female personnel and labor relations managers in 1980 was $13,978, 58 percent of the average for males.[2] A comparison of earnings for women and men in 1982 found the gap for personnel and labor relations workers to be the largest for any occupational category (Norwood, 1982, p. 4).

A 1981 survey of members of IAPW (the organization that had been surveyed in 1969 and 1976) found 21.6 percent of them in policy-

---

[1] The IRRA *Membership Directory* in 1972 reported only 33 women members from the combined fields of business management/administration and business personnel/IR, a little more than 5 percent of the total. In 1979, a number of members employed in the latter category alone had risen to 70 and in 1984 to 97, constituting 16 percent of the total membership classified in business personnel/IR, while the percentage in business management/administration reached 14 percent.

[2] U.S. Census 1980, Equal Opportunity Tape.

making positions (3.8 percent with the title of vice president for human resources or its equivalent and 17.8 percent in the top personnel management position of the employing organization). An additional 30.9 percent of the respondents were managing one of the specific personnel functions. As compared with 1969, career prospects for women in personnel seemed to be brighter. Fewer were involved in employment and welfare/service functions (34 percent, as compared with 53 percent 12 years earlier) and more in the administrative, technical, and managerial aspects of the field (37 percent, up from 28 percent). On the other hand, only 2.5 percent performed the labor relations function, which remained a male preserve. The authors observed that underrepresentation of women in labor relations seemed to reflect "a reluctance to use women in such conflict laden roles until they have proven themselves in other capacities."

Analysis of factors contributing to upward mobility for personnel women in the 1980s yields the following advice to aspirants: (1) start in a technical aspect like affirmative action, human resources information systems, compensation, or even employment (which had been reported as a dead end in earlier studies); (2) take on other technical assignments to broaden your background (except for statistical and training and development work); and (3) avoid welfare/service jobs.

In addition, IAPW respondents advised women entering the field to find a mentor to offer advice and encouragement, seek a role model, and learn about organizational politics in order to be successful in achieving recognition in the personnel profession (Doll et al., 1982).

While evidence is incomplete (e.g., there are no studies comparing the career patterns of women and men), women seem to be on their way to regaining the role in personnel and human resource management that they held in the early years of this profession. However, progress has been uneven, with advancement largely in the administrative and technical areas of the personnel function and relatively little change on the labor relations side. Women are not visible in the prestigious decision-making circles of labor policy committees in the Business Round Table, National Association of Manufacturers, and U.S. Chamber of Commerce, and they rarely represent employers at the bargaining table.

It appears that the avenues of advancement open to women are today, as in the past, mainly in the sex-segregated areas of specialization considered suitable for the application of "feminine" qualities—that is, detail work and helping individuals with problems. Labor-management relations, which in most settings is adversarial, is seen to demand characteristics of assertiveness, confrontation, and manipulative bargaining which continue to be regarded as "masculine."

What types of organizations are providing the most supportive environment for women? The most recent survey of IAPW members suggests that women fare better in personnel departments of large organizations, both government and profit making (Doll et al., 1982). This result conflicts with those of earlier studies which found women doing relatively better with smaller employers, including those in the nonprofit field (Kay, 1969). What accounts for the change?

Women seeking a professional career in personnel fare relatively better in government than in private industry. Recent statistics reveal that almost half of all personnel-related positions are held by women. However, when these data are examined by category, a degree of sex segregation is found to exist even in the government. Women hold approximately two-thirds of the jobs classified as "personnel staffing" and 45 percent of those in "personnel management," but only 23 percent of those in "labor relations." Also, the median salary for women falls approximately 20 percent below that for men in every personnel category (U.S. Office of Personnel Management, 1982, Table 3).

Future research on the role of women as employer representatives in personnel and labor relations should draw on hypotheses offered and evidence amassed in the voluminous literature on women in management.[3] Among the questions raised by scholars and practitioners and applied to various levels of management are: (1) how do women compare with men in their career patterns, and (2) what does it take to succeed? A study of chief executive officers, for example, reported that women think they have to work harder and show a willingness to take greater risks than men. They also need a firm grounding in organizational politics (Magerson and Kaladradse, 1984). Are these generalizations also applicable to women in personnel? How effective is sex-segregated training—for example, special workshops for women?[4] What are the most effective strategies for upward mobility?

Gary N. Powell (1980) observes that women tend to be relegated to "velvet ghettos" in management, that is, functions which are stereotypically female, calling for social sensitivity and interpersonal skills. He poses a choice of strategies for achieving recognition in management: (1) capitalize on "feminine" characteristics to achieve a reputation in the "velvet ghetto" type of function that leads to broader influence in the organization; (2) adopt a "masculine" stereotypical style—assertive, aggressive, "take charge"—as a personal standard of behavior (as he reports most recent MBA graduates do) in order to compete with men for the most desirable jobs; and/or (3) plug into a

---

[3] For bibliographies on this subject, see Farley (1983) and Levitt (1980).
[4] This area of research is suggested in Larwood and Lockheed (1979).

network, whether achieving acceptance in the "old boy" group or forging a new network of women with similar interests. What strategies are currently employed by women in personnel and which are most effective?

Given the recent influx of college-educated women into the personnel field, what are the differences in the barriers encountered and the opportunities available to recent college graduates as compared with women of earlier generations who were hired and promoted in the traditional modes?[5] For example, one study found that middle managers preferred older, nonaggressive women, while upper management looked for young, aggressive dynamos, constituting a "catch-22" for the latter who were never promoted to the level to be considered by top management (Harlan and Weiss, 1981). Does this phenomenon apply to career advancement in personnel?

Finally, what are the barriers to women aspiring to a career in corporate labor relations, and how are they overcome? Studies of "success stories," male and female, might yield valuable insights on these questions.

The literature documents the rise and decline of women in personnel as reflecting changes in the functions performed and how these were viewed as relating to the personal and sex-stereotypical qualifications of males and females. In looking toward the future, what changes, if any, can be anticipated in personnel and labor-management relations, and how will these affect the acceptability of women as employer representatives and strategists? For example, what is the impact of a shift to more cooperative labor-management relations, including quality circles, employee involvement, and labor-management committees? Comparative case studies of the role of women within existing relationships (cooperative and adversarial) might be worthwhile. What are the implications of recent changes in the personnel function that have come about as a result of federal and state regulations—for example, affirmative action and occupational safety and health legislation which are monitored by personnel departments and call for specialists in the law? How about the increasingly complex compensation and fringe-benefit plans and record-keeping systems that involve computer expertise?

If organizations are becoming more people-oriented, as suggested by leading business and social science writers, will there be a return to the days when personnel was "women's work"? Or are the increased

---

[5] Brown (1979) points out that most of the management research mixes the generations together, failing to take into account differences in education, expectations, and changes in employer policies during the past 10 to 15 years.

technical and analytical demands of the personnel job weighted in the "male" direction?

Government Regulatory Agencies

Labor legislation is another aspect of industrial relations in which women historically played a leadership role. Dedicated women organized the Women's Trade Union and Consumer Leagues that spearheaded the drive for protective labor legislation.

Frances Perkins, teacher and social worker, became the first woman cabinet member and the only woman to serve as Secretary of Labor in United States history. She played a decisive role, at the state level, in securing factory inspection and worker compensation and, at the national level, in putting into place unemployment insurance, wage and hour regulations, and Social Security.

Her experience as a woman who was nationally prominent in industrial relations, a "man's field," illustrates the barriers that existed at the time. Her biographer, George Martin (1976) concluded that what interested people was "not her qualifications but her sex." Her appointment was denounced by major power groups including the AFL. When asked by a reporter whether being a woman was a handicap, she replied crisply, "Only in climbing trees" (Martin, 1976, p. 211). Nonetheless, she was not invited to cabinet meetings at times when they were scheduled as dinners in men's clubs (p. 284). As the first woman Secretary of Labor, she did not feel free to hire another woman in a key job even when the woman had superior qualifications (p. 427). In 1941, *Time* magazine reported, "[O]f all the game in the Roosevelt preserve, Secretary of Labor Perkins has been the most frequently chased and most savagely harried." After Pearl Harbor, Roosevelt received volumes of mail protesting that a woman held this key role in wartime, and he responded by setting up the War Labor Board and the War Manpower Commission outside the jurisdiction of the Labor Department. A prominent labor leader characterized her as "basically a social worker"—the "soft type" who would just "try to appease," not the desired dynamic Secretary of Labor who would "make decisions" (p. 362). A fellow cabinet member, reacting to her disagreement on an issue, said, "I suppose that was to be expected of a woman" (p. 388). Her strategy for dealing with male prejudice was "to remind them of their mothers," thereby relieving their anxieties and resentments, and she dressed the part (p. 146).

Frances Perkins, although the most prominent, was not alone among women who helped to bring about labor legislation and who achieved recognition during the 1920s and 1930s. Women headed the Women's Bureau and the Children's Bureau, for example, and held key positions in the formative years of the National Labor Relations Board (Gross, 1974). During the Depression and war years, women continued to be involved at middle to top levels in labor-related agencies. After the war their visibility declined, and governmental regulation of labor came to be regarded as a "male" field.

Title VII, affirmative action, and the raised consciousness of women may account for the upturn in the 1970s. Although there has never been another woman Secretary of Labor, women are increasing their participation in the governmental regulatory agencies that deal with labor issues. The National Mediation Board and the National Labor Relations Board have been chaired by women in recent years, and most of the labor-related agencies have at least one woman on their policy-making boards. As of this writing, there are two female labor commissioners at the state level.

One current member of the National Labor Relations Board is a woman, as is the general counsel. Of 1,035 professionals, 31 percent are women. Males continue to predominate in the supervisory positions (90 percent) and among administrative law judges (93 percent). The number of women new hires more than doubled between 1972 and 1980 when women constituted 45 percent of the total, reflecting a deliberate recruiting policy.[6]

Within the U.S. Department of Labor, women hold more than 30 percent of the labor-management administrator positions, including compliance officers, supervisors, and assistant regional administrators, in field offices across the country.[7] Twenty-one percent of the wage and hour enforcement officials are women, while women hold only 8 percent of the jobs in apprenticeship and training, a traditionally male field (U.S. Office of Personnel Management, 1982). The top jobs—regional directors, assistants, and deputy commissioners—are still held by men.

Numbers of women in government regulatory agencies are increasing. Whether women who are entering these positions will reach the executive levels remains to be seen.

In-depth research is needed on current career ladders for women in this field in which women were at one time among the leaders and initiators. What are the barriers, if any, to acquiring high-level labor-related jobs through civil service examinations? Through political appointment?

---

[6] Office of the General Counsel, National Labor Relations Board, "FY '84 Report of Accomplishments and FY '85 Affirmative Action Plan Update," Breakdown of Hiring—FY 1972–FY 1980.

[7] Linda Lafferty, Federal Services Impasses Panel, 1985.

Labor Education

Labor education is an area in which women were unquestionably the pioneers. The Women's Trade Union League developed the first educational program for unionists and offered the first staff training. The special schools for women workers, established in the 1920s, were later opened to men. From this movement came Hilda Smith, the director, and other women who played a dominant role in the massive labor education program that was funded by the U.S. government during the 1930s.[8] In these formative years, women who were social workers and teachers were the innovators in bringing education to workers. They were accepted leaders in an era when social reform was emphasized.

As the function of labor education changed, the involvement of women dropped. Responding to the growth of unionism and the evolution of systems of industrial relations, labor education shifted its emphasis to training for collective bargaining.[9] Not coincidentally, most labor educators in the post-World-War-II period were men.

The number of women staff members of universities with labor education programs has increased in the past 10 years, from 10 percent in 1973 to 33 percent in 1984–1985. But women still tend to be grouped at the bottom; few have reached the top. The AFL-CIO education director is a woman and 10 of 57 education departments of AFL-CIO unions are headed by women. Two of the 43 university labor education programs have a female director. None of the women staff members of university labor education programs (except the two who are directors) has reached the rank of full professor, and only 16–17 percent of the associate and assistant professors in these centers are women.[10] The positions women hold are generally untenured and their median salary is below that of men.[11] What are the continuing barriers to the advancement of women in this field which they once dominated?

Labor Unions and Employee Associations

There are historical records of women who were activists and exceptional leaders,[12] but unions have traditionally been led by men. Full-time staff positions in unions have always been filled from the

---

[8] Wertheimer (1981), Summary Discussion by Larry Rogin, pp. 265–68.

[9] See Gray (1966) for a history of labor education and its shifts in content.

[10] Report by Anne Nelson, "Women's Representation on the Staff of UCLEA Institutions," prepared for the University and College Labor Education Association Annual Meeting, March 1985.

[11] "Summary Report, Committee on Salary and Benefits," University and College Labor Education Association, 1984–1985 Academic Year.

[12] See Foner, Chapter 6 of this book.

ranks of the membership by those who first demonstrated their abilities and loyalty as volunteers. Almost all of them were men. In the early years, local union business agents were male, as were all of the national officials. The first woman appointed as an AFL organizer held her job for only six months during which she encountered male resistance to her role (Wertheimer, 1977, pp. 286–87). Women officers and staff emerged in the garment and industrial unions. Nonetheless, the vast majority of union leadership posts continued to be held by men.

What are the career prospects for women in unions today? "Women in Unions: Current Issues," Chapter 7 of this book, estimates that 32 percent of the current full-time staff of national unions are female and reports that the relative representation of women in union staff positions doubled over the past decade. Women's opportunities for appointment to staff positions are even greater in the burgeoning state government and professional employee associations.[13] Today the relative number of women employees of unions and employee organizations in professional roles appears to be about the same as in other sectors of the industrial relations field, including personnel management.

What types of functions are women staff members performing? Private-sector unions, like employers, rarely utilize women as spokespersons at the bargaining table. At the national level, women are most often found in support roles in research, education, publications, and public relations. The number of women directing specialized departments of the AFL-CIO has increased in recent years. Even more dramatic has been their growing prominence in staff associations. In 1984, women directed union legal and legislative departments in addition to the research, public relations, and publications roles which they held in earlier years.[14] Observation suggests a similar pattern at state, regional, and local levels. As with public-sector employers, women are more likely to be found in both line and staff positions in public-sector unions.

To what extent are union staff positions available as a career option for college-trained women? While promotion from within has been traditional in unions, with expertise being acquired at the bargaining table, on the picket line, or in the everyday administration of local unions, increasing numbers of professional positions have been opening up to "outsiders." A 1977–1978 survey (Gray, 1981, note 40) found that almost all unions (81 percent of the respondents) searched outside for specialized talent to fill technical positions, and a growing number

---

[13] See Needleman and Tanner, Chapter 7 of this book.
[14] Gifford (1984) and *Monthly Labor Review* (August 1978).

(28 percent of the respondents) were recruiting outside membership ranks for organizers and even for core service positions where the individual would represent the national union in grievance handling and administration. Unions are beginning to recruit on campuses, following the corporate practice, and several offer internships to try out students who aspire to union work (Gray, 1981). That labor union career opportunities are improving for women is evidenced by the increasing number elected to office at both national and local levels and the growth in numbers hired for specialized staff positions. For both categories, specialized training is increasingly recognized as an asset.

Among IRRA members who list their occupation as "union," approximately 20 percent are female. Almost all report a college education, ranging from B.A. to Ph.D.; most have a degree in industrial relations or labor studies. More than half are in elected or appointed positions with responsibility for representing the members in collective bargaining and/or union administration. Not surprisingly, research is a major job responsibility, followed by education. Most of these IRRA members are employed by the American Federation of Teachers, the National Education Association, the American Federation of State, County and Municipal Employees, and various independent unions in the public sector. Several IRRA members work for the Service Employees International Union, the Office and Professional Employees International Union, and the Teamsters, with others scattered among professional and industrial unions (Industrial Relations Research Association, 1984).

Opportunities for a union career for college graduates continue to be relatively rare compared with their opportunities in personnel management and government. For example, less than 10 percent of the graduates of Cornell's ILR school have found jobs in labor organizations, and reports from other IR centers generally indicate that relatively few of their graduates are employed in unions. Nonetheless, prospects are improving. The fact that the two women members of the AFL-CIO Executive Council entered their unions from the "outside" and have college degrees may be a harbinger of future trends.

Most of the literature in this area deals with barriers to women's participation and ascent to leadership in unions.[15] Studies of the careers of "successful" or achieving women who are full-time union officials would be useful as a guide to future aspirants.

Labor Dispute Settlement

Women have been among the mediators from the time when third-party dispute settlement was introduced in the field of labor

---

[15] See Needleman and Tanner, Chapter 7 of this book.

relations. Frances Perkins, as the New York State Industrial Commissioner and U.S. Secretary of Labor, intervened for the governor and later for the president to settle strikes in the public interest (Martin, 1976). In the 1920s when the U.S. Conciliation Service was established, a woman was appointed as a full-time professional mediator (Wertheimer and Nelson, 1978, p. 24). Later, a number of women were recruited by the War Labor Board for dispute resolution during World War II, and later Anna M. Rosenberg was appointed an assistant secretary in the Department of Defense.

Nonetheless, the vast majority of "neutrals," mediators, arbitrators, and fact-finders have been and continue to be men. Of the 387 IRRA members who list their principal occupation as arbitrator, only 14 percent are women (Industrial Relations Research Association, 1984). The National Academy of Arbitrators, which admits only the elite who are firmly established in the dispute-settlement field, has only 25 women among a total of 607 members—about 4 percent. The American Arbitration Association currently lists 192 women on its Labor Panel, approximately 6 percent of the total.[16] No statistics are available with respect to their usage. The Federal Mediation and Conciliation Service employs 13 women as full-time mediators (less than 6 percent of the total in this category). Fragmentary evidence indicates that women's representation on state mediation agency panels is about the same.[17]

Public-sector labor relations, which has multiplied the use of third parties in dispute settlement, has also expanded opportunities for women as neutrals. Approximately 30 percent of the professional staff members of the New York State Public Employment Relations Board are women, as are 12 percent of the ad hoc panel members.[18]

Women who have aspired to acceptance as third-party neutrals have encountered sex-stereotyping. As one arbitrator put it, "Selection is still done in one's own image" (Wertheimer and Nelson, 1978). Since sex stereotypes prevail in other aspects of life, it is not surprising that women might be viewed as fragile or as sex objects at the bargaining table, as reported by a federal mediator (Yager, 1983). Female neutrals report experiences that illustrate barriers to acceptance. For example, interviews for neutral positions focus on ability to stay up all night, to cope with rough people, or to take "obscene" language. Skepticism about a woman's ability to fill a role that was regarded as "man's work" is openly expressed in a pledge to try the aspirant "in an

---

[16] Letter from Robert Coulson, President, American Arbitration Association, August 9, 1985.

[17] Interviews with knowledgeable officials and observers.

[18] Letter from Harold Newman, Chairman, New York State Public Employment Relations Board.

emergency if no man is available." Lower compensation is described as "enough for a woman" (Wertheimer and Nelson, 1978, pp. 3, 15, 28). A dissent to the point of view that sex plays a role in arbitrator selection is entered by a former mediation official who conducted a survey of users and arbitrators in western New York, the majority of whom said that sex and ethnic characteristics were unimportant considerations. However, the surveyor noted that this view was not shared by female arbitrators.[19]

Strategies for achieving acceptability, as recommended by those who have succeeded, include apprenticeship training with an experienced arbitrator, acquiring labor relations experience as an advocate, getting to be known as a teacher in programs that attract labor and management representatives, building experience and a reputation in legal practice, or acquiring dispute settlement expertise in new fields such as community, divorce, and prison mediation (Wertheimer and Nelson, 1978, pp. 9–39).

To implement these ideas, the American Arbitration Association and Cornell University's School of Industrial and Labor Relations mounted a special training program for women who aspired to be arbitrators. Key components of the program, which included classroom sessions, were practical on-the-job exposure to the field as an intern with an experienced arbitrator and hands-on practice in writing decisions which were reviewed and critiqued by a professional. This two-year program produced 20 graduates, more than half of whom are currently practicing as professional neutrals.

Like other facets of the industrial relations field, dispute settlement involves an increasing number of women but continues to be predominantly a male occupation. The vast majority of the practitioners are men, and they are the ones usually selected for prestigious roles in "public interest" disputes and as permanent umpires under major collective bargaining contracts. On the positive side is the increasing recognition as evidenced by their election to leadership roles in the National Academy of Arbitrators and the Society for Professionals in Dispute Resolution. As in the case with women in unions, more is known about the barriers than about factors leading to success. What is needed are studies of the women who "made it," both in the earlier years and today.

College Faculties

Among the early university teachers of industrial relations and writers on the subject were such women as Lois McDonald at New

---

[19] "Labor Comment" by Ed Kelley, reporting a survey by Eric Lawson, *Buffalo Evening News*, July 3, 1982; p. 2.

York University and Theresa Wolfson at Brooklyn College. Women on university campuses have been pressing for affirmative action in appointment and tenure decisions since the early 1970s (Lester, 1977). Nonetheless, there are few women among the tenured faculties of industrial relations research institutes and none is headed by a woman. In 1984, among members of the IRRA involved in research, teaching, or administration in industrial relations, 12 percent of the individuals identified as "academic" were women. The percentages in each discipline ranged from 9 in psychology to 24 in "other and unspecified." Among student members, 38 percent were female (Industrial Relations Research Association, 1984).

Women are a small minority of the IR teachers and researchers, but their numbers, as in other sectors, are growing. With increasing female enrollment in graduate study of industrial relations, this trend should accelerate. Studies of the experience of IR centers in faculty recruitment and tenure review might yield valuable clues with respect to academic career prospects of current Ph.D. candidates.

Experience of Women With Professional Training in Industrial Relations

The past 10 years has brought a dramatic increase in the number and percentage of women pursuing academic degrees in the field of industrial relations. In 1954–1955, most students enrolled in IR graduate degree programs were male, with female percentages at the leading institutions ranging from 0 to 9; 10 years later the representation of women had increased to a range of 6 to 30 percent. The 1970s brought a striking change in IR student enrollments. By 1984–1985, half of all reported students enrolled in university IR graduate programs were female.[20]

Enrollment at the undergraduate level seems to have followed the same trend. Records for Cornell, the university with the largest IR enrollment, show that the proportion of female students remained at about 15 percent for the years 1950 through 1970, doubled in the 1970s, and rose to more than 50 percent in 1984–1985. Undergraduate labor studies programs that enroll adults, mostly from unions (approximately 75 currently offer degrees) also report a significant increase in the numbers and percentages of women registrants over this time period.[21] While increasing enrollment is consistent with the general upward trend in female enrollment in higher education, the relative number of women currently enrolled in IR professional training

[20] Reports from IR centers.
[21] Interviews with directors.

exceeds that for law and equals the proportion enrolled in business and management degree programs.[22]

Confronting a record of limited opportunities for women in industrial and labor relations, what inspires rising numbers of them to enroll for professional training in the field? What are their prospects? How do the careers of women compare with those of men who have similar training?

In an attempt to find answers to these questions, a questionnaire was mailed to males and females who completed degree requirements at Cornell's ILR program (B.S., M.S., M.I.L.R., and Ph.D.) in 1955, 1965, and 1975, soliciting information about career goals, jobs, salaries, barriers, and factors leading to success.[23]

Most (69 percent) of the female respondents found jobs in the ILR field immediately following graduation. Among the 1955 and 1965 respondents, a few went to work for unions and others were employed in corporate personnel departments. The female graduates of 1975, as compared with the earlier graduates, reported a wider variety of job opportunities, including neutral and government as well as personnel work; none reported a union position. Males who graduated in 1955 and 1965 were less likely than the women to go immediately into IR jobs. Some went on to law schools, others into the army, or they took non-IR business positions. Corporate personnel was the major IR-related occupation of the 1955 and 1965 male graduates, followed by governmental and academic employment; one went to work for a union. Among males graduating in 1975, a smaller percentage opted for law school or non-IR positions. Government was the leading employer of men who found IR-related work, followed by corporate and nonprofit organizations.

Males who graduated in 1955 and 1965 reported average starting salaries that were 15 percent higher than those reported by their female classmates. This sex differential in starting salaries had virtually disappeared for the class of 1975.[24]

After 20 to 30 years in the field, female graduates of 1955 and 1965 who responded to the questionnaire were no longer employed in union and corporate personnel jobs. They had shifted to nonprofit personnel, law, neutral, and academic work. In contrast, male graduates of the

---

[22] The U.S. Department of Labor's *Report on the United Nations Decade for Women, 1976–1985: Employment in the United States*, July 1985, gives statistics on enrollment of women in higher education (Table 12, p. 134), reporting it up from 33 percent in 1976 to 45 percent in 1980. For law, the percentage rose from 26 to 34; for business and management, from 33 to 45.

[23] A total of 387 questionnaires were mailed; 108 were returned—79 from males, 29 from females. Of these respondents, 56 were currently employed in the IR field—36 males and 20 females.

[24] Placement records for recent graduates from ILR and other university IR centers (contacted by mail and telephone) confirm the finding that there is little difference in starting salaries for men and women.

same years were still to be found in union, corporate personnel, government, and academic positions, but two-thirds of them were practicing law or working in non-IR positions as managers of their own businesses. For the 1975 class there was little difference in the occupational distribution of males and females. Approximately one out of four in each group (27 percent of the males, 23 percent of the females) was practicing law. Two out of five of both sexes were working outside the IR field (38 percent of the males, 41 percent of the females). One in 12 was employed in personnel work, with females more likely to work in nonprofit organizations and males in corporations. Two of the men were consultants and three of the women were practicing neutrals.

Women ILR graduates who responded to the questionnaire were more likely than men to change their career goals over the 10- to 30-year period since their graduation. Two-thirds of the women and about half the men found jobs in fields different from their original goals. Reasons for the shift differed between the sexes, men citing "changing interests" and greater economic opportunities as the two motivating factors, while women listed "family responsibilities" with the same frequency as "changing interests."

After 20 or more years on the job there continued to be a 15 percent salary gap between the men and women who graduated in 1955 and 1965. For the class of 1975 the differential in salaries for professionals with 10 years' experience had narrowed to 9 percent.

When asked about barriers to achieving their objectives, women listed "discrimination" and "family restrictions," while men cited "mobility" (which could include the influence of family responsibilities), "organizational politics," and "money."

There was also a striking difference by sex in replies to the question about what factors lead to advancement. Women perceived getting ahead on the job as coming from hard work, ability, and an ILR education. Men tended to attribute success partly to these factors, but added the influence of "luck" and "contacts."

Women cited their experiences in applying for IR jobs and working in business and unions to illustrate the discrimination and prejudice they encountered. For example, one 1955 female graduate aspired to a union career and found a position which was "occupied by women only," a "dead-end, low paid job with little status." She concluded that the jobs that were her goal—organizer or political activist—were seen as "man's work." Another early graduate found prejudice in business to be "open and gross" and met with what she characterized as an "absolute refusal to hire, promote, or utilize" her talents and skills. Family responsibilities constitute a major handicap to many respondents. For example, one woman who left the IR field to become a businesswoman expressed her belief that if she had not married, she would be vice president of the company where she was employed.

When asked whether sexual stereotypes had helped or hindered their careers, males responded that the characteristics associated with the masculine image—for example, "rational, decisive, power oriented, competitive"—had helped (the response from a majority of the 1975 graduates) or had no significant influence (a majority of the 1955 and 1965 graduates). In contrast, a majority of the women reported that stereotypes associated with their sex—"empathy, people oriented, collaborative"—had a negative influence on their careers.

Given a choice in strategies for getting ahead in industrial relations, women look to "mentoring" and "networking" and, to a lesser extent, "awareness training." Adopting male strategies was overwhelmingly rejected by these respondents.

Have women achieved equality with men? Women ILR graduates responded five to one that women have not yet achieved equality with men in the industrial relations field. On the other hand, almost all expressed the belief that career prospects for women have improved over the past 20 years. Recent graduates were more likely than the others to perceive equality of opportunity. In the class of 1975, approximately one-fifth of the women assessed career prospects of women and men as equal, while all of the female respondents from earlier classes saw inequality.

In comparison with their female counterparts, male ILR graduates are more inclined to believe that women have achieved equality (40 percent of those expressing an opinion). Like the women, they underscored improvement of career chances over the past 20 years. A few of the male respondents (1955 and 1965 classes) denounced the questionnaire for raising these and other questions that they interpreted as implying sex discrimination in this field.

Experience reported by this sample of Cornell ILR graduates suggests that the opportunity gap between males and females in the profession of industrial relations (as measured by type of job available and rates of pay) has narrowed over the past 20 years, but full equality has yet to be achieved.

Summary and Conclusions

An increasing number of young, professionally trained women aspire to careers in the field broadly defined as industrial relations. The numbers employed in IR-related jobs have risen sharply in recent years. Newcomers are faring better than their predecessors, and the status and salary gaps have narrowed relative to their male counterparts. Nevertheless, men earn more and have better chances for advancement to the top levels in all segments of the field. "Velvet ghettos," which segregate work by gender, still exist. Collective bargaining remains largely a male domain.

Looking backward, it appears that the rise and fall in the participation of women in industrial relations reflects shifts in the functions the professionals are called upon to perform as well as changes in the motivation and abilities of women to compete for jobs in this field.

What all of this suggests is that we need to know more about industrial relations functions in order to assess the career prospects of the young women who are currently preparing to enter the profession. Also needed is research that compares the work experience of men and women, examines the barriers to upward mobility, and assesses alternative strategies for overcoming these barriers. Awaited is an in-depth study of the motivations and expectations of young, professionally trained women with regard to IR jobs. It would be useful to have an econometric analysis of the salary gender gap to pinpoint the explanatory factors.

The most important need is for comparative studies of organizations in a variety of industries and organizations with differing policies and industrial relations functions to provide insights with respect to the environments most favorable to achieving equality of opportunity for careers in this profession.

References

Brown, Linda Keller. "Review Essay: Women and Business Management." *Signs: Journal of Women in Culture and Society* 5 (Winter 1979): pp. 266–68.

Doll, Williams, Dale Sullivan, Jack L. Simonetti, and Jacqueline A. Ervin. "Fast Tracks to Success for Women in Personnel." *Personnel* (May-June 1982): pp. 12–22.

Farley, Jennie. *The Woman in Management: Career and Family Issues.* Ithaca: New York State School of Industrial and Labor Relations, Cornell University, 1983.

Gifford, Courtney D. *Directory of U.S. Labor Organizations: 1984–85 Edition.* Washington: BNA Books, 1984.

Gray, Lois S. "Unions Implementing Managerial Techniques." *Monthly Labor Review* 104 (June 1981): pp. 3–13.

———. "The American Way in Labor Education." *Industrial Relations* 5 (February 1966): pp. 53–66.

Greenwald, Douglas, ed. *Encyclopedia of Economics.* New York: McGraw-Hill Book Co., 1980.

Gross, James. *The Making of the National Labor Relations Board: A Study in Economics, Politics and the Law.* Albany: State Univ. of New York Press, 1974.

Harlan, Ann, and Carol Weiss. "Final Report from Moving Up: Women in Managerial Careers." Working Paper No. 86. Wellesley, MA: Wellesley College Center for Research on Women, 1981.

Industrial Relations Research Association. *Membership Directory.* Madison, WI: IRRA, 1972, 1984.

Kay, M. Jane. "What Do Women in Personnel Do?" *Personnel Journal* 48 (October 1969): pp. 810–12.

Larwood, Laurie, and Marlene Lockheed. "Women as Managers: Toward Second Generation Research." *Sex Roles* 5 (1979): pp. 559–66.

Lester, Richard A. "Labor Market Discrimination and Individualized Pay: The Complicated Case of University Faculty." In *Equal Rights and Industrial Relations*, eds. Leonard J. Hausman et al. Madison, WI: Industrial Relations Research Association, 1977. Pp. 197–233.

Levitt, Judith A. *Women in Management, 1970–1979, A Bibliography*. Chicago: C.P.L. Bibliographies, 1980.

Lynch, Edith. "Women at Work in Personnel." *Personnel Journal* 34 (January 1956): pp. 295–97.

Magerson, Charles, and Andrew Kaladradse. *How American Chief Executives Succeed: Implications for Developing High Potential Employees*. AMA Survey Report. New York: American Management Association, 1984.

Martin, George. *Madam Secretary: Frances Perkins*. Boston: Houghton-Mifflin Co., 1976.

Merkel, Muriel. "Profile of the Professional Personnel Woman." *Personnel Journal* 42 (March 1963): pp. 127–34.

Miller, Frank B., and Mary Ann Coghill. "Sex and the Personnel Manager." *Industrial and Labor Relations Review* 18 (October 1964): pp. 32–44.

Norwood, Janet. "The Female-Male Earnings Gap: A Review of Employment and Earnings Issues." Report 675, U.S. Department of Labor, Bureau of Labor Statistics, September 1982.

Powell, Gary N. "Career Development and the Woman Manager—A Social Power Perspective." *Personnel Journal* (May-June 1980): pp. 22–32.

U.S. Office of Personnel Management, Compliance and Investigation Group, Office of Workforce Information. *Federal Civilian Workforce Statistics*, September 30, 1982.

Wertheimer, Barbara M. *We Were There: The Story of Working Women in America*. New York: Pantheon Books, 1977.

Wertheimer, Barbara M., ed. *Labor Education for Women Workers*. Philadelphia: Temple University Press, 1981.

Wertheimer, Barbara M., and Anne N. Nelson, eds. *Women as Third Party Neutrals: Gaining Acceptability*. Proceedings of a Conference, New York State School of Industrial and Labor Relations, Cornell University, 1978.

Yager, Paul. "A Manager of Neutrals' Perspective." In *Emerging Issues in the Work Force: The Female Perspective*. Conference Proceedings, Corsi Institute, Pace University, June 14, 1983, unpublished.

CHAPTER 9

Women in Professions:
Academic Women

MARIO F. BOGNANNO*

Few women became university faculty members in the past, and those who were in academic jobs often found themselves in non-tenure-track positions and at lower rank and salary than their male colleagues. There are signs, however, that the status of women in academe is changing and that public policy is a major factor encouraging change.

This chapter is a review of the employment status of women faculty in higher education. The dimensions discussed include employment levels, rank, pay, and faculty women's representation in top administrative positions. Where research findings permit, comparisons are made with male faculty within discipline, rank, productivity, and length of continuous service classifications in an attempt to assess whether sex (female) adversely affects hiring, pay, and promotion decisions in academe. Key judicial decisions are reviewed as part of the discussion of discrimination against women in higher education. The final section of the chapter includes both an overall assessment of the employment status of women professors and suggestions of areas where more research is needed.

Employment Status Comparisons

This century's most significant social development is perhaps the dramatic entry of women into the U.S. labor force, and the increasing number of women in academe is an important part of this general phenomenon.

Numbers and Distribution of Faculty Women in America

In 1870, women represented 12 percent of the 5,553 total faculty in 563 higher education institutions across the United States. By 1970

* Professor and Director, Industrial Relations Center, University of Minnesota.
  Note: The author thanks Bruce Goodman and Lisa Novotny, M.A.-IR students at the University of Minnesota, for their research assistance and Karen S. Koziara for her helpful ideas in the preparation of this chapter.

the percentage had doubled (25 percent of 825,000 total faculty at 2,525 institutions), and by 1980 had increased further (33.3 percent of the 1,127,000 total faculty in 3,152 institutions) (see Table 1). This trend is not inconsistent with the finding that female access to academic jobs is more open now than it was in the past. Although few studies focus on this aspect of academic employment, one 1982 study does hazard the finding that "young women with Ph.D.s are no longer at a significant disadvantage in finding employment with high-quality universities" (Ferber and Green, 1982, p. 553). Ahlburg and Lee (1986), who examined the mobility of academics in industrial relations, reached a similar conclusion. Using a sample of Ph.D. faculty members of the Industrial Relations Research Association in 1984, they report regression coefficients relating gender and the rankings of universities at which these scholars took first and second faculty jobs. The coefficient estimates showed no significant gender differences.

Data on full-time faculty by academic rank in 1982–1983 reveal that, relative to their male counterparts, faculty women were less likely to be full professors (36 versus 12.1 percent), while the opposite is true for assistant professors, lecturers, instructors, and in nonranked classifications at two-year institutions (1 of 3 males versus 2 of 3 females). However, the percentage of male associate professors is

TABLE 1

Historical Summary of U.S. Faculty in Higher Education
by Sex, Selected Years, 1969–1970 to 1980–1981

Year	Total Institutions	Total Faculty	Men	Women	% of Faculty Who Are Women
1869–1870	563	5,553[a]	4,887[a]	666[a]	12.0
1969–1970	2,525	825,000	619,000	206,000	25.0
1971–1972	2,720	881,665	639,251	242,414	27.5
1976–1977	2,785	1,073,119	729,169	343,950	32.0
1977–1978[a]	2,826	1,090,000	740,000	350,000	32.1
1978–1979	3,134	1,097,000	732,000	365,000	33.3
1979–1980	3,152	1,127,000	751,000	376,000	33.3
1980–1981	3,321	1,179,000[a]	784,000[a]	395,000[a]	33.5

Source: Professional Women and Minorities, A Manpower Data Resource Service, Scientific Manpower Commission, 5th ed. (August 1984), p. 131. Data summarized from The Digest of Education Statistics, Series 1973 through 1983–1984 editions, National Center of Education Statistics.

Note: Totals include full- and part-time teaching and nonteaching faculty, all ranks combined. Higher education as used here includes public and private secular and church-related, two-year and four-year, undergraduate and advanced degree-granting universities and colleges.
[a]Estimate.

higher (27.5) than the percentage of females at that rank (21.9) (see Table 2).

Significant differences between the sexes also exist in tenure status. Data for full-time faculty show about 70 percent of all male and 50 percent of all female faculty were tenured. This difference is partly explained by the intersex variations in academic ranks just cited. The foregoing suggests that women faculty do not enjoy the relative levels of academic prestige, achievement, and job security that their male counterparts enjoy. Whether gender plays a significant role in determining rank and tenure is examined in a later section.

Within academic disciplines, 78.1 percent of all male faculty and 63.5 percent of total female faculty are employed in science/engineering fields (see Table 3). For the humanities, however, these figures are 36.5 percent for women but only 21.9 percent for men. It is generally recognized that salaries and, perhaps, opportunities for promotion vary across academic disciplines. Whether there is sex differentiation *within* a discipline, after accounting for other factors affecting salary and rank, is discussed in a later section.

Women also have been making inroads into previously male-dominated positions in higher education administration. Significant

TABLE 2

Full-Time Faculty in Public and Private Higher Education
by Rank, Sex, and Percent with Tenure, 1982–1983

| Rank | Men | Women | % Men by Rank | % Women by Rank | Percent With Tenure | | |
					Total	Men	Women
Professor	97,715	11,617	36.0	12.1	95.6	95.7	94.3
Associate Professor	74,717	20,939	27.5	21.9	82.1	82.2	81.7
Assistant Professor	58,103	32,652	21.4	34.1	26.8	25.5	29.2
Instructor	12,863	13,993	4.7	14.6	9.0	9.7	8.5
Lecturer	3,305	2,989	1.2	3.1	11.0	11.2	10.8
No academic rank[a]	24,850	13,608	9.2	14.2	77.2	80.1	71.9
All ranks combined	271,554	95,798	100.0	100.0	65.4	70.4	51.0

Source: Professional Women and Minorities, A Manpower Data Resource Service, Scientific Manpower Commission, 5th ed. (August 1984), p. 118. Unpublished data compiled by the National Center for Education Statistics.

Note: Includes only institutions reporting tenured faculty members.

[a] There are 38,458 faculty under this category, of which 35,087 are from public two-year institutions, 741 are from private two-year institutions, and 2,630 are from four-year public and private universities and colleges.

TABLE 3
Academically Employed Ph.D.s, by Field and Sex,
and Percent with Tenure, 1983

Field	Men	Women	% of Total Men (206,700)	% of Total Women (43,300)	% With Tenure Men	% With Tenure Women
EMP	65,200	3,900	31.5	9.0	64.8	38.9
Life sciences	47,800	10,900	23.1	25.2	62.2	32.1
Behavioral/social sciences	48,400	12,700	23.4	29.3	69.6	45.4
Total: Science/engineering	161,400	27,500	78.1	63.5	65.5	39.2
Eng./Amer. Lit.	11,600	5,200	5.6	12.0	79.0	54.7
History	12,100	2,000	5.9	4.6	80.4	51.7
Other languages	7,700	4,500	3.7	10.4	76.6	50.6
Other humanities	13,900	4,100	6.7	9.5	73.2	46.8
Total: Humanities	45,300	15,800	21.9	36.5	77.2	51.1

Source: Professional Women and Minorities, A Manpower Data Resource Service, Scientific Manpower Commission, 5th ed. (August 1984), pp. 114–15. Data obtained from *Science, Engineering and Humanities Doctorates in the United States,* 1983 Profile (Washington: National Academy of Sciences/National Research Council, 1984).
Note: Includes part-time and full-time faculty and nonfaculty staff whose primary work is teaching, basic research, applied research, development, or design.
EMP = engineering, mathematics, computer sciences, physics/astronomy, chemistry, and earth/environmental sciences. Life sciences = agricultural sciences, medical sciences, and biological sciences. Behavior/social sciences = psychology and social sciences. Other humanities = library and archival sciences, linguistics, archeology, American studies, religious studies, and general humanities.

changes in the number of women in senior administrative positions took place between 1975 and 1980 (Touchton and Shavlik, 1984). There were 1,625 senior women administrators employed by 2,689 accredited institutions of higher education in 1975, an average of 0.6 per institution. By 1983 the number of senior women administrators had nearly doubled to 3,084, an average of 1.1 in 2,824 institutions (see Table 4). Women administrators in both 1975 and 1983 held positions in primarily academic programs and offices, followed by student affairs. While this trend is noteworthy, women occupy only a minor fraction of top leadership positions in higher education. Any hope for a more balanced representation of women in leadership positions must lie in the future as the expected effects of post-1972 affirmative action programs established in higher education institutions continue to be realized.

TABLE 4
Changes in Total Number of Senior Women Administrators
by Type of Position, 1975 and 1983

Position Title	1975		1983		Change 1975–1983	
	Women	% of Total	Women	% of Total	Number	%
Executive vice president	11	.7	35	1.1	24	218
Vice president (other than academic)	7	.4	32	1.0	25	357
Chief academic officer	194	11.9	373	12.1	179	92
Chief business officer	137	8.4	241	7.8	104	76
Chief development officer	61	3.7	210	6.8	149	244
Chief public relations officer	142	8.7	322	10.4	180	128
Chief student life officer	290	17.8	454	14.7	164	56
Dean of women	215	13.2	86	2.8	− 129	− 60[a]
Deans/Directors of academic programs	539	33.2	1,232	39.9	693	128
Other[b]	29	1.8	99	3.2	70	241
Total	1,625	99.8[c]	3,084	99.8[c]	1,459	90
Number of accredited institutions[d]	2,689		2,824		135	

Source: Judy Touchton and Donna Shavlik, "Senior Women Administrators in Higher Education—A Decade of Change, 1975–1983," Preliminary Report, Office of Women in Higher Education, American Council on Education, November 14, 1984.

[a] The number of women in this position declined over the eight-year period because many institutions eliminated the title in the 1960s and 1970s.

[b] Includes deans and directors in areas not represented in above categories.

[c] Does not total to 100 percent due to rounding.

[d] Includes only those institutions accredited by the six major regional accrediting associations: Middle States Ass'n of Colleges and Schools (MSA); New England Ass'n of Schools and Colleges (NEASC); North Central Ass'n of Colleges and Schools (NCA); Northwest Ass'n of Schools and Colleges (NASC); Southern Ass'n of Colleges and Schools (NACS); and Western Ass'n of Schools and Colleges.

In the position of chief executive officer (CEO), change has been slow but promising. As shown in Table 5, women held 148 CEO positions in 1975, or 5.2 percent of the total (Touchton, 1980). Eight years later, that number had increased to 254, giving women 9.1 percent of the presidencies of public and private universities and colleges. The greatest gains were in public institutions where there was a fivefold increase in the number of women presidents in eight years. Therein women held 1.1 percent of the CEO positions in 1975 and 5.7 percent of these same positions in 1983. Most women presidents head four-year private institutions.

TABLE 5
Women Chief Executive Officers in U.S. Colleges and Universities,
1975–1983

Type of Institution	1975		1982		1983		Change 1975–1983	
	Women CEOs	% of Total	Women CEOs	% of Total	Women CEOs	% of Total	Number	%
Private	132	4.7	166	5.9	169	6.0	37	28
4-year	98	3.5	127	4.5	124	4.4	26	27
2-year	34	1.2	39	1.4	45	1.6	11	32
Public	16	.6	78	2.8	85	3.0	69	431
4-year	5	.2	25	.9	28	1.0	23	460
2-year	11	.4	53	1.9	57	2.0	46	416
Total	148	5.2	244	8.7	254	9.1	106	72

Source: Judy Touchton, "Women CEOs in Higher Education: Getting to the Top," Office of Women in Higher Education, American Council on Education (May 1984).

Note: Only institutions accredited by the six major accrediting associations in the United States and outlying areas are included (N = 2,800). The total number of women CEOs reflects both new appointments and women presidents of newly accredited institutions.

Relative Salaries of Male and Female Faculty

Salaries of women faculty lag behind those paid to male faculty, but this gap is smaller than that which is typical of women and men in general (*AAUP Bulletin: Academe*, various years; Fuchs, 1986; O'Neill, 1985). Table 6 shows that in 1976 women faculty earned 90.4, 95.2, and 95.7 percent of male earnings at the full, associate, and assistant professor ranks, respectively. By 1985 the gap had widened to 88.1, 92.9, and 91.9 percent per rank.

These figures indicate that the gross salary differentials existing between women and men professors in 1976 stubbornly persisted in higher education in 1985. As was shown previously in Table 2, women faculty do not enjoy as favorable a distribution across ranks as do their male counterparts, but even *within* ranks, women's salaries lag behind those of men.

These rank and salary data, in combination, invite explanation. It is expected that individual differences in discipline, education, years of continuous service, academic performance, and relevant demographic factors should account for some of the observed gender-based differences in rank and in salary. Of course, the critical question is whether gender remains as an independent and significant determinant. If it does, then the discrimination hypothesis cannot be dismissed. This conclusion would also suggest the need for affirmative action programs designed to correct sex-biased employment decisions in higher education. The power of this argument would be strengthened

TABLE 6
Weighted Average Salaries of Faculty in Higher Education,
by Rank and Sex, Selected Years, 1975–1985[a]
(in dollars)

	Professor	Associate Professor	Assistant Professor	Instructor	Lecturer
1975–1976					
Men	$22,970	$17,260	$14,240	$11,620	n/a
Women	20,770	16,440	13,630	11,030	n/a
Women's salary as a percent of men's	90.4	95.2	95.7	94.9	n/a
1976–1977					
Men	24,290	18,340	15,120	12,300	n/a
Women	22,290	17,540	14,440	11,630	n/a
Women's salary as a percent of men's	91.3	95.6	95.5	94.5	n/a
1977–1978					
Men	25,190	19,060	15,690	13,010	14,960
Women	22,970	18,110	14,950	12,160	12,940
Women's salary as a percent of men's	91.2	95.0	95.3	93.5	86.5
1978–1979					
Men	26,600	20,190	16,630	13,820	15,620
Women	24,160	19,200	15,820	13,020	13,870
Women's salary as a percent of men's	91.2	95.1	95.1	94.2	88.8
1980–1981					
Men	31,140	23,530	19,340	15,550	n/a
Women	28,250	22,290	18,300	14,780	n/a
Women's salary as a percent of men's	90.7	94.7	94.6	95.0	n/a
1982–1983					
Men	35,960	27,270	22,550	18,340	20,970
Women	32,010	25,470	20,940	17,030	18,260
Women's salary as a percent of men's	89.0	93.3	92.8	92.9	87.1
1983–1984					
Men	37,860	28,610	23,870	19,410	22,050
Women	33,730	26,870	22,050	17,960	19,150
Women's salary as a percent of men's	89.1	93.9	92.4	92.5	86.8
1984–1985					
Men	40,390	30,410	25,370	19,880	23,430
Women	35,590	28,240	23,320	18,500	20,450
Women's salary as a percent of men's	88.1	92.9	91.9	93.1	87.3

Source: AAUP Bulletin: Academe. "Annual Report on the Economic Status of the Profession," Vols. 62–65, 67, 69–71 (1976–1985).
[a] "Weighted" refers to weighting average salary by number in each group. Samples include between 1,278 and 2,598 institutions providing data by sex. Figures have been rounded to the nearest $10.

by a finding that young women assistant professors publish virtually as much as their male counterparts. It would be further strengthened if it could be shown that affirmative action does not reduce the quality of the faculty as a whole—an argument sometimes leveled against such programs. While general findings are not available, these were two of the conclusions drawn by Ferber, Loeb, and Lowry (1978) in their study based on data from a major university.

Discrimination in Earnings and Promotions

Few seriously challenge the assertion that sex (female) discrimination is a fact of academic life. The causal evidence presented in the previous section certainly shows that faculty women have not fared as well as male faculty in terms of ranks, tenure, top administrative positions, and earnings. However, there is a need to establish the degree to which the observed female-male differences are attributable to gender as opposed to factors other than discrimination. This is a complex empirical issue.

Ceteris Paribus Assumption

Discrimination can be shown to exist only when women who have identical characteristics (e.g., ability, education, experience, performance, and tastes) as men faculty are accorded inferior employment treatment. Numerous studies have attempted to meet this requirement in varying degrees with both national and university-specific samples. Virtually all of these studies found that earnings decisions are governed, in part, by gender.

This finding holds up when female and male information is pooled in a single regression model with gender as an independent variable and male and female economic rewards are analyzed in separate regression runs. When gender (female $= 1$) is entered as a dummy variable after controlling for other influences, its coefficient invariably was found to be negative and statistically significant. Similarly, under the two-regression alternative, the earnings determination structures (i.e., sets of estimated coefficients) for women and men were found to be significantly different. This approach predicts what the earnings of women would be if they were paid in the same way as men. The difference between this predicted value and women's actual pay measures the extent to which women are paid less than men with identical characteristics.

The Human Capital Argument

Part of the literature on the economic status of women uses various methods to examine theorems and empirical conclusions derived from human capital theory. The theory's holding is simple—namely, that earnings differentials are caused by human capital differentials.[1] An assumption is that women accumulate less human capital (i.e., knowledge and skills derived from on-the-job training and continuous work experience) than men. The theory suggests that women will choose not to invest in as much human capital (e.g., by attending less expensive graduate programs and/or taking teaching rather than research jobs) if they anticipate a lower return on their investment due to career interruptions. This suggests, in turn, that the female-male salary differential may be virtually nonexistent at the beginning of a woman's career, that it widens as she drops out of her career, and that it then narrows gradually in later life after she permanently resumes her career (Johnson and Stafford, 1974).

Using 1970 National Science Foundation data on Ph.D.s, Johnson and Stafford found that female faculty earn less than male faculty. Attribution is assigned both to sex discrimination and to differences in female and male human capital investment, in step with the aforementioned theory. Moreover, the female-male salary profiles suggested by this theory could not be dismissed by the evidence.

Ferber and Kordick's 1978 study analyzing national data for the years 1958–1963 and 1967–1972 attenuates the above findings to some extent. After controlling for numerous other variables such as discipline, age, academic performance indexes, hours worked, and percent of time worked (excluding rank), they also found that gender negatively affects salary. However, in contrast to the Johnson and Stafford findings, they discerned that the labor force participation of Ph.D.-holders is only marginally lower for women than for men, that Ph.D. women are no more likely than men to take jobs in teaching institutions where the opportunity to accumulate human capital is less, and that while women have a flatter salary profile than men, the salaries of faculty women do not seem to "catch up" with those of men in the later stages of their careers. Related attenuations are also drawn based on an analysis of data from a major university (Ferber, Loeb, and Lowry, 1978).

The analytical tug-of-war illustrated by this brief comparison is noted only to recognize that the proportion of the faculty salary gap attributed to human capital and other arguments as opposed to discriminatory causes is a matter of continuing investigation. Differences in the models estimated and in the data used naturally lead to differences in results. Thus, the task of making strict comparisons is difficult at best. More central to this review, however, is the observa-

---

[1] As this issue relates to women in general, a recent empirical study (O'Neill, 1985) is suggested to the reader.

tion that even after human capital and other variables are taken into account, gender-based wage discrimination is invariably shown to exist.

Other Empirical Findings

Many faculty salary, rank, and promotion studies were published during the 1970s and 1980s. The Johnson and Stafford (1974) study referenced above that used National Science Foundation data concluded that 40 percent of the wage disadvantage faculty women endure over a 35-year work life is attributable to discrimination. Another study (Ferber and Green, 1982) that analyzed data from the University of Illinois, Urbana-Champaign, found that 48 percent of the differential between the mean salary of faculty men and women could be attributed to discrimination (omitting rank from the analysis).

Another study of an unnamed university examined the relationship between salary and a host of independent variables including age, race, years at the university, current education, department, work, and sex (Gordon, Morton, and Braden, 1974). With pooled female-male data, this study found that faculty women earned 9.5 percent less than men, ceteris paribus. The two-regression approach yielded a sex-based difference in salary of 11.4 percent. Using a data set from another university, Hoffman (1976) conducted a study that replicated the models used by Gordon, Morton, and Braden. However, in this analysis, rank was alternatively included and excluded. When it was included, the gender (female = 1) coefficient was − 7.4 percent; when it was excluded, this coefficient changed to − 16.2 percent. The two-regression approach yielded a similar sensitivity to the inclusion/exclusion of a rank variable. In this instance, the percent difference between mean male and female salaries that can be attributed to discrimination when using the male salary structure jumped from 29 to 56 percent, respectively. The findings of other studies are similar (Ferber and Green, 1982; Bayer and Astin, 1975).

Clearly, rank is related to faculty salaries. However, if promotions in rank are also open to sex-discriminatory decisions, then a case can be made to omit the rank variable from any model that attempts to measure the degree of gender-based salary discrimination. The question begging an answer, of course, is whether gender plays a role in the rank or promotion decision-making process. Using national data, Bayer and Astin (1975) found few differences in the structure of separate equations used to predict the rank of women and men professors. A university-based study of the status of new hires during the 1975–1978 period concluded that some, albeit weak, evidence exists showing that women are more likely to receive a lower rank than men with equivalent qualifications (Ferber and Green, 1982).

Among the studies noted above, and others, it has been a general finding that, in addition to gender, variables such as experience and qualifications, teaching and research productivity, and external market conditions (as measured by discipline and/or the mean pay of assistant professors in a given department) are also important determinants of faculty pay.[2] Interestingly, while the results are mixed as to whether the sex-based salary gap is closing, at one university it appears as though the availability (and also the subsequent distribution) of post-1972 affirmative action salary disbursement money has had the effect of equalizing pay (Koch and Chizmar, 1976).

It is premature to conclude that university-based affirmative action programs have been effective on an across-the-board basis. The overall findings of sex discrimination in pay and promotion as garnered from 1960 and 1970 in-house and national data sets, regardless of the variables selected for use in the analysis, seem to argue for the continuation and enhancement of administrative programs designed to purge sex discrimination from academe.

Antidiscrimination Policies

Gender as well as other forms of discrimination in the employment areas of hiring, promotion, and pay are banned by federal and state statutes. Under federal law, most cases of sex discrimination in higher education are brought under Title VII of the Civil Rights Act of 1964 (which was amended in 1972 to include academe) or under Title IX of the Higher Education Act of 1972. To a lesser extent, remedies have also been sought under the Equal Pay Act of 1963. Responsibility for enforcing Title VII rests with the Equal Employment Opportunity Commission (EEOC). Indeed, some argue that the EEOC, along with consent decrees and remedies available at the state level, have offered female faculty a greater margin of success than have suits brought in the federal courts.

Sex discrimination is complex and multifaceted and thus, admittedly, difficult to measure or quantify. Nevertheless, as already noted, the preponderance of the statistical studies that have been made of this untidy area of employment in higher education suggest the presence of discrimination against women faculty. Discriminatory practices diminish economic efficiency and cause productivity to be less than it would be in its absence. In the next section, antidiscrimination policies and court rulings are briefly reviewed. One can only conjecture as to their overall effectiveness. It would seem that this is an area requiring more scientific investigation.

---

[2] See, for example, Tuckman and Tuckman (1976), Reagan and Maynard (1974), Ferber and Loeb (1973), Katz (1973), Koch and Chizmar (1973), and LaSorte (1971).

Faculty Litigation

The empirical literature reviewed above suggests that gender (female) has played an independent and statistically significant role in promotion and pay decision-making in higher education. Thus, it is not surprising that hundreds of judicial decisions involving sex discrimination in academe have been handed down, including some involving hiring decisions. Moreover, thousands of charges have been filed by female faculty with the EEOC, and still more have been processed through institutional grievance procedures or otherwise settled through out-of-court agreements (LaNoue, 1981).

Establishing a Prima Facie Case

Establishing a prima facie case for sex discrimination is difficult. The strategy of establishing a case based on "disparate treatment" (i.e., proving intent to discriminate) has met with mixed success because sex discrimination is seldom explicit and in academe many employment decisions are decentralized and reached in closed-door sessions. A showing of "disparate impact" (i.e., proving that a facially neutral employment policy favors one group over another) has been easier to establish. Both strategies involve the use of statistics, but the courts have not laid out the analytical methodologies and statistical applications that they find most probative (Vladeck and Young, 1978). Even where statistical discrimination is shown, a disparate-treatment claim requires additional proof of the presence of a sex-biased motive. In contrast, when disparate impact is shown, the higher education institution has the burden of proving the academic justification for the policy in question.

Judicial Restraint

In addition to the technical complexities required to prove sex discrimination in academe, the courts have shown some reluctance to review the merits of sex-discrimination claims in higher education. Rather, their preference was to ensure that the faculty plaintiff's record was evaluated in good faith and that the professor received procedural due process.[3] Moreover, one author observed that four years elapsed following passage of the 1972 Higher Education Amendment to Title VII before a single female faculty member received a salary adjustment under court order (LaNoue, 1981, 1982). The primary reason for this reluctance stems from the high level of subjectivity inherent in the nature of faculty hiring, promotion, tenure, and pay decisions. The courts have noted, for example, that the tenure decision

---

[3] *Johnson v. University of Pittsburgh*, 435 F.Supp. 1328, 1332 (W.D. Pa. 1977).

can carry with it a lifelong employment commitment and, thus, their intrusion into the assessment of academic decisions through the requirement of, say, rigid and objective standards of performance evaluation could seriously compromise any higher education institution's goal of academic excellence.[4]

Nothing in Title VII suggests that higher education is unique and should be treated any differently from industry-at-large in the area of sex discrimination. Thus, as one might expect, the early hands-off pattern established by the courts is changing (LaNoue, 1981; Vanderwaerdt, 1981). For example, in *Sweeney v. Board of Trustees of Keene State College*,[5] a female faculty member was denied promotion to the rank of full professor twice before receiving it. The trial court in this case found that the college had discriminated against her and awarded promotion back-dated two years, with back pay and attorney's fees. The college appealed, but the First Circuit Court of Appeals upheld the decision of the lower court. Of greater significance is the court's statement of misgiving with the hands-off approach that other courts previously had applied to hiring, promotion, tenure, and salary decisions involving colleges and universities.

Many scholars believe that *Sweeney* and its progeny marked the beginning of a new era in academic discrimination cases—a beginning that was augmented by court-approved settlements and consent decrees like those reached at Rutgers in 1976, Brown University in 1977, and the University of Minnesota in 1979.[6] Moreover, as implied in the previous section, the EEOC and other judicial forums have not demonstrated the same degree of reluctance to intervene in sex-based employment-status issues as have the courts (Vanderwaerdt, 1981).

The Rajender *Consent Decree*

The impetus for the *Rajender* decree began in 1973. Shymala Rajender, with a Ph.D. in chemistry, held a postdoctoral research appointment in the Chemistry Department at the University of Minnesota from 1966 to 1969. From 1969 through 1972, she was employed by the department as a temporary assistant professor. In 1972 her contract was not renewed. Thereafter she filed Title VII sex-discrimination charges against the University of Minnesota. Her initial complaint was later amended and became a class-action suit on behalf of female faculty members and applicants.

---

[4] Two leading cases advancing the doctrine of judicial restraint are *Faro v. New York Univ.*, 502 F.2d 1229, 8 EPD ¶ 9632 (2d Cir. 1974) and *Green v. Board of Regents of Tex. Tech Univ.*, 335 F.Supp. 249 (N.D. Tex. 1971), *aff'd*, 474 F.2d 594 (5th Cir. 1973).
[5] 569 F.2d 169, 175, 176, 16 FEP 378 (1st Cir. 1978).
[6] Respectively, the citations are as follows: *Bennun v. Board of Governors of Rutgers Univ.*, 413 F.Supp. 1274, 12 FEP 1393 (D.N.J. 1976); *Lamphere v. Brown Univ.*, 553 F.2d 714, 16 FEP 941 (1st Cir. 1977); and *Rajender v. University of Minnesota*, 24 FEP 1051 (D. Minn. 1979).

Rajender showed that the Chemistry Department had not hired a woman into a regular faculty position for 60 years and that the last woman hired had retired in the 1940s. Moreover, during her six years with the department, only one woman had been invited to the campus for a job interview. The department had invited 26 men but only the one woman to job interviews on the campus since 1971, and 17 men and zero women were offered tenure-track positions.

Seven years later the case of *Rajender v. University of Minnesota*[7] was settled out of court. Rajender, now a patent attorney in San Francisco, was awarded $100,000. More critically, the decree also called for the following: (1) a quota on the Chemistry Department, whereby two of the next five tenure-track openings must be filled by women; (2) an augmented universitywide affirmative action program focusing on academic employment and requiring aggressive advertising of vacancies directed at women, with employment notices carrying the phrase, "The University of Minnesota specifically invites and encourages applications from women and minorities"; (3) field-specific affirmative action goals and timetables based on national statistics to define "available pools" of female Ph.D.s and data on departmental hiring and underutilization rates; (4) a preferential hiring policy requiring that a woman applicant receive preference over the male counterpart if the two are "approximately equal" in their qualifications for the position and if the employing department is underutilizing female faculty vis-à-vis their relative availability; (5) a seven-member committee to consult with the University administration on equal employment issues; (6) a grievance procedure for claimants, which provides for an internal review of the charge before it may proceed to trial; and (7) a court-appointed "Special Master" with the power to resolve all past or future sex-discrimination claims, including the power to award cash damages, make faculty appointments, and oversee hiring practices until 1989.

Under the decree, faculty women were given until December 31, 1981, to make claims retroactive to March 1972. After that, all claims must be based on alleged contemporary sex discrimination.

As of September 15, 1985, 322 claims alleging sex discrimination were filed under the *Rajender* decree. Of these, 189 individual claims have been settled (only 9 of which went to trial before the Special Master), 93 individual claims were dismissed or withdrawn, 8 cases remain unsettled, and 32 petitions for policy change were still pending.

The *Rajender* litigation, administration of the *Rajender* decree, and the settlements reached under it were costly. As of October 17,

---

[7] 546 F.Supp. 158, 29 FEP 513 (D. Minn. 1982).

1985, the University of Minnesota spent slightly more than $7,000,000 as a result of this suit, and the financial burden will no doubt continue to grow. Presumably, the magnitude of these dollar outlays and the national publicity that the *Rajender* case received would have the effect of putting other higher education institutions on notice that sex discrimination can be a losing proposition. Of more importance, sex discrimination may cause upheaval in otherwise academically sound, peer-based policies for hiring, promoting, tenuring, and paying faculty (Broad, 1980).

As one might expect, women's share of full-time regular faculty positions at the University of Minnesota has grown steadily since 1980. In the fall of 1981, 16.6 percent of those positions were held by women; the figure in the fall of 1985 was 18.7 percent. It seems that the decree's demand for an aggressive program for affirmative action may be paying dividends.

Sexual Harassment

Until recently, the legal standing of sexual harassment under Title VII was a matter of some controversy. In June 1986, however, the Supreme Court unanimously held that Title VII authorizes sexual harassment suits based on claims of a "hostile or offensive working environment," *even if* the plaintiff does not suffer any economic loss in employment benefits, such as pay or promotion, and *even if* sexual favors are not demanded in exchange for a more favored condition of employment. Moreover, the Court seemed to affirm the EEOC guideline that employers may be liable for supervisors' conduct.[8]

In the hope of getting at some measures of the incidence of sexual harassment on the campuses, surveys involving faculty were recently conducted at the University of Arizona (Metha and Nigg, 1983) and Harvard University (Verba, DiNunzio, and Spaulding, 1983). The research included information on both perceptions and experiences.

Regardless of the definition of the behaviors used, a large enough share of faculty women on both campuses reported incidents of sexual harassment for the authors to call for stronger institutional policies and programs. Adverse perceptions and experiences were far more numerous among women than among men faculty. Both studies recommended using publicity to raise sensitivity on the campus to the negative effects of sexual harassment. Moreover, since many victims of harassment were not aware of their own university's policies for dealing with problems of this nature, and since others feared reprisals, one study pointed out the "need for well-publicized, trusted, easily used,

---

[8] *Meritor Sav. Bank v. Vinson*, 477 U.S.___, 40 FEP 1822 (1986).

and effective channels of complaints" (Verba, DiNunzio, and Spaulding, 1983, p. 70).

A necessary step in shaping institutional policies and programs to prevent and redress damages arising out of sexual harassment cases is agreement on how it is to be defined. Definitions of sexual harassment vary from campus to campus (Crocker, 1983; Somers, 1982). Nevertheless, higher education is not immune from either the problem or the necessity for framing specific policies and programs to rid the academic environment of this impediment to open academic and professional exchange.

For example, in 1981 the University of Minnesota formally established a sexual harassment policy. This policy draws on the EEOC's definition and makes clear that the University will not tolerate such behavior. In part, the policy notes: "Sexual harassment in any situation is reprehensible. It subverts the mission of the University and threatens the careers of students, faculty, and staff. . . . Academic and career relationships may be poisoned by the subtle and destructive overtones of this problem" (University of Minnesota, 1981, p. 1).

The policy was amended in 1984 to include a section on "consensual relationships" between faculty, faculty and student, or supervisor and subordinate. This extension cautions that if a sexual harassment charge is lodged and the case involves a consensual relationship where a power differential exists between the two parties, it will be extremely difficult to prove immunity on the grounds of mutual consent. Shortly after the policy was amended, C. Peter Magrath, then president of the University of Minnesota, stated in a letter to the university community: "It should be clearly understood that the policy does not forbid such relationships, but we believe that we would be shirking our responsibility if we did not warn individuals of the possible pitfalls in such relationships" (Magrath, 1984).

The University's 1981 and 1984 actions also created formal procedures for filing, investigating, and resolving complaints. Sexual harassment experience at the University of Minnesota suggests that (1) harassment is a more common problem for students and clerical workers than for faculty women; (2) sexual harassment comes in many forms; and (3) male faculty are often cited in harassment complaints. The University is averaging about 20 complaints a year. Sanctions leveled against respondents range from verbal warnings to terminations. One of the more interesting sanctions involved billing the budget of a department for the tuition, fees, and related educational expenses incurred by a student now pursuring her studies at another university, because it was deemed impossible for her to continue with her major at the University of Minnesota (University of Minnesota, 1986).

A Final Assessment

Analytical studies to date suggest that gross negative female-male earnings differentials existed in the 1960s and 1970s. Moreover, this negative difference, though smaller, persisted even after controlling for nondiscriminatory determinants of earnings such as discipline, education, years of continuous service, academic performance, and other meritorious factors. Though not as strong, there is also some evidence drawn from these early data bases to suggest that sex discrimination may have been present in decisions that impinge on promotions and tenure.

Whether the employment status of female faculty has measurably improved relative to male faculty since the 1960s and 1970s is hard to determine. Unadjusted, aggregate female-male cross-tabulations covering the 1980s suggest that while the share of female faculty in the academic labor force and in leadership positions within higher education institutions seems to be inching upward, negative gaps persist in the rank, tenure, and earnings areas of employment status. The extent to which these gaps are governed by the sex variable is a subject demanding empirical research that draws on contemporary national and institutional data bases.

Moreover, there is a paucity of analytical studies that relate hiring processes and decisions specifically to the sex variable. We hope that any subsequent research along the lines suggested here will also attempt to measure the employment effects of affirmative action programs. In a broad sense, it is important to learn more about the impact of affirmative action on both the employment status of female faculty and the overall welfare of academe itself. The significance of this recommendation lies in the fact that it is sometimes argued that the principles of equal employment opportunity and academic excellence are more competitive than they are complementary.

Little is known about on-campus sexual harassment, its presence, causes, and consequences. As a burgeoning area of sex-discrimination concern, this subject awaits rigorous analysis. The survey research being used to study sexual harassment leaves a great deal to be desired. Little attention has been given to the problems of retrospective self-reports, selectivity bias, and other distorting features. There is a need for studies on sexual harassment that stand on scientifically received principles of empirical methods. Also, there is an unmet need for baseline studies within academic institutions that will be of secular value as subsequent attempts are made to measure the extent and the degree to which progress is being made to stop it.

In summary, it appears as though female faculty may be somewhat better off than women in general vis-à-vis their relevant male counterparts. However, employers in higher education have not done a particularly good job of distinguishing themselves from industry in general. No doubt there will be other examples of situations that produce positive shock effects, as the *Rajender* decree did. Nevertheless, there is concern that when research findings based on data from the 1980s begin to come in, they too will show the presence of sex discrimination against women in academe.

References

Ahlburg, Dennis A., and Michael B. Lee. "The Labor Market for Industrial Relations Academics: Job Status and Mobility." Unpublished paper, Industrial Relations Center, University of Minnesota, 1986.

American Federation of State, County and Municipal Employees (AFSCME). *On the Job Sexual Harassment: What the Union Can Do.* Washington: AFSCME, 1981.

AAUP Bulletin: Academe. "Annual Report on the Economic Status of the Profession." Volumes 59, 62–65, 67, 69–71 (1973–1985).

Baxter, Ralph H., Jr. "Judicial and Administrative Protections Against Sexual Harassment in the Workplace." *Employee Relations Law Journal* 7 (1982): pp. 587–93.

Bayer, Alan E., and Helen S. Astin. "Sex Differentials in the Academe Reward System." *Science* 188 (May 23, 1975): pp. 796–802.

Broad, William J. "Ending Sex Discrimination in Academia." *Science* 208 (June 6, 1980): pp. 1120–22.

Crocker, Phyllis L. "An Analysis of University Definitions of Sexual Harassment." *Signs: Journal of Women in Culture and Society* 9 (Summer 1983): pp. 696–707.

Faley, Robert H. "Sexual Harassment: Critical Review of Legal Cases with General Principles and Preventive Measures." *Personnel Psychology* 35 (1982): pp. 583–600.

Ferber, Marianne A., and Carole A. Green. "Traditional or Reverse Sex Discrimination? A Case Study of a Large Public University." *Industrial and Labor Relations Review* 35 (July 1982): pp. 550–64.

Ferber, Marianne A., and Betty Kordick. "Sex Differentials in the Earnings of Ph.D.s." *Industrial and Labor Relations Review* 31 (January 1978): pp. 227–38.

Ferber, Marianne A., and Jane W. Loeb. "Performance, Rewards, and Perceptions of Sex Discrimination among Male and Female Faculty." *American Journal of Sociology* 78 (January 1973): pp. 995–1002.

Ferber, Marianne A., Jane W. Loeb, and Helen Lowry. "The Economic Status of Women Faculty: A Reappraisal." *Journal of Human Resources* 13 (Summer 1978): pp. 385–401.

Fuchs, Victor R. "Sex Differences in Economic Well-Being." *Science* 232 (April 1986): pp. 459–64.

Gordon, Nancy M., Thomas E. Morton, and Ina C. Braden. "Faculty Salaries: Is There Discrimination by Sex, Race, and Discipline?" *American Economic Review* 64 (June 1974): pp. 419–27.

Hoffman, Emily P. "Faculty Salaries: Is There Discrimination by Sex, Race, and Discipline? Additional Evidence." *American Economic Review* 66 (March 1976): pp. 196–98.

Howard, Susan. "Title VII Sexual Harassment Guidelines and Education Employment." *Project on the Status and Education of Women* (August 1980): pp. 1–4.

Johnson, George E., and Frank P. Stafford. "The Earnings and Promotion of Women Faculty." *American Economic Review* 64 (December 1974): pp. 888–903.

Katz, David A. "Faculty Salaries, Promotions, and Productivity at a Large University." *American Economic Review* 63 (June 1973): 469–77.

Koch, James V., and John F. Chizmar. "Sex Discrimination and Affirmative Action in Faculty Salaries." *Economic Inquiry* (March 1, 1976): pp. 16–24.

———. "The Influence of Teaching and Other Factors Upon Absolute Salaries and Salary Increments at Illinois State University." *Journal of Economic Education* 5 (Fall 1973): pp. 27–34.

LaNoue, George W. "Review of Books by Richard A. Lester and Pezzullo-Brittingham." *Academe* 68 (January-February 1982): pp. 29–30.

———. "The Federal Judiciary, Discrimination, and Academic Personnel Policy." *Policy Studies Journal* 10 (September 1981): pp. 105–23.

LaSorte, Michael A. "Academic Women's Salaries: Equal Pay for Equal Work?" *Journal of Higher Education* 42 (April 1971): pp. 265–78.

Livingston, Joy A. "Responses to Sexual Harassment on the Job: Legal, Organizational, and Individual Actions." *Journal of Social Issues* 38, No. 4 (1982): pp. 5–22.

Magrath, C. Peter, President, University of Minnesota. Letter to University Community, January 10, 1984, regarding the Rajender Consent Decree.

———. Letter to University Community, June 29, 1984, regarding the University's Policy on Sexual Harassment.

Metha, Arlene, and Joanne Nigg. "Sexual Harassment on Campus: An Institutional Response." *Journal of NAWDAC* (Winter 1983): pp. 9–15.

Miranda Assoc., Inc. "Sexual Harassment: Why, and How to Define." Adapted from "An Analysis of University Definitions of Sexual Harassment," by Phyllis L. Crocker (1984).

O'Neill, June. "The Trend in the Male-Female Wage Gap in the United States." *Journal of Labor Economics* 3, Pt. 2 (January 1985): pp. 91–116.

Project on the Status and Education of Women, Association of American Colleges. "On Campus With Women," 13, No. 1, 3, and No. 3, 5 (1983–84).

Reagan, Barbara B., and Betty J. Maynard. "Sex Discrimination in Universities: An Approach through Internal Labor Market Analysis." *AAUP Bulletin* 60 (March 1974): pp. 13–21.

Safran, C. "What Men Do to Women on the Job: A Shocking Look at Sexual Harassment." *Redbook* (November 1976): pp. 149, 217–18, 220, 222–23, and (March 1981): pp. 47–51.

Scientific Manpower Commission. *Professional Women and Minorities,* 5th ed. (August 1984): pp. 114–15, 118–31.

Somers, Amy. "Sexual Harassment in Academe: Legal Issues and Definitions." *Journal of Social Issues* 38, No. 4 (1982): pp. 23–32.

Tangri, Sandra S., Martha R. Burt, and Leanor B. Johnson. "Sexual Harassment at Work: Three Explanatory Models." *Journal of Social Issues* 38, No. 4 (1982): pp. 33–54.

Touchton, Judy. "Women CEOs in Higher Education: Getting to the Top." Office of Women in Higher Education, American Council on Education (May 1980).

Touchton, Judy, and Donna Shavlik. "Senior Women Administrators in Higher Education—A Decade of Change, 1975–1983." Preliminary Report, Office of Women in Higher Education, American Council on Education (November 14, 1984).

Tuckman, Barbara H., and Howard P. Tuckman. "The Structure of Salaries at American Universities." *Journal of Higher Education* 47 (January-February 1976): pp. 51–64.

University of Minnesota. "Sexual Harassment Review Board: Annual Report, 1985–86." University Senate Minutes, May 15, 1986, pp. 77–83.

————. "Sexual Harassment Policy and Procedures." Senate Committee on Faculty
    Affairs, Senate Consultative Committee, April 16, 1981, revised May 17, 1984.
Vanderwaerdt, Lois. "Higher Education Discrimination and the Courts." *Journal of
    Law and Education* 10 (October 1981): pp. 467–83.
Verba, Sidney, Joseph DiNunzio, and Christina Spaulding. "Unwanted Attention:
    Report on a Sexual Harassment Survey." Unpublished Report to the Faculty
    Council of the Faculty of Arts and Sciences, Harvard University, September
    1983.
Vladeck, Judith P., and Margaret M. Young. "Sex Discrimination in Higher Educa-
    tion: It's Not Academic." *Women's Rights Law Reporter* 4, No. 2 (Winter 1978):
    pp. 59–78.

Chapter 10

Minority Women in the Workplace

Julianne Malveaux*
Phyllis Wallace**

The term "doubly disadvantaged" has been frequently used to describe the economic status, and especially the labor market status, of minority women. This double disadvantage is defined as membership in both a minority group and the gender group that has the least amount of economic power. But the term ignores another source of disadvantage for minority women—the labor market disadvantage experienced by her spouse or by members of her family unit. Indeed, as black male employment-population ratios have declined to below 60 percent in 1984 (compared with white male employment-population ratios of more than 70 percent), and as the number of black females heading households has risen to over 42 percent, the family status of black women may be perceived as a third labor market disadvantage (although this is less true for nonblack minority women).

Who are these "doubly disadvantaged" minority women? Almquist and Wehrle-Einhorn (1978) described them as black, "of Spanish origin," American Indian, and "of Asian origin." In a 1978 article that provides some information about the diverse experiences of these women, they estimated the proportion of minority women in the labor force as between 16 and 18 percent. This number had increased by 1984. The nearly 6 million black women in the labor force represent 12 percent of the female labor force, and the 2.6 million Hispanic women (or women of Spanish origin) represent 5 percent of the labor force. Although the Bureau of Labor Statistics (BLS) does not report data on the status of American Indian or Asian women, the recent influx of Vietnamese and Cambodians suggests that the number of these women in the labor force is increasing as well. Based on the 1978 figures cited above, and on the current number of black and Hispanic

* Visiting Research Associate, Institute of Industrial Relations, University of California, Berkeley.
** Professor, Sloan School of Management, Massachusetts Institute of Technology.
Note: Some of Malveaux's work on this chapter was done while she was recipient of support from the Henry A. Murray Center, Radcliffe College; her work as Research Associate, University of California, Berkeley is supported by the National Research Council.

women in the labor force, we estimate the proportion of minority women to be 20 percent of all women in the labor force.[1]

Although the number of minority women in the workplace is sizable, the reader who is interested in their labor market status will frequently be frustrated by finding that discussions of their unique status are almost totally absent from the social science literature. The purpose of this chapter, then, is to review what research there is and to identify and elaborate on the gaps in this research area. Because economic researchers occasionally comment in passing about the status of black women, this review does not purport to be exhaustive. Instead, we hope to raise some of the more important research questions and to highlight trends in the current labor market status of minority women as well as to discuss these trends and their implications for policy. We conclude with our suggestions for future research.

Research on Minority Women: "Some of Us Are Brave"

Marianne Ferber (1982) referred to a tendency toward generalization when she noted that studies concerned only with men tended to be "globally" labeled, while those that refer to women state so clearly. She buttressed her case by mentioning such global titles as "Work Roles and Earnings" and "Economics of Affirmative Action" that refer only to men. Similarly, our review of research on women in the workplace uncovered titles like "Women in Law," "Women and Work: Issues of the 1980s," and "Women, Work, and Wages." These articles or books deal briefly, if at all, with minority women. Hull, Scott, and Smith (1982) reinforce Ferber's point as it relates to black women in the title of their book, *But Some of Us Are Brave: Black Women's Studies.*[2]

Among the few researchers who have directly addressed the position of minority women in the labor market are Phyllis Wallace in her 1980 monograph, *Black Women in the Labor Force*, Julianne Malveaux in a number of her recent studies, and the authors of the essays in *The Black Woman*, a book edited by La Frances Rogers-Rose (1980). A more usual pattern has been to address the status of black women in passing, if at all, in larger studies of women in the labor force or in studies of the labor market status of the black population. Thus,

---

[1] Table 9 in *Employment and Earnings* (U.S. Department of Labor, Bureau of Labor Statistics, January 1985) reports 49.7 million women in the labor force in 1984, of whom 5.9 million were black and 2.6 million were Hispanic. Black and Hispanic women constitute 17 percent of the female labor force. Almquist and Wehrle-Einhorn (1978) report 700,000 Asian-American women in the labor force in 1970. Assuming an annual growth rate of 7 percent since 1970, there would be 1.4 million Asian women, roughly 3 percent of the total, in the labor force in 1984.

[2] The full title of the Hull, Scott, and Smith book is *All the Women Are White, All the Blacks Are Men, But Some of Us Are Brave: Black Women's Studies.*

research on black women seems to have "slipped between the cracks" in studies on blacks and on women.

If research on women in the workplace has neglected the status of black women, it has almost completely ignored the work status of other minority women. Maxine Baca Zinn's 1982 review essay, "Mexican-American Women in the Social Sciences," makes a few references to the labor market status of Mexican, Chicana, or Latina women,[3] and Rosemary Cooney (1975) has studied the labor market participation of Mexican-American women. Our literature search yielded almost nothing on Asian women.[4]

Lack of data is one limiting factor facing researchers attempting to study the labor market status of minority women. There are labor market indicators and data on occupational and industrial status from the Current Population Survey (CPS) as well as BLS data on a monthly or quarterly basis. While the BLS has collected detailed data on blacks and whites since the 1960s, detailed annual data on Hispanic workers has been available only since 1976.

The size of minority populations and the sampling techniques used by the BLS are other limiting factors facing researchers. When unpublished BLS data are used, for example, in a discussion of occupational shifts by age and race, cell sizes are frequently too small to support conclusive results. Similarly, nearly half of the 1984 median age figures for full-time workers by two-digit occupations were reported on cells too small to make accurate comparisons for black and Hispanic women.

On the other hand, research can be designed to overcome many of these sample size limitations. For example, the National Longitudinal Surveys have oversampled for blacks, making it possible to review the labor market behavior of black women over time. Census data, though collected only every 10 years, provide a rich data source for studies of the labor market status of nonblack, non-Hispanic minorities. Chiswick (1983) found the 1/1,000 1970 Census sample large enough to analyze the labor market status of Asian men, and Carliner (1981) used that sample to study the labor force participation of married women in nine ethnic groups. Almquist and Wehrle-Einhorn (1978) also used these data to examine the status of minority women in the labor force.

---

[3] Writers have used the term "Chicana," "Mexican-American," and "Latina" synonymously, although the "Latina" designation is broader and may include other Latin-American women such as Nicaraguans and Salvadorans. The Bureau of Labor Statistics uses the term "Hispanic" to designate women of Mexican, Cuban, and Puerto Rican origin (all groups reported separately in the data) as well as women of other Hispanic origin—those from Latin America, for example.

[4] A bibliography in Kim's 1983 book lists several sources of information on Asian-American women. One article, *Amerasia Journal* (1977), suggests that researchers might examine those regions in which the Asian population is high, such as the San Francisco-Oakland area. The Committee on Women in Asian Studies, University of Minnesota, has also developed a list of information sources on Southeast Asian women abroad and in the United States.

Although the current Census data are a rich source for the study of the labor market status of minorities, changes in the kinds, classifications, and locations of data collected may make comparisons over time difficult. Briggs, Fogel, and Schmidt (1977) noted that the 1970 Census collected data for the Spanish-surnamed (or Hispanics) in only 5 southwestern states, although data on the Mexican-American population are collected for all 50 states.

While the size of data sets that include minority women may certainly impede the study of their labor market status, the myopic collection of all data on women is an equally important impediment. Many researchers have accepted the view that "all women are white" and therefore failed to code their data by race. For example, Catalyst Career and Data Center (1980) gathered data on 816 two-career couples but did not code by race. Similarly, Ann Harlan, in her 1976 study of women who received the MBA from Harvard, failed to code by race.

Shirley Harkess (1985) reviewed the literature on women's occupational experiences in the 1970s and uncovered several shortcomings in existing research. She noted that "very, very few" researchers "chose as their focus the systematic analysis of minority women's occupational experiences." Yet she seems to accept the premise that "all women are white" when she noncritically reports the results of several studies that use large data sets but do not differentiate results by race.

As a case in point, Harkess discusses Cynthia Epstein's 1981 book, *Women in Law*, without observing the cursory treatment given black women attorneys. Epstein's treatment of black women is particularly troubling because some of her earlier work (1973) focused on the status of black women professionals. However, her discussion of women's participation in bar associations ignores the role of black women in black bar associations such as the National Conference of Black Lawyers and the National Bar Association. Instead, she confines her observations to white women's participation in women's and in alternative bar associations like the National Lawyers Guild. While the Epstein discussion is exclusionary, it is of limited importance because it concerns the status of just 1 percent of the black women in the workplace.[5]

The Harkess review cited several other studies that are flawed by their failure to examine the position of minority women. One is Langwell's (1982) study of physicians that describes "men" and "women" physicians but ignores racial differences among them. Another is the DeTray and Greenberg (1977) study of more than 10,000 Michigan teachers where race is mentioned, but where the authors choose, for

---

[5] According to BLS data, of the 3.8 million full-time wage and salaried workers in the labor force, 4,000 are black women lawyers and judges.

the sake of "brevity," to concentrate on gender differences. Given the history of blacks in the teaching profession (elementary and secondary school teaching was one of the few professional occupations in which blacks were employed prior to 1960), such further investigations would have been illuminating. A third example mentioned by Harkess is Link and Settle's 1979 study of the labor supply of nurses. Using a sample of nearly 5,000 married registered nurses, these researchers find significant differences in their labor supply by race and, although these results are reported with others in tabular form, the finding is neither discussed further nor interpreted in the body of the article.

The Labor Force Participation of Minority Women

Is the labor market position of minority women sufficiently different from that of white women that different labor market results need to be routinely reported in research on women? Table 1 sets forth the differences in their labor force participation, unemployment rates, and occupational status, showing that the unemployment rates of black and Hispanic women are higher than those of whites. Although the gap between the labor force participation rates of all black and white

TABLE 1
Selected Data on the Labor Market Status of Women by Race, 1984

	Black Women	Hispanic Women	White Women
Labor force participation rate	55.2	49.9	53.3
16–19 years old	35.0	42.2	55.4
20 and over	57.6	50.8	53.1
20–24	60.7	n/a[a]	72.5
25–34	71.5	n/a	69.8
35–44	73.7	n/a	69.6
45–54	64.5	n/a	62.7
55–64	46.1	n/a	41.2
65 plus	8.0	n/a	7.5
Unemployment rate	15.4	11.0	6.5
16–19 years old	42.6	22.8	15.2
20–24	25.6	12.5	8.8
25 and over	11.2	9.2	5.2
Part-time status			
Percent part-time	22.8	n/a	29.1
Percent part-time for economic reasons	10.5	n/a	6.7
Percent voluntary part-time	12.4	n/a	22.3

Source: U.S. Department of Labor, Bureau of Labor Statistics, *Employment and Earnings* (January 1985), Tables 3, 39, 44.
[a] n/a = not published for Hispanic workers.

women has narrowed over the past 20 years,[6] young black women continue to have lower labor force participation rates than white women in
the same age group. Hispanic women have been increasing their labor
force participation, but their rates continue to be lower than those of
either black or white women.

In her 1980 review of the pre-1980 economic literature on differences in the labor force participation of black and white married
women, Wallace speculated that at the same time the participation gap
between the two groups was narrowing, the factors that explain participation may also have been changing. In particular, although there
was no consensus in the five studies she reviewed (*Dual Careers*, 1975;
Jones, 1973; Bell, 1974; Bowen and Finegan, 1969; Cain, 1966), factors
such as the presence of young children, size of husband's income, and
education emerged as significant in some of the studies. But as black
male labor force participation has declined and the number of black
female family headships has increased (thus increasing the pressures
for black women to participate in the labor force), the rate of change in
the level of black female labor force participation has slowed (and even
declined among black women under age 25).

Studies of black women's labor force participation highlight some
of the issues that should be examined in studies of the participation of
other minority women. Cooney (1975) rejects the notion that "cultural"
differences explain the lower labor force participation of Hispanic
women and suggests that the gap between white and Mexican-American participation rates should be attributed to socioeconomic factors.
She notes in particular that Mexican-Americans are young, have more
children, have younger children, and have less education than their
white counterparts. She also reports that the participation rate of
Mexican-American women increased by 41.8 percent between 1960
and 1970, a rate considerably greater than that of either black (3 percent) or white (26.6 percent) women.[7] The trend Cooney reported in
1975 has continued. Between 1970 and 1984, Mexican-American
female labor force participation rose by 40 percent, compared with
22 percent for white women and 11 percent for black women.

Among non-Mexican Hispanic women, Cuban women have even
higher participation rates than the Mexican women; in fact, their participation rate, 55.6 percent, also exceeds that of either black or white
women. On the other hand, Puerto Rican women have participation

---

[6] See Table A-4 of the *Employment and Training Report of the President* for annual civilian
labor force participation rates.

[7] Cooney (1975) incorrectly reports black female labor force participation at 58.1 percent in
1970 and the participation increase as 24 percent. According to the *Employment and Training
Report of the President*, the black female participation rate was 48.2 percent in 1960 and
49.2 percent in 1970.

rates lower than those of any other group (37.7 percent). Newman (1978) observed that the low Puerto Rican participation rates in the 1970s (when they declined to 27.5 percent in 1977) were not explained by differences in education or fertility, and he speculated that, since half of the Puerto Rican population lives in New York City, the decline might be attributed to the city's deteriorating economic climate during that decade.[8] He supports this speculation by noting that two-thirds of the Puerto Rican women employed in New York City worked in clerical and operative jobs, the two occupations in which employment levels decreased the most during the 1970s.

Like Cooney, Zinn (1982) has criticized the social science literature on Mexican-American women for its "overreliance on culture." Cooney's adjustments in labor force participation rates, coupled with the dramatic increase in the participation rate of Mexican-American women, suggests that a cultural explanation of economic status is inappropriate. Mirande and Enriquez's 1979 study of Mexican-American women takes a quite different approach, relying on a cultural argument to explain low Chicana labor force participation.

Although there is little research on other minority women, one can foresee similar "cultural" arguments being used to explain their participation rates, especially those of American Indian and Asian-American women. This point has not been raised in the current literature, however. Almquist and Wehrle-Einhorn (1978) report (from Census data) that the 1970 labor force participation rates of Asian women were higher than those of black women in that year. Japanese-American and Chinese-American women had participation rates of 49 percent, while the participation rate of Filipino-American women was 55 percent. Using the same data, but restricting his inquiry to married women, Carliner (1981) found that Asian women's participation rates were slightly lower than those of black women, but still more than 50 percent. In his study of the female labor force participation of nine ethnic groups, he reports "the signs and significance of coefficients were generally as expected, but there were wide variations among ethnic groups." One of the more interesting differences was that fertility had a negative effect on the labor supply of all but American Indian and Asian (Chinese, Japanese, and Filipino) women.

While the labor force participation rates of black and white women appear to be increasing and the gap between the rates is narrowing, the difference between the participation rates of white and minority teenagers (ages 16–19) is increasing. Much of the research on

---

[8] Puerto Rican male participation rates are also lower than those of other Hispanic men. In 1984 it was 72.3 percent, compared with 80.5 percent for all Hispanic men, 81.8 percent for Mexican-American men, and 80.4 percent for Cuban-American men.

this group has focused on the high unemployment rate of young men, but, in fact, employment-population ratios for black teen women are even lower and have been for some time. The labor force participation rates of teen Hispanic women are higher than those of black teen women, but lower than those of white teen women.

The low participation rates of young women are a larger problem for black than for white women, especially since young men are a larger proportion of the black population (24 percent) than of the white population (18 percent). After identifying some dimensions of young black women's high unemployment and low participation rates, and controlling for such dimensions as differences in research methods, geographic concentration, family background, or educational attainment, Malveaux (1981) concluded that, within similar groups, young black women experience more unemployment and less participation. Sandell and Shapiro (1980) say that part of the wage (but not employment) difference between young black and white women is due to black women's underinvestment in human capital and, interestingly, that public employment is associated with a 12 percent wage premium. Proportionately more black female teenagers were employed in the public sector in the late 1970s. But, while wage premiums and high employment levels are associated with positive employment situations for young black females, these opportunities have been less available in the 1980s. According to Smith (1980), teen unemployment is often not a significant problem when a young woman plans to attend college, for any possible "scarring" or negative effect on her future wage position can be ameliorated by educational attainment. Yet, despite black gains, the educational gap between blacks and whites remains. Wilkerson (1985) details barriers to access to education for young black women, including the fact that most of them who are college-bound come from families with incomes below $12,000.

In her 1974 study of unemployment among black female teenagers, Wallace raised questions about their labor force participation and work expectations. Many of the youth employment experiments of the late 1970s provided information on the response of young black women to training and education programs.[9] But a number of questions remain. Future research on youth unemployment must examine more closely the work experience of young women. We need an explanation of the low participation rates of young minority women, and we need to know whether these low rates have serious long-term consequences.

---

[9] The Youth Incentive Entitlement Pilot Projects provided minimum-wage jobs for 16- to 19-year-old youths from low-income and welfare households. See Gueron (1984).

During the 1970s, the gap between the participation rates of black and white women over age 25 narrowed, while Hispanic women's participation rate rose rapidly. Given these changes and a changing social environment, it would be interesting to reestimate models that explain labor force participation using current data. If the "convergence" notion holds, similar factors will explain participation rates. If, on the other hand, differences in the status of white and minority women remain important, the factors explaining participation will be as varied as they were in 1970–1975, the years providing data points in many of the existing studies.

Convergence in the Wages of Black and White Women?

Table 2 reports wage differences among women by race. While the median wage for a white female full-time worker is $264 weekly (or $13,728 a year), the median weekly wage for a similarly situated black

TABLE 2
Median Weekly Wage for Women Full-Time Workers
by Race and Selected Occupations

	Black Women	Hispanic Women	White Women
All occupations	$242	$224	$264
Managerial/professional	359	365	378
Executive/administrative	350	357	358
Engineers	457	530	553
Health assessment (nurses, technicians)	370	370	404
College teachers	428	328	456
Other teachers	359	389	374
Technical, sales, administrative support	255	252	256
Technicians	297	307	317
Sales occupations	181	199	215
Administrative support	256	256	256
Secretaries	249	258	258
Service occupations	180	163	180
Private household workers	143	148	124
Food service	171	156	165
Health service	199	181	202
Cleaning service	183	166	193
Precision, production, craft, and repair workers	245	231	256
Operators, fabricators, and laborers	206	182	211
Machine operators and assemblers	206	178	210
Farming	149	190	179

Source: U.S. Department of Labor, Bureau of Labor Statistics, unpublished data on black and Hispanic women, 1976–1984.

woman is $242 (or $12,584 a year). A Hispanic woman working full-time earns $224 a week (or $11,648 annually). The earnings of black women are 92 percent of what white women earn, while Hispanic women's earnings are 85 percent of white women's earnings.

The similarity in the full-time earnings of black and white women has led several researchers to conclude that a "convergence" has occurred, and they now question whether race or gender is more important in explaining the labor market status of black women. Gender tends to be their choice.

Richard Freeman has been a key proponent of the "convergence" theory, and in his book, *The Black Elite* (1976), he demonstrates that black and white male college graduates begin their first jobs at nearly identical wage levels. Although his work is clearly cross-sectional, a subsequent study (Freeman, 1981) suggests that affirmative action gains have been maintained despite the cyclical economic impacts of the 1970s.

Smith (1979) also addressed "The Convergence to Racial Equality in Women's Wages." Labeling the wage growth experienced by black women as "extraordinary" and documenting a wage ratio that narrowed from 34 percent in 1947 to 97 percent in 1975 (for workers), he shows that the characteristics of black and white women have become more similar since the 1950s. He cited a reduction in the proportion of black women who work part-time, shifts in occupational distribution, and migration as factors that partially explain the narrowing of the wage gap between black and white women.

A key aspect of the work of both Smith and Welch (1978) and Freeman (1976) is the "vintage hypothesis" that views the status of cohorts of young blacks as becoming increasingly similar to cohorts of young whites. Comparisons of young (ages 25–34), college-educated, two-earner couples in the Northeast, for example, revealed racial earnings parity. But comparisons frequently fail to note that such families are but a small proportion of the overall black population, and they also frequently fail to point out that blacks who were ages 16–24 in 1984 seem to have experienced few of the "vintage" effects that older black cohorts encountered. Darity (1982) addresses the employment gap between black and white youth and questions the applicability of the "vintage" hypothesis to these youths.

Malveaux (1981) also looks at change and convergence, though from an occupational perspective. Describing those black women who were ages 25–34 in 1968 as a "golden cohort," she documents their progress by comparing their occupational status with that of black women who were 35–44 in 1978. Her conclusion is that an affirmative action climate was at least partially responsible for the gains, but she questions their durability when she views the employment and occupational status of young black women.

The 1979 Smith observations have been echoed in other research. Mellor and Stamos (1982) report weekly earnings in 1981 to support their claim that racial-ethnic differences among women were less than those among men. Smith and Ward (1984) restate Smith's earlier conclusions and say that "the disparity between black and white women has almost vanished." But Darity and Myers (1980) challenge the Smith conclusion and the "convergence" notion, asserting that biases arise in relative income studies when zero-wage individuals are not included.

When Darity (1980) adjusts female income ratios to include women with zero incomes, he finds no "dramatic" narrowing of the income gap between black and white women. If only those women with positive incomes are compared, the ratio of the black to white female wage rises from 61 percent in 1953 to 92 percent in 1977. But if all women are included in the calculation, the narrowing is more modest. Darity reports that the adjusted black female income was 84 percent of the adjusted white female income in 1953. This percentage fluctuated with the business cycle between 1953 and 1963, dropping to 72 percent in 1955. The percentage did not decline between 1963 and 1972; instead it rose to 101 percent in 1972, matching white female income. The adjusted female income ratio was down to 94 percent in 1977.

Darity's examples illustrate the weakness of the income ratio as an aggregate measure. The ratio measures several things—the increased labor force participation of white women which reduces the number with zero incomes, and the occupational shift among black women, most of which took place prior to 1972, the year when black women's income level matched that of whites. Ultimately, however, the flatness of the increase and the decline in the ratio of black to white female income in recent years measure a lack of progress, not convergence.

In another criticism of the Smith approach, Shulman (1984) notes that "Smith is implicitly restricting his definition to that of wage discrimination." He goes on to say that there has been qualified progress in the economic status of blacks, especially black wage-earners, but he argues convincingly that there are still differences in labor market outcomes by race. His conclusion is that if the group experiences of blacks and whites do not become more similar, then the experiences of some cohorts, no matter how small, cannot be used to "rationalize the lack of progress among others."

Bates (1984), too, is critical of the convergence arguments and suggests that the economic well-being of blacks may be declining.

Although he deals only indirectly with the status of black women, he does cite a shift out of private household employment as a key factor in their improved labor market status.

Even though Smith's "convergence" conclusions are not universally accepted, his work has influenced research on/the labor market status of black women. In the report of their study of young black women, Lyon and Rector-Owens (1981) claim that they found low levels of discrimination in the labor market, and they attribute any remaining status differences to the fact that white women bring more "advantages" to the labor market than do black women. Rather than including the traditional human capital variables such as education and experience in their model, they use IQ, family background, and parents' socioeconomic status, and, on the basis of their conclusions that most labor market differences are due to "individual differences," they question whether the labor market is the appropriate place to equalize outcomes.

The problem with work in this area is that the investigators assume that measured IQ (as opposed to actual intelligence), family background, and parents' socioeconomic status are exogenous variables not influenced by labor market outcomes. Lyon and Rector-Owens shift the locus of change from the public policy arena to the individual, and instead of suggesting a positive step, such as affirmative action programs, toward a solution to labor market inequality, they propose that workers find better family backgrounds, better parents (or parents with higher socioeconomic status), and better IQs. Better jobs and better labor market outcomes might conceivably help this process along.

While some researchers rely on human capital variables to explain differences in the labor market status of black and white women, and others use family background variables as explanatory factors, Madhaven, Green, and Jung (1985) posit that "factors associated with an institutional framework will add to the explanatory power of the model." In their attempt to explain their dependent variable, the racial wage ratio, they use the human capital variables, earnings, education, and experience, and add two additional independent variables—political power (or the ratio of blacks in elected offices to their population in the state to the ratio of white elected state officials relative to the state's white population) and a dummy variable measuring the enforcement of fair employment laws.

Although the Madhaven, Green, and Jung model does not explain wage variations in professional and private household work, it does account for a considerable portion of the wage variation in managerial, service, clerical, and craft and kindred occupations. The political power variable is significant only for managers, but the variable that measures enforcement of fair employment laws is significant across occupations. On the basis of their results, Madhaven, Green, and Jung conclude that enforcement of the fair employment legislation has been helpful in closing the wage gap between black and white women.

In any case, it is likely that discussions of the "convergence" of black and white women's wages is inappropriate, as both are affected by occupational segregation that "crowds" most women into what we define as "typically female" jobs. There is little doubt that race discrimination is a factor in explaining differences in the occupational status of black, white, and Hispanic women.

In an attempt to untangle the effects of race and gender in the labor market, Almquist (1975) suggests that comparisons between black and white men or black and white women measure "pure race" effects, while comparisons between white men and white women or black men and black women measure "pure sex" effects. She goes on to say that an "interaction" between race and sex occurs when the difference between black women and white men is greater than the combined race and sex effects. While her article raises interesting questions about untangling the effects, and while she uses her interaction concept to show that black women's unemployment rates are higher than either race or sex effects would predict, her work is but a first step in the untangling process. Readers would have benefited had she gone beyond her discussions of income and unemployment to examine occupational differences by race and sex.

The Darity criticism of convergence theories as well as Almquist's discussion of untangling provide an interesting point from which to consider the implications of wage convergence. If full-time minority women and white women workers had the same median wage levels, would that signal the absence of discrimination? Possibly not, especially when minority women experience more unemployment than do white women. Would convergence suggest the further need for public policy remedies to improve the labor market status of black women? Would convergence signal a reduction in the poverty of black families, especially those headed by black women? Comparing the wages of black and white women deals with just one outcome in a labor market process that has several potential outcomes. A black woman may receive a wage equal to that of a white woman, but she also faces the possibility of being unemployed or working part-time for economic, rather than voluntary, reasons. Further, the comparison of black and white women, both potential victims of discrimination, may obscure the larger gap that needs to be closed—the gap between the wages of minority women and white men.

Occupational Status of Women Workers: Convergence or Key Differences?[10]

The status of low-wage black women casts some doubt on the convergence notion. Differences in employment rates, in occupational distribution, and in the number of full- and part-time workers suggest that conclusions about the status of black women must take these factors, among others, into account. In particular, more black women work part-time for economic reasons, while more white women are voluntarily employed part-time. Many of the occupations in which black women are overrepresented are those where the proportions of economic part-timers is high.

Historically, black women have been heavily overrepresented in the labor market as private household workers. In fact, until the 1960s, the term "occupational distribution" may have been an exaggeration as far as black women were concerned. In 1940, 70 percent of all black women worked in domestic and personal service jobs, 60 percent of these jobs being in private homes. Only 16 percent worked in agriculture and 14 percent were employed in manufacturing and professional jobs. The percentage of black women in private household work had declined to 36 percent by 1960, and by 1981 there were only 6 percent in that classification.

The literature on occupational segregation is helpful in explaining the occupational status of black women. Bergmann (1974) advanced the theory that women were "crowded" into "typically female" occupations, which removed them from competition with men and forced their wages down. The concentration of women in particular occupations provided some support for this theory. The Women's Bureau of the U.S. Department of Labor reported that in 1975 nearly 40 percent of all women workers were employed as secretaries, retail sales workers, elementary school teachers, waitresses, typists, cashiers, seamstresses and stitchers, and registered nurses. Rytina (1981) reported that 51 percent of all women working in 1980 were in occupations that were more than 80 percent female.

Some researchers object to the causality implied in the term "occupational segregation" and suggest instead that women "choose" employment in typically female occupations.[11] Others have refuted these claims empirically.[12] We use the term "occupational segregation" deliberately and with full knowledge of the debate over whether or not women choose segregated jobs. Given the extreme crowding

---

[10] Much of the information presented in this section is from Malveaux (1984a).
[11] See Polachek (1979).
[12] See England (1982).

that black women faced, especially prior to 1960, we see little "choice" involved in black women's occupational distribution.

Occupations have been described in the literature as "typically female," "typically male," and "mixed." The strictest definition of these terms is offered by Jusenius (1976) who suggests that a five percentage point interval around the percentage of women in the labor market represents the cushion between "typically male" and "typically female" jobs. Women were 43 percent of the labor force in 1981. Thus, "typically female" jobs are defined as those in which the proportion of women exceeds 48 percent; "typically male" jobs are those in which the proportion of women is less than 38 percent; "mixed" jobs are those in which the proportion of women ranges between 38 and 48 percent.

Black women moved out of private household jobs and into clerical positions between 1960 and 1981; they also increased their representation in retail sales and maintained significant representation in nondurable goods manufacturing and in service work. Proportionately more black women increased their representation in "traditionally female" professional jobs such as nursing and noncollege teaching, and they began to penetrate "traditionally male" professional and managerial jobs as well.

In Table 3, which shows the occupational distribution of black, Hispanic, and white women as of 1981, the similarity of women's occupational patterns is clear. It is equally clear that there are important differences between minority women and white women as well as occupational differences among minority women. While the proportions of black and white women in the professions are comparable, Hispanic women are underrepresented in professional occupations— even in the "typically female" professional jobs: the health professions and noncollege teaching.

There are proportionately fewer black and Hispanic female managers than white female managers; also, there are proportionately fewer black females than Hispanic females in managerial positions. In this comparison, it is also useful to note the differences among the Hispanics: Mexican-American have the lowest proportional representation of all Hispanic ethnic groups in this category. In sales work, white women had the highest proportional representation of the three groups, with Hispanic women second; the proportional representation of black women was about half that of whites. The largest proportions of women workers of all races are employed in clerical jobs, but both black and Hispanic women lag behind white women in representation in this occupation.

TABLE 3
Occupational Distribution of Women by Race, 1981[a]

	Black Women	Hispanic Women	Mexican Women	White Women
Professional, Technical, and Kindred Workers	15.4%	8.8%	7.5%	17.3%
Engineers	0.1	0.1	0.1	0.2
Physicians, dentists	0.4	0.2	0.1	0.3
Other health professions	4.4	2.1	1.6	4.7
Noncollege teachers	4.7	2.6	2.6	5.4
Engineering, science technicians	0.5	0.5	0.5	0.5
Other salaried	5.1	3.3	2.6	5.8
Other self-employed	0.2	0.2	0.1	0.5
Managerial and Administrative, except Farm	4.1	4.8	3.9	7.8
Salaried manufacturer	0.2	0.4	0.2	0.6
Salaried, other industry	3.3	3.5	3.1	6.0
Self-employed, retail	0.4	0.5	0.3	0.8
Self-employed, other	0.2	0.4	0.3	0.5
Sales	3.2	5.1	5.0	7.3
Retail	2.5	3.8	3.9	5.2
Other	0.8	1.2	1.1	2.1
Clerical	29.5	31.9	31.3	35.5
Bookkeeper	1.9	2.5	2.3	4.5
Office machine operator	2.2	1.7	1.6	1.6
Secretaries	8.2	9.4	8.7	12.0
Other clerical	17.3	18.3	18.6	17.5
Craft and Kindred	1.5	2.4	2.4	1.9
Carpenter	b	0.1	0.1	0.1
Other construction	0.1	0.2	0.2	0.1
Foremen	0.4	0.8	0.6	0.5
Machine jobsetters	0.9	0.1	0.2	0.1
Other metal workers	0.8	b	b	0.1
Auto mechanics	b	0.1	b	b
Other mechanics	0.1	0.2	0.2	0.1
Other craft	b	1.1	1.2	1.0
Operatives, except Transport	14.2	22.2	22.6	9.1
Mine workers	b	b	b	b
Motor vehicle equipment	b	0.2	0.2	0.2
Other durable manufacturing	4.1	7.6	7.9	3.4
Nondurable manufacturing	7.2	11.1	10.5	4.1
Other operatives	2.5	3.3	4.1	1.4
Transport Equipment Operatives	0.7	0.4	0.5	0.7
Driver deliverers	0.6	0.3	0.4	0.7
All others	0.8	0.1	0.2	0.1
Nonfarm Laborers	1.3	1.6	2.3	1.2
Construction	b	0.1	0.2	b
Manufacturing	0.5	0.6	0.9	0.3
All other	0.8	1.0	1.3	0.9
Private Household Workers	9.7	3.7	2.8	1.8
Service, except Private Household	23.7	17.8	18.2	16.1
Cleaning	5.6	4.5	5.0	1.8
Food	6.8	6.1	6.8	7.3

TABLE 3 (*Continued*)

	Black Women	Hispanic Women	Mexican Women	White Women
Health	7.4	3.6	3.3	3.7
Personal	3.3	3.3	3.0	3.1
Protective	0.5	0.3	0.2	0.3
Farmers and Farm Managers	0.1	0.1	b	0.5
Farm Laborers/Foremen	0.5	1.6	1.1	0.8
Paid	0.4	1.5	1.1	0.4
Unpaid family	b	0.1	b	0.4

Source: U.S. Department of Labor, Bureau of Labor Statistics, unpublished data on black and Hispanic women, 1976–1984.
    a Percentages of workers in each racial-ethnic group by occupation. Totals should add to 100.
    b Less than 0.05 percent.

More minority women than white women have blue-collar jobs. The second highest concentration of black women is in service occupations, and a significant proportion of them work as operatives and in private household jobs. Similarly, the second highest concentration of Hispanic women is in operative (or manufacturing) occupations. More Hispanic than white women are employed in service and in private household jobs.

The *Amerasia Journal* (1977) published some estimates of the occupational status of Asian women in the San Francisco Bay area, and while the writers do not suggest that their data are typical of all Asian women, their observations are interesting nonetheless. The *Amerasia Journal* reported a "sizeable" number of Asian women in "lower-ranking professional occupations" and a representative number in clerical work; their representation was uneven among bank tellers, bookkeepers, and file clerks. The writers also noted a heavy concentration of Asian women sewers and stitchers and very few Asian women managers.

Almquist and Wehrle-Einhorn (1978) also provide some information on the occupational status of women by race and ethnicity and report that the occupational distributions of Asian women are somewhat similar to those of white women except for a much higher proportion of Filipino women professionals (32 percent compared with 16 percent for white women) and a much higher level of Chinese women operatives (23 percent compared with 14 percent for white women, 17 percent for black women, and 40 percent for Puerto Rican women). More detailed data on Asian women are needed if we are to compare their status with that of white and other minority women.

Almquist and Wehrle-Einhorn (1978) also include the status of American Indian women in their study, finding that fewer are in professional, managerial, sales, and clerical jobs than either white or, generally, other minority women. There are proportionately more American Indian women operatives (19 percent) than white women operatives, but their representation in this occupation was comparable to that of other minority women. As many American Indian as black women worked in service jobs, and their representation among private household workers was second only to that of black women. Here again, the data are scarce and more are needed.

Although many occupations have remained as "typically female" in 1984 as they were in 1960,[13] the percentage of women in these jobs has declined over the years. If we define two-digit occupations[14] as typically female depending on the percentage of women in those jobs, the proportion of black women in typically female jobs declined from 81.7 percent in 1968 to 77.4 percent in 1981. Similarly, the proportion of white women in typically female jobs fell from 77.7 percent to 72.4 percent between 1968 and 1981.

Black and white women differ both because more black women work in typically female jobs and because they are more likely than white women to be employed as operatives, private household workers, and service workers—all typically female blue-collar jobs. While the proportion of white women in female jobs declined steadily between 1968 and 1981, the proportion of black women in jobs of that type decreased only until 1975 and then leveled off. There was a change, however, in the distribution of black women in typically female jobs. In 1977 most black women were working in blue-collar occupations, but by 1981 the majority had white- or pink-collar jobs. In other words, while white women moved out of typically female occupations between 1977 and 1981, black women moved from one set of typically female jobs to another. In 1977 there were approximately the same number of Hispanic women in typically female white-collar jobs as in blue-collar jobs, but by 1981 more Hispanic women were found in the white-collar occupations.

There is another dimension of occupational segregation that is frequently overlooked as far as minority women are concerned. Not only are they crowded as women, they are also crowded as minority women and thus experience a degree of occupational segregation that is based on gender as well as race.

In her 1982 study, Malveaux explored the dual dimension of this occupational segregation and developed a concept of "black women's

---

[13] For example, 97.7 percent of all secretaries were women in both 1964 and 1984.
[14] Occupational data presented in the tables are based on pre-1982 BLS and Census classifications. As later data are reported differently, they must be adjusted to be comparable with those we have used—an exercise we chose not to attempt. See Rytina (1981) for more detail on methods of classification.

crowding" that attempts to measure the extent to which black women work in occupations that are "crowded" by black women. She compares the representation of black women in detailed occupations with their 5.4 percent representation in the 1981 labor force. She then defines jobs as having a representative number of black women if that number is between 50 and 150 percent of the proportion of women in the labor force—that is, jobs where between 2.7 and 8.1 percent of all workers are black women. This enabled her to determine "degrees" of black women's crowding. Crowding "by a factor of four," for example, means that black women are four or more times their labor force proportion in that particular occupation. Table 4, which shows the extent of black women's crowding as of 1981, indicates that nearly 60 percent of all black women were working in "typically black female" jobs. Nearly 30 percent worked in jobs in which black women were overrepresented by a factor of four or more.

What kinds of jobs are "typically black female"? Black women are overrepresented by a factor of three or more among dieticians, prekindergarten teachers, social workers, registered nurses, and lab technicians. A quarter of black female clerical workers are employed in 5 (of 48) occupations where they are overrepresented by a factor of four: file clerks, typists, keypunch operators, calculating machine operators, and social welfare clerical assistants. They are not overrepresented in

TABLE 4
Employment Among Black Women Workers
Ranked by Percentage of Black Women Employed, 1981

Percent of Black Women in Occupation	Number of Occupations	Percent Black Women Employed
51+		0.1
46.0–50.0	3	4.5
37.9–45.9	0	0.0
32.5–37.8	2	1.2
27.1–32.4	2	0.5
21.7–27.0	1	5.0
16.3–21.6	15	16.8
10.9–16.2	24	12.4
8.2–10.8	21	19.4
5.5–8.1	38	14.6
2.8–5.4	68	16.9
0.0–2.7	254	8.5
Total	429	99.9[a]

Source: Unpublished data, Bureau of Labor Statistics, from Current Population Surveys, annual averages 1981. Also in Malveaux (1982).
[a] Total may not add to 100 due to rounding.

the same clerical jobs where white women are heavily overrepresented, such as bank tellers, secretaries, or receptionists, all occupations that are more than 95 percent female. In service jobs, black women are overrepresented as cleaning and health service workers, but only proportionately represented among food service workers. Finally, although black women are overrepresented by a factor of nine as private household workers, this is an improvement over the situation 20 years ago.

This analysis of detailed occupations leads to the conclusion that black women experience not only more, but also a different kind of occupational segregation than white women. While the concept of "black women's crowding" is a good starting point for a discussion of these differences, it needs further development and precision. Even jobs in which black women are overrepresented by a factor of four or five may be typically female jobs because of the size of the white female population. Thus, the interaction between jobs that are typically female and typically black female must be studied more carefully. Further, the economic consequences of holding typically black female jobs must be examined. Finally, the occupational status of nonblack minority women also must be investigated systematically. If each group of minority women is concentrated in different enclaves of typically female jobs, issues of crowding and of reduced wage competition become more important.

In an extension of her earlier work on the occupational segregation of women, Andrea Beller (1984) explains some of the occupational changes that Malveaux (1982) also identified. In this study she uses the Duncan and Duncan (1955) index of similarity as a measure of the percentage of women or men who would have to change jobs in order to have the same occupational distribution as the other group. Beller documents a decline in the segregation index for both whites and nonwhites. For nonwhites, the major changes toward less segregation by gender occurred in the labor and service occupations; few shifts were noted in the professions. Among white women, fewer were entering traditionally female white-collar jobs and more were employed in occupations that have been classified as traditionally male. The representation of minority women in private household work had declined.

While Beller's discussion adds some precision to our conclusions about changes in the occupational concentration of black women, the fact that she compares nonwhite women with nonwhite men and ignores the forces that have shaped the black male occupational distribution flaws her analysis. Nonwhite women should be compared with white men since the occupational distribution of black men has been affected by racial crowding. More black than white males work in jobs that are typically female,[15] and this may be because, in the past, black men have been excluded from the professional, managerial, and craft jobs where most white men find employment. Thus, Beller's conclusion about the decline in occupational stratification among nonwhites must be interpreted with caution.

Although it has been apparent for some time that the occupational status of minority women has been changing, few researchers have analyzed what changes actually are taking place. As mentioned in the discussion of the Harkess (1985) review, they frequently have focused broadly on women in occupations and made sweeping conclusions that presumably apply uniformly to white women and women of color. A few exceptions are worth noting. Malveaux (1980) studied private household work as a black women's occupation that is declining in size. However, since many women do not report their employment in jobs of this type, the occupation may be more important than its relative size suggests. Priscilla Douglass (1981) studied the careers of black blue-collar working women, Cheryl Leggon (1980) has written about the "contradictions in status" of black women professionals, and Ann Burlew (1981) compared black women in traditional and nontraditional professions. Despite a growing body of literature on black managers and women managers, most studies of black managers focus on men, not women. An exception is Karen Fulbright's 1985 study of barriers to occupational mobility in a sample of more than 150 black women managers.

There are even fewer studies of the occupational status of nonblack minority women. Using the labor market segmentation theory, Guadalupe Friaz (1983) examined the occupational structure in high tech firms in the Silicon Valley where many Mexican-American women are employed. Maria Patricia Fernandez-Kelly's (1982) study of women factory workers at the Mexican border has implications for the status of Mexican-American women elsewhere in the United States. And Elaine Kim's 1983 analysis of the diverse lives and occupations of 12 Asian women is a first step toward more systematic work on occupations of this minority group.

Implications of the Labor Market Position of Minority Women

Some of the occupational differences between white women and their black and Hispanic counterparts in the labor force have been cited in previous sections of this chapter. Here we ask: What are the

---

[15] Table 1 of Malveaux's (1982) paper shows that 13.7 percent of all men, but 16.5 percent of black men, worked in occupations that were more than 70 percent female; 36 percent of all men, and 43 percent of black men, worked in occupations that were more than 50 percent female.

implications of these differences? Do black and Hispanic working women experience more poverty than do white working women? Table 5 displays estimates of the proportion of working women who are poor or near poor, by race.

These estimates are derived by designating those occupations with median earnings of less than $180 a week in 1981 (or less than $9,300 annually, the poverty line for that year) as occupations where workers were poor. Those occupations with median earnings of less than $223 per week (or less than 125 percent of the poverty line) are termed "near poor." These figures must be interpreted with caution, both because some workers earn more and some less than the median wage, and because the weekly earnings levels are estimated assuming full-time, full-year employment. Part-time employment is high in many low-wage occupations.[16]

The poverty of minority women workers becomes an even more serious dilemma when it is recognized that large numbers of them are family heads. Female headship is most prevalent among black families—42 percent of black families were headed by females in 1982, compared with 22 percent of Hispanic and 12 percent of white fami-

TABLE 5
Working Women in Poverty, by Major Occupation, 1981[a]
(numbers in thousands)

Occupation	Black Women		Hispanic Women		White Women	
	Poor	Near-Poor	Poor	Near-Poor	Poor	Near-Poor
Service	965	205	279	52	4755	792
Private household	317	0	73	0	671	0
Operative	253	481	149	284	921	2,232
Clerical	215	628	80	233	1,534	4,548
Sales	117	5	65	3	1,580	96
Laborers	5	54	3	24	79	325
Transport operatives	0	6	0	8	0	57
Total	1,872	1,379	649	604	9,540	8,050
Percent of total women	35.6	26	32.4	30.2	26	21.9
Total poor or near-poor	61.6		62.6		47.9	

Source: Malveaux (1984a).

[a] Poverty status is determined by using median weekly full-time earnings of workers at the detailed occupational level. As noted in the text, these numbers are estimates, as some women work less than full-time, and some women earn more than median occupational earnings. Since detailed data were unavailable for Hispanics in 1981, poor and near-poor status estimates are based on the proportion of white and black poor women in occupations.

---

[16] Thirty-seven percent of service workers are employed part-time; 16 percent work part-time for economic reasons. See Malveaux (1984a) for more detail on part-time work by occupation.

lies. Female headship in and of itself is not a problem, but the low wages and occupational status of women mean that large numbers of female-headed families are poor families. Fifty-six percent of the black families headed by women were poor in 1982, as were 55 percent of Hispanic families and 36 percent of white families.

Although families headed by minority women experience propor-tionately more poverty than do families headed by white women, the emerging "feminization of poverty" literature sweeps broadly past racial differences to discuss poverty as a "women's issue." Pamela Sparr (1984) takes issue with this approach, noting that industrial shifts have caused an increase in the poverty levels of minority men as well. Paths to poverty may differ by race, with more white than black women entering poverty because of divorce. While the level of poverty rose through 1983, the proportion of poor families headed by women actually declined after 1980. Poverty among families headed by men rose during the 1980–1983 period.

Corcoran, Duncan, and Hill (1984), using the Panel Study of Income Dynamics to measure poverty trends and determinants, find that human capital variables explain but a third of the wage gap between white men and white women, and only a quarter of the gap between white men and black women, and they suggest instead that family structure and composition provide an explanation for a signifi-cant amount of poverty. Divorce is one of the most important causes, they say, while remarriage "sharply improves economic status." Inter-estingly, remarriage occurs more frequently for white than for black women.

Because Corcoran, Duncan, and Hill are using longitudinal data to examine poverty, they are able to refute the "culture of poverty" hypothesis. Although they do find a very small number of persistently poor in their sample—a group that they identify as one that does not "easily fit into the underclass stereotype"—a third of the remaining long-term poor are elderly and others live in households headed by women (70 percent by black women). Corcoran, Duncan, and Hill also are able to refute the notion of long-term welfare dependency, noting that just 2 percent of the population in their sample received welfare payments for 8 of the 10 years between 1969 and 1978.

Corcoran, Duncan, and Hill's conclusion is consistent with Lopes and View's (1983) finding that women who receive public assistance do so for an average of 22 months. It may be that poor wages and working conditions of some typically female jobs create an AFDC "merry-go-round": women holding such jobs work as long as they can and are forced to accept public assistance when financial obligations become too great for them to handle with small paychecks. Although the status of minority women on public assistance is not the primary focus here, we need to know much more about the relationship between work and welfare. Both the work/welfare demonstration (Gueron, 1984) and supported work projects (Manpower Demonstration Research Corporation, 1980) yielded some information about this nexus. From a small number of interviews in the latter study, Danziger (1981) was able to conclude that participation in supported work programs was a positive experience for the women who made the successful transition from welfare to steady employment.

An implication of women's poverty status is the status of their children. Corcoran, Duncan, and Hill highlight this critical issue when they note that 30 percent of the white children and 70 percent of the black children experienced poverty at some time during the 10-year period they studied. The families of 30 percent of the black children and 2 percent of the white children had poverty-level incomes at some time during 6 of the 10 years. Poverty data reported by the Department of Commerce in 1983 indicate that 42 percent of Hispanic children under age 5 experienced poverty in 1982, as did nearly half of black children and 18 percent of white children in that age group.

Data on the poverty status of Asian and American Indian women are not available in the same form as comparable data on black, Hispanic, and white women. Yet Sorkin (1978) is able to raise questions about the extent of American Indian poverty in his discussion of their economic status both on and off the reservations. From work by Chiswick (1983) and Almquist and Wehrle-Einhorn (1978) we can guess that Asian women and their children experience less poverty than do the other ethnic groups, although we know that first-generation Southeast Asians have been dependent on public assistance while they were adjusting to living in the United States.

The issue of children's poverty may seem to be only tangentially related to the labor market status of minority women, but since many researchers seem to be convinced that family background variables are useful in explaining current labor market status, it is entirely possible that poverty resulting from the labor market status of minority women affects the future labor market experience of their children.

Among the researchers who have studied the "intersection of work and family," a few have noted the effects it has had on minority women. This research is of interest because it supplements what we know about minority women in the labor market with information about their extra-labor-market experiences. The fact that most minority men have not had access to a "family wage" (Zinn, 1982) forced many minority women into the labor market and makes the study of the intersection of work and family all the more compelling. For many minority women, especially those with children, labor market participation requires that they develop coping strategies.

McAdoo (1980) found that, in their efforts to cope, the majority of black women used a "kin help exchange" strategy, with child care being the service most frequently given and received. In a later book (1981), she reported high levels of stress among single mothers, most of it associated with finances and adequate child care. She calls this finding significant because "oppressive" stress levels may prevent them from dealing with the developmental needs of their children. At least part of this stress might be alleviated if child care were available.

In her research on the child-rearing goals and strategies of black female domestics, Dill (1980) also examined the family/work interaction and found that, despite their limited resources, the women she studied had strong educational goals for their children. Dill notes that her work might be viewed more as "personal histories" had not "racial and sexual barriers" been the reason for the high concentration of these women in private household employment. Too, her discussion of the relationship between black domestics and their white employers raises interesting questions about how black and white women relate to each other.

Strategies to Improve the Labor Market Status of Minority Women

Either supply-side or demand-side strategies may be used to improve the status of minority women. Human capital theory suggests that supply-side policies, including programs designed to improve the productivity of individual minority women, would be an appropriate choice. Several variations of this strategy exist, including apprenticeship training for women preparing to enter skilled blue-collar jobs, educational access programs that facilitate college entry and attendance for both minority women and men, employment and training programs for workers wishing to learn the skills required in new occupations, and youth employment programs that teach new skills and job-search techniques. While we have a lengthy history and a number of evaluations of supply-side strategies that indicate in which areas they have been successful, it is important to note that they have their limitations. These programs do not guarantee workers jobs, nor do they combat those structural aspects of the labor market that produce lower wages, higher unemployment, and crowded occupations for minority women.

The structural, or demand-side, strategies—those that attempt to change institutions, terms, and conditions of work through litigation, organization, legislation, and evaluation—may be more successful in improving the labor market status of minority women. These institutions and the terms and conditions of work can include pay, work status (full- or part-time, public- or private-sector employment), work environment (with special attention to hazardous work conditions), and related issues.

Affirmative action legislation attempted to deal with inequality in the labor market by making discriminating behavior illegal and requiring open access to jobs on a nondiscriminatory basis. Wallace (1982) and Lloyd and Niemi (1979) describe the development of affirmative action legislation and the role of the Equal Employment Opportunity Commission in enforcing it.

No sooner had affirmative action legislation been passed and the EEOC given enforcement powers than the attacks on the process began.[17] At the same time a growing number of researchers were assessing the outcomes of affirmative action laws.[18] Wallace (1976) carefully documented the results of the AT&T consent decree and reported that managerial women were the greatest gainers in that case. Beller (1982a) found that equal opportunity policies helped college-educated women who were new labor market entrants get nontraditional jobs.

What did minority women gain from affirmative action? Will strict enforcement of the legislation improve the labor market status of minority women over time? Wallace (1980, p. 104) writes that "black women as well as other women will benefit greatly from full implementation of laws against sex discrimination. Once there is equal pay for equal work, no differentiation between males and females on fringe benefits, a limitation on separate lines of progression and seniority systems, appropriate maternity and pregnancy leave policies, earnings of women will be increased." In a 1981 paper, Malveaux notes an improvement in the occupational status of the cohorts of black women who were ages 25–34 in 1968 and 35–44 in 1978 and suggests that this occupational advancement is a result of affirmative action. She also finds that the pace of occupational improvement, especially in managerial jobs, was strong in the 1968–1972 period, but weakened between 1972 and 1977.

While affirmative action may have benefited some black women, especially professionals, managers, and unionized workers,[19] the policy was ill-suited to improve the labor market status of more than a third of the black female labor force who are low-skilled, low-wage workers. And while the position of Hispanic women has not been analyzed, it is likely that their experience is similar to that of black women. Although affirmative action as a strategy to improve the labor market status of minorities never achieved wide popularity, it was

---

[17] Glazer's (1975) attack is representative.
[18] See, for example, Beller (1982a), Freeman (1981), and Flanagan (1976).
[19] See Wallace (1984).

accepted as policy up to the early 1980s. Since then, response to the law has become increasingly hostile and enforcement has been weak or nonexistent.

Another strategy, comparable worth, developed out of frustration as women found, after two decades of equal opportunity laws, their wages had increased only slightly relative to those of men. Most researchers attributed the persistence of the pay gap to the occupational segregation that women experience. Comparable worth is based on the concept that "equal pay for equal work" is not enough. Rather, what is required is "equal pay for jobs of equal value." Remick (1981), after documenting the fact that typically male and typically female jobs are evaluated differently, recommends "the application of a single bias-free point factor evaluation system within a given establishment, across job families, both to rank order and to set salaries."

Comparable worth is a relatively new way of dealing with pay inequities in the workplace. Is it a useful strategy for improving the status of black women? Noting the large number of black women who work both in clerical jobs and in the public sector, Malveaux (1985a) concludes that they are likely to benefit from comparable worth legislation and litigation. However, comparable worth may have limits as a strategy for minority women as its greatest impact is likely to be on women employed in the public sector. Minority women whose public-sector service jobs are now contracted out have nothing to gain from comparable worth.

Perhaps what is required to improve the status of minority women in the workplace is a series of demand-side strategies, including unionization and legislation designed both to create jobs and to improve the terms and conditions of employment.

Research Needs and Policy Prescriptions

The research reviewed in this chapter reveals that there are many similarities and many differences in the status of minority women and white women. While most research has focused on similarities and, in fact, failed to focus on nonwhite women, the small but growing literature on minority women makes it clear that we need to know much more about their experience in the workplace and the factors that determine their participation and predict their labor market status.

To date, more has been written about black women than about other minority women. But demographers indicate that the Hispanic minority is currently growing more rapidly than any of the other groups, and thus we need to know more about the factors that determine the participation of Hispanic women in the workplace, more about their experiences of discrimination in the labor market, and more about how the human capital they bring to the labor market affects their status once there. The Asian minority, though small, also is growing. The 1/1,000 1980 Census tapes will be a rich source of data on the labor market status of these women.

Although human capital differences explain some of the wage gap between black women and white men, more research on the impact of particular human capital variables may be useful. If education continues to be even slightly important in determining labor market status, research on educational access must continue.

Is the labor market so segmented that other minority women are overrepresented in their own occupational ghettos? Research on patterns of employment, especially in individual firms, may reveal some answers to this question. And if such patterns exist, how do we change them? More careful analysis of the effects of certain federal policies on minority women (not on either minorities or women) is needed so that we have the information necessary to modify existing policies or develop new ones that would improve the status of minority women. Policy analysis also must be clear on the uneven effects that public policy designed to help women in general may have on minority women.

We need to know more about the occupational experiences of minority women in specific occupations. Some work has been done on black private household workers, professionals, and managers as well as on Chicana electronics assembly workers, but what about their experiences in clerical, service, and operative jobs—occupations in which they are heavily represented? We need to compare the experiences of union and nonunion minority women and their experience in jobs in both the public and private sectors if we are ever to understand why some of them earn wages above the poverty level—but most do not. And we need to know more about what factors were important determinants of the success of some black women, as they may be useful predictors in shaping programs that will aid young women in their efforts to duplicate these successes. We also need studies of the internal labor markets of firms that hire these workers so that we can learn whether the impact of work rules and other institutional factors are different for minority women than for others.

The work/welfare nexus is a challenging issue and will require investigation as long as minority women and children are disproportionately represented among welfare recipients. The "work and welfare" experiments that have been conducted and the evaluations of them have been based primarily on the human capital premise that the problem can be at least partially solved by "improving" the productivity characteristics that welfare women bring to the labor market and then helping them find jobs. But if we view the problem from an institutional perspective we would ask why so many women work under "revolving door" conditions, and we would examine the jobs they have when not on welfare to find out why pay and benefits in these jobs are so low.

As additional research on minority women becomes available, how will we compare the status of minority women with that of others? We believe that comparing the work experiences of minority women with those of white women is the wrong approach because it obscures discrimination that both groups face in the labor market. We prefer the Corcoran, Duncan, Hill (1984) comparison of the status of minority women with that of white men. At the same time, even in a discrimination-free environment, family considerations make it likely that there will be labor market differences between men and women. More work needs to be done on the "untangling" process that Almquist began in her 1975 study.

Because minority women (especially blacks and Hispanics) have crowded the bottom of the labor market, our efforts to shape public policy to improve their status must necessarily concentrate on that segment of the market. Must there be a "bottom," or how fully can we guarantee decent wages, hours, and employment conditions to all workers? If minority women do not occupy this "bottom," then who will? What are the policy implications? It is very important to understand that the labor market status of minority women is closely related to the status of many others—especially minority men and minority children. As we come closer to understanding what determines the labor market status of minority women, and to designing policy to equalize the status of all groups, we come closer to racial and ethnic equality, and thus to a fairer, more equal society.

References

Almquist, Elizabeth M. "Untangling the Effects of Race and Sex: The Disadvantaged Status of Black Women." *Social Science Quarterly* 56 (June 1975): pp. 129–42.

Almquist, Elizabeth M., and Juanita L. Wehrle-Einhorn. "Doubly Disadvantaged: Minority Women in the Labor Force." In *Women Working*, eds. A. Strongberg and S. Harkess. Palo Alto, CA: Mayfield Press, 1978. pp. 63–88.

Amerasia Journal. "Selected Statistics on the Status of Asian-American Women." 4 (1977): pp. 133–40.

America, Richard F., and Bernard Anderson. *Moving Ahead: Black Managers in American Business.* New York: McGraw-Hill Book Co., 1978.

Bates, Timothy. "Black Economic Well-Being Since the 1960s." *Review of Black Political Economy* 12 (Spring 1984): pp. 5–39.

Bell, Duran, Jr. "Why Participation of Black and White Wives Differs." *Journal of Human Resources* 9 (Fall 1974): pp. 465–79.

Beller, Andrea. "Trends in Occupational Segregation by Sex and Race, 1960–1981." In *Sex Segregation in the Workplace: Trends, Explanations, and Remedies*, ed. Barbara F. Reskin. Washington: National Academy Press, 1984. Pp. 11–26.

———. "The Impact of Equal Opportunity Policy on Sex Differentials in Earnings and Occupation." *American Economic Review* 72 (May 1982a): pp. 171–75.

———. "Occupational Segregation by Sex: Determinants and Changes." *Journal of Human Resources* 17 (Summer 1982b): pp. 371–92.

Bergmann, Barbara. "Occupational Segregation, Wages and Profits When Employers Discriminate by Race or Sex." *Eastern Economic Journal* (April-July 1974): pp. 103–10.

Bowen, William G., and T. Aldrich Finegan. *The Economics of Labor Force Participation.* Princeton, NJ: Princeton University Press, 1969.

Briggs, Vernon, Walter Fogel, and Fred Schmidt. *The Chicano Worker.* Austin: University of Texas Press, 1977.

Burlew, Ann K. "The Experiences of Black Females in Traditional and Nontraditional Professions." *Psychology of Women Quarterly* (1981): pp. 192–203.

Cain, Glen G. *Married Women in the Labor Force: An Economic Analysis.* Chicago: University of Chicago Press, 1966.

Carliner, Geoffrey. "Female Labor Force Participation for Nine Ethnic Groups." *Journal of Human Resources* 16 (Spring 1981): pp. 285–93.

Catalyst Career and Family Center. *Corporations and Two Career Families.* Washington: Catalyst, 1980.

Chiswick, Barry R. "An Analysis of the Earnings and Employment of Asian-American Men." *Journal of Labor Economics* 1 (April 1983): pp. 197–214.

Cooney, Rosemary. "Changing Labor Force Participation of Mexican-American Wives: A Comparison With Anglos and Blacks." *Social Science Quarterly* 56 (September 1975): pp. 252–61.

Corcoran, Mary, Greg J. Duncan, and Martha S. Hill. "The Economic Fortunes of Women and Children: Lessons from the Panel Study of Income Dynamics." *Signs: Journal of Women in Culture and Society* 10 (Winter 1984): pp. 232–48.

Danziger, Sandra. "Post-Program Changes in the Lives of AFDC-Supported Work Recipients: A Qualitative Assessment." *Journal of Human Resources* 16 (Fall 1981): pp. 637–48.

Darity, William. "The Human Capital Approach to Black-White Earnings Inequality: Some Unsettled Questions." *Journal of Human Resources* 17 (Winter 1982): pp. 72–93.

———. "Illusions of Black Progress." *Review of Black Political Economy* 10 (Winter 1980): pp. 153–68.

Darity, William, and Sam Myers. "Changes in Black-White Income Inequality, 1968–78: A Decade of Progress?" *Review of Black Political Economy* 10 (Summer 1980): pp. 354–79.

DeTray, Dennis N., and David H. Greenberg. "On Estimating Sex Differences in Earnings." *Southern Economic Journal* 44 (October 1977): pp. 348–53.

Dill, Bonnie Thornton. "The Means to Put My Children Through: Child Rearing Goals and Strategies Among Black Female Domestic Servants." In *The Black Woman*, ed. La Frances Rogers-Rose. Beverly Hills, CA: Sage Publications, 1980. pp. 107–34.

Douglass, Priscilla H. "Black Working Women." Harvard University, 1981.

Dual Careers: A Longitudinal Study of Labor Market Experience of Women. Vol. 1, by John R. Shea et al. Columbus: Center for Human Resource Research, Ohio State University, 1970. Vol. 2, by John R. Shea et al. Washington: U.S. Government Printing Office, 1973. Vol. 3, by Carol Jusenius and Richard L. Shortlidge, Jr. Columbus: Center for Human Resource Research, Ohio State University, 1975. Vol. 4, by Herbert S. Parnes et al. Columbus: Center for Human Resource Research, Ohio State University, 1976.

Duncan, Otis Dudley, and Beverly Duncan. "A Methodological Analysis of Segregation Indexes." *American Sociological Review* 20 (April 1955): pp. 210–17.

Employment and Training Report of the President. Washington: Government Printing Office, 1976-1982.

England, Paula. "The Failure of Human Capital Theory to Explain Occupational Sex Segregation." *Journal of Human Resources* 17 (Summer 1982): pp. 358–70.

Epstein, Cynthia Fuchs. *Women in Law*. New York: Basic Books, 1981.

————. "Positive Effects of the Multiple Negative: Explaining the Success of Black Professional Women." *American Journal of Sociology* 78 (January 1973): pp. 912–35.

Ferber, Marianne. "Women and Work: Issues of the 1980s." *Signs: Journal of Women in Culture and Society* 8 (Winter 1982): pp. 273–95.

Fernandez-Kelly, Maria Patricia. "Feminization, Mexican Border Industrialization and Migration." Working Paper No. 3, Center for the Study, Education, and Advancement of Women, University of California, Berkeley, 1982.

Flanagan, Robert. "Actual versus Potential Impact of Government Anti-Discrimination Programs." *Industrial and Labor Relations Review* 29 (July 1976): pp. 486–507.

Freeman, Richard. "Have Black Labor Market Gains Post-1964 Been Permanent or Transitory?" Discussion Paper 849, Institute of Economic Research, Harvard University, September 1981.

————. *The Black Elite*. New York: McGraw-Hill Book Co., 1976.

Friaz, Guadalupe. "Segmented Markets in Silicon Valley High Tech Firms: Implications for Production Workers." Paper presented at Allied Social Science Associations meetings, December 1983.

Fulbright, Karen. "The Myth of the Double Advantage: Black Women in Management." Ph.D. dissertation, Massachusetts Institute of Technology, 1985.

Giddings, Paula. *When and Where I Enter: The Impact of Black Women on Race and Sex in America*. New York: William Morrow Co., 1982.

Glazer, Nathan. *Affirmative Discrimination*. New York: Basic Books, 1975.

Gueron, Judith. "Lessons from a Job Guarantee: The Youth Incentive Entitlement Pilot Projects." In *Findings from the San Diego Job Search and Work Experience Demonstration*. New York: Manpower Demonstration Research Corporation, 1984. pp. 26–34.

Harkess, Shirley. "Women's Occupational Experiences in the 1970s: Sociology and Economics." *Signs: Journal of Women in Culture and Society* 10 (Spring 1985): pp. 59–96.

Harlan, Ann. "A Comparison of Careers for Male and Female MBAs." Paper presented at the Academy of Management meeting, August, 1976.

Harlan, Ann, and Carol L. Weiss. "Sex Differences in Factors Affecting Managerial Career Advancement." In *Women in the Workplace: Management of Human Resources*, ed. Phyllis A. Wallace. Dover, MA: Auburn House, 1982. pp. 495–516.

Hull, Gloria, Patricia Bell Scott, and Barbara Smith, eds. *But Some of Us Are Brave: Black Women's Studies*. Old Westbury, NY: Feminist Press, 1982.

Jones, Barbara. "The Contribution of Black Women to the Incomes of Black Families: An Analysis of the Labor Force." Ph.D. dissertation. University of Illinois at Urbana-Champaign, 1973.

Jusenius, Carol. "The Influence of Work Experience and Typicality of Occupational Assignment of Women's Earnings." In *Dual Careers*, Vol. 4, eds. Herbert S. Parnes et al. Columbus: Center for Human Resource Research, Ohio State University, 1976. Pp. 97–118.

Kim, Elaine. *With Silk Wings: Asian American Women at Work.* San Francisco: Asian Women United of California, 1983.

Ladner, Joyce. *Tomorrow's Tomorrow: The Black Woman.* Garden City, NY: Doubleday, 1971.

Langwell, Kathryn M. "Factors Affecting the Incomes of Men and Women Physicians: Further Explorations." *Journal of Human Resources* 17 (Spring 1982): pp. 261–75.

Leggon, Cheryl B. "Black Women Professionals: Dilemmas and Contradictions of Status." In *The Black Woman,* ed. La Frances Rogers-Rose. Beverly Hills, CA: Sage Publications, 1980.

Link, Charles R., and Russell F. Settle. "Labor Supply Responses of Married Professional Nurses: New Evidence." *Journal of Human Resources* 14 (Spring 1979): pp. 235–76.

Lloyd, Cynthia B., and Beth T. Niemi. *The Economics of Sex Differentials.* New York: Columbia University Press, 1979.

Lopes, Marguerite, and Janice View. *Women, Welfare and Enterprise.* Washington: American Enterprise Institute, 1983.

Lyon, Larry, and Holly Rector-Owens. "Labor Market Mobility Among Young Black and White Women." *Social Science Quarterly* (1981).

Madhaven, M.C., Louis C. Green, and Ken Jung. "A Note on Black-White Wage Disparity." *Review of Black Political Economy* 13 (Spring 1985): pp. 39–50.

Malveaux, Julianne. "An Activist's Guide to Comparable Worth." *North Star* 1 (April 1985a): pp. 23–31.

———. "The Economic Interests of Black and White Women: Are They Similar?" *Review of Black Political Economy* 14 (Summer 1985b): pp. 5–27.

———. "Low Wage Black Women: Occupational Descriptions, Strategies for Change." Unpublished paper, NAACP Legal Defense and Education Fund, 1984a.

———. "The Status of Women of Color in the Economy: The Legacy of Being Other." Paper presented at the National Conference on Women, the Economy, and Public Policy. Washington: Women's Research and Education Institute, 1984b.

———. "Recent Trends in Occupational Segregation by Race and Sex." Paper presented to the Committee on Women's Employment and Related Social Issues, National Academy of Sciences, May 1982.

———. "Shifts in the Occupational and Employment Status of Black Women: Current Trends and Future Implications." In *Black Working Women: Debunking the Myths, A Multidisciplinary Approach.* Berkeley: University of California-Berkeley Women's Center, 1981. Pp. 133–68.

———. "From Domestic Workers to Household Technicians: Black Women in a Changing Occupation." In *Black Women in the Labor Force,* ed. Phyllis A. Wallace. Cambridge, MA: MIT Press, 1980. Pp. 85–98.

Manpower Demonstration Research Corporation. *Summary and Findings of the National Supported Work Demonstration.* New York: 1980.

McAdoo, Harriette Pipes. "Stress and Support Networks of Working Single Black Mothers." In *Black Working Women: Debunking the Myths, a Multidisciplinary Approach.* Berkeley: University of California-Berkeley Women's Center, 1981. Pp. 169–96.

———. "Black Mothers and the Extended Family Support Network." In *The Black Woman,* ed. La Frances Rogers-Rose. Beverly Hills, CA: Sage Publications, 1980. Pp. 125–44.

Mellor, Earl, and George D. Stamos. "Usual Weekly Earnings: Another Look at Intergroup Differences and Basic Trends." *Monthly Labor Review* 105 (April 1982): pp. 15–24.

Mirande, Alfredo, and Evangeline Enriquez. *La Chicana*. Chicago: University of Chicago Press, 1979.

Newman, Morris J. "A Profile of Hispanics in the U.S. Work Force." *Monthly Labor Review* 101 (December 1978): pp. 3–14.

Polachek, Solomon. "Occupational Segregation Among Women: Theory, Evidence, and a Prognosis." In *Women in the Labor Market*, eds. Cynthia Lloyd et al. New York: Columbia University Press, 1979. Pp. 137–57.

Remick, Helen. "The Comparable Worth Controversy." *Public Personnel Management* 10 (Winter 1981): pp. 371–83.

Rogers-Rose, La Frances, ed. *The Black Woman*. Beverly Hills, CA: Sage Publications, 1980.

Rytina, Nancy. "Occupational Segregation and Earnings Differences by Sex." *Monthly Labor Review* 104 (January 1981): pp. 49–53.

Sandell, Steven, and David Shapiro. "Work Expectations, Human Capital Accumulation, and the Wages of Young Women." *Journal of Human Resources* 16 (Summer 1980): pp. 335–53.

Shulman, Steven. "The Measurement and Interpretation of Black Wage and Occupational Gains: A Re-Evaluation." *Review of Black Political Economy* 12 (Spring 1984): pp. 59–69.

Smith, James P. "The Convergence to Racial Equality in Women's Wages." In *Women in the Labor Market*, eds. Cynthia Lloyd et al. New York: Columbia University Press, 1979. Pp. 173–215.

Smith, James P., and Michael P. Ward. *Women's Wages and Work in the Twentieth Century*. Santa Monica, CA: Rand Corporation, 1984.

Smith, James P., and Finis Welch. *Race Differences in Earnings: A Survey and New Evidence*. Santa Monica, CA: Rand Corporation, March 1978.

Smith, Martin M. "Early Labor Market Experiences of Youth and Subsequent Wages." Paper presented at Western Economics Association meetings, June 1980.

Sorkin, Alan. "The Economic Basis of Indian Life." *American Indian Today, The Annals of the American Academy of Political and Social Science* 436 (March 1978): pp. 1–12.

Sparr, Pamela. "Re-Evaluating Feminist Economics." *Dollars and Sense* (September 1984): pp. 12–14.

U.S. Bureau of the Census. *Money Income and Poverty Status of Families and Persons in the United States, 1982*. Current Population Reports, Series P-60, No. 140. Washington: U.S. Government Printing Office, 1983.

U.S. Department of Labor, Bureau of Labor Statistics. *Employment and Earnings* (January 1985).

————. Unpublished data on black and Hispanic women, 1976–1984.

U.S. Department of Labor, Women's Bureau. *Handbook on Women Workers*. Washington: U.S. Government Printing Office, 1975.

Wallace, Phyllis A. "Title VII and the Economic Status of Blacks." Sloan Working Paper WP# 1578-84, MIT, July 1984.

————. *Black Women in the Labor Force*. Cambridge, MA: MIT Press, 1980.

————. *Pathways to Work: Unemployment Among Black Teenage Females*. Lexington, MA: Lexington Books, 1974.

Wallace, Phyllis A., ed. *Women in the Workplace, Management of Human Resources*. Boston: Auburn House, 1982.

————. *Equal Employment Opportunity and the AT&T Case*. Cambridge, MA: MIT Press, 1976.

Wilkerson, Margaret. "A Report on the Occupational Status of Black Women During the UN Decade of Women, 1976–85." *Review of Black Political Economy* 14 (Fall-Winter 1985–1986): pp. 83–96.

Zinn, Maxine Baca. "Racial-Ethnic Family Strategies: Costs, Continuities, and Changes." In *Women and Structural Transformation: The Crisis of Work and Family Life*, ed. Beneria Lourdes. In press.

————. "Mexican-American Women in the Social Sciences." *Signs: Journal of Women in Culture and Society* 8 (Winter 1982): pp. 259–72.

CHAPTER 11

From Midlife to Retirement:
The Middle-Aged Woman Worker

Lois B. Shaw*
Rachel Shaw**

The middle-aged woman worker has received little attention in the social science literature on employment. Research on women and work has been preoccupied to a great extent with the conflict between child-rearing and paid employment. Women's work in the period when children are grown and no longer require much care has been relatively neglected. In addition, the voluminous literature on older workers has been overwhelmingly focused on men, particularly in the areas of job displacement and early retirement.

There are several reasons for this neglect of older women workers. First, middle-aged women, ages 40–64, are generally not perceived to be a group that presents a social problem. Whereas displaced older men, unemployed youth, or working mothers may appear to pose some kind of threat to social peace or traditional values, middle-aged women have appeared to have few problems. Although for a time the media showed some interest in the "empty nest syndrome," or labor market reentry, these situations were viewed as problems for the individual but not for society. Closely related to the lack of societal interest in any problems that older women workers might have is the fact that women at this age are a heterogeneous group; until recently middle-aged women have not been sufficiently dissatisfied (or been sufficiently articulate about their dissatisfactions) to form pressure groups to promote their own interests. In the 1970s this situation began to change; because of their own experiences as older divorced women and widows, some women organized political action groups to promote awareness of the plight of the "displaced homemaker" and to advocate legislation that would help these older women gain the confidence and skills necessary for reentering the labor market. Finally, researchers in the social sciences may have a tendency to focus

* Economist, U.S. General Accounting Office.
** Institute for Social Research, University of Michigan.

on problems that have a personal meaning for them. If this is the case, the fact that the majority of social scientists are men and the majority of women social scientists are young would lead to the problems of older women receiving less attention than those of other groups.

Despite this past neglect of research on older women and work, the subject is very likely to receive more attention in the future. The problems of an aging society are already creating some concern. The costs of Social Security and medical care for the aged will impose increasing burdens on the working-age population, an issue that policy-makers will be called upon to address. Employers are concerned about the quality of the work force and possible labor shortages in an aging population. Women constitute more than 40 percent of the labor force, so it appears probable that interest already finding expression in studies of older male workers must soon be extended to women. Furthermore, a majority of the population age 65 and older are women, and they represent about 70 percent of the elderly living below the poverty line. The labor market position of women from midlife onward is crucial in determining how financially independent these women will be in old age.

The baby boom generation will reach midlife in the near future, and over the next 20 years the number of middle-aged women will increase markedly. These women have much more experience with social activism and include a much larger contingent of highly educated and articulate women than their counterparts today. For this reason, too, we expect that research on women's working lives from midlife onward will receive more attention than at present. We hope that our review of what is already known and where the most glaring gaps in our knowledge are can contribute to this future effort.

An Overview of Middle-Aged Women Workers Today

In defining the period from midlife to retirement, we do not want to draw a rigid line at either end of the age range. Midlife could easily be defined as age 40 or less; at the other end of the age range, retirement at age 62 or before is increasingly common, but some women will work until age 70 or even beyond. Much of the research reported here focuses on ages 40–64, but earlier and later ages are included when the research seems relevant.

Any discussion of a particular life-cycle stage must begin with the problem of distinguishing age, period, and cohort effects.[1] Research on middle-aged women has focused on those who are in this age range

---

[1] A more complete description of the problems of identifying age, period, and cohort effects may be found in Palmore (1978). For a brief but well-presented conceptualization of the problem, see Rhodes (1983).

currently; these women are members of a particular cohort with a past history unlike that of any other. Although comparison with middle-aged women in the past is possible, little of the research we describe has been of this nature. Therefore, some of what we may see as problems for middle-aged women generally may, in fact, be specific to the particular cohort being studied. Similarly, these women have reached middle age at a period with its own characteristics that may be unlike those in the future when succeeding cohorts reach midlife. Finally, some features of the years from midlife to old age represent biological aging effects that will not vary markedly from one cohort to another. However, even in this case, childhood nutrition, access to health care, and differences in life events may have effects on the aging process. Other age-connected factors such as the maturing of children will have common features across cohorts, but their effects will also vary with possible changes in social definitions of responsibilities to adult children and differences in the age when childbearing ends.

Historical Background

To gain a perspective on cohort effects for women who are now in the 40–64 age range, it is useful to begin with a brief discussion of the historical background for women born between 1921 and 1945. The oldest of these women were growing up during the Depression of the 1930s and reached adulthood as World War II was beginning. Because of the war, marriage and childbearing were often postponed, and these women had somewhat smaller families than the succeeding cohorts. Women born in the early 1930s were growing up during the war years, and most of their childbearing occurred during the postwar baby boom, a period during which the climate of opinion was hostile to working women and traditional roles were strongly encouraged (Chafe, 1972). Women born in the early 1940s were still in their early twenties at the time of the beginning of the women's movement and the passage of equal employment opportunities legislation in the 1960s. Although they had grown up during the years when traditional roles were advocated, they were still young adults when these roles began to be debated and challenged. The quite different life experiences of women born within this 25-year period suggest the need for extreme caution in extrapolating into the future the findings from research on these cohorts.

Work Patterns

In 1983, about two-thirds of women ages 45–54 and nearly three-fourths of those 35–44 were employed at some time during the year. However, the percentages of women in these age ranges who had worked full-time for at least 40 weeks during the year were between 40 and 45 percent, about 12 percent had worked part-time for at least 40 weeks, and the rest (13 percent of those 45–54 and 17 percent of those 35–44) had worked for fewer than 40 weeks. Thus, although the majority of women workers in these age ranges worked full-time for at least 40 weeks per year, a substantial minority worked only part-time or part of the year. Beyond age 55, the percentages of women employed at some time during the year falls to 54 percent at ages 55–59, 40 percent at ages 60–64, and only 10 percent at age 65 and beyond; the percentages working full-time for 40 weeks or more falls to 32, 21, and 3 percent, respectively.[2]

These figures for a one-year period show considerable diversity in the work patterns of middle-aged and older women. Even more diversity might be expected over a longer period. The only means of characterizing the work patterns of women over the life-cycle stage under examination here is to have access to longitudinal data, in which the same persons are reinterviewed over time, or to collect detailed retrospective work histories. Fortunately for our purposes, the mature women's cohort of the National Longitudinal Surveys of Labor Market Experience (NLS) provides data on 15 years of the work experience of women who were ages 45–59 in 1982. Beginning in 1967, these surveys have followed a nationally representative sample of women who have been interviewed at one- or two-year intervals. More than 5,000 women were interviewed in 1967, and in 1982 about 3,000 women remained in the sample.[3]

A recent analysis using the NLS reveals that slightly over one-fifth of these women had worked fairly continuously over the preceding 15-year period. Another quarter were women with an increasing work attachment, mainly labor market reentrants who had worked intermittently or not at all in the early years, but had been steadily employed in the last five years of the period. Only 13 percent of women ages 45–59 had never worked during the 15 years, and approximately the same percentage had only very casual and short-term employment, making in total about one-quarter who had only minimal work involvement or none at all. Women who had intermittent work records constituted about 22 percent of the sample; another 5 percent had stopped working after being employed regularly for a number of years (Shaw,

---

[2] All figures are calculated from U.S. Bureau of the Census (1985a), Table 14.
[3] The National Longitudinal Surveys have also interviewed three other age-sex groups over the same period, and a new youth survey was begun in 1979. A comprehensive description of the surveys may be found in Center for Human Resource Research (1983).

1986a). Even these broad categories oversimplify the diversity of work patterns at midlife.[4]

Although the group that could be described as reentrants is the largest single one, the intermittent-worker group is nearly as large, and continuous workers are also a sizable group among midlife women. The reentrant is probably thought to be the typical middle-aged woman worker, even though only a minority of middle-aged women fit this description. This perception may have its origin in the fact that returning to work after childbearing is a fairly recent phenomenon. Before World War II, most married women left the labor market at marriage and did not return to work unless they were widowed or the family's economic situation required them to work (Treiman, 1985; Robinson, 1980), but during and after World War II many married women began returning to work after rearing children. Myrdal and Klein (1956) took note of this new pattern and helped to popularize the idea of women's second career after the child-rearing years. Indeed, the NLS mature women's survey was initiated with the idea of collecting data to illuminate the problems that women might encounter in reentering the labor force after staying home to rear children (Parnes, 1975).

Labor market reentry was brought to public attention in the 1970s when women's groups began to publicize the problems of the "displaced homemaker" and to lobby for legislation that would provide job counseling and training for labor market reentrants who fit this definition.[5] The displaced homemaker was pictured as a woman who had spent many years out of the labor market as a homemaker and had been displaced from her homemaker role through widowhood, divorce, or husband's disability. She was represented as having no recent work experience and few marketable skills. She did not qualify for welfare because her children were grown, but she was too young to receive Social Security.

Both the idea of a second career and the stereotype of the displaced homemaker pictured reentry as a once-for-all event; a woman stays at home until her children are in school, until her children have left home, or until she loses her husband. Then she returns to work. But any examination of women's work records, such as those contained

---

[4] As might be expected, considerable variation was found within the 45–59 age range; compared with the average woman, those who were 45–49 were more likely to be either reentrants or intermittent workers and were less likely to have little or no work involvement, while those who were 55–59 were less likely to be reentrants or intermittent workers and more likely to have retired after following a continuous or intermittent work pattern in earlier years.

[5] As a result of this political activity, a number of states and ultimately the federal government passed displaced-homemaker legislation. See Shields (1981) for an interesting description of the displaced-homemaker movement written by one of its organizers.

in the NLS, quickly changes one's view that most women's lives have been so neatly blocked off into child-rearing years followed by reentry and then continuous employment. For example, 45 percent of the women in the NLS sample had worked at some time between the birth of their first and last child (Dex and Shaw, 1986). More than 20 percent of white women first returned to work within the first year after their first child was born, and 40 percent had worked by the time their first child was 6. The corresponding figures for black women were 40 and 60 percent (Mott and Shaw, 1986). However, the great majority of women who returned to work before their first child reached school age had additional absences from the labor force. Even women who returned much later had further work interruptions. Overall, only about 20 percent of women worked fairly continuously from the time they first returned to work.[6] As these figures suggest, reentry is usually not a single event.

A second problem with the stereotypic view of reentry is the perception that the reentrant is usually middle-aged. However, only about one-quarter of women who are now middle-aged remained out of the labor force for as long as 15 years after their first child was born (Dex and Shaw, 1986);[7] thus, most women's first reentry more commonly occurred when they were in their twenties or thirties rather than their forties or fifties. As the data quoted previously suggest, the middle years appear to be a period when some women have already become established as continuous workers, others are becoming established after a period of intermittent employment, and still others continue to work intermittently.

Because of the focus on reentrants, other work patterns of midlife women have not received as much attention as they deserve. Intermittent work patterns, especially, are followed by a relatively large group and should be studied further. Why do some women follow this pattern? Do they work only when some financial crisis impels them? Are they women who work in secondary-sector unstable jobs that are unsatisfactory and lead to job changing? One study of middle-aged women who had irregular employment patterns over a six-year period found a variety of reasons for work interruptions, including family

---

[6] These figures are based on Mott and Shaw (1986) and on unpublished tabulations from the NLS. Another major longitudinal data set, the Panel Study of Income Dynamics, appears to show more women following the single work interruption pattern. Corcoran (1979) found that only 17 percent of women ages 30–44 in 1975 had experienced more than one work interruption since leaving school. However, since her sample was limited to women who had worked at least 500 hours in the previous year, many of the women most likely to have intermittent work patterns would not have been included. The sample she describes is also somewhat younger than the NLS women, and the work-history information is retrospective, which may lead to understating past spells of employment.

[7] However, it is possible that some women who returned in the early years after their first child's birth experienced longer work interruptions after other children were born.

needs, layoffs, working at temporary or seasonal jobs, and health problems. In addition, a family's move to a different city or state often leads to a work interruption for the wife (Shaw, 1983a).

Part of the difficulty in studying work patterns stems from lack of data or inadequacy of the sources available. Even the NLS, which is the most detailed source available, has gaps in some years and is difficult to use. Furthermore, although new methods of studying longitudinal data are being developed, useful ways of characterizing the many work patterns are difficult to devise.[8] Yet in the absence of better descriptions, we may be tempted to continue to think in over-simplified terms of reentry as one event and of women's work lives as proceeding simply from work to child-rearing to reemployment.

Earnings and Occupations

In 1980 women workers in the 45–64 age range were somewhat less likely to be found in professional or managerial jobs than were women who were ages 25–44; 20 percent of the older women compared with 27 percent of younger women held these jobs. The older group was also more likely to hold low-paid retail sales or service jobs; 27 percent of older women, compared with 21 percent of younger women, held these kinds of jobs.[9] Among only year-round full-time workers, the average annual earnings of women in their thirties were somewhat higher than those of women in their forties and fifties; younger women averaged about $17,000 compared with $15,500 for older women in 1983 (U.S. Bureau of the Census, 1985b, Table 48). These differences probably reflect the higher levels of education of the younger women, partially offset by the greater amount of work experience of the older workers.

When women's earnings are compared with those of men of the same age, we see increasing differentials with age. Again considering only year-round full-time workers, at ages 25–34 women's earnings are about 73 percent of men's, but by ages 35–44 the ratio falls to 61 percent and from age 45 onward to about 55 percent. For the youngest age group, the ratio increased from 62 to 73 percent between 1967 and 1982, but little change occurred for older women (see Blau and Ferber, Chapter 2 of this book). Similarly, compared with their older counterparts, younger women were less likely to work in predominantly female occupations and showed more movement into predominantly male occupations over the decade of the 1970s (Beller, 1984).

---

[8] Event history analysis solves some of the problems of analyzing events such as spells of working or work interruptions that begin and end at irregular intervals (Tuma, Hannan, and Groeneveld, 1979). However, the problem of characterizing multiple work spells has not been satisfactorily addressed.

[9] Calculated from Table 280, U.S. Bureau of the Census (1984a).

Attitudes Toward Work

Women who are currently middle-aged express a fairly high degree of satisfaction with their jobs; about 60 percent say they like their work very much (Shaw, 1986a). Researchers have consistently found a positive association between age and overall job satisfaction for both women and men (Rhodes, 1983), although the reason for older workers being more satisfied than younger workers is not clear. Job satisfaction might increase with age because increasing work experience brings greater job rewards or because older cohorts have less education or different life experiences which cause them to have lower expectations than their younger counterparts. Glenn, Taylor, and Weaver (1977) found evidence that, for men, part of the association between age and job satisfaction was the result of greater job rewards at older ages, but the higher job satisfaction of older women could not be explained in this way.

Studies of changes in individual workers' job satisfaction over time have not found that satisfaction increased with age. In fact, a study of four NLS cohorts showed a decrease in job satisfaction over a five-year period for all groups, including middle-aged women (Andrisani, 1977a). Because different age groups of both women and men all showed decreasing satisfaction, this result may have been related to the period of the late 1960s and early 1970s when these data were collected. In a later analysis of NLS data, Shaw (1986a) found that women who were in their fifties reported lower levels of job satisfaction at that age than they reported 15 years earlier, but women in their late forties showed no change over the same period. In addition, women who were 55 and over were found to have lower satisfaction than those who were under 55.[10] Thus, there is no evidence that women's job satisfaction has increased as they have grown older, at least among women who are currently middle-aged. If middle-aged women generally have higher levels of job satisfaction than younger women, lower expectations would appear to be a plausible explanation.

Job satisfaction has been found to be highly correlated with occupational status for men and women of all ages (Andrisani, 1977a). However, all women may not find occupational status equally important. Appelbaum (1981) examined differences between two categories of women in their late thirties and forties in the NLS sample: those who had taken long and short absences from the labor force in order to raise children. She found that for those who were out of the labor force for a longer period, job satisfaction was positively related to husbands'

---

[10] Some researchers have shown lower job satisfaction after age 60, but others have found a positive association between age and job satisfaction throughout the age spectrum (Rhodes, 1983). However, most studies have not looked for sex differences at these older ages.

approval of their working and negatively related to presence of pre-school children in the home. For those reentering the work force after a short absence, this was not the case. The latter group's satisfaction was affected by earnings and social status on the job, which was not true for the first group. These findings support the view that older women who have been primarily oriented toward raising children may be satisfied with their jobs because they do not have high expectations, but that as women come to work more continuously in the future, they will tend to be less satisfied unless their jobs carry the occupational status and earnings they aspire to.

In a study of job-preference attributes (Lacy, Bokemeir, and Shepard, 1983), both men and women, when asked to rank-order five job attributes, listed meaningful work first, followed by promotion, income, security, and hours. Middle-aged and younger women differed very little in their rankings of job attributes. Women who like the content of their jobs are much more likely to be highly satisfied with their work than women who find pay to be the most attractive feature of their jobs (Andrisani, 1978). In 1982 about half of middle-aged women in the NLS mentioned job content as the factor they liked most about their jobs.[11] As with overall job satisfaction, considerable research shows higher levels of satisfaction with job content at older ages (Rhodes, 1983).

Work commitment is frequently measured by asking the individual if he or she would continue to work even if provided with a comfortable income for life. Both sex and age have been found to be related to commitment to work. Men have consistently been found more likely than women to want to work in the absence of economic need (Lacy, Bokemeir, and Shepard, 1983; Andrisani, 1977b). Older people are generally found to be less committed to working than younger people. Lacy, Bokemeir, and Shepard found that 58 percent of women age 40 and over said they would continue to work even if there were no economic reason to do so; the corresponding figure for women under 40 was 70 percent. Although Andrisani (1977b), using NLS data, found no difference in work commitment between middle-aged and younger women in 1967, by 1982 NLS women who were in their fifties were somewhat less likely to want to continue working than were women still in their forties.[12] Thus, it appears that women's work commitment remains high while they are in their forties, but begins to decline as they grow older and approach the conventional age for retirement.

---

[11] These figures were calculated from NLS data tapes.
[12] Figures calculated from NLS data tapes.

Why They Work

Most workers probably have a mixture of economic and non-economic motives for working. Ferree (1984) notes a frequent assumption that middle-class women work for noneconomic reasons, while working-class women's motives are economic. A woman who "must" work for the money is assumed not to want to work at all; this picture overlooks the mixture of motives that most workers hold for working. Although we will be discussing economic and noneconomic motives separately, we realize that they may not be so neatly separable in fact. For example, a woman may work in order to have control over income that she may spend for her own purposes. Her reason for working could be considered economic, but the benefits to her may also include a feeling of independence or fewer marital arguments over expenditures. However, because there is a large literature devoted solely to economic reasons, we have found it convenient to consider economic and noneconomic reasons separately.

Economic Reasons

Only a small amount of the extensive research on the factors affecting women's labor force participation has focused on middle-aged and older women. Most research has either used samples of women in the childbearing years or samples of women undifferentiated by age. However, researchers on older women have found that many of the same factors that influence younger women's employment influence older women as well.[13] The lower the family's income from other sources, such as husband's earnings and assets, the more likely women at all ages are to be employed. The higher labor force participation of unmarried women compared with their married counterparts is largely due to their lack of other sources of income.

Caring for young children causes many women to leave the labor force, but few middle-aged women have preschool children and most have only teenage or grown children. Unlike the situation for young women, it appears that middle-aged women who still have children at home or in college are more likely to work than are women who no longer have dependent children (Gitter, Shaw, and Gagen, 1986; Bowen and Finegan, 1969). These findings support Oppenheimer's (1982) view that a "life-cycle squeeze" occurs for many families at the time when all of their children are in high school or college, the period when the cost of raising children is at a maximum. Oppenheimer believes that this period of financial stringency has been especially pro-

---

[13] Research that investigates the economic factors influencing middle-aged women's work includes Gitter, Shaw, and Gagen (1986), Shaw (1983a, 1983c), Long and Jones (1980), Heckman (1979), Blau (1978), Cain and Dooley (1976), Sweet (1973), and Bowen and Finegan (1969).

nounced in recent years as the very large families born during the baby boom have reached this stage. Thus, it appears that when children are old enough so that women can work fairly easily, women's employment is influenced by the adequacy of income for family needs, and needs will be greater the larger the family or the greater its ambitions for the children.[14]

As Oppenheimer points out, the employment of the wife also often means that a family in which the husband's income is modest can enjoy a standard of living equal to that of a family in which the husband has a higher-status job and the wife does not work. She speculates that if families judge their "success" by that of other families, the increase in the percentage of working wives will cause increasing pressures for the wife in a one-earner family to go out to work. However, it is possible that with smaller families in the future, the period of financial stringency when women are middle-aged will be reduced.

If middle-aged women are influenced to work because of economic pressures, their response to these pressures will be determined in part by how good their job prospects are. At all ages, women are more likely to work the greater their potential earnings, which in turn depend to a considerable extent on their education and past work experience. The economic interpretation of the relationship between potential earnings and employment is that the higher the earnings a woman could obtain by working the more costly it is for her to remain at home. Opportunities in the local labor market also affect women's employment. Women are less likely to be employed if they live in places where the local unemployment rate is high or the industrial composition of the area provides few jobs in occupations that are typically filled by women (Cain and Dooley, 1976; Bowen and Finegan, 1969).

Noneconomic Reasons

Although a great deal of research has established the relationship between education, past work experience, potential earnings, and employment, it is possible that the economic explanation for these relationships is not the whole story. Jobs that require more education and offer higher wages are generally more interesting than low-wage jobs, and the content of the job compares more favorably with housework. Therefore, it is not clear how much of the observed relationship between potential earnings and employment is due to the economics of working in the marketplace versus working at home.

---

[14] Sweet (1973) also found that women respond not so much to husband's earnings as to income adequacy measured by the ratio of husband's earnings to the level of family needs, which in turn depend on family size and composition.

The quality of the job could be an especially important consideration for the middle-aged woman who no longer has the absorbing work
of raising small children, but only routine housework to compare with a
possible job. Spitze and Spaeth (1979) found that married college
graduates without children were more likely to work if they did not like
housework, but that attitudes toward housework did not affect the
work activity of mothers of young children. [15] In another study, middle-
aged women who disliked housework were found to be more likely to
reenter the labor market than were their counterparts who expressed a
strong liking for housework (Shaw, 1983c). In addition, middle-aged
working women express a higher level of satisfaction with their jobs
than with housework, and a much lower level of satisfaction with
housework than women who are not employed (Shaw, 1986a). In a
cross-national study which asked women to compare their jobs with
doing housework, a third of the women employed as operatives liked
the work on their jobs better than housework, and a clear majority of
retail sales and clerical workers preferred their jobs (Agassi, 1979).
Although not extensive, all of this research suggests that many women,
especially when they no longer have children to consider, choose
between paid employment and work in the home at least partly on the
basis of which kind of work appears more satisfying.

Considerable research has shown a relationship between women's
attitudes toward the appropriateness of women working (role attitudes)
and their actual employment (Waite, 1978). However, as employment
becomes an increasingly common role for them, fewer women are
likely to be deterred from selecting work by a belief that women's place
is in the home. Furthermore, much of the disapproval of women
working is focused on women with small children; at present there is
probably little social disapproval of women working after their children
are grown. For women just reaching midlife, increasingly favorable
opinions about working women have probably facilitated their increasing employment (Shaw, 1985). However, studies of women in the NLS
have shown a decrease in the significance of the effect of role attitudes
on employment as the women have grown older (Statham and Rhoton,
1983).

Although there have been no large-scale quantitative investigations of other motivations for midlife women's employment, research
using in-depth interviews such as those conducted by Rubin (1979)
suggests that a need for new roles and interests and for greater inde-

---

[15] The sample used by Spitze and Spaeth was interviewed in the 1960s and consisted of
women who had recently completed college. At present these same women would be in their
forties and have teenage or grown children. Whether their attitudes toward housework and their
work responses would be the same after raising children as they were earlier is, of course,
uncertain.

pendence have caused many middle-aged women to seek work. Divorce or widowhood, while usually making employment necessary for financial reasons, may also increase the need to find new interests and roles. As previously mentioned, more than half of middle-aged women workers say they would continue to work even if they could live comfortably without doing so. Even if women sometimes misjudge what they would actually do if their economic circumstances were to improve, the fact that so many express this attitude toward work gives some indication of the importance of their noneconomic motives for working.

Why Their Pay Is So Low

A great deal of research has been devoted to determining what causes the pay differential between men and women. A related literature seeks to explain the occupational segregation of the sexes and the extent to which pay differentials are related to differences in occupation. Although some of this research has utilized data on women of all ages, considerable research has focused on women at midlife, the stage when maximum differences in pay are observed. The major reasons advanced for the pay differential are the human capital or differential productivity explanation and explanations that involve discrimination by sex or age. Of course, these explanations are not mutually exclusive.

Human Capital Explanations

Differences in the amount and kind of education and job training that men and women have acquired by midlife undoubtedly account for part of the lower earnings of women (see Blau and Ferber, Chapter 2 of this book). Two other aspects of human capital theory are particularly relevant for today's middle-aged women. First is the theory that job-related skills will "depreciate" during periods away from work. Although considerable research shows a negative association between time spent out of the labor force and wages, it seems doubtful whether, for most women who are now middle-aged, this negative relationship can be attributed to a loss of work-related skills during periods spent at home.[16]

Most of these women held clerical, sales, or service jobs before they had children. In a study of women in their thirties and forties who experienced work interruptions between 1967 and 1979, about half were found to have left jobs that require less than six months to learn;

---

[16] Researchers who find very large wage losses include Mincer and Ofek (1982) and Mincer and Polachek (1974, 1978). Much smaller estimates, in some cases statistically insignificant, have been found by Corcoran, Duncan, and Ponza (1983), Shaw (1982), Ferber and Birnbaum (1981), Corcoran and Duncan (1979), and Sandell and Shapiro (1978).

another quarter held jobs requiring less than a year to learn (Shaw, 1982). In any event, it is not always clear why work skills would have been lost while at home because many jobs that middle-aged women hold require skills such as interacting with people, teaching and caring for children, cleaning, and basic literacy that are also used at home or in volunteer work. Only a few of the commonly held occupations of middle-aged women, such as nursing and some kinds of clerical work, might require some retraining to regain old skills or learn to use new equipment not formerly available.

A second strand of human capital research has sought to explain occupational segregation on the basis of women's voluntary choices of jobs in which their skills will not depreciate during the years they spend at home.[17] Put together, these two strands of human capital research offer a dismal picture of the work situation of middle-aged women. On the one hand, the low pay of middle-aged women is said to be due to their having chosen low-skilled occupations in which their human capital would not depreciate, but on the other, the same group of women are shown to have lower wages—said to be due to human capital depreciation the longer they stay out of the labor force. The occupational-choice explanation of the lower wages of middle-aged women may have some validity; rather than carefully preparing themselves for occupations they could resume later, many of today's middle-aged women probably did not plan to work at all after they had children.[18] Furthermore, given the climate of opinion when they might have prepared for a later return to the labor market, it seems more likely that most women saw only certain traditionally female occupations as suitable. But if most women prepared only for traditional jobs or did not plan to resume employment, it also seems unlikely that the modest skills they acquired should depreciate rapidly. If these women have received lower wages after work interruptions, it seems more likely that a lack of recent references, a lack of information about the job market, or a lack of confidence in their own abilities are more likely explanations than a deterioration of their basic job-related skills (Corcoran, Duncan, and Ponza, 1983; Strober, 1979).

Sex Discrimination

When considering women who are now middle-aged, it is important to remember that, when they were younger, these women often faced much more overt sex discrimination than is now possible. For

---

[17] For a review of this literature, see Blau and Ferber, Chapter 2 of this book.

[18] A study using a national sample of white wives of childbearing age in 1955 found that less than half expected to continue working or to return to work in the future (Sobol, 1963). These women are now in the age range we are considering here.

example, medical schools appear to have maintained low quotas for women until the 1960s (Walsh, 1977). Only after the equal opportunities legislation of the 1950s did it become illegal for employers to specify the sex of applicants for job openings listed in newspapers. Women who are now in their fifties and sixties were already well past the age of making initial vocational choices before a wider range of occupations became available; women in their forties may have benefited more from the legislation, but in their case, too, most had completed their education before enforcement of this new legislation became effective. Although sex segregation of occupations has decreased during the 1970s, the decrease has been considerably greater for young women than for middle-aged women (Beller, 1984). However, opportunities for moving into management positions have shown some increase for older women as well as their younger counterparts (Shaw, 1986a).

Race Discrimination

Although the position of minority women in the labor market is discussed in depth in the Malveaux and Wallace chapter in this volume, the especially disadvantaged position of older black women should be mentioned here. Black women who are age 50 or older were past high-school age at the time of the school-desegregation decision of the Supreme Court in 1954. Less than half of black women who are 45 and over have completed high school (U.S. Bureau of the Census, 1985a, Table 13). The racial discrimination that their parents and they themselves suffered when they were growing up and reaching adulthood has precluded most of this generation from obtaining even the modest clerical and white-collar jobs that white middle-aged women hold. Only one-third of black women ages 45–59 held white-collar jobs of any kind in 1982, as compared with about two-thirds of their white counterparts (Shaw, 1986a).

Age Discrimination

Public-opinion polls show widespread agreement that older workers face age discrimination. A 1981 survey of more than 500 employers found that a majority agreed with this public perception, although only a fifth were willing to admit that older workers faced barriers in being hired, trained, or promoted in their own companies (McConnell, 1983). The extent of such discrimination and its importance for older women's employment is not known. Some of the difficulties in conducting research in this area are similar to those encountered in research on sex discrimination; if systematic differences in pay or in length of time unemployed are found between younger and older workers, we do not know whether these differences are due to unmeasured differences in the productivity of the two groups or to discrimination. Furthermore, at older ages workers who can find only poorly paid work or no work at all may be more likely to leave the labor force entirely; comparisons between the two groups may then fail to include some of the most disadvantaged in the older groups.

A survey of the extensive literature on the job performance of older workers is beyond the scope of this chapter. Review of this literature (Doering, Rhodes, and Schuster, 1983; Rhodes, 1983) shows mixed results even within occupational categories such as clerical work, with some studies showing performance decreasing, increasing, or unrelated to age, as well as an inverted U-shaped association. Across occupations, some of the differences in age-related performance probably depend on the nature of the job. Rhodes questions the reliability and validity of the criteria of performance used in many of these studies. Of course, even a finding of a negative statistical association between age and performance for a group would not rule out the possibility of age discrimination in individual cases.

As for other productivity-related characteristics such as absenteeism, no clear-cut relationship between avoidable absence and age was found for women (Rhodes, 1983). For unavoidable absence, there was either a positive or nonsignificant relationship between age and absenteeism. The relationship between age and accidents was more frequently negative, while both duration of disability and fatalities were positively associated with age.

Even if good measures of productivity existed, defining what should be considered discrimination still presents difficulties. For example, should failure to offer training for a new position to an older worker be considered discrimination? A company may view such training as a poor investment because of the shorter time during which the company might reap the benefits of this training. Here, it is probably possible to compare actual expected tenure of employees after training. Because younger workers are more likely than older workers to quit for another job, such a comparison may reveal whether the company is basing its policy on reasonable expectations of the pay-off to training an older worker or to an age-stereotyped view of who should receive training.

One line of research has attempted to document age discrimination through asking employers (or potential employers, such as students in business administration) to answer questions on whether hypothetical job candidates with certain characteristics would be hired or considered for promotion; typically, respondents are given descriptions of potential employees who differ only by age. In many cases older workers were less likely to be hired or considered for training or promotion.[19] However, the age at which older workers begin to be at a disadvantage differs; for example, Craft et al. (1979) found no evidence for age discrimination until age 60. Most of these studies have been confined to men, but a study asking personnel specialists to rate secretaries found no age-related differences in recommendations for promotion or salary increase (Schwab and Heneman, 1978). On the other hand, employers surveyed in Illinois were less willing to hire 55-year-old hypothetical applicants than 25-year-old applicants for semi-skilled jobs even though the descriptions of competence were identical (Haefner, 1977). The same employers preferred men to women; unfortunately, a cross-tabulation of hiring practices by sex and age was not undertaken. Although these results provide some evidence of age discrimination, the samples used were often small and the occupations covered were diverse, so that generalizability to other occupations and to the nation as a whole is not possible.

A few multivariate statistical analyses have attempted to determine whether wages decline with age, after controlling for other worker characteristics. A study of male workers displaced from their jobs found that older workers remained unemployed longer than younger workers, but except for those age 65 and over, older displaced workers who found jobs did not return to work at lower wages than their younger counterparts (Shapiro and Sandell, 1983). Other studies have found that after their fifties the earnings of men decline with age (Hanoch and Honig, 1983; Wanner and McDonald, 1983). However, some of this decline may be associated with part-time employment and job-changing after retiring from a regular job (Gustman and Stein-meier, 1985). Very few studies of this nature have been undertaken for women. In the study previously mentioned, Hanoch and Honig (1983) did not find an adverse age effect on the wages of unmarried women. In a study of earnings and promotion of workers in a large company, Rosenbaum (1984) found that, after controlling for level of the first job, the age when men first joined the company had a negative effect on their advancement; a smaller but still significant age effect was found for women as well. These findings suggested that the age at which an employee reached a certain level may have been used as an indicator of future performance.

Another approach to studying age discrimination is through examination of complaints and lawsuits filed under the Age Discrimination in Employment Act (ADEA). In 1981 approximately 9,000 age-discrimination charges were filed with the Equal Employment Oppor-

---

[19] See Rosen and Jerdee (1977) and other research cited in Doering, Rhodes, and Schuster (1983).

tunity Commission; about 36 percent of the charges were filed by women. Since women constituted about 40 percent of the labor force age 40 and over in 1981, their complaint rate was slightly lower than that for men (McConnell, 1983). About half of the charges were filed because of termination. Only 17 percent of the cases involved hiring or promotion, which are probably much more important for women than for men because middle-aged women are more frequently looking for work or in the early stages of resuming a work career.

In a study of a sample of actual lawsuits under ADEA, Schuster and Miller (1984) found that women were more likely to be involved in job-status cases (those involving hiring, promotion, wages, and fringe benefits) and men more frequently brought cases involving termination and involuntary retirement. Women were more likely to win their suits than were men; 52 percent of women, but only 29 percent of men, won their lawsuits. The authors speculate that this result may have been due to women having the additional protection of legislation against sex discrimination, to courts being more responsive to job-status claims, or to companies being less attentive to performance appraisal at the clerical-worker level where most women plaintiffs were employed than at the professional and managerial levels that account for most male plaintiffs.

Taken together these lines of research suggest that age discrimination is of considerable importance for older women workers. The cases that are probably most important for women are informal age limits on hiring for certain positions, but this kind of discrimination may be difficult for individuals to detect because most people have little information about other applicants and the qualifications of those finally chosen. Discrimination involving promotion or wage and fringe benefits may be easier to learn about, though still not easy to remedy.

Age limits in apprenticeship programs, scholarships, and fellowships may mean that women who spend their twenties and early thirties rearing children are considered too old for some kinds of training when they return to work (Roos and Reskin, 1984). Many jobs listed in want ads formerly had specified age limits, but such advertising is now illegal. The importance of allowing for later-than-usual entry into various occupations can be illustrated by the case of Great Britain, which has no legislation on age discrimination. Upper age limits for entering such fields as science, librarianship, and social work are common. Entry into clerical work is less frequently restricted, but an employer may specify age limits if he chooses (Jolly, Creigh, and Mingay, 1980). As a result, women who reenter the labor force after childbearing are likely to be restricted to occupations they formerly held or to work not requiring special skills. This situation may be one of the factors accounting for the marked downward occupational mobility that occurs after British women begin childbearing, whereas among American women little downward mobility is observed (Dex and Shaw, 1986). Even though such formal age limits are illegal in the United States, employers' attitudes on appropriate ages for certain positions may limit some older women's opportunities.

Education and Training for Better Jobs

Skills that women use at home are often poorly rewarded in the labor market; acquiring specialized skills through additional education and training offers prospects for better pay. It is well established that higher levels of education lead to higher earnings for women as well as men. Noncollege training of various types also appears to yield at least modest increases in earnings for older women (Shaw, 1983b; Appelbaum, 1981). Studies of government training programs for disadvantaged workers have found that they increase the earnings of women, especially those with little labor market experience (Bassi, 1983; Congressional Budget Office and National Commission for Employment Policy, 1982). However, with some exceptions, these programs appear to have been less successful in training women for more than entry jobs (Harlan, 1985).

Many midlife women return to school or participate in occupational training programs. A recent study using the NLS found that about 22 percent of women who were ages 45–59 in 1982 had attended college at some time during the previous 15 years (Morgan, 1986).[20] Women who attended college were more likely than other women to be employed, which suggests that many attended in order to improve their employment prospects. Many women also completed high school at older than traditional ages. About 4 percent of middle-aged women who had graduated from high school but had not gone to college had received their high school diplomas at age 35 or later; nearly 10 percent of black women had graduated at these ages.

The extent of older women's involvement in other kinds of job training is difficult to determine, partly because any definition of what should be counted as job-related training is somewhat arbitrary. A study of middle-aged women in 1981 found that during the previous four years about 16 percent of employed women reported participation in some kind of noncollege occupational training that was not provided by their employers. About one-quarter reported having participated in on-the-job training. However, much of this training was of quite short duration, averaging 8 to 12 weeks (Shaw, 1983b).

---

[20] This study found that women who had completed their degrees at age 35 or later accounted for about one-quarter of associate degrees, 16 percent of bachelor degrees, and over 60 percent of higher degrees held by all women in the 45–59 age group.

Although these data show fairly high levels of participation in education and training programs by middle-aged women, it is not clear how well women's needs are being served by the programs available. Even though many women had obtained college degrees at older than traditional ages, the great majority of women in the NLS who had attended college during the 15 years of the surveys did not obtain a degree (Morgan, 1986). In some cases these women may have wanted to take only a limited number of courses for a specific purpose—for example, for recreation or to renew a teaching credential. However, some women may have become discouraged by the problems they encountered. Educational institutions have traditionally been less than sensitive to the needs of part-time and older students. Returning women students, who are often employed and must attend part-time, may face such problems as lack of financial aid for part-time students, inflexibility in the scheduling of courses, time limits on degrees, and limited access to services of counseling, career placement, and financial offices, which are usually not open in the evening.[21] The older woman student may also have to deal with her own lack of confidence, uncertainty over career directions, a sense of isolation, or opposition from family members.

Recognizing some of the barriers faced by returning women students, many universities have opened centers for the continuing education of women. These centers typically offer such services as support groups, assertiveness training, and career and personal counseling (Girard, Sweeney, and Sorce, 1979). Several hundred such centers were in existence at both two-year and four-year colleges by the late 1970s, but many schools still do not address the needs of reentering women (Osterkamp and Hullet, 1983; Tittle and Denker, 1980).

The problem of upgrading the job skills of disadvantaged older women is a difficult one. Most federally funded job-training programs for disadvantaged persons have focused on youth. Displaced homemaker programs provide the only government-sponsored employment and training services specifically geared to the needs of middle-aged women.[22] Displaced homemakers are defined as women who must become primary breadwinners following divorce, separation, widowhood, or husband's inability to work and who experience difficulty

---

[21] See Astin (1976) and Tittle and Denker (1980) for good overviews of the institutional barriers faced by older women students.

[22] A few middle-aged women have received training through the Work Incentive (WIN) program, a job-training and placement program for recipients of Aid to Families With Dependent Children. However, a study of WIN programs found that older women were underrepresented among participants; only 13 percent of female participants were age 40 or over compared with one-third of nonparticipants (U.S. General Accounting Office, 1982). Some older women who have been displaced from long-term jobs are eligible for training through the displaced-worker program of the Job Training Partnership Act. In addition, some older women have undoubtedly participated in other government programs that are not limited to special groups.

in finding jobs that will enable them to be self-supporting. In 1978 amendments to the Comprehensive Employment and Training Act (CETA) made displaced homemakers a target group for employment and training programs and authorized funds for demonstration projects serving displaced homemakers. Federal support for displaced home-maker programs was weakened in 1982 when CETA was replaced by the Job Training Partnership Act, which made funding for the pro-grams optional. Recently, however, some additional support was made available through the Carl D. Perkins Vocational Education Act, which set aside funds for single parents and homemakers (U.S. Con-gress, 1985).[23] In 1984, 24 states also supported displaced homemaker programs.

A survey of displaced homemaker centers in 1984 by the national Displaced Homemaker Alliance found over 400 centers nationwide, usually supported at modest levels by a combination of federal, state, and private funds.[24] Services offered by the centers include personal and career counseling, peer support groups, training in job-search skills, and job-placement services. A few centers offer their own short training courses for jobs such as word processing and nurse's aide, but most offer only information and assistance in enrolling in local training programs sponsored by educational and other institutions. Many cen-ters report that displaced homemakers need financial assistance to cover basic living expenses if they are to enroll in training programs, but funds for this purpose are very limited. With further cuts in funding, it is unlikely that existing programs can be expanded or improved. In any event, further research is needed on what kinds of programs are most likely to help disadvantaged older women obtain better jobs.

Retirement

Some research has begun on women and retirement, the upper end of the middle-age spectrum. The recent crisis in the Social Security system and the recognition of future consequences of an aging society have brought questions about workers' retirement to the fore.

---

[23] Exact definitions of who qualifies as a displaced homemaker differ. Some programs have lower age limits of 35 to 40 years, but many serve younger women as well. Income qualifications are found in most state and federally funded programs, often drawn at or slightly above the federally established poverty line. Many women are ineligible because their incomes exceed these levels, even by small amounts. Privately funded programs sometimes serve middle-class women as well as the economically disadvantaged. Under the Perkins Vocational Education Act, states may set their own definitions of homemakers, but must emphasize assistance to those in greatest financial need. Because there are no age limits and single parents are eligible, these funds will also be open to younger women and to men who are single parents (U.S. Congress, 1985).

[24] More detailed results of this survey may be found in U.S. Congress (1985). In this publication the Office of Technology Assessment analyzed survey results supplied by the Dis-placed Homemaker Network and, in addition, interviewed directors of 20 established centers.

A marked tendency for men to retire at earlier ages than formerly has focused attention on the causes of their early retirement. However, labor force participation rates of women in the 55–64 age range have declined by no more than two percentage points from a peak of about 43 percent reached in 1969 and 1970—a very modest decline, not exciting much attention. In addition, the habit of considering women as secondary workers and a widespread feeling that retirement would present no problems for women who could easily resume their former housewife roles have until recently inhibited research in this area. An unfortunate consequence of these attitudes toward women and retirement is that data sources for studying women's retirement decisions are less plentiful than those available for studying men. Both the Social Security Administration's Retirement History Survey (RHS) and the NLS mature men's sample have been used extensively to study the influences on men's age of retirement. The RHS contains a representative sample of women who were heads of household at the time of the survey's first interview, but wives in the same age range were not interviewed.[25] The NLS mature women's sample has been used to study women's retirement plans, but the oldest of these women are only now reaching age 60, and only a few have actually retired.

Much of the research on age of retirement has focused on the effects of the Social Security system and employer-provided pensions on the timing of retirement. Most empirical work on retirement has found that pension eligibility and size of pension are important predictors of the age of retirement. On balance, the availability of Social Security benefits has probably promoted earlier retirement as well.[26] The effect of health on men's retirement has been the subject of considerable controversy. Although very few researchers would deny that health may affect retirement in some cases, the relative importance of health and alternative sources of income in retirement is a matter of dispute.[27] Certainly it seems plausible that increases in

---

[25] The Social Security Administration did not interview married women because preliminary interviews led them to believe that "for most married women of this generation 'retirement' had no meaning apart from their husbands' stopping work" (Irelan, 1972). The generation referred to was women who were 57–63 years of age in 1969, the first year of the survey. This survey has been used extensively to study the retirement of unmarried women, and wives of the men's sample have also been studied, even though the data on their work are not as extensive as those for their husbands.

[26] A review of this research may be found in Fields and Mitchell (1984). Aaron (1982) contains a good discussion of the effects of the Social Security system on age of retirement, offering a somewhat different view from Fields and Mitchell's.

[27] Much of the debate revolves around the inadequacy of the self-reported measures of health available from most surveys. Probably some workers may prefer to report health problems as the reason they are not working because this reason is socially acceptable. However, the extent of this problem is uncertain (Wolfe, 1984), and whether women, who have other acceptable reasons for not working, would have the same incentives as men to overuse health as a reason for not working has not been considered. A balanced review of this debate may be found in Daymont and Andrisani (1983) and Parnes (1983). A statement of the opposing positions may be found in Myers (1982) and Kingson (1982).

disability payments and earlier eligibility for Social Security have made it possible for some workers in poor health to retire earlier than they would have if no alternative source of income had been available.

Only a small fraction of the extensive research on the effects of pensions, Social Security, and health on retirement has used samples of women. Some studies of unmarried women have provided evidence that, as in the case of men, both health and pension or Social Security eligibility or potential income from pensions were of major importance in determining when they retire (Hanoch and Honig, 1983; O'Rand and Henretta, 1982; Hall and Johnson, 1980) or plan to retire (Shaw, 1986b).[28] In a study using the NLS mature women's sample, married women's plans for retirement were found to be strongly influenced by their own pension and Social Security eligibility, and most women who would later become eligible for pensions planned to postpone retirement until they became eligible (Shaw, 1984).

Several studies have attempted to determine how dual-earner couples time their retirement or make plans for retiring (Shaw, 1984; Shaw and Gagen, 1984; Anderson, Clark, and Johnson, 1980; Clark, Johnson, and McDermed, 1980; Henretta and O'Rand, 1980). Generally some evidence for reciprocal influences has been found: women are more likely to retire or plan to retire if their husbands are retired, and husbands also appear to be influenced by their wives' retirement.

It is not clear how these factors will influence older women's labor force participation as more women come to have their own pensions. If pension eligibility begins before age 60, women's labor force participation in the 55–64 age range might decline, but if the age of eligibility were to be increased in the future, women might work longer. Because husbands are usually older than their wives, it is also possible that a strong desire to retire together would cause men to remain at work longer if more wives had pensions and chose to work until they became eligible to retire. However, a study of the effect of wives' pensions on husbands' retirement found no evidence for such an effect (Shaw and Gagen, 1984).

The role of poor health in causing women to leave the labor force at an early age has not been the subject of the extensive debate accorded the subject of men's health. Although they live longer than men, on average, middle-aged women generally appear to report more health-related problems and more severe levels of disability than men of the same age (Feldman, 1983; Levitan and Taggart, 1977). Poor health, in general, appears to cause middle-aged women to leave the

---

[28] Hanoch and Honig (1983) found that being eligible for a larger Social Security benefit decreased older women's labor force participation, whereas eligibility for a private pension did not. However, their pension variable probably did not adequately measure whether a woman was already eligible for pension benefits.

labor force (Gitter, Shaw, and Gagen, 1986; Chirikos and Nestel, 1983, 1985; Hanoch and Honig, 1983; Shaw, 1983a). Black women in the generation that is currently middle-aged have more severe health problems than white women and are more likely to leave the labor force because of poor health (Chirikos and Nestel, 1983, 1985; Shaw, 1983a). One study found that women are less likely to receive disability payments than men, but more likely to leave the labor force when they are beneficiaries (Better et al., 1979).

Economic theory predicts that workers will retire when the benefits from retirement, monetary and psychological, exceed the costs. This formulation suggests that more attention should be paid to the worker's satisfaction or dissatisfaction with the job and the value the worker puts on the additional leisure time that would become available with retirement. Although some research has found that job satisfaction affects men's retirement (Morgan, 1980; Parnes and Nestel, 1974) and women's plans for retirement (Shaw, 1986b), the question of how jobs might be redesigned to induce workers to remain in the labor force longer has been the subject of considerable speculation but little research. Exceptions are reports on individual companies offering part-time work options to retired employees (see, e.g., Buchman, 1983).

Different surveys have produced quite different results about how many retirees are interested in part-time work and whether workers approaching retirement would like to work part-time if pension and Social Security rules were changed to encourage continued employment (Rones, 1980). Not only is there considerable doubt about workers' views, there is little information about whether men and women differ in this respect. Furthermore, research in this area may be premature. It does not appear that labor shortages will be a problem for many employers in the near future; only when the baby boom generation reaches retirement age may employers become willing to provide incentives for workers to remain at work longer than they do at present.

More important at this time is the question of older workers displaced from their jobs by plant closings, layoffs due to declining demand, and the elimination of some kinds of jobs. For workers approaching retirement age, displacement may lead to early retirement (Shapiro and Sandell, 1984; Bould, 1980). Although the effects of displacement on older male workers has received considerable attention, very little is known about the situation of older women. A recent study using a special survey of workers displaced between 1979 and 1984 (Flaim and Sehgal, 1985) found that only 36 percent of women and 44 percent of men ages 55–64 were reemployed by 1984, compared with 53 percent of all women and 64 percent of all men. However, older men were more likely to be unemployed and looking for work, while older women were more likely to stop looking for work. Women who do find new jobs may be less likely than men to suffer large pay cuts, primarily because women are less likely to have been employed in high-paying jobs such as those in the automobile and steel industries and more likely to have lost relatively low-paying jobs such as those in apparel or textiles.[29]

The few case studies of displaced older workers that include women also appear to indicate that many older women, like older men, experience difficulty in finding new jobs (Bluestone and Harrison, 1982). Displaced male workers have a greater tendency to retire after displacement during years when the national unemployment rate is high (Shapiro and Sandell, 1984). Female displaced workers probably behave similarly. A study using the NLS mature women's cohort found that older women were more likely to withdraw from the labor force between 1977 and 1982 if they lived in areas with above-average unemployment rates (Gitter, Shaw, and Gagen, 1986). However, few of these women said they had been laid off from their previous jobs; probably most were intermittent workers who were unable to find work again after leaving jobs for other reasons.

Conclusions

This review of research on middle-aged women workers reveals important gaps in our knowledge about women workers and their problems at this life-cycle stage. We do not know whether family reasons, personal preferences, or lack of job opportunities cause some women to follow intermittent work patterns after they no longer have small children. Research on age discrimination has not been a high priority and what research there is has been more concerned with older men than older women. Displacement of older workers due to plant closings or technological change has focused primarily on men. Research on age of retirement also has been overwhelmingly concerned with explaining the trend toward earlier retirement among men.

Even if research on middle-aged women workers were more complete, an additional problem is that some of the research we have today will soon become dated. Ten years from now the characteristics of middle-aged women workers will have changed considerably from those we have described. The oldest women—those who grew up

---

[29] In dissertation research now in progress at Ohio State University using the NLS, Mary Gagen finds small but significant wage losses among displaced women workers. Those who were reemployed earned on average about 5 percent less than their counterparts who remained with the same employer or changed employers voluntarily.

during the Depression or World War II years and were raising their children during the baby boom years of the 1950s—will have retired, to be replaced by their daughters, born in the baby boom years. Compared with women who are currently middle-aged, in the future more women in this age group will be college-trained and many more will have worked continuously or with only short work interruptions throughout their adult lives. This greater work experience will come about because women who are now in their thirties are on average having fewer children and returning to work much sooner after child-bearing than women of the previous generation.

In addition to these differences between generations, the economic climate may be different for middle-aged women in the future. Some of today's middle-aged women reentered the labor market or sought better jobs after years of intermittent work at the very time when labor markets were crowded with young workers entering the labor force for the first time; thus, some middle-aged women must have faced competition from younger workers for entry-level jobs (Grant and Hamermesh, 1981). In the future the number of new entrants will decline and older women will face less competition from this source; on the other hand, competition for high-level jobs may be keen among their own large age cohort. Conditions on the demand side of the labor market are even more uncertain. If technological change eliminates many clerical jobs, as some researchers predict, women's employment opportunities could be drastically reduced.[30] It is also uncertain whether societal commitment to affirmative action will be maintained in the future.

What do these considerations suggest about future research needs? First, because of a tendency for social change to receive more attention than social continuity, it is possible that differences between generations have been exaggerated. Undoubtedly more women in the future will work continuously than at any time in the past, but women who follow this work pattern will probably remain a minority. For example, in a study of work experience during the 5 to 10 years after the first birth for women who were ages 24–34 in 1978, Mott and Shapiro (1982) found that only 12 percent of these women had followed a fairly continuous work pattern, 30 percent had not worked at all or had not worked for as long as six months in any year, and the remainder—over half of all women—had followed a work pattern intermediate between these extremes.

---

[30] Economist Wassily Leontieff has estimated that the full introduction of office automation would reduce the percentage of the labor force employed in clerical jobs from 18 to 12 percent (quoted in *Scientific American*, September 1984, p. 82).

In the future more middle-aged women than at present may be childless or have only one child.[31] Childless women especially will add to the ranks of continuous workers, but even so the majority of middle-aged women will continue to have experienced periods of intermittent work or, in a declining number of cases, long work interruptions while raising children. We need to monitor the changes that may occur in work patterns during the child-rearing years as well as the period after children are grown. If average work interruptions are shorter and more women work continuously, the decline in the wage gap observed at younger ages should begin to be seen at older ages as well. It will also be important to observe the progress of those women who do work continuously.

The effect of new office technologies on women workers will become an important area for research in the future. Effects of job displacement on older women workers, a topic which has not been adequately studied at present, may become even more important in the future. It is often assumed that an aging population will mean that older workers will be more valued by employers as the supply of young workers diminishes, but this outcome depends on the overall demand for labor and what kinds of workers are needed. Company policies that may be biased against older workers, especially in hiring, need to be examined. Finally, more of the research on retirement, on changes in pension and Social Security systems, and on incentives for later retirement need to consider how proposed changes affect women.

References

Aaron, Henry J. *Economic Effects of Social Security*. Washington: Brookings Institution, 1982.

Agassi, Judith Buber. *Women on the Job: Attitudes of Women Toward Their Work*. Lexington, MA: D.C. Heath, 1979.

Anderson, Kathryn, Robert L. Clark, and Thomas Johnson. "Retirement in Dual Career Families." In *Retirement Policy in an Aging Society*, ed. Robert L. Clark. Durham, NC: Duke University Press, 1980. Pp. 109–27.

Andrisani, Paul J. "Job Satisfaction among Working Women." *Signs: Journal of Women in Culture and Society* 3 (Spring 1978): pp. 588–607.

———. "Levels and Trends in Job Satisfaction, 1966–72." In *Work Attitudes and Labor Market Experience*, by Paul J. Andrisani et al. Philadelphia: Center for Labor and Human Resource Studies, Temple University, 1977a. Pp. 60–102.

---

[31] About 11 percent of women who are now ages 40–59 have no children, and another 11 percent have one child. Although the percentage of women ages 25–34 who expect to remain childless is approximately the same as the percentage for middle-aged women, 20 percent of women ages 30–34 and nearly half of those ages 25–29 are still childless. Probably considerable numbers in both groups will not realize their plans. About 15 percent of women in the 25-34 age group expect to have only one child (U.S. Bureau of the Census, 1984b).

_____. "Work Attitudes and Labor Market Experience: Other Findings." In *Work Attitudes and Labor Market Experience*, by Paul J. Andrisani et al. Philadelphia: Center for Labor and Human Resource Studies, Temple University, 1977b. Pp. 135–61.

Appelbaum, Eileen. *Back to Work: Determinants of Women's Successful Reentry.* Boston: Auburn House, 1981.

Astin, Helen S. *Some Action of Her Own: The Adult Woman and Higher Education.* Lexington, MA: D.C. Heath, 1976.

Bassi, Laurie J. "The Effects of CETA on the Postprogram Earnings of Participants." *Journal of Human Resources* 18 (Fall 1983): pp. 539–56.

Beller, Andrea H. "Trends in Occupational Segregation by Sex and Race, 1960–1981." In *Sex Segregation in the Workplace: Trends, Explanations, Remedies*, ed. Barbara F. Reskin. Washington: National Academy Press, 1984. Pp. 11–26.

Better, S., P. Fine, D. Simon, G. Doss, W. Walls, and D. McLaughlin. "Disability Benefits and Disincentives to Rehabilitation." *Milbank Memorial Fund Quarterly* 57 (Summer 1979): pp. 412–27.

Blau, Francine D. "The Impact of the Unemployment Rate on Labor Force Entries and Exits." In *Women's Changing Roles at Home and on the Job*, Special Report No. 26. Washington: U.S. Department of Labor, Employment and Training Administration, 1978. Pp. 263–86.

Bluestone, Barry, and Bennett Harrison. *Deindustrialization of America: Plant Closings, Community Abandonment, and the Dismantling of Basic Industry.* New York: Basic Books, 1982.

Bould, Sally. "Unemployment as a Factor in Early Retirement Decisions." *American Journal of Economics and Sociology* 39 (April 1980): pp. 125–36.

Bowen, William G., and T. Aldrich Finegan. *The Economics of Labor Force Participation.* Princeton, NJ: Princeton University Press, 1969.

Buchman, Anna M. "Maximizing Post-Retirement Labor Market Opportunities." In *Policy Issues in Work and Retirement*, ed. Herbert S. Parnes. Kalamazoo, MI: W.E. Upjohn Institute for Employment Research, 1983. Pp. 109–29.

Cain, Glen G., and Martin D. Dooley. "Estimation of a Model of Labor Supply, Fertility, and Wages of Married Women." *Journal of Political Economy* 84 (August 1976): pp. S176–S200.

Center for Human Resource Research. *The National Longitudinal Surveys Handbook.* Columbus: Ohio State University, revised 1983.

Chafe, William H. *The American Woman.* New York: Oxford University Press, 1972.

Chirikos, Thomas N., and Gilbert Nestel. "Further Evidence on Economic Effects of Poor Health." *Review of Economics and Statistics* 67 (February 1985): pp. 61–69.

_____. "Economic Consequences of Poor Health in Mature Women." In *Unplanned Careers: The Working Lives of Middle-Aged Women*, ed. Lois B. Shaw. Lexington, MA: D.C. Heath, 1983. Pp. 93–108.

Clark, Robert L., Thomas Johnson, and Ann A. McDermed. "Allocation of Time and Resources by Married Couples Approaching Retirement." *Social Security Bulletin* 43 (1980): pp. 3–6.

Congressional Budget Office and National Commission for Employment Policy. *CETA Training Programs: Do They Work for Adults?* Washington: Congressional Budget Office, 1982.

Corcoran, Mary E. "Work Experience, Labor Force Withdrawal, and Women's Wages: Empirical Results Using the 1976 Panel of Income Dynamics." In *Women in the Labor Market*, eds. Cynthia B. Lloyd, Emily A. Andrews, and Curtis L. Gilroy. New York: Columbia University Press, 1979. Pp. 216–35.

Corcoran, Mary E., and Greg J. Duncan. "Work History, Labor Force Attachment, and Earnings Differences Between Races and Sexes." *Journal of Human Resources* 14 (Winter 1979): pp. 3–20.

Corcoran, Mary E., Greg J. Duncan, and Michael Ponza. "A Longitudinal Analysis of White Women's Wages." *Journal of Human Resources* 18 (Fall 1983): pp. 497–520.

Craft, James A., Samuel I. Doctors, Yitzchak M. Shkop, and Thomas J. Benecki. "Simulated Management Perceptions, Hiring Decisions and Age." *Aging and Work* 2 (Spring 1979): pp. 95–102.

Daymont, Thomas N., and Paul J. Andrisani. "The Health and Economic Status of Very Early Retirees." *Aging and Work* 6 (1983): pp. 117–35.

Dex, Shirley, and Lois B. Shaw. *British and American Women at Work: Do Equal Opportunities Policies Matter?* London: Macmillan Ltd., 1986.

Doering, Mildred, Susan R. Rhodes, and Michael Schuster. *The Aging Worker.* Beverly Hills, CA: Sage Publications, 1983.

Feldman, Jacob J. "Work Ability of the Aged Under Conditions of Improving Mortality." *Milbank Memorial Fund Quarterly/Health and Society* 61 (1983): pp. 430–44.

Ferber, Marianne A., and Bonnie G. Birnbaum. "Labor Force Participation Patterns and Earnings of Clerical Workers." *Journal of Human Resources* 16 (Summer 1981): pp. 416–25.

Ferree, Myra Marx. "Sacrifice, Satisfaction and Social Change: Employment and the Family." In *My Troubles Are Going to Have Trouble With Me*, eds. Karen Brodkin Sachs and Dorothy Remy. New Brunswick, NJ: Rutgers University Press, 1984. Pp. 61–79.

Fields, Gary S., and Olivia S. Mitchell. *Retirement, Pensions, and Social Security.* Cambridge, MA: MIT Press, 1984.

Flaim, Paul O., and Eileen Sehgal. "Displaced Workers of 1979–83: How Well Have They Fared?" *Monthly Labor Review* 108 (June 1985): pp. 3–16.

Girard, Kathryn, Joan Sweeney, and Patricia Sorce. "Results from the Second Needs Survey of Campus-Based Women's Centers, 1978–79." Amherst: National Women's Centers Training Project, University of Massachusetts, 1979.

Gitter, Robert J., Lois B. Shaw, and Mary G. Gagen. "Early Labor Market Withdrawal." In *Midlife Women at Work: A Fifteen-Year Perspective*, ed. Lois B. Shaw. Lexington, MA: D.C. Heath, 1986. Pp. 87–97.

Glenn, Norval D., Patricia A. Taylor, and Charles N. Weaver. "Age and Job Satisfaction Among Males and Females: A Multivariate, Multisurvey Study." *Journal of Applied Psychology* 62 (1977): pp. 189–93.

Grant, James H., and Daniel S. Hamermesh. "Labor Market Competition Among Youth, White Women, and Others." *Review of Economics and Statistics* 63 (August 1981): pp. 354–60.

Gustman, Alan L., and Thomas L. Steinmeier. "The Effect of Partial Retirement on the Wage Profiles of Older Workers." *Industrial Relations* 24 (Spring 1985): pp. 257–65.

Haefner, James E. "Race, Age, Sex, and Competence as Factors in Employer Selection of the Disadvantaged." *Journal of Applied Psychology* 62 (1977): pp. 199–202.

Hall, Arden, and Terry R. Johnson. "The Determinants of Planned Retirement Age." *Industrial and Labor Relations Review* 33 (January 1980): pp. 241–54.

Hanoch, Giora, and Marjorie Honig. "Retirement, Wages, and Labor Supply of the Elderly." *Journal of Labor Economics* 1 (1983): pp. 131–51.

Harlan, Sharon L. "Federal Job Training Policy and Disadvantaged Women." In *Women and Work: An Annual Review*, Vol. 1, eds. Laurie Larwood, Ann H. Stromberg, and Barbara A. Gutek. Beverly Hills, CA: Sage Publications, 1985. Pp. 282–310.

Heckman, James J. "New Evidence on the Dynamics of Female Labor Supply." In *Women in the Labor Market*, eds. Cynthia B. Lloyd, Emily A. Andrews, and Curtis L. Gilroy. New York: Columbia University Press, 1979. Pp. 66–97.

Henretta, John C., and Angela O'Rand. "Labor Force Participation of Older Married Women." *Social Security Bulletin* 43 (1980): pp. 10–26.

Irelan, Lola M. "Retirement History Study: Introduction." *Social Security Bulletin* 35 (1972): pp. 3–8.

Jolly, J., S. Creigh, and A. Mingay. *Age as a Factor in Employment*. Department of Employment Research Paper No. 11. London: Her Majesty's Stationery Office, 1980.

Kingson, Eric. "The Health of Very Early Retirees." *Social Security Bulletin* 45 (September 1982): pp. 3–9.

Lacy, William B., Janet L. Bokemeir, and Jon M. Shepard. "Job Attribute Preferences and Work Commitment of Men and Women in the United States." *Personnel Psychology* 36 (1983): pp. 315–29.

Levitan, Sar, and Robert Taggart. *Jobs for the Disabled*. Baltimore: Johns Hopkins Press, 1977.

Long, James E., and Ethel B. Jones. "Labor Force Entry and Exit by Married Women: A Longitudinal Analysis." *Review of Economics and Statistics* 62 (February 1980): pp. 1–6.

McConnell, Stephen R. "Age Discrimination in Employment." In *Policy Issues in Work and Retirement*, ed. Herbert S. Parnes. Kalamazoo, MI: W.E. Upjohn Institute for Employment Research, 1983. Pp. 159–96.

Mincer, Jacob, and Haim Ofek. "Interrupted Work Careers: Depreciation and Restoration of Human Capital." *Journal of Human Resources* 17 (Winter 1982): pp. 3–24.

Mincer, Jacob, and Solomon Polachek. "An Exchange: The Theory of Human Capital and the Earnings of Women: Women's Earnings Reexamined." *Journal of Human Resources* 13 (Winter 1978): pp. 118–34.

―――. "Family Investments in Human Capital: Earnings of Women." *Journal of Political Economy* 82 (March-April 1974): pp. S76–S106.

Morgan, James N. "Retirement in Prospect and Retrospect." In *Five Thousand American Families—Patterns of Economic Progress*, Vol. VIII, eds. Greg J. Duncan and James N. Morgan. Ann Arbor, MI: Institute for Social Research, 1980. Pp. 73–106.

Morgan, William R. "Returning to School at Midlife: Mature Women with Educational Careers." In *Midlife Women at Work: A Fifteen-Year Perspective*, ed. Lois B. Shaw. Lexington, MA: D.C. Heath, 1986. Pp. 51–71.

Mott, Frank L., and David Shapiro. "Continuity of Work Attachment Among Young Mothers." In *The Employment Revolution*, ed. Frank L. Mott. Cambridge, MA: MIT Press, 1982. Pp. 80–101.

Mott, Frank L., and Lois B. Shaw. "The Employment Consequences of Different Fertility Behaviors." In *Midlife Women at Work: A Fifteen-Year Perspective*, ed. Lois B. Shaw. Lexington, MA: D.C. Heath, 1986. Pp. 23–36.

Myers, Robert. "Why Do People Retire Early?" *Social Security Bulletin* 45 (September 1982): pp. 10–14.

Myrdal, Alva, and Viola Klein. *Women's Two Roles*. London: Routledge and Kegan Paul, 1956.

Oppenheimer, Valeria Kinkaid. *Work and the Family*. New York: Academic Press, 1982.

O'Rand, Angela M., and John C. Henretta. "Delayed Career Entry, Industrial Pension Structure, and Early Retirement in a Cohort of Unmarried Women." *American Sociological Review* 47 (June 1982): pp. 365–73.

Osterkamp, Darlene, and Phyllis Hullet. "Re-Entry Women and Part-Time Students: An Overview With Relevant Statistics." Educational Resource Information Center, 1983.

Palmore, Erdman. "When Can Age, Period, and Cohort Effects Be Separated?" *Social Forces* 57 (September 1978): pp. 282–95.

Parnes, Herbert S. "Health, Pension Policy and Retirement." *Aging and Work* 6 (1983): pp. 244–49.

———. "The National Longitudinal Surveys: New Vistas for Labor Market Research." *American Economic Review* 65 (May 1975): pp. 244–49.

Parnes, Herbert S., and Gilbert Nestel. "Early Retirement." In *The Pre-Retirement Years: Five Years in the Work Lives of Middle Aged Men*. Columbus, OH: Center for Human Resource Research, 1974. Pp. 153–96.

Rhodes, Susan R. "Age-Related Differences in Work Attitudes and Behavior: A Review and Conceptual Analysis." *Psychological Bulletin* 93 (March 1983): pp. 328–67.

Robinson, J. Gregory. "Labor Force Participation Rates of Cohorts of Women in the United States: 1890–1979." Paper presented at the Population Association of America meetings, Denver, 1980.

Rones, Philip L. "The Retirement Decision: A Question of Opportunity?" *Monthly Labor Review* 103 (November 1980): pp. 14–17.

Roos, Patricia A., and Barbara F. Reskin. "Institutional Factors Contributing to Sex Segregation in the Workplace." In *Sex Segregation in the Workplace: Trends, Explanations, Remedies*, ed. Barbara F. Reskin. Washington: National Academy Press, 1984. Pp. 235–60.

Rosen, Benson, and Thomas H. Jerdee. "Too Old or Not Too Old." *Harvard Business Review* 55 (November-December 1977): pp. 97–105.

Rosenbaum, James E. *Career Mobility in a Corporate Hierarchy*. Orlando, FL: Academic Press, 1984.

Rubin, Lillian B. *Women of a Certain Age*. New York: Harper & Row, 1979.

Sandell, Steven, and David Shapiro. "The Theory of Human Capital and the Earnings of Women: A Reexamination of the Evidence." *Journal of Human Resources* 13 (Winter 1978): pp. 103–17.

Schuster, Michael, and Christopher S. Miller. "An Empirical Assessment of the Age Discrimination in Employment Act." *Industrial and Labor Relations Review* 38 (October 1984): pp. 64–74.

Schwab, Donald P., and Herbert G. Heneman. "Age Stereotyping in Performance Appraisal." *Journal of Applied Psychology* 63 (1978): pp. 573–78.

Shapiro, David, and Steven H. Sandell. "Effects of Economic Conditions on the Labor Market Status and Experiences of Older Male Workers." Paper presented at the Eastern Economic Association meetings, New York, March 1984.

———. "Age Discrimination and Labor Market Problems of Displaced Older Workers." National Commission for Employment Policy Report Series RR-83-10. Washington: National Commission for Employment Policy, 1983.

Shaw, Lois B. "Introduction and Overview." In *Midlife Women at Work: A Fifteen-Year Perspective*, ed. Lois B. Shaw. Lexington, MA: D.C. Heath, 1986a. Pp. 1–22.

_____. "Looking Toward Retirement: Plans and Prospects." In *Midlife Women at Work: A Fifteen-Year Perspective*, ed. Lois B. Shaw. Lexington, MA: D.C. Heath, 1986b. Pp. 113–33.

_____. "Determinants of the Increasing Work Attachment of Married Women." *Work and Occupations* 12 (February 1985): pp. 41–57.

_____. "Retirement Plans of Middle-Aged Married Women." *Gerontologist* 24 (February 1984): pp. 154–59.

_____. "Causes of Irregular Employment Patterns." In *Unplanned Careers: The Working Lives of Middle-Aged Women*, ed. Lois B. Shaw. Lexington, MA: D.C. Heath, 1983a. Pp. 45–59.

_____. "Effects of Education and Occupational Training on the Wages of Mature Women." Special Report to the U.S. Department of Labor. Columbus: Center for Human Resource Research, Ohio State University, 1983b.

_____. "Problems of Labor Market Reentry." In *Unplanned Careers: The Working Lives of Middle-Aged Women*, ed. Lois B. Shaw. Lexington, MA: D.C. Heath, 1983c. Pp. 33–44.

_____. "Effects of Age, Length of Work Interruption, and State of the Economy on the Reentry Wages of Women." Paper presented at the Western Economic Association meeting, Los Angeles, 1982.

Shaw, Lois B., and Mary G. Gagen. "Retirement Decisions of Husbands and Wives." Special Report to the U.S. Department of Labor. Columbus: Center for Human Resource Research, Ohio State University, 1984.

Shields, Laurie. *Displaced Homemakers: Organizing for a New Life*. New York: McGraw-Hill, 1981.

Sobol, Marion G. "Commitment to Work." In *The Employed Mother in America*, eds. F. Ivan Nye and Lois W. Hoffman. Chicago: Rand McNally, 1963. Pp. 40–63.

Spitze, Glenn D., and Joe L. Spaeth. "Employment among Married Female College Graduates." *Social Science Research* 8 (June 1979): pp. 184–98.

Statham, Anne, and Patricia Rhoton. "Attitudes towards Women Working: Changes over Time and Implications for the Labor-Force Behavior of Husbands and Wives." In *Unplanned Careers: The Working Lives of Middle-Aged Women*, ed. Lois B. Shaw. Lexington, MA: D.C. Heath, 1983. Pp. 77–92.

Strober, Myra. "Comment." In *Women in the Labor Market*, eds. Cynthia B. Lloyd, Emily S. Andrews, and Curtis L. Gilroy. New York: Columbia University Press, 1979. Pp. 271–77.

Sweet, James A. *Women in the Labor Force*. New York: Seminar Press, 1973.

Tittle, Carol Kehr, and Eleanor Rubin Denker. *Returning Women Students in Higher Education: Defining Policy Issues*. New York: Praeger, 1980.

Treiman, Donald J. "The Work Histories of Women and Men: What We Know and What We Need to Find Out." In *Gender and the Life Course*, ed. Alice J. Rossi. New York: Aldine, 1985. Pp. 213–32.

Tuma, Nancy B., Michael T. Hannan, and Lyle P. Groeneveld. "Dynamic Analysis of Event Histories." *American Journal of Sociology* 84 (1979): pp. 820–54.

U.S. Bureau of the Census. *Characteristics of the Population Below the Poverty Level, 1983*. Current Population Reports, Series P-60, No. 147. Washington: U.S. Government Printing Office, 1985a.

_____. *Money Incomes of Households, Families, and Persons in the United States, 1983*. Current Population Reports, Series P-60, No. 146. Washington: U.S. Government Printing Office, 1985b.

_____. *Characteristics of the Population*. 1980 Census of Population, Vol. 1, Ch. D. Washington: U.S. Government Printing Office, 1984a.

————. *Fertility of American Women, June 1983*. Current Population Reports, Series P-20, No. 395. Washington: U.S. Government Printing Office, 1984b.

U.S. Congress, Office of Technology Assessment. *Displaced Homemakers: Programs and Policy—An Interim Report*. Washington: U.S. Government Printing Office, 1985.

U.S. General Accounting Office. *An Overview of the WIN Program: Its Objectives, Accomplishments, and Problems*. Washington: U.S. General Accounting Office, 1982.

Waite, Linda J. "Projecting Female Labor Force Participation from Sex-Role Attitudes." *Social Science Research* 7 (December 1978): pp. 299–318.

Walsh, Mary Roth. *"Doctors Wanted: No Women Need Apply": Sexual Barriers in the Medical Profession, 1835–1975*. New Haven, CT: Yale University Press, 1977.

Wanner, Richard A., and Lynn McDonald. "Ageism in the Labor Market: Estimating Earnings Discrimination Against Older Workers." *Journal of Gerontology* 38 (1983): pp. 738–44.

Wolfe, Barbara. "Editorial." *Journal of Health Economics* 3 (1984): pp. 187–93.

CHAPTER 12

International Comparisons: Problems and Research in the Industrialized World

ALICE H. COOK*

The United Nations Women's Decade, 1976–1985, was marked by three great meetings, attended by thousands of the world's women, gathered in both intergovernmental and nongovernmental forums in Mexico City, Copenhagen, and Nairobi. Discussions ranged widely to cover women's personal, family, and work problems. All workshops, committees, and plenums had to do with the status of women and the hope to build a world free of sex bias. Labor market policy played a significant role in each of the meetings. The achievement of a non-sex-biased labor market emerged as a major goal.

The purpose of this chapter is to look at achievements and failures in attaining this goal in the Western market economies. This is a task that, when thoroughly addressed, is as complex and manifold as the field of labor relations itself. Women are now a major factor in the labor forces of the industrialized nations that include not only those in Western Europe and North America, but Japan, Australia, and New Zealand.

The number of women in the various national labor forces has risen rapidly over the postwar years. In the United States, for example, 35.6 percent of all women between the ages of 25 and 34 in 1946 worked for salaries or wages. In 1970, it was 50.4 percent; by 1984, it was 68.6 percent, and for 1985, 70.2 percent.[1] The same report notes that of the 2 million jobs created in 1985, 70 percent went to women. While figures in other countries are not generally quite so startling, the United States leads a trend that is clearly marked throughout the capitalist economies.

Yet despite the evidence of the continuously growing importance of women's role in the labor forces of these countries, the characteristics of their work, their earnings, their participation rates in

---

* Professor Emerita, Cornell University.
[1] U.S. Department of Labor, Bureau of Labor Statistics, January 1986.

various sectors of the economy, their career guidance, and vocational training still set them apart from men to such a degree that the issues of the causes and persistence of sex bias become paramount in considering their status.

It is not possible within the confines of a single chapter to deal with all the problems of women's work, for the list specific to women is a long one. It includes, among other issues, the "double burden" (work and family roles), job segregation, shorter hours, part-time work, reentry, vocational training and guidance, health and safety, and participation in trade unions. Among the remedies that have been advocated or implemented and to some degree evaluated are child care, parental leave, training projects directed at bringing women into male-dominated occupations, affirmative action in hiring and promotion, the abolition of protective legislation, and flextime schedules.

We first take up the status of these work-related issues and then turn to an evaluation of the research done in these areas. We ask to what degree the research findings have resulted in the adoption of policy that responds to and goes some way to remedy the revealed inequalities. In a third section we move to discuss briefly some areas of labor relations that now need to be studied if sex bias is to be completely eliminated in these societies.

Before turning to the review, however, it is well to note the kinds of research bodies that have been addressing these issues so as better to identify the sources of information and the likely sponsors of future studies.

Sources of Representative Research

A number of international agencies play a dominant research role in comparing the trends among nations and in setting intergovernmental norms of policy and approach. Foremost among these is the International Labour Office (ILO) with its membership of most of the countries in the United Nations. For the industrialized countries, to which we direct attention, the Organisation for Economic Cooperation and Development (OECD) with 28 members and the European Economic Community (EEC), including 12 nations, are most influential. The EEC has a variety of subgroups concerned with these problems. They include the European Parliament, the Social Fund, the Community's High Court, its Vocational Training Center (European Center for the Development of Vocational Training, CEDEFOP), and its Office for Women's Affairs.[2]

---

[2] Two periodicals report regularly on equality measures as they develop within the member states of the EEC. One comes from the women's affairs office of the EEC, *Women of Europe*, and includes from time to time supplements reporting on studies sponsored by the office. The other is *CREW Reports* (Center for Research on European Women) issued about six times a year. It has correspondents in all the EEC countries who report on governmental and private organizations' activities in support of EEC directives.

Each country has established offices, or in some cases ministries, on Women's and Family Affairs. In addition, provincial or even city governments within the countries have Equality Offices that often conduct research projects on many aspects of women's work. In several countries, advisory committees to government agencies exist to promote study of the status of women and to prepare legislation. Some are empowered to set up educational and vocational programs to correct inequities. They frequently carry out careful evaluative studies of these experiments. In France the National Center for Scientific Research had one of the first divisions in a national research agency devoted to work on women's problems. In both Sweden and West Germany the labor market boards have research arms concerned to an important degree with women's employment questions. In Germany it is the Institute for Labor Market and Vocational Research; in Sweden research emanates from the board itself.[3]

In addition to these governmental and quasi-governmental institutions, women's autonomous organizations in many countries, including Denmark, Belgium, and the Netherlands, have centers for research on women's problems. As women's studies programs have taken root in European universities, some of them have begun to produce research reports as well.

One must note in this connection the indisputable fact that women scholars are responsible in a major way for the work that has been done on these issues. Without their initiative and persistence, women's work problems would probably have remained as invisible, unanalyzed, and unremedied as they have been from the industrial revolution onward.

Some nonfeminist centers devoted to labor relations research have done studies dealing with women's work. Among these are the Institute for Work Environment Research at Trondheim, Norway, the Arbetslivcentrum in Stockholm, and the Wissenschaftszentrum in Berlin. In this category fall also the trade union research centers, such as the European Trade Union Confederation (ETUC) Research Office in Brussels and national union and labor-party-related centers, notably in Germany in the Wirtschaftswissenschaftliches Institut in Duesseldorf and the Friedrich-Ebert Foundation in Bonn.

Current Practice and Policy

When we look at the problem of women and work over the past two decades with the help of work produced from the sources men-

---

[3] The German Institut fuer Arbeitmarkt- und Berufsforschung der Bundesanstalt für Arbeit issues from time to time its *Literaturdokumentation*, a bibliography on labor market and vocational research with a section on "Working Women's Activity." The bibliography is international, although stronger on the German-language side than the French, English, Dutch, or Scandinavian, and contains nearly 1,400 entries that speak to the volume of activity in labor market research on women.

tioned above as well as other sources, characteristic similarities become evident.

Female Labor Force Participation Rates

Female labor force participation rates (LFPRs) had a constantly rising trend in the majority of countries. In some—Denmark, Sweden, Norway, and the United States—the increase was very rapid; in others—Austria, Italy, Germany, and Switzerland—the overall increase was slow and interrupted by occasional declines, although these declines seem not to have been reactions to cyclical fluctuations. According to an OECD report (1984): "(a) decline occurred in 1980–81 only in Spain and the United Kingdom. . . . Thus the discouraged worker effect seems to have been less strong among women in that recession than during the first oil crisis, which supports the argument of women's rising labour force commitment" (pp. 17–18). Of countries with relatively slow rates of increase, Austria, Italy, France, and Japan had always had a comparatively high percentage of women working for wages or salaries. While their LFPR did not grow rapidly, it remained relatively high (see Table 1). An ILO 1985 study including 1980 figures by world regions shows that women's LFPR increased 5.7 percentage points between 1975 and 1980 in European market countries and 6.9 percent in North America. Unfortunately, figures for Japan, New Zealand, and Australia are masked with the overall statistics for Asia and Oceania, respectively.

In the early years of the women's massive movement into the labor market, scholars wanted answers to the question of why women worked when, presumably, they had a choice to remain at home. One set of answers came in response to an inquiry initiated by the Women's Division of the German Trade Union Federation (DGB). To its questionnaire carried in a popular women's magazine in 1970, more than 9,000 replies were received. Many men joined their wives in making the responses. The overwhelming majority of these responses made clear that women were not working merely to fill time or to earn "pin money," but because they share the same economic incentives that brought men to the labor market: the need to support families and to provide them with a better standard of living and education. Comparable studies with similar results were carried out in other Common Market countries and in Australia (Bevege, James, and Shute, 1982; Organisation for Economic Cooperation and Development, 1982), Japan (Women's and Minors' Bureau, Ministry of Labor, 1983), Germany (Deutsches Institut fuer Arbeit und Berufsforschung, 1984), and Austria (Bartunek, Boehm, and Gross, 1984). For Scandinavia, see Hvidfeld, Jorgensen, and Nielsen (1982) and Wistrand (1981), and for a comparative survey of five European countries, see Eurostat (1981)

TABLE 1
Labor Force Participation Rate, by Sex
(Selected Years, 1960–1984)

| Country | Year | Labor Force Participation | | |
		Total	Female	Male
Austria	1975	58.4	42.4	76.3
	1979		30.5[a]	54.0[a]
	1982		32.2[a]	56.3[a]
Canada[b]	1960	56.2	30.2	82.2
	1968	57.7	37.1	78.7
	1974	61.1	42.9	78.7
	1979		47.9	78.1
	1983		52.6	76.7
Federal Republic of Germany	1960	60.0	41.2	82.7
	1968	57.1	38.6	79.1
	1976	53.2	37.7	72.1
	1982[c]	54.1	39.1	70.9
France	1960[d]	62.0	43.3	84.2
	1968[d]	58.8	41.4	78.5
	1976[d]	58.7	43.8	75.3
	1982[c]	55.6	42.4	69.8
Italy[c]	1982	51.6	33.6	70.9
Sweden	1960	63.2	43.4	83.3
	1968	62.4	46.9	78.9
	1976	65.3	55.2	75.8
	1980		64.6	78.4
United Kingdom[e]	1960	60.7	38.7	86.0
	1968	60.2	40.8	81.7
	1976	61.5	45.8	79.0
	1983[c]	59.1	44.5	75.0
United States[d]	1960	59.4	37.7	83.3
	1968	59.6	41.6	80.1
	1976	61.6	47.3	77.5
	1981	64.0	52.1	77.0

Sources: Ratner (1980); Commission of the European Community, Women in Statistics, Supplement No. 4 to Women of Europe (Brussels), January 1984; Austrian Federal Ministry of Social Affairs, "Case Study Austria, 1979–1984," prepared for Seminar on the Economic Role of Women in the ECE Region, Vienna, October 1984; Status of Women, Canada, "Women and the Economic Crisis," Seminar, p. 19; "Sweden," in Cook, Lorwin, and Daniels (1984), p. 265; U.S. Department of Labor, Office of the Secretary, Women's Bureau, Time of Change: 1983 Handbook on Women Workers, Bull. 298 (Washington: 1983): pp. 9–11.

[a] Labor force divided by total population. The use of the total population lowers the participation rate relative to other countries, as can be observed with the unusually low male LFPR.

[b] Working age is 15 and over.

[c] Working age is 15 and over and civilian population is 15 and over.

[d] Working age is 16 and over.

[e] Working age was raised from 15 to 16 in 1973.

and Organisation for Economic Cooperation and Development (1984, pp. 41–42).

Early in the 1970s, Pross's study (1973) of the then six Common Market countries raised the additional question of whether women's increased market activity had brought improvements in equality of work. Her inquiry covered 7,000 women throughout the EEC. The findings made clear that the problems of inequality for working women began in the home and were supported by both family and labor market law and practice. Together with Evelyne Sullerot's work on *Women, Society and Change* (1971) and Andrée Michel's *Les Femmes dans la société marchande* (1978), they laid the groundwork for analysis of women's place in the labor market of the early 1970s. They further demonstrated the presence of widespread discrimination and outlined problems that needed to be addressed if equal rights were to be achieved by women workers.[4]

Psychologists and sociologists were concerned with the conflict women presumably felt between going to work and their primary loyalty to home and family. The term "sex role" originated in Sweden to delineate the boundaries and differences between men's and women's worlds in both the home and the workplace. It brought to consciousness the facts of separation between the sexes in both worlds. Rita Liljeström, in her study of *Sex Roles in Transition* (1975), used the experience in one Swedish county where women were being placed in nontraditional jobs to examine the reactions of both men and women to these new roles—this crossing of the line between what had been separate worlds of work. She included interviews with husbands to ascertain the degree of change in the places of both men and women in the family as a result of women working in these occupations.

The "Double Burden"

The "double burden" became an independent subject of research. The actual areas of responsibility that women retained for work in the home, the additional hours they devoted to these tasks, the fact that housework has always been unpaid, and the degree to which this nonvaluation of women's household work contributed to the low value placed on similar tasks when performed for pay were all taken into consideration. Indeed, the very existence of the "double burden" for married—and many unmarried—working women was the starting point for much of the attention given to the poor conditions they met when they left the home for work outside it (Adams and Adams, 1980; Cook, 1978; Myrdal and Klein, 1956).

---

[4] See also Cook (1978).

Among the subjects of research that stemmed from the acknowledgment that women's lives were doubly burdened were time-use studies. Comparative studies (Goldschmidt-Clermont, 1982, 1983; Szalai, 1972) and individual country studies (Walker and Gauger, 1973; Girard, 1970) supplemented one another. They uniformly demonstrated that household tasks throughout the world are rigidly gender-segregated, that women devote 30 or more hours per week to household work than men do—indeed, that men and teenage children contribute only minutes a day to what is perceived to be their share in maintaining the household, and that women are consequently working a total or 70 or more hours a week. Moreover, other family members' household tasks increased by only a few minutes a day when the wife and mother worked outside the home.

The Value of Household Work

The value of household work has nowhere been included in reckoning the total gross national product (GNP). Measurements of its value based on the skills involved were early undertaken in the Colleges of Home Economics. Since in those days these schools were largely committed to professionalizing housework, their studies were directed to raising its status and improving its efficiency, altogether lightening the load of the housewife. Although some feminists raised the slogan of "wages for wives" as far back as the 1920s, the home economists paid little attention to this outcome of their work. Their estimates of value varied, but they tended to be conservative since they took women's earnings for similar work outside the home as their measure. In any case, these studies had little, if any, practical effect on the evaluation or payment of women's household work.

Chief attention in practical terms in the current period has been in the courts. Here, widowed husbands have brought cases asking for loss and damages arising from the accidental death of their wives. The effort has not been to repay the female spouse for her labors in the home while she was performing them, but to recompense her deprived husband who has lost her services. Courts in Britain, Japan, and the United States have awarded widowers for these losses at fairly high amounts. An investigation of the evidence entered into such pleadings as compared with the findings of the home economists ought to provide an interesting and even ironic study for a researcher interested in both law and consumer economics. The long and short of it all is, however, that the contribution women make to the economy through their work in the home is still not entered in the sum of the GNP.

The ILO, out of its concern for development aid for rural women, has noted that census practices "tend to under-report these [household] activities," and official data fail to provide "an accurate picture of women's economic contribution." It is therefore important to learn that

the 13th International Conference of Labour Statisticians, held in 1982, adopted a new definition of the "economically active population," based on the UN system of accounts, in which production and processing of primary products, *whether for the market, for barter or for own consumption, the production of all other goods and services for the market, as well as own consumption of these goods and services by households* that otherwise produce them for the market [will be taken into consideration]. (Emphasis added. ILO, 1985, p. 5.)

This new definition of economic activity, if in fact widely accepted in national statistical summaries of income, could greatly influence the status of women's work not only at home but in the market as well.

Perhaps as a consequence of such considerations, historical examinations have thrown light on hitherto neglected aspects of the home/work dichotomy, job segregation by gender, and its relationship to women's traditional assignment to home duties. Historians and sociologists have tracked the origins of what has come to be called "invisible" work in the home and its effects on values and remuneration in the fields of paid work. Studies on the origins and treatment of housework have been particularly plentiful in Britain and the United States (Kessler-Harris, 1982; Strasser, 1982; Vanek, 1978; Hartmann, 1974; Oakley, 1974; Lopata, 1971). Tracing the relationship of housework on the segregation of women's paid work into female-dominated categories has disclosed the powerful continuance from the early days of the industrial revolution to the present of what Kessler-Harris calls "the domestic code" still dominating women's home and work lives.

These studies have enriched work on specific aspects of labor market equality or inequality. Some have focused on the legal code (Bulletin of Comparative Labour Relations, 1979); most have dealt with an array of labor market inequities (Farley, 1985; Ireland, Working Party on Women's Affairs and Family Reform, 1985; Bartunek, Boehm, and Gross, 1984; Kohlstad, 1982; Enquête Kommission, 1979; Cook, 1978; Australia, National Commission on Discrimination in Employment and Occupations, 1975; Japan, Commission to Research the Problem of Equality between Men and Women at Work, 1975; Elliott et al., undated). An EEC study in 1984 pinpointed sectors where women were most at risk. Its summary reads in part:

The first thing to emerge is that, generally speaking, women who work in the public sector feel far less vulnerable than the rest of the female work force. However, . . . the majority of those doing administrative work (in an office) expect technological developments to have an effect on their work and those who teach often feel ill-prepared for any change.

In the private sector, women who work on the shop floor feel more vulnerable than the rest on almost all counts. They feel more exposed to unemployment and subject to greater discrimination as regards wages, regardless of the size of the firm. In large and medium-sized companies, it is access to vocational training, and above all, promotion they see as being difficult. Lastly in the big companies, they are very aware of the probable effect of technological change (65%), they feel ill-prepared to cope with it and fear their jobs will be threatened. . . . Women in office jobs feel discriminated against as far as their salaries are concerned and when it comes to promotion. They believe technological developments will [mean] they will need retraining. (Commission of the European Community, 1984, p. 94.)

Unemployment

Although women's employment has steadily increased and will continue to do so, women's unemployment rates in most countries have exceeded those of men (see Table 2). Canada and the United Kingdom are the major exceptions to what is otherwise an almost universal rule. (In both countries the unemployment rates of both men and women are unusually high.) While some labor market analysis attributes women's higher rates of unemployment to their low level of

TABLE 2
Unemployment Rate, 1976 and 1981 (percent)

Country	Year	Male	Female
Austria	1975	1.5	2.8
	1981	1.6	2.3
	1985	3.8	3.5[a]
Canada	1976	6.3	8.4
	1981	7.0	8.3
Federal Republic of Germany	1976	3.4	4.9
	1981	3.8	5.9
France	1976	2.8	7.1
	1981	5.0	10.9
Italy	1976	4.2	12.0
	1981	5.3	14.2
Sweden	1976	1.3	2.1
	1981	2.3	2.7
United Kingdom	1976	6.1	2.8
	1981	10.9	6.0
United States	1976	6.6	8.6
	1981	7.2	7.9
	1984	5.9	6.2[b]

Source: Organisation for Economic Cooperation and Development, *Historical Statistics, 1960–1981* (Paris: 1981).
[a] Bartunek, Boehm, and Gross, Austrian Federal Ministry of Social Affairs (1984), p. 33.
[b] U.S. Department of Labor, Bureau of Labor Statistics (January 1986).

"work commitment"—that is, their tendencies to higher rates of absenteeism and lower rates of productivity—and their "preference" to remain at home following the birth of a child and during its preschool years, much of the support for this line of argument disappeared as more and more mothers of young children entered and continued in the labor market, only taking legal maternity leave away from work. To be sure, Japan and Ireland represent exceptions to this rule. In both cases a strong tradition calls for women to leave work on marriage or the birth of a first child, returning, if at all, only after children are well established in secondary school. (Japan's high LFPR is largely explained, particularly in recent years, by the return of women over 40 to the labor force.) In Japan, young women in the upper level of the economy find it almost impossible to continue working following maternity leave because of the shortage of child-care facilities for children under 2 or 3 years of age and because the lifetime system of employment in that sector leaves little room for older women (Cook and Hayashi, 1981).

Women's susceptibility to high rates of unemployment now appears to be traceable to their more recent addition to the labor force, resulting in low seniority where that is used as a fairness guide in layoffs and dismissals. Their lower levels of training, some part of which is attributable to discrimination both at the apprentice level and in access to on-the-job training, play a part as well. Finally, the dispensability of their routine jobs to automation and the new technology contributes to the unemployment totals (Bouillaguet-Bernard, Gauvin-Ayel, and Outin, 1981; Standing, 1981; Nauhaus, 1979; Daeubler-Gmelin, 1977).

Where unions or works councils have some veto over selection of workers for layoffs, evidence accumulates that employers and fellow workers frequently agree in the judgment that since women "do not really need to work," they should properly be laid off before men. This view rests on the belief that men are still universally the heads of families while women are not. It overlooks, however, the effects of the rising divorce and abandonment rates on young mothers whose spouses and companions leave them. They become single heads of families in increasing numbers, at least for several years between legal or companionate marriages.

Technology

The introduction of sophisticated technology has always raised fears of unemployment or displacement among both male and female workers. One of the exceptions to this generalization occurs in Japan where the security of lifetime employment in the upper sector of the economy allows employers to introduce not only new machinery, but new processes at will because they bear the costs of retraining and, in effect, guarantee continued employment. This circumstance, however, does not hold where women employees are concerned, since it is assumed that they will in any case remain with the company only until marriage or the birth of their first child. The reaction of EEC women noted in the citation from the 1984 study testifies to the widespread concern about technology's effect both on employment and on training.

One effect, as the feminization of banking and insurance illustrates, is that the simplification of work that technology brings about in tasks below the level of middle-management tends to encourage employers to displace men with women, as they increase the division of labor so as to redefine jobs as low-paid and dead-end, many of which can be performed part-time. A concomitant development allows women to work at computers in their homes, with the advantage of setting their own times and presumably fitting work in between the demands of the household. Opponents insist these conditions will only, in fact, isolate women from the society of the workplace, make them almost impossible to organize, subject them to all the drawbacks of part-time work, and relieve companies of responsibility for maintaining standards of adequate lighting, safety, and job load.

A 1983 study of technological change and office jobs in OECD countries has shown that although the new technology was obviously laborsaving, it has not resulted in widespread female job loss so far. It has, however, led to a considerable reallocation of female labor within enterprises and to changes in job content (Werneke, 1983). Although much of this adjustment takes place as the result of natural turnover and does not lead to dramatic layoffs of large numbers of workers, Paukert warns that "the process of job reduction by 'natural wastage' markedly reduces employment opportunities for young people and for women wishing to re-enter the labor market" (Paukert, 1984a). She notes further that in some countries these changes have led to decided increases in part-time work, as new employment opportunities have become available for women. The deep recessions in Europe have, moreover, somewhat slowed the introduction of technology so that the full impact of changes remains to be evaluated.

Women Are Poor

The rising number of young women who are single heads of families is only one element contributing to what has been identified as "the feminization of poverty." It is a characteristic of women's low economic and social status in all countries with which we are concerned. In testimony before a U.S. Congressional committee studying "the poverty rate increase," Patricia Johnson, director of Family and Children Services in the State of Georgia, spoke of "the alarming proportion of women and children in female-headed households living lives of want and deprivation." The reasons she put forth were that "four out of five working women have low paid jobs with little future . . . [and] half of America's women have jobs with no pension plans. . . . The cost of medical care has risen faster than any other consumer cost item." In addition, a substantial number of poor women are elderly and thus subject to increased medical cost as they become more infirm. She noted, too, the high proportions of black women in these statistics (Johnson, 1983; Pearce, 1979).

Where pensions are linked to income, low-paid employment over a lifetime must result in low pension income. The result is that women who have never worked outside the home often receive more retirement income as widows than women who have worked all their lives for wages (U.S. Department of Health and Human Services, 1980; Spector, 1979).[5]

But it is not just women on welfare or unemployed or elderly who are poor. Women everywhere are typically engaged in low-paid jobs with low training and promotional opportunities. In fact, the structural changes that the Western economies have undergone in the past few decades, which have resulted in the shift from manufacturing to the service trades as the main providers of employment, have had a decided effect on lowering the incomes of the majority of workers in these occupations, and these are women. Thus, while women's employment opportunities have far exceeded those of men as this shift has taken place, jobs are no less gender-separated than they were at the beginning of the century and remain relatively almost as low paid.

Pay Equity

The differentials between men's and women's pay represent a disadvantage to women in every country (see Table 3). They are a product of the kinds of work women are assigned to in their segregated jobs. They are linked to the fact that women are given jobs that appeal to employers as suited to their sex: suited because they are related to housework which is their "natural sphere"; to small muscle activity, considered less worthy of recompense than "hard physical labor"; to repetitive work calling for little responsibility or creativeness because it is work that does not require them to put its demands ahead of those

---

[5] The EEC in 1978 adopted a directive (Council Directive of 17 December 1978 on the progressive implementation of equal treatment of men and women in matters of social security: 79/7/EEC), requiring member states within seven years to have revised their pension systems so as to conform to equal treatment standards for men and women. Most states within the Community began studies and other preparation to bring them into conformity with the Directive. Unfortunately, when the critical year 1985 arrived, it was England—as has so often been the case in recent years with EEC equal-treatment reforms—that refused to go along with full implementation of the program and thus stymied adoption for the present.

TABLE 3

Wage Differentials Between Women and Men
(Nonagricultural; Percent Women/Men)

Country	1973	1975	1977	1979	1981	1983
Austria	63.1	64.4	63.1			.77.5
Australia	70.0		82.0			
Denmark (hourly)	79.2	83.2	85.2	84.7	84.5	
Federal Republic of						
Germany	70.3	72.3	72.7	72.6	72.5	
France						
Manual	75.8		74.6			
Nonmanual	58.0		66.2			
Italy						
Manual	75.5	80.0	83.1			
Nonmanual	61.9		68.8			
Sweden						
Manual	84.1	85.2	87.4	89.3	90.1	
United Kingdom	62.5	67.6	71.9	70.7	69.5	
Nonmanual	45.1		54.6			
United States	56.6	57.0	58.9	59.7	59.2	64.3

Sources: Centre for Social Development and Humanitarian Affairs, Department of International Economic and Social Affairs, "Some Aspects of the Role of Women in Economic Development, Part II," unpublished paper prepared for the *Seminar on the Economic Role of Women in the ECE Region*, Vienna, October 1984, pp. 19, 21; Ratner (1980); Cook, Lorwin, and Daniels (1984), p. 90; U.S. Department of Labor, Women's Bureau, *Time of Change: 1983 Handbook on Women Workers*, Bull. 298 (Washington, 1983); Eurostat (1981).

of family. "Women's jobs" are also judged less valuable than men's, as already noted, because, unlike men, women are not presumed to support families. Thus, a bundle of contradictory wage theories are tied together so that if one does not explain women's low wages, another will.

For many years the demand for "equal pay for equal work" was raised to deal with the differential remuneration of men and women. One of the very early ILO conventions met the problem in this way. But by 1952, the ILO had adopted Convention 100 that called for "equal pay for work of equal value." In 1963, the EEC's founding charter, the Treaty of Rome, reverted to equal pay for equal work as the norm that should obtain within the Community. This phrase was, however, reinterpreted to mean equal pay for work of equal value, a fact made very clear by rulings of the High Court and by the wording of the Directive itself.[6] Slowly governments have recognized that the

---

[6] In a sharp rebuke to the British government, the Court in 1979 made clear that equal pay for work of equal value could not be limited to broadly similar work and stated that "member states

extreme job segregation in every country makes equal pay for equal work a goal that would at best benefit not more than 20 percent of working women. Table 4 shows the steps that selected countries have taken to live up to the various equal pay goals, while Table 3 indicates that at least three non-Community countries have moved closer to achieving equal pay—Sweden, Austria, and Australia—than have three members of the Community—France, Germany, and England. The United States, however, is by far at the bottom of the list (Paukert, 1984a, 1984b; Gregory and Duncan, 1981; Pfarr and Bertelsmann, 1981; Sloane, 1980; Bouteiller, 1975; Takahashi, 1975; Pettman, 1977).

Vocational Training

One of the most aggressive undertakings of the EEC in respect to women's equal treatment at work is its investment in studies and model programs in this field. The central organization carrying out this work, CEDEFOP (Berlin), produces a steady stream of comparative and single-country studies. Moreover, the Community has designated a substantial (but recently declining) portion of its Social Fund for such projects. Many ministries of labor, with and without help from the EEC, have initiated their own studies of need (Botezat, 1977), experimental programs (Hegelheimer, 1979), and evaluations of these programs (Fairbanks, 1979; Hegelheimer, 1979; *Literaturdokumentation,* various issues).

A 1980 CEDEFOP conference of persons sponsoring innovative programs for women looked at "social, material, and occupational situation, development of employment, work organization, and training"; at "the functioning of the vocational guidance and placement services"; and at the attitudes of employers, male workers, and the employment services about such programs. In each of these three workshops, conference participants raised questions for further consideration and proposed specific measures that might be undertaken by each of the concerned elements: trainers, counselors, employers, fellow workers, and employment agencies. Achievements were to be measured against the goal of attaining equality in the labor markets in respect to access to jobs, promotion, compensation, training, and retirement, all of which are presumably now guaranteed by law in all Community states.

Reentry

Women's work generally, until the mid-1970s, could still be described with some accuracy by an "M" curve—that is, by a graph

---

must endow an authority [in this case, the Equal Opportunities Commission] with the requisite jurisdiction to decide whether work has the same value as other work" (Rights of Women, Europe, 1982, p. 62).

TABLE 4
National Equality Policy: Principal Machinery for Implementation

Country	Method	A	B	C	Year	Title	Enforcement Machinery
Austria	EPb		x		1979	Law on Equal Treatment of Women and Men in Determining Remuneration	Equality Commission
	EOc	x				Under consideration by tripartite panel	
Canada	EP		x		1978	Human Rights Act	Human Rights Commission
					1970	Canadian Labour Code amended	Labor Standards Branch
					1966–1967	Consolidated into Labour Code	Department of Labour
					1956	Female Employees Equal Pay Act	
Denmark	EO		x		1978	Human Rights Act	Human Rights Commission
	EP		x	x	1978	Act of Equal Treatment for Men and Women	Civil courts
					1976	Equal Remuneration Act	Labor tribunals
					1975		Council for Equality
					1973	National Collective Agreement	Labour courts to enforce collective agreements
	EO		x		1978	Act of Equal Treatment for Men and Women	Civil courts
					1975		Council for Equality
Federal Republic of Germany	EP		x		1982	Act Respecting Equality of Treatment for Men and Women at the Workplace	Labour courts
					1952	Law of Enterprises	
	EO		x		1982	Act Respecting Equality of Treatment for Men and Women at the Workplace	Labour courts

TABLE 4 (Continued)

Country	Dominant Method of Implementation[a]			Principal Implementing Measures		
	A	B	C	Year	Title	Enforcement Machinery
France	x	x		1983	Law on Equality in the Employment Field between Men and Women	Labor inspectors, industrial tribunals
				1972	Act No. 72–1143 respecting equal remuneration for men and women, implemented through Directive, in 1973	Labor inspectors in Ministry of Labor
				1950	Law establishing equal pay in collective bargaining	
				1946	Constitutional guarantee of equality between the sexes	
		x		1983	Law on Equality in the Employment Field between Men and Women	Labor inspectors, industrial tribunals
Italy	x	x		1977	Antidiscrimination Act	Works inspectorate, conciliation, or collective bargaining
				1978	Constitution	Equal Opportunities Commission
		x		1977	Antidiscrimination Act	Works inspectorate, conciliation, or collective bargaining; Equal Opportunities Commission

TABLE 4 (Continued)

Country	Dominant Method of Implementation[a]			Principal Implementing Measures		
	A	B	C	Year	Title	Enforcement Machinery
Sweden	EP	x	x	1979	Equal Treatment in Working Life Act	Equality Ombud
				1979	Wage Solidarity Agreement	Labor court—enforce collective bargaining
	EO	x	x	1983	Collective agreement to promote equal opportunity	None
				1979	Equal Treatment in Working Life Act	Equality Ombud
				1976	Equal Opportunities Ordinance for Public Employees	
United Kingdom	EP	x		1983	Equal Pay (Amendment Regulation) (equal value) and Industrial Tribunals (Rules of Procedure) (Equal Value Amendment) Regulations	Industrial Tribunal; Central Arbitration Committee; Advisory Conciliation and Arbitration Service
				1975	Sex Discrimination Act	Equal Opportunity Commission; Industrial Tribunal
	EO	x		1970	Equal Pay Act (inactive)	Equal Opportunity Commission; Industrial Tribunal
				1975	Sex Discrimination Act	

TABLE 4 (*Continued*)

Country	Dominant Method of Implementation[a]			Principal Implementing Measures		
	A	B	C	Year	Title	Enforcement Machinery
United States	EP	x		1963	Equal Pay Amendments to Fair Labor Standards Act	Originally Department of Labor; currently, Equal Employment Opportunity Commission
	EO[d]	x		1972	Amendments to Title VII	Department of Labor Equal Employment Opportunity Commission
				1964	Executive Order 11246	Equal Employment Opportunity Commission
				1964	Title VII of the Civil Rights Act	Equal Employment Opportunity Commission

Sources: Ratner (1980); Cook, Lorwin, and Daniels (1984); Cynthia Goodwin, *Equal Pay Legislation and Implementation: Selected Countries* (Ottawa, Canada: Minister of Labour, 1984); Austria, "Case Study Austria, 1979–1984," prepared for *Seminar on the Economic Role of Women in the ECE Region*, Vienna, October 1984; Ylva Ericsson, "The Economic Role of Women in Sweden, *Seminar*.

[a] A = by Constitution; B = by legislation; C = by collective bargaining.
[b] Equal pay.
[c] Equal opportunity.
[d] As of August 1985, more than two dozen states had gone beyond equal-pay-for-equal-work to equal-pay-for-work-of-comparable-worth.

depicting their entry into the labor market, their work until marriage or the birth of their first child, their retirement from work for the years of child-rearing, and their return to work after their children were well along in school. Statistics from that period indicate that women tended to withdraw from the labor market between 30 and 44 years of age, with the average period lasting about 20 years, and then to return to work, although in reduced numbers, between ages 45 and 49 (Botezat, 1977, pp. 27–28; Foelsing, 1973). Programs for these women reentering the labor force were fairly widespread, consisting of retraining and updated training (Yohalem, 1980).

In the late 1970s and early 1980s, women's employment dip in their middle years tended to flatten out. With each succeeding year women's work life, particularly in Scandinavia, the United States, and France, corresponds more closely to men's in its uninterrupted nature (Organisation for Economic Cooperation and Development, 1984, pp. 23–30). The growing number of mothers of preschool children who are in the labor market further attests to this trend. By 1980 a somewhat broader set of "re-integration" issues was replacing the single focus on "reentry" (Hvidfeld, Jorgensen, and Nielsen, 1982).

Part-Time Work

Although with increasingly high levels of education and the rapid introduction of early phased retirement, a rising number of part-time workers are men, women continue to represent more than 90 percent of this category of workers. Indeed, part-time work is the most immediate response women make when faced with the overload of the double burden. Its occurrence is particularly high in the countries where the rates of female labor force participation are high, notably in Scandinavia (although Finland is an exception to this rule). With few exceptions, part-time work falls outside the laws covering fringe benefits, such as private pension programs, health and welfare provisions offered by employers, and many protective measures provided by law, custom, or union contracts. Part-time workers, moreover, are rarely offered opportunities for in-firm training or promotion and are generally lower paid than full-time workers. In many countries part-time work is simply not defined or recognized, and hence workers in these categories have little access to either legal or union protections.

Unions on the whole have been reluctant to welcome part-time workers. To be sure, exceptions can be found, particularly in sectors such as food service and retail sales where customer demand fluctuates widely during the day. Among these are white-collar workers in the private sector in Austria, retail employees in Belgium and Sweden, and lunchroom workers and custodians in the public service in Great Britain. In Germany, however, even the Women's Division of the

DGB has insisted upon opportunities for full-time work in preference to advocating protections for part-time workers. Sweden makes a distinction between short part-time and long part-time—that is, less or more than 20 hours a week—and includes the latter category with full-time workers so far as legal and contractual relations are concerned. Critics, nevertheless, focus on how part-time work perpetuates the norm that while women do some paid work, they must and do concentrate on doing all the family upaid work. "It contributes to preserving the traditional division of labor within the family, and to keeping alive a job market system that fails to take into consideration that people are obliged to spend time doing other things than working," said Mai-Britt Carlsson, in 1976 the chief women's officer of Sweden's white-collar federation (TCO), as she addressed the Canadian Congress of Labour.

Despite all the drawbacks of part-time work, some governments, nominally in the interest of easing women's double burden, endeavor to increase its introduction (Casey, 1983). There is no doubt that in response to these opportunities, thousands of women even gratefully accept part-time work despite its drawbacks, so desperate is their need for additional income and so demanding the circumstances they face at home.

Hours

Part-time work is, of course, one way of shortening hours of work, although the price of doing so is very high. A variety of other proposals and experiments for shorter hours have been put forward, not least by working men. Indeed, the major thrust of union demands in Europe within the past decade has been toward achieving shorter hours with no loss in pay. German metal workers have been in the forefront in conducting long and severe strikes through which they first achieved no direct shortening of hours, but rather a few extra vacation days in the year. A second round of work actions, when settled by an arbitrator, resulted in the achievement of a somewhat shorter work-week.

Union leaders justify shortening the workweek or year by the resulting creation of jobs. Women support job-creation goals as well, but even across national boundaries they join in the hope that their own special needs can be met in the process. They opt for shorter workdays rather than shorter workweeks. With a shorter day they can better meet the demands of home and work. They believe, too, that men and their children could benefit from the added hours such a reform would give fathers at home. Uniformly, they have had little success in achieving these demands. Only the Swedes have given parents of children under school age the option of working six hours per day.

Gösta Rehn, a Swedish economist, prepared a paper for OECD in 1974 in which he took a longer, more radical view of the question. He looked at lifetime allocation of working and nonworking time and proposed "promoting diversification and variability—in one word—flexibility in the regulation and allocation of time, work, study and leisure [including retirement], allowing for the greatest possible freedom of choice." He would allow every worker, in the course of his or her lifetime, paid periods of freedom from work every few years. They might serve women as maternity leaves or for retraining. They might be used simply for rest and recreation, for reading and systematic study—indeed, for what the individual most wanted. Despite the fact that this "modest proposal" was put forward with practical consideration for how its costs might be borne by existing social security schemes, it has received little serious consideration.

Several country studies as well as some comparative ones have greatly helped in understanding women's special concerns with shorter hours. The reorganization of working time has played a significant part in debates in the European Parliament on the situation of European working women. In January 1984, H. Wieczorek-Zeul, chair of the committee on part-time work, echoed the Rehn proposal as a solution to the need young families have for a reduction in the working day. She said, in part, "Why should the reduction always be made at the end of working life through the lowering of the retirement age? It could also be suggested that free time should be provided where it is urgently needed; in families with small children, i.e., for employees between the ages of 25 and 40" (European Economic Community, European Parliament).

Other approaches to the hours problems that respond to women's needs include flextime schedules, job sharing, and dual-career couples' arrangements for sharing home and work responsibilities. Many governments and private employers of white-collar workers have, in fact, introduced flexible work schedules experimentally, usually around some core hours of required attendance. They have found, whether by scientific research methods or simply by referendums of their employees, enthusiastic acceptance of the program not only among women, but among men as well. Flextime in white-collar employment is probably more widespread in Europe in both public and private sectors than in North America. Japan has not copied this Western innovation.

Dual-career families have been the subject of research in Britain by Rhona and Robert Rapoport (1978) and in Norway by Erik Grønseth (1974). In both cases the populations studied were very small and suggested that these approaches to sharing the double burden worked best and perhaps only in professional families. Job sharing has been more widely used. It frequently involves two women sharing a full-time job and child care. Employers have been more willing to open up such opportunities in periods of high employment than in recessions (Cook, 1978, pp. 37–38).

Protective Legislation

The long accepted remedy for women's inferior position in the labor market was for the hand of government to protect them in their inherent weakness. Working hours were thus generally limited to day and evening hours, while night work was forbidden; women could not work underground, and in some countries not at heights; they could not lift weights above a given amount, usually 20–25 pounds; they could not be exposed to certain toxins or dangerous working conditions. In all countries except the United States they were entitled or mandated to take maternity leaves with pay in stated weeks before and after delivery of the child. These protections were adopted primarily to ensure the birth of healthy children, although they applied to all working women even beyond childbearing age.

Employers saw the demands for equality in working conditions as an opportunity to release them from the obligations these laws put upon them. Women's organizations saw the laws as limiting women's employment, and particularly their earning opportunities. Government lawyers saw possible conflicts between equality legislation and the maintenance of a code of statutes related only to women and urged their repeal. Most of these groups, however, accepted the retention of laws pertaining to the protection of maternity as one justifiable exception to general abandonment of the protections on working women's conditions (Kamerman, 1980; Enquête Kommission, 1979; Hanami, 1979).

The ILO approached the issue very tentatively. Its Convention concerned with protective laws for women (mainly involving night work and exposures to toxic substances) continues to the present to be justified "from the maternity point of view." Its Recommendation No. 123, a modernization of protective legislation, is on the Employment of Women With Family Responsibilities. An amendment to it would cover all workers, not just women (International Labour Organisation, 1980, 1985).

Unions, however, widely throughout Europe continue strong support for the existing protective laws and do so, as they have done since their inception, to protect their own standards for men. Originally they feared that the growing employment of women at low wages and under exploitive conditions would endanger the gains of men unless some floor were built under them. Later they saw women as hard to organize because they were short-term, intermittent members of the labor force and consequently uncommitted to work as a lifetime career. These elements made them unreliable members if they joined unions. But quite aside from all that, most women worked in sectors where unions either had not tried to organize or had had little success. Like their parent bodies, most women's divisions of unions have also opposed the lifting of protective legislation, seeing it as the only protection that four-fifths of the working women have.

Only Sweden and the United States have abolished these laws, seeing them as incompatible with equality policies laid down in law or collective bargaining. In Sweden this abolition explicitly excluded the maternity protections. In the United States where there are none, this exception did not arise. As for toxic exposure, the growing view of unions and other interested groups is to protect both men and women rather than to forbid such jobs to women and pay men bonuses for doing them.

Women in Trade Unions

The history of women in the labor movements, both in the parties and in the unions, is remarkably similar throughout the Western world. Whether this is a product of the international character of the socialist movement, beginning with the First International, is not clear and has not been the subject of more than cursory investigation.

Unions usually were the creation of the socialist parties and, during the late 19th century, gradually separated into distinct although allied institutions. Both parties and unionism were made up almost entirely of men who saw the role of women as ideally in the home and free of the necessity of working for wages.[7] The family wage, an early demand of union men, would bring about this "liberation" for women. But migration of displaced agricultural workers and their families to cities and to work in the factories took place in such numbers that the unions could not hope to organize the mass of unskilled workers feeding into the new factories. The unions retreated to the manageable task of organizing chiefly skilled workers. In these unions women could find no place. Indeed, this early stage of unionism was characterized by its lack of attention or even its hostility to working women so that organization of women, when it existed at all, was in women's unions. Examples are the matchworkers of London under the leadership of Eleanor Marx; the organization of women textile workers in separate unions from those of the male spinners, weavers, and fixers in Germany and England; and the creation of miscellaneous unions of women

[7] Exceptions were usually made, however, where women's work was needed—in nursing, communications, and even in manufacturing in busy seasons.

workers in many trades, as occurred in Denmark (Dubeck, 1980), Ireland, and certain regions in Britain, Italy, Germany, and France.[8]

But as semiskilled and even unskilled workers were organized, women could not be left out. Women's divisions were set up to take care of their special needs and interests, including advocating the passage of protective laws. Women's problems on the whole were seen as calling for political answers. Therefore, much of the responsibility for improvement of their conditions was turned over to the labor and socialist parties as these established bases in national parliaments. This view permitted the unions to abdicate much of the responsibility for dealing with women's problems.

The modern flood of women into the labor market was presaged by women's taking over men's work during the two world wars. These events remained somewhat isolated phenomena, however, because everyone, including the women workers, fully understood that, with demobilization, men would properly reclaim "their jobs." In Japan in a single day soon after the end of the war, tens of thousands of women were dismissed by the national railroad system. In the United States, the Women's Bureau carried out studies after World War II of what was happening to the women displaced from tank and munitions factories and shipyards. It found them, after holding out as long as they could for equivalent, well-paid skilled jobs, returning bitterly to laundries, restaurants, and clothing and shoe factories with great loss in wages and status. In labor history, tradition has extended a powerful hand over reform. Unions on the whole have been among the last of the labor market institutions to recognize the ever-increasing influx of women into the work force as a permanent feature. Progress has been intermittent, yet more consistent among the peak organizations than at the workplace.

Early on, the German DGB designated 1972 as the Year of the Working Woman. Programs suggested by the Women's Divisions of the Confederation and its national unions were placed in whole or in part on national union agendas; a woman was elected first vice president of the Confederation. Each of the 17 national unions pledged in that year to improve the wage scales that distinguished between light and heavy work and which had replaced the "women's wages" outlawed in 1957 by the High Labor Court. In the same year the Swedish unions abandoned their women's divisions in favor of a department on family policy in which men as well as women would sit.

By the mid-1970s several international labor bodies were examining women's place in the unions as part of the whole movement toward

---

[8] See individual country chapters in Cook, Lorwin, and Daniels (1984).

equality that was already accepted by labor market policy-makers. Both the ICFTU Täljøviken Report (International Confederation of Free Trade Unions, 1977) and the ETUC White Paper (European Trade Union Confederation, 1976) were documents that served as guides to national confederations and their affiliates in raising issues for bargaining and legislation and in outlining the kind of strategies that might be adopted to ensure an equal role for women in the labor organizations.

In the past 10 years, appraisals of the role of women in trade unions have appeared in most Western countries (Cook, Lorwin, and Daniels, 1984; Berg, 1981; Wistrand, 1981; Dubeck, 1980; Hunt and Adams, 1980; Qvist, 1980; Losseff-Tillmans, 1978). Most students of the issues have been critical of the slow progress of unions in implementing the resolutions and models offered by the international and national confederations of which they are a part, and at the continuing deep bias against women among union leaders and fellow workers in almost every country (Pini, 1977).

Migrant and Foreign Workers

As the European economies boomed in the late 1960s and 1970s, many countries, including Sweden, Germany, France, and Switzerland, actively recruited foreign labor from Greece, Yugoslavia, Turkey, Spain, and Portugal as well as southern Italy (the latter governed by the EEC rules on free movement of labor within the Community). They wanted these outsiders to take over jobs that native workers were more and more rejecting because they were either ill-paid or dirty, or both. Almost alone, Sweden, in accepting such workers, expected them to bring their families with them. Other countries recruited only the workers themselves, most but not all of whom were male, under annual contracts. Germany brought in many Greek and Turkish women, also without families, to staff the textile and clothing industries. Britain's foreign workers came on a somewhat different basis since most of them migrated from Commonwealth countries with a right to a British passport. It was not long however, before extended families joined these migrants, often resulting in tragic experiences of displacement, particularly for women. They became alienated from their own children who were attending local schools, and they found employment under highly exploitive conditions. They clustered in slum housing in inner cities in what became foreign enclaves.

An inquiry this writer made at the ILO in 1976 revealed that it had not at that time undertaken any studies of these women workers and their problems. Researchers were handicapped in attempting to include them in broader studies of working women because of their traditional isolation within the family and their subordination to their husbands. Their somewhat exotic languages and their life in the enclaves of their own compatriots further contributed to their inaccessibility. Among the first to champion their struggles in Germany were Marxist scholars who looked at several women's wildcat strikes in the Frankfurt area and the behavior of unions in relation to them. Most recently it has become unmistakably clear that these so-called migrants are permanent, although they are only rarely aided by unions. One exception is the Metal Workers of the DGB which, a decade ago, established a "Guestworkers" department, headed by a Turk. He admitted, however, in the early 1980s that his department has had no success whatever in reaching women migrants although they numbered several tens of thousands.

Religious and welfare agencies were the first to try to reach these women and to understand and minister to their problems. Reports of conferences dealing with these issues have appeared (Guyot et al., 1978). The aim of a 1975 study (Kellner) was to distinguish the work motivation and behavior of migrant women in the workplace. A more inclusive study (Muenscher, 1986) was recently completed. The German Labor Market Research Center's *Literaturdokumentation* includes the scanty list of foreign publications on this subject.

Health and Safety

Although safety hazards were first regulated in the first third of this century and industrial accidents were insured under workers' compensation laws, industrial disease was much more slowly identified as a health hazard. Women frequently received special treatment in this regard, again as mothers or putative mothers of offspring whose lives might be damaged by having toxins inhaled or ingested during pregnancy. Early industrial toxicologists warned that men were as disastrously subject to lead, benzene, dust, and chemicals as women and proposed that prohibitions for one sex ought not exclude the other. Slowly, as national centers for research and regulation of industrial disease became more numerous and better staffed, studies made clear that many areas previously thought of as "clean" were instead places where unique hazards, both physical and mental, might exist. White-collar unions as well as industrial disease research centers took up such issues as damage to eyes and bodies from constant use of video display terminals. Stress, whether derived from work demands or the double burden, became recognized as an important source of physical and mental illness.

In the mid-1970s the Swedes set up a national Center on the Quality of Working Life (Arbetslivcentrum), supported by a minute employer tax on every working person in the country. In the decade since its founding it has established something of a record for its wide-ranging research. Unfortunately, little of it has been directed specifically to the hazards and exposures of women's work and very little to comparing women's and men's reactions to the same occupations. One exception was a study by the Swedish psychologist, Bertil Gardell, of men and women bus drivers in the city of Stockholm.

Cooperation of Trade Union Women With the Women's Movement Organizations

Organizations within the new women's movement are often charged with lack of interest in and knowledge of working women in ranks below those of the professionals. If this charge can be really substantiated, the issues on the agendas of women's groups within the trade unions would be hard to explain, for they largely duplicate the feminist programs. To the extent that the unions as a whole have loosened their affiliations with the socialist and anticlerical parties, they have approached the issue of abortion with considerable hesitation. This has, however, failed to deter many women's trade union groups from joining in demonstrations and lobbying efforts to persuade the legislatures to legalize abortion. In Italy an alliance of feminist groups with trade union women brought about laws protecting abortion in that overwhelmingly Catholic country. Similarly, trade union groups have supported the establishment of "women's houses" as refuges for battered and abused women. On issues outside the collective bargaining agendas, trade union women in most countries recognize that only through coalitions with other women can they achieve goals of equality.

The German trade union women are full and active affiliates of the German Women's Council (Deutscher Frauenrat), the umbrella confederation of all women's groups in the country, including professionals, religious bodies, and homemakers. Indeed, the heads of the trade unions' women's divisions have several times been elected chairs of the entire organization. Moreover, they have used this affiliation to generate support for their own wage and equality demands. The "openness" that characterizes Italian unions enables them to accept, as full-fledged members, women outside their occupational jurisdictions and thus to enlarge support for women's issues.[9] Similarly, Australian trade union women and the major autonomous women's organization, WEL, have enjoyed close cooperation.

Scandinavian labor women who are more separatist have been able to call on a cooperative social-democratic government to support

---

[9] See chapters on Italy and Germany in Cook, Lorwin, and Daniels (1984).

their goals during most of this century and have perhaps needed to rely less on coalitions.

Progress in Practice and Policy

Equal Employment Opportunity

Labor market policy over the past 15 years has made many significant efforts to adapt to the problems outlined in the previous sections. Equal employment opportunity, however variously defined and interpreted, is now the accepted goal in every country. The common elements of such a policy include attention to the recruiting and hiring process, some—usually uneven—concern with opening up training opportunities for women in the nontraditional occupations, some emphasis on wider and longer-range career guidance in the employment offices, concern with equalizing the age of men and women for compulsory retirement and for pension entitlements on retirement, and some recognition that the provision of child care is essential if women are to have equal access to full-time employment.

In 1976 the European Council issued its Directive on Equal Treatment in Employment (Council Directive of February 9, 1976, on the implementation of the principle of equal treatment for men and women as regards access to employment, vocational training and promotion, and working conditions [76/207/EEC]). It directed the member states to "carry out a first examination and if necessary a first revision of the laws, regulations and administrative provisions referred to therein within four years of notification of this directive." The first positive steps, including remediation, were thus to have been achieved by 1980. The Directive served the useful purpose of placing the issue before all the parliaments and resulted in a variety of initial steps toward the goal of freeing labor markets of sex bias (see Table 4). Practice, however, continues to fall short of anything like the purpose set forth in the Directive.

Enforcement of equal opportunity legislation rests in many cases with especially created commissions bearing a variety of names and with varying powers. In several countries departments of labor have full jurisdiction over the entire labor code, including now its equal opportunity sections. Countries with a special system of labor courts rely on these institutions for eventual and final enforcement. Some encourage initial action through collective agreements. In the case of Japan, the latest country to adopt such legislation (May 1985), the statute is written in voluntary terms to *encourage* employers to accept its guidelines, while the Women's Bureau of the Ministry of Labor plays the multiple role of stimulator, educator, and inspector, but not enforcer of the law.

Affirmative action programs such as those required in the United States of contractors to the federal government and affecting agriculture, environment, education and research, and manufacturing and construction firms have not been adopted in other countries. "Positive discrimination," however, is explicitly provided for in the British antidiscrimination law and is the subject of discussion and evaluation in a number of other countries.

Vocational Training

Among the Community's members, new agencies have been set up to provide transition programs for young people. The program is a response to the very high and growing unemployment of youth, both boys and girls, in all EEC countries. Two sets of plans have been adopted under the general title of "Transition of Young People from Education to Adult and Working Life." The first lays down policies to guide the forthcoming projects; the second, the action program, had established 30 pilot projects by October 1984. Girls are to be treated as a special target group because "the range of opportunities open to women entering the labour market is in practice restricted": (1) they are consistently underrepresented in vocational training; (2) they form a greater proportion of the unskilled, low-paid labor force; and (3) they are overrepresented in the lower-status jobs in certain occupations (European Center for the Development of Vocational Training, *Programme News*, (#1, p. 11). Yet, of the projects listed in nine countries, none by title is directed specifically to young women. An evaluative study, "Girls in Transition," however, refers to projects in Germany, Denmark, France, Greece, Italy, and the Netherlands, while a Danish study done at the University of Aarhus in 1980 examines the work experience of young women in that country (European Community Action Programme, 1984).

These projects, it should be noted, are not necessarily aimed at bringing young women into nontraditional occupations. Nevertheless, in Britain, Germany, Sweden, Belgium, and France—and probably in a good many other countries as well—official training agencies are directing projects that identify nontraditional occupations needing trained personnel and setting up projects that include pretraining selection, counseling, and support systems for young women going into these occupations. Many of these programs include "bridge" educational opportunities for those who missed elements of basic education when they dropped out of secondary school at an early stage.

Reentry programs have on the whole been cut back in view of the high unemployment rates in the EEC countries. Austria and Sweden, which have on the whole controlled unemployment at a very low rate (around the 2 percent level), continue to place emphasis on training and retraining of women, including the middle-aged, as the preferred alternative to paying unemployment and welfare compensation.

Despite all these efforts, there has been no significant effect on the existing gender-segregation of jobs. "Women's work" continues to designate a distinctive category of work characterized by low pay, low training opportunities, and a low ceiling on promotional opportunities (Paukert, 1984a).

Equal Pay

"Pay equity"—that is, equal payment for jobs of equal worth to the employer—is the present response to dealing with the pay differentials between men and women that obtain in every country (see Table 3). By placing emphasis on measuring unlike jobs through some method of job evaluation, the value of women's work can be compared with that of male workers in the same agency or firm and placed on a similar wage scale with that of men. This approach was incorporated in the British antidiscrimination act dealing with equal pay; it has become the rule for compensating work in federal employment in Canada and is now adopted also in the provinces of Quebec and Manitoba in their public service. In the United States, some 30 states have adopted or are on the way to implementing programs for public employees, as are more than 100 cities and other local governments (Cook, 1985). Australia has used its system of labor arbitration in wage setting to apply the principles of pay equity federally and in most states (Gregory and Duncan, 1981).

Sweden did not address the problem as one of sex bias. Rather, its highly disciplined trade unionists adopted a policy of what they called the "solidarity wage." Its aim was to narrow the gap between low- and high-paid workers and depended on the cooperation of the well-paid union members if the low-paid categories—largely women—were to benefit. Years of consistent bargaining on this issue have brought wages of blue-collar women to 88 percent of those of males and raised the salaries of women white-collar workers to more than 70 percent of men's wages.

The German Minister of Labor under the Social-Democratic government of Helmut Schmidt in the early 1970s authorized a study of the so-called "light work" or "light wage" categories very largely occupied by women at the bottom of the 10-point German wage scales (Helberger, 1980; Rutenfranz and Rohmert, 1975). This undertaking was stimulated by the DGB's designation of 1972 as the Year of the Working Woman. The report issued in 1975 provided for a system of job evaluation that decidedly upgraded the value of women's typical work activities. Its methodology was new and complex and required several months of study by both unions and employers. The unions eventually endorsed it, but more than a year later the employers rejected it. With a change in government to one headed by the conservative parties, the report went into deep freeze and has never been implemented. Nevertheless, a number of German unions have considerably revised their wage scales so as to eliminate or upgrade the "light wage" categories (Cook, 1980).

The 1975 EEC Directive on Equal Pay is still a controversial issue in several member countries where equality commissions or similar national institutions must operate with small staffs and low budgets and are basically unable to enforce what equal pay legislation has been adopted in those countries. Many borderline issues and requests for interpretation of the Directive go to the Community's High Court for adjudication (Rights of Women, Europe, 1982).

Women and Trade Unions

In several countries, but chiefly in Sweden, the implementation of public policy in matters of work and working conditions rests in the first instance with the initiative of unions and is considered their responsibility. Indeed, the Swedish unions opposed legislation on equal employment opportunity as an invasion of their prior claim to regulate these matters in collective bargaining. Both LO and TCO, the two major labor confederations, entered into equality pacts with management in the mid-1970s that called for the establishment of joint workplace committees to monitor these issues. This author's inquiry five years later brought the response from several observers that almost nothing had been accomplished at the local level and that considerable stimulation of such programs by the national unions would be needed if they were to become common practice. The Arbetslivcentrum, however, now has a study of the subject in progress.

In Germany, the Women's Division and the women officers in the various national unions have kept up a steady drumbeat urging women to bring their complaints of discrimination to the unions and to raise the level of consciousness in the works councils about women's issues. The Division's publication, *Frauen und Arbeit*, reports and advocates these issues. Its quadrennial conventions precede the DGB Congress of Labor, to which it sends drafts of policy proposals on these matters. Women's issues are, however, rarely the subject of serious and sustained collective bargaining. The enthusiasm that peaked in 1972 has not again reached those heights.

Since unions are the established labor market institutions set up to represent workers' interests and are recognized in all the market economies as bargaining partners with management for the regulation of working conditions, the degree to which women have an influential role within them is significant. The conclusions of most researchers in the field is that the unions have been slower than other labor market agencies to recognize and act upon the issues raised by women's increased labor force participation (Cook, Lorwin, and Daniels, 1984; Berg, 1981; Hunt and Adams, 1980). This criticism applies not only to the outcome of union-management negotiations, but to the roles women play within the unions themselves. To be sure, notable exceptions exist, such as those in the National Union of Public Employees in Britain, the private-sector white-collar workers in Austria, the leadership training programs for trade union women conducted by the Institute for Education and Research on Working Women in New York, U.S.A., and the "150 hours" education programs in the universities in Italy.[10]

On the whole, however, and despite recommendations stemming from the international trade union bodies (ICFTU and ETUC as well as many of the International Trade Secretariats), women—again, with notable exceptions—cannot be said to play an influential role in union life. They seldom appear on bargaining teams, where the crucial work of the unions takes place. While a substantial number are named or elected to local union office, their proportions of officerships in regional, national, and international bodies grows smaller as the hierarchy pyramid narrows toward the top.

Child Care

The epitome of a woman's double burden is her responsibility for her children. Because child neglect is abhorrent to all social systems, public policy seeks to deal with child care. Usually it does so in one of two ways: the conservative approach is to persuade women to remain at home caring for their children by the provision of some substitute for the earnings they might receive in work outside the home (France). The other approach is to provide non-means-tested child allowances. This inducement was in some cases linked to the number of children in the family and thus was meant to affect population policy as well. Some countries increased the amount of the allowances with family size (Germany). The Swedes at first recognized the prior responsibility of mothers for child care by making these grants payable to them. Equality goals have now prescribed that a "designated parent" will receive the quarterly grant. The United States pays only for children of single mothers and means-tests such payments.

These issues of child support have on the whole become distinct from those of child care. The latter generally refers to provisions for care of children outside the home when the mother herself goes to

---

[10] See appropriate chapters in Cook, Lorwin, and Daniels (1984).

work. For the most part it refers to care of preschool children. Thus, the public school becomes the major child-caring institution for children above the age of 6 or 7. But in countries such as Israel, Germany, and France, where the full-day school is only exceptionally experimented with, the family is still responsible for providing the midday meal and afternoon supervision of school children. If women are to conform to the male standards of full-time employment, child care has to be full-day care—sometimes evening or night-shift care. Children's illnesses, summer vacations, and school holidays that are not work holidays raise their own problems.

Social policy varies from leaving the matter almost entirely to private local initiative or even to individual personal arrangements with family members or neighbors, to planning at the national level. Depending on the amount of public support or private charity available to working parents, the costs of child care can run from prohibitive to manageable. Nowhere except in France is it free, in the sense in which primary and secondary education are available to school-age children. Kamerman and Kahn are the outstanding authors of comparative studies in this area. A host of national studies provide guidance as well. Yet even in countries that have done careful planning— mainly Sweden, Norway, and Finland—subsidized places fall far short of the number of children in families where both parents work outside the home. Attempts to increase available care include programs under which employers would either supply care or provide a fringe benefit for the purchase of care. Some unions are bargaining on this issue. Parental leaves are designed to meet the need for the most expensive kind of child care, that of the infant. Family day care which some research has shown is the kind a majority of parents prefer is nevertheless controversial because of the problems of standard setting and inspection. Scandinavian countries have adopted programs of licensing and training of day "mothers." Its local children's bureaus pay the child carers and collect the fees from the parents.

For all its problems, progress can be measured from the early years when charitable women volunteered to "mind"—or provide "minding" for—the children of their less fortunate sisters, the poor women who had to work in factories or domestic service, to the present when preschool experience is seen as part of social education, particularly useful for children even of the highest economic status without siblings in their own age range. The attitudinal shift has been from "doing good" for the disadvantaged to providing an educational element for all working families—from private charity to social policy.

Part-Time Work

The advantages and disadvantages in working part-time are the subject of considerable controversy. Women's organizations, employers, and trade unions are taking very different views about it. What is clear is that so long as women's home responsibilities go unshared, part-time work will appeal to thousands of them as the practical choice for combining household and paid work. The ongoing economic recession in Europe has had the effect of increasing many part-time work opportunities, at the same time that full-time employment opportunities decrease. In many countries the growth in employment of women in the service trades has been mainly in part-time work.

The EEC "Women's Action Programme" (European Economic Community, 1982) warns that one consequence of this increase can be the intensification of women's job segregation and, with it, the ongoing limitation on occupations that women can readily enter. The EEC's attempt to issue a directive on the reorganization of working time, including part-time work, was ready for approval by the commissioners when, in the fall of 1983, its implementation was defeated, again by the refusal of the British government's representative to give his approval to the draft (CREW Reports, 1983).

Summary

Policy has responded to women's growing presence in the labor market by setting equal opportunity as a widely accepted goal for women as well as for men. However laggard many countries and labor market institutions have been, the goal remains. Even its detractors do not expect it to go away. While the Scandinavian countries have done most to implement equality programs across the board with the backing of unions, employers, conservative as well as liberal and socialist parties, and the powerful Labour Market Board (AMS, 1977), other countries have dealt with only bits and pieces of a full equality program. In the degree they have done so, it has not always resulted in a clear-headed or consistent policy. Thus, from country to country, policy varies from piecemeal and overly general to total and detailed. If Sweden is at one end of this scale, Japan and Ireland are at the other.

Although the double burden is widely recognized as the distinct barrier to women's achievement of equality, the only major remedy so far proposed for easing it is child care. In turn, the form this takes, its costs, its availability, and its quality vary considerably. Even so, it is much more available in every country than it was 10 or 15 years ago and it holds a distinct place in the educational system.

Equality in the home is not a matter that readily lends itself to legislation or other social policy solutions. The division of labor in the home that gives major responsibility to women is deeply embedded in long-standing traditions, shaped and adopted in economic history to meet premodern conditions. It is, moreover, a powerful element in the paternalism pervading all phases of modern life. Paternalistic traditions have shaped the thinking and behavior of employers, unions, and women's fellow workers. Equality in unions creates a special challenge, for unions have presented themselves to their members and to the public as significant agents of change and pillars of political and economic democracy. Yet, on the sex-equality issue they have shown themselves to be reluctant in accepting women as equals in the organizations and have been only tardily responsive to women's needs in bargaining with employers. The recent advocacy of the American United Mine Workers for parental leave as a result of consistent pressure from its growing number of women members gives an indication of the possible.

While statutory approaches can rarely reach attitudes, it is important that administrators of equal opportunity programs begin to scrutinize labor market policies and practices across the board for the measures of paternalism that are assumed in setting the norms of working life.[11] In this area many of the social sciences have a contribution to make.

Research Needs and Prospects

A vocal and self-conscious women's movement has appeared in all the democratic world. In a minuscule form it exists even in such traditional countries as Japan and Ireland. Its extent and intensity and its universal concern for the problems of women at work have traversed national boundaries, and the many groups have worked among themselves symbiotically to influence institutions and governments in similar directions. How this all occurred—what models excited international attention, what initiatives were stimulated by intergovernmental agencies or by autonomous groups, what guidelines and directives have contributed most to practical application—remains unstudied. Even limited comparative studies in which accomplishments in three or four countries were evaluated would be useful. Critical studies of policy formation in individual countries would supply students of social policy with the basic data for theoretical and practical evaluation.

Institutes devoted to social policy have sprung up in several countries. They attempt not only to evaluate existing programs, but to recommend adoption of new or revised policy. Much of this has

---

[11] Two issues to which the women's movements internationally have in recent years called attention received almost immediate and widespread support, once they were identified. They were sex harassment in the workplace and wife and child abuse in the home. Only a few years back these were both looked upon as entirely personal matters. Yet the positive responses both have received among lawmakers and judges suggest that their time had come. Action to combat these problems may contribute more effectively to change traditional patriarchic attitudes and behavior than all the policy statements on equal employment opportunity.

necessarily been fragmented into studies of discrete measures and institutions. Yet, with all this, relatively little attention has been paid to issues of major importance to women. Exceptions are the issues of part-time work, of child care, and of the pay differentials between men and women. Studies of technology and work are increasing. A major area that remains relatively untouched is that of health and safety in the workplace, as it may be revealed in work on the differential or similar impact of toxic exposures, stress, fatigue, monotony, and noise on men and women.

A holistic approach to questions raised by women's growing occupational activity is rare indeed. Sweden and Norway are almost alone in having approached the problem from a single focus. Interestingly enough, it was the rather old-fashioned view of what is best for children that controls the way they look at the long list of individual problems discussed here. In Sweden, where more than 25 percent of the children are born out of marriage, and where a decision was made to call on married women to work instead of continuing to import foreign workers, it was inevitable that women would enter the labor market. They needed to earn a living wage, to have flexible working hours, and to work part-time in employment that was legally covered by the social security system. Enhancement of the quality of work life—a goal of the 1970s—contributed to women's "commitment to work." The state's commitment to equality in the labor market was part of its turn to recruiting married women and motivated the consistent way in which the Labour Market Board shaped individual policies and developed programs to realize them. The result was that with the abandonment of protective legislation came a rethinking of maternity policy to include both parents, the establishment of the right of parents of preschool children to work shorter hours, the planning of public work projects to include not just heavy construction but the extension of health and child welfare programs in which large numbers of women could work, and the reconsideration of prerequisites for what had hitherto been women's jobs in the care of children and the infirm, in health care, and in teaching to attract men and enable them to qualify for admission.

The "big" questions that now could challenge research on social policy are:

- What are the underlying considerations in national societies that motivate them to adopt equality programs?
- How have these been rationalized and accepted?
- What goals are they shaped to achieve? How are they integrated with one another?
- Do they embody traditional, paternalistic assumptions, or

- Do they emerge from a commitment to fundamental change in the relations of men and women, such that the whole of family life as well as work life will be built upon a total concept of equality?

The new theoreticians of feminism could provide help in approaching these questions, but their thinking has not so far been much used to penetrate the world of the public policy-makers dealing with labor market equality. The time is now.

References

Adams, Carolyn Teich, and Katherine Teich Adams. *Mothers at Work: Public Policies in the United States, Sweden and China.* New York: Longmans, 1980.

Alexander, Ralph A., and Gerald V. Barrett. "Equitable Salary Increase Judgments Based upon Merit and Non-Merit Considerations: A Cross-National Comparison." *International Review of Applied Psychology* 31 (1982): pp. 443–54.

Arbetsmarkmadsstyrelsen (AMS) (National Labour Market Board). "Equality in the Labour Market: Programme Adopted by the Labour Market Board, September 1977." Solna, Sweden: AMS, 1977.

Australia. National Commission on Discrimination in Employment and Occupations (NCDEO). "Toward Equal Opportunity in Employment." Canberra: NCDEO, February 1975.

Bartunek, Ewald, Christian Boehm, and Inge Gross. *The Economic Role of Women in Austria: Statistical Data.* Vienna: Austrian Federal Ministry of Social Affairs, 1984.

Berg, Anne Marie. "Union Growth, Feminist Issues." Oslo: Institute for Social Research, 1981. (Unpublished)

Bevege, Margaret, Margaret James, and Carmel Shute. *Worth Her Salt: Women at Work in Australia.* Victoria, Canada: Hale & Ironmonger, 1982.

Botezat, Liselotte. *Die Vorbereitung der Frau fuer Familie und Beruf.* Internationale Studie 1. Teil, "Die Situation der europaeischen Frau in Familie und Beruf." Vienna: Berufspaedagogisches Institut des Bundes, 1977.

Bouillaguet-Bernard, P., A. Gauvin-Ayel, and J.L. Outin. *Femmes au travail: prospérité et crise.* Paris: 1981.

Bouteiller, Jacques. "Male and Female Wage Differentials in France: Theory and Measurement." Hull, England: International Institute of Economics, 1975.

Bulletin of Comparative Labour Relations. *Women and Labour: A Comparative Study.* Deventer, The Netherlands: Kluwer, 1979.

Bundesanstalt fuer Arbeit (BfA). *Zur Struktur der Teilzeitbeschaeftigung.* Nuernberg: BfA, 1976.

Canada. Ministry of Supply and Services. *Part-time Work in Canada.* Ottawa: Ministry of Supply and Services, 1983.

Casey, Bernard. "Governmental Measures to Promote Part-Time Working: Experiences in Belgium, France, Great Britain, the Netherlands, and the FRG." Berlin: Wissenschaftszentrum, 1983.

Clark, G. *Working Patterns: Part-time Work, Job Sharing and Self-Employment.* London: Manpower Services Division, January 1982.

Commission of the European Community (CEC). *European Women in Paid Employment.* Brussels: CEC, 1984. (V/1240/84)

Commission to Research the Problem of Equality between Men and Women at Work. *About Equality between Men and Women at Work.* Tokyo: Prime Minister's Office, 1975.

Cook, Alice H. *Comparable Worth: A Casebook of State and Local Experiences.* Honolulu: Industrial Relations Center, University of Hawaii, 1985. *Supplement,* 1986.

_____. "Women and Work in Industrial Societies: Where Are We and Where Are We Going?" In *Urbanism and Urbanization: Views, Aspects, Dimensions,* ed. Noel Iverson. Leiden: E.J. Brill, 1984.

_____. "Collective Bargaining as a Strategy for Achieving Equal Opportunity and Equal Pay: Sweden and Germany." In *Equal Employment Policy for Women,* ed. Ronnie S. Ratner. Philadelphia: Temple University Press, 1980. Pp. 53–78.

_____. *The Working Mother: Problems and Programs in Nine Countries.* Ithaca, NY: Industrial Relations Press, Cornell University, 1975. Revised 1978.

Cook, Alice H., and Hiroko Hayashi. *Japanese Working Women: Discrimination, Resistance and Reform.* Ithaca, NY: Industrial Relations Press, Cornell University, 1981.

Cook, Alice H., Val R. Lorwin, with Arline Kaplan Daniels, eds. *Women and Trade Unions in Eleven Industrialized Countries.* Philadelphia: Temple University Press, 1984.

CREW Reports. "Reorganization of Working Time—UK Torpedoes Commission Proposals." Brussels: Council for Research on European Women, September–November 1983.

Daeubler-Gmelin, Herta. *Frauenarbeitslosigkeit oder Frauen zurueck an den Herd?* Hamburg: Rowohlt, 1977.

Deutsches Institut fuer Arbeit und Berufsforschung. *Ausgewaehlte Aspekte der Frauenerwerbsarbeit: Quintessenzen.* Nuernberg: Bundesanstalt fuer Arbeit, 1984.

Drew, Ellen. "Full Employment or Part-Time Working?" *Equal Employment Opportunities* (London) 3, 1985.

Dubeck, Inge. "Female Trade Unions in Denmark." *Scandinavian Journal of History* 5 (1980).

Elliott, R., P. Glucklich, E. Maclennan, and C. Pond. *Women in the Labour Market: A Study of the Impact of Legislation and Policy toward Women in the UK Labour Market during the 1970s.* A Report for the Project, "Regulation Theory of the Labour Market Related to Women and Handicapped," by Guenther Schmid, Klaus Semlinger, and Renate Weitzel. Bonn: Deutsche Forschungsgemeinschaft, undated. (Unpublished)

Enquête Kommission. "Frau und Gessellschaft." *Oeffentliche Anhoerung zum Thema, Durchsetzung der Gleichberechtigung.* Bonn: Deutscher Bundestag, September 5, 6, and 7, 1979.

Equal Opportunities Commission (EOC). *Towards Equity: A Casebook of Decisions on Sex Discrimination and Equal Pay, 1976–1981.* Manchester: EOC, 1982.

European Center for the Development of Vocational Training (CEDEFOP). *Programme News* #1 (October 1984) and *Programme News* #2 (April 1985).

_____. *Innovative Training and Employment for Women.* Report of Seminar held in Brussels 15–17 September 1980. Luxembourg: CEDEFOP, 1983. (HX-35/82 110/EN-C)

_____. *Bildungs- und Arbeitsmarktpolitische Massnahmen zur beruflichen Foerderung von Frauen in der Bundesrepublik Deutschland.* Berlin: CEDEFOP, 1979a.

_____. *Training and Labour Market Policy Measures for the Vocational Promotion of Women in France.* Berlin: CEDEFOP, 1979b.

_____. *Women and Vocational Training.* Berlin: CEDEFOP, 1979c.

European Community Action Programme (ECAP). *About Work Experience: An Inventory of Published Materials.* Brussels: ECAP, February 1985.

————. "Transition of Young People from Education to Adult Working Life." *Working Document: Policies for the Transition*. Brussels: ECAP, March 1984. (Doc: 21 WD 84 EN)

European Economic Community (EEC). "EEC's Women's Action Programme: Equal Opportunities, 1982–1985." Supplement #9, *Women of Europe*. Brussels: EEC, 1982.

European Economic Community (EEC), European Parliament. *The Situation of Women in Europe*. Brussels: EEC, 1984.

European Industrial Relations Review (London). "Equal Pay: Commission's Report on Equal Pay in Denmark, Ireland, and the UK." (May 1974).

European Trade Union Confederation (ETUC). *Women at Work: White Paper on Working Women in Europe*. Brussels: ETUC, 1976.

Eurostat. *The Economic and Social Position of Women in the Community*. Brussels: European Economic Community, 1981.

Fairbanks, Jill. *Evaluation of Wider Opportunities for Women ("WOW") Courses: Final Report*. London: Manpower Services Commission, 1979.

Farley, Jennie T., ed. *Working Women in Fifteen Countries*. Ithaca, NY: Industrial Relations Press, Cornell University, 1985.

Foelsing, Ulla. "Zum Problem der Rueckkehr von Frauen in den Beruf." *Informationen fuer die Frau*. Bonn: Deutscher Frauenrat, December 11, 1973.

Fogerty, Michael, Rhona Rapoport, and Robert N. Rapoport. *Sex, Career, and Family*. London: Allen and Unwin, 1971.

Germany. *Bericht der Bundesregierung ueber Benachteiligung von Frauen in und ausserhalb des Arbeitslebens*. Bonn: Bundesminister fuer Jugend, Familie und Gesundheit, Arbeitsstab Frauenpolitik, Oktober 1983.

Girard, Alain. "Working Hours and Time Schedules: The Time Budget of Married Women in Urban Centers (France)." In *Employment of Women*, OECD Regional Trade Union Seminar, September 1969. Paris: Organisation for Economic Cooperation and Development, September 1970.

Gladh, Lillemore, and Siv Gustafsson. *Labor Market Policy Related to Women and Employment in Sweden*. Stockholm: Arbetslivcentrum, 1981.

Goldschmidt-Clermont, Luisella. "Output-related Evaluation of Unpaid Household Work: A Challenge for Time Use Studies." *Home Economics Research Journal* 12, No. 2 (1983): pp. 127–32.

————. *Unpaid Work in the Household: A Review of Economic Evaluation Methods*. Women, Work and Development Series #1. Geneva: International Labour Office, 1982.

Gregory, R.D., and R.C. Duncan. "Segmented Labor Market Theories and the Australian Experience of Equal Pay for Women." *Journal of Post-Keynesian Economics* 3 (Spring 1981): pp. 403–28.

Grønseth, Erik. "The Familial Institution: The Alienated Labor-Producing Appendage." Paper presented at World Congress of Sociology, Toronto, 1974. Oslo: Institute of Sociology, University of Oslo, 1975. (Skriftserie #15)

————. "Working-sharing Families: Adaptations of Pioneering Families With Husband and Wife in Part-time Employment." Oslo: Institute of Sociology, University of Oslo, 1974. (Skriftserie #22)

Guyot, Jean, et al. "Des Femmes immigrées parlent." Geneva: Churches' Committee on Migrant Workers, 1978.

Hanami, Tadashi. "Protection or Equality?" *Japan Labour Bulletin* 18 (December 1979): pp. 7–10.

Hartmann, Heidi. "Capitalism and Women's Work in the Home." Ph.D. dissertation, Yale University, 1974.

Hegelheimer, Barbara. *Bildungs- und Arbeitspolitische Massnahmen zur beruf lichen Foerderung von Frauen in der Bundesrepublik Deutschland.* Berlin: European Center for the Development of Vocational Training, 1979.

Helberger, Christof. "Work Analysis as a Means for Achieving Pay Equity for Working Women: The Federal Republic of Germany." In *Equal Employment Policy for Women,* ed. Ronnie S. Ratner. Philadelphia: Temple University Press, 1980. Pp. 458–83.

Holter, Harriet, ed. *Patriarchy in a Welfare Society.* Oslo: Universitetsforlaget, 1984.

Holter, Harriet, and Hildur Ve Hendriksen. "Social Policy and the Family in Norway." In *Sex Roles and Social Policy,* eds. Jean Lipman-Blumen and Jessie Bernard. London: Sage Publications, 1979.

Hunt, Judith, and Shelley Adams. *Women, Work and Trade Union Organisation.* London: Workers Educational Association, 1980.

Hvidfeld, K., K. Jorgensen, and R. Nielsen, eds. *Strategies for Integrating Women in the Labor Market: Report from the European Seminar.* Copenhagen: European Women's Studies in Social Science, Vol. 1, 1982.

Institute for Labor Market and Vocational Research (Institut fuer Arbeits und Berufsforschung der BfA, Nuernberg). *Literaturdokumentation zur Arbeitsmarkt- und Berufsforschung.* Sonderhaft 4, "Frauenerwerbstaetigkeit." Nuernberg: Bundesanstalt fuer Arbeit, 1984.

International Confederation of Free Trade Unions (ICFTU). "Integration of Women into Trade Union Organizations: The Täljøviken Report." Brussels: ICFTU, 1977.

International Labour Organisation (ILO). "Occupational Segregation Prevalent on Global Basis." Geneva: ILO, May 1985.

_____. *Equal Opportunities and Equal Treatment for Men and Women Workers: Workers with Family Responsibilities.* Geneva: ILO, 1980.

_____. *Special National Procedures Concerning Non-Discrimination in Employment: A Practical Guide.* Geneva: ILO, 1975.

_____. *Part-Time Employment: An International Survey.* Geneva: ILO, 1973.

Ireland. Working Party on Women's Affairs and Family Reform. *Irish Women: Agenda for Practical Action.* Dublin: The Stationery Office, February 1985.

Jaekel, Monika. "Results of the European Study Concerning Maternity Leave, Parental Leave, Home Care Support Measures in Finland, Sweden, Hungary, Austria and Germany." Munich: Deutsches Jugendinstitut, 1982.

Japan. Women's and Minors' Bureau, Ministry of Labour. "Outline of the Status of Female Labour in 1982." Tokyo: Ministry of Labour, 1983.

Johnson, Patricia. "Poverty Rate Increase." Testimony before the U.S. Subcommittee on Public Assistance and Unemployment Compensation of the Committee on Ways and Means, 98th Congress, 1st Session, October 18, 1983.

Kamerman, Sheila. *Parenting in an Unresponsive Society: Managing Work and Family Life.* New York: Free Press, 1981.

_____. "Maternal and Parental Benefits and Leaves: An International Review." New York: Columbia University Center for the Social Sciences, 1980. (Impact on Policy Series, Monograph 1)

_____. "Child Care Programs in Nine Countries: A Report Prepared for the OECD Working Party on the Role of Women in the Economy." Washington: U.S. Department of Health, Education, and Welfare, Office of Human Development/ Office of Child Development, 1976. (HEW Publication OHD 30080)

Kamerman, Sheila, and Alfred J. Kahn. *Income Transfers for Families with Children: An Eight-Country Study.* Philadelphia: Temple University Press, 1983.

_____. *Child Care, Family Benefits and Working Parents.* New York: Columbia University Press, 1980.

Kamerman, Sheila, and Alfred J. Kahn, eds. *Family Policy: Government and Families in Fourteen Countries*. New York: Columbia University Press, 1978.

Kamerman, Sheila, Alfred J. Kahn, and Paul Kingston. *Maternity Policies and Working Women*. New York: Columbia University Press, 1983.

Kellner, Wolfburg. "Motivation and Verhalten tuerkischer Gastarbeiterinnen." *Arbeit und Leistung* 26, No. 6 (1975).

Kergoat, Danielle. "Ouvriers: Ouvrière?" *Critique de l'économie politique*, No. 5 (Octobre-Novembre 1978).

Kessler-Harris, Alice. *Out to Work: A History of Wage-Earning Women in the United States*. New York: Oxford University Press, 1982.

Klein, Viola. *Women Workers: Working Hours and Services*. Paris: Organisation for Economic Cooperation and Development, 1965.

Kohlstad, Eva. "Three Years With an Act on Equality." *Equal Opportunities International* (London) 1, No. 4 (1982).

Liljestrøm, Rita. *Sex Roles in Transition*. Stockholm: Swedish Institute, 1975.

Lopata, Helen Z. *Occupation Housewife*. New York: Oxford University Press, 1971.

Losseff-Tillmans, Gisela. *Frauenemanzipation und Gewerkschaften*. Wuppertal: Hammer, 1978.

Meggender, Oskar. "Politik der Gleichstellung von Mann und Frau am Beispiel Schwedens." *Frauen und Arbeit* 7/85. Duesseldorf: DGB, 1985.

Michel, Andrée, ed. *Les Femmes dans la société marchande*. Paris: Presses Universitaires de France, Sociologie Aujourd'hui, 1978.

Muenscher, Alice. *Auslaendische Familien und Frauen*. Munich: Deutsches Jugendinstitut, 1986.

Myrdal, Alva, and Viola Klein. *Women's Two Roles: Home and Work*. London: Routledge and Kegan Paul, 1956.

Nauhaus, Brigitte. *Probleme der Frauenarbeitslosigkeit in der gegenwaertigen Krise*. Koeln: Pahl-Rugenstein, 1979.

Nollen, Stanley D., Brenda Broz Eddy, and Virginia Rider Martin. *Permanent Part-Time Employment: The Manager's Perspective*. New York: Praeger, 1978.

Oakley, Ann. *Housewife*. London: Allen Lane, Penguin Books, Ltd., 1974.

Organisation for Economic Cooperation and Development (OECD). "The Concentration of Female Employment in the Australian Labor Market, 1972–1980." Paris: OECD, January 1982.

——————. *Women and Employment: Politics for Equal Opportunity*. Paris: OECD, 1980.

——————. *Demographic Trends, 1950–1990*. Paris: OECD, 1979.

Paukert, Liba. *The Employment and Unemployment of Women in OECD Countries*. Paris: Organisation for Economic Cooperation and Development, 1984a.

——————. "The Pay Differential for Women: Some Comparisons for Selected EEC Countries." Vienna: United Nations Economic Commission for Europe, September 17, 1984b.

Pearce, Diana. "Women, Work, and Welfare: The Feminization of Poverty." In *Working Women and Families*, ed. Karen Wolk Feinstein. Beverly Hills, CA: Sage Publications, 1979. Pp. 103–24.

Pettman, Barrie O., ed. *Equal Pay for Women: Progress and Problems in Seven Countries*. London: Hemisphere, 1977.

Pfarr, Heide M., and Klaus Bertelsmann. *Lohngleichheit zur Rechtssprechung bei Geschlechtsspezifischer Entgelddiskriminierung*. Schriftenreihe des Bundesministeriums fuer Jugend, Familie und Gesundheit, Vol. 100. Stuttgart: Kohlhammer Verlag, 1981.

Pini, Claudia. *Das Arbeitnehmerpatriarchat*. Koeln: Kiepenheuer & Witsch, 1977.

Pross, Helga. *Gleichberechtigung im Beruf? Eine Untersuchung von 7,000 Arbeitnehmerinnen in der EWG.* Frankfurt: Athenaeum Verlag, 1973.

Qvist, Gunnar. "Policy Towards Women and the Women's Struggle in Sweden." *Scandinavian Journal of History* (1980): pp. 51–74.

Rapoport, Robert, and Rhona Rapoport (with Janice Brumstead). *Working Couples.* New York and London: Harper Colophon Books, 1978.

Ratner, Ronnie S., ed. *Equal Employment Policy for Women.* Philadelphia: Temple University Press, 1980.

Rehn, Gösta. "Lifetime Allocation of Time." Paris: Organisation for Economic Cooperation and Development, 1974. (MS/S/74.4)

Rights of Women, Europe. *Women's Rights and the EEC: A Guide for Women in the UK.* London: 1982.

Rutenfranz, Josef, and Walter Rohmert, "Arbeitswissenschaftliche Beurteilung der Belastung und Beanspruchung an unterschiedlichen industriellen Arbeitsplaetzen." Bonn: Bundenministerium fuer Arbeit and Sozialordung, 1975.

Sloane, Peter J., ed. *Women and Low Pay.* London: Macmillan, 1980.

Smith, Ralph E., ed. *The Subtle Revolution: Women at Work.* Washington: Urban Institute, 1979.

Spector, William D. "Women's Retirement Income." In *Working Women and Families,* ed. Karen Wolk Feinstein. Beverly Hills, CA: Sage Publications, 1979. Pp. 247–76.

Standing, Guy. "The Notion of Voluntary Unemployment." *International Labour Review* 120 (September-October 1981): pp. 563–79.

Strasser, Susan M. *Never Done: A History of American Housework.* New York: Pantheon, 1982.

Sullerot, Evelyne. *Women, Society and Change.* London: World University Library, Weidenfelt and Nicholson, 1971.

Szalai, Alexander, ed. *The Use of Time: A Multinational Study.* Paris: Mouton, 1972.

Takahaski, Nobuko. "Women's Wages in Japan and the Question of Equal Pay." *International Labour Review* 111 (January 1975): pp. 31–68.

U.S. Department of Health and Human Services. *Social Security Programs Throughout the World.* Washington: U.S. Government Printing Office, 1980.

U.S. Department of Labor, Bureau of Labor Statistics. "Major Indicators of Labor Market Activity, Seasonally Adjusted." Reported in BNA *Daily Labor Report,* No. 6 (January 9, 1986): p. B–3.

Vanek, Joann. "Housewives as Workers." In *Working Women: Theorties and Facts in Perspective,* eds. Ann Stromberg and Shirley Harkess. Palo Alto, CA: Mayfield Publishing Co., 1978. Pp. 392–414.

Wahlund, I. "Salaried Employees' Working Hours. Length of Working Hours and Location. Working Conditions, Health and Leisure." Stockholm: TCO, 1981.

Walker, Kathryn, and William Gauger. *The Dollar Value of Household Work.* Social Sciences, Consumer Economics and Public Policy, #5, Information Bull. No. 60. Ithaca, NY: State College of Human Ecology of Cornell University, June 1973.

Werneke, Diane. *Microelectronics and Office Jobs: The Impact of the Chip on Women's Employment.* Geneva: International Labour Organisation, 1983.

Wistrand, Birgitta. *Swedish Women on the Move.* Stockholm: Swedish Institute, 1981.

Yohalem, Alice. *Women Returning to Work.* Montclair, NJ: Alanheld Osmun, 1980.

CHAPTER 13

Women and Work: The Evolving Policy

KAREN SHALLCROSS KOZIARA*

Yahweh spoke to Moses . . . "a man between twenty and sixty years of age shall be valued at fifty shekels—a woman shall be valued at thirty shekels. . . ."

Leviticus, Chapter 27

This chapter traces the evolving public policy treatment of women workers from early industrialization to the present. Included is an analysis of the development and impact of labor market policies affecting working women, an identification of recurring themes, a discussion of current policy, and suggested topics for further research.

Historical Perspective

The evolution of public policy treatment of women workers can be divided into four distinct periods. The first extends from the early 1800s to the turn of the century. The first laws directed at women workers, most of which limited access to certain occupations, and the first efforts to achieve protective legislation occurred during these years. The second, from 1900 to 1920, saw attempts to enact and establish the constitutionality of hours regulation, the first generation of protective legislation. The third, from 1930 to 1963, was characterized by the growing acceptance of workplace protections, but not equal treatment, for both men and women. The fourth began in 1963 with enactment of the Equal Pay Act. It includes efforts to protect and promote equality, and may be termed the second generation of protective policy.

As discussed in Marshall and Paulin, Chapter 1 of this book, few women worked for wages prior to the development of early factories. Those who did work were usually widowed, unmarried, black, or married to husbands unable to support them. They most often were employed in domestic occupations, such as cook and housekeeper and other extensions of women's work in the home. In the early 1800s, for

---

* Professor of Human Resource Administration, Temple University.

example, soldiers were poorly paid, and it was common for soldiers' wives to work for pay laundering the clothes of unmarried soldiers. With the development of the textile industry in the 1830s and 1840s, many single women entered the labor force, and increasing numbers of them took factory jobs as industrialization advanced.

Little labor legislation of any type existed during this early period. However, restrictions existed on the entry of women into some professions and occupations. Occupations frequently restricted to men were mining and smelting, work in places serving liquor and, sometimes, work on moving machinery (Baer, 1978). These restrictions were arguably "protective," but they also reflected commonly held notions that women were to be wives and mothers, not paid workers. For example, in 1872 the Supreme Court approved an Illinois refusal to allow women to practice law. The decision reasoned:

> the family institution is repugnant to the idea of a woman adopting a distinct and independent career from that of her husband. . . . It is true that many women are unmarried and not affected by any of the duties, complications, and incapabilities arising out of the married state, but these things are not exceptions to the general rule. The paramount destiny and mission of women are to fulfill the law of the Creator, and rules of civil society must be adapted to the general condition of things, and cannot be based upon exceptional cases.[1]

During the 19th century's second half, factory women worked long hours at low pay in substandard conditions. Women earned substantially less than men, at least partly because their wages were depressed by the large numbers of women willing to work in the few occupations open to them. Other explanations include the belief of many factory women that their employment was temporary, thus reducing their incentive to address wage inequities between men and women; the views held by some employers that women were worth less than men because they were inherently inferior workers (McGlen and O'Connor, 1983); and paternalistic wage setting which rewarded head-of-household status.

In the 1860s, women's suffrage leaders, including Susan B. Anthony and Elizabeth Cady Stanton, wanted to improve the status of employed women. This goal reflected both a philosophical commitment to improving women's economic and political positions and the hope that working women would be a new source of support for the suffrage movement. However, because the movement focused on political issues and most suffragists wanted to have little to do with poor and immigrant women, attempts to combine the suffrage movement with efforts to organize working women were short-lived. Toward the end of the century women associated with the progressive movement

---

[1] *Bradwell v. Illinois*, 83 U.S. 130, 141–42 (1872).

recognized the importance of dealing with the problems of working women, but their attempts to organize working women were largely unsuccessful. These middle-class reformers then concentrated their efforts on getting protective legislation to aid working-class women (McGlen and O'Connor, 1983).

These efforts were harbingers of things to come. The history of the development of public policy tailored for women workers consistently shows the importance of the active advocacy of women's groups, labor unions, other interest groups, and supportive politicians to the enactment of laws and their implementation.

By 1896, 13 states had laws restricting working hours for women, but only three of them were enforceable. Several limited penalties to employers who "compelled" women to work more than the legal maximum, others outlawed only "willful" violations, and one was found unconstitutional. All but one limited coverage to women in manufacturing. Some states had hour laws that covered men and women, but most women were not affected by this legislation because, in theory, they were covered by laws with higher standards (Brandeis, 1952).

Some courts ruled these general hours laws to be an unconstitutional infringement on the right of individuals to contract their labor. In 1905 the Supreme Court found a New York 10-hour law for bakers invalid because "[t]he act is not . . . a health law, but is an illegal interference with the right of individuals, both employers and employees, to make contracts regarding labor upon such terms as they may think best. . . ."[2] This decision brought into question the constitutionality of laws limiting women's hours.

In spite of these setbacks, political pressure for effective and enforceable protective legislation for women grew in the early 1900s. This pressure came from the National Women's Trade Union League, the National American Woman Suffrage Association's reawakened interest in working women, and the National Consumers' League (NCL), a middle-class reform organization dedicated to helping working-class women.

The NCL used education to convince the public and the courts of the necessity of legislation to protect working women's health and family stability, and it was a determined advocate of the constitutionality of women's hours laws. Its general counsel, Louis Brandeis, submitted a lengthy statistical brief, probably the first of its kind, to show the Supreme Court the negative impact of long work hours on women's health and reproductive ability (McGlen and O'Connor, 1983).

---

[2] *Lochner v. New York*, 198 U.S. 45, 75 (1905).

This brief may have influenced the Court. In 1908 it found an Oregon hours law for women constitutional, and the opinion included references to the need for women to have special protections. It read in part "that [a woman's] physical structure and a proper discharge of her maternal functions—having in view not only her own health, but the well-being of the race—justify legislation to protect her from the greed as well as the passion of man."[3]

More state legislation regulating working hours for women followed this decision. Between 1909 and 1917, 19 states passed their first laws limiting the hours women worked, and 20 states raised standards in existing laws. During the same period 5 states introduced restrictions on night work for women. By 1933 all but 6 states had maximum hours laws for women (Brandeis, 1952).

Minimum wage laws for women made slower progress, due in part to a 1923 Supreme Court decision invalidating a Washington, D.C., law creating a board to set minimum wages for women.[4] Additional opposition to protective legislation came from employers and some women's organizations, including the National Women's Party, which saw protection as incompatible with equal rights for women. It was not until the early 1930s that state minimum wage laws became a reality (Brandeis, 1952).

Until the New Deal the federal role in labor market regulations was minimal. However, in 1920 Congress approved the establishment of the Women's Bureau in the U.S. Department of Labor. Its charge—to investigate and improve the condition of working women—reflected the Progressive Party's belief that women workers needed a government advocate to protect them for future family obligations. The Women's Bureau conducted studies documenting the often regrettable conditions in which women worked, supported protective legislation, tried to implement reform through persuasion, and was one of the advocates of equal pay for equal work in the 1960s (Sealander, 1983).

There was a marked increase in federal labor market regulation during the Depression and the New Deal. Included in the New Deal legislation were the National Labor Relations Act (NLRA), the Fair Labor Standards Act, and the Social Security Act. Although these laws covered both men and women, their inclusion of both did not indicate wide acceptance of equal treatment for women workers. During the Depression the federal government enacted legislation limiting federal employment to one family member, an action that had a greater impact on women than on men. Laws in 26 states prohibited the

---

[3] *Muller v. Oregon*, 208 U.S. 412, 422 (1908).
[4] *Adkins v. Children's Hosp.*, 261 U.S. 525 (1923).

employment of married women in some occupations, as did many public school systems (McGlen and O'Connor, 1983).

World War II and the increased demand for workers ended most of these restrictions. However, federal action to guarantee equality for women in the work force was notably absent. The government did provide federally funded day-care centers, but these efforts reached only a few of those needing child care. Furthermore, there were no federal guarantees of equal employment opportunity or equal pay for equal work.

Additionally, some laws that appeared to treat men and women the same actually provided more benefits for men than for women workers. For example, until 1975 the Social Security Act reflected the traditional assumption that men were the major breadwinners by providing benefits for widows, but not for widowers.[5] In a similar vein, it is not clear that NLRA coverage has benefited women as much as men. Historically, more men than women have joined unions, a disparity usually thought to reflect factors other than the NLRA. However, it is possible that NLRA protections have not been sufficient to allay fears of employer reprisals on the part of some women workers, particularly clerical employees working in close proximity to management (Koziara and Insley, 1982).

The 1963 Equal Pay Act and Title VII of the 1964 Civil Rights Act ushered in the second generation of protective legislation for women. These laws, unlike the original protective legislation, are designed to protect women from unequal treatment rather than to provide them with special treatment.

Equal Pay for Equal Work

Although the Equal Pay Amendments to the Fair Labor Standards Act did not become law until 1963, efforts to guarantee women equal pay for performing work equal to men's jobs date back to Knights of Labor support of equal pay for equal work in the 1800s. The principle of equal pay for equal work first received government attention during World War I. The National War Labor Board, in response to pressure from women's organizations and unions, applied the equal pay for equal work principle in 50 cases. However, organized support was insufficient for there to be wide application of the equal pay principle, and in most industries there continued to be large differences between wages paid to men and to women (Fisher, 1948).

Women's organizations and labor unions renewed the equal pay campaign during World War II. In 1942 the War Labor Board issued

---

[5] *Weinberger v. Wisenfeld*, 420 U.S. 636 (1975).

an order permitting employers to equalize wages of men and women without Board consultation. In addition, the Board heard equal pay cases and issued rulings requiring equal wages for equal work. Nonetheless, many employers violated the equal pay principle. Equal pay legislation was introduced in Congress a number of times following the end of the war, but did not have enough political support to become law (Fisher, 1948). The equal pay campaign had more success at the state level, and by 1963, 22 states had enacted equal pay legislation.

Organized labor's support for efforts to get federal equal pay legislation is an indication of both the interest of female union members in equal pay and the labor movement's desire to prevent general wage scales from being undermined by low-wage women workers (Stencel, 1981). Other supporters of equal pay legislation included representatives of civic, social, professional, and government organizations as well as women's groups. They argued that to permit wage discrimination based on sex was immoral, unjust, contrary to the interests of the broader community, and economically inefficient. The major opponents of the legislation came from industry, and they argued that equal pay was too costly, that higher rates of absenteeism and turnover made women more expensive to employ than men, that equal pay might increase female unemployment, that the law would interfere with established collective bargaining relationships, and that, in order to gain flexibility, the issue should be left to the states (U.S. Senate, Subcommittee on Labor, 1963).

The bill that became the Equal Pay Act was introduced in 1962 and required equal pay for work of "comparable character." In a series of amendments the term "comparable character" was replaced by "equal work." The intent behind this change was to narrow the concept of equal pay. As explained by Representative Goodell (R., New York), "We went from 'comparable' to 'equal,' meaning the jobs should be . . . very much like or closely related to each other. We do not expect the Labor Department people to go into an establishment and attempt to rate jobs that are not equal" (109 Congressional Record, 1963, p. 9197).

The Equal Pay Act prohibits employers from discriminating on the basis of sex in setting wages for work requiring equal skill, effort, and responsibility and performed under similar working conditions in the same establishment. However, wage differentials based on seniority, merit systems, incentive pay systems, or any factor other than sex are permissible. It applies to all employers and employees covered by the Fair Labor Standards Act's minimum wage and overtime provisions as well as to exempt employees such as executives, administrators, and professionals.[6]

---

[6] 29 U.S.C. §206(d).

The initial administrative responsibility for the Equal Pay Act was assigned to the Wage and Hour Division of the Department of Labor. Enforcement began slowly, at least in part because of "federal district judges' . . . lifelong impressions on the role of women in society," and the resulting feeling that bringing cases to court would be futile (Sangerman, 1971). Not until 1971 was it announced that the Equal Pay Act would be enforced with the same vigor as other sections of the Fair Labor Standards Act. Credit for the policy change went to the women's movement and supportive decisions in appellate courts. Of particular importance in the enforcement of the Equal Pay Act were Equal Employment Opportunity Commission (EEOC) guidelines, discussed later, superseding state protective legislation limited to women.

The Act had a significant and useful impact both because it was the only law directly concerned with equal pay and because an established and experienced agency was charged with its administration. Perhaps more important, as a Department of Labor solicitor responsible for equal pay cases said, "Without the Equal Pay Act to keep the issue of sex discrimination in the forefront in the courts, the problem would have been lost among the other areas of employment bias covered by EEOC" (Cook, 1975, p. 171).

An ongoing issue in enforcement of the Equal Pay Act is what constitutes equal work. The initial impression after the law's enactment was that changing content descriptions of men's jobs to include work not normally done by women would serve as a defense against unequal pay charges, and consultants spent much time writing "compliance job descriptions" (Sovereign, 1984, p. 235). However, the courts require that the work in question be "substantially" equal, but not necessarily identical.[7] Actual job demands rather than job descriptions determine the skill, effort, and responsibility required by a job, and when wage differentials exist between men and women doing substantially equal work, the burden of proof is on the employer to show that differentials are not based on sex. Extra duties taking up little time and of little importance are not an adequate justification for wage differentials.[8]

Average wage differentials in litigated equal pay cases are about 15 percent (Cooper and Barrett, 1984, p. 84), and Equal Pay Act enforcement has to its credit a number of significant back-pay awards, an indication of its importance in remedying wage discrimination. The Act has also been a factor in consent decrees, including the EEOC's

---

[7] *Shultz v. Wheaton Glass Co.*, 421 F.2d 259, 9 FEP Cases 502 (3d Cir. 1970), *cert. denied*, 398 U.S. 905, 9 FEP Cases 1408 (1970).
[8] *Brennan v. Board of Educ.*, 374 F.Supp. 817, 9 FEP Cases 951 (D.N.J. 1974).

1974 settlement with the American Telephone and Telegraph Co. (Greenberger, 1980).

The 1979 government reorganization transferred enforcement responsibility for the Equal Pay Act from the Wage and Hour Division to EEOC, and in 1981 the Commission published some controversial modifications of existing equal pay guidelines. Major changes included an enlarged definition of the meaning of "establishment," a more restrictive definition of acceptable "red circle" rates, and more restrictions on the calculation of life cycles (Greenlaw and Kohl, 1982). Although the overall impact of these changes is not yet clear, they create ambiguity about how the EEOC will apply them. Typically, ambiguous rules increase the need for litigation and slow the compliance process.

Regardless of these administrative changes, and no matter how rigorously the Act is enforced, the Equal Pay Act will not reduce income differences between men and women that result from occupational differences. The persistence of the gap between male and female incomes even after enactment of the Act was generally not anticipated by its supporters. This unintended outcome is a major reason for the developing interest in the comparable worth issue, discussed in a later section.

Title VII of the 1964 Civil Rights Act

New York State enacted the first fair employment practices law in 1945, and by 1964, 22 states had similar legislation. During the same time period a number of bills that would have provided equal employment opportunity were introduced in Congress. These efforts to mandate fair employment practices focused on outlawing discrimination based on race, religion, and sometimes age. A few included sex as an illegal basis for employment discrimination, but most did not.

Section 703 of Title VII of the 1964 Civil Rights Act did not include sex as a protected category in its original form. Congressman Smith (D., Virginia) introduced the amendment adding sex to the text of the bill the day before it was passed by the House of Representatives. Smith said that his intent in offering the amendment was serious and that it was indisputable that women face employment discrimination. However, to show that women had rights entitled to protection, he read parts of a letter from "a lady with a real grievance" who wrote, "Why the Creator would set up such an imbalance of spinsters, shutting off the right of every female to have a husband of her own is, of course, known only to nature. . . . [T]his is a grave injustice to womankind and something that Congress and President Johnson should take immediate steps to correct" (U.S. Equal Employment

Opportunity Commission, 1968). Many supporters of this amendment later voted against Title VII, and it is generally believed that the purpose of the amendment was to kill the legislation.

Although the sex amendment had a tongue-in-cheek introduction and produced levity in the House, most congresswomen gave it determined support. Their active participation in the debate over the amendment resulted in the event being known as "ladies' afternoon in the House." Supporters of the amendment pointed out that discrimination against women was well known and that to provide equal employment opportunities for racial minorities but not for women would be illogical and would mean that "down at the bottom of the list there would be a white woman with no rights at all" (U.S. Equal Employment Opportunity Commission, 1968).

The amendment generated some opposition. One objection was that it might endanger the law's primary objective of eliminating racial discrimination. Indeed, there was some fear that one amendment would lead to a plethora of amendments that would eventually scuttle the bill. Another concern was that sex and race discrimination were too dissimilar to include in the same legislation. In support of this position, the Women's Bureau of the U.S. Department of Labor referred to the conclusion of the President's Commission on the Status of Women that "[d]iscrimination based on sex . . . involves problems sufficiently different from discrimination based on other factors to make separate treatment preferable" (U.S. Equal Employment Opportunity Commission, 1968, p. 3,214).

There is not much evidence of opposition, nor is there much legislative history on what Congress intended the amendment to mean. The legislative history does discuss the Bennett amendment, indicating that it was meant to protect the Equal Pay Act's provisions in the event that the two laws conflicted. There was also a brief discussion of the inclusion of sex as a bona fide occupational requirement (BFOQ) exception to the law. The exceptions alluded to include an elderly woman wanting a female nurse, a college looking for a dean of men or a dean of women, and a masseur in the congressional gymnasium. However, an interpretive memo from Senators Clark (D., Pennsylvania) and Case (R., New Jersey), the floor managers of the bill in the Senate, suggested the provision was to be a "limited exception."

Racial equality was the primary focus of the 1964 Civil Rights Act. EEOC policies reflected this focus, and its administrative efforts concentrated on race discrimination. Lack of attention to women, and descriptions of the sex amendment as a "fluke," angered many women, including Congresswoman Griffiths (D., Michigan), who had actively supported the amendment's passage, and the emerging feminist movement. Two EEOC members informally suggested to some active feminists that EEOC responded to public pressure and that women's groups could use political action to change EEOC policy. The National Organization for Women (NOW) was organized on the heels of this suggestion, with active and meaningful implementation of Title VII's prohibition of sex discrimination as a major objective (Zelman, 1982).

Implementation

Title VII makes it illegal for employers to discriminate in any aspect of employment on the basis of sex unless sex is a BFOQ necessary to business operation. In addition, Section 708 states that compliance with state law is not an admissible excuse for violating the law's antidiscrimination requirements. This provision raised questions about whether state legislation protecting women was discriminatory. Protective legislation did single out women for special treatment, but many people thought these laws were important to maintain because they had a favorable effect on women's working conditions.

The legal issue was complicated by political issues. On the one hand, some supporters of equality for women felt that protective legislation perpetuated the status of women as second-class citizens. On the other, protective legislation had long had politically important supporters, such as the Women's Bureau of the Department of Labor and the AFL-CIO, which had not presented their views during the abbreviated legislative debate on the amendment adding sex to Title VII. Initially, EEOC considered these protective laws to be BFOQ exceptions to Title VII justifying employment discrimination against women. Support for a move from this protectionism toward full employment equality for women developed slowly (Zelman, 1982). It was not until 1969 that EEOC revised its sex discrimination guidelines to specify that Title VII superseded state protective laws that did not take into account capacities and preferences of individual women, and thus discriminated against rather than protected women.

EEOC's policy on classified job advertising was also a thorny issue. This reflected some EEOC confusion on how to handle sex discrimination issues, open opposition to Title VII's sex provisions, and lack of a clear feminist consensus on employment issues. In addition, EEOC's authority to regulate advertising extended only to employers, not to the providers of advertising services. Civil rights advocates had worked hard and effectively to educate the public on the importance of discontinuing help-wanted columns designated "white" and "colored." In contrast, doing away with "sex"-designated help-wanted columns met public ridicule and significant opposition from the newspaper industry. EEOC developed a policy for the "convenience of readers" which permitted male and female columns as long as such advertising announced on each page that employers covered by

Title VII could not discriminate on the basis of sex (Zelman, 1982). The 1969 EEOC revised guidelines on sex discrimination finally ended advertising using male and female help-wanted designations.

As indicated earlier, Title VII provides that sex may be used as the basis for employment decisions when it is a BFOQ necessary to business operations. A broad interpretation of the BFOQ exception would have reflected widely held norms of the appropriate gender distribution of jobs and substantially reduced the impact of including sex in Title VII as a category of forbidden employment discrimination. However, the BFOQ provision was interpreted narrowly. To rely on the BFOQ exception, an employer must show "reasonable cause to believe . . . that all or substantially all women would be unable to perform safely and efficiently the duties of the job involved."[9]

In practice, it is difficult for employers to show that the gender of a job incumbent is necessary for efficient operations. For example, the argument that being female was a BFOQ for airline cabin attendants because of customer preference, company history, and efficiency in the hiring process was rejected by the Supreme Court. The decision reads, "The primary function of an airline is to transport passengers safely from one point to another. . . . No one has suggested that having male stewards will so seriously affect the operation of an airline as to jeopardize or even minimize its ability to provide safe transportation. . . ."[10]

There are few legitimate BFOQ exceptions, but some are made for artistic, safety, and privacy reasons. The Supreme Court permitted a male-only policy for prison guards in an Alabama maximum security prison because of conditions in the prison and the possibility of substantial security problems.[11] A requirement that nurse's aides for female guests in a nursing home be female is also a valid BFOQ.[12]

Society's ambivalence toward working women has been so strong that it was thought that adding sex to Title VII protected groups would result in the legislation's defeat. Despite the law, sex discrimination in employment still exists. However, Title VII significantly changed employer practices and increased employment opportunities for women workers. The law prohibits sex discrimination in job advertising, recruiting, interviewing, hiring standards, and job assignments. Illegal practices include sex-specific job advertisements, height and weight requirements that are not job-related, refusing to hire women but not men who have children, and a host of more subtle employment practices.

[9] *Weeks v. Southern Bell Tel. & Tel. Co.*, 408 F.2d 228, 1 FEP Cases 656, 661 (5th Cir. 1969).
[10] *Diaz v. Pan Am. World Airways, Inc.*, 442 F.2d 385, 3 FEP Cases 337, 339 (5th Cir. 1971).
[11] *Dothard v. Rawlinson*, 433 U.S. 321, 15 FEP Cases 10 (1977).
[12] *Fesel v. Masonic Home of Del., Inc.*, 447 F.Supp. 1346, 17 FEP Cases 330 (D.Del. 1978).

Policy often has unintended and unexpected consequences, and Title VII has had its share. Apparently Congress did not foresee current sex discrimination issues such as pay equity, sexual harassment, those related to pregnancy, and disparity in pension payments. Although the question of equal pay for jobs of comparable value was discussed in the Equal Pay Act hearings, it was not addressed in Title VII's legislative history. There is no mention of sexual harassment and little discussion of pregnancy discrimination. Pregnancy, sexual harassment, and pensions and retirement are discussed in the following sections; pay equity is the subject of a later section.

Pregnancy

Prior to Title VII, pregnant employees had few protected employment rights. Mandatory unpaid pregnancy leave policies were common, with reemployment rights not guaranteed. Sometimes employers made unpaid leaves available; sometimes they did not. Paid maternity leaves were rare. The legality of these policies changed considerably with the enactment of Title VII, as will be described in this section.

Mandatory unpaid leaves were among the first employer pregnancy-related policies to face legal challenge. In 1970 two teachers informed their local school boards of their pregnancies. Both were compelled to take mandatory unpaid pregnancy leaves beginning, as the school boards' rules required, at the end of the fifth month of pregnancy. The school boards defended the rules as being necessary to maintain continuity in classroom instruction, to protect the health of the teachers and their unborn children, and to guarantee physically capable teachers in the classroom.

The Supreme Court pointed out that because the fifth month of pregnancy would begin at different times in the school year for different teachers, it could actually inhibit continuity of classroom teaching. In addition, the ability of any one teacher to work past a predetermined date in her pregnancy was an individual matter. Thus, the mandated-leave rules violated the 14th Amendment because they "employ irrebuttable presumptions that unduly penalize a female teacher for deciding to bear a child."[13]

Currently, mandatory pregnancy leaves are illegal unless the employer can show an underlying business necessity for the practice. This exception has been interpreted narrowly. However, airline companies are permitted to have forced-leave pregnancy rules designed to reduce possible safety risks to passengers.

---

[13] *Cleveland Bd. of Educ. v. LaFleur*, 414 U.S. 632, 6 FEP Cases 1253, 1260 (1974).

In 1972 the EEOC issued guidelines providing that pregnancy should be covered in disability benefit plans in the same way as other temporary disabilities. However, disability benefit plans, which are designed to provide income protection for disabled employees, vary widely in their content, and some employers do not have them at all. When the EEOC guidelines were challenged before the Supreme Court in 1976 in *General Electric Co. v. Gilbert*,[14] the Court ruled that disability plans that did not include pregnancy benefits did not violate Title VII. It reasoned that because women were entitled to all the benefits to which men were entitled, the exclusion of pregnancy benefits from a disability plan did not discriminate against women.

This decision was extremely controversial because it had the effect of providing men with income protection from all disabilities while not providing women with income protection from an important cause of disability. The result of the decision was a major lobbying effort aimed at getting Congress to protect disability benefits for pregnant workers. Congress did nullify the decision in 1978 by adding the Pregnancy Discrimination Amendment to the Civil Rights Act.

This amendment to Title VII makes it illegal to discriminate on the basis of pregnancy, childbirth, or related medical conditions in hiring, promotion, suspension, training, discharge, or other terms and conditions of employment. Although it does not require special accommodation for pregnant employees, it does specify that the primary consideration should be the ability of pregnant employees, as well as other employees, to do the work required by the employer.

In practice this means that an employer cannot refuse to hire someone simply because she is pregnant, and employees who become pregnant must be treated in the same way as employees with other temporary disabilities. If an employer uses transfers to light work to accommodate people with temporary disabilities, similar accommodations should be made for pregnant workers. Likewise, unpaid leaves should be available to pregnant employees on the same basis and for the same duration as they are for employees with other temporary disabilities.

Many questions remain about how specific issues should be handled under this law. One is the legal status of discharges and involuntary transfers of pregnant employees. In general, involuntary transfers and discharges violate the law if they occur primarily because the employee is pregnant. Interrogation of a saleswoman about her reproductive plans, combined with threats of being removed from her lucrative account if she became pregnant and her actual transfer when she was pregnant, violated the law. However, transferring an

---

[14] 429 U.S. 125, 13 FEP Cases 1657 (1976).

employee involuntarily because she could not do the lifting required by the job during her pregnancy is legal.[15]

Another question involves what constitutes a legitimate leave policy. It is unlawful to deny a reasonable leave of absence to pregnant employees, and employer policies about leaves, including accrual of seniority and other employee benefits, and the availability of extensions, should be applied to pregnancy in the same way they are to other disabilities. In some cases, however, employers showing business-necessity reasons were found not to have violated the law by refusing to reinstate a returning employee. For example, an employer who found it impractical to hire a temporary replacement in order to be able to guarantee a continuing job opening did not violate the law by refusing reinstatement.[16] EEOC guidelines require that an employee returning from a pregnancy leave be given recall preference if she cannot be reinstated in her former job.

Although the Pregnancy Discrimination Amendment provides important new protections for working women, some issues remain unresolved. Many employers, especially those with large numbers of low-income women in their labor force, have restrictive leave policies. Others require employees to miss no more than 15 days of work a year. Restrictive leave policies, even when equally available to men and women, provide so little leave for childbirth that they result in hardship for or termination of pregnant employees. Some observers argue that although these policies are facially neutral, they have a disparate impact on women workers and thus violate Title VII. In their view, equal treatment is not sufficient protection for pregnant workers.[17] An opposing view is that even restrictive leave plans are not discriminatory if they are applied even-handedly. An outgrowth of this issue is interest in legislatively guaranteed parental leaves, a proposal discussed in a later section.

The legality of fetal protection policies is also an unsettled issue. Early Title VII decisions found that policies that protected women by excluding them from some jobs reflected Victorian-romantic paternalism.[18] However, court decisions are inconsistent on the legality of policies barring women who are pregnant or of childbearing age from jobs that may involve exposure to safety or health hazards. These policies have been found to be legal in several recent cases.[19]

---

[15] Bureau of National Affairs, Inc., *Employee Relations Weekly*, December 12, 1984, p. 1493.
[16] *Newmon v. Delta Air Lines*, 374 F.Supp. 238, 7 FEP Cases 26 (N.D. Ga. 1973); *Satty v. Nashville Gas Co.*, 384 F.Supp. 765, 10 FEP Cases 73 (D. Tenn. 1974), *aff'd*, 522 F.2d 850, 11 FEP Cases 1 (6th Cir. 1975).
[17] Bureau of National Affairs, Inc., *Employee Relations Weekly*, September 16, 1985, p. 1136.
[18] *Weeks v. Southern Bell Tel. & Tel. Co.*, supra note 9.
[19] Bureau of National Affairs, Inc., *Employee Relations Weekly*, December 12, 1984.

Laws in 19 states prohibit employment discrimination based on pregnancy, but their provisions vary. Many, like the Alaska law, have qualifications, such as forbidding discrimination unless the job's "reasonable demands" require distinctions based on pregnancy. In contrast, Minnesota law requires the accommodation of pregnant employees unless it would place undue burdens on the employer. In addition, California, Hawaii, New Jersey, New York, Rhode Island, and Puerto Rico have laws providing pregnant workers with disability benefits similar to workers' compensation.[20] However, these benefits are not available to pregnant workers in most states.

The remaining unresolved legal issues and the differences in state laws with respect to pregnancy suggest that confusion continues about appropriate legal protections for pregnant workers. The proportion of working women who have children and continue to work is increasing, and these issues will not go away.

Sexual Harassment

Although a number of studies show sexual harassment to be widespread, only recently has this issue, once little discussed except by joke or innuendo, reached the courts. Surveys show that about 40 percent of the respondents reported unwanted sexual harassment, and between 1 and 2 percent said that they were coerced into sexual relations, the most extreme form of sexual harassment. About 30 percent reported severe sexual harassment, including phone calls and sexual pressure; the remainder described less severe forms, such as vulgar jokes and requests for dates. The emotional effects of harassment include anger, fear, humiliation, shame, guilt, helplessness, and alienation. Some victims of sexual harassment also reported physical effects (MacKinnon, 1982; Silverman, 1976). Although the victims may be more likely than nonvictims to respond to these surveys, the studies suggest that few organizations are free of sexual harassment.

Employers formerly were not legally responsible for regulating the sexual conduct of employees either at work or after work hours. Some had rules against romantic relationships between employees, but many considered personal relationships to be private and beyond employer regulation.

Title VII does not specifically outlaw sexual harassment, but cases in which it is alleged come to the federal courts as sex-discrimination claims. Initially the courts dismissed claims that sexual harassment was a form of sex discrimination. In one case, a court found that a supervisor's sexual advances to be "a personal proclivity, peculiarity, or

---

[20] *Id.*, at 1499.

mannerism" and not the employer's legal responsibility. It also stated that the supervisor's behavior was not based on gender because the actions could have been directed at either male or female employees, and it went on to say that if the court found the questioned behavior to be sex discrimination, it would lead to "a potential federal lawsuit every time any employee [ ] made amorous or sexually oriented advances toward another."[21] In a similar case, where the ruling was that sexual harassment was neither sexual discrimination nor employment-related, the opinion read, "the supervisor was male and the employee was female. But no immutable principle of psychology compels this alignment of parties. . . . While sexual desire animated the parties, or at least one of them, the gender of each is incidental to the claim of abuse."[22]

Subsequently another federal court ruled that a male supervisor's retaliation against a woman employee who refused his advances was a reaction based on sex,[23] and in yet another decision the court explained: "But for her womanhood . . . [her] participation in sexual activity would never have been solicited. To say she was victimized in her employment simply because she declined the invitation is to ignore the asserted fact that she was invited only because she was a woman subordinate. . . ."[24]

In a later decision a supervisor's sexual harassment was defined as illegal although it was unknown to the employer who had a sexual-harassment policy.[25] In another case tasteless behavior and jokes that led to an employee's resignation were declared illegal, the court ruling that the former employee was entitled to reinstatement and that each of the supervisors who had been aware of the situation should pay a $1,500 fine.[26]

In the wake of federal court decisions finding sexual harassment to be a form of illegal sex discrimination, the EEOC prohibited it in its 1980 guidelines. The Commission's definition of sexual harassment as "unwelcome sexual advances, requests for favors and other verbal or physical conduct of a sexual nature" applies in three types of circumstances: (1) when submission to sexual conduct is made explicitly or implicitly a condition of an individual's employment; (2) when submission to or rejection of sexual conduct is used in making employment decisions such as retention and promotion; and (3) when sexual conduct interferes with job performance or creates an intimidating, hos-

---

21 *Corne v. Bausch & Lomb, Inc.*, 390 F.Supp. 161, 10 FEP Cases 289, 291 (D. Ariz. 1975).
22 *Tomkins v. Public Serv. Elec. & Gas Co.*, 422 F.Supp. 553, 13 FEP Cases 1574, 1576 (D.N.J. 1976).
23 *Williams v. Saxbe*, 413 F.Supp. 654, 12 FEP Cases 1093 (D.D.C. 1976).
24 *Barnes v. Castle*, 561 F.2d 983, 15 FEP Cases 345, 350 (D.C. Cir. 1977).
25 *Miller v. Bank of Am.*, 600 F.2d 211, 20 FEP Cases 462 (9th Cir. 1979).
26 *Kyriazi v. Western Elec. Co.*, 461 F.Supp. 894, 18 FEP Cases 924 (D.N.J. 1978).

tile, or offensive work environment. The guidelines also make employers responsible for the actions of supervisors regardless of whether or not the employer has knowledge of the illegal conduct (U.S. Equal Employment Opportunity Commission, 1980).

The guidelines protect both men and women from unwelcome sexual advances. However, the vast majority of the cases involve the harassment of women. To a certain extent this reflects differences in occupational distribution between men and women and the greater likelihood that women will have male supervisors rather than vice versa. Sexual harassment is at least partly a power issue, as subordinates rarely harass supervisors. In fact, in a number of cases involving sexual harassment of a man, the unwelcome advances came from a female supervisor.

The EEOC guidelines also deal with situations in which an employee uses sexual favors to win promotions or other employment advantages at the expense of more qualified employees. In these cases the more qualified employees can be defined as sexually harassed and may claim sex discrimination.

An ongoing problem is how to determine when sexual harassment exists. In a *Harvard Business Review* survey, readers generally agreed that it existed when an employee was not able to go into the boss's office without being pinched or patted or when a boss told an employee, "It would be good for your career if we went out together." However, there was less certainty about whether the following situations were sexual harassment: (1) "Whenever I go into the office the supervisor eyes me up and down, making me feel uncomfortable," or (2) "My supervisor puts his hand on my arm when making a point" (Collins and Blodgett, 1981).

Because many people who become romantically involved first meet at work, another problem is determining whether a particular sexual activity was unwelcome or had been consented to. Because of such difficulties, and because harassment usually involves individuals rather than broad classes of employees, the EEOC recommends that courts use a case-by-case approach that permits a review of all surrounding circumstances.

Employers often can limit their liability if they take immediate action to correct instances of sexual harassment. More and more of them are attempting to eliminate harassment by implementing programs that often include policy statements from top management, training, and procedures for handling complaints about sexual misconduct.

The Supreme Court reinforced the wisdom of having such programs when it made clear in 1986 that sexual harassment is an illegal form of sex discrimination. It ruled that sexual harassment could result in a "hostile or offensive" work environment even if sexual favors were not demanded for more favored treatment or the plaintiff did not suffer economic losses in terms of employment. The Court also appeared to look favorably on the EEOC guidelines indicating that employers may be held liable for supervisors' conduct.[27]

Pensions and Retirement

Defining nondiscriminatory benefit standards for pension and retirement plans is a complex task, one reason being that men and women have different life expectancies. Many defined-contribution pension plans, in which employees and employers make specific contributions that determine benefit levels, formerly adjusted for life-expectancy differences either by requiring women to make larger contributions than men or by providing women with smaller periodic benefits, presumably over a longer time period, than men. These plans were interpreted as not violating the Equal Pay Act as long as employers were providing equal contributions for male and female workers.

However, in 1978 the Supreme Court ruled that requiring women to contribute more than men to employer-based retirement programs violated Title VII. This decision made it illegal to deduct more from a female's wage than from a male's to pay for the same periodic benefit.[28] A subsequent Supreme Court ruling required that "[a]ll retirement benefits derived from contributions made after the decision today must be calculated without regard to the sex of the beneficiary."[29] This means that men and women who made equal contributions will receive equal periodic benefits. The result will be lower contribution levels or higher periodic benefit levels for women in defined-contribution plans.

Defined-benefit plans, in which benefits are based on prior earnings or years of service, are more common than defined-contribution plans. One estimate suggests that only 24 percent of all retirement plan participants are covered by defined-contribution plans (Burkhauser, 1983). Benefits based on prior earnings or service years result in lower benefits for women with discontinuous work histories, women who entered the labor force in midlife, and women working in low-paying, traditionally female occupations.

A recent study of people who retired in 1977–1978 found median annual pensions paid to women to be 56 percent lower than those paid to men. Women's pension benefits were worth $2,240 annually in 1984 dollars and replaced 18 percent of their preretirement income. In

---

[27] *Meritor Sav. Bank v. Vinson*, 477 U.S. ___, 40 FEP Cases 1822 (1986).
[28] *City of Los Angeles Dep't of Water & Power v. Manhart*, 435 U.S. 702, 17 FEP Cases 395 (1978).
[29] *Arizona Governing Comm. v. Norris*, 463 U.S. 1073, 32 FEP Cases 233, 235 (1983).

contrast, men's annual pension benefits were worth $5,050 in 1984 dollars and replaced an average of 22 percent of their preretirement earnings. Median benefit levels for people with less than 10 years of service were $590 annually as compared with $6,340 median benefits for people with 35 or more years of service. These findings show the great impact of years of service on benefit levels and underlines the effect of discontinuous service and late labor market entry on women's pension earnings (U.S. Department of Labor, 1985).

In addition, women are more likely than men to work part-time and to be ineligible for employer-based pension plans, or to work for employers who do not have pension plans. For these women Social Security may be their only source of retirement income.

The 1984 Retirement Equity Act addresses some retirement issues affecting women workers. It makes it easier for women to become eligible for pension benefits by lowering the minimum participation age to 21 and by requiring that nonvested pension participants do not incur a break in service if they return to work for the employer within five years. It also requires a spouse to sign a consent if waiving joint and survivor benefits. This means that spouses may not be excluded unknowingly from retirement benefits.

This law makes it somewhat easier for women to become eligible for pension benefits. It does not, however, address the differences in the retirement income of men and women based on wages, length of service, and part-time work. Thus, there is continuing interest in developing policies designed to enhance women's retirement income.

Evaluating Title VII

There is little doubt that Title VII has improved the employment status of women. It was instrumental in changing employer staffing policies and providing women access to positions previously denied them. Its breadth enables it to encompass issues such as sexual harassment and the treatment of pregnant workers, unanticipated at the time of its enactment. However, the income gap between men and women workers persists, and women remain heavily concentrated in a few occupations. Therefore the relevant question is not whether, but how much impact Title VII has had. Related questions are whether it should have been more effective and whether its effectiveness can be enhanced.

As discussed earlier, in the years immediately following the enactment of Title VII little effort went into enforcing its sex-discrimination provisions. This reflected the general belief at the time that race discrimination was a more important problem than sex discrimination. It was also because the EEOC treated state protective legislation as a BFOQ exception legitimizing sex discrimination. External pressure shifted the Commission's focus to include women's employment issues in the late 1960s, and in 1969 EEOC stipulated that Title VII superseded state protective legislation. However, these changes did not end criticism of EEOC administration.

Scarce resources and limited personnel constrained EEOC's effectiveness during the early 1970s, resulting in the development of a case backlog that grew steadily to reach a total of 130,000 in 1977 (U.S. Civil Rights Commission, 1977). The EEOC was also criticized for focusing on individual complaints rather than using class-action suits to combat systemic discrimination (Bergmann, 1976). Class-action suits address discrimination affecting an entire group of employees rather than an individual. As a result of this focus, one study of EEOC administration concluded, "[F]irst-hand observations suggest that the EEOC is unlikely to have had a major impact" on minority employment opportunities (Butler and Heckman, 1977).

The EEOC was reorganized in 1977 with an increase in budget and authorized positions. "Rapid charge processing" reduced the case backlog significantly, and the agency began to focus on systemic discrimination. Commission staffing peaked between 1979 and 1981, and in the latter year the backlog was about 15 percent of what it had been in 1977.

EEOC budgets and staffing declined after 1981, as did systemic discrimination investigations, while the number of cases dismissed for having "no cause" to proceed increased (Burbridge, 1984). In 1984 EEOC instituted a policy of filing suit in every discrimination case in which reasonable cause was found and conciliation had failed. This policy was aimed at making the EEOC a "credible" enforcement agency, but critics suggested that failure to distinguish among cases based on relative importance made little administrative sense and could result in an enormous growth in agency caseload.[30] In 1984 the agency also decided not to actively pursue the question of comparable worth in the courts.

In 1985 the EEOC announced a "remedies policy" of seeking individual relief for identified victims of discrimination rather than numerical remedies in the form of goals and timetables in class-action suits. Goals and timetables were characterized as a "cop-out," allowing companies to hide behind affirmative action, in contrast to effecting remedies that directly change employer practices.[31] These recent policy changes do not appear likely to increase EEOC's impact on employment discrimination.

---

[30] Bureau of National Affairs, Inc., *Employee Relations Weekly*, July 29, 1985, p. 941.
[31] Bureau of National Affairs, Inc., *Employee Relations Weekly*, November 18, 1985, p. 1423.

Thus, it might be said that Title VII has had a mixed administrative history, with the agency's role and effectiveness heavily influenced by political forces. One study identified EEOC's major contributions as (1) the establishment of the principle of a narrow definition of sex as a BFOQ; (2) its guidelines on recruiting and selection, pregnancy, employee benefits, and sexual harassment; and (3) its role in framing remedies and consent decrees (O'Farrell and Harlan, 1984). A number of studies have attempted to evaluate its impact on wages and employment. However, cross-sectional analyses are somewhat inconclusive because of Title VII's broad coverage which makes identification of an appropriate control group difficult (Brown, 1982).

Other studies have used time-series analyses, but they face all the limitations inherent in longitudinal analysis. Among other problems, it is difficult to isolate the impact of policy from the impact of changes in labor markets, labor force participation rates, other governmental policies, and social norms and expectations. Regardless of their limitations, these studies generally show that the labor market position of minorities improved more rapidly after 1964 than trends prior to 1964 would have predicted. Another general finding is that the employment status of male and female black workers improved more rapidly than that of white women (Brown, 1982).

Pay Equity

During the past few years comparable worth, or pay equity, has become a major equal employment opportunity issue. The basis of the controversy is whether employers should pay equal wages for jobs segregated by sex but of equal value to the employers, as measured by job-comparison criteria. Comparable worth raises fundamental questions about wage setting. What should be the basis for wages? Should wages reflect supply and demand forces in the labor market? Should organizations be required to set wages using internally equitable criteria that reflect the contributions of individuals? If so, how should the value of individual contributions be measured? Should employers be required to explain and defend the wage-setting process? Some answers to these questions are philosophical. However, pay equity involves income distribution and thus is an important economic and political issue. Wages also have important psychological and sociological dimensions. They are symbols of status, progress, and self-worth. It is not surprising that some opponents believe that pay equity will have unpredictable and undesirable consequences. Nor is it surprising that advocates see the issue in moral and ethical terms and as a fundamental and necessary part of equal employment opportunity.

Although the 1963 Equal Pay Act and Title VII became law more than two decades ago, women working full-time earn on average about 40 percent less than men who work full-time. Much research indicates that the concentration of women workers in low-paying occupations is the major explanation for this pay gap. About 80 percent of the women in the labor force work in 25 of 420 distinct occupations, and most of the jobs in these 25 occupations are filled by women. For example, about 99 percent of all secretaries, 85 percent of all registered nurses, 82 percent of all librarians, and 86 percent of all clerks are women (U.S. House of Representatives, 1983). The comparable worth debate focuses on these and similar female jobs.

Pay-equity adjustments have the potential of affecting the wages of many working women as well as the wages of men in predominantly female occupations. Thus, many employers are concerned about the economic consequences of comparable worth, including increased costs, the negative impact of possible price increases, and possible unemployment within jobs allocated comparable worth increases. Advocates of comparable worth predict that it will enhance both the economic and the political position of working women, and that increasing the compensation for female jobs may increase the status of these jobs and women's work in general.

Because of its possible impact, pay equity is of great interest to many employers, women's organizations, unions, government officials, and individual workers. Currently pay equity is being addressed in the courts, through legislation, and at the bargaining table. The status of pay equity in the courts and as a legislative issue are discussed in the following sections. (Pay equity as a bargaining issue is considered in Needleman and Tanner, Chapter 7 of this book.)

Litigation

The Equal Pay Act makes it illegal for employers to pay men more than women for doing the same job. Courts have generally ruled that the Equal Pay Act requires jobs to be essentially similar, rather than comparable, if they are to be the basis for wage-discrimination suits.[32] As a result, differences in wages that men and women receive for dissimilar jobs are beyond the scope of the Equal Pay Act.

In contrast, Title VII is broader in scope and prohibits discrimination in any of the terms and conditions of employment. A legal issue is whether it is broad enough to question the legality of paying unequal wages for jobs that have comparable worth to the employer. A com-

---

[32] See, e.g., *Christensen v. Iowa*, 563 F.2d 353, 16 FEP Cases 232 (8th Cir. 1977); and *Lemons v. City and County of Denver*, 620 F.2d 228, 22 FEP Cases 959 (10th Cir. 1980).

plicating factor is the Bennett amendment, which states that any wage differential authorized by the Equal Pay Act is not a Title VII violation.

The Supreme Court addressed this issue in *County of Washington v. Gunther*.[33] The County of Washington, Oregon, paid substantially lower wages to female prison guards than to male guards. It used its own evaluation of external labor markets to set wages, and the female guards alleged that the county intentionally discriminated by setting their wages lower than those of the male guards in comparison with market wages. The Supreme Court ruled that the Bennett amendment makes the Equal Pay Act's affirmative defenses applicable in Title VII suits, but does not limit wage suits to the Equal Pay Act's equal-work standard.

Although the Court decided not to limit suits involving discriminatory wage claims to the equal-work standard, it stressed that it did not decide the case using a comparable-worth standard. The basis of the decision was intentional wage discrimination. Thus, the decision was narrowly drawn. Comparable-worth cases are not precluded by the Bennett amendment, but the circumstances under which such claims will be found legitimate are still uncertain.

In a subsequent decision, the Ninth Circuit Court of Appeals concluded that nursing school faculty could not establish prima facie discrimination simply by showing they were paid less than other faculty. Evidence that the wage disparity was more than likely to result from intentional discrimination was necessary to establish a valid suit. Furthermore, "[i]ntuitively, evidence of a pay disparity between jobs that are only comparable says very little about discrimination" and the comparable-worth theory "would plunge us into uncharted and treacherous areas."[34]

More recently the same court ruled that it is not illegal for an employer to set wages for male-dominated jobs higher than for female-dominated jobs due to market forces. At issue was whether Washington State engaged in illegal discrimination by not making pay-equity adjustments based on a 1974 study showing gender wage inequities. The court reasoned that Title VII "does not permit the federal courts to interfere in the market based system" of setting wages.[35] The American Federation of State, County and Municipal Employees (AFSCME), which had initiated the suit, announced that it would appeal the decision. In late 1985 the state and AFSCME reached a settlement that provided for $41.4 million in equity adjustments in 1986 and additional annual adjustments over the next seven years. The

---

[33] 452 U.S. 161, 25 FEP Cases 1521 (1981).
[34] *Spaulding v. University of Wash.*, 740 F.2d 686, 35 FEP Cases 217 (9th Cir. 1984).
[35] *American Fed'n of State, County and Municipal Employees v. Washington*, 770 F.2d 1401, 38 FEP Cases 1353 (9th Cir. 1985).

union indicated that the settlement was an effort to show the public the "pervasiveness of sex-based wage discrimination" and agreed to withdraw the case from appeal.[36]

The Washington case was noted in a subsequent court ruling on whether the State of California discriminated by paying less for female-dominated jobs than for male-dominated jobs. The court decided that the Washington State case did not foreclose Title VII's application to wage disparities between job classes filled primarily by women and job classes filled primarily by men where there is a discriminatory animus, even though the wages may have had their origins in market rates.[37]

These cases clearly show the uncertain legal status of pay equity as a Title VII issue. This lack of clarity partly reflects pay equity's recent emergence as a legal issue. However, these recent decisions focus on discriminatory intent as critical in evaluating claims of discrimination. Because discriminatory intent is ambiguous and the judgments are necessarily subjective, the legal status of comparable worth will remain unclear in the near future. Thus, it is likely that pay-equity claims will be a continuing focus of litigation and efforts to negotiate out-of-court settlements.

Legislation

Nearly every state has taken some action on the question of pay equity, as have many municipalities and counties. Most common is legislation authorizing pay-equity or job-evaluation studies. Seven states—Idaho, Iowa, Minnesota, New Mexico, South Dakota, Washington, and Wisconsin—are implementing pay-equity adjustments for state employees. Minnesota also has a local government pay-equity law requiring cities, counties, and school districts to undertake pay-equity efforts. At the federal level, it has been proposed that a study of pay equity for federal employees should be designed and implemented.

The costs of pay-equity adjustments vary by jurisdiction because of differences in numbers of people affected, size of adjustments required, and methods of implementation. New Mexico allocated $3.3 million to increase salaries in the lowest paid job classifications. Women held 86 percent of these positions, and the remaining 14 percent of the jobs were held primarily by Hispanic and Native American men. The estimated cost for full implementation over a number of years is $40 million. Implementation may take up to six years in Iowa, at an estimated cost of $35 million, although additional allocations may be necessary (National Committee on Pay Equity, 1985).

---

[36] Bureau of National Affairs, Inc., *Employee Relations Weekly*, January 6, 1986, p. 7.
[37] *California State Employees Ass'n v. California*, No. C-84-7275 (N.D. Calif., 1985).

The cost of implementing Minnesota's pay-equity law covering state employees is put at 4 percent of the payroll budget and required an initial two-year allocation of $21.7 million. About 8,000 employees received pay-equity adjustments. Those benefiting the most were clerical workers, all of whom received pay-equity increases, and health-care workers, half of whom received adjustments. The average annual increase was $1,600 (Minnesota Commission on the Economic Status of Women, 1985b).

The cost of these adjustments is one reason for the opposition to pay-equity legislation. Another is the belief that government should not get involved in wage-setting because wages that are above the market-wage level interfere with the market allocation process and may result in unemployment. It is also argued that pay-equity laws are unnecessary because sufficient legislation currently exists to guarantee equal employment opportunities.

To date, most pay-equity efforts have focused on public-sector employers, partly because they are politically visible and because many of them are large organizations with diverse job titles, making wage comparisons between predominantly male and predominantly female jobs possible. In addition, the possible employment effects of pay-equity adjustments are less of an issue in the public than in the private sector. Finally, the contention that government should not be involved in wage setting is less relevant when government is the employer and wages are public knowledge.

One reason for the growth of pay equity as a political issue is pressure from coalitions of advocate organizations including status-of-women commissions, organizations of working women, labor unions, female legislators, and other supportive legislators and groups. These coalitions lobby and attempt to increase public understanding of the pay-equity issue. Nonetheless, pay equity remains a complex and often misunderstood issue.

Although public-sector pay-equity legislation will continue to be opposed, opposition to private-sector legislation will be even more determined. In fact, some opponents of pay-equity legislation in the public sector are employers concerned that the legislation will have spillover effects on the private sector.

Affirmative Action

President Johnson's Executive Order 11246, signed in 1965, prohibited discrimination by government contractors on the basis of race, creed, color, and national origin, but not sex. The failure to include gender drew little attention prior to the signing of the order, but subsequently a number of women's organizations, including the

National Organization for Women (NOW) and the American Association of University Women, lobbied to expand the order to include sex (Freeman, 1982, p. 51). Sex was added in 1967 by Executive Order 11375. Although Title VII already covered most government contractors, and the Department of Labor did not issue guidelines for this order until 1970, Executive Order 11375 was important because its clear message was that including sex in Title VII was not a "fluke," but intentional federal policy (Zelman, 1982).

In 1970 the Office of Federal Contract Compliance (OFCC) announced orders requiring contractors to engage in "affirmative action" to improve the employment position of minority workers. These efforts were to include setting goals for minority employment and developing hiring timetables. Sex was added to these orders in 1971.

Theoretically, noncompliance has severe consequences. Violators can lose federal contracts and be debarred from future contracts. However, fewer than 30 government contractors have been debarred, more than half during the Carter Administration (Reskin and Hartmann, 1986). The severity of the debarment penalty results in its being little used. Not only does it penalize the contractor, but it also raises a variety of political issues. Local politicians actively oppose having locally based employers lose government contracts, and the government contracting agency resists going without contracted goods or services. The enforcement tools most commonly used are compliance reviews and conciliation aimed at encouraging voluntary compliance, but threats of contract delays or cancellations can be used by compliance officers in the conciliation process.

Early affirmative action focused on black workers, particularly in the construction industry. It was not until early 1978 that affirmative action goals and timetables were required in construction for sex as well as for race and national origin (Greenberger, 1980). Similar trends emerged in other industries. In shipbuilding, for example, an industry heavily dependent on government contracts, compliance efforts, despite male resistance, resulted in some women moving into non-traditional jobs, "but only on a token basis" (Marshall et al., 1978).

One explanation for the lack of affirmative action attention to women is the paucity of female advocates in these industries. In higher education, however, women's organizations, including NOW and the Women's Equity Action League, filed complaints in the early 1970s against numerous universities holding government contracts. This action resulted initially in a requirement that these institutions show that they were attempting to recruit, but not necessarily hire, women faculty. White male professors and several Jewish organizations charged that this requirement was reverse discrimination, and the

Department of Health, Education, and Welfare (HEW), the administering agency, responded by actually giving priority to these reverse discrimination complaints and sending the complaints of faculty women to the EEOC (Freeman, 1982). In a resulting court case, HEW and the Department of Labor admitted that they had failed to adequately enforce the sex-discrimination prohibitions and entered into a consent order requiring more stringent standards.[38] The decentralized and often subjective university decision-making process is a continuing barrier to affirmative action in academia.

In 1978 compliance activity was consolidated in the Office of Federal Contract Compliance Programs (OFCCP) in the Department of Labor. OFCCP targeted several industries, including construction, for special enforcement attention, with the result that the employment of women in traditionally male occupations increased (Reskin and Hartmann, 1986). This experience, along with other evaluations of affirmative action, shows how important active enforcement and monitoring are to effective affirmative action efforts.

Early statistical evaluations of the impact of affirmative action plans, like the plans themselves, focused on black men. Studies based on recent data suggest that affirmative action has a positive impact on the employment status of minority workers. One shows black men gaining more than women, black women making more progress than white women, and compliance reviews having a positive impact on minority employment (Leonard, 1984). A study focusing on female quit rates found that affirmative action enforcement reduced turnover among women, but not men, perhaps because of its positive impact on female job satisfaction (Osterman, 1982). Somewhat different results came from as yet unpublished Department of Labor-sponsored studies which found that affirmative action had a positive impact and that it was particularly pronounced among women workers. Between 1974 and 1980 the percentage of women working for firms covered by OFCCP regulations increased by 15.2 percent, while the percentage of women working for other organizations increased by 2 percent.[39]

Changes in Executive Order 11246 proposed by the Reagan Administration would permit employers to set voluntary goals and timetables that "do not operate to discriminate or grant a preference to any person on account of race, color, sex, religion or national origin." This proposal has many critics, including civil rights and women's

---

[38] *Women's Equity Action League v. Califano*, Civ. Action No. 74-1720, (D.D.C. December 19, 1977).

[39] "Study Says Affirmative Action Rule Expands Hiring of Minorities," *New York Times*, June 19, 1985.

rights advocates as well as some employer organizations, including the National Association of Manufacturers.[40]

Regardless of Executive Order 11246's future, the role of OFCCP changed considerably during the early 1980s. Budget cuts resulted in staff cuts of 52 percent between 1979 and 1985. There were similar decreases in compliance reviews, back-pay agreements, and debarments from federal contracts. A number of requirements were relaxed. For example, the requirement that contractors receiving more than $10,000 have affirmative action plans was changed to eliminate contractors with fewer than 50 employees, and there are proposals to increase that limit (duRivage, 1985).

Child Care

The increase in the number of working mothers is a notable recent change in the labor force. The increase was 20 percent between 1970 and 1984. Seventy-one percent of employed mothers work full-time, and about 65 percent of those with children under 3 years of age are full-time employees. Approximately 56 percent of U.S. children have employed mothers, with black children somewhat more likely than white children to have working mothers (Minnesota Commission on the Economic Status of Women, 1985a). As a result, public concern is growing about the provision of adequate child care, particularly for very young children for whom there are few child-care facilities.

The most common child-care arrangements are care in another's home (40.2 percent), care in own home (30.6 percent), and care in child-care centers (14.8 percent). About 75 percent of the care in another's home is provided by nonrelatives; most care provided in children's own homes is by a relative. About 7 million children ages 13 and under care for themselves for part of each day while parents work (Minnesota Commission on the Economic Status of Women, 1986).

About 96 percent of the 2 to 3 million child-care workers in the United States are women, the majority of whom earn less than the minimum wage. Continuity of care (low staff turnover), low staff/child ratios, and staff training are important indicators of the quality of child care. However, a Bureau of Labor Statistics study ranked child-care center workers as one of the top 10 categories with the highest turnover. The national turnover rate was 42 percent in 1980, and the vast majority of these workers had less than five years of experience (Minnesota Commission on the Economic Status of Women, 1986).

Adequate child care is not just a matter of convenience for working parents. Many of them, including myself, know the frustration in

---

[40] Bureau of National Affairs, Inc., *Employee Relations Weekly*, October 14, 1985, p. 1253.

attempting to find appropriate child care. Moreover, a recent study of employees varying in occupation, age, race, marital status, and number of children found that child-care problems have a negative impact on employee performance (Fernandez, 1985).

Nonetheless, the federal government historically and currently has had a limited role in providing child care. There has been some federal funding of day-care programs for use by women in antipoverty and training programs and to encourage women receiving Aid to Families With Dependent Children payments to train for and find paid employment. OFCCP recognizes the provision of child care as a form of affirmative action, but does not require that it be provided by government contractors. The major federal child-care policies revolve around tax credits to parents of amounts from 20 to 30 percent of their child-care expenses and tax incentives to employers (Reskin and Hartmann, 1986).

Although federal efforts to provide these services are limited, some local governments are developing innovative approaches to child care. In 1985 San Francisco and Contra Costa counties in California joined with six corporations to increase the availability of quality child care. Both the counties and the corporations committed funds to the project, and the money will be used to establish pilot child-care resource and referral programs.[41]

In another local effort, the city of San Francisco passed an ordinance requiring real estate developers to underwrite child-care costs. Under this 1985 ordinance, office developers may either provide space for on-site child-care facilities, contribute an amount based on floor space to a city-sponsored "Affordable Child Care Fund," or use some combination of these two options. When developers choose the on-site option, the space will be used by a nonprofit child-care provider without charges for rent, utilities, property taxes, and other building services. Noncomplying developers may have building occupancy permits denied.[42]

Because of its design, this ordinance will result in phased evolutionary change in child-care availability. A state law permitting local communities to pass this type of legislation made this ordinance possible. Depending on its success, it may serve as a model for other communities. It may also encourage other creative approaches to the provision of child care.

Parental Leave

Like child care, parental leave has increased in importance because of numbers of working mothers. Although employers are

---

[41] Bureau of National Affairs, Inc., *Employee Relations Weekly*, April 29, 1985, pp. 516–17.
[42] San Francisco Downtown Plan, Sections 165 and 315; San Francisco Municipal Code, Section 314.

required by law to treat pregnancy leave the same as leave for other purposes, they are not required to have unpaid leave programs. Some employers permit employees to combine leaves from options including paid leave of a specific duration, unpaid leave, and flexible arrangements such as part-time work. Other employers provide leave, paid or unpaid, for a specific period, and returning employees are expected to resume full-time duties. Although they are less common, some employers provide adoptive-parent and fraternal leaves. There are no comprehensive data on the average length of leaves, but some unpaid leaves are as brief as two weeks. Anecdotal information suggests that paid and extended leave is less available for low-income women than for women employed in professional and technical occupations or those covered by collective bargaining contracts. It also suggests that generous and flexible leave policies have a positive impact on employee morale, and perhaps productivity.

California and Montana have laws requiring employers to provide job-guaranteed extended maternity leave. In California, employers must grant pregnancy leave of up to four months with reinstatement rights to the same or similar job. The law has been challenged on the grounds that it violates Title VII by discriminating against men on the basis of pregnancy. In January 1987 the Supreme Court ruled that California's pregnancy disability leave statute does not violate Title VII.[43]

Similar legislation has been introduced in Congress and in several state legislatures. The House bill (H.R. 2020) would provide unpaid job-guaranteed leave for parents of a newborn or a newly adopted child. This legislation would both guarantee parental leave and create a uniform policy for employers and employees to use in their planning. This type of legislation is common in Western Europe.

This proposal again raises the question of whether women workers—in this case pregnant workers—should have special workplace protections. On the one hand, the argument is that pregnancy is a special condition and needs a special policy in order to protect working women. On the other hand, it is argued that the feminist movement has equal treatment as a goal and that protective legislation has historically worked to the detriment of working women (Adams and Winston, 1980).

Why has the United States moved so slowly to provide child-care assistance and parental-leave guarantees? Child care and parental leave are quite different issues. Child care is typically both more expensive and of much longer duration than parental leave, especially unpaid leave. However, it is useful to link the two, particularly given

---

[43] *California Fed. S.&L. Ass'n v. Guerra*, 42 FEP Cases 1073 (1987).

that even the relatively inexpensive option of unpaid leave is not guaranteed by law. One possibility, which has as its support the failure of the Equal Rights Amendment, is that this society still has as its model a two-parent family in which the woman works only when there are no children who need care. Although this model is becoming less and less descriptive of reality, it endures at least partially because of tradition.

Another explanation is that social policy in the United States is typically a reaction to an identified problem rather than a proactive effort to stimulate social change (Adams and Winston, 1980). One response to this explanation might be to question why child care and parental leave have not been perceived as identifiable problems in need of policy attention. A possible answer is that the increasing number of employed mothers is a recent phenomenon and policy has simply lagged behind labor force changes. A contributing factor is that somehow families have managed "to cope" with parental leave issues and child care on an individual basis. Only recently have the financial and emotional costs of individual coping begun to be recognized.

In addition, the policy-formation process in the United States is fragmented, and policy change usually requires an extended period of coalition formation, compromise, and consensus-building. Coalition formation around child care and parental leave may have been slowed because both issues affect people during only part of their working lives, not all people are affected, and the people who are affected are not affected at the same time. Too, some potential allies on work and family issues are separated by philosophical differences about the legality of abortion.

However, there are signs of change in public attitudes toward these issues. Many employers do have parental leave policies, the number of employers providing child-care assistance is increasing, and some groups are actively working for policy changes. For example, the Family Policy Panel of the Economic Policy Council of the United Nations Association of the United States of America in 1986 came out in support of maternity leave with partial income replacement, federal assistance for child care, and the creation of a national commission on contemporary work and family patterns. Panel members included the presidents of Sarah Lawrence College and six international unions, and former President Gerald Ford.

Work and family issues are beginning to get media attention. In February 1986 the television program "20/20" included a segment in which Barbara Walters interviewed family members and discussed "What happens when Mom has to work?" The program emphasized the stress associated with having both parents work, indicated that stress was even greater in one-parent families, and concluded that child care was the number-one problem families face. This recent attention to family and work issues in the media and among organizations suggests that an emerging coalition is forming to encourage new policy approaches to family, child care, and work.

Future Research

Comparable worth is currently attracting considerable research interest. Initially, the focus was on providing empirical evidence of the impact of gender differences in occupational distribution on wages. As the issue grew in policy importance, a number of research efforts concentrated on comparing the worth of dissimilar jobs. This research continues and generally shows about a 15 to 20 percent gap between wages for predominantly male and predominantly female jobs of comparable worth to the employer. A new research theme is how job content might be measured and compared more effectively. Future research will also analyze the impact of comparable worth adjustments on internal organizational issues such as turnover and job satisfaction as well as the income and employment effects of pay-equity adjustments.

Nonetheless, Title VII and affirmative action are at the core of current public policy affecting women workers. Changing administrative policies affect the implementation of Title VII and affirmative action, and research on this topic as well as on the employment effects and the impact of enforcement will continue to be valuable. Studies of employer responses to changes in affirmative action and EEOC guidelines and enforcement also will be important to policy-framers.

Parental leave and the provision of child care are the policy and research issues of the future. These issues raise some basic questions. Is equal treatment enough? Or should public policy go further than equal treatment in protecting the people who bear and raise children? These questions have research implications. What workplace accommodations are most needed by parents? How can policies be designed to address these needs and take employer needs into account as well?

Proposals to guarantee parental leave suggest even more research questions. How generally available are extended job-guaranteed pregnancy leaves? What is the typical length of these leaves? How well do they meet the needs of affected families? What adjustments would employers be faced with if they were required to provide guaranteed leaves of several months, and how can policy be designed to assist employers in implementing extended leaves? Are adjustments more difficult for small employers than for large employers, or for employers in some industries? Answers to these questions would be useful in helping develop parental-leave legislation.

Perhaps policy efforts directed toward providing quality child care would benefit most from extensive research. How can government approach this issue creatively? Who should bear the costs? An assessment of alternative child care models will both assist policymakers and bring attention to this important issue.

Conclusions

An overview of the public-policy treatment of women workers shows that it responds to, rather than encourages, changes in the labor force status of women workers. When policy changes do occur, they result from coalition-building, research support, and political pressure from women's organizations and other interested groups, including the labor movement. The inclusion of sex discrimination in Title VII appears to be an aberration from this pattern. However, political pressure was instrumental in achieving enforcement of the prohibition of sex discrimination.

The evolution of laws covering women workers reflects slowly changing norms about the role of women in society. The hope of those supporting early efforts to get protective legislation was that it would protect women from the negative impact working might have on their families and on childbearing. These norms made it difficult to see women workers as deserving treatment equal to that of men. The norms change slowly, and society is just beginning to accept the reality that women spend more of their lives as workers than as wives or mothers.

Policy changes are currently under consideration in two new areas—the relationship between work and family and pay equity. Both policies are based on the often unspoken recognition that men and women still have different roles in our culture. Culture influences job choice and family roles. As a result, a review of the policy treatment of women workers finds us searching for answers about how to balance equal opportunity with the different roles and needs of men and women workers.

Our challenge, as a society, is to attempt to build consensus on these issues. This is complicated by the recognition that policy almost always has unanticipated consequences, some positive and some negative. For the near future, as in the past, it appears that labor market policies affecting women workers will change slowly in response to political pressure and as part of the consensus-building process. It is hoped that the process will include attention to the development of standards for evaluating policies affecting women workers. For policy to be good for women, should it also be good for men and children? And can policy be framed that benefits families, employers, and society as well? Answers to these questions will challenge us and perhaps change us as well.

References

Adams, Carolyn Teich, and Kathryn Teich Winston. *Mothers at Work: Public Policies in the United States, Sweden, and China.* New York: Longman, 1980.

Baer, Judith A. *The Chains of Protection.* Westport, CT: Greenwood Press, 1978.

Bergmann, Barbara R. "Reducing the Pervasiveness of Discrimination." In *Jobs for Americans,* ed. Eli Ginzberg. Englewood Cliffs, NJ: Prentice Hall, 1976. Pp. 142–61.

Brandeis, Elizabeth. "Labor Legislation." In *History of Labor in the United States, 1896–1932,* ed. John R. Commons. New York: Macmillan Co., 1952. Pp. 475–62.

Brown, Charles. "The Federal Attack on Labor Market Discrimination: The Mouse That Roared." In *Research in Labor Economics,* Vol. 5, ed. Ronald G. Ehrenberg. Greenwich, CT: JAI Press, 1982. Pp. 55–59.

Burbridge, Lynn C. *The Impact of Changes in Policy on the Federal Equal Employment Opportunity Effort.* Washington: Urban Institute, 1984.

Burkhauser, Richard V. "Pension Plan Equity: Second-Round Consequences." *Journal of Policy Analysis and Management* 3 (Fall 1983): pp. 613–18.

Butler, Richard, and James J. Heckman. "The Government's Impact on the Labor Market Status of Black Americans: A Critical Review." In *Equal Rights and Industrial Relations,* eds. Leonard J. Hausman et al. Madison, WI: Industrial Relations Research Association, 1977. Pp. 235–81.

Collins, Eliza G.C., and Timothy B. Blodgett. "Sexual Harassment . . . Some See It . . . Some Won't." *Harvard Business Review* 59 (March-April 1981): pp. 84–85.

Cook, Alice. "Equal Pay: Where Is It?" *Industrial Relations* 14 (May 1975): pp. 158–77.

Cooper, Elizabeth A., and Gerald V. Barrett. "Equal Pay and Gender: Implications of Court Cases for Personnel Practices." *Academy of Management Review* 9 (January 1984): pp. 84–94.

duRivage, Virginia. "The OFCCP Under the Reagan Administration: Affirmative Action in Retreat." *Labor Law Journal* 36 (June 1985): pp. 360–68.

Fernandez, John F. *Child Care and Corporate Productivity.* Lexington, MA: Lexington Books, 1985.

Fisher, Marguerite. "Equal Pay for Equal Work Legislation." *Industrial and Labor Relations Review* 2 (October 1948): pp. 50–57.

Freeman, Jo. "Women and Public Policy: An Overview." In *Women, Power and Policy,* ed. Ellen Boneparth. New York: Pergamon Press, 1982. Pp. 47–73.

———. *The Politics of Women's Liberation.* New York: David McKay, 1975.

Greenberger, Marcia. "The Effectiveness of Federal Laws Prohibiting Sex Discrimination in Employment in the United States." In *Equal Employment Policy for Women,* ed. Ronnie Steinberg Ratner. Philadelphia: Temple University Press, 1980. Pp. 108–28.

Greenlaw, Paul S., and John P. Kohl. "The EEOC's New Equal Pay Act Guidelines." *Personnel Journal* (July 1982): pp. 517–21.

Koziara, Karen S., and Patrice J. Insley. "Organizing Low-Income Women in New Ways: Who, Where, and Why." In *Proceedings of the 34th Annual Meeting, Industrial Relations Research Association, 1981.* Madison, WI: IRRA, 1982. Pp. 381–89.

Leonard, Jonathan S. "Employment and Occupation Advance Under Affirmative Action." *Review of Economics and Statistics* 66 (August 1984): pp. 366–85.

MacKinnon, Katherine. "Sexual Harassment: The Experience." In *The Criminal Justice System and Women*, eds. Barbara R. Price and Natalie J. Sokoloff. New York: Clark Boardman, 1982.

Marshall, Ray, et al. *Employment Discrimination: The Impact of Legal and Administrative Remedies*. New York: Praeger, 1978.

McGlen, Nancy E., and Karen O'Connor. *Women's Rights: The Struggle for Equality in the 19th & 20th Centuries*. New York: Praeger, 1983.

Milkovich, George T., and A. Broderick. "Pay Discrimination: Legal Issues and Implications for Research." *Industrial Relations* 21 (Fall 1982): pp. 309–17.

Minnesota Commission on the Economic Status of Women (MCESW). *Employed Mothers*. Newsletter No. 94. St. Paul: MCESW, September 1985a.

——. *Pay Equity: The Minnesota Experience*. St. Paul: MCESW, 1985b.

——. *Child Care Workers*. Newsletter No. 98, St. Paul: MCESW, January 1986.

National Committee on Pay Equity. "1984 Survey of Public Sector Employers," 1985. (Unpublished).

O'Farrell, Brigid, and Sharon Harlan. "Job Integration Strategies: Today's Programs and Tomorrow's Needs." In *Sex Segregation in the Workplace: Trends, Explanations, Remedies*, ed. Barbara F. Reskin. Washington: National Academy Press, 1984. Pp. 267–91.

Osterman, Paul. "Affirmative Action and Opportunity: A Study of Female Quit Rates." *Review of Economics and Statistics* 64 (November 1982): pp. 604–12.

Reskin, Barbara F., and Heidi Hartmann. *Women's Work, Men's Work: Sex Segregation on the Job*. Washington: National Academy Press, 1986.

Sangerman, Harry. "A Look at the Equal Pay Act in Practice." *Labor Law Journal* 22 (May 1971): pp. 259–65.

Sealander, Judith. *As Minority Becomes Majority: Federal Reaction to the Phenomenon of Women in the Work Force, 1920–1963*. Westport, CT: Greenwood Press, 1983.

Silverman, Dierdre. "Sexual Harassment: Working Women's Dilemma." *Quest: A Feminist Quarterly* 3 (Winter 1976).

Sovereign, Kenneth L. *Personnel Law*. Reston, VA: Reston Publishing Co., 1984.

Stencel, Sandra. "Equal Pay Fight." In *The Women's Movement: Agenda for the '80s*, Editorial Research Reports. Washington: Congressional Quarterly, Inc., 1981. Pp. 3–19.

U.S. Civil Rights Commission. "To Eliminate Employment Discrimination: A Sequel." In *The Federal Civil Rights Enforcement Effort—1977*. Washington: U.S. Government Printing Office, 1977. P. 211.

U.S. Department of Labor. *Findings from the Survey of Private Pension Benefit Amounts*. Washington: U.S. Government Printing Office, 1985.

U.S. Equal Employment Opportunity Commission. *EEOC Sex Discrimination Guidelines*. Washington: U.S. Government Printing Office, 1980.

——. *Legislative History of Titles VII and XI of Civil Rights Act of 1964*. Washington: U.S. Government Printing Office, 1968.

U.S. House of Representatives, Subcommittee on Human Resources. "Forward." Hearings on Human Resources, September 16, 21, 30, December 2, 1983.

U.S. Senate, Subcommittee on Labor. Equal Pay Hearings, 1963.

Zelman, Patricia G. *Women, Work, and National Policy: The Kennedy-Johnson Years*. Ann Arbor, MI: UM Research Press, 1982.

Index